**Latinas/os in New Jersey**

# Ceres: Rutgers Studies in History

*Lucia McMahon and Christopher T. Fisher, Series Editors*

New Jersey holds a unique place in the American story. One of the thirteen colonies in British North America and the original states of the United States, New Jersey plays a central, yet underappreciated, place in America's economic, political, and social development. New Jersey's axial position as the nation's financial, intellectual, and political corridor has become something of a signature, evident in quips about the Turnpike and punchlines that end with its many exits. Yet, New Jersey is more than a crossroad or an interstitial "elsewhere." Far from being ancillary to the nation, New Jersey is an axis around which America's story has turned, and within its borders gather a rich collection of ideas, innovations, people, and politics. The region's historical development makes it a microcosm of the challenges and possibilities of the nation, and it also reflects the complexities of the modern, cosmopolitan world. Yet, far too little of the literature recognizes New Jersey's significance to the national story, and despite promising scholarship done at the local level, New Jersey history often remains hidden in plain sight.

Ceres books represent new, rigorously peer-reviewed scholarship on New Jersey and the surrounding region. Named for the Roman goddess of prosperity portrayed on the New Jersey State Seal, Ceres provides a platform for cultivating and disseminating the next generation of scholarship. It features the work of both established historians and a new generation of scholars across disciplines. Ceres aims to be field-shaping, providing a home for the newest and best empirical, archival, and theoretical work on the region's past. We are also dedicated to fostering diverse and inclusive scholarship and hope to feature works addressing issues of social justice and activism.

For a complete list of titles in the series, please see the last page of the book.

# Latinas/os in New Jersey

## Histories, Communities, and Cultures

EDITED BY ALDO A. LAURIA SANTIAGO AND ULLA D. BERG
With a foreword by Olga Jiménez de Wagenheim

**Rutgers University Press**
New Brunswick, Camden, and Newark, New Jersey
London and Oxford

Rutgers University Press is a department of Rutgers, The State University of New Jersey, one of the leading public research universities in the nation. By publishing worldwide, it furthers the University's mission of dedication to excellence in teaching, scholarship, research, and clinical care.

Library of Congress Cataloging-in-Publication Data

Names: Lauria-Santiago, Aldo, editor. | Berg, Ulla D., editor.
Title: Latinas/os in New Jersey : histories, communities, and cultures / edited by
    Aldo A. Lauria Santiago and Ulla D. Berg.
Description: New Brunswick : Rutgers University Press, [2025] | Series: Ceres :
    Rutgers studies in history | Collection of essays by Johana Londoño and 21 others. |
    Includes bibliographical references and index.
Identifiers: LCCN 2024026985 | ISBN 9781978826175 (paperback) | ISBN 9781978826182
    (cloth) | ISBN 9781978826199 (epub) | ISBN 9781978826212 (pdf)
Subjects: LCSH: Hispanic Americans—New Jersey—Social conditions—20th century. |
    Hispanic Americans—New Jersey—Social conditions—21st century. | Hispanic
    Americans—Political activity—New Jersey—History—20th century. | Hispanic
    Americans—Political activity—New Jersey—History—21st century. | New Jersey—
    Race relations—History—20th century. | New Jersey—Race relations—History—
    21st century. | Immigrants—New Jersey—History.
Classification: LCC F145.S75 L37 2025 | DDC 305.868/07307490904—dc23/eng/20240826
LC record available at https://lccn.loc.gov/2024026985

A British Cataloging-in-Publication record for this book is available from the British Library.

This collection copyright © 2025 by Rutgers, The State University of New Jersey
Individual chapters copyright © 2025 in the names of their authors

All rights reserved

No part of this book may be reproduced or utilized in any form or by any means, electronic or mechanical, or by any information storage and retrieval system, without written permission from the publisher. Please contact Rutgers University Press, 106 Somerset Street, New Brunswick, NJ 08901. The only exception to this prohibition is "fair use" as defined by U.S. copyright law.

References to internet websites (URLs) were accurate at the time of writing. Neither the author nor Rutgers University Press is responsible for URLs that may have expired or changed since the manuscript was prepared.

∞ The paper used in this publication meets the requirements of the American National Standard for Information Sciences—Permanence of Paper for Printed Library Materials, ANSI Z39.48-1992.

rutgersuniversitypress.org

We dedicate this book to the memory of Hilda Hidalgo.

Hidalgo was a Puerto Rican community activist, feminist lesbian, and Rutgers professor, who provided leadership to many institutions and movements and became one of the most important Puerto Rican leaders in New Jersey in the 1970s and 1980s. Hidalgo was born in Rio Piedras, Puerto Rico, in 1929 to a middle-class family. She interrupted her university studies to become a nun. After leaving the church, she completed her college degree in education at the University of Puerto Rico in 1957. She then completed a master's in guidance counseling from the Catholic University in Washington, DC. In 1960, she moved to Newark to work with the Girl Scouts. There she became an anti-racism activist and joined Congress of Racial Equality, Americans for Democratic Action, and the New Frontier Democrats. She partook in organizing against police violence in Newark, and among many other involvements picketed the construction site of Rutgers University Newark to protest the lack of minorities in the construction industry. She also served as a mediator between the National Guard and the residents of the Central Ward during the 1967 Newark riot. When Black students occupied a Rutgers building in 1969, she served as the mediator.

Around the same time, she became involved in ASPIRA and soon directed the Newark branch, an involvement that lasted for many years. She joined the United Community Corporation, the most important anti-poverty coalition and agency in Newark, initially led by the dean of the Rutgers law school, William Heckert. In 1967 she left the Girl Scouts and joined the Child Services Association where she became the director. Hidalgo continued her activism in anti-poverty work and focused on how to expand the participation of Latinos in the United Community Corporation and other anti-poverty programs. She participated in the founding of La Casa de Don Pedro in Newark and was leader of the Puerto Rican Congress during the 1970s. Along the way, in 1969, she moved to work at the newly inaugurated Livingston College at Rutgers as a professor of urban studies while enrolling in a PhD program at Union Graduate school. She worked at Rutgers in various capacities for eight years and organized the BA in social work. From Livingston she transferred to Urban Studies at the Newark Campus. From there she helped create specialized MSW and MPA programs. She became director of the first Puerto Rican Studies program at Rutgers-Newark.

After Rutgers she served as commissioner of the Department of Education in New Jersey in the early 1990s. In retirement in Florida she continued to be active in gay and lesbian rights organizations. She died in 2009, leaving behind a legacy of community research, multi-sited activism, civic engagement, and educational innovation. In 2010 a street was named after her on the Rutgers-Newark campus, Hilda Hidalgo Way.[1]

---

[1] Interview with Dr. Hilda Hidalgo, Griselda Cueto et. al, May 9, 1987, Newark Public Library, p17229coll54_629; Hilda Hidalgo Papers Finding Aid, Newark Public Library; Kelly Heyboer, "Rutgers, Newark Name Street after Professor Who Was a Pioneer for Gay, Hispanic Rights," September 22, 2010, NJ.com, https://nj.com/news/2010/09/rutgers _university_newark_name.html.

# Contents

Foreword     ix
OLGA JIMÉNEZ DE WAGENHEIM

Introduction: Framing Latinos in New Jersey:
From Invisibility to Empowerment     1
ALDO A. LAURIA SANTIAGO AND ULLA D. BERG

**Part I    Spaces and Places**

1    Latino New Jersey: A Demographic and Geographic Portrait     11
RAYMOND SÁNCHEZ MAYERS, LYNA L. WIGGINS, ELSA CANDELARIO, AND LAURA CURRAN

2    Latino Segregation across New Jersey Counties:
Are Latino Groups Becoming More or Less Residentially
Segregated during the Last Four Decades?     28
GIOVANI BURGOS, ALEX F. TRILLO, AND ANIL VENKATESH

3    The Gateway Reconsidered: The Paradox of Latinx
Barrioization in a Connected Metropolis     58
JOHANA LONDOÑO

4    From Havana on the Hudson to Bolivar's Enclave:
Change, Solidarity, and Conflict in Pan-Latinx Space     75
ALEX F. TRILLO AND JENNIFER AYALA

5    "Aggressive Newark": Puerto Ricans, Brazilians, and
Structuring Feelings under Neoliberalism     98
ANA Y. RAMOS-ZAYAS

## Part II  Histories

**6**  Peruvians in Paterson, New Jersey, 1920–1950  117
GIANNCARLO MUSCHI

**7**  "A Recoger Tomates": Puerto Rican Farmworkers in the Garden State, 1940s–1980s  134
ISMAEL GARCÍA COLÓN AND WILLIAM SUÁREZ GÓMEZ

**8**  Puerto Ricans in New Jersey: Migration, Settlement, and Work, 1940s–1980s  159
ALDO A. LAURIA SANTIAGO

**9**  A Century of Cuban Music in New Jersey  199
BENJAMIN LAPIDUS

## Part III  Experiences

**10**  Mexican Immigrants Fighting for Educational Justice: Community Activism to Save a New Brunswick Public School  229
LILIA FERNÁNDEZ

**11**  Forgotten Voices: Gender and Social Networks in Paterson's Peruvian Community  252
ELENA SABOGAL

**12**  "La Iglesia Católica es Mi Comunidad": A Union City Latinx Destination from Arrival to Old Age  268
MELANIE Z. PLASENCIA

**13**  Parque Oaxaca/Jotería: Trans Latina History in New Brunswick from Urban Renewal to the Coronavirus Pandemic  288
DANIELA VALDES

## Part IV  Institutions

**14**  Reverse Diasporas: Immigrant Detention, Deportation, and Latinx Communities in New Jersey and South America  313
ULLA D. BERG

**15**  Latinx LGBTQ Students and Placemaking in School: Voguing and Ball Culture at Elizabeth High, 1989–1994  332
YAMIL AVIVI

**16**  From Puerto Rican to Latino Studies at Rutgers University: Fifty Years of Student Activism  351
KATHLEEN LÓPEZ

Notes on Contributors  373
Index  377

# Foreword

OLGA JIMÉNEZ DE WAGENHEIM

At last there is a book that focuses on the historical presence and major contributions Latinos/as have made to the economy, society, and culture of the state of New Jersey since the early twentieth century.

The various chapters included in the book discuss the national diversity of the Pan Latino community and the places where they settled throughout the state, as well as highlight the opportunities and challenges each group encountered, and how the community contributed to its own and the surrounding community's development.

In the case of Puerto Ricans, for instance, a large number of the migrants were brought in on labor contracts during the 1940s and early 1950s to help harvest various crops in the southern part of the state. Initially, the migrants returned home after the job was done but, in time, thousands of them found work in nearby towns and cities and moved to New Jersey permanently.

The earliest group of Peruvians who settled in Paterson, according to chapter 6, began arriving in the 1920s, and tended to have connections to American corporations that were doing business in several port cities of Peru, while others were seamen who eventually chose Paterson as their new home. The Peruvians who came between the 1940s and 1960, were attracted by jobs in the city's silk industry.

The earliest Cubans to settle in Hudson County, New Jersey, according to chapter 9, arrived prior to the Cuban revolution and tended to be rural workers from the region of Santa Clara. These actually welcomed Fidel Castro when he paid a visit to Union City prior to becoming Cuba's maximum leader. By contrast, the Cubans who arrived shortly after the Cuban revolution were mostly urban migrants who were fleeing the Castro government. As political refugees, they were generally welcomed and aided by the U.S. government in ways no other Latino group had been. Many of the new migrants who arrived in Hudson County settled in Union City just as Germans and other Europeans were leaving the city.

Chapter 12 focuses on the significant roles played by the Catholic Church in helping the Cubans adjust to the new environment they encountered in an English-speaking society. Though that chapter focuses mostly on the Cuban community, one could argue that many Latinos in other communities benefited from similar church programs. In my own study of Puerto Ricans in Dover, I found that the Catholic Church was instrumental in providing Masses in Spanish at the Dover church, offering English classes during the evenings for working adults, and helping to set up pre-kinder programs for the community's children.

Most chapters discuss the economic conditions each group encountered at various times, and the ways they dealt with the opportunities available during the industrial bonanza of the war years, and how they adjusted when the industrial jobs disappeared.

A couple of the chapters discuss the language challenges most Latinos faced, and the racial and ethnic biases some groups faced while they tried to support their families, educate their children, and trying to fit in. Chapter 11 focuses on the important roles women played in the Peruvian community, though they were hardly recognized. The same could be said of other migrant groups, where women played significant roles that were, for the most part, ignored by the patriarchal societies they came from.

In general, the book offers wonderful insights into a Latino community about which little had been written. The fact that this book is dedicated to the late Hilda Hidalgo is significant, given that she was a pioneer leader in many of the struggles that resulted in the establishment of organizations that led to political empowerment, improvement of social services, and educational programs including the creation of the Puerto Rican Studies Department, and a master of arts social work program at Rutgers University.

In the process Hidalgo mentored many of us. I first met Hilda Hidalgo in the early 1970s, when I moved with my family to New Jersey after obtaining a master's degree in Latin American history from the State University of New York at Buffalo (SUNY-Buffalo). I met Hilda on the recommendation of Professor Maria Canino, then director of the Puerto Rican Studies Department at Rutgers-New Brunswick. I had met Canino at a Puerto Rican Women's Conference I had organized at SUNY-Buffalo. Shortly after I met Hilda, she recommended me to teach a course she had developed for the Sociology Department at Rutgers-Newark called Puerto Rican Life Styles. After obtaining a PhD in Latin American and Caribbean history, I remained at Rutgers-Newark for another twenty-seven years.

Following in Hidalgo's footsteps, and with her help, I established a Puerto Rican studies program at Rutgers-Newark during the mid-1970s. Hidalgo ran the program during one of my sabbatical leaves. That program in turn led me to research the Puerto Rican community in Dover, New Jersey, and later to pursue the idea of creating an archival research center at the Newark Public Library (NPL) in order to begin documenting the Latino communities in the state.

A fortuitous collaboration with Ingrid Betancourt, a highly regarded member of the NPL staff, led to the creation of the New Jersey Hispanic Research and Information Center (NJHRIC) at the NPL in 2001. Years earlier, with the support of several Latino leaders, Betancourt had created the Sala Hispanoamericana, a resource center with books and other materials in Spanish, in order to better serve the Hispanic community in Newark and other cities.

One of the tiers of the NJHRIC is the Puerto Rican Community Archives, where I donated dozens of oral histories conducted by students in the courses I offered at Rutgers, as well as books and archival materials on various subjects pertaining to Puerto Ricans I had accumulated for nearly thirty years. Creating the archival component of the NJHRIC required having a trained archivist to manage it. That job was shortly thereafter entrusted to Yesenia López, a Rutgers-Newark graduate, who took it upon herself to train in the field after a brief apprenticeship under the guidance of now retired head archivist Nelida Pérez at Centro de Estudios Puertorriqueños at Hunter College.

I am not sure whether any of these ventures would have been undertaken by us in Newark had it not been for the lessons we learned from Hilda Hidalgo. I am glad this book is dedicated to her memory.

**Latinas/os in New Jersey**

# Introduction

## Framing Latinos in New Jersey: From Invisibility to Empowerment

ALDO A. LAURIA SANTIAGO AND
ULLA D. BERG

New Jersey is a state that barely knows itself. It is also a state that hardly *wants* to know itself. Scholarship on New Jersey is frequently framed by themes drawn from deeply rooted ideas that originate in eighteenth-century colonial history or simplistic derivations from the state's peculiar late twentieth-century economic development.[1] Phrases and terminologies commonly express these ideas, often with substance but also as cliches: empty, gateway, corridor, ethnic, divided, unintegrated, corrupt, postindustrial, posturban, postsuburban, larger New York. In New Jersey's dominant discourses and professional knowledge economies, any visibility offered to postwar immigrants is squeezed into (and often out of) these frames built through narratives of enduring contrasts and liberal successes.

These frames created by ideas of continuity and development may be potentially inclusive of many aspects of the histories of Latinos in the state but, more often than not, they are limiting and exclusive. This volume parts from the assumption that any knowledge about Latino communities in New Jersey has to simultaneously reference these enduring narratives, but also challenges the

1

limitations they impose. We suggest that the immigrant paradigm encloses any possibility of a truly integrated knowledge of Latino (and other) communities, as originators and owners of an organic New Jersey experience.[2] As a result, and enhanced by the persistent marginality of its urban centers and the political weakness of its urban (and non-White) working-class sectors, New Jersey has simultaneously welcomed and hidden its Latino population in the state's cultural, political, and educational spaces.[3] Consequently, despite the production of some knowledge about Latinos in the last twenty years, Latinos have remained peripheral, incidental, local, and even evanescent, to major narratives about the state.[4]

Predictably immigration resonates with a framework that emphasizes development in the form of economic growth, employment and access to housing, welfare state resources, and public education is understandable. These are foreseeable, even obligatory, characteristics of the migratory and generational experience of most Latinos in New Jersey. These immigrant vectors may be framed in slightly different ways depending on which of New Jersey's postwar development stages (industrial, postindustrial, administrative, distributional/service) or regional economies (industrial, affluent/suburban, rural/agricultural) is under scrutiny, but they provide the basis of the diversity of places, moments, and experiences represented in this book's chapters.[5]

Inevitably, suburbanization, housing and labor market dynamics, public school systems, and the complexities of the state's changing economic landscape are all part of New Jersey success stories and frame many of the themes analyzed in the chapter contributions. Yet other less visible stories and dynamics of exploitation, poverty, immigrant detention and deportation, violence, racism, urban decline, police brutality, and socioeconomic marginalization do not so easily fit New Jersey's persistent metanarratives. Several contributors address these themes as well.

The scholarly literature on Latinos in New Jersey is scant and until recently included no more than a few in-depth monographs and only a few dozen social science, education, and public-health studies. Pioneers of Puerto Rican studies like Maria Josefa Canino Arroyo, Hilda Hidalgo, Olga Jiménez de Wagenheim, Gloria Bonilla-Santiago, and Kal Wagenheim carried out the first studies in the 1970s and 1980s, often as part of community-oriented pedagogies linked to programs in Puerto Rican studies. Mostly written by women, these works had a persistent focus on class, gender and sexuality, and the contribution of Latinas.[6] One dissertation on Cubans in New Jersey took decades to be published as a book, joining one other study of Cubans, while an important book on Puerto Ricans in Philadelphia included significant content on Camden.[7] The all-too-thin literature on the urban crisis in New Jersey often includes discussions of Puerto Rican urban communities with some attention to Camden and Newark.[8] Yet Perth Amboy, Paterson, Jersey City, and other places remain largely unexamined. The Catholic Church and the religious practices of Latinos also received some attention.[9] The growing presence of South Americans beginning in the

1980s and of Mexicans in the 1990s was noticed by the press but produced very limited scholarly research. Since the 2000s a small highly specialized but growing literature has addressed questions of health, diet, bilingual education, and educational outcomes.[10] In some of these fields Peter Guarnaccia, a now retired Rutgers University professor, played a pioneering role.[11] New Jersey entered the twenty-first century with little knowledge of its Hispanic or Latino populations at the same time that a massive third generation was already entering its educational and other institutions.

The chapters in this book represent the, by now, mature fields that intersect in the interdisciplinary arena of Latino studies. With roots in the Puerto Rican and Chicano studies programs of the 1960s and 1970s, Latino studies emerged in the 1980s as a dialog about the growing diversity of people with shared roots in the American spaces colonized by Spain and with Spanish-language cultures.[12] An emphasis on culture and politics was followed by a historical turn and later a diverse social science and ethnographic literature.[13] By the turn of the twenty-first century Latino studies matured in its interdisciplinary complexity, regional coverage, and rejection of facile oppositional concepts, inevitably losing some of the political baggage that gave origin to the discipline.

Despite its diverse demographics, New Jersey lags far behind other states and regions with similar or even smaller Latino demographics and communities. The Southwest, New York City, Chicago, and even New England and Florida have denser literature on Latinos. We are only beginning to catch up despite having one of the earliest programs in Puerto Rican studies in the United States (at Rutgers) with a decades-long trajectory of research, activism, and pedagogy, and a major Ivy League university in the state. The state that claims the renowned poet of Puerto Rican and Caribbean descent, William Carlos Williams (1883–1963), as its own does not even understand his origins.[14]

This book is an initial attempt to *create* Latino studies of New Jersey and to begin making up for the decades-long invisibility. The book is divided into four parts: Spaces and Places, Histories, Experiences, and Institutions. While these categories overlap in the individual contributions, they served us well as an organizing structure for the book. "Space and Places" both offers an overview of Latino demographics in New Jersey and accounts for the many kinds of Latino spaces and the social and racial processes that shape them, especially in northern New Jersey. "Histories" offers accounts of Puerto Rican, Cuban, and Peruvian migration and settlement through the perspectives of economic history, labor history, and cultural history. "Experiences" offers insights into the social struggles of different constituencies and social groups including Mexican immigrants fighting for educational justice in New Brunswick, Peruvian women's participating in public life and community organizing in Paterson, church-centered community-building activities among elderly Latinos in Union City, and Trans Latinx experiences during the COVID-19 pandemic. Finally, "Institutions" focuses on different institutional settings where the state's Latino population have been educated and disciplined with long-lasting effects in the state and beyond.

Precisely because of this complex history and the limited scholarship available, this book represents only an initial and incomplete effort. Readers will note the absence of chapters or substantial discussions of Dominican-descent communities, of Salvadorans, Hondurans, and Guatemalans, and of Ecuadorians and Colombians. Geographical coverage is also partial, with an emphasis on familiar Latino spaces and stories. The racial, class, linguistic, and ethnic diversity within the Latino category will need significant development in future works, particularly in regard to indigeneity and Afro-Latinidad.[15]

Other pieces are missing as well. There are many Latino experiences in the neglected and impoverished urban spaces of New Jersey. The decades of the 1980s, 1990s, and even early 2000s is nearly invisible and forgotten, with stories of housing discrimination, police abuse, and school failures, some of which are noted but not fully developed in the contributions to this book. New Jersey also has a growing Latino middle class populating the state's many suburban communities and revitalizing main streets across the state with a variety of ethnic businesses. We also need more elements to understand New Jersey's peculiar Latino politics, which has produced many Latino mayors (mostly democratic) and one of the few Latino U.S. senators. And moving beyond narrow examinations of Latino communities and Latin American national-origin groups, we need more research on how Latinos relate to other immigrant groups, to African Americans, to White New Jerseyans, and to the state's unionized and social service sectors.[16]

Disclaimers aside, what the book does well, and how it benefits from the maturity of Latino studies at a national level, is worthy of attention. There is much we have learned in the last decades about handling knowledge and research about diverse but regionally focused Latino populations and histories. We no longer uncritically assume pan-Latino formations, identities, or solidarities unless they can be identified empirically. Class, racial, and gender diversities and differences within the communities have also been acknowledged and are well represented in this book. Cultural identities are no longer strictly counterposed to experiences of incorporation or assimilation into the U.S. mainstream especially for second-generation Latinos. The importance of generational distinctions and of national origin cultures and transnational connections remain part of the cases examined in this book.

Despite the noted invisibility, we have learned that New Jersey has two majority Latino counties—Hudson and Passaic—and a third that is well on its way. Here, the dynamics are denser and more comparable with other similar national-level spaces, but comparisons are rarely made. The distinction between urban and rural contexts so common in other regional Latino literatures are also challenged in New Jersey. What used to be suburbs and what used to be cities now flow into each other with an uneasy sociological haze. Generational upward mobility, the increasing presence of Latino groups of mixed origin, and the integration especially through educational institutions, that are so visible in the chapters presented in this book, suggest that New Jersey might have lessons for the national level.

The field calls for further research and more dedicated researchers, and the institutions in the state should learn more clearly that they need to support these efforts beyond the now-standard institutional diversity, equity, and inclusion frameworks in which Latino scholars and communities often end up as invisible and under resourced as before. This book should encourage substantial investment in young scholars that will bring New Jersey up to speed in Latino studies and help erase or at least complexify some of the facile generalizations made about the state and its communities. There is much we do not know about how this process should proceed. Yet the presence right now of hundreds of thousands of people of Spanish-speaking descent across multiple generations, and many more to come, are a call for projects of visibility, recovery, documentation, and participation. That it might one day contribute also to empowerment will depend on these communities themselves.

## Notes

1. Richard Francis Veit and Maxine N. Lurie, *New Jersey: A History of the Garden State* (New Brunswick, NJ: Rutgers University Press, 2012).
2. The literature on immigrant New Jersey has shifted slowly from discussions of southern U.S. and European groups to non-European groups, especially South Asian immigrants. See Robyn Magalit Rodriguez, *In Lady Liberty's Shadow: The Politics of Race and Immigration in New Jersey* (New Brunswick, NJ: Rutgers University Press, 2017); Noriko Matsumoto, *Beyond the City and the Bridge: East Asian Immigration in a New Jersey Suburb* (New Brunswick, NJ: Rutgers University Press, 2018). But generic approaches that frame Latinos as only the latest part of the continuity of immigration into New Jersey persist.
3. Harold Aurand Jr., "Suburban Erasure: How the Suburbs Ended the Civil Rights Movement in New Jersey," book review, *Pennsylvania History* 81, no. 4 (2014): 537–540.
4. Perhaps the most consistent tracing of the diversity and continuity of the Latino communities in New Jersey since the 1970s has been produced by journalists.
5. James W. Hughes and Joseph J. Seneca, *New Jersey's Postsuburban Economy* (New Brunswick, NJ: Rutgers University Press, 2015); Stephen A. Salmore and Barbara G. Salmore, *New Jersey Politics and Government: The Suburbs Come of Age* (New Brunswick, NJ: Rutgers University Press, 2013).
6. For a discussion of the research projects organized by Canino (and other department chairs) see chapter 16 by Kathleen López in this volume, and the Department of Puerto Rican Studies Archival Project. Maria Josefa Canino-Arroyo, "Reflections on Latino Advocacy and Welfare Reform in New Jersey," *Centro: Journal of the Center for Puerto Rican Studies* 15, no. 1 (April 2003): 177–195. Publications by these authors include Kal Wagenheim, *New Jersey's Hispanic Population: An Overview of Quality of Life* (1980); Olga Jimenez de Wagenheim, "New Jersey's Puerto Ricans Corralling Their History," *Hispanic Outlook in Higher Education*

(July 4, 2005): 25; Olga Jimenez de Wagenheim, "From Aguada to Dover: Puerto Ricans Rebuild Their World in Morris County, New Jersey, 1948 to 2000," in *The Puerto Rican Diaspora: Historical Perspectives*, ed. Carmen Teresa Whalen and Victor Vázquez-Harnandez (Philadelphia: Temple University Press, 2005), 106–127; Brenda Bell and Hidalgo Hilda, *Puerto Rican Lifestyles and the American Urban Experience: An Update of the Survey of 120 Puerto Rican Families in Newark* (Newark, NJ: Mayor's Policy and Development Office, 1976); Hilda Hidalgo and Joan L. McEniry, *Hispanic Temas: A Contribution to the Knowledge Bank of the Hispanic Community* (Newark, NJ: Puerto Rican Studies Program, Rutgers—The State University of New Jersey, 1985); Hilda Hidalgo, *Lesbians of Color: Social and Human Services* (New York: Haworth Press, 1995); Hilda Hidalgo, *The Puerto Ricans in Newark, N.J.* (Newark, NJ: Aspira, 1971); Gloria Bonilla-Santiago, *Hispanics in New Jersey: A Survey of Women Raising Families Alone* (New Brunswick, NJ: Rutgers University Press, 1988); Gloria Bonilla-Santiago, *Latina Farm Workers and Families in the United States: Breaking Ground and Barriers* (1993); Gloria Bonilla-Santiago, *Organizing Puerto Rican Migrant Farmworkers: The Experience of Puerto Ricans in New Jersey* (New York: P. Lang, 1988); Gloria Bonilla-Santiago, "Puerto Ricans Harvest a Victory," *Progressive* 49, no. 12 (1985): 17–18; Gloria Bonilla-Santiago, *A People in Two Communities: Puerto Ricans on the Island and in the United States* (Washington, DC: National Puerto Rican Coalition, 1992); Gloria Bonilla-Santiago, *Hispanics in New Jersey: A Survey of Women Raising Families Alone* (Newark, NJ: Rutgers University Press, 1988).

7   Yolanda Prieto, *The Cubans of Union City: Immigrants and Exiles in a New Jersey Community* (Philadelphia: Temple University Press, 2009); Eleanor Meyer Rogg and Rosemary Santana Cooney, *Adaptation and Adjustment of Cubans, West New York, New Jersey* (Bronx, NY: Hispanic Research Center Fordham University, 1980); Carmen Teresa Whalen, *From Puerto Rico to Philadelphia: Puerto Rican Workers and Postwar Economies* (Philadelphia: Temple University Press, 2001).

8   Howard Gillette, *Camden after the Fall: Decline and Renewal in a Post-Industrial City* (Philadelphia: University of Pennsylvania Press, 2005); Brad R. Tuttle, *How Newark Became Newark: The Rise, Fall, and Rebirth of an American City* (New Brunswick, NJ: Rivergate Books, 2009); Kevin J. Mumford, *Newark: A History of Race, Rights, and Riots in America* (New York: New York University Press, 2007); Julia Rabig, *The Fixers: Devolution, Development, and Civil Society in Newark, 1960–1990* (Chicago: University of Chicago Press, 2016). See also David Listokin, Dorothea Berkhout, and James W. Hughes, *New Brunswick, New Jersey: The Decline and Revitalization of Urban America* (New Brunswick, NJ: Rutgers University Press, 2016).

9   Yolanda Prieto, *The Catholic Church and the Cuban Diaspora* (Washington, DC: Caribbean Project Center for Latin American Studies, Georgetown University, 2001); Ana Maria Díaz-Stevens, "Postwar Migrants and Immigrants from the Spanish-Speaking Caribbean: Their Impact upon New Jersey Catholic History," *New Jersey History* 113, no. 1/2 (1995): 60–81. See also Larissa Ruiz Baia, "Rethinking Transnationalism: Reconstructing National Identities among Peruvian Catholics in New Jersey," *Journal of Interamerican Studies and World Affairs* 41, no. 4 (1999): 93–109.

10  Maria J. Zarza and Rachel H. Adler, "Latina Immigrant Victims of Interpersonal Violence in New Jersey: A Needs Assessment Study," *Journal of Aggression, Maltreatment and Trauma* 16, no. 1 (2008): 22–39; Nia Parson, Rebecca Escobar, Mariam Merced, and Anna Trautwein, "Health at the Intersections of Precarious

Documentation Status and Gender-Based Partner Violence," *Violence against Women* 22, no. 1 (2016): 17–40; Sandra E. Echeverría, Punam Ohri-Vachaspati, and Michael J. Yedidia, "The Influence of Parental Nativity, Neighborhood Disadvantage and the Built Environment on Physical Activity Behaviors in Latino Youth," *Journal of Immigrant and Minority Health* 17, no. 2 (April 2015): 519–526; Michele Ochsner, Elizabeth Marshall, Lou Kimmel, Carmen Martino, Rich Cunningham, and Ken Hoffner, "Immigrant Latino Day Laborers in New Jersey: Baseline Data from a Participatory Research Project," *New Solutions: A Journal of Environmental and Occupational Health Policy* 18, no. 1 (2008): 57–76; Pauline Garcia-Reid, "Examining Social Capital as a Mechanism for Improving School Engagement among Low Income Hispanic Girls," *Youth and Society* 39, no. 2 (2007): 164–181; Chris Rasmussen, "Creating Segregation in the Era of Integration: School Consolidation and Local Control in New Brunswick, New Jersey, 1965–1976," *History of Education Quarterly* 57, no. 4 (2017): 480–514; Debbie Salas-Lopez, Linda Janet Holmes, Dawne M. Mouzon, and Maria Soto-Greene, "Cultural Competency in New Jersey: Evolution from Planning to Law," *Journal of Health Care for the Poor and Underserved* 18, no. 1 (2007): 35–43.

11  Igda E. Martínez Pincay and Peter J. Guarnaccia, "'It's Like Going through an Earthquake': Anthropological Perspectives on Depression among Latino Immigrants," *Journal of Immigrant Health* 9 (2007): 17–28; Peter J. Guarnaccia, Pilar Parka, Aura Deschamps, Glen Milstein, and Nuri Argiles, "Si Dios Quiere: Hispanic Families' Experiences of Caring for a Seriously Mentally Ill Family Member," *Culture, Medicine and Psychiatry* 16 (1992): 187–215; Peter J. Guarnaccia, Teresa Vivar, Anne C. Bellows, and Gabriela V. Alcaraz, "'We Eat Meat Every Day': Ecology and Economy of Dietary Change among Oaxacan Migrants from Mexico to New Jersey," *Ethnic and Racial Studies* 35, no. 1 (2012): 104–119.

12  The flagship journal of the field is *Latino Studies*. The Center for Puerto Rican Studies' *Centro Journal* and *Aztlan: A Journal of Chicano Studies* are the oldest. For reviews of the history of the field see Pedro A. Cabán, "From Challenge to Absorption: The Changing Face of Latina and Latino Studies," *Centro Journal* 15, no. 2 (Fall 2003): 126–145; Pedro Cabán, "Moving from the Margins to Where? Three Decades of Latino/a Studies," *Latino Studies* 1, no. 1 (March 2003): 5; María E. Pérez y González and Virginia Sánchez Korrol, *Puerto Rican Studies in the City University of New York: The First 50 Years* (New York: Centro Press, 2021). The field also has a good number of surveys and readers: Chon A. Noriega, Eric Avila, Karen Mary Davalos, Chela Sandoval, and Rafael Pérez-Torres, eds., *The Chicano Studies Reader: An Anthology of Aztlán, 1970–2015* (Los Angeles: UCLA Chicano Studies Research Center Press, 2016); Ramon A. Gutiérrez and Tomás Almaguer, *The New Latino Studies Reader: A Twenty-First-Century Perspective* (Oakland: University of California Press, 2016); Ana Y. Ramos-Zayas and Mérida M. Rúa, *Critical Dialogues in Latinx Studies: A Reader* (New York: New York University Press, 2021); Marcelo M. Suárez-Orozco and Mariela Páez, *Latinos: Remaking America* (Berkeley: University of California Press, 2002); Richard Delgado and Jean Stefancic, *The Latino/a Condition: A Critical Reader* (New York: New York University Press, 2011).

13  The literature on Latinos in the United States is now massive, with thousands of monographs and diversity of ways of addressing language, ethnicity, race, and color lines within Latino communities. Historical research has grown the most and displaced studies of culture. Monographs like this one addressing a region or state began in the 1970s and include texts like Ruben Orlando Martinez, *Latinos in the*

*Midwest* (East Lansing: Michigan State University Press, 2011); David A. Badillo, *Latinos in Michigan* (East Lansing: Michigan State University Press, 2003); Debra J. Schleef and H. B. Cavalcanti, *Latinos in Dixie: Class and Assimilation in Richmond, Virginia* (Albany: State University of New York Press, 2009); Andrés Torres, *Latinos in New England* (Philadelphia: Temple University Press, 2006); Heather A. Smith and Owen J. Furuseth, *Latinos in the New South: Transformations of Place* (Burlington, VT: Ashgate, 2006); David E. Hayes-Bautista, *La Nueva California: Latinos in the Golden State* (Berkeley: University of California Press, 2004); Gabriel Haslip-Viera and Sherrie L. Baver, *Latinos in New York: Communities in Transition* (Notre Dame, IN: University of Notre Dame Press, 1996). Some notable textbook-like surveys include Juan González, *Harvest of Empire: A History of Latinos in America* (New York: Penguin Books, 2022). There are also ethnic-group-specific historical surveys: Zaragosa Vargas, *Crucible of Struggle: A History of Mexican Americans from Colonial Times to the Present Era* (New York: Oxford University Press, 2011); Lorrin Thomas and Aldo Lauria-Santiago, *Rethinking the Struggle for Puerto Rican Rights* (New York: Routledge, 2019); Marc S. Rodriguez, *Rethinking the Chicano Movement* (New York: Routledge, 2014).

14 Peter Ramos, "Cultural Identity, Translation, and William Carlos Williams," *MELUS* 38, no. 2 (2013): 89–110; Armando Rendon, "William Carlos Williams: Latino Poet," *Somos en Escrito* 16 (September 2018), https://www.somosenescrito.com/writings-escritos/flashback-william-carlos-williams-latino-poet.

15 The majority of the state's indigenous population are now from countries like Mexico, Guatemala, and Ecuador.

16 Ana Ramos-Zayas's study of Puerto Ricans and Brazilians in Newark is one of the only book-length ethnographies that describes and analyzes intra-Latinx relations in New Jersey, including how these groups imagine one another. See Ana Y. Ramos-Zayas, *Street Therapists: Race, Affect, and Neoliberal Personhood in Latino Newark* (Chicago: University of Chicago Press, 2012). A recent book by Mercy Romero explores the substantial relationships and social life between the vacant lots that make up the largely African American and Puerto Rican Cramer Hill neighborhood in Camden where Romero grew up. See Mercy Romero, *Toward Camden* (Durham, NC: Duke University Press, 2021).

# Part 1
# Spaces and Places

# 1
# Latino New Jersey

## A Demographic and Geographic Portrait

RAYMOND SÁNCHEZ MAYERS,
LYNA L. WIGGINS, ELSA CANDELARIO,
AND LAURA CURRAN

The face of New Jersey is changing. From large cities to small townships, Hispanic retail establishments—restaurants, bodegas, botanicas, and others—line the main streets and business districts of these communities.[1] Latino/a children make up a majority of the public elementary school populations in cities from Camden to New Brunswick to Paterson. Rutgers, the State University of New Jersey, has large Latino/a student bodies on all of its campuses, especially Camden and Newark. Indeed, the Rutgers-Newark campus has a large enough Hispanic student body to be classified as a Hispanic-serving institution of higher learning.[2]

This chapter will explore the extent and diversity of the Latino/a population in New Jersey, including its geographic distribution and some of its demographic characteristics. While a variety of sources have been used in this chapter, for the most part data from the U.S. Decennial Censuses of 1970 to 2020 was used to inform this work. However, at the time of this writing, only limited data from the 2020 census had been released. So, other sources such as the U.S. Census

Bureau's American Community Survey's (ACS) five-year estimates have also been used. However, these data may exclude some of the undocumented Hispanics who live and work in New Jersey.

The Latino population currently comprises the largest minority group in the United States and accounted for 18.7 percent of the U.S. population (approximately 62.1 million people) in the 2020 decennial census.[3] The number of Latinos under eighteen years of age is projected to nearly double by 2060. Interestingly, the United States ranks second in the world in the size of its Hispanic population. Only Mexico, with 128 million persons, has a larger Hispanic population than the United States. U.S. Latinos are highly diverse, and differ based on race, color, language, national origin (representing twenty different countries in Central and South America, the Caribbean, and Spain), generation, and immigration status, among other social, cultural, and economic differences.

## Trends Over Time

Ten states have the largest percentage of Latinos, and New Jersey is one of them, ranking number eight.[4] In 1970, Latinos represented only 4 percent of the New Jersey population with a population of 289,000; this number has been increasing ever since (see figure 1.1). By 1990, there were 740,000 Latinos, representing 10 percent of the population. In 2000, there were over a million Latinos in the state (1.1 million), 13 percent of the state's population. The 2010 census saw an increase to 1.5 million, 18 percent of the population of New Jersey. In 2020, Latinos made up 22 percent of the population of New Jersey, slightly higher than the national average of 19 percent, and representing over two million persons. The cumulative increase from 1970 to 2020 is 594 percent. This expansion is based on the growth in immigration but also second- and third-generation people who are either born in, or move into, the state.

Immigration to New Jersey is an important factor in the growth of the Hispanic population. A very large number of Latinos in New Jersey are foreign-born (42%), while 38 percent were born in New Jersey (see figure 1.2). In the United States as a whole, 34 percent of Latinos are foreign born. While the number of Latinos increased by over a million people in New Jersey between 1980 and 2010, the latest 2020 census figures reflect a slowing pace of new Latino immigrants settling in New Jersey and is the smallest increase since 1980.

New Jersey also has a large number of unauthorized immigrants to the state. It is difficult to ascertain the true number of unauthorized immigrants, mainly because many of them are not likely to respond to census surveys and most of the data come from sample surveys conducted by the U.S. Census Bureau's annual ACS. Be that as it may, estimates have been derived from those persons who have completed the surveys as well as data from the U.S. Office of Immigration Statistics.[5] As of 2018, estimates of the unauthorized population of New Jersey ranged from 425,000 to 460,000.[6] Using the Migration Policy Institute's

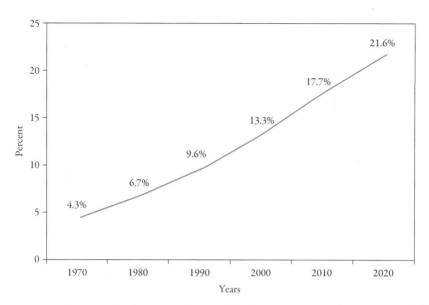

FIGURE 1.1 Changes in the Latino population of New Jersey, 1970–2020. (Sources: Campbell Gibson and Kay Jung, "Historical Census Statistics on Population Totals by Race, 1790 to 1990, and by Hispanic Origin, 1970 to 1990 for the United States, Regions, Divisions, and States." Working Paper No. 56. (Washington DC: U.S. Census Bureau, Population Division, September 2002); Sen-Yuan Wu, "The Changing Face of New Jersey is More Diverse Than Ever," New Jersey Department of Labor and Workforce Development, Labor Market and Demographic Research, NJ Labor Market News, Issue 2, March 22, 2011; U.S. Census Bureau, "2015–2019 ACS 5-Year Estimates." Table C24010I; U.S. Census Bureau, "2020 DEC Census," Redistricting Data (Public Law 94–171) Table P2: Hispanic or Latino and Not Hispanic and Latino by Race, for New Jersey.)

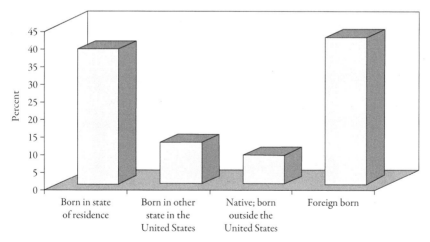

FIGURE 1.2 Place of birth of Latinos in New Jersey. (Source: U.S. Census Bureau, "2015–2019 ACS 5-Year Estimates," Table B06004I, *Place of Birth (Hispanic or Latino) in the United States: New Jersey*, 2021).

estimate of 425,000 unauthorized persons, 42 percent of them were from Mexico, Dominican Republic (7%), Guatemala (7%), and El Salvador (7%). Another 19 percent were from South America.[7] New Jersey has one of the highest overall rates of unauthorized immigrants in its population of all states.

## Current Status

In the 2020 census, the majority of Latinos identified themselves as White (60.1%), while a smaller number (3.9 percent) identify as Black or African American. A sizable group (29.1%) report their race as "Some other race alone," a practice that is growing among Puerto Ricans and second-generation Latinos. Usually, when asked to define this race, they reply "Hispanic" or "Latino."

While a majority of Latinos in the United States are Mexican or Mexican American (>60%), this is not the case in New Jersey and is a reflection of the different immigration histories and migration patterns of Latinos in the state, despite the fact that Mexicans were the fastest growing group in the 2010 period. The largest Latino groups in New Jersey are people who identify as Puerto Ricans, who make up 26.5 percent of the Latino population, South Americans (22%), and Dominicans (16.3%) (see figure 1.3). Of those South Americans, those from Colombia and Ecuador made up the largest number. From a regional perspective, while there are no majority Latino counties as yet, there are approximately twenty cities and towns that are 50 percent or more Latino.

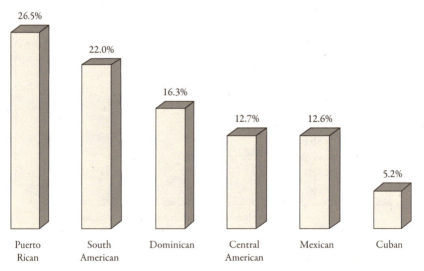

FIGURE 1.3 National origin of Latinos in New Jersey. (Source: U.S. Census Bureau, "2015–2019 ACS 5-Year Estimates," Table B03001. *Hispanic or Latino by Specific Origin*, 2021.)

Latino New Jersey • 15

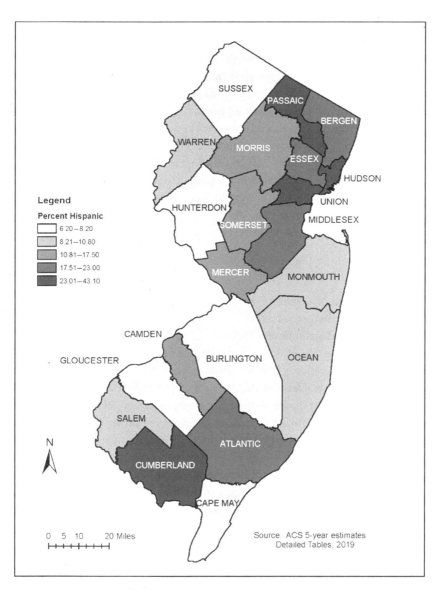

FIGURE 1.4 Percent Hispanic by county, 2019.

However, there are regional differences around the state. As can be seen in figure 1.4, the Latino population ranges from a high of 42.7 percent for Passaic County to a low of 7.3 percent in Gloucester County. Other counties where almost a quarter or more of the population is Latino include Hudson (40%), Cumberland (34%), Union (34%), and Essex (24%). Even within counties, there is clustering of Latino communities in certain towns and cities. So, for example, Perth Amboy in Middlesex County is 78 percent Latino, while Union City in Union County is 76 percent Latino. To the south, Latinos make up 49 percent of the population of Bridgeton in Cumberland County and 51 percent of the population in Camden City, Camden County.[8]

There is also clustering of the various Latino groups by country of origin. For example, 71 percent of Cubans reside in five counties in central and northern New Jersey. Seventy-eight percent of South Americans are clustered in six counties in northern New Jersey, while 70 percent of Central Americans are in six counties in central and northern New Jersey as well. A majority of Dominicans (78%) reside in just four counties in northern New Jersey and one county in the central part of the state. Sixty-one percent of Mexicans are in six counties as well, but more dispersed—two counties in the south, two counties in central New Jersey, and two counties in north New Jersey. Puerto Ricans are the most dispersed, being found in large numbers all over the state, but especially counties in south New Jersey and some northern counties as well (see figures 1.5–1.8).

## Age Patterns

The median age for New Jersey in 2019 for all races and ethnicities was forty years, compared to a median age of thirty-two years old for Latinos. As can be seen in figure 1.9, the age distribution of Latinos and non-Latino Whites and Blacks is very different. For example, 32 percent of Latinos are nineteen years or younger compared to 21 percent for Whites, while 52 percent of non-Hispanic Whites are forty-five years or older compared to only 30 percent for Latinos. Blacks fall in the middle between these two groups. That is, 26 percent of Blacks are under nineteen years of age, and 38 percent of them are over forty-five years of age. Almost twice as many Latino children are under the age of five (9%) as compared to non-Hispanic Whites (5%) and Blacks (6%). School-aged children ages five to nineteen make up 23 percent of Latinos, while non-Hispanic White children comprise 16 percent and Black children 20 percent of that population. Those aged sixty-five years and over are 8 percent of Hispanics compared to 21 percent of non-Hispanic Whites, and 12 percent of Blacks. Clearly, Latinos/as in New Jersey are a younger population.

## Family Structure and Composition

Latinos have higher birth rates than Whites or Blacks. Nationally, the birth rate in 2019 per one thousand population is 9.8 for Whites, 13.4 for Blacks, and 14.6 for Hispanics.[9] The birth rate for Hispanic women in New Jersey in 2019 was similar to the national average, 14.8. However, this varies across the state from a high of twenty live births per one thousand in Mercer and Salem Counties to a low of 10.0 in Sussex County.[10] Interestingly, in only two counties did other groups exceed the birth rate of Hispanic women. In Hudson County, Whites and Asians exceeded the Hispanic birth rate, while in Sussex County, Blacks and Asians had higher birth rates. These differences may be due to the settlement

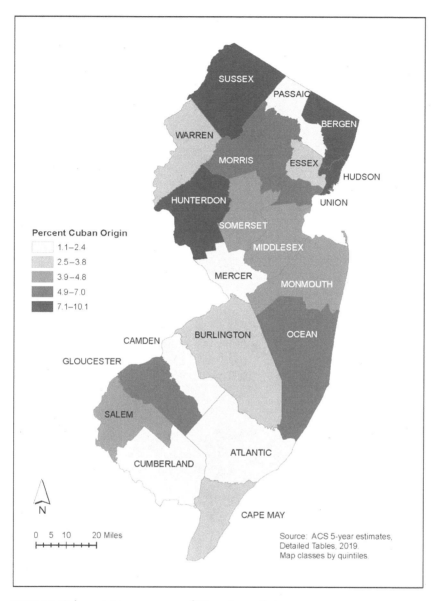

FIGURE 1.5 Cuban origin as percentage of Hispanic population.

patterns of the varying Latino groups in the state as birth rates may differ among the various Latino groups. Overall, Hispanic women do have higher birth rates than other racial/ethnic groups. In 2019, 28 percent of all births in the State of New Jersey were to Hispanic women.[11]

One area of concern is teen pregnancy rates. While teen pregnancy rates have been declining for decades, they still remain high for Hispanic young women in New Jersey. For non-Hispanic White females aged fifteen to seventeen years

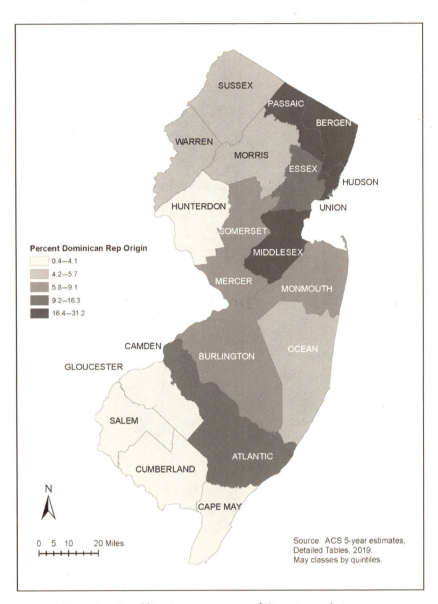

FIGURE 1.6  Dominican Republic origin as percentage of Hispanic population.

old, the birth rate per one thousand in 2019 was less than one (.07) and for Black females the rate was 6.6, while for Hispanic females of the same age the birth rate was 10.8. This is viewed as a public health issue because children born to teen mothers are at higher risk for poor birth outcomes.[12]

Hispanics are less likely to be married than the general New Jersey population. Forty-five percent of Hispanic males over the age of fifteen years have never been married compared to 37 percent of New Jersey males over the age of fifteen years

Latino New Jersey • 19

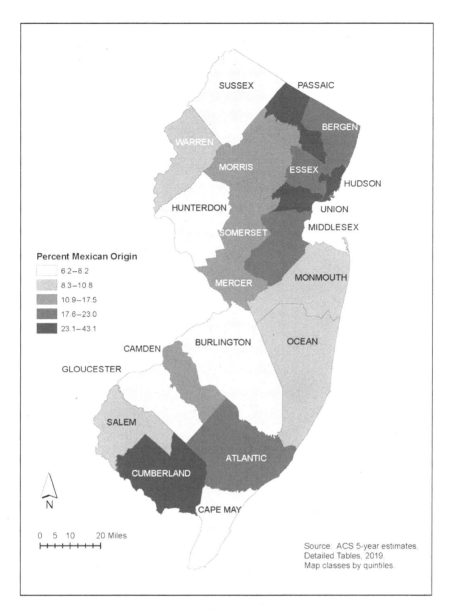

FIGURE 1.7  Mexican origin as percentage of Hispanic population.

(see table 1.1). And 39 percent of Hispanic females over age fifteen years have never been married compared to 31 percent of New Jersey females. Forty-four percent of Hispanic males are married compared to 52 percent of all New Jersey males over age fifteen years. Fewer Hispanic females are married, 40 percent, compared to 47 percent for all New Jersey females. While only a small percentage of the total, more Hispanic males and females are separated than the general New Jersey population. And more Hispanic females are divorced than any other group.[13]

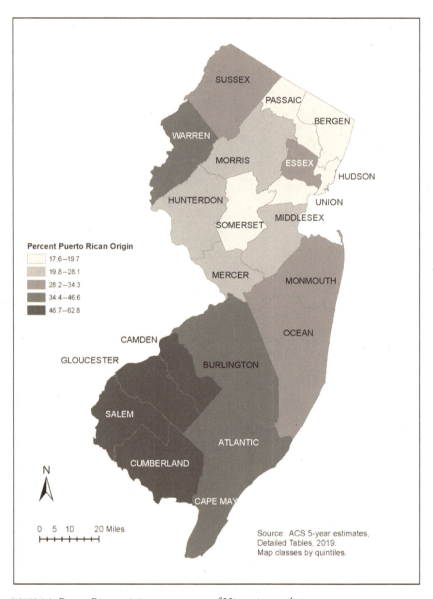

FIGURE 1.8  Puerto Rican origin as percentage of Hispanic population.

## Education and Employment

As a whole, Hispanics in New Jersey tend to be less educated than non-Hispanic Whites and Blacks. Of most concern is the fact that about 27 percent of males and 24 percent of females have less than a high school diploma (see table 1.2). Fifteen percent have less than nine years of schooling. Thus, about a fourth of Hispanics over the age of twenty-five years are lacking this basic credential. Hispanic males

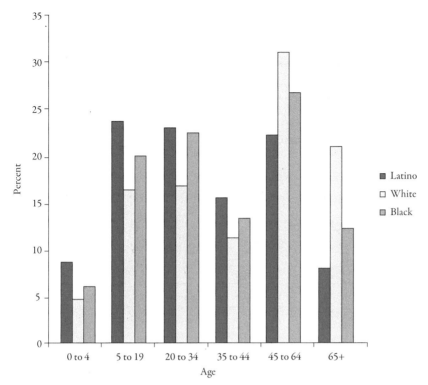

FIGURE 1.9 Age distribution of Latinos, Whites, and Blacks in New Jersey, 2019. (Source: U.S. Census Bureau, "2015–2019 ACS 5-Year Estimates," Table B01001B, *Sex by Age (Black or African American Alone)*, 2021; U.S. Census Bureau, "2015–2019 ACS 5-Year Estimates," *Sex by Age (Hispanic or Latino)*, Table B01001I, 2020k; *Sex by Age (White Alone, Not Hispanic or Latino)*, 2021).

and females are on par with Whites in having some college or associate's degrees, but lag behind both Whites and Blacks with bachelor's or higher degrees. In addition to less educational attainment, Hispanics also have higher school dropout rates, although this varies by sex as well as country of origin.

While still higher than most other groups, the dropout rate for Hispanics fell nationally from 2010 to 2019 from 16.7 to 7.7 percent.[14] The rates for sex differ, as the rate for Hispanic males is 9 percent and for females 6 percent. The rates for native-born and foreign-born Hispanics differ as well. Foreign-born students are much more likely to drop out of school (17%) versus native-born students (6%). The three highest dropout rates are for Guatemalans (20%), Hondurans (18%), and Salvadorans (12%).[15] In New Jersey, the dropout rate for Hispanics overall in 2018 was 8 percent compared to 5 percent for Blacks and 2 percent for Whites.

Immigrants come to the United States mostly motivated by work opportunities and also because of their age characteristics. Hispanics in the labor force

Table 1.1
Marital status of New Jersey Hispanics and general New Jersey, population over fifteen years of age

|  | Hispanics (%) | New Jersey (%) |
|---|---|---|
| Male: |  |  |
| Never married | 45.1 | 37.0 |
| Now married (except separated) | 44.1 | 52.1 |
| Separated | 2.6 | 1.5 |
| Widowed | 1.3 | 2.6 |
| Divorced | 6.9 | 6.8 |
| Female: |  |  |
| Never married | 39.0 | 31.4 |
| Now married (except separated) | 40.3 | 47.2 |
| Separated | 4.1 | 2.1 |
| Widowed | 5.4 | 9.2 |
| Divorced | 11.1 | 10.1 |

SOURCES: U.S. Census Bureau, "2015–2019 ACS 5-Year Estimates," Table B12001; U.S. Census Bureau, "2015–2019 ACS 5-Year Estimates," Table B12002I.

Table 1.2
Educational attainment for the population, twenty-five years and over—New Jersey, 2019

|  | Hispanic | White, non-Hispanic | Black or African American |
|---|---|---|---|
| Label | % | % | % |
| Male: | (N = 539.035) | (N = 1,732,065) | (N = 360,161) |
| Less than high school diploma | 27.1 | 5.9 | 12.5 |
| High school diploma, includes equivalency | 33.8 | 26.2 | 37.6 |
| Some college or associate's degree | 22.1 | 23.1 | 28.3 |
| Bachelor's degree or higher | 17.0 | 44.8 | 21.6 |
| Female: | (N = 549,907) | (N = 1,887,077) | (N = 433,187) |
| Less than high school diploma | 24.1 | 5.6 | 11.3 |
| High school diploma, includes equivalency | 30.1 | 27.9 | 30.9 |
| Some college or associate's degree | 24.1 | 23.1 | 31.3 |
| Bachelor's degree or higher | 21.7 | 43.5 | 26.5 |

SOURCE: U.S. Census Bureau, "2015–2019 ACS, 5-Year Estimates," Table C15002B, Sex by Educational Attainment for the Population 25 Years and Over (Black or African American Alone); U.S. Census Bureau, "2015–2019 ACS, 5-Year Estimates," Table C15002I, Sex by Educational Attainment for the Population 25 Years and Over (Hispanic or Latino); U.S. Census Bureau, "2015–2019 ACS, 5-Year Estimates," Table C15002H, Sex by Educational Attainment for the Population 25 Years and Over (White Alone, Not Hispanic or Latino).

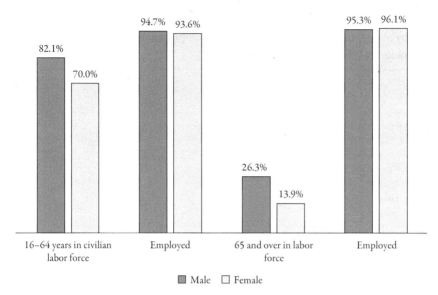

FIGURE 1.10 Employment status of Hispanics in New Jersey, 2019. (Source: U.S. Census Bureau, "2015–2019 ACS, 5-Year Estimates," Table C23002I. *Sex by Age by Employment Status for the Population 16 Years and Over (Hispanic or Latino)*, 2021).

in New Jersey have high rates of employment. Eighty-two percent of Hispanic males and 70 percent of Hispanic females between the ages of sixteen and sixty-four years are in the civilian labor force. Of those, more than 90 percent are employed (see figure 1.10). The unemployment rate is low both for males (5.3%) and females (6.4%). Of Hispanics over the age of sixty-five years, there is a high rate of labor force participation for males especially. Twenty-six percent of males over sixty-five years old are in the labor force as are 14 percent of Hispanic females. Of those Hispanic seniors, both males and females have employment rates of around 95 percent.

As would be expected given the gendered nature of work, Hispanic males and females predominate in different occupations. More females are in management, business, science, and arts occupations, service occupations, and sales and office occupations. Twenty-nine percent of Hispanic women are in management, business, science, and the arts (see table 1.3). Within this category, large numbers are in management, education, and health care. Twenty-eight percent are in service occupations, mainly healthcare support, food preparation, buildings and grounds cleaning and maintenance, and personal care. Of the 28 percent in sales and office occupations, most are in office and administrative support. Another 14 percent are in production or material moving occupations.

Twenty-seven percent of Hispanic males are in production, transportation, and material-moving occupations. These occupations include factory work,

**Table 1.3**
**Sex by occupation for the Hispanic civilian employed population sixteen years and older in New Jersey**

|  | Male (%) (N = 498,747) | Female (%) (N = 418,784) |
|---|---|---|
| Management, business, science, and arts occupations | 20.7 | 28.8 |
| Service occupations | 19.2 | 27.8 |
| Sales and office occupations | 11.3 | 28.2 |
| Natural resources, construction, and maintenance occupations | 22.0 | 0.8 |
| Production, transportation, and material moving occupations | 26.8 | 14.4 |

SOURCE: U.S. Census Bureau, "2015–2019 ACS, 5-Year Estimates," Table C24010I.

delivery truck drivers, passenger vehicle drivers, and others. Twenty-two percent of Hispanic males are in construction and maintenance occupations compared to less than 1 percent for Hispanic females. These occupations include (besides construction) installation, maintenance, and repair. Twenty-one percent of males are in management, business, science, and arts occupations, many in management, computer science, and engineering. In the service occupations, many Hispanic males are in food preparation and serving, and building and grounds cleaning and maintenance.

## Income

Partly due to their educational status as well as immigration status, Hispanics make less than the median income in both New Jersey and the United States in general. For example, the median income for the Unites States in 2015–2019 was $62,843. New Jersey is a high-income state, so the median income was higher, $82,545.[16] The median income for Hispanics during this period was $57,068. Among non-Hispanic Whites, Blacks, and Asians in New Jersey, only Blacks made less than Hispanics, and Asians made more than twice as much as Hispanics. In fact, Asians had the highest median income of any group in New Jersey.

Not only do 50 percent of Latino households make less than $58,000, a high number of them also live in poverty. For example, the poverty rate in New Jersey in 2019 was 10 percent, for non-Hispanic Whites, 8 percent, while the poverty rate for Latinos was 18 percent.[17] There is an even sharper contrast when we look at childhood poverty rates. The poverty rate for children under five years of age in New Jersey was 16 percent, lower than the national average of 20 percent in 2019. However, for Latino children under five years old, the poverty rate was 25 percent. This means that one in four Latino children are living in poverty in New Jersey. Only non-Hispanic Blacks have a slightly higher poverty rate.

## Health Insurance Status

Most Hispanics in New Jersey are covered by health insurance, and this is particularly true for those under nineteen years of age. This may be due to social insurance programs such as the Children's Health Insurance Program, which covers children under the age of eighteen years. For those in this age group, 94 percent of Hispanic children are covered by health insurance, very similar to the rates for White and Black children. The same is true for those over the age of sixty-five years. Over 95 percent of Hispanic elderly, non-Hispanic Whites, and Blacks are covered by some form of health insurance such as Medicare or Medicaid. The difference lies in the age group nineteen to sixty-four years old, many of whom are in the labor force. Only 74 percent of Hispanics in this age category are covered by health insurance. This may be because they work in low-wage jobs that do not offer insurance or, because of their immigration status, do not qualify for Medicaid.

## Conclusion

As we have discussed in this chapter, Latinos are a large and growing population in New Jersey. Many different Latin American and Caribbean countries of origin are represented in the state, with large numbers of Puerto Ricans, Mexicans, Dominicans, Central and South Americans clustered in various areas. The educational attainment of Hispanics is less than non-Hispanic Whites; however, the dropout rate for Hispanics has decreased dramatically over the last twenty years. More Hispanics are going on to higher education; however, there are still a number of immigrants with low levels of education, that is, less than high school diplomas. They often work in low-wage jobs, which contributes to the high poverty level of Hispanics. Large Latino populations, with large percentages of immigrants means that bilingual Spanish/English-speaking workers, such as teachers, nurses, doctors, other health personnel, social workers, and others, will be in high demand to serve this population.

## Notes

1   The term "Hispanic" was first used in the 1970 decennial census. Prior to that, questions were asked regarding country of origin. In 1997, the federal government, through the U.S. Office of Management and Budget, issued revisions to the Standards for Classification of Federal Data on Race and Ethnicity. This mandated how Hispanics would be defined by all official government agencies and is the basis for the current Census Bureau definition for Latino or Hispanic. The Census Bureau defines Latino or Hispanic as "a person of Cuban, Mexican, Puerto Rican,

South or Central American, or other Spanish culture or origin, regardless of race." Notice that this definition does not include Brazilians or other ethnic groups of Central or South America who are not of Spanish origin. As the Office of Management and Budget mandates these terms, the U.S. Census Bureau follows their use. So, in this chapter we will use the two terms, Hispanic and Latino, interchangeably. Office of Management and Budget, Office of Information and Regulatory Affairs, "Revisions to the Standards for the Classification of Federal Data on Race and Ethnicity. Federal Register, 62 (210), Thursday, October 30, 1997," 58782–58790.

2 "A Hispanic-Serving Institution (HSI) is defined as an institution of higher education that—(A) is an eligible institution; and (B) has an enrollment of undergraduate full-time equivalent students that is at least 25 percent Hispanic students at the end of the award year immediately preceding the date of application." U.S. Department of Education, White House Hispanic Prosperity Initiative, "Hispanic Serving Institutions: Biden–Harris Administration Awards More Than $40 Million to Support Hispanic-Serving Institutions," September 21, 2023, https://sites.ed.gov/hispanic-initiative/hispanic-serving-institutions-hsis/.

3 U.S. Census Bureau, "2020 DEC Census Redistricting Data (Public Law 94-171)." Table P2, Hispanic or Latino, and Not Hispanic and Latino by Race. Last modified December 8, 2021. https://data.census/gov/table?g=010XX00US$0400000&y=2020&d=DEC+Redistricting+Data_(PL+94-171)&tid=DECENNIALPL2020.p2.

4 U.S. Census Bureau, "2020 DEC Census."

5 Bryan Baker, *Estimates of the Unauthorized Immigrant Population Residing in the United States January 2015—January 2018*. (Washington, DC: Department of Homeland Security, Office of Immigration Statistics, January 2021), www.dhs/gov/immigration-statistics.

6 Migration Policy Institute, "Profile of the Unauthorized Population: New Jersey," accessed 2019, www.migrationpolicy.org/data/unauthorized-immigrant-population/state/NJ#; Baker, *Estimates of the Unauthorized Immigrant Population*.

7 Migration Policy Institute, "Profile of the Unauthorized Population."

8 U.S. Census Bureau, "Quick Facts, Hispanic or Latino Origin for the United States, Regions, Divisions, States, and for Puerto Rico: 2000."

9 Joyce A. Martin, Brady E. Hamilton, Michelle J. K. Osterman, and Anne K. Driscoll, "Births: Final Data for 2019," *NCHS National Vital Statistics Reports* 70, no. 2 (March 23, 2021).

10 New Jersey Department of Health, "New Jersey State Health" 2021, https://www-doh.state.nj.us/doh-shad/indicator/view/AgeSpecBirthRate.RE.html.

11 Martin et al., "Births: Final Data for 2019."

12 New Jersey Department of Health, "New Jersey State Health Assessment Data," 2021, https://www.doh.state.nj.us/doh-shad/indicator/summary/TeenBirths.html.

13 U.S. Census Bureau, "2015–2019 ACS 5-Year Estimates," Table B12001. Sex by Marital Status for the Population 15 Years and Over. Last modified December 8, 2021, https://data.census.gov/cedsci/table?q+Hispanics%20New%20Jersey&tid=ACSDT5Y2019.B12001&hidePreview+true.

14 Veronique Irwin, Jijun Zhang, Xiaolei Wang, Sarah Hein, Ke Wang, Ashley Roberts, Christina York, Amy Barmer, Farrah Bullock Mann, Rita Dilig, and Stephanie Parker, *Report on the Condition of Education 2021* (NCES 2021-144). (Washington, DC: U.S. Department of Education, National Center for Education Statistics, 2021), https://nces.ed.gov/pubsearch/pubsinfo.asp?pubid=2021144.

15 Cristobal DeBrey, Thomas D. Snyder, Anlan Zhang, and Sally A. Dillow, *Digest of Education Statistics 2019* (NCES 2021–009). (Washington, DC: National Center

for Education Statistics, Institute of Educational Sciences, U.S. Department of Education, February 2021), Table 219.82.

16 Gloria Guzman, *Household Income by Race and Hispanic Origin: 2005–2009 and 2015–2019, American Community Survey Briefs* (Washington DC: U.S. Census Bureau, ACSBR-007, December 2020).

17 U.S. Census Bureau, "2015–2019 ACS 5-Year Estimates," Table B17001B, Poverty Status in the Past 12 Months by Sex by Age (Hispanic or Latino), https://data.census.gov/cedsci/table?g=0400000US34&tid=ACSDT5Y2019.B17001B&hidePreview=true. U.S. Census Bureau, "2015–2019 ACS 5-Year Estimates," Table B17020I, Poverty Status in the Past 12 Months by Sex by Age (Hispanic or Latino), https://data.census.gov/cedsci/table?q=poverty%20status%20hispanic%20new%20jersey&tid=ACSDT5Y2019.B17020I&hidePreview=true; U.S. Census Bureau, "2015–2019 ACS 5-Year Estimates," Table B17001H, Poverty Status in the Past 12 Months by Sex by Age (White Alone, Not Hispanic or Latino), https://data.census.gov/table?q=B17001H&g=040XX00US34&tid=ACSDT5Y2019.B17001H.

# 2
# Latino Segregation across New Jersey Counties

Are Latino Groups Becoming More or Less Residentially Segregated during the Last Four Decades?

GIOVANI BURGOS, ALEX F. TRILLO, AND ANIL VENKATESH

The previous chapter details the unprecedented growth of the Latino population in New Jersey. One of the most striking patterns is that every county in the state has experienced a notable increase in the Latino population from the year 2010 to 2020 with at least some representation for all ten of the largest Latino ethnic groups in the region.[1] These demographic shifts include significant growth in urban, suburban, and rural areas coupled with an expectation that the Latino population in all counties will continue to grow through the year 2030.[2] Such rapid demographic changes raise important research questions and inspire fierce public debates about the integration, or lack thereof, of minority groups into the dominant White society.

As the Latino population grows, there is an uptick in the rhetoric about the benefits of *ethnic diversity* across the United States and the assumption that the

United States is an integrated society.[3] For instance, in a recent NBC news article that highlights the latest 2020 Census findings, the vice president of UnidosUS states that the "increase in diversity the data show is the source of the nation's strength."[4] In a similar spirit, the U.S. Census Bureau website highlights increased ethnic diversity in their advertisement for the 2020 Census redistricting data.[5] However, a key drawback of such framing is that it equates diversity with integration and ignores a large body of work on residential segregation. The segregation literature reveals that Latinos are becoming more residentially segregated from non-Hispanic Whites (hereafter Whites), more isolated, and less integrated in some places. And where segregation levels decrease, the drops are slight, at best, and continue to be high. As we discuss below, diversity and segregation are two very different processes and it is important to differentiate between the two terms.[6] If Latinos in the United States are becoming more segregated, then it might be premature to celebrate the nation's diversity.

The distinction between diversity and segregation is crucial given that segregation stems from past and present acts of discrimination in the housing market.[7] On the one hand, these exclusionary acts of discrimination tend to solidify social and economic disadvantages in minority communities. On the other hand, widespread housing discrimination ensures systematic advantages in the neighborhoods where Whites live.[8] Perhaps, not surprisingly, segregation has been called the "structural linchpin" of racial stratification.[9]

Unfortunately, we know little about how segregation levels have changed over time and across New Jersey counties among Latinos of different ethnic backgrounds. This dearth of county and subethnic research is unfortunate given that counties better reflect housing markets and determine the disbursement of goods and services.[10] Because segregation is considered an important social determinant of life chances in the United States, documenting these trends in Latino population dynamics contributes to our understanding of racial and ethnic inequality, and the life prospects of Latino ethnic groups in New Jersey, more specifically.[11]

This chapter has three overarching goals. First, we explain what segregation is and why it is important to study. This includes an introduction to the Racialized Place Inequality Framework (RPIF), which is a multilevel theoretical model that can help trace the connections between residential segregation and limited life chances of racialized groups and individuals.[12] Second, we use census data to answer the following research questions: Has Latino segregation from Whites in New Jersey increased or decreased over the last forty years (1980–2020)? In which New Jersey counties has Latino segregation increased or decreased during this time period? And what are the changes in segregation levels during this same time span for the largest Latino ethnic groups across the state and in each county? Third, we chart a course for future research, and highlight how the RPIF can be used to inform the study of Latino segregation in New Jersey and beyond.

Our broader concern is with understanding how racism can harm Latino life chances and well-being.

## Background: What Is Residential Segregation?

Segregation represents the unequal distribution of Whites and minorities living in a specified geographical area, such as counties, cities, states, or metropolitan areas. In general, census tracts are commonly used to create measures called segregation indices, which capture the levels of integration in a larger geographic area, such as a county, state, or metropolitan area.[13] For instance, when racial (i.e., African Americans, Asian Americans, Native Americans) and racialized ethnic minorities (e.g., Hispanics, Puerto Ricans, Mexicans) share a large geographic area (e.g., county) with Whites, but reside in separate neighborhoods (i.e., tracts) from Whites, the area is considered highly segregated. Conversely, an area is viewed as integrated (or to have low levels of segregation) when minorities live in the same neighborhoods as Whites. In the segregation literature, a common proxy for neighborhoods is census tracts. Census tracts are small, numbered subdivisions within each county that do not cross county boundaries. On average, census tracts encompass several blocks of houses, contain about 4,000 individuals, and range from a minimum of 1,200 to a maximum of 8,000 people.[14]

The most common measure of segregation, the *dissimilarity index*, is calculated by contrasting the population of each census tract with the overall population of the larger geographic unit in which the tracts reside, such as a city, county, state, or metropolitan area. When calculated across tracts within counties, each county receives its own segregation score. In the state of New Jersey, for example, there are twenty-one counties (see figures 2.1 and 2.2) and a segregation score can be computed for each county. We can thus assess whether Hudson County is more segregated than its neighboring Union County, or any other county in New Jersey, or the United States. It is important to note that segregation is a structural characteristic of place and not an attribute of individuals. In this chapter, we present segregation indices for each of the twenty-one New Jersey counties. We will return to this point below, to explain how living in segregated places can shape minority experiences and limit life chances.

Segregation scholars have identified at least five dimensions of segregation and over two dozen measures or indices of segregation.[15] For brevity, we explain the two dimensions that are most common and that appear in our analysis: *evenness* and *exposure*. Evenness represents the differential distribution of groups (such as Latinos and Whites) across neighborhood units (e.g., census tracts) in an area such as a county. If the distribution of Whites and Latinos in each census tract is the same as the distribution across the entire county, the county unit is integrated, or not segregated. Conversely, if the distribution of the two groups in many of the census tracts is different from the distribution of these groups across the entire county, the county is considered segregated. Evenness takes on its

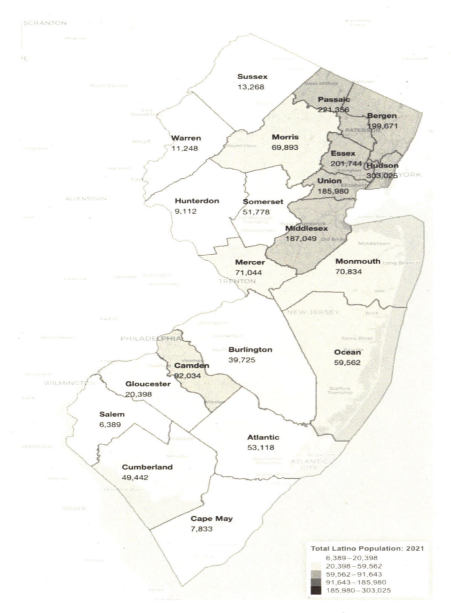

FIGURE 2.1 Total Latino population in New Jersey counties, 2017–2021. (Source: American Community Survey Data)

largest value when, for instance, Latinos and Whites live in separate census tracts within a county. A detailed explanation and graphical representation of these dimensions is provided by Iceland et al. and it is publicly available online.[16]

The most widely used measure of evenness is the index of dissimilarity, which varies from zero (no/low segregation) to one (perfect or extremely high

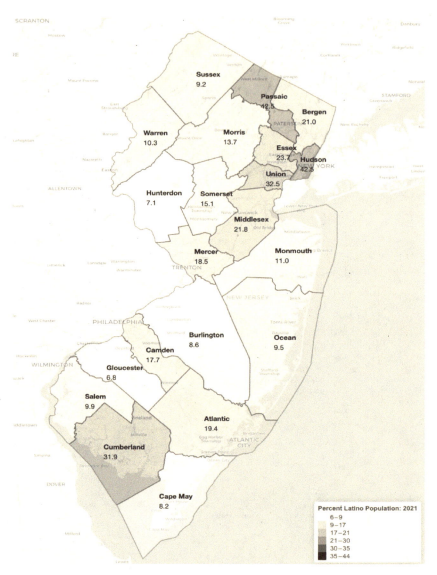

FIGURE 2.2  Percent Latino population in New Jersey counties, 2017–2021. (Source: American Community Survey Data)

segregation). Segregation indices can be reported in decimal form or as a multiple of one hundred. Thus, a segregation score of 60 percent and 0.60 are equivalent and the decision on how to present the score is made by the researcher. On average, many counties in the United States have dissimilarity scores between fifty and one hundred for African Americans and Latinos, two of the most segregated groups. Conceptually, dissimilarity scores represent the proportion of minority group members that need to move within a county so that every census tract has the same proportion of Latinos as the county as a whole. Thus, a dissimilarity value of 0.61 means that 61 percent of Latinos would need to move from their tract so that each tract has the same representation of Latinos as the whole county.

The second most common dimension of segregation is exposure, which represents the likelihood that Latinos and Whites in a given area, for example, would come into contact with members of the same group or a different group. There are two common measures of exposure. The *exposure index* captures the probability that Latinos will come into contact with Whites in a particular area, while the *isolation index* captures the likelihood that Latinos will come into contact with other Latinos of the same group, as opposed to Whites, in their neighborhoods. Both indices range from zero to one. Higher values on the isolation index represent higher segregation, because minorities are more likely to be isolated from Whites or more exposed to each other.

While there is no consensus as to what constitutes high levels of segregation, scholars use the term *hypersegregation* to describe a group that has a high score on multiple dimensions of segregation. Denton notes that the original criteria for categorizing areas as hypersegregated was 0.6 for indices of evenness and 0.7 for isolation.[17]

## Why Study Segregation: The RPIF

Segregation has been described as the lynchpin of American race relations because it results from systemic acts of discrimination in the housing market that solidify racial and ethnic inequalities onto the geographical spaces where racialized minorities live.[18] Before the passage of the Fair Housing Act of 1968, housing discrimination was widely practiced with impunity in the South under the Jim Crow laws that separated Whites from non-Whites in housing, education, marriage, and healthcare, among other institutional arrangement.[19] These boundaries were at times enforced in violent ways.[20] Known as *de jure segregation* (Latin for "derived from law") Jim Crow laws affected Latinos as well and those considered non-White.

Outside the South, Whites found creative ways to maintain separation from non-Whites through a set of housing discrimination practices known as *de facto segregation* (i.e., as matter of fact or practice, but not law). De facto discriminatory behaviors largely occurred through habits and customs, including implicit and explicit biases in the selling, and renting, of homes.[21] Some of the more egregious kinds of de jure and de facto segregation were central to the suburbanization process that took hold in the United States in the 1940s. From racially restrictive covenants that prevented selling homes to African Americans, to the *redlining* process that either refused bank loans to folk

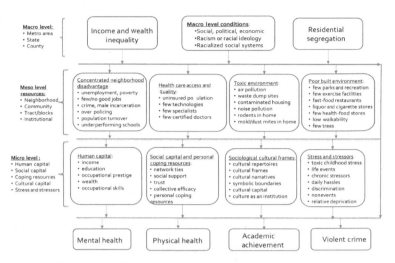

FIGURE 2.3 The Racialized Place Inequality Framework.

living in neighborhoods with Black residents, to banks disproportionately giving minorities subprime loans that increased the chances of foreclosure, these acts of discrimination and exclusion still affect where racial groups live today and even account for intergenerational racial wealth gaps.[22] These inequalities are further exacerbated by contemporary real estate practices where realtors steer minorities away from White neighborhoods.[23] Many municipalities have zoning ordinances in place that preclude the building multifamily units, which disincentivizes developers from building affordable housing that minorities can afford in White areas.[24] And banks continue to provide substandard and predatory loans to vulnerable minorities, which makes stable homeownership precarious.[25]

What are the implications of these practices of de jour and de facto segregation? The RPIF is theoretically and analytically useful for answering this question.[26] The RPIF (figure 2.3) is a multilevel model that captures how structural characteristics of places affect experiences and life chances such as the health of individuals, the academic achievement of students, and the propensity of people to engage in violent behavior. The basic idea behind the RPIF is that residential segregation is a macro-level indicator of racism that sets into motion systemic advantages for some groups (usually Whites) and disadvantages for others (often African Americans and Latinos). The disadvantages include, but are not limited to, neighborhood conditions, such as poor air quality, high rates of violence, lack of school resources, lack of access to quality health care, and poor built environment. Segregation indirectly can affect human capital (i.e., the skills and credentials individuals accumulate), their social capital and personal coping resources (e.g., social support networks and information brokers that residents come in contact with, and the sense of self-efficacy one has), cultural frames of how groups and individuals respond to local institutional conditions, and stress, including feelings of relative deprivation and experiences with discrimination.

## Research on Latino Segregation Patterns

So, what do we know about segregation and particularly Latino residential segregation thus far? For New Jersey, there is a dearth of research at the county level across time. Most studies either examine segregation for the state as a whole, include New Jersey as part of a larger metropolitan area, or examine just a limited slice of metro areas within the state. For example, Acevedo-Garcia reports persistent and moderately high segregation for Latinos across multiple metropolitan areas such as Atlantic City, Newark-Elizabeth, Paterson–Clifton–Passaic, Camden, the Newark suburbs, Jersey City, and Trenton for 1980 and 1990.[27] Crowder confirms hypersegregation vis-à-vis Whites for Puerto Ricans, Cubans, Mexicans, South Americans, and Central Americans at the New York/New Jersey metropolitan area level, in 1990.[28] Although informative, this body of work does not address the time period (1980–2021), level of analyses (county), or ethnic group detail we explore in this chapter. While some scholars argue that Latino residential segregation is decreasing, our review of the literature reveals a more nuanced scenario, given the growth and dispersion of the Latino population.

First, traditional studies that examine segregation at the metropolitan area level show that dissimilarity scores for Latinos have remained in the moderate to high range between 1970 and 2010.[29] When using measures of exposure, these same studies still show that Latino segregation is steady, or even increasing.[30]

Second, Latino segregation patterns differ based on geography, which is noteworthy given the dispersion of Latinos across many different parts of the country, including the recent trend of Latinos settling in the suburbs, and the increasing ethnic diversity of the Latino population. Researchers find that hypersegregation is common in larger and rapidly growing metro areas with greater levels of income inequality and in the deindustrialized towns of the Northeast and Midwest.[31] These demographic shifts have resulted in the growth of multiple Latino hubs throughout the Northeast region, which often began as Puerto Rican industrial enclaves, then transformed into postindustrial mixed Latino communities that are sustained by local service economies that serve ethnic communities, proximity to suburban sprawl service economies, and proximity to larger urban centers.[32]

Third, current trends in employment opportunities and White housing preferences further shape Latino segregation patterns in suburbs and other new frontiers. Gentrification lures one segment of White families from the older suburbs into urban centers, while another segment of White families pushes further into suburban sprawl and the newer *exurbs*. Meanwhile, more middle-class employment opportunities are also moving to the suburbs and exurbs, inspiring a service economy and demands for more workers.[33]

Finally, demographic characteristics that proxy for structural inequalities also affect segregation scores. For example, places with large Latino populations that have greater shares of undocumented residents have higher levels of segregation, as do populations with larger numbers of Black Latino members.[34] And, of the few studies contrasting Latino subgroups, one found decreases in dissimilarity scores for Mexicans, Cubans, and Puerto Ricans between 1980 and 2010, and for Dominicans and Salvadorans only between 2000 and 2010.[35] However, all 2010 dissimilarity scores were still exceptionally high for each group, while several groups experienced a decrease in interaction scores between 1980 and 2010. This includes Mexicans, who make up 75 percent of the Latino population. The Martin study we referenced earlier finds that segregation is thus greatest in the Northeast and Midwest postindustrial towns, but less for groups like Mexicans concentrated in the west, and for Cubans concentrated in South Florida.[36]

## Implications for New Jersey?

While studies focusing on segregation in New Jersey are quite limited, the literature suggests several patterns for New Jersey. One possibility is that the outward movement of Latinos into other parts of New Jersey reflects a classic spatial assimilation process and integration with Whites. This would mean that Latino movement into the outer counties should result in declining segregation. Some suburban and exurban counties might show persistent or increasing levels of segregation that are associated with White flight from those counties. One possible type of destination fitting this scenario are the older, deindustrialized and semi-industrialized hubs, some of which were already Latino enclaves.[37] Examples include Perth Amboy in Middlesex County, Patterson in Passaic County, and Bridgeton in Cumberland County. Another possibility is that Latinos are finding opportunities in economically declining suburbs where housing is more affordable. As gentrification in cities and suburban sprawl out to the exurbs continues to inspire a White flight out of the older, smaller homes built in the 1940s and 1950s, these worn suburbs become an affordable alternative to gentrifying cities and other land grabs of valuable real estate. Such movement into the suburbs and other outer areas is fueled by the emergence of self-sustaining suburban enclaves that provide job opportunities, the emergence of service economies that serve the more affluent suburban residents, proximity to the bigger cities, and the relocation of good paying jobs to suburbs.[38]

Finally, New Jersey's Latino population is more ethnically diverse than most states. Each group's unique history and the nature of their migration means that ethnic group differences are also a rough proxy for differences in race, class, citizenship status, time and context of arrival, and the geographic locations they have access to. Thus, while we expect Latinos as a whole to experience some challenges in accessing White communities, we also expect some ethnic group variation in the process, and in segregation levels across the state and across counties. For example, groups like Cubans and Colombians with greater class and racial privileges should be able to access more towns and neighborhoods in Bergen County. Therefore, it is possible that segregation among Cubans and Colombians is decreasing. Dominicans are more racially visible and tend to migrate with less economic resources. Consequently, segregation levels might be increasing among Dominicans. Mexicans and Central Americans are more likely to be undocumented—or face stereotypes about being undocumented—and may also be limited to enclaves that offer a safe haven, which may lead to increasing levels of discrimination for these groups and high levels of segregation.

## Data and Methods

We use two sources of data in this chapter from the U.S. Census Bureau. The first data come from the 1980–2010 Decennial Censuses, which collected large amounts of demographic information including individuals' racial background (e.g., Black, White, Asian) and ethnic background (e.g., Dominican, Mexican, Peruvian). The counts of Latinos can be documented for the whole nation, down to smaller geographical areas, such as states, counties (e.g., Hudson, Camden), and census tracts.[39] Researchers can then determine, for example, how many Latinos live in the United States, in New Jersey, Hudson County, or a census tract. For the 1980, 1990, 2000, and 2010 Censuses, we use data from Summary File 1.

Our second set of data come from the 2017–2021 American Community Surveys.[40] Unlike the Decennial Census, the five-year American Community Survey data are based on representative samples aggregated over five years. This technique produces estimates of the whole population that are more precise with a smaller margin of error than the yearly samples for a large array of social and demographic variables including race and ethnicity.

It is important to note some minor data details produced by the way census data collection has evolved. From the 1980 and 1990 Censuses, our data contains census tracts counts for Mexicans, Puerto Ricans, Cubans, Dominicans, other Spanish or Hispanic, and non-Hispanic Whites. Starting in the year 2000, the Census Bureau expanded its data collection efforts to include other Latino groups from Central America and South America. We calculate segregation indices for the different Central American groups, including people from Costa Rica, Guatemala, Honduras, Nicaragua, Panama, and El Salvador. For South Americans, we include indices for Latinos from Argentina, Bolivia, Chile, Colombia, Ecuador, Paraguay, Peru, Uruguay, and Venezuela. We consider our findings exploratory until the 2020 Census data are fully released.

We use two of the most common measures of segregation, namely the index of dissimilarity ($D$) and the isolation index ($xPx$).[41] In the calculation of our indices, Whites serve as the comparison group. The index of dissimilarity is a measure of evenness.[42] Evenness is maximized, and segregation is minimized, when every census tract has the same relative number of Latinos and Whites as the county as a whole.[43] $D$ takes on its largest value of one when Latinos and Whites do not have census tracts in common within a county, and it takes on a value zero when every tract has the same relative number of Latinos and Whites as the county as a whole.[44] The dissimilarity score is interpreted as the percentage of Latinos that would have to move census tracts for each tract to have the same percentage of Latinos as the whole county. For instance, a Latino–White dissimilarity index of 0.80 indicates that 80 percent of Latinos would need to move tracts to obtain parity with their county representation, and so on.

Our second measure of segregation is the isolation index.[45] Isolation is a measure of exposure and is interpreted as the probability that Latinos share a census tract with other Latinos. It ranges from zero, or low segregation, to one, high segregation. As Massey and Denton note, isolation "measures the extent to which minority members are exposed to one other, rather than to majority members" and "attempt to measure the experience of segregation as felt by the average minority" person.[46]

We use these two measures since they each have limitations. Whereas $D$ is sensitive to small population sizes and produces indices that are biased upward (i.e., estimates tend to be inflated), isolation is sensitive to the size of the minority population.[47] An area like a county can have low levels of dissimilarity, whereby Latinos and Whites are evenly distributed across neighborhoods but have little interaction with each other.[48] This can happen in a scenario where there is a large minority population. Note, however, that in figure 2.4 we focus on the dissimilarity index only because of space limitations.

## Results

To answer the question of how segregation has changed from 1980 to 2019 across New Jersey counties for Latinos as a whole, we begin by ranking the counties on White–Latino dissimilarity scores from the most segregated to the least segregated, relative to other counties in the state. Figure 2.4 categorizes counties that dropped at least one position in rank from 1980 to 2021 (left panel), counties that moved up the rankings in dissimilarity by at least one point (center panel), and counties that are within one point during this entire time period, or stable counties (right panel).

One of the most interesting patterns to emerge from figure 2.4 is that county ranks in dissimilarity are dynamic and change over the years. For instance, among the counties that fell in rank, Camden ranked number one in dissimilarity from 1980 to the year 2000. In 2010 and 2021, Camden dropped two spots and became the third highest ranking county, only to be overtaken by Passaic and Essex Counties starting in 2010. In the middle panel of figure 2.4, meanwhile, counties such as Salem, Somerset, Bergen, and Hunterdon, have seen dramatic increases in their relative dissimilarity ranking. In 1980, Salem County ranked

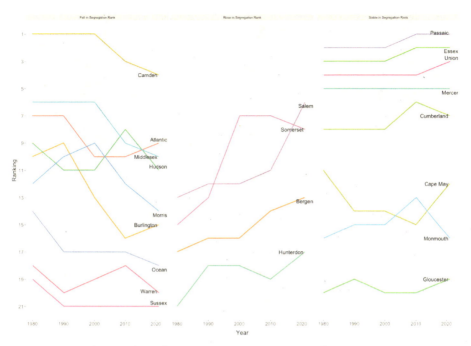

FIGURE 2.4 Relative ranking of New Jersey counties on Latino–White segregation (dissimilarity scores), 1980–2021.

thirteenth in dissimilarity in 1980 but, by 2021, it ranked sixth. Somerset County ranked fifteenth in 1980 and it now occupies the eighth most segregated county rank. Bergen county ranked seventeenth in 1980 and ranks thirteenth in 2021. These shifts in rank, especially in counties where the exurbs are located, indicate that Latinos are a population on the suburban move where housing is more affordable.

Figure 2.4, however, does not tell us if segregation is increasing or decreasing, it just captures how counties rank in comparison to each other over the years. In figures 2.5 and 2.6, we look at more precise changes in dissimilarity and isolation scores, respectively. We group the counties under the same scheme as those found in figure 2.4, or counties that fell in rank, those that increased in rank, and stable in rank counties. Which counties have experienced increases or decreases in segregation?

In terms of dissimilarity, figure 2.5 shows that among the counties that dropped in rank, dissimilarity levels trended downward, except for Sussex and Warren Counties. The reason Warren County fell in rank in figure 2.5, is because of the slight decreases in segregation from 2010 to 2021. Among the counties that increased in rank (center panel) from 1980 to 2019, figure 2.5 reveals dissimilarity levels increased over the forty-year period for Bergen, Hunterdon, Salem, and Somerset Counties. And among the counties that had stable rank (right panel),

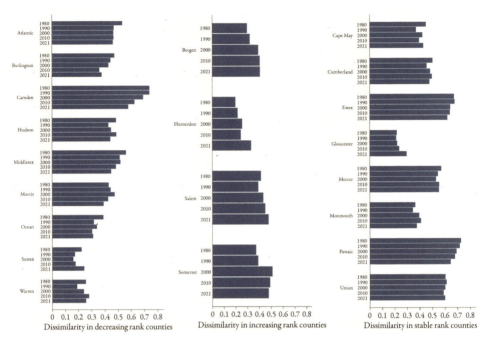

FIGURE 2.5  Dissimilarity across New Jersey counties, 1980–2021, categorized by county change in ranking.

figure 2.5 also shows that dissimilarity levels are relatively stable. In general, counties that are moving up in rank on dissimilarity are also experiencing increases in dissimilarity. On the left panel of figure 2.5, there are two possibilities for why segregation might be decreasing: Whites are gentrifying neighborhoods closer to Philadelphia and New York, and Latinos are moving to the outer suburbs in search of more affordable housing. Some Black and Latino families are pushed out.

When we look at isolation levels in figure 2.6, a different picture emerges. The overall trend across all counties is that Latinos are becoming more isolated. These increases in isolation over time are consistent with those found in our literature review above and are not surprising. As the Latino population significantly grows in a county with small Latino populations, isolation levels are also expected to increase, indicating they are congregated in the same neighborhoods within a county. This appears to be the case in places like Burlington, Warren, Sussex, and Gloucester. In the counties with more Latinos, like Passaic, Middlesex, Union, and Hudson, the isolation scores were high, but also increased. This also suggests that the Latino population is growing in these counties in the same neighborhoods.

In figures 2.7 to 2.10, we examine how dissimilarity levels have changed for Latinos of different ethnic backgrounds from 1980 to 2021. Data collection for Central and South Americans and Dominicans began in the year 2000.

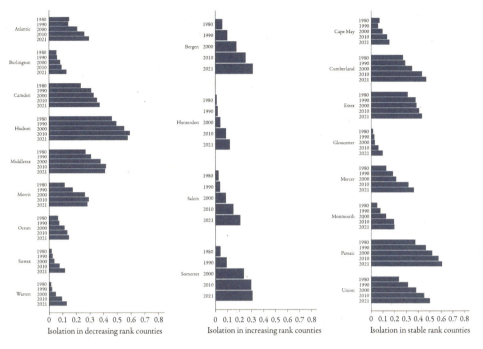

FIGURE 2.6 Isolation across New Jersey counties, 1980–2000, categorized by county change in ranking.

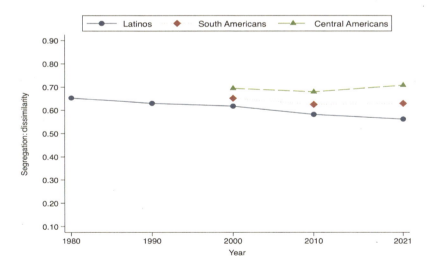

FIGURE 2.7 Segregation (dissimilarity) levels for all Latinos, South Americans, and Central Americans in New Jersey, 1980–2021.

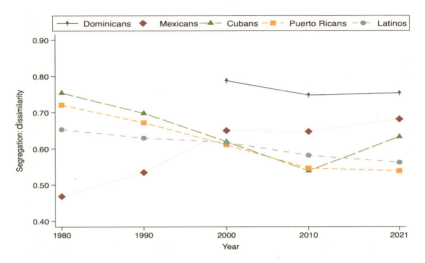

FIGURE 2.8 Segregation (dissimilarity) levels for all Latinos, Caribbean Latinos, and Mexicans in New Jersey, 1980–2021.

Figure 2.7 shows dissimilarity for the pan-ethnic groups Latinos, South Americans, and Central Americans. For Latinos as a whole, there has been about an eight-point drop in dissimilarity between 1980 and 2021. Still, the dissimilarity levels remain high among Latinos. Among Central and South Americans, dissimilarity slightly increased from 2010 to 2021. Figure 2.8 reveals that dissimilarity levels for Dominicans, Mexicans, and Cubans are on the rise in New Jersey from 2010 to 2021, after dropping consistently from 1980 to the year 2010. For Puerto Ricans, dissimilarity scores steadily decreased from 1980 to 2010 and are holding steady between 2010 and 2021. Figures 2.9 and 2.10 show dissimilarity levels for Central Americans and South Americans. Both figures reveal an initial drop in dissimilarity from 2000 to 2010, but a rapid increase in dissimilarity from 2010 to 2021. Overall, dissimilarity levels are increasing from 2010 to 2021 for every group, except Puerto Ricans.

In figure 2.11 to 2.14, we replicate the same analysis but look at the isolation index. Taken as a whole, these figures show that between 1980 and 2021, isolation levels have increased for Latinos, South Americans, Central Americans (figure 2.11), Dominicans and Mexicans (figure 2.12), all Central American groups (figure 2.13), and all South American Groups (figure 2.14). Isolation levels only decreased for Puerto Ricans and Cubans between 1980 and 2010, but we observed a slight increase in isolation for Puerto Ricans and Cubans between 2010 and 2021 (figure 2.12).

Taken as a whole, from 1980 to 2021, we observe increases in isolation level for most Latino groups, except for Puerto Ricans and Cubans. As noted above, isolation indices are sensitive to the size of the Latino population. One of the

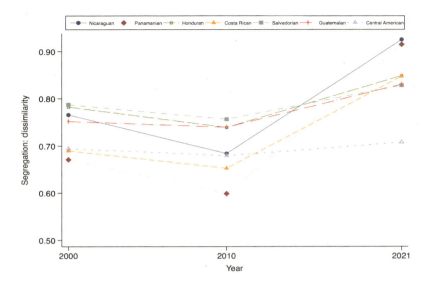

FIGURE 2.9  Segregation (dissimilarity) levels for Central Americans in New Jersey, 2000–2021.

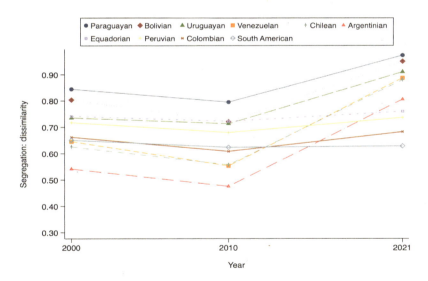

FIGURE 2.10  Segregation (dissimilarity) levels for South Americans in New Jersey, 2000–2021.

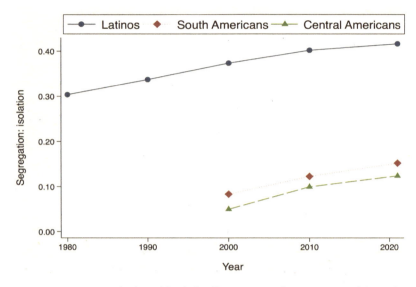

FIGURE 2.11  Segregation (isolation) levels for all Latinos, South Americans, and Central Americans in New Jersey, 1980–2021.

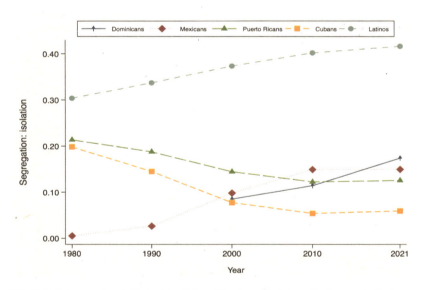

FIGURE 2.12  Segregation (isolation) levels for all Latinos, Caribbean Latinos, and Mexicans in New Jersey, 1980–2021.

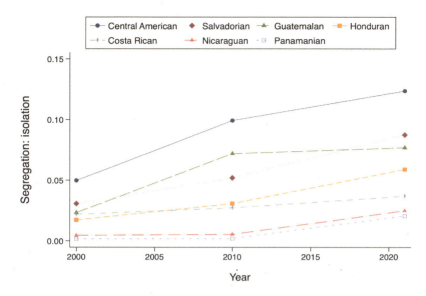

FIGURE 2.13 Segregation (isolation) levels for Central American groups in New Jersey, 2000–2021.

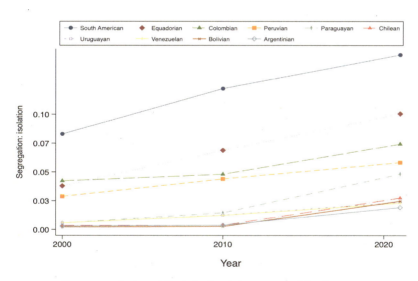

FIGURE 2.14 Segregation (isolation) levels for South Americans in New Jersey, 2000–2021.

## Table 2.1
## Total Latino population in New Jersey counties, 1980–2021

| County | 1980 population | 1990 population | 2000 population | 2010 population | 2021 population | Percent change 1980 vs. 2021 |
|---|---|---|---|---|---|---|
| Atlantic | 7,590 | 16,117 | 30,729 | 46,241 | 53,118 | 600 |
| Bergen | 28,514 | 49,776 | 91,377 | 145,281 | 199,671 | 600 |
| Burlington | 8,658 | 12,819 | 17,632 | 28,831 | 39,725 | 359 |
| Camden | 20,626 | 36,022 | 49,166 | 73,124 | 92,034 | 346 |
| Cape May | 1,190 | 1,855 | 3,378 | 6,054 | 7,833 | 558 |
| Cumberland | 12,525 | 18,348 | 27,823 | 42,457 | 49,442 | 295 |
| Essex | 76,584 | 97,777 | 122,347 | 159,117 | 201,744 | 163 |
| Gloucester | 2,407 | 4,131 | 6,583 | 13,712 | 20,398 | 747 |
| Hudson | 145,163 | 183,465 | 242,123 | 267,853 | 303,025 | 109 |
| Hunterdon | 908 | 1,732 | 3,371 | 6,722 | 9,112 | 904 |
| Mercer | 10,580 | 19,665 | 33,898 | 55,318 | 71,044 | 571 |
| Middlesex | 34,138 | 59,776 | 101,940 | 148,975 | 187,049 | 448 |
| Monmouth | 12,915 | 22,407 | 38,175 | 60,939 | 70,834 | 448 |
| Morris | 10,952 | 19,814 | 36,626 | 56,482 | 69,893 | 538 |
| Ocean | 8,444 | 13,950 | 25,638 | 47,783 | 59,562 | 605 |
| Passaic | 62,123 | 98,092 | 146,492 | 185,677 | 221,356 | 256 |
| Salem | 1,005 | 1,436 | 2,498 | 4,507 | 6,389 | 536 |
| Somerset | 4,080 | 10,187 | 25,811 | 42,091 | 51,778 | 1,169 |
| Sussex | 1,764 | 2,911 | 4,822 | 9,617 | 13,268 | 652 |
| Union | 40,756 | 67,797 | 103,011 | 146,704 | 185,980 | 356 |
| Warren | 961 | 1,784 | 3,751 | 7,659 | 11,248 | 1,070 |
| Total | 491,883 | 739,861 | 1,117,191 | 1,555,144 | 1,924,503 | 11,333 |

SOURCES: U.S Census Bureau, 1980 to 2010 U.S. Decennial Censuses; U.S Census Bureau, "American Community Survey 2017–2021 5-Year Data Release," December 8, 2022. https://www.census.gov/newsroom/press-kits/2022/acs-5-year.html.

reasons we see such dramatic increases in isolation levels is the astronomical growth in the Latino population in every county, as revealed in chapter 1 and also captured in table 2.1. Notice that between 1980 and 2021, the percent change in each county grew by more than 100 percent. Table 2.1 reveals that whereas the Latino population grew by 109 percent in Hudson County between 1980 and 2021, it grew by 1,070 percent in Warren County.

To examine more detailed segregation patterns by group and county, tables 2.2 to 2.4 show percent change in segregation levels between 2000 and 2021. We report changes for counties with one thousand or more Latinos, as larger populations produce more reliable estimates. Table 2.2 shows the changes in dissimilarity and isolation for Latinos, Mexicans, Puerto Ricans, and Cubans. Table 2.3 shows dissimilarity results for Dominicans and Central Americans, and table 2.4 captures dissimilarity changes for South American groups. Column 2 of table 2.2 reveals that among the Latino category, the pattern is mixed, with some counties showing lower levels of dissimilarity in 2021 than in 2000,

## Table 2.2
### Percent change in dissimilarity and isolation for largest Latino groups in New Jersey, 2000 vs. 2021 change

| | Dissimilarity % Change | | | | Isolation % Change | | | |
|---|---|---|---|---|---|---|---|---|
| County | Latinos | Mexican | Puerto Rican | Cuban | Latino | Mexican | Puerto Rican | Cuban |
| Atlantic | −0.94 | 6.57 | 0.53 | 0.00 | 41.87 | 41.87 | 19.97 | 0.00 |
| Bergen | 3.71 | 42.89 | 19.10 | 35.16 | 77.67 | 77.67 | 116.09 | 99.29 |
| Burlington | −12.03 | 53.25 | −3.34 | 0.00 | 57.16 | 57.16 | 66.99 | 0.00 |
| Camden | −16.10 | 11.58 | −16.68 | 0.00 | 13.33 | 13.33 | −18.15 | 0.00 |
| Cape May | 1.61 | 0.00 | 7.16 | 0.00 | 59.77 | 0.00 | 28.94 | 0.00 |
| Cumberland | −1.23 | −4.34 | −7.68 | 0.00 | 34.28 | 34.28 | 11.16 | 0.00 |
| Essex | −3.41 | 6.86 | −6.04 | 9.49 | 12.09 | 12.09 | −26.91 | 81.33 |
| Gloucester | 34.37 | 0.00 | 28.39 | 0.00 | 212.20 | 0.00 | 185.93 | 0.00 |
| Hudson | −1.22 | 1.05 | −3.82 | −4.80 | 4.60 | 4.60 | −2.85 | −17.85 |
| Hunterdon | 30.11 | 0.00 | 37.58 | 0.00 | 187.12 | 0.00 | 118.77 | 0.00 |
| Mercer | 4.41 | 20.37 | −2.85 | 0.00 | 69.86 | 69.86 | 11.53 | 0.00 |
| Middlesex | −13.84 | −7.87 | −16.65 | 71.62 | 9.04 | 9.04 | −21.93 | 156.49 |
| Monmouth | −4.97 | 12.55 | 1.90 | 127.53 | 55.70 | 55.70 | 26.08 | 515.19 |
| Morris | −17.69 | 21.66 | 2.65 | 174.69 | 6.60 | 6.60 | 1.85 | 601.76 |
| Ocean | −8.57 | 3.91 | 5.34 | 146.57 | 29.09 | 29.09 | 43.96 | 473.39 |
| Passaic | −6.88 | 0.10 | −10.65 | 40.36 | 16.53 | 16.53 | −20.81 | 467.23 |
| Salem | 10.26 | 0.00 | −3.73 | 0.00 | 136.45 | 0.00 | 89.45 | 0.00 |
| Somerset | −6.34 | 18.57 | 13.97 | 152.71 | 30.57 | 30.57 | 92.51 | 349.33 |
| Sussex | 51.68 | 0.00 | 62.23 | 0.00 | 201.07 | 0.00 | 222.80 | 0.00 |
| Union | −0.37 | 19.70 | −2.59 | −12.07 | 30.92 | 30.92 | 6.18 | −3.34 |
| Warren | 7.02 | 0.00 | 18.21 | 0.00 | 160.84 | 0.00 | 215.35 | 0.00 |

NOTE: Cells with 0.00 do not have a reliable sample size (≤ 1,000 minority group per county) and results are omitted.

such as Atlantic (−0.94), Burlington (−12.03), Camden (−16.10), Middlesex (−13.81), among others. Table 2.2 also shows that isolation levels increased across the board with some exceptions. Puerto Ricans became less isolated in Camden (−18.15), Essex (−26.91), Hudson (−2.85), Middlesex (−21.93), and Passaic (−20.81) Counties. Cubans only a decrease in isolation in Hudson (−17.85) and Union (−3.34) Counties. These findings highlight the importance of disaggregating the data by ethnicity, moving away from the widespread practice of ethnic lumping, and aggregating the analyses level at larger geographical levels, such as states and metropolitan areas.

Table 2.3 shows dissimilarity scores for Dominicans and Central Americans, and table 2.4 shows dissimilarity scores for South Americans. Turning to table 2.3, Dominicans experienced decreases in dissimilarity in Middlesex (−17.8) and Passaic (−2.2) Counties. In almost every county, Central Americans experience increases in dissimilarity between 2000 and 2021. The patterns are more mixed

## Table 2.3
### Percent change in dissimilarity for Dominicans and Central Americans in New Jersey counties, 2000 vs. 2021

| County | Dominican | Central American | Costa Rican | Guatemalan | Honduran | Nicaraguan | Panamanian | Salvadorian |
|---|---|---|---|---|---|---|---|---|
| Atlantic | 3.75 | -3.19 | 0.00 | 0.00 | 0.00 | 0.00 | 0.00 | 0.00 |
| Bergen | 9.59 | 14.70 | 0.00 | 4.06 | 0.00 | 0.00 | 0.00 | 21.24 |
| Burlington | 0.00 | 4.89 | 0.00 | 0.00 | 0.00 | 0.00 | 0.00 | 0.00 |
| Camden | 0.10 | 0.63 | 0.00 | 0.00 | 0.00 | 0.00 | 0.00 | 0.00 |
| Cape May | 0.00 | 0.00 | 0.00 | 0.00 | 0.00 | 0.00 | 0.00 | 0.00 |
| Cumberland | 0.00 | 0.00 | 0.00 | 0.00 | 0.00 | 0.00 | 0.00 | 0.00 |
| Essex | 0.83 | 9.90 | 0.00 | 19.94 | 0.00 | 0.00 | 0.00 | 7.01 |
| Gloucester | 0.00 | 0.00 | 0.00 | 0.00 | 0.00 | 0.00 | 0.00 | 0.00 |
| Hudson | 0.23 | 12.53 | 0.00 | 39.99 | 21.18 | 0.00 | 0.00 | 12.37 |
| Hunterdon | 0.00 | 0.00 | 0.00 | 0.00 | 0.00 | 0.00 | 0.00 | 0.00 |
| Mercer | 0.00 | -1.23 | 0.00 | 5.09 | 0.00 | 0.00 | 0.00 | 0.00 |
| Middlesex | -17.80 | 12.74 | 0.00 | 0.00 | 8.42 | 0.00 | 0.00 | 10.44 |
| Monmouth | 0.00 | 16.76 | 0.00 | 0.00 | 0.00 | 0.00 | 0.00 | 0.00 |
| Morris | 0.00 | 13.04 | 0.00 | 0.00 | 6.41 | 0.00 | 0.00 | 0.00 |
| Ocean | 0.00 | 0.00 | 0.00 | 0.00 | 0.00 | 0.00 | 0.00 | 0.00 |
| Passaic | -2.20 | 2.02 | 30.95 | 0.00 | 0.00 | 0.00 | 0.00 | 0.00 |
| Salem | 0.00 | 0.00 | 0.00 | 0.00 | 0.00 | 0.00 | 0.00 | 0.00 |
| Somerset | 0.00 | 0.65 | -0.98 | 0.00 | 0.00 | 0.00 | 0.00 | 0.00 |
| Sussex | 0.00 | 0.00 | 0.00 | 0.00 | 0.00 | 0.00 | 0.00 | 0.00 |
| Union | 2.96 | 7.80 | 45.93 | 13.15 | 8.15 | 0.00 | 0.00 | 5.99 |
| Warren | 0.00 | 0.00 | 0.00 | 0.00 | 0.00 | 0.00 | 0.00 | 0.00 |

NOTE: Cells with 0.00 do not have a reliable sample size (≤1,000 minority group per county) and results are omitted.

## Table 2.4
### Percent change in dissimilarity for South Americans in New Jersey counties, 2000 vs. 2021

| County | South American | Argentinian | Bolivian | Chilean | Colombian | Ecuadoran | Paraguayan | Peruvian | Uruguayan | Venezuelan |
|---|---|---|---|---|---|---|---|---|---|---|
| Atlantic | 15.90 | 0.00 | 0.00 | 0.00 | 11.20 | 0.00 | 0.00 | 0.00 | 0.00 | 0.00 |
| Bergen | −3.66 | 82.80 | 0.00 | 0.00 | 3.73 | 14.72 | 0.00 | 20.88 | 0.00 | 0.00 |
| Burlington | 0.00 | 0.00 | 0.00 | 0.00 | 0.00 | 0.00 | 0.00 | 0.00 | 0.00 | 0.00 |
| Camden | 0.00 | 0.00 | 0.00 | 0.00 | 0.00 | 0.00 | 0.00 | 0.00 | 0.00 | 0.00 |
| Cape May | 0.00 | 0.00 | 0.00 | 0.00 | 0.00 | 0.00 | 0.00 | 0.00 | 0.00 | 0.00 |
| Cumberland | 0.00 | 0.00 | 0.00 | 0.00 | 0.00 | 0.00 | 0.00 | 0.00 | 0.00 | 0.00 |
| Essex | 4.14 | 0.00 | 0.00 | 0.00 | 28.48 | 3.25 | 0.00 | 10.62 | 0.00 | 0.00 |
| Gloucester | 0.00 | 0.00 | 0.00 | 0.00 | 0.00 | 0.00 | 0.00 | 0.00 | 0.00 | 0.00 |
| Hudson | 6.50 | 30.92 | 0.00 | 50.56 | 0.02 | 17.70 | 0.00 | 20.35 | 0.00 | 0.00 |
| Hunterdon | 0.00 | 0.00 | 0.00 | 0.00 | 0.00 | 0.00 | 0.00 | 0.00 | 0.00 | 0.00 |
| Mercer | 10.97 | 0.00 | 0.00 | 0.00 | 0.00 | −2.68 | 0.00 | 0.00 | 0.00 | 0.00 |
| Middlesex | 11.82 | 0.00 | 0.00 | 0.00 | 37.43 | 46.41 | 0.00 | 15.10 | 0.00 | 0.00 |
| Monmouth | 56.09 | 0.00 | 0.00 | 0.00 | 78.38 | 0.00 | 0.00 | 0.00 | 0.00 | 0.00 |
| Morris | −17.75 | 0.00 | 0.00 | 0.00 | −9.99 | 0.01 | 0.00 | 0.00 | 0.00 | 0.00 |
| Ocean | 34.55 | 0.00 | 0.00 | 0.00 | 0.00 | 0.00 | 0.00 | 0.00 | 0.00 | 0.00 |
| Passaic | −9.84 | 0.00 | 0.00 | 0.00 | −3.83 | 4.29 | 0.00 | −6.71 | 0.00 | 0.00 |
| Salem | 0.00 | 0.00 | 0.00 | 0.00 | 0.00 | 0.00 | 0.00 | 0.00 | 0.00 | 0.00 |
| Somerset | −12.24 | 0.00 | 0.00 | 0.00 | −1.95 | −15.52 | 0.00 | 0.00 | 0.00 | 0.00 |
| Sussex | 0.00 | 0.00 | 0.00 | 0.00 | 0.00 | 0.00 | 0.00 | 0.00 | 0.00 | 0.00 |
| Union | 0.57 | 0.00 | 0.00 | 0.00 | 3.11 | 7.82 | 0.00 | 5.26 | 15.16 | 0.00 |
| Warren | 0.00 | 0.00 | 0.00 | 0.00 | 0.00 | 0.00 | 0.00 | 0.00 | 0.00 | 0.00 |

NOTE: Cells with 0.00 do not have a reliable sample size (≤ 1,000 minority group per county) and results are omitted.

for South Americans in table 2.4 and we will leave it up to the reader to explore those patterns.

## Conclusion

In the late 1960s, a group of African Americans in Mount Laurel, New Jersey—a small agricultural town outside Philadelphia in Burlington County—organized against new zoning ordinances that would have prevented Blacks from staying in Mount Laurel and newcomer minorities from moving in. The council's intent was to maximize property tax revenue by making the area more attractive to affluent Whites. Among the tools they used was the adoption of ordinances and zoning restrictions on the building of townhomes, multifamily, and mobile home units that had the potential to make housing affordable for African Americans and other racialized minorities and facilitate desegregation.[49]

The outcome of African American pushback and civil rights organizing on new development guidelines was the 1975 Mount Laurel Doctrine in which the New Jersey Supreme Court found these discriminatory practices unconstitutional.[50] To date, this doctrine is considered one of the most seminal decisions since *Brown v. Board of Education* in that it prohibits exclusionary zoning practices that discriminate against the poor and minorities by states and municipalities. While the doctrine was aimed at economic discrimination, civil rights proponents and the court understood that racial and ethnic minorities tend to be economically poorer due to structural racism, and so the doctrine would help efforts to desegregate towns and cities by both class and race.[51]

Yet, despite this law and many other legal battles, our results affirm that residential segregation continues to be a typical feature of Latino life in New Jersey.[52] Statewide, we observed that isolation levels have increased in every county in New Jersey between the post-Jim Crow 1980s and the contemporary colorblind diversity epoch of 2021. And, as the Latino population has spread across the different counties of the state, Latinos of every ethnicity continue to experience increasing levels of isolation in almost every county.

Although the results were mixed when we measured segregation using the index of dissimilarity, they do not paint a rosy and optimistic picture for the future either. We found that dissimilarity levels between Whites and Latinos increased in four counties from 1980 to 2021 (Bergen, Hunterdon, Salem, and Somerset) as captured in figure 2.5. In counties that had stable levels of segregation over this time span, most had moderately high (above 0.3) or high (above 0.5) levels of dissimilarity (Cape May, Cumberland, Essex, Gloucester, Mercer, Monmouth, Passaic, and Union). Even among counties that saw dissimilarity levels drop between 1980 and 2021 in figure 2.5 for Latinos (Atlantic, Burlington, Camden, Hudson, Middlesex, Morris, Ocean, Sussex, and Warren), dissimilarity levels remain moderately high or high. These high levels of segregation are not indicative, in our opinion, of spatial assimilation. This is especially the case since we also found isolation and dissimilarity levels increasing since 2010 for almost all Latino ethnic groups.

In line with past studies, our findings suggest that geographic factors, such as population size of the counties and the existence of postindustrial towns, contribute to persistent segregation. Our data show that larger, more populated counties have consistently moderate to high segregation scores, even where there are slight dips. Passaic and Hudson Counties are examples, the latter of which has slightly decreased only because of the influx of White middle-class residents that have displaced minority residents.

In the counties with smaller, outer industrial towns, or hubs, Latinos are likely congregated away from Whites. This might be in places with long-standing Latino communities such as Perth Amboy in Middlesex County, or Dover in Morris County. In both cases, Latinos are relegated to marginalized parts of the county, or parts that have become more desirable in the gentrification process. By disaggregating the Latino umbrella (i.e., pan-ethnic) category, we also learned that not all groups are experiencing segregation in the same way. From 1980 to 2010, Cuban and Puerto Rican segregation was on the decline, though neither group fell below the moderate level of segregation, and isolation slightly increased from 2010 to 2021 for both groups. Newer data since 2010 show that segregation for groups from Central and South America begins and remains at very high levels, even for those we assume to have more race and class privileges. At the same time, Mexican segregation has consistently inched upward across all counties from 1980 to 2021. These patterns point to the limitations of the Mount Laurel Doctrine, which has undergone several modifications since 1975 and continues to face hostile resistance from New Jersey Republicans and Democrats alike. They also send a sign of caution that the Latino experience in New Jersey is vulnerable to the negative implications of residential segregation and related aspects of social inequality.

Given the uncertain future of desegregation efforts and the sobering result of our descriptive analysis, we conclude this chapter by highlighting directions for future research and some recommendations on how to apply our findings to contemporary social problems. At the forefront of our research is a concern for how segregation can impact Latino well-being. Here we try to spell out some of the connections.

First, and foremost, it is important to continue documenting levels of segregation across different geographical units. Most studies document segregation levels across metropolitan areas. Our research offered a more geographically refined analysis of counties. But even our assessment pushes us to think about census tracts vis-à-vis cities, towns, or even zip codes. As Pinto-Coelho and Zurberi show, a place can appear diverse and integrated at the city level, but this does mean that all groups have the freedom to reside in all parts of that city.[53] Such divides inevitably lead to disparate experiences in terms of local resources. Our hunch is that places like Passaic and Bergen Counties register as being increasingly segregated because the Latino populations continue to grow, but only have access to particular towns like Patterson or Hackensack, while White residents go further out into the more exclusive suburbs. It is also possible that there are divides within Paterson and Hackensack that exacerbate the disparities.

Second, and to our broader point, it is critical to examine how segregation affects the life chances and well-being of racialized minorities, including Latinos. Most studies that document segregation levels across metropolitan areas note that it is important to study segregation because people living in segregated areas may be at a systematic disadvantage when compared to people living in more integrated places. The first task at hand is to trace the pathways through which segregation, along with other forms of structural inequalities, limit the life chances of individuals.

As we highlighted in figure 2.3, the RPIF is a multilevel model that can be used to theoretically examine how segregation affects the prospects of communities and individuals. This model considers segregation as a macrostructural characteristic of place, that can be measured at the metropolitan, state, and county levels.[54] For example, counties with higher levels of segregation increase the chances that minorities live in neighborhoods with social and economic disadvantage, poor access to health care, toxic environments, and poor built environment at the mesolevel of analyses. In turn, people living under those conditions have lower levels of human capital, social capital, and higher levels of stress. Segregation also impacts people's understanding of the world and how they deal with adversity through cultural understanding and cultural frames—more on this below. Through these mechanisms, directly and indirectly, segregation negatively impacts the mental health of individuals, their physical health, academic achievement, and violence, including victimization. Many county-level government functions such as parks and youth programs are often compromised by extreme segregation levels, and individuals and groups living in integrated communities tend to enjoy more of these services and benefits than their more segregated neighbors.[55] Segregation tends to limit the life chances of minorities across generations.[56] In sum, future research should seek to make connections between the various levels of segregation and a range of life outcomes for Latinos, such as health, socioeconomic status, and even the chances of interracial marriages (i.e., integration) between Latinos and other groups.[57]

Third, future research should continue to make these connections not just for Latinos as a whole, but for each Latino ethnic group. While there is some salience to the term Latino and group members share unique strands of history, culture, and contemporary experiences, the groups also have differences that mediate the segregation processes. In all likelihood, these ethnic differences will appear in analyses that try to make connections between segregation, life chances, and well-being.

Finally, our findings and the RPIF can be used to inform academic and public debates that obscure the persistence of structural racism. Earlier we noted that the results of our analysis contradict the popular spatial assimilation theory, which assumes that all immigrants that come to the United States will eventually move up the economic ladder and out to the suburbs to integrate with Whites. Yet, while this theory describes the experiences of earlier immigrants from Northern Europe, it clearly does not apply to Latinos who have arrived under different circumstances.

Another example is the inappropriate conflation of the concept's diversity and integration. Increasingly, we see celebrations about the United States and New Jersey becoming a *diverse melting pot* of cultures as the population of Black and Brown people continues to grow.[58] For instance, after learning that Jersey City was ranked as the most diverse small city in the United States, Mayor Steven Fulop touted this ranking as representing a welcoming atmosphere for minority newcomers.[59] The problem with this line of thinking is that the term *diversity* is inappropriately being used to suggest that Jersey City is also *residentially integrated (or not segregated)* and that some degree of racial and ethnic equality has been achieved. But diversity and integration are two different phenomena such that places like Jersey City or Bergen County can be both diverse and segregated.[60] Diversity occurs when the proportion of Latinos in the total population of a geographic unit increases. But integration (e.g., low dissimilarity) only happens when those Latinos are evenly spread across all tracts of the geographic entity (i.e., county), or when the likelihood of running into another Latino in your neighborhood is not greater than the likelihood of running into Whites (low isolation). If the counties of New Jersey are becoming more diverse and segregated at the same time, then it might be premature to celebrate diversity and we still have much civil rights work to do. One place to begin might be encouraging your local congressperson to see through the objectives of the Mount Laurel Doctrine.

## Appendix: Computational Formulas

The index of dissimilarity ($D$) is captured by the follow formula:

$$D = \frac{1}{2}\sum_{i=1}^{n}\left|\frac{w_i}{W} - \frac{l_i}{L}\right|$$

where $n$ is the number of census tracts in the county, starting with the first census tract; $w_i$ is the number of Whites in tract I; $l_i$ is the number of Latinos in tract I; W is the county total White population, and L is the county total Latino population.

The isolation index as captured by the following formula:

$$\sum_{i=1}^{n}\left[\left(\frac{x_i}{X}\right)\left(\frac{x_i}{t_i}\right)\right]$$

where $x_i$ is the minority population of tract I; $t_i$ is total population of area I; and X is the sum of all $x_i$ or the total minority population in the county.

## Notes

1. Colleen O'Dea, "See How and Where New Jersey Changed," *NJ Spotlight News*, August 13, 2021; Peter Chen, "How New Jersey's Population Changed since 2010 and What It Means for Redistricting," New Jersey Policy Perspective, August 18, 2021, https://www.njpp.org/publications/report/how-new-jerseys-population-changed-since-2010-and-what-it-means-for-redistricting/.
2. New Jersey State Data Center, *Population by Race and Hispanic or Latino Origin New Jersey, Counties and Selected Municipalities: 1980, 1990 and 2000* (Trenton, NJ: State of New Jersey: Division of Labor Market and Demographic Research, 2001), 16; State of New Jersey, Department of Labor and Workforce Development, "Population and Labor Force Projections for New Jersey: 2010 to 2030," accessed February 2, 2020, https://nj.gov/labor/labormarketinformation/assets/PDFs/content/njsdc/2013WU%20PopLFProj2030.pdf.
3. Teri West, "Jersey City Ranked the Most Diverse U.S. City in 2020," NJ.com: True Jersey (Hudson), February 22, 2020, https://www.nj.com/hudson/2020/02/jersey-city-ranked-the-most-diverse-us-city-in-2020.html; Eric Jensen, Nicholas Jones, Megan Rabe, Beverly Pratt, Lauren Medina, Kimberly Orozco, and Linsay Spell, "The Chance That Two People Chosen at Random Are of Different Race or Ethnicity Groups Has Increased since 2010," U.S. Census Bureau, August 12, 2021, https://www.census.gov/library/stories/2021/08/2020-united.
4. Suzanne Gamboa, "Latinos Account for Over Half of the Country's Population Growth," *NBC News*, August 12, 2021, https://www.nbcnews.com/news/latino/latinos-account-half-countrys-population-growth-rcna1667.
5. Nicholas Jones, Rachel Marks, Roberto Ramirez, and Merarys Ríos-Vargas, "2020 Census Illuminates Racial and Ethnic Composition of the Country," U.S. Census Bureau, August 12, 2021, https://www.census.gov/library/stories/2021/08/improved-race-ethnicity-measures-reveal-united-states-population-much-more-multiracial.html.
6. See Joanna Marie Pinto-Coelho and Tukufu Zuberi, "Segregated Diversity," *Sociology of Race and Ethnicity* 1, no. 4 (2015): 475–489.
7. Emmanuel Martinez and Lauren Kirchner, "Denied: The Secret Bias Hidden in Mortgage-Approval Algorithms," *The Markup*, August 25, 2021.
8. Patrick J. Bayer, Hanming Fang, and Robert McMillan, "Separate When Equal? Racial Inequality and Residential Segregation," *SSRN Electronic Journal* 660 (2015).
9. Douglas S. Massey, "Residential Segregation Is the Linchpin of Racial Stratification," *City and Community* 15, no. 1 (2016): 4–7.
10. Denise E. O'Donnell, "Managing Costs and Improving Public Safety" (presentation, National Association of Counties: 2013 Legislative Conference, Washington, DC, March 3, 2014).
11. Jessica Trounstine, *Segregation by Design: Local Politics and Inequality in American Cities* (New York: Cambridge University Press, 2018).
12. Giovani Burgos, Fernand I. Rivera, and Marc A. Garcia, "Contextualizing the Relationship between Culture and Puerto Rican Health: Towards a Place-Based Framework of Minority Health Disparities," *CENTRO: Journal of the Center for Puerto Rican Studies* 29, no. 3 (2017): 10–49.
13. Barrett A. Lee, Sean F. Reardon, Glenn Firebaugh, Chad R. Farrell, Stephen A. Matthews, and David O'Sullivan, "Beyond the Census Tract: Patterns and Determinants of Racial Segregation at Multiple Geographic Scales," *American Sociological Review* 73, no. 5 (2008): 766–791.
14. "Census Tracts," U.S. Census Bureau, accessed May 1, 2021, https://www2.census.gov/geo/pdfs/education/CensusTracts.pdf.

15 Douglas S. Massey and Nancy A. Denton, "The Dimensions of Residential Segregation," *Social Forces* 67, no. 2 (1988): 281–315; Sean F. Reardon and David O'Sullivan, "Measures of Spatial Segregation," *Sociological Methodology* 34, no. 1 (2004): 121–162.
16 John Iceland, Daniel H. Weinberg, and Erika Steinmetz, *Racial and Ethnic Residential Segregation in the United States 1980–2000* (Washington, DC: U.S. Census Bureau, Special Report, CENSR-3, August 2002).
17 Nancy A. Denton, "Hypersegregation," in *The Blackwell Encyclopedia of Sociology*, ed. George Ritzer (Oxford: Blackwell, 2007), DOI: 10.1111/b.9781405124331.2007.x.
18 See Lawrence D. Bobo, "Racism in Trump's America: Reflections on Culture, Sociology, and the 2016 US Presidential Election," in "The Trump/Brexit Moment: Causes and Consequences," *British Journal of Sociology* 68, no. S1 (November 2017): S85–S104; Ronald R. Sundstrom, "Residential Segregation and Rethinking the Imperative of Integration," in *The Routledge Handbook of Philosophy of the City*, ed. Sharon M. Meagher and Samantha Noll (New York: Routledge, 2020), 216–228.
19 Margery A. Turner, and Stephen L. Ross, "Discrimination in Metropolitan Housing Markets: National Results from Phase I Hds 2000," Urban.org, November 2002.
20 Viviana López Green and Samantha Vargas Poppe, "Toward a More Perfect Union: Understanding Systemic Racism and Resulting Inequity in Latino Communities," *UnidosUS*, April 2021, https://unidosus.org/publications/2128-toward-a-more-perfect-union-understanding-systemic-racism-and-resulting-inequity-in-latino-communities/?&utm_source=twitter&utm_medium=social&utm_campaign=racialequity&utm_content=publication&utm_term=organic.
21 Justin P. Steil, Jorge De la Roca, and Ingrid Gould Ellen, "Desvinculado y Desigual: Is Segregation Harmful to Latinos," *ANNALS of the American Academy of Political and Social Science* 660, no. 1 (2015): 57–76.
22 Alisha Jarwala, "The More Things Change: Hudley V. Gorewitz and 'Change of Neighborhood' in the NAACP's Restrictive Covenant Cases," *Harvard Civil Rights–Civil Liberties Law Review* 55 (2020): 707–731; Gregory D. Squires and Frank Woodruff, "Redlining," in *The Wiley Blackwell Encyclopedia of Urban and Regional Studies*, ed. Anthony M. Orum (Hoboken, NJ: John Wiley and Sons, 2019), 1–8; Martinez and Kirchner, "The Secret Bias"; Derek S. Hyra, Gregory D. Squires, Robert N. Renner, and David S. Kirk, "Metropolitan Segregation and the Subprime Lending Crisis," *Housing Policy Debate* 23, no. 1 (2013): 177–198; Yancey Roy, "State Senate to Subpoena Real Estate Agents, Firms in Housing Probe," *Newsday*, December 12, 2019; Dorothy A. Brown, *The Whiteness of Wealth: How the Tax System Impoverishes Black Americans—and How We Can Fix It* (New York: Crown, 2021).
23 Ann Choi, Bill Dedman, Keith Herbert, and Olivia Winslow, "Long Island Divided," *Newsday*, November 2019; Roger W. Shuy, "Racial Steering in Real Estate," in *Fighting Over Words: Language and Civil Law Cases* (New York: Oxford University Press, 2008), 145.
24 Jon Vogel, "Exclusionary Zoning and Fear: A Developer's Perspective," in *The Dream Revisited*, ed. Ingrid Gould Ellen and Justin Peter Steil (New York: Columbia University Press, 2019), 104–107; Jonathan Rothwell and Douglas S. Massey, "The Effect of Density Zoning on Racial Segregation in US Urban Areas," *Urban Affairs Review* 44, no. 6 (2009): 779–806; Richard D. Kahlenberg, "The 'New Redlining' Is Deciding Who Lives in Your Neighborhood," *New York Times*, May 22, 2021.
25 Gregory D. Squires and Derek S. Hyra, "Foreclosures: Yesterday, Today, and Tomorrow," *City and Community* 9, no. 1 (2010): 50–60; Debbie G. Gruenstein Bocian, Keith S. Ernst, and Wei Li, "Race, Ethnicity and Subprime Home Loan Pricing," *Journal of Economics and Business* 60 (2008): 110–124.

26 Burgos et al., "Contextualizing the Relationship."
27 Dolores Acevedo-Garcia, "Has Residential Segregation Shaped the Epidemiology of Tuberculosis among United States Minorities? The Case of New Jersey, 1985–1992" (Princeton University, ProQuest Dissertations Publishing, 1996).
28 Kyle Crowder, "Residential Segregation of West Indians in the New York/New Jersey Metropolitan Area: The Roles of Race and Ethnicity," *International Migration Review* 33, no. 1 (1999): 79–113.
29 Maria Krysan and Kyle Crowder, *Cycle of Segregation* (New York: Russell Sage Foundation, 2017); John Iceland, Daniel Weinberg, and Lauren Hughes, "The Residential Segregation of Detailed Hispanic and Asian Groups in the United States: 1980–2010," *Demographic Research* 31 (2014), 393–624; Douglas S. Massey and Jacob S. Rugh, "Segregation in Post-Civil Rights America: Stalled Integration or End of the Segregated Century?" *Du Bois Review* 11, no. 2 (2014): 205–232; Michael E. Martin, *Residential Segregation Patterns of Latinos in the United States, 1990–2000* (Oxford: Routledge, 2006).
30 Iceland et al., "Residential Segregation"; Massey and Rugh, "Segregation in Post-Civil Rights America."
31 Massey, "Residential Segregation."
32 Martin, *Residential Segregation Patterns*.
33 Kasey Zapatka, John Mollenkopf, and Steven Romalewski, "Reordering Occupation, Race, and Place in Metropolitan New York," in *Urban Socio-Economic Segregation and Income Inequality*, ed. Maarten van Ham, Tiit Tammaru, Rūta Ubarevičiene, and Heleen Janssen (Cham, Switzerland: Springer, 2021).
34 Matthew Hall and Jonathan Stringfield, "Undocumented Migration and the Residential Segregation of Mexicans in New Destinations," *Social Science Research* 47 (2014): 61–78; Nancy A. Denton and Douglas S. Massey, "Racial Identity among Caribbean Hispanics: The Effect of Double Minority Status on Residential Segregation," *American Sociological Review* 54, no. 5 (1989): 790.
35 Iceland et al, "Residential Segregation."
36 Martin, *Residential Segregation Patterns*.
37 Martin, *Residential Segregation Patterns*.
38 Zapatka, Mollenkopf, and Romalewski, "Reordering Occupation."
39 See "Standard Hierarchy of Census Geographic Entities," U.S. Census Bureau, November 2020, https://www2.census.gov/geo/pdfs/reference/geodiagram.pdf.
40 "American Community Survey 2017–2021 5-Year Data Release," U.S. Census Bureau, December 8, 2022, https://www.census.gov/newsroom/press-kits/2022/acs-5-year.html
41 See Lee et al., "Beyond the Census Tract."
42 Otis Dudley Duncan and Beverly Duncan, "A Methodological Analysis of Segregation Indexes," *American Sociological Review* 20, no. 2 (1955): 210–217; Michael J. White and Ann H. Kim, "Residential Segregation," in *Encyclopedia of Social Measurement*, ed. Kimberly Kempf-Leonard (New York: Elsevier, 2005), 403–409.
43 Massey and Denton, "The Dimensions of Residential Segregation," 284.
44 See Appendix for the computational formula.
45 Wendell Bell, "A Probability Model for the Measurement of Ecological Segregation," *Social Forces* 32, no. 4 (1954): 357–364.
46 Massey and Denton, "The Dimensions of Residential Segregation," 287–288.
47 William J. Carrington and Kenneth R. Troske, "On Measuring Segregation in Samples with Small Units," *Journal of Business and Economic Statistics* 15, no. 4 (1997): 402–409.

48  Massey and Denton, "The Dimensions of Residential Segregation."
49  Douglas S. Massey, Len Albright, Rebecca Casciano, Elizabeth Derickson, and David N. Kinsey, *Climbing Mount Laurel: The Struggle for Affordable Housing and Social Mobility in an American Suburb* (Princeton, NJ: Princeton University Press, 2019).
50  Vanita Karla, Martina Manicastri, and Tanushree Bansal, *Exclutionary Zoning: New Jersey's Blueprint for Overcoming Segregation* (Cherry Hill, NJ: Fair Share Housing Center, 2023), https:www.fairsharehousing.org/wp-content/uploads/2023/04/Dismantling-Exclusionary-Zoning_New-Jerseys-Blueprint-for-Overcoming-Segregation.pdf.
51  For example, New Jersey Division on Civil Rights, *New Jersey Fair Housing Report: Housing Discrimination Enforcement and Initiatives in 2007* (Trenton, NJ: New Jersey Office of the Attorney General, Department of Law and Public Safety, 2007); Vincent J. Reina, Wendell E. Pritchett, and Susan M. Wachter, *Perspectives on Fair Housing* (Philadelphia: University of Pennsylvania Press, 2020).
52  Richard Rothste, *The Color of Law: A Forgotten History of How Our Government Segregated America* (New York: Liveright Publishing, 2017).
53  See Pinto-Coelho and Zuberi, "Segregated Diversity," 475–489.
54  Burgos et al., "Contextualizing the Relationship."
55  Krysan and Crowder, *Cycle of Segregation*. See James H. Carr and Nandinee K. Kutty, *Segregation: The Rising Costs for America* (New York: Routledge, 2008).
56  Justin P. Steil, Len Albright, Jacob S. Rugh, and Douglas S. Massey, "The Social Structure of Mortgage Discrimination," *Housing Studies* 33, no. 5 (2018): 759–776; Gregory D. Squires, *The Fight for Fair Housing: Causes, Consequences, and Future Implications of the 1968 Federal Fair Housing Act* (New York: Routledge, 2018).
57  Giovani Burgos and Fernando I. Rivera, "Residential Segregation, Socioeconomic Status, and Disability: A Multilevel Study on Puerto Ricans in the United States," *CENTRO: Journal of the Center for Puerto Rican Studies* 24, no. 2 (2012): 14–47; William Vélez and Giovani Burgos, "The Impact of Housing Segregation and Structural Factors on the Socioeconomic Performance of Puerto Ricans in the United States," *CENTRO: Journal of the Center for Puerto Rican Studies* XXII, no. 1 (2010): 174–197; Anthony De Jesús, Giovani Burgos, Melissa Almenas, and William Velez, "Puerto Rican Intergroup Marriage and Residential Segregation in the US: A Multilevel Analysis of Structural, Cultural, and Economic Factors," *Journal of Human Behavior in the Social Environment* 24 (2014): 156–178.
58  For example, Adam McCann, "Most & Least Ethnically Diverse Cities in the U.S." *WalletHub*, February 17, 2021.
59  West, "Jersey City."
60  Pinto-Coelho and Zuberi, "Segregated Diversity."

# 3

# The Gateway Reconsidered

The Paradox of Latinx
Barrioization in a Connected
Metropolis

JOHANA LONDOÑO

The term "gateway" has made headlines since 2015 when the New York/New Jersey Gateway Development Corporation's program—intended to enhance transportation between Newark and New York City and considered to be the most important transportation project in the nation—began to face numerous financial hurdles.[1] The objective of this chapter is to demonstrate that the concept of the gateway is much older than a twenty-first-century transportation planning project might suggest, having long been used as a concept to connect both states. Moreover, the concept has evolved over time in how it has been used to describe socioeconomic space. These variations reflect and contribute to larger socioeconomic changes in the metropolitan area that affect low-income populations, such as the mostly immigrant, Latinx population of Union City, New Jersey, which is the focus of this chapter.

In the New York/New Jersey area, planning, real estate, policy, and media professionals and scholars in immigration studies, urban planning, architecture, and geography have deployed the term gateway to denote spatial entryways that serve a wide-range of functions: immigration, recreational space, urban development, beautifying architecture and urban design, and engines of metropolitan economic growth. In this chapter, I show that the gateway concept has recently been used to generate gentrification from New York City to Union City. The city-designated gateway lies on the fringe of Union City and it is the site of new and expanding gentrifying residential and commercial developments. Considering this added meaning, the term gateway demands a reckoning of how its various connotations have led to its involvement in the twinned processes of gentrification—elevating real estate costs and urban marginalization.

This chapter asks: How does the gateway, as an idea and built space, act as both an opening, a through way, and a closing, barrioizing force affecting where Latinx residents of the city can establish a sense of belonging and cultural expression?[2] At the crux of the chapter is the understanding that gateways lead somewhere, and where they lead is politically significant as it shifts attention there in ways that can possibly affect real estate values in the metropolitan area. Those values dictate who does and does not gain access to housing and the kinds of commercial options available. Using maps, urban planning documents, and observation of architectural and social space as sources, as well as primary and secondary texts, this chapter shows how the idea of the gateway has been deployed to transform Union City into a place open to gentrifiers and the developers hoping to attract them while simultaneously visually enclosing this city's low-income population and limiting their ability to equally engage with the ever-expanding metropolitan area.

This chapter argues that despite the term's often-positive associations with place and movement and immigrant assimilation found in various scholarly and professional circles, and urban development, the use of the gateway is at times complicit in the invisibility of low-income racialized places and the immobility that remains a feature of urban inequality, especially for people of color and, more specifically, in this chapter, Latinx locals.

## What Is in a Term? A Keywords Approach to Gateway

My analysis of the "gateway" concept and its impact on the metropolitan area follows a cultural studies "keywords" approach that was first laid out by literary scholar Raymond Williams in *Keywords: A Vocabulary of Culture and Society*. Williams introduces a method for writing about words that moves beyond meanings provided in the dictionary. He argues that doing so synthesizes definitions found in both general, public usage and specialized academic settings.[3] Williams's method can be seen in Stuart Hall et al.'s, *Policing the Crisis*. That text examines the word "mugging" to better understand its racial and economic connotations. In a more recent example, the editors of *Keywords for American Cultural Studies* write that keywords "tell different stories about how the meanings of words change through time and across space, how they have shaped our thinking, and how they could be deployed in relation to future debates."[4] Additionally, the editors for *Keywords for Latina/o Studies* describe the ability of this approach to transform an object of study: keywords can "reinterpret, challenge, contest, and complicate the field named 'Latina/o studies.'"[5] This chapter's keywords approach attempts to have a similar effect. I critically examine how the gateway language has evolved to describe and intervene in the development of urban space and, in particular, to delimit Latinx space in Union City.

To fully comprehend the extent of the gateway's impact on the city, it is necessary to go beyond the neighborhood or city limits and contextualize the use of the gateway in Union City in a larger metropolitan scale. This wider scale aims to reveal how the political, economic, and cultural power centralized in New York City emanates outward to affect the gentrification of Hudson County. I have argued elsewhere that Union City's proximity to New York City requires that it be studied relationally, not only as a bounded community history.[6] For several years now, scholars have pushed the boundaries of community histories by taking a transnational turn.[7] The metropolitan scale I propose to examine the gateway and its effects on Union City also attempts to offer an expansive and relational framework.

## Gateway: A History and Contradiction in Terms

The term gateway has been applied to the New Jersey/New York area to reference its historical location as a passing point and settlement for immigrants arriving to the ports of New York City since the nineteenth century. One of the earliest identified sources, an 1854 annual report of the Methodist Episcopal Church, proclaimed that "the gateway to the continent is the great city of New York, through which come immigrants of all nationalities, of all languages, of all religions."[8] Fifteen years after the major immigrant processing center of Castle Island opened (1855) and before Ellis Island opened (1892), an 1870 report on "emigration in New York" noted that the city was the "main gateway through which the vast tide of emigration enters, and New York State the great thoroughfare over which it pours to be diffused over the Union."[9]

The diffusion "over the union" referenced above greatly reshaped the demographics of New Jersey. According to Douglas Shaw, "In every census since 1840" New Jersey "has been one of the states with the highest proportion of residents born outside the country." New York City's port of entry, and to some extent Philadelphia's port, had a major impact on New Jersey's population and its urbanization in the nineteenth century.[10] Largely due to immigration, "Newark's population increased from seventeen thousand in 1840 to seventy-two thousand in 1860. Jersey City expanded from a village of three thousand to a city of thirty thousand during the same period and reached 120,000 after another twenty years."[11] The New York City gateway, as described above, was thus the starting point for immigrant urban clusters but also, eventually, and as implied in the storied narratives of European immigrants and their economic mobility, a future stepping stone to a more "American" experience defined by suburban landscapes.

In the postwar era, European immigrants, and more so their descendants, would move to suburbs where they would typify the so-called American dream and middle-class American standardization.

Through the 1930s and into the 1950s with the construction of the Lincoln Tunnel's multiple tubes underway, the Hudson County area, and Union City with its proximity to the tunnels, was recognized as part of "the major gateway to the central business sector of the region."[12] With New York City designated the "central business sector," the outlying area's increased articulation but nonetheless secondary role in the metropolitan area was cemented. This resonates with how geographers Sören Scholvin, Moritz Breul, and Javier Revilla Diez describe the gateway as a world city, a key point of global capital, connected to a metropolitan economy in addition to global networks.[13]

The term gateway has been used to present New York City as an originating site for the economic development of the nation and even the world. Indeed, for over a century, the New York City gateway also signaled U.S. imperial efforts. The *New York Times* proclaimed the city in 1886 an "imperial gateway."[14] The "young metropolis," it explained further, "reposed with ample room for expansion, with water front unparalleled, and waiting to levy toll on the commerce of a hemisphere for the privileges it was to be allowed, and for the service the city could perform in its processes of exchange."[15] Today, the New York/New Jersey gateway continues to be a site of global industry and exchange. According to the North Jersey Transportation Planning Authority, the region is home to "the largest seaport on the East Coast (and third largest in the United States)" where large quantities of imports and exports are handled.[16] Moreover, and perhaps a better barometer of the "imperial" character of the metropolitan area, Wall Street and some of the nearby articulated trading centers (i.e., Jersey City), are the core of U.S. financial markets: Wall Street is home to the world's two largest stock exchanges. The privileged global economic standing of the United States has its symbolic center in New York City.

The concept of the gateway has also been used to market the New York metropolitan area as a tourist destination. In regard to regional tourism, the "Gateway National Recreation Area," created in 1972, covers twenty-seven thousand disconnected acres from Sandy Hook in New Jersey to Breezy Point in New York City. The park, according to its website, "is both the gateway from the ocean into New York Harbor, and the gateway to the National Park Service for millions of visitors every year."[17] In the hearings that led to the creation of the recreation area, then Commissioner of Parks and Recreation for the State of New York said, "The Gateway idea is a bold and exciting step in the right direction. It symbolizes the needed recognition by the Federal Government that it must help meet recreation needs in urban areas. The New York metropolitan area, ... which represents the Gateway to the entire Nation, is the ideal place for such a new Federal commitment."[18] The word gateway in this statement hinted at previous meanings afforded to the term. The commissioner suggested that the metropolitan area's immigration gateway had led to urban concentrations—most of which were described as poor (without any specific racial or ethnic qualifiers) by others who shared statements at the hearing—that were deprived of open green space and thus in need of the new recreation area. In regard to international tourism, the region's immigrant experience was unstated but nonetheless implied as an advantage. The 1983 Gateway Improvement task force and the 1991 New York City Gateway Program, created by business elites and the Port Authority of New York and New Jersey, were initiatives that sought to make various tourist amenities available in multiple languages with the intention of luring international visitors to the city at a time when tourist competition with cities across the country was increasing.[19]

Despite the ongoing framing of New York City as an immigrant gateway, throughout the end of the twentieth century, New York could no longer claim to be the nation's primary immigrant destination. Ethnic studies scholars have stressed how these narratives of immigration history are Eurocentric and neglect the Mexican and Asian immigration that entered through the west coast.[20] Additionally, starting in the 1970s when Newark International Airport began to offer overseas flights, New York City was no longer a prerequisite stop for immigrants entering the metropolitan area. Though in the 2000s sociologist Audrey Singer referred to New York as "a continuous gateway" because of its ongoing status as an immigrant destination, she noted elsewhere that suburbs were also becoming gateways.[21]

Perhaps due to these changes in the metropolitan area, New Jersey began to assume the gateway label for its own areas. According to the official website of the state, six counties (Passaic, Bergen, Hudson, Essex, Union, and Middlesex) in New Jersey—the state's most urban, most densely populated, and most ethically and racially diverse—are the "Gateway Region." Touted as a tourist destination, this gateway region includes cities with early U.S. historical architecture, large shopping malls, and large art venues, such as the New Jersey Performing Arts Center in Newark.[22] While some cities, such as Newark, which is sometimes known as the "gateway city," figure prominently in the state website's list of go-to places in the region, other cities including Union City are omitted.

In the twentieth century, the term figured prominently as a means for placemaking in New Jersey. Parks (e.g., Gateway Park-and-Ride in Jersey City and Gateway in Hoboken), residential developments (e.g., Gateway in Jersey City and Gateway at 1700 Park Avenue in Weehawken), and office buildings (e.g., the Gateway office, retail, and hotel complex in Newark), were designated gateways. Planners for Union City, and nearby Hoboken and Jersey City, discussed the importance of gateway entrances and corridors in their respective master plans—documents that outline development patterns, zoning ordinances, and the urban planning prerogatives of a city.

Curiously, in looking at the etymology of the word gateway in the *Oxford English Dictionary*, the most constant and earliest definition available regards the built environment not the above-named connections to immigration, industrial ports, imperial trade, recreation, tourism, or urban development. Specifically, since the eighteenth century the word has described gate architecture. According to the *Oxford English Dictionary*, a gateway is (1) "A passage that is or may be closed by a gate" and (2) "a frame or arch in which a gate is hung; a structure built at or over a gate, for ornament or defence."[23]

Contemporary urban planning has elaborated on this rather simple definition of the architectural gateway and developed it into a design element that largely includes a physical marker or set of markers (not always a gate with typical bars) that convey the identity of a place and encourage movement through that place. Design guidelines created for city governments, such as those discussed above and across the United States, discuss the benefits of gateways. Urban planner Michael Barrette notes that the gateway is "an entrance corridor that heralds the approach of a new landscape and defines the arrival point as a destination. The goal of gateway planning is to arrange this landscape so that it rewards the viewer with a sense of arrival and a positive image of the place."[24] In this view, the gateway's main audience is the outsider not the local resident. Urban planner Suzanne Sutro Rhees adds that it can also benefit the local neighborhood. She states that "the new emphasis on gateways and corridors reflects a growing trend toward 'place-making'—creating identifying landmarks that, in a national landscape grown increasingly homogeneous, help the traveler to distinguish one place from another, and give residents and businesses a renewed sense of civic pride." She adds that gateways are the "successors to the monuments of the early 20th century City Beautiful movement."[25] The parallel is interesting. The City Beautiful movement was a design approach that influenced the building of grand classicist landscapes in U.S. cities to instill order and civic pride in what were perceived to be the unruly spaces of immigrants, racialized migration, and poverty.[26] It has been critiqued for its idealism, for implying that built space can change morals and uplift society. Jane Jacobs called it "architectural design cults, rather than cults of social reform."[27] Gateways may be critiqued along the same lines. Even if the planners who promote gateways do not outright proclaim a social agenda, social consequences are nonetheless evident especially when intervening in public spaces that immigrants and low-income racialized people use. According to Robyn Moran and Lisbeth A. Berbary, top-down placemaking, as seen in city-designated gateways, is a kind of "unmaking," a way to undo the environments of low-income people of color.[28]

The emergence of planned gateways in northern New Jersey reflects the ongoing centralization of New York City in the metropolitan area, whereby the surrounding areas serve as a gateway opening up to the central city. In these examples, the gateway—as an idea and built space—seeks to create a place that leverages its proximity to New York City. These shifting gateway roles mirror metropolitan changes in real estate value over the last ninety years—northern New Jersey transforms its built environment to appeal to the needs of New Yorkers. It also speaks to northern New Jersey's hopeful, emulative desire to be known as a gateway similar to, not only for, New York City.

## The Gateway as Placemaking in Union City

The 2009 Master Plan for Union City, prepared by planning consultants Heyer, Gruel & Associates, promoted the design of gateways that identified the city "as a diverse cultural center."[29] It recommended treating the center of the city over I-495—the route that grants access to the Lincoln Tunnel and feeds vehicles to and from midtown Manhattan—"as the primary gateway" with "iconic architecture, pedestrian-friendly active streetscapes, public parks, with additional housing opportunities will undoubtedly have a positive impact on the long-term future of Union City."[30] Italian American architect and planner Julius Panero, a professor at the Fashion Institute of Technology and resident of the city and member of the Master Plan subcommittee, proposed filling in the I-495 overpass to create a park and residential housing. Considering how starved for green space Union City is, and its status as one of the most densely populated cities in the nation, this would have been an interesting idea. But ultimately the I-495 has only had minimal infill. In 2012, the city rezoned the area surrounding I-495 "as the City's Parks-Air Rights District with the intent to create hardscape park space above the freeway and minimize the spatial division the corridor creates."[31] The rezoning also allowed for small buildings of "an accessory nature," but not the residential buildings envisioned by Panero.[32] As of 2021, a large park has yet to be built due to "significant exterior regulatory and jurisdictional hurdles, as well as substantial cost considerations."[33] However, various sculptures, used as place markers, have been erected on the small portions of land that new infill provided.

The gateway section on the westernmost end of the city was renamed the Plaza of the Arts in 2010. The plaza sits on Bergenline Avenue, the city's main commercial corridor and an area that in the early 2000s was the target of city gentrification efforts to mainstream and standardize signage that caters to Latinx consumers. The Urban Enterprise Zone Program, a state initiative that had primarily served to lower the tax rate in this low-income city, encouraged local business owners to replace their colorful, hand-painted, and sometimes three-dimensional, signage with burgundy or navy blue awnings.[34] On the north and south, the plaza is sandwiched between two streets that are heavily navigated by public transportation and private vehicular traffic going to and out of the Lincoln Tunnel. Some of this traffic has as its destination or origin Union City, other traffic simply passes through. The sculpture, with which the plaza was inaugurated, includes the words "Art UC" (short for Union City) on top of an open trapezoid that frames the midtown Manhattan skyline on one side (figure 3.1). The sculpture was designed by Cuban Lucio Fernandez, the city's Commissioner of Public Affairs and a multidisciplinary artist. There is also a sculpture of a red

FIGURE 3.1 Art UC sculpture. (Photo by Johana Londoño)

heart placed by the fencing that acts as a barrier between the street and I-495 humming down below. To make the plaza possible, Fernandez told a local newspaper that the city eliminated street parking, extended sidewalks, and added "new lighting, planters and benches."[35] According to Fernandez, the idea came to him after artists approached the city requesting an open space for exhibiting and selling art but it was also intended to offer people "a nice place to see the New York skyline."[36] The focus on the arts is a curious one. Though the city's early twentieth-century concentration of burlesque and German breweries and the 1930s-built Park Performing Arts Center, which sits a few blocks to the west of the plaza, had once made it an entertainment and nightlife destination, this historically industrial city had not since been particularly known for its creative industries. The art the plaza appealed to was a hodgepodge of new art galleries and artists moving into the city or nearby as part of gentrification.

The gateway section on the easternmost end of the city, nearest to the opening of the Lincoln Tunnel, was named Embroidery Plaza in 2014 in honor of the area's historic garment industry. Swiss and German migrants had imported embroidery machinery in the late nineteenth century and later migrants, first from Cuba and then from all over Latin America and the Caribbean, had worked in this industry since the 1960s and until the 1990s when it nearly all but disappeared. In honor of those workers and the industry as a whole, the plaza includes two Singer sewing machines, each on top of a steel frame that has a large rock nestled at the bottom. The rock is presumably a reference to the Palisades Cliffs on which Union City sits. An additional sculpture adorns the plaza, the

*Embroidery Tree* made from parts of an embroidery machine, designed by fashion designer Amy Cheung, made by Marco Designs, a local carpentry company, and painted by graffiti artist Aldo Sanchez "Zar."[37] The art is accompanied by a no-frills, now faded, poster with text describing the history of the garment industry in the city.

Passing by the plazas on numerous occasions, I have primarily seen it used by older Latino men who sit on benches, seemingly unperturbed by the exhaust of the many cars, buses, and public shuttles that drive through, and local Latinx passerby crossing the center of the city. Indeed, it is difficult, just by seeing all the Latinx people who navigate this city, to attribute demographic change to the creation of these modest plazas, but it is rather easy to link them to two of the major progentrification, placemaking trends of the turn of the twenty-first century. The Plaza of the Arts appeals to art-led gentrification popularized among city officials and planners in the early 2000s by Richard Florida's publications on the "creative class" and its description of its effects on urban development. Sociologist Sharon Zukin had, years before, documented the artist–gentrifier dynamic in her book, *Loft Living*, on the Soho neighborhood of Manhattan.[38] The Embroidery Plaza's attempt to honor the local garment industry also has ties to one of the most prevalent gentrification processes of the late twentieth and early twenty-first centuries, namely the reconversion of old warehouses and factories in deindustrialized cities in the United States. Zukin also spoke to this process in her above-named book. "Industrial heritage," as described by historians Steven High and Fred Burrill, "is valued by condominium developers and the new creative class."[39] This is evident in Brooklyn's former Domino sugar factory now turned into 325 Kent apartments, Jersey City's Dixon Crucible Company factory now turned into Dixon Mill apartments, and a Lipton Tea factory in Hoboken converted into the Hudson Tea Buildings, to name but a few. Even more relevant, the Thread building, a fifteen-story condominium that opened in 2014 in Union City, a few blocks away from Embroidery Plaza on Park Avenue, is a direct reference to the industry that dominated the city. Developed by W Developers, a developer of luxury buildings in Tribeca, Brooklyn Heights, and Long Island City, the building towers over a city of mostly two- and three-story houses and what remains of low-scale factory buildings.[40] Though the condominium was not part of the city's master plan, it echoes its mission and magnifies the gentrification imperatives of new development in the city. A *New York Times* heading announcing the building's arrival—"Hoboken Comes to Union City"—gestured toward the hopeful Hobokenization of the area, a common sign of gentrification on this side of the Hudson River.

Indeed, various other high-rise residential developments have been erected on Park Avenue at the edge of the city, north of the easternmost designated gateway and parallel to the luxury waterfront development that has risen in the last forty years. Like the Thread building, new luxury developments fall in the

Urban Enterprise Zone. This, the very tax-reducing program that erased some Latinx signage from the city's main commercial boulevard, also made new luxury development eligible for tax abatements.[41] Much of this development, which caters to young professionals, is named to reference New York City and the Hudson River.[42] The Hudson View and the Skyline, to name a few, are new apartment buildings that soar over the low-scale landscape of Union City, acting as a visual barrier that denies the Manhattan skyline to residents living in the interior of the city.

More recently, gray-colored developments and freshly painted gray exteriors in houses that are about to go or are on sale have also cropped up on Park Avenue and adjacent side streets. I have also noticed gray exteriors on trendy restaurants and coffee shops. Others in cities such as San Francisco have also noticed that gray is the palette of gentrification.[43]

With these forms of placemaking, the gateway and nearby developments seem to want to reverse the feeling of transitoriness and in betweenness at the center of what I call a Jersey affect, though unsuccessfully.[44] Movement in and out of the state and the places that border it—New York and Pennsylvania—dominate representations of New Jersey. Opening shots to the HBO series *The Sopranos*, one of the state's most popular media depictions, shows the main character moving out of the Lincoln Tunnel and into northern New Jersey. Frank Sinatra's rendition of the 1977 song, "New York, New York," merely hints toward his humble beginnings in nearby working-class Hoboken while proclaiming his object of desire across the Hudson River. Bruce Springsteen's 1975 song "Born to Run," also implies a need to leave, "this town rips the bones from your back / It's a death trap, it's a suicide rap / We gotta get out while we're young." While the placemaking initiatives discussed above intend to create positive associations with the environment that minimize this feeling of transitoriness, the desire to be on the other side of the river is still there, ingrained in the marketing of new developments.

To better understand the complex implications of the placemaking evident in Union City, it is apt to point out the internal contradiction in the word gateway. It is both a gate and a way, but sometimes it acts more as one than the other. "Way" notes the availability of passage, the possibility of moving through. It reminds us that this gate is not going to enclose or anchor permanently. The "gate," however, represents the possibility of enclosure. It refuses to foreclose on the idea of containment. Writing on gated communities in Puerto Rico, sociologist Zaire Dinzey-Flores writes that gates have a dual purpose. For the wealthy, gates are erected to keep the undesirable out, specifically poor and Black people, and keep inhabitants safe. In low-income communities, however, gates are meant to keep inhabitants contained, to avoid spreading what elites believed to be improper behavior. Gates are tools of social segregation.[45] Because the materiality of the gateway may not always present as a gate with bars, its ability to segregate may not be immediately evident. It is my contention, however, that in Union City the gateway and its related developments segregate urban space and do not always include low-income Latinx residents of the area.

The "way" in gateway is mostly that for gentrifiers. In Union City, it even insinuates a hopeful, socioeconomic parity with wealthy Manhattan across the river. But it acts as a "gate" for low-income people who may not be able to remain in or capitalize on the places they have produced as members of local communities. The low-income residents of Union City are faced with the limitations of barrioization and the negative effects of gentrification—displacement. Though gentrification is not as obvious in Union City as it is elsewhere in the county (e.g., Jersey City and Hoboken) or across the Hudson River, the gentrification aspirations of local government officials and property owners are evident in the above-named developments that have emerged in the last twenty years.[46]

## "Gate" Or a "Way"? Latinx Experiences in the Gateway

Some Latinx people have been key exponents of the gentrification imperatives underlying the city's (and the county's) gateway development. Through their actions and discourse they trumpet the "way" of gentrification and suggest the places and people who do not contribute to the process. Real estate professionals, property owners, or business owners who are long-term Cuban residents or Cubans who grew up in Union City and have returned to take advantage of new development are repeatedly interviewed in articles documenting the city's urban change. Grisselle Martinez, a real estate agent in Hoboken, was quoted in 2008 by a local northern New Jersey newspaper *The Record*, saying:

> I came from Cuba into the United States at the age of 3, and I've lived in Union City for 37 years. . . . I am seeing an amazing enhancement of our neighborhoods—it's just a transition that is unreal. I have a lot of people who are priced out of Hoboken rolling over into Union City. They are finding it's culturally diverse with everything at your doorsteps: transportation, restaurants, shopping.[47]

Jose Ortega, a realtor in Rutherford, New Jersey, and first-generation Cuban American raised in Union City, was quoted in a *New York Times* real estate section article in 2018, noting that Union City was "an emerging market" for millennials because "you're closer to Times Square from Union City than from Brooklyn."[48]

Cubans, have been the longest-standing Latinx residents of Union City, beginning to arrive in as far back as the 1920s. They were poor, rural immigrants looking for work and not all were anti-communists. In fact, in the 1950s Fidel Castro visited the city while on a tour to raise money for his revolution. By 1959, the year that Castro took over Cuba, there were two thousand Cubans living in

Union City. Their arrival was most opportune for city elites. Although the opening of the Lincoln Tunnel had seemingly positioned the city to become a bedroom community for Manhattan, White flight to more suburban areas of New Jersey, particularly that of White descendants of German, Italian, Serbian immigrants, dashed any hopes the real estate sector had for maintaining property values. White flight also affected the local embroidery industry, which was already impacted by increasing international trade. A leader of the embroidery industry worried that Union City would become a "ghost town."[49] In this context of crisis, Cuban political exiles were welcomed in Union City.[50]

Catholic charities, along with existing Cuban residents, helped redirect thousands of Cubans arriving in Miami to Union City. The federal Cuban refugee program poured money into the new areas where migrants settled in the 1960s and facilitated mortgages and other forms of assistance for refugees. In Union City, Cubans bought houses and opened stores.

By the 1970s, Union City leaders and business owners, and real estate actors were thankful for the Cuban residents and customers. One clothing shop owner was quoted in the *New York Times* as saying "We have Mr. Castro to thank for" the surge in business.[51] A lieutenant for the city's police department claimed that had it not been for Cubans, Union City would be a parking lot.[52] The garment industry also celebrated the new Cuban arrivals. This is in stark contrast to how Puerto Ricans and other Latinx people in nearby working-class Jersey City and New York City would be treated. Local Puerto Rican and Black people were sometimes denied the very small business loans that Cubans were granted.[53] Indeed, Cuban Union City was a relatively privileged place compared to Puerto Rican neighborhoods nearby. A 1975 *New Yorker* article addressed the racial politics of this preferential treatment:

> When people in Union City say how fortunate it is that the Cubans are mainly middle-class, they mean middle-class not compared to the Italians who came in 1910 but compared to the Puerto Ricans who come anytime. The Cubans are celebrated not merely for revitalizing the stores but for staying out of the streets.... The fact that Union City is filled to bursting with Cubans means, among other things, that it has no room for blacks. People in Union City talk about the Cubans having saved the town from dying, but in fact a city that straddles the approach to the Lincoln Tunnel does not die in the sense of disappearing, the way a Western town that lost its silver mine might die. It becomes the South Bronx. In conversations about Cubans in Union City, Hoboken is often mentioned. It could be that what Cubans are really seen as saving Union City from is not death but Puerto Ricans.[54]

"Staying out of the streets" indirectly references the political organizing among Puerto Rican youth in the late 1960s and early 1970s. The Young Lords, a radical Puerto Rican youth group inspired by the Black Panthers, for example, had branches in Jersey City and Hoboken. And in 1970 and 1971 Puerto Rican protests against police brutality led to the creation of tenants' rights groups.[55] No such political organizing has been readily documented for Union City at this time, making Cubans in Union City a preferred migrant group among city elites.[56]

The large numbers of Black Cubans who arrived with the Mariel boatlift, as well as Colombians, Ecuadorians, and Dominicans who arrived in the 1980s, altered the ways city elites thought of Union City's Latinx populations. These groups did not have the same economic basis and monetary assistance as earlier Cuban refugees. In some instances, they were looked down upon by White Cubans and other long-standing residents for not having the same resources. And yet, Union City and neighboring towns were among some of the last to deindustrialize in the metro area thanks to the steady supply of these low-wage Latin American, specifically women workers.[57]

As deindustrialization took root in the 1990s, however, racially diverse, low-income Latinxs were not able to stave off the stigma of barrioization implicit in the mention of "the South Bronx" in the previous quote. Union City, with almost 65,000 people, nearly 52,000 of whom identified as Hispanic or Latino (of various nationalities and increasingly Mexican and Caribbean) in the 2010 Census, faces declining public transportation and high poverty rates. As high-rise buildings emerge on the city's designated gateway, visually enclosing it, the city's spatial segregation has gotten worse.

City officials have started to address this, although in ways that do not directly acknowledge the effects on the low-income population of the area. In a letter to his constituents, Union City mayor and state senator, Brian Stack, condemned high-rise buildings below the Palisades Cliffs in cities such as Weehawken and Hoboken that have capitalized on their waterfront access by building luxury condominiums with Manhattan views. He wrote "the Commissioners and I have strongly opposed the construction of outrageous structures that have attempted to be built below Union City which would come directly in front of the Palisades Cliffs destroying our views, but more importantly, our quality of life."[58] Stack and Nicholas Sacco, mayor of North Bergen and also state senator, have proposed the Palisades Protection Act to advance their position. In Union City, however, some redevelopment areas are allowed to build higher than four stories "where," according to the mayor, "the development would bring other benefits to the residents of Union City."[59] Thus far, this building exception seems to benefit private developers and their tenants. A councilwoman in Hoboken, who opposes the act, noted the irony, saying that in Union City "portions of the Palisades have literally been gutted entirely to accommodate projects built directly into the same cliffs these bills state they are trying to protect."[60]

Union City is an example of how gateway development can act as both a closing, barrioizing force, a gate, and a throughway. The "gate" and its extended gentrification is doing the work of visually barrioizing the population that mid-twentieth-century policies of racist disinvestment and segregation had done for nearby Puerto Rican and Black residential populations. Union City has no discernible antigentrification protests despite ongoing worries of affordability and displacement.[61] In this context of minimal vocal resistance from low-income residents, the use of the built environment as markers of exclusion is important to consider.

## Conclusion

This chapter's aim has been to critically analyze buzzwords that are commonplace and seem neutral, such as the term gateway. Union City's gateway and its nearby urban development references the area's proximity to New York City in a way that moves with and beyond the immigrant, tourist, and connotations applied to earlier versions of the gateway concept. The migration element is still there, but immigrants are not necessarily moving out of the "gateway" by their own volition as mid-century Whites did in pursuit of the American dream: instead we see a simultaneous pushing out and enclosure of Latinx people due to gentrification while the mobility—both socioeconomic and geographic—associated with the gateway is most readily available to gentrifiers. In other words, the gateway concept has experienced a shift and now serves as a sign of gentrification-led, socioeconomic, and visual exclusion of low-income Latinx people, a majority of whom are immigrants.

## Notes

1 The Gateway, as it is simply known, is a multibillion-dollar infrastructure project that aims to improve the transit options available between Newark and Manhattan's Penn Station. It specifically intends to build a new tunnel under the Hudson River and rehabilitate already existing tubes. The project took its cue from an Amtrak proposal known as the Gateway program. The project's predecessor, the Access to the Region's Core project, was terminated by New Jersey governor, Chris Christie, in 2010. Though considered to be the most urgent infrastructure project in the United States, financing for the project has partly stalled because President Trump's administration refused to commit to fund the project that the Obama administration had greenlit. As of 2021, the Biden administration, with Pete Buttigieg as Secretary of Transportation, has renewed confidence in the project and it is expected that various phases of the project will be carried out. Emma G. Fitzsimmons, "Corporation to Oversee New Hudson Rail Tunnel, with U.S. and Amtrak Financing Half," *New York Times*, November 11, 2015, https://www.nytimes.com/2015/11/12/nyregion/corporation-to-oversee-new-hudson-rail-tunnel-with-us-and-amtrak-financing-half.html; Nat Bottigheimer, "The Gateway Tunnel

Is on the Ballot," NJ.com, October 29, 2020, https://www.nj.com/opinion/2020/10/the-gateway-tunnel-is-on-the-ballot-opinion.html.
2  My use of barrioizing or barrioization in this chapter echoes that of Raúl Homero Villa who refers to barrioization as the process by which real estate practices, public policy, and racial discrimination limit Latinx residential and commercial spaces to a ghetto-like cluster. In this chapter, I also emphasize the visual effects of urban development and gentrification that also barrioize, and the stigma of Latinx urban concentrations that results. Raúl Homero Villa, *Barrio Logos: Space and Place in Urban Chicano Literature and Culture* (Austin: University of Texas Press, 2000).
3  Raymond Williams, *Keywords: A Vocabulary of Culture and Society* (New York: Oxford University Press, 1976), xxvi.
4  Bruce Burgett and Glenn Hendler, "What Is a Keyword?" in *Keywords for American Cultural Studies*, 2nd edition. (New York: New York University Press, 2014), https://keywords.nyupress.org/american-cultural-studies/keywords-an-introduction/.
5  Deborah R. Vargas, Nancy Raquel Mirabal, and Lawrence La Fountain-Stokes, eds., *Keywords for Latina/o Studies* (New York: New York University Press, 2017), 4.
6  Johana Londoño, "Critical Latina/o Urban Studies in Metropolitan Perspective: The Case of Latina/o Majority Union City, NJ," *Occasion* 9 (August 2015): 1–13.
7  Nina Glick Schiller and Ayse Caglar, eds., *Locating Migration: Rescaling Cities and Migrants* (Ithaca: NY: Cornell University Press, 2011).
8  "Annual Report of the Methodist Episcopal Church," (N.p.: n.p., 1854).
9  Friedrich Kapp, *Immigration and the Commissioners of Emigration of the State of New York* (New York: Douglas Taylor, 1870).
10  Douglas Shaw, *Immigration and Ethnicity in New Jersey History* (Trenton: New Jersey Historical Commission, Department of State, 1994), 10.
11  Shaw, *Immigration and Ethnicity*, 19.
12  Warren Lovejoy, "Authority Trans-Hudson River Vehicular Origin and Destination Survey," Port of New York, *Port Development Department Planning Division, Public Roads* 31, no.4 (1960): 94.
13  Sören Scholvin, Moritz Breul, and Javier Revilla Diez, "Revisiting Gateway Cities: Connecting Hubs in Global Networks to Their Hinterlands," *Urban Geography* 40, no. 9 (2019): 1291–1309.
14  "New York City's Growth," *New York Times*, January 1, 1886.
15  "New York City's Growth."
16  North Jersey Transportation Planning Authority, *Plan 2040*, accessed June 14, 2020.
17  "Gateway National Recreation Area," National Park Service, accessed June 14, 2020, https://www.nps.gov/gate/.
18  *Hearings before the Subcommittee on Parks and Recreation of the Committee on Interior and Insular Affairs United States Senate*, Ninety-Second Congress, May 12 and 17, 1971 (Statement of Sal J. Prezioso, Commissioner of Parks and Recreation, New York, Representing Governor Rockefeller), 64.
19  Sarah Bartlett, "New Goal for New York: Tourist-Friendly Image," *New York Times*, September 29, 1991.
20  George J. Sanchez, *Becoming Mexican American : Ethnicity, Culture, and Identity in Chicano Los Angeles, 1900–1945* (New York: Oxford University Press, 1995); Erika Lee, *At America's Gates: Chinese Immigration during the Exclusion Era, 1882–1943* (Chapel Hill: University of North Carolina Press, 2003).
21  Audrey Singer, *The Rise of New Immigrant Gateways* (Washington, DC: Brookings Institution Press, 2004); Audrey Singer, Susan W. Hardwick, and Caroline B. Brettell, eds. *Twenty-First Century Gateways: Immigrant Incorporation in Suburban America* (Washington DC: Brookings Institution Press, 2008).

22 "A Dozen Adventures in NJ's Six Regions," Official Tourism Website of New Jersey, accessed June 14, 2020, https://www.visitnj.org/dozen-adventures-njs-six-regions.
23 *Oxford English Dictionary*, s.v. "gateway." July 2023, https://doi.org/10.1093/OED/1074801168.
24 Michael Barrette, "Planning Basics for Gateway Design," *Zoning News*, December 1994, 1.
25 Suzanne Sutro Rhees, "Gateways: Creating Civic Identity," *Planning Commissioners Journal*, no. 21 (1996): 9.
26 Howard Gillette Jr., *Civitas by Design: Building Better Communities, from the Garden City to the New Urbanism* (Philadelphia: University of Pennsylvania Press, 2012), 16.
27 Jane Jacobs, *Death and Life of Great American Cities* (New York: Knopf Doubleday, 1961), 375.
28 Robyn Moran and Lisbeth A. Berbary, "Placemaking as Unmaking: Settler Colonialism, Gentrification, and the Myth of 'Revitalized' Urban Spaces," *Leisure Sciences* (February 2021): 1–17.
29 Heyer, Gruel & Associates, "City of Union City, Hudson County, Master Plan Reexamination Report," February 2018, 5. Accessed March 1, 2021, https://www.ucnj.com/_Content/pdf/plans/2018-Union-City-Master-Plan-Reexamination-Report.pdf. 5.
30 Heyer, Gruel & Associates, "City of Union City," 78.
31 Heyer, Gruel & Associates, "City of Union City," 15.
32 Heyer, Gruel & Associates, "City of Union City," 18.
33 Heyer, Gruel & Associates, "City of Union City," 27.
34 For more on the connections between gentrification in Union City and Urban Enterprise Zone, see Johana Londoño, *Abstract Barrios: The Crises of Latinx Visibility in Cities* (Durham, NC: Duke University Press, 2020), 202–203.
35 Karina Arrue, "Union City Unveils Plaza of the Arts Next Week," *Jersey Journal*, November 24, 2010, https://www.nj.com/hudson/2010/11/union_city_unveils_plaza_of_th.html.
36 Deanna Cullen, "Local Artists' Communal Grounds," *Hudson Reporter*, December 5, 2010, https://archive.hudsonreporter.com/2010/12/05/local-artists-communal-grounds/.
37 "Embroidery Plaza Dedication Ceremony," *Hudson Reporter*, May 29, 2014, https://archive.hudsonreporter.com/2014/05/29/embroidery-plaza-dedication-ceremony/; Michaelangelo Conte, "Union City Dedicates Plaza That Honors History as 'Embroidery Capital of the World,'" *Jersey Journal*, May 31, 2014, https://www.nj.com/hudson/2014/05/embroidery_square_dedicated_in_union_city.htm.
38 Sharon Zukin, *Loft Living: Culture and Capital in Urban Change* (New Brunswick, NJ: Rutgers University Press, 1989).
39 Steven High and Fred Burrill, "Industrial Heritage as Agent of Gentrification," *National Council on Public History* (blog), February 19, 2018, https://ncph.org/history-at-work/industrial-heritage-as-agent-of-gentrification/.
40 "New Jersey Gold Coast's 'City by City'—Welcomes First Luxury High-Rise," *Union City Reporter*, March 23, 2008.
41 Johana Londoño, "Aesthetic Belonging: The Latinization and Renewal of Union City, New Jersey," in *Latino Urbanism: The Politics of Planning, Policy, and Redevelopment*, ed. David R. Diaz and Rodolfo D. Torrez (New York: New York University Press, 2011), 56; "Attention Property Owners: Union City's Newly Revised Tax Incentive Program for Tax Payers," August 3, 2006. Accessed August 13, 2021, https://www.ucnj.com/_Content/pdf/forms/tax/TAX-ABATEMENT.pdf

42  Mary Amoroso, "Now It's Union City's Turn," *The Record*, April 20, 2008.
43  Annie Vainshtein, "How San Francisco Lost Its Color," *San Francisco Chronicle*, October 11, 2019.
44  It is telling that these new placemaking practices and progentrification developments mostly exist in the eastern part of the city. In contrast, moving west from the Art Plaza and then north onto Kennedy Boulevard, a main artery lying at the edge of the city, the growth of drive-through banks and fast-food restaurants replacing aging residential structures and underused property are more reminiscent of a typical New Jersey suburban landscape. These new developments signal that they are not for pedestrians, which considering that nearly 19.6 percent of the total population lives in poverty is a likely majority of residents. But neither does it include urban amenities, such as outdoor seating, cafés, and boutiques that Manhattan-led gentrification encourages on the city's eastern border.
45  Zaire Dinzey-Flores, *Locked In, Locked Out: Gated Communities in a Puerto Rican City* (Philadelphia: University of Pennsylvania Press, 2013) 14, 26.
46  Londoño, *Abstract Barrios*, 186.
47  Amoroso, "Now It's Union City's Turn."
48  Jill P. Capuzzo, "Union City, NJ: Close to the City, But Still Affordable," *New York Times*, May 9, 2018.
49  "'Worry about Us,' Lace Area Pleads," *New York Times*, February 3, 1955; Londoño, *Abstract Barrios*, 190.
50  Yolanda Prieto, *The Cubans of Union City: Immigrants and Exiles in a New Jersey Community* (Philadelphia: Temple University Press, 2009), 9.
51  Jesus Rangel, "A Touch of Havana Brings Life to Union City," *New York Times*, February 22, 1988.
52  Alfonso Narvaez, "50,000 Cubans Add Prosperity and Problems to New Jersey," *New York Times*, November 24, 1970.
53  Ramón Grosfoguel and Chloé S. Georas. "Latino Caribbean Diasporas in New York," in *Mambo Montage: The Latinization of New York*, ed. Agustín Laó-Montes and Arlene Dávila (New York: Columbia University Press, 2001), 112. Grosfoguel and Georas cite Denise Margaret Cronin, "Ethnicity, Opportunity and Occupational Mobility in the United States" (PhD diss., State University of New York, Stony Brook, 1981).
54  Calvin Trillin, "U.S. Journal: Union City, N.J.," *New Yorker*, June 30, 1975, 95.
55  Dylan Gottlieb, "Hoboken Is Burning : Yuppies, Arson, and Displacement in the Postindustrial City," *Journal of American History* 106, no. 2 (September 2019): 397.
56  For more on how Latinx political organizing differs among these cities, see Londoño, *Abstract Barrios*, 197.
57  Patricia Fernández Kelly and Saskia Sassen, "Recasting Women in the Global Economy: Internationalization and Changing Definitions of Gender" in *Women in the Latin American Development Process*, ed. Christine E. Bose and Edna Acosta-Belén (Philadelphia: Temple University Press, 1995), 99–124.
58  Daniel Israel, "Protecting Historic Views," *Hudson Reporter*, March 4, 2021. https://hudsonreporter.com/2021/03/04/protecting-historic-views/.
59  Israel, "Protecting Historic Views."
60  Marilyn Baer, "Hoboken Council Opposes Palisades Cliffs Protection Act," *Hudson Reporter*, January 8, 2021, https://hudsonreporter.com/2021/01/08/hoboken-council-opposes-palisades-cliffs-protection-act/.
61  For more on how the Cuban population that dominated the city for decades shaped the political context, see Londoño, *Abstract Barrios*, 198.

# 4
# From Havana on the Hudson to Bolivar's Enclave

Change, Solidarity, and
Conflict in Pan-Latinx Space

ALEX F. TRILLO AND JENNIFER AYALA

Pupusas, comida criolla, Colombian antojitos, botanicas, dress shops, pastelerias, and, of course... McDonald's. These are some of the places we pass, as riders hop off and on the local guaguita at almost every block of the Bergenline corridor. Near Celia Cruz Way, three young Dominican girls climb on board. One is a few cents short, but the driver just shrugs and says "la proxima." Several blocks later, it happens again with a Honduran man who is headed to work in Manhattan.... As we approach 32nd street, two Colombian women are chiding the Ecuadorian driver for not closing the windows to preserve the

AC-chilled air. "Señor, por qué no se cierra las ventanas? Tenemos aire!" ... In the middle, a Black Cuban man dressed in white watches calmly.
—Alex Trillo's field notes, 2010

It's like Bolivar got to realize his dream of Latin American nations coming together in this one little spot ... sort of.
—Merci, who migrated from Cuba in 1995

Situated near the Hudson River separating New York City from New Jersey, Bergenline Avenue is a three-mile commercial strip and the center of a vibrant, pan-Latinx *geographic* community.[1] The avenue spans four municipalities that share a contiguous pan-Latinx population, bound by relatively common histories, cultural practices, and intense social ties between them.

In the 1940s, a handful of Puerto Ricans, first, then Cubans made their way to what was then a mostly German and pan-European community built on textile factories and microbusinesses. In the late 1960s, when Bergenline was enduring the effects of suburbanization and White flight, an influx of nearly forty thousand postrevolution Cuban refugees joined their fellow Caribbeans and transformed the area into Havana on the Hudson. By the 1990s, shifts in the economy and immigration patterns further transformed Bergenline into the *pan-Latinx* space it is today.[2] As of 2020, 77 percent of the residents are descended from nineteen different Latinx countries sharing just a few square miles of space. For some, a stroll down Bergenline conjures up the legacy of Simon Bolivar, the Venezuelan political leader who advocated for a united Latin America.

As descendants of Cuban and Cuban/Ecuadorian migrants, we often move through Bergenline's Havana-tinged, *pan-Latinized* spaces wondering: (1) *How did this happen?* And (2) *Does everybody really get along?* These questions resonate with us personally as Bergenline still grounds our sense of what it means to be *northern Cubans*, a unique experience that is worth documenting as part of New Jersey's Latinx immigrant history.[3] Our questions also compel us to think more broadly about the meanings ascribed to the umbrella term "Latinx," and how well it characterizes Bergenline and the everyday experiences that people of Latin American descent have here today. That is, do the range of Latinxs affiliated with the community today experience the kind of solidarity that was common during the Cuban years, or in more homogeneous Latinx communities? Or do the various groups function as silos, perhaps in competition or conflict with each other?

Debates about pan-Latinx conflict, solidarity, and the salience of common Latinx identity across subgroups are not new, but we think the Bergenline context presents unique contours to examine. The spatial dynamics that bring so many groups into one space, the local history, and the nuances of Cuban settlement patterns that still affect the community today all yield unique opportunities for cultivating a collective Latinx identity.[4] Our sense is that everyday life on pan-Latinx Bergenline does manifest into a system of pan-Latinidad that cultivates some degree of Latinx solidarity by default, and that there are spaces in the community that further contribute to a common identity. But we also suspect that the final answers to our questions do not fit neatly into binary constructions where Latinxs are framed as either one cohesive social group, or a set of loosely connected nationalities reproducing colonial hierarchies and fighting each other for resources.[5] Here we empirically explore some of the spaces and nuances between these two formulations.

The remainder of this chapter has three goals: (1) to describe the Cubanization of Bergenline, (2) to describe the contemporary pan-Latinized Bergenline and its connections to the Cuban era, and (3) to apply what Gilda Ochoa calls *the continuum of conflict and solidarity* between Latinx groups to understand how groups get along today.[6] To situate readers, we begin with a detailed description of the community and the current population counts, followed by an overview of the Havana on the Hudson years that likely shaped some of the current dynamics. We then use census data and field notes to further describe Bergenline's unique pan Latinx character today, including some potential bases for solidarity, division, and conflict. Finally, we complement our analysis with excerpts from open-ended interviews to demonstrate fluctuating moments on the community–conflict continuum.

## Bergenline and Its Diversity

Table 4.1 presents Bergenline populations by region and for each individual Latinx ethnic group across the three main towns of the Bergenline corridor—Union City, West New York, and North Bergen. We reported at the outset that 77 percent of all Bergenline residents are of Latinx origin exceeding the 75 percent threshold for what demographers call a *hyper-barrio*.[7] We also noted that Bergenline Latinxs represent nineteen different nations with notable presence from ten of them. This combination of *vertical* and *horizontal diversity,* and the absence of a numerically dominant group is quite unique.[8]

Another unique aspect of pan-Latinidad on Bergenline dynamic is the tight geographic confines of the community that create population density and persistent interaction between diverse residents, businesses, and other organizations. Union City and West New York are among the most densely populated municipalities in the United States at over fifty-two thousand people per square mile. The North Bergen census tracts that straddle Bergenline are identical to the other two

**Table 4.1**
**Group diversity on Bergenline: Union City, West New York, and North Bergen**

| | Total Population | Percent of total | All Latinxs, % | Union City, % | West New York, % | North Bergen, % |
|---|---|---|---|---|---|---|
| HISPANIC/LATINX | 134,647 | 77 | – | 76.1 | 77.3 | 68.2 |
| Not Hispanic/Latinx | 47,860 | 23 | – | 23.9 | 22.7 | 31.8 |
| CARIBBEAN | 56,338 | 31 | 42 | 32 | 29 | 31 |
| Cuban | 18,577 | 10 | 14 | 9 | 11 | 12 |
| Dominican | 24,901 | 14 | 19 | 16 | 13 | 12 |
| Puerto Rican | 12,860 | 7 | 10 | 7 | 5 | 8 |
| CENTRAL AMERICAN | 25,535 | 14 | 19 | 15 | 17 | 10 |
| Costa Rican | 348 | <1 | <1 | <1 | <1 | <1 |
| Guatemalan | 5,438 | 3 | 4 | 2 | 4 | 4 |
| Honduran | 5,583 | 3 | 4 | 4 | 3 | 2 |
| Nicaraguan | 583 | <1 | <1 | <1 | 1 | <1 |
| Panamanian | 355 | <1 | <1 | 1 | <1 | <1 |
| Salvadoran | 13,130 | 7 | 10 | 9 | 9 | 4 |
| Mexican | 11,345 | 6 | 8 | 6 | 10 | 3 |
| SOUTH AMERICAN | 37,359 | 21 | 28 | 21 | 18 | 22 |
| Argentinean | 859 | 1 | 1 | <1 | 1 | 1 |
| Bolivian | 287 | <1 | <1 | <1 | <1 | <1 |
| Chilean | 527 | <1 | <1 | <1 | <1 | <1 |
| Colombian | 12,240 | 7 | 9 | 5 | 7 | 8 |
| Ecuadorian | 15,718 | 9 | 12 | 9 | 8 | 9 |
| Paraguayan | 83 | <1 | <1 | <1 | <1 | <1 |
| Peruvian | 5,358 | 3 | 4 | 4 | 2 | 3 |
| Uruguayan | 487 | <1 | <1 | <1 | <1 | 1 |
| Venezuelan | 1,785 | 1 | 1 | 1 | 1 | 1 |
| OTHER HISPANIC/ LATINX | 4,070 | 2 | 3 | 2 | 3 | 2 |
| Total | 182,507 | – | – | 68,226 | 52,662 | 61,619 |

SOURCES: U.S. Census Bureau, "2019 ACS 5-Year Data." Retrieved on January 15, 2023 from data.census.gov.

cities. The streets are narrow and filled with multifamily housing, and the small microbusinesses that cater to everyday needs, producing an endless stretch of small businesses that practically blend together. These concentrations bring different Latinxs together into close proximity on a recurring basis.

An unofficial center-point is the ad hoc bus depot on the Plaza of the Arts Bridge in Union City, which stretches from the Celia Cruz Salsa Park at Thirty-Second Street to Thirtieth Street on the lower side.[9] From there, a combination of New Jersey Transit and privately owned *guaguitas* (jitney buses) can take Route

495 east directly into the Lincoln Tunnel and New York City, any number of backstreets north toward the George Washington Bridge, south toward Jersey City, or out to the nearby western/northwestern suburbs that older Latinx Bergenliners have been moving into over the last thirty years. Most guaguitas service the Bergenline corridor before branching off to outer destinations, while others run on parallel avenues.

Uptown Bergenline stretches from Thirty-Second in Union City to Seventy-Ninth in North Bergen. The strip between Thirty-Second and Forty-Eighth Streets is one way, headed south. Here the street is narrower and the shops are smaller. At Forty-Ninth Street and the West New York border the avenue then becomes a wider, two-way street with slightly bigger stores and homes. Noting the small sliver of Guttenberg from Sixty-Eighth and Seventy-First Streets, the avenue then transitions to North Bergen with the commercial intensity fading around Seventy-Ninth Street at Boulevard East Park. Subtle differences noted, this section between Thirty-Second and Seventy-Ninth Streets is regularly packed with shoppers, commuters, cars, and what seems like an endless stream of guaguitas that mostly say "Bergenline" regardless of where they are going.

Downtown Bergenline is commercial until Fifteenth Street near the William Musto-Union City Museum area, though it is much less intense. The last fifteen blocks have occasional small markets but are far more residential with the avenue ending at Washington Park on the border of Jersey City Heights. But what the lower section of Bergenline might lack in commercial activity is made up for by Summit Avenue between the Jose Marti STEM Academy at Eighteenth Street down to Washington Park and the border of Jersey City Heights and parts of New York Avenue, Hudson Street, Broadway, Palisade, and Park Avenues. Likewise, many of the seventy-nine cross streets branch off Bergenline like overflow spaces for more small businesses; Thirtieth, Forty-Eighth, and Sixtieth Streets in particular are major commercial and travel corridors. The fact that Bergenline is the longest commercial strip in the nation outside Las Vegas is perhaps overshadowed only by the fact that its complimentary commercial strips could likely populate another three-to-four-mile stretch just like it.

## Little Havana on the Hudson: The Cuban Years

To those who are familiar with the area and the Cuban Diaspora, Bergenline still conjures up memories of a community overflowing with Criollo restaurants, bakeries, clothing stores, and other Cuban-themed businesses. From the late 1960s through the mid-1980s, nearly forty thousand Cubans refugees made their way to Hudson County, settling mainly in Union City and West New York.[10] By the 1970s, Bergenline and the surrounding streets were transformed from a community struggling through population decline into the second largest Cuban American enclave in the United States. Just as it once was home to German, Swiss, Austrian, and other Europeans in the early 1900s, the avenue became the place for Cuban Americans to find work, housing, eat, shop, and take care of everyday tasks in stores that functioned in a particular kind of Spanish and Spanglish. As one Italian/Irish American lifetime Hudson resident fondly recalled from his childhood in the late 1960s, "I woke up one day and everything was Cuban."[11]

Social scientists have chronicled Cuban migration and how post 1959 revolution refugees in particular have been able to *Latinize* places like Miami, Union City, and West New York.[12] Those who arrived between 1959 and 1979 generally had more education, skills, capital, and racial privileges than most Latinx migrants. Many did encounter discrimination, but they also received economic, logistic, legal, and symbolic support that made the acclimation process much easier compared to other immigrant groups.[13] As part of the Cold War with the Soviet Union, the United States had an interest in Cubans doing well and not wanting to return to communism. Their white-ish appearance and middle-class backgrounds made Cubans a relatively welcomed group by politicians, business owners, and real estate owners alike.[14]

The most comprehensive analysis of Cubans in the northeast is Yolanda Prieto's book, *The Cubans of Union City*.[15] As with other Latinx communities in the area, Prieto's participants reveal that a handful of Puerto Ricans helped Cubans settle in Union City in the 1940s.[16] In turn, those early Cubans made Bergenline an alternative to the more crowded Miami. The new Cubans faced some resistance from Italian and Irish residents, but they were also welcomed as new clients in the housing market and the many businesses that filled the avenue. Cubans also received significant federal, state, and county resources to facilitate the transition.[17] For example, the Cuban Adjustment Act of 1966 created a fast track to citizenship.[18] Federal monies were transferred to the Small Business Administration and local social service agencies.[19] Cubans quickly made use of this assistance to capitalize on a variety of opportunities. Networks helped each new wave of arrivals find housing, jobs, health care, and educational opportunities that helped ease the transition. They helped each other open new businesses like restaurants, construction companies, doctors' offices, and furniture stores. They set up informal credit lines for newcomers to do things like refurbish and furnish new homes. Bound by a common resentment of Castro and less desire to return to Cuba than their Miami counterparts, Cuban solidarity and external resources were powerful tools for making Bergenline a new home. By the early 1970s, it was as if a slice of Havana had literally been transplanted into Bergenline, even though most of the Cubans there were from other parts of the island.[20]

Cuban business success on Bergenline was complemented by the local embroidering industry and its position vis-à-vis New York City. When large numbers of Cuban refugees began to arrive in 1968, depopulation in Hudson County had begun to affect small businesses and the real estate market. In the background, New York City and much of the northeast were about to experience deindustrialization, the loss of unionized manufacturing jobs, and the further decline of U.S. cities. But Bergenline's dual position as both part of the northeast manufacturing sector and an affordable alternative to it meant that factories in the area would last about a decade longer than in most other places.[21] Many factories began to deunionize, but Cubans still benefitted from the jobs as supplementary work, especially for women in multiworker households.[22] Between the entrepreneurial opportunities, factory work, and a handful of professionals like doctors, Union City, West New York, and the edges of North Bergen and Weehawken created a relatively stable enclave economy.

By the 1990s, the decline of embroidering jobs began to take a toll. Newer waves of Latinxs from South and Central America, Mexico, the Dominican Republic, and even the newer economic migrants from Cuba did not encounter the same assistance programs and economic opportunities as the earlier refugees did. Local small businesses became more important sources of employment and affordable shopping. At the same time, the new sprawling service economy would send more Bergenline residents to work in Manhattan and the suburbs. By that point, many of the older Cubans were established and had begun to move on to nearby Bergen County or Florida.[23]

At the same time, the benefits of citizenship coupled with the power of numbers, and political opportunities allowed Cubans to set in motion a political dynasty that is still taking shape today. One of Prieto's most important observations was that, compared to Miami, Cuban refugees that came to Bergenline were more working class and had stayed in Cuba through the first decade of the Castro government. This meant that they had experienced some of the challenges with the transition and a new system, while realizing how unlikely things were to change in Cuba. Hence, the Bergenline refugees were more likely to have social ties to the island, but less likely to imagine ever going back. As a result, in contrast to Miami where the hope of taking back the island persisted, Bergenline Cubans tended to be more concerned with local affairs.[24]

The political process in Hudson County has been dominated by the Democratic Party for decades, functioning largely as a multiethnic, patronage-politics machine, penetrable via the indoctrination of new groups by the ethnic group in control, and by new ethnic groups ultimately seizing on opportunities often created by corruption scandals. While Cubans in Miami were inclined to align with the Republican Party, most in New Jersey understood that the Democratic Party was essential for addressing local needs such as work conditions, social services, and access to the political process.[25] When the Cuban population surged around Bergenline, they also became targets for patronage and co-optation. In Union City, it was Mayor William Musto, an Italian American, who was compelled by Cuban politico Juliana Valdivia to pay attention to Cubans and elevate Robert Menendez. Valdivia ran an informal Office of Hispanic Affairs during Musto's tenure, and she understood that serving Cubans in this way would help him stay in office. A *New York Times Magazine* article about politics and the changing demographics on Bergenline quoted her: "When Musto lost in 1970 ... he came to know white rice, black beans, and [chicharron] for the first time!"[26]

In 1982, Mayor Musto picked Menendez to run for Union City school board. But on the eve of the elections, Musto was indicted for corruption. Menendez chose to splinter off from Musto and challenge him. In a miraculous New Jersey political corruption moment, Musto, under indictment, still won the election and appointed his successor, Arthur Wichert, before stepping down. Menendez went on to take control of the school board—a position that yielded a significant number of patronage jobs and added support—en route to winning his bid for Union City mayorship the following election in 1986.[27] Menendez then became the local representative in the State Assembly and the State Senate, stockpiling a great deal of power in the Hudson County Democratic Organization along the way. He then continued in the U.S. House of Representatives in 1993 and the U.S. Senate in 2006, while maintaining ties to local politics and the machine in Hudson County.

In West New York there was a parallel process that helped another up and coming Cuban American politico, Albio Sires. In the 1980s, Italian American mayor, Anthony DeFino, failed to build relations with the growing Cuban community in the same way Musto had.[28] Sires shifted from the Republican Party to align with Menendez and the powerful Democratic machine to win the West New York mayorship in 1994. This put Sires in a position to follow Menendez into the State House of Representatives in 2000, and the U.S. Congress in 2006. Together they continue to run pro-immigrant platforms and command a good deal of resources for the state, county, and Bergenline area, even though many residents cannot vote. On the street level, Menendez has maintained a strong presence and is admired by residents from different Latin American countries.

Yet as the Bergenline pan-Latin community matures and signs of gentrification set in, it will be important for researchers and pundits to sort out what becomes of Cuban political domination and the political power of newer groups. In 2022, Robert Menendez Jr. was tapped to run for Sires's seat in Congress, while Sires recaptured mayorship of West New York in 2023, further solidifying the Cuban dynasty and pro-immigrant positions. But in 2024, Menendez Sr. was indicted for his own corruption schemes. Menendez Jr. was able to hold on to his congressional seat in 2024, even as his father was being dropped by Democrats, including the powerful Hudson County Democratic Organization (HCDO), where he wielded power for so long. At the time of this writing, Menendez Sr. has been convicted and agreed to resign from the U.S. Senate.

For now, Union City Mayor Brian Stack, an Irish-American, has elevated his standing with the HCDO while assembling a diverse, pan-Latinx coalition of commissioners to help engage with his Latinx constituents. Stack's on-the-ground approach and unique brand of patronage politics has endeared him to many in the pan-Latinx community. The situation is similar in North Bergen under Italian-American Nicholas Sacco, even though Sacco has become less central to the HCDO and lost his second job as a state congressperson. These strategies of essentially pandering to pan-Latinidad via patronage and low-level social service provision for immigrant communities might continue to work so long as there is no dominant Latinx group on Bergenline, or until the new housing developments shift power to a less Latinx gentrifier class.

## Conflict and Solidarity in the Bolivarian Enclave

So does solidarity appear in other aspects of Bergenline? Is it undermined by history and power imbalances? Both? In this section we focus on the built environment and its role in Bergenline's pan-Latinidad, focusing specifically on pan-Latinx language dynamics. We contrast this example of solidarity with more demographic data that tells a different story. Our goal is to elicit more of the nuances of everyday life on Bergenline and to set a backdrop for interview responses.

Table 4.1 showed that the Latinx population on Bergenline is proportionally greater and more diverse than Miami, where Latinxs make up 70 percent of the population, 50 percent of which are Cubans.[29] Our overview of the Bergenline area helped explain the geography and the tight-knit confines that bring different groups into proximity with each other. Another unique feature of Bergenline pan-Latinidad that also speaks to the conflict–solidarity continuum is the built environment. Tight-knit streets that were once filled with signs and sounds of Cubanness have become one contiguous collage of multiple nations and some blended into a hybrid. The Havana on the Hudson businesses that were born out of immigrant economic strategies remain central to the new pan-Latinx owners and workers in the new service-based economy.[30] Most serve everyday needs of residents by providing clothing, immigration services, health care, furniture, and food. To contend with increasing rents and more ethnic group demands, many of the larger stores have been subdivided into smaller ones. The result is that the commercial signs of individual ethnic groups and umbrella terms are nonstop for about seventy-nine blocks. Within a few short blocks it is possible to walk past a Cuban-, Colombian-, Ecuadorian-, Mexican-, or Central American–themed establishment. Sprinkled throughout are Argentinian and individual Central American (Honduran, Salvadoran, etc.) themed stores, as are Latino, Hispanic, and similar labels like "Criollo" or "Spanish."[31] All are marked with formal and informal signage.

Linguists often refer to the totality of public signage as the linguistic landscape.[32] Linguistic landscapes are important because they reflect the language preferences of a group, even if those preferences do not comport with codified language standards. Linguistic landscapes are also important because they become a source of language and perception learning for community members. From a structural perspective, the linguistic landscape on and around Bergenline advances a pan-Latinx cultural solidarity. This happens via the seventy-nine-block collage of signs representing different nations and pan-ethnic terminology, and through *translanguaging*—the blending of named languages into one ongoing system.[33] On Bergenline there are signs that are bilingual, signs that are in different examples of Spanglish, and signs that blend different Spanishes—words and phrases that are unique to one or more Spanish-speaking countries. These practices are not limited to signs. Conversations on the streets and inside stores span multiple group accents and idioms, with some groups occasionally borrowing from others.

The built environment and linguistic landscape add to Bergenline's pan-Latinx space in which locals bring themselves and interact with the environment and each other, creating new iterations of Latinidad and cultural solidarity, yet still grounded in their own. Yet, in contrast to the overarching population diversity in Table 4.1, politics, and the language synthesizing on the streets, a deeper examination of census data shows that Bergenline Latinxs are not all participating in the community on equitable terms. For example, from Table 4.2, column (a), all Caribbean groups and Colombians tend to be proportionally more female (>50%) in line with the general U.S. population. The rest, however, tend to be less than 50 percent female with Guatemalans at just 35.1 percent. Likewise with age in column (b), Cubans are the oldest group with a median age of 51.9 years, followed by Peruvians at 42.1 years, and Colombians at 38.5 years old. The remaining groups fall between mid- to low 30s, while Mexican median age is just 26.6 years. In most groups, women tend to be older than men, with the greatest divide between Dominican males (26.7 years old) and females (35.9 years old). For Mexicans and Guatemalans, the men and women are relatively the same age.

Column (c) reports a more poignant measure of inequality—the percentage of group members aged 25 years and older that have completed at least one year of college. South Americans are most likely to report having a year or more of college (42.7%), though Ecuadorian and Peruvian men score lower. Caribbeans also score higher on education (35.5%) though Puerto Ricans are somewhat lower at 25.5 percent. Mexicans and Central Americans are least likely to have completed one year of college (24.1% and 22.4% respectively). Salvadorans are an exception with 35.5 percent completing one year of college, while the least likely to reach one year is Guatemalan women (18.1%).

Another key measure of inequality is median household income. From column (d), Caribbeans have the lowest overall income, with Cubans and Dominicans earning $36,560 and $36,814 respectively. This could be related to age and the fact that many Cubans that remain in the area are retired and living in smaller households, while Dominicans are more likely to be economic migrants that enter the United States with fewer resources and are more vulnerable to

Table 4.2
**Sociodemographics: similarity/differences for ten largest groups**

|  | a. Sex[i] m/f |  | b. Age median |  |  | c. College >1 year |  |  | d. Income median HH | e. Born outside United States |
|---|---|---|---|---|---|---|---|---|---|---|
|  | %f | %All | %m | %f | %All | %m | %f | All | % of group |
| **HISPANIC/LATINX** | **50.0** | **34.6** | **32.5** | **37.1** | **33.5** | **31.9** | **35.1** | **43,476** | **61** |
| **CARIBBEAN** | **53.3** | **39.0** | **36.5** | **40.4** | **36.5** | **35.3** | **37.4** | **39,680** | **57** |
| Cuban | 51.4 | 51.9 | 50.7 | 53.6 | 36.0 | 35.6 | 36.3 | 36,560 | 70.7 |
| Dominican | 55.5 | 31.0 | 26.7 | 35.9 | 38.3 | 37.6 | 38.9 | 36,814 | 65.0 |
| Puerto Rican | 52.2 | 33.7 | 32.2 | 36.2 | 25.5 | 25.4 | 25.5 | 41,263 | 3.0 |
| **CENTRAL AMERICAN** | **45.4** | **31.7** | **30.9** | **33.0** | **22.4** | **26.9** | **30.1** | **46,700** | **69.8** |
| Guatemalan | 35.1 | 31.0 | 31.2 | 29.6 | 20.4 | 21.6 | 18.1 | 43,532 | 79.0 |
| Honduran | 42.8 | 31.6 | 31.1 | 31.9 | 14.3 | 14.4 | 14.1 | 45,244 | 71.6 |
| Salvadoran | 48.8 | 31.8 | 30.3 | 33.1 | 35.3 | 34.9 | 35.8 | 49,271 | 66.7 |
| Mexican | 46.0 | 26.7 | 26.6 | 26.6 | 24.1 | 25.3 | 22.4 | 49,271 | 63.0 |
| **SOUTH AMERICAN** | **49.5** | **37.9** | **35.7** | **39.9** | **42.7** | **38.1** | **46.6** | **51,506** | **70.6** |
| Colombian | 52.4 | 38.5 | 34.2 | 42.0 | 40.8 | 42.2 | 39.5 | 50,698 | 70.6 |
| Ecuadorian | 44.2 | 36.3 | 34.3 | 39.0 | 28.6 | 24.5 | 32.9 | 48,636 | 67.6 |
| Peruvian | 48.9 | 42.1 | 41.7 | 43.7 | 37.5 | 31.4 | 42.6 | 48,862 | 79.2 |

NOTES: i U.S. Decennial and ACS Census data are limited to male–female dichotomies; m = male, f = female, HH = household.
SOURCE: U.S. Census Bureau, "2015 ACS 5-Year Data." Retrieved on January 15, 2020 from data.census.gov.

anti-Black racism. Puerto Ricans have been subject to similar barriers as Dominicans but have access to citizenship: they have a somewhat higher household median income of $41,263. Despite less college experience, Central Americans have a higher median household income than Caribbeans. Guatemalan household income is $43,532, Hondurans are slightly higher at $45,244, and Salvadorans at $49,271. Meanwhile, South American as a whole have the highest median household income at $51,506. For the largest three groups, Colombian household income is $50,698, while Peruvians and Ecuadorians are at $48,862 and $48,636 respectively.

Lastly, column (e) reports the percentage of group members that were born outside the United States. This measure tends to correlate with language, citizenship, and familiarity with the home country. The scores are interesting because, more than other measures, they reflect diverse experiences within each regional group. The Caribbean scores are, of course, affected by Puerto Ricans who are U.S. citizens. All other groups score relatively highly with roughly 63 to 79 percent being born outside the United States. Dominicans, Salvadorans, Mexicans, and Ecuadorians are on the lower end of the proportion born outside the United States, all in the mid-60 percent range. Cubans, Colombians, and Hondurans are all around 70 percent, while Peruvians and Guatemalans are both at the upper end with 79 percent.

What can we make of the coexistence of similarities and differences inside tight-knit pan-Latin spaces? Gilda Ochoa writes: "Cross-Latina/o relationships . . . are not fixed and cannot be presumed. Instead, they are constructed and negotiated within the context of several simultaneous and interacting phenomenon and within various locations . . . just as the matrix of macro[structural] factors influence . . . institutions that might shape cross-Latina/o relationships, cross-Latina/o relationships are experienced and lived from the bottom-up—through microscopic, everyday interactions by individuals and Latina/o organizations that might work to change institutions and macro factors."[34]

In the broadest sense, Latinxs share common histories, language, migration challenges, and common interests that can be nurtured by a community. It is also true that they migrate at different times, for different reasons, with different sets of resources. The geographic community functions as one institution as does the business community, schools, and some churches. Whether or not Latinxs of different backgrounds coalesce in solidarity or remain divided is not so much a yes or no question as a series of ebbs and flows shaped by multiple contextual factors and ongoing iterations of social interaction in which actors have degrees of agency. Or, as one resident said when asked if different Latinx groups in the area get along and help each other: "depende de la situacion . . . [pauses and looks outside at the Avenue] y la persona!" In the following section we share more ethnographic insights and in-depth interviews with community residents to examine some of the different manifestations of history, structure, and everyday life on Bergenline.

FIGURE 4.1. Guaguitas on Bergenline at Forty-Eighth Street, facing south. (Photo by Alex Trillo)

## Residents on Living in Bergenline's Pan-Latinx Space

This chapter began with reference to a guaguita ride down Bergenline Avenue. Like much of the local business community on Bergenline and in other immigrant communities throughout New Jersey, the creation and use of the guaguita system is another pragmatic, entrepreneurial response to local needs for transportation. Currently, there are around 6,500 of these jitney buses operating across the northern half of the state. They largely serve immigrant enclaves and other minoritized communities in Passaic, Bergen, and Hudson Counties. Bus owners are mostly immigrant-owned companies like Spanish Transportation Services, while they lease them to independent drivers, most of whom are South American, Dominican, or Middle Eastern.

The guaguitas are another mechanism that brings Latinx Bergenliners together into shared space and produces cultural solidarity. The buses are smaller and more intimate and operate mostly in Spanish. They let some customers slide and occasionally overcharge others. They might make an unmarked stop if you need it. Edwin, a twenty-seven-year-old Dominican man from North Bergen shared:

> I really like them because they remind me of the public transportation I used to take in the Dominican Republic. They have music in them, and . . . drivers

talk to the passengers making jokes and things like that.... It's not this rigid thing where you just pick me up, drop me off... they make political campaigns... They put flyers of whatever politician they are supporting. You cannot see that in New Jersey Transit.... [And] you will always talk and joke with people from different countries.

Another place we observed cultural solidarity was in community language practices. Earlier we described some of the linguistic landscape dynamics such as the blending of Spanishes and Spanglishes as pragmatic forms of transculturation. When we asked about Latinx diversity and what it was like to live with so many different groups, our respondents spoke directly about language blending as a form of cultural solidarity. For example, Julio, a twenty-four-year-old White-appearing male who migrated from Cuba to New Jersey as a teenager, talked specifically about different Spanishes and his acclimation process:

JULIO  Like we Cubans speak very fast... and... cut words.... Even communication with my Colombian friends, Dominican friends, sometimes it got a little complicated. It was like a barrier, even in Spanish, a language we all spoke, sometimes it was complicated, my friends all asked me, told me please talk slower... or specific words they would say I wouldn't understand... even though we are all Hispanics... we are all different...
INTERVIEWER  Do you remember a specific word or situation where this happened?
JULIO  I would say from Dominicans the word "vaina." It's used for so many things! [*collective laugh*]... We [Cubans] don't use it at all. For us it's like a little thing that grows on a tree, then it falls off, and has seeds in it.... For them it's like everything!... I think it was so hard for me to understand because in one sentence you can have so many vainas at the same time that you can lose track of what they were talking about in the first place... [*laughs*] now [vaina] is normal for all of us.[35]

Julio's comments capture his transition away from being strictly culturally Cuban into solidarity with his non-Cuban Latinx friends and something more pan-Latinx. These shifts are created out of everyday interactions with friends from different backgrounds. For people who live on Bergenline, it is the type of interaction that can happen when one enters a grocery store, a restaurant, botanicas that serve spiritual-health needs, or in Sunday mass. These repeated interactions lead to a fusion of language that fills and extends the transcultural space from one that is Cubanized to something pan-Latinx. The repetition of these kinds of interactions eventually solidifies in language and other forms of cultural solidarity. Yet even though Julio provides some insight into cultural solidarity and the forging of a pan-Latinx identity, he does so without abandoning his dedication to being Cuban. Julio at once talks about "We Cubans" with the same fluidity he has with "we Hispanics." This duality is in many ways how Latinxs live and experience everyday life on Bergenline.

Milly, a twenty-five-year-old Afro-Colombian woman, expressed similar tensions between cultural solidarity and group individuality in a way that emanates from the unique pan-Latinx geographic community and the normalization of pan-Latin interactions:

> Bergenline is like the library. You can go there and check out whatever you want.... It never clicked until I went to college and I was like, wow! [*laughs*] Because, in the moment it just felt natural . . . during those moments we were living each other's culture, without realizing.... All of these things [trying things] . . . we were just doing naturally—I was inventing sandwiches . . . we were all trying each other's stuff . . . living each other's culture without realizing it . . . because it was in one place . . . we didn't have to go anywhere. It was little effort to do it. It was happening in . . . each other's houses . . . going out to eat . . . hanging out in school . . . church . . . and we actually were a majority.[36]

Our in-depth interviews also revealed that there were acts of solidarity that had more material implications in line with the ways Prieto described Puerto Ricans helping Cubans, or Cubans helping each other in earlier eras.[37] We learned from respondents like Edwin that many organizations including churches have transitioned to become pan-Latinx organizations that serve current community needs:

> I don't really go with her. I think mostly she goes with the woman downstairs from our old apartment. She's Dominican, too. But the people there [at the church] are from everywhere. I think the priest is Cuban. But she's always talking about Puerto Ricans, Salvadorans, you know how Latinxs are. We always identify people by country . . . but they're always doing things together where they bring food . . . do community service projects . . . and its never just Dominicans.[38]

We also learned about some of the ways Latinxs help each other across ethnic lines in entrepreneurial activities, again putting the avenue and the commercial core at the center of the community. This was the case with one Dominican restaurant owner downtown named Zaida:

> We had one place on Summit. It was always busy but it's very small, only a few tables. People used to wait in line down the street. And this man, a Cuban guy, lawyer, he used to wait every day and tell me: You need a bigger place! So one day he said to come with him, that he wanted to show me something. And he brought me here and introduced me to the owner of this deli owned by a

Cuban guy. That he was sick and retiring and did we want to take this place. That's how we got here. And now I own the building![39]

In another store owner interview with Jorge, we learned how a long-standing Cuban restaurant was sold to two Salvadoran brothers who had been working there as servers.

> The original owner was a Cuban ... and opened in 1976. My brother and I worked here and another place down the street as waiters. ... When the owner retired, he asked if we wanted to buy the restaurant. This was around 1996. We thought he was joking but everybody was working here for a long time and he didn't want to disrupt anything. ... So he helped us with the financing because that's the only way it would work.[40]

While it is difficult to know the exact motivations for Cubans and other Latinxs to help the newer Dominican and Salvadoran owners, these interviews suggest to us that there is at least some degree of solidarity between them. In these cases, social networks across ethnic lines do play a role in creating entrepreneurial opportunities that otherwise might not be possible. It is Zaida's and Jorge's perception that the Cubans were being helpful and trying to create some continuity. There were other examples of this kind of helpfulness when our respondents talked about Cuban teachers in schools, priests and other important actors in the church, or when growing up.

## Divides, Tensions, and Conflict

Of course, our observations, interviews, and other data sources did illustrate that Bergenline is more complicated than pan-Latinx solidarity. Some of what we observed in the built environment reinforces what we saw in the census data. For example, the number and general aesthetics of restaurants and other stores show signs that some groups have more resources than others. In politics, while Cubans dominate the top levels of government, some groups have a significant presence on city councils. And in our interviews, we observed overt forms of what Marie Mallet and Joanna Pinto-Coelho call secondary marginalization, where members of one minoritized group contribute to the minoritization of another group, or otherwise take advantage of them.[41] Moreover, in some cases we found that solidarity and tension coexisted as we observed in Milly and Julio.

One example of group tension has to do with community reactions to a sighting of the Mexican patron saint, La Virgen de Guadalupe, in a tree trunk on Bergenline in 2012.[42] The story resurfaced when we asked Julio about groups getting along. For decades, the Cuban saint, Caridad del Cobre, was the most popular religious figure in the community, decorating botanica windows, restaurant walls, trinket stores, and community murals. The initial sighting followed an automobile accident in which a Mexican man was killed on that same block.[43] Residents, politicians, clergy, and others with connections to the neighborhood affectionately took note. The story received both local and national media attention, reaching the *New York Times, Los Angeles Times,* and CNN en Español. The garden box became decorated with fresh flowers, candles, and similar offerings. The crowds came from the neighborhood and from many of New Jersey's surrounding Latinx communities in Bergen County, Passaic, Newark, New Brunswick, and Perth Amboy. Some were Mexican, but they were also Dominican, Cuban, Ecuadorian, Colombian, Honduran, and Salvadoran. They took pictures, left prayer beads, flowers, candles, and overtly challenged those who came in opposition or skepticism.[44]

But not all residents were comfortable with Guadalupe. To some it might have even seemed like a challenge to Caridad del Cobre's status as the patron saint of Bergenline, or to Cuban elitism. And so it was peculiar when the tree mysteriously caught fire in 2013. According to Julio:

I walk past there every day because it's close to my house ... so I chose it to write an essay for my theology class. It was interesting because people kept saying it was the candle like they wanted to believe it was an accident. But it's very hard for a candle to burn a tree, you know ... The truth is that some people were upset. The mayor had to spend a lot of money on security because people were throwing things and trying to damage it. They had the police and then they put the fence. They knew some people didn't like it.[45]

Our interviews also revealed more direct examples of secondary marginalization in the way older groups perceive newer ones. For example, when we asked about changes on Bergenline, Yolanda, a fifty-nine-year-old Cuban woman had this to say:

I'm an immigrant. . . . But when you see those [new] immigrants they're living out of ... social security, medicare ... they have (this is a topic I don't like but I will express it), and they're living out of the government, they have a million children, they're undocumented, but when you see their car they're driving a Mercedes Benz or they're carrying purse I cannot even afford and they're full of jewelries ... I don't think that's fair ... [*pause*] [In Cuba] when they found out we were leaving the country, they took my father away from home for five years to work in the country like he was a prisoner. I was only allowed to see him once a month. And here, we came, and he was making $1.25 an hour to survive. OK. That was his first job making the record players, they were made of plastic, he would come home all burned on his hands. We [Cubans] never went to welfare, we never went to any place.... And I see all these people, they're getting all the benefits without paying their dues.[46]

Yolanda's perceptions are common among older Cubans, though certainly not universal. Research comparing Cuban American refugees with newer, post-Mariel migrants shows that refugees are less connected to the island, more pro-American, and conservative.[47] Yolanda and many refugees *became American* and extended their affinities for the Republican Party at a time when cities were in decline, conservatives became less favorable of immigration due to globalization and less demand for migrant labor,[48] and anti-immigrants and anti-minority narratives were on the rise. Unfortunately, some Cuban American refugees gloss over the resources they received to help settle in the United States, while buying into the false correlation that urban centers changed because of the influx of populations of color, including those that now share Bergenline. It is, in this flawed perspective, the new immigrant's fault that luxury stores have left, and things look shabby. The more realistic explanations are deindustrialization, White flight, centralized shopping malls, and the fact that newer groups have less racial privilege and fewer resources, including access to citizenship.

But these patterns of incorporation are not a given and can shift where old (Cuban) refugees come in contact with newer (Cuban) migrants in situations where newer migrants can sensitize the older ones to their unique struggles and the island.[49] This kind of interaction seems more likely to happen inside the tight confines of Bergenline's pan-Latinx space between elder Cubans and immigrants from other Latin American countries, as was the case with restaurant owners, Jorge and Grissel. By being in common spaces such as a workplace, church, school, or political activities, the pan-Latinx geographic community compels more possibilities for solidarity in everyday life.

These tensions and situational differences comport with the conflict–solidarity continuum and what we observed on Bergenline. In brief, contextual factors can shape—and eventually shift—immigrant outlooks and thus how different groups interact with each other. In this sense, the pan-Latinx community and all its functions are a key backdrop for bringing Bergenliners into shared spaces, socializing them into pan-Latinidad practices, and even prompting them to further participate. But these interactions are qualified by a number of background factors, such as generational cohort and exposure to other experiences. Older Cubans and others that knew the Havana on the Hudson years may define themselves apart from newer residents, but there are situations that can alter this dynamic to continue the supportive aspects of the enclave in pan-Latinx form. In contrast, younger generations that grow up on Bergenline live fluidly across ethnic lines. These experiences are facilitated by school but also by just hanging out on the avenue, eating in restaurants or riding the guaguitas. These younger people all conveyed a particular affinity with their pan-Latinx practices, even claiming them as "their normal."

## Discussion and Conclusion

This chapter set out to understand Bergenline Avenue—a place we have described as a unique pan-Latinx geographic community in northern New Jersey. We began by geographically situating Bergenline as a densely populated place anchored by the commercial strip on the edge of New York City. We described how three municipalities traversing Bergenline—Union City, West New York, and North Bergen—are all bound by similar population dynamics, culture, and overlapping social ties. Our guiding questions were: How did this happen? Is there solidarity inside pan-Latinx space or do social differences fuel conflict that undermines cohesiveness? A key point in this chapter is that Bergenline as a place constitutes a unique pan-Latinx community that creates some solidarity by default, apart from whether or not Latinxs from different nations, generations, or cohorts would self-identify as such. The pan-Latinidad manifests from population diversity, density, and the built environment that inspires interaction, but also reflects and shapes language and other cultural practices.

To understand the formation of Bergenline we provided an overview of the Cuban years, which figure prominently in the pan-Latinx community it is today. Key to the Cuban experience was early connections to Puerto Ricans who were migrating to many parts of New Jersey, the unique opportunities around Bergenline as the Cuban Revolution of 1959 happened, global politics and the resources Cubans had access to, and the power they could leverage to make Bergenline into Havana on the Hudson. Rather than following a straight-line assimilation model, the Cuban transculturation of Bergenline, coupled with political inroads, make the pan-Latinx community more possible, even now as Cubans move out into the suburbs or Florida.

We also examined the dynamics of pan-Latinx Bergenline, the experiences that residents and business owners have there, and the way groups perceive each other. One result is that there are varieties of solidarity across groups and that the totality of these interactions adds to the systemic pan-Latinx identity. In this sense, the community with all its places for interaction *is* an institution and part of Ochoa's solidarity–conflict *sancocho* that facilitates solidarity.[50]

On that note, we also learned that cultural solidarity is not a constant on Bergenline. Depending on the context and who is involved, relations can be positive, negative, or vacillate between both. One interesting and less problematic example is that Latinxs in pan-Latinx space appear likely to exist in a state of duality—if not a continuum—between their home and pan-Latinx cultures. That is, they simultaneously embrace moments of solidarity and commitment to home nations. Folks such as Milly and Julio speak of "we" Latinxs and "we" Colombians or Cubans often in the same sentences. Edwin sees his fellow bus riders as a collective that reminds him of the Dominican Republic. This coexistence of a U.S. pan-Latinx and transnational identity speaks also to a unique pattern of social incorporation into U.S. society that challenges a traditional assimilation model that describes earlier European immigrants. Latinxs have been theorized to either become more American, more integrated with an urban underclass, or isolated within their own groups, but not as part of a pan-Latinx group.

Some troubling divisions also emerged when we looked at demographics, asked respondents to reflect on the neighborhood, and delved into the story of the Guadalupe apparition. While younger generation 1.5 and second-generation folks are inclined to engage in cultural solidarity, older and longtime residents have some inclination to take a negative view of newer immigrants and the incorporation of their icons. This perspective seems to vary based on the extent to which the older residents are engaged with newcomers in common spaces like school, work, or politics.

Despite the leveling of Latinx populations and the pan-Latin character of the community, we surmise that Cubans still play a critical role on Bergenline and that the foundation for this centrality hinges on at least two factors. One is the formation of Havana on the Hudson and the local New Jersey context. That Cubans benefitted from and leveraged local opportunities in business and politics continues to keep Cubans in key positions. The second is the different settlement patterns between groups and what Bergenline means to each of them, which is not always the same. Outside of Cubans, each group on Bergenline has other enclaves throughout the New York metro region: Colombians in Queens and Elizabeth, Peruvians in Passaic, Dominicans in Washington Heights, and Puerto Ricans in Harlem and Jersey City. For Latinxs other than Cubans, Bergenline is often an alternative. Many non-Cuban respondents did say their families lived elsewhere in New York or New Jersey before coming to Bergeline. On that note, any attempt to understand Bergenline's pan-Latinidad requires covering a lot of territory, and this chapter barely scratches the surface. It remains to be seen how the unique contours of Bergenline contrast with Latinx group experiences in other parts of New Jersey.

Finally, we cannot ignore some of the pending changes throughout Hudson County and the New York City metro area. Johanna Londoño's *Abstract Barrios: The Crises of Latinx Visibility in Cities* has pointed to initial signs of gentrification and the erasure of the pan-Latinx aesthetic we have described on Bergenline. On the one hand, Latinx communities in the region such as East Harlem, Williamsburg Brooklyn, and the Lower East Side, have experienced this erasure and depletion of cultural resources that follows. In neighboring Jersey City and Hoboken there are scarce remnants of once thriving Puerto Rican communities. On the other hand, having had some time to watch these projects unfold, our sense is that they are slow in coming to Bergenline. One reason is that so much governance and development that causes aesthetic changes is inconsistent. Another possibility is that the long-term effects of Cuban transculturation, complimented by the spirit and resources of newer groups, may delay the process compared to the other communities we have mentioned. This is one of many topics to further explore.

# Notes

1 Dennis Poplin, *Communities: A Survey of Theories and Methods of Research* (New York: Macmillan, 1979).
2 We use Latinx here as the group label for Latinos, Latinas, Latines, and Hispanics, as a reminder that gender exclusion and other forms of marginalization remain unresolved.
3 Northern Cubans is a term used by some Cuban Americans in the northeast to distinguish from Miami Cubans.
4 J. S. Onésimo Sandoval and Bienvenido Ruiz, "Pan-Latino Neighborhoods: Contemporary Myth or Reality?" *Sociological Focus* 44 (2011): 295–313. This shows that Latino neighborhood diversity is increasing, but that greater density is associated with less diversity.
5 Cristina Beltrán, *The Trouble with Unity: Latino Politics and the Creation of Identity* (Oxford: Oxford University Press, 2010).
6 Gilda Ochoa, "Entre Nosotros: Theorizing, Researching, and Constructing Cross-Latina/o Relations in the United States," in *Latina/os in the United States: Changing the Face of America*, eds. Havidan Rodriguez, Rogelio Sanz, and Cecilia Menjivar (New York: Springer, 2007), 263–276.
7 J. S Onésimo Sandoval and Joel Jennings, "Barrios and Hyper Barrios: How Latino Neighborhoods Changed the Urban Built Environment," *Journal of Urbanism: International Research on Placemaking and Urban Sustainability* 5, no. 2–3 (2012): 111–138. Demographers use the term hyper-barrio for a neighborhood that is 75 percent or more Latino.
8 Onésimo Sandoval and Jennings, "Barrios and Hyper Barrios."
9 See Johana Londoño, chapter 3 of this volume for a photo of the Plaza.
10 Yolanda Prieto, *The Cubans of Union City: Immigrants and Exiles in a New Jersey Community* (Philadelphia: Temple University Press, 2009); Eleanor M. Rogg and Rosemary Santana Cooney, *Adaptation and Adjustment of Cubans: West New York, New Jersey* (New York: Fordham Hispanic Research Center, 1980).
11 Interview with a Weehawken resident who grew up in Union City, June 2017.
12 Alejandro Portes, "The Social Origins of the Cuban Enclave Economy of Miami," *Sociological Perspectives* 30, no. 4 (2018): 340–372; Alex Stepick, Guillermo Grenier, Max Castro, and Marvin Dunn, *This Land Is Our Land: Immigrants and Power in Miami* (Los Angeles: University of California Press, 2003).
13 Ramón Grosfoguel and Chloé S. Georas, "Latino Caribbean Diasporas in New York," in *Mambo Montage: The Latinization of New York City*, ed. Agustín Laó-Montes and Arlene Dávila (New York: Columbia University Press, 2001), 97–118.
14 Johana Londoño, *Abstract Barrios: The Crises of Latinx Visibility in Cities* (Durham, NC: Duke University Press, 2020).
15 Prieto, *Cubans of Union City*.
16 Londoño, *Abstract Barrios*, finds evidence that the first Cuban in the area arrived from New York City in the 1920s.
17 Prieto, *Cubans of Union City*.
18 William L. Mitchell, "The Cuban Refugee Program," Social Security Administration Bulletin, March 1962, https://www.ssa.gov/policy/docs/ssb/v25n3/v25n3p3.pdf.
19 Denise M. Cornin, "Ethnicity, Opportunity, and Occupational Mobility in the United States" (PhD diss., State University of New York, Stony Brook, 1981); Prieto 2009.

20 Prieto, *Cubans of Union City*.
21 Silvio Laccetti, *Report to the State of New Jersey* (Hoboken, NJ: Stevens Institute of Technology, 2016).
22 Francis Martel, "Hanging by a Thread: Surviving Globalism and Losing Factory Culture in the Embroidery Capital of the World," *Breitbart*. Retrieved on January 15, 2021 from https://www.breitbart.com/union-city/.
23 Elizabeth Llorente, "Cuban-Americans Leaving New Jersey for the South," *Baltimore Sun*, March 22, 2022, https://www.baltimoresun.com/news/bs-xpm-2002-03-22-0203220043-story.html.
24 Prieto, *Cubans of Union City*.
25 Prieto, *Cubans of Union City*.
26 Jeff Stein, "An Army in Exile," *New York Magazine*, September 1979.
27 Fred Snowflack, "CONTEXT: In 1974, Menendez Seemed Mature Beyond His Years," *Insider NJ*, November 16, 2017, https://www.insidernj.com/context-1974-menendez-seemed-mature-beyond-years/.
28 Joseph Sullivan, "Town Mayor for 22 Years Is Facing Recall Vote," *New York Times*, January 20, 1993.
29 U.S. Census Bureau, "2020 Decennial Redistricting Data, Table P2." Retrieved on January 15, 2023 from data.census.gov.
30 Michael Martin, *Residential Segregation Patterns of Latinos in the United States, 1990–2000* (London: Routledge, 2007).
31 "Spanish" has been commonly used by Latinxs in the New Jersey/New York City context. It is based on language, not nation.
32 Rodrigue Landry and Richard Y. Bourhis, "Linguistic Landscape and Ethnolinguistic Vitality: An Empirical Study," *Journal of Language and Social Psychology* 16, no. 1 (1997): 23–49.
33 Ofelia García and Li Wei, *Translanguaging: Language, Bilingualism and Education* (New York: Palgrave Macmillan, 2014).
34 Ochoa, "Entre Nosotros," 267.
35 Interview with Julio, May 2018.
36 Interview with Milly, May 2021.
37 Prieto, *Cubans of Union City*; Liz Robbins, "In 'Havana on the Hudson,' Few Are Left to Celebrate Castro's Death," *New York Times*, November 16, 2016.
38 Interview with Edwin, January 2018.
39 Interview with Zaida, October 2019.
40 Interview with Jorge, December 2021.
41 Marie L. Mallet and Joanna M. Pinto-Coelho, "Investigating Intra-Ethnic Divisions among Latino Immigrants in Miami, Florida," *Latino Studies* 16, no. 1 (2018): 91–112.
42 Nate Schweber, "In New Jersey, a Knot in a Tree Trunk Draws the Faithful and the Skeptical," *New York Times*, July 22, 2012.
43 "West New York Residents Believe Likeness of Virgin Mary Has Appeared in Tree," CBSNews.com, July 13, 2012, https://www.cbsnews.com/newyork/news/west-new-york-residents-believe-likeness-of-virgin-mary-has-appeared-in-tree/.
44 "Imagen de Virgen une a hispanos de West New York," *El Nuevo Herald*, January 15, 2013, www.elnuevoherald.com%2Fnoticias%2Famerica-latina%2Farticle202020280.html&usg=AOvVaw2pE4cu13qv9-55fOEkoSDo; Schweber, "In New Jersey," noting that the city spent "$1,000 a day for police officers to prevent vandalism, defuse confrontations, and keep traffic moving."
45 Gennarose Pope, "Hundreds Descend on West New York to Pray after Image of Virgin Saint Spotted in Tree," *HudsonReporter*, July 12, 2012, https://archive

.hudsonreporter.com/2012/07/12/hundreds-descend-on-west-new-york-to-pray-after-image-of-virgin-saint-spotted-in-tree/.
46 Interview with Yolanda, May 2020.
47 Susan Eckstein and Lorena Barberia, "Grounding Immigrant Generations in History: Cuban Americans and Their Transnational Ties," *International Migration Review* (Fall 2002): 36, 3.
48 Margaret Peters, *Trading Barriers: Immigration and the Remaking of Globalization* (Princeton, NJ: Princeton University Press, 2017).
49 Eckstein and Barberia, "Grounding Immigrant Generations in History."
50 Ochoa, "Entre Nosotros"; see also Melanie Z. Plascencia "Age-Friendly as Tranquilo Ambiente: How Sociocultural Perspectives Shape the Lived Environment of Latinx Older Adults," *Gerontologist* 62, no. 1 (February 2022): 110–118, for a similar perspective.

# 5
## "Aggressive Newark"

### Puerto Ricans, Brazilians, and Structuring Feelings under Neoliberalism

ANA Y. RAMOS-ZAYAS

The first thing that I learned here [in the United States] was the trouble with black people. Very antagonistic, aggressive. They are like that, with that attitude, and they are proud of it! I never saw something like that in Brazil. I never saw people like that there, with that attitude. People are afraid of black people here. Because it's like they are going to hit you out of nowhere. And you can't show them you're afraid because they'll fight you even more, they're like guys.
—Ana Tereza Botelho, age nineteen, Brazilian living in Ironbound

I think Hispanic families are very open. They will accept anyone as long as they give us respect... because we are

ourselves [racially] mixed, so we're used to that. My aunt is married to a black guy and my family is crazy about him. He eats our food, dances salsa, he says a few words in Spanish.... It's harder with the [Black] women because they get very jealous of us. They think we steal their men, because you see more couples of a black man and a Puerto Rican woman than the other way around. That we're prettier, have prettier hair. They do give you a lot of attitude, to see what you do. They can be very aggressive, like they live on an edge, and you have to analyze the situation, which way it's going to go.
—Migdalia Rivera, age eighteen, U.S.-born Puerto Rican living in North Broadway

I met Ana Tereza and Migdalia while doing fieldwork at the high schools they attended in two neighborhoods in Newark, New Jersey—the Ironbound, a largely Portuguese area with a growing influx of Brazilian migrants, and North Broadway, a predominantly Puerto Rican neighborhood with a significant presence of African Americans and Caribbean and South American immigrants. Like the other U.S.-born Latino and Latin American migrants whom I met in Newark in the first decade of the 2000s, Ana Tereza and Migdalia consistently raised, without any prompting, the volatility, uncertainty, and illegibility that characterized their everyday relationships with, and affective perceptions of, African Americans, particularly African American women.

Migdalia was oftentimes confused for African American. She had arrived from Puerto Rico a year before I met her in a bilingual class at the Ironbound high school: "I have no problem with Black guys. They always try to speak a little Spanish, say 'mamichula' and things like that [*laughed*]. But I can't stand Black women. They are arrogant and like to fight. They look at you, at the fact that you speak Spanish, and they hate you for that. They don't like your color.... They have their own style, way of walking, machúas [unfeminine, butch]." Likewise, Ana Tereza, a dark-skinned Brazilian woman who had arrived from Belo Horizonte in the late 1990s, declared: "The thing that I learned here was the trouble with Black people. You are looking at someone and they're like 'What you looking at?'—very aggressive. And don't think it's the guys that I'm talking about. Nooooo ... it's the women!" The conversation with Alexandra made me go over my fieldnotes and transcripts again, only to realize the many references to "girls being jumped," "lesbian gangs," or "aggressive Black lesbians" in the hundreds of pages of data I had. I had dismissed some of the data as "urban legend" before realizing how ubiquitous these narratives of violence and sexuality were to the fabric of systems of difference, race, affect, and relationships among young people in Newark.

Most of them emphatically condemned African American women's "attitude" as vulgar, unfeminine, and contrary to an aesthetic of self-care and comportment to which both Latinas and Latin American women aspired, and to which they attributed success in all aspects of life, from securing jobs to finding boyfriends. They offered characterizations of Black women as affectively inadequate, excessively kinetic, and over-the-top or flashy fashion, hair, or nail styles. Like other Newark residents with whom I spoke over the years, Ana Tereza and Migdalia formulated a surprisingly cohesive characterization of "Blackness" as a deeply emotive and gendered idiom, appraised in a visceral and spectacular way, not unlike an audience's response to an over-the-top, exaggerated television talk show.

Through quotidian observations, these young U.S.-born Latinos and Latin American migrants assessed the interactive styles of African American women in ways that were surprisingly congruent with mainstream corporative and managerial views of "emotional intelligence," a prerogative of the upwardly mobile, productive individual.[1] There was a general sense that the emotional style of African American women was more difficult to commodify because of their presumed inability to hide temperamental outbursts, a quality that would render them unmarriageable and unemployable in most of the service-sector, customer-oriented jobs available to working-class women of color in Newark. Likewise, among recent Latin American migrants, a politicized Black consciousness elicited feelings of anger rather than appreciation for the United States. In the cosmologies of many of these migrants, a Black/White U.S. racial model, which in their view was obsessed with race, was to blame for the emotional handicap—the "aggressiveness"—of African Americans and, consequently, their presumed material failure in a city like Newark.

Nevertheless, young Latinos and Latin American migrants also acknowledged the importance of acquiring a form of racial knowledge that would enable them to better navigate Newark's urban landscape. They recognized that African Americans possessed a desired form of urban competency, and the modernity, hipness, and cosmopolitanism globally associated with Blackness. Acquiring and internalizing the knowledge of how race operates in social exchange became a deeply emotive process for Latinos in Newark, as individuals both phenomenologically experienced these emotions and projected them onto others, particularly African Americans, to render them legible. Quotidian interactions in schools, neighborhoods, commercial venues, or the streets and public transportation oftentimes propelled a therapeutic (and psychoanalytical) engagement, a heightened gaze of Black bodies and mannerisms. These interactions and the historical, political, and economic contexts enabled a sort of urban emotional commonsense.

In Newark, aggression frequently served as a meta-sentiment that dominated quasi-therapeutic readings and assessments of emotional adequacy. Fred Myers uses the term "meta-sentiment" to refer to a specific regulatory emotion that some communities place outside the person, as a "control feeling," to teach individuals what to feel and what not to feel, what kind of self to be and not be.[2] In this sense, distinctions between emotions at a micro (social psychological) level oftentimes get confused with emotions at a structural and cultural level. Latin American migrants and U.S.-born Latinos deployed these readings in their everyday encounters with, visual attention to, and narrative understanding of African Americans. The alignment between emotions and the needs of state and market has reinvigorated the discourse of personal responsibility in everyday racial encounters.

Under neoliberalism, racialized groups were incited to develop complementary scales to measure their marketability, attractiveness, and desirability, as well as their "worthiness" of U.S. citizenship, in accordance with the urban renewal goals of cities and surveillance projects of the nation-state.[3] Variously racialized populations assessed their own emotional style against the emotional competency of others, so that groups were able to explain material conditions as consequences of the "attitudes" or "way of being" of other minority groups, rather than the structures on which these conditions were played out. Because of the multilayered nature of emotions, these assessments were prone to creating a slippery sense that political economy did not really matter. The illusion of "immediacy" and "intimacy" derived from emotions rendered them powerful tools in advancing neoliberal objectives.

Emotions were an integral part of the historical unfolding of politically significant events, institutions, and practices in Newark, New Jersey. In Newark, "anger" and "aggression" became dominant emotions inscribed through the interpretation, narration, and policy outcome of salient historical events in Newark's urban landscape. I am inspired here by Raymond Williams's dynamic integration of two seemingly oppositional phenomena: "feelings" as a kind of experience that is inchoate and derives from who we are without us being able to articulate it, and "structure," which suggests that this level of experience has an underlying logic rather than being haphazard. Williams introduces the term "structures of feeling" to distinguish the lived experiences of a community from the institutional and ideological organization of society. He shows that the relations of production and the pursuit of a hegemonic cultural configuration relied on the systemic or institutional regulation of individual emotion, as well as on the emotive articulation of those very regulatory systems.[4] The institutional operation of the Newark Renaissance, like other urban development projects that privilege real estate, commercial, and touristic interests, requires that cities are associated with a right (middle-class or neoliberal-friendly) emotional style for their success. Neoliberal measures coexist with certain anti-poverty government initiatives and together constitute the operational aspects, institutional components, and emotional requirements of the Newark Renaissance.

## The Feel That Sells Newark: From "Aggressive" City to Neoliberal-Friendly Emotional Regime

The neoliberal policies of the 1980s and 1990s implicitly required that a normative style of emotional management—in which characterizations of the city as aggressive or angry were concealed or redressed—be instituted if attractive real estate, well-attended artistic venues, and the promotion of tourism were to be successful urban-development strategies. Therefore, examining the emergence and control of aggression in Newark requires an analysis of historical moments that aimed to solidify particular social structures; in this sense, it also requires an examination of how old and new forms of capitalist development entered synergistic interaction with a politics of individual agency.

Newark's perceived pathology was not based on just any form of illness but specifically on mental illness and an emotional inadequacy projected onto its racialized populations. An emotional regime was established in Newark according to which the welfare of certain populations, particularly the Black "underclass," was attributed to their inappropriate emotional style—an embodied form of the city's aggressiveness. Visions of racial violence and urban decay that crystallized in our collective memory around the time of the 1967 riots still dominate the popular imagination and function as a dividing line in Newark's collective historical consciousness. Among some Newark residents, everyday social exchanges, memories, images, and daily uses of the built environment in Newark frequently evoke images of the riots or the "rebellion," as well as speculations about "those [former Newark residents] who left" or "angry blacks."[5] Those who stayed came to witness an urban change that altered most, if not all, aspects of their lives and identities at a most intimate level. To them, the riots provided the precise date to affix to the death of Newark.

Rarely was "slum clearance," rather than the 1967 riots, the entry point into everyday narratives of Newark's "decay."[6] Nevertheless, Newark has been rightly called "a living laboratory for nearly every bad planning idea of the twentieth century."[7] Accounts of the lived experiences of space must consider how place is produced and conceived in light of citywide policies, urban planning, and, in the case of Newark, the "slum clearance" in the 1950s and 1960s. Urban renewal attempts within the city destroyed whole neighborhoods, replacing low-rise, vernacular residences with mismanaged public housing projects. The new interstate highways linking Newark to adjacent suburbs cut the city into pieces, dividing and isolating neighborhoods, and increasing levels of segregation. Along with most major industrial centers in the United States, Newark had fallen from grace by the 1960s. Affectively charged images that attribute a negatively-judged anger to Black residents dominated Newark's representation in the national media, obliterating historical evidence of urban decay that predated the riots.[8] The centrality of these images that permanently attached anger to Black bodies led to multiple levels of discourse—from national narratives to everyday neighborhood conversations—and contributed to a particular kind of emotive inscription or feel associated with Newark.

Since the 1980s, and once again inspired by the interest of corporations and private developers, the Newark city government made the development of a downtown—under the banner of the "Newark Renaissance"—a priority. Unlike other midsize cities stumbling from the loss of their manufacturing bedrock, Newark's location ten miles from Manhattan, its surrounding wealthy suburbs, expanding seaport, international airport, and commuter rail lines were commonly cited as blessings that could allow the city to become an urban renewal success. Newark began to be marketed as an important gateway in the heart of the most economically powerful metropolitan region in the United States.[9]

By the 1990s, Newark had become a prime example of an aspiring neoliberal city. Selective state retrenchment and deregulation, along with the privatization of public spaces and privileging of free market approaches to development, provided the basis on which arguments for efficient technologies of government were fostered under neoliberal economic and urban policies. The opening of the first Starbucks in Newark in 2000 became evidence of governmental success, as documented in an article that describes how the mayor at the time, Sharpe James, "christened an espresso machine during the opening of a Starbucks on Broad Street, [while] 40 travel agents toured the city's sites [sic] and sounds. The two separate events merged when agents stopped to have samples of mango tiazzis, mochas and lemon and chocolate sweets at the trendy coffeehouse."[10] Like downtown revival projects in other U.S. cities, the Newark Renaissance has largely relied on the promotion of the arts to ameliorate the deeply seeded consequences of deindustrialization and recession by creating a profitable commercial machine focused on leisure, tourism, and conspicuous consumption as an antidote to urban decline.[11]

## Imaginaries of White Flight, Belonging, and Displacement

In the 1970s, high schools were premier sites of tension between African American students and the largely working-class, European Whites who had remained in Newark. At Barringer High School in North Broadway, White teenagers, who comprised about one-fourth of the student body in 1972, reportedly found themselves "engulfed by a whirlwind of blackness," as they experienced a curriculum that now included Black history and literature, and Black Pride cultural events, including the playing of Swahili music over the school's public address system, and which some White students found "as offensive and threatening as blacks would find 'Dixie.'"[12] Newark White ethnics represented what Michael Novak called "the rise of the unmeltable ethnics," a European nationality pride that emerged in the 1970s in response to civil rights achievements and what Whites viewed as a totalizing Black Pride movement.[13] Similarly, Shipler describes a Newark resident who reaches back to his Italian roots, arguing that as a minority ethnic group, Italians should be given the same kind of representation on public bodies and in federal programs that Blacks have won for themselves in cities where they are the minority. This same man condemned middle-class Italian politicians whom he called "Uncle Marios who think black."[14] These early manifestations of what later might have been labeled in reactionary circles as "reverse discrimination,"[15] inspired "emotional, hate-filled"[16] conversations in the Italian social clubs of North Broadway in the 1970s, as well as heated discussions about employment prospects in a perilous city.

In a city where race relations had been configured according to a southern-style Black–White dyad, the arrival of Puerto Ricans, the first Latinos to arrive in significant numbers in Newark, altered the racial landscape of the city. Old-time Puerto Rican residents continuously recalled the great tensions between Italians and Puerto Ricans and felt that Italians had an even harder time accepting Puerto Ricans as they did relating to Blacks. Puerto Ricans began appearing, along with Blacks, as the purported beneficiaries of new local and federal initiatives. In speculating about the job openings that would result from the construction of Newark Airport, an Italian interviewee complained that "they held up construction for a year already... being that it's being built in Newark they want 50 percent of the working force minorities, if they're qualified or not, because they're black or Puerto Rican. That means if I'm a qualified man, a bricklayer, I'm gonna lose a fuckin' job because I'm gonna be replaced by a shine that has no qualifications."[17] While some of these families "stuck it out in Newark" and even put up signs declaring "This house is NOT For Sale," these decisions caused great rifts in families who "have lived all their lives in Newark, their parents having arrived there from Italy, but their block has become mostly Puerto Rican, and crime has increased in recent years."[18]

When Abel Cabrera, a Puerto Rican resident of North Broadway and the uncle of a student at Barringer High School, who had been a nationalist activist in the 1970s, warned me that he wanted to say something "off the records," he didn't even wait for a response: "Well, I'm going to tell you something off the records. If you mention I told you, I'll deny it. But what happened was that, after the riots, all the wealthy Jewish people living in the mansions in the South Ward left. They collected the insurance money for their businesses and, instead of reinvesting in Newark they headed out and never returned." Abel was possibly referring to the fact that by 1972, barely five years after the Newark riots, only six thousand Jews remained in Newark out of a total of one hundred thousand Jewish residents in Essex County.[19]

The salience of historically inspired narratives, including hyperbolic stories of powerful but benevolent mafia lords and prosperous but malevolent Jewish deserters, have captured individual and community imaginations and contributed to an emotional commonsense in/of the city. The riots and slum clearance projects not only consolidated a Black political elite, in light of increasing White suburbanization, but also revealed competing tensions and steep class divisions among European ethnics in their connection to the privilege of their whiteness. At the time of Kenneth Gibson's mayoral victory in 1970, many of the White residents who had remained in Newark, as well as those who had moved to the suburbs but perhaps maintained occupational ties to the city, "expressed great panic at the possibility that 'angry Blacks' would 'take over.'"[20] According to an account in the *New York Times*: "The City of Newark [is] angry and anguished as Negroes take over political life amidst bitter racial tensions.... Negroes are now 60% of the population, with an ever-increasing white minority of mostly Italians, so that Newark may become the first all-black major U.S. city.... Puerto Ricans and Cubans are 10% of the population but have been politically passive."[21]

Such configurations and repositioning of whiteness and White privilege made an inadequate emotional persona the main cause of Newark's poverty and decay. As seen in the previous section, the Newark Renaissance aimed to redress these racialized images of aggression by adopting a message of respectability, as key to generating in Newark a "feel that sells," an emotional landscape that is attractive to potential White, middle-class investors. Among Puerto Ricans in North Broadway, this urban emotional commonsense was met through the development of not-for-profit service organizations that have largely relied on "self-help" or "building self-esteem" rhetoric in order to challenge a perpetual view of Puerto Ricans as "delinquent citizens."[22] Among Brazilians in the Ironbound neighborhood, a commercialization of "Brazilian culture" was deployed in the context of ethnic restaurants, stores, and festivals, as well as in the circulation of life stories of overcoming and conquering hardship.

Although Newark remains one of the few U.S. cities with a majority Black population, the presence of some European ethnic groups, particularly Portuguese in the Ironbound and some Italians in North Broadway, and the increasing numbers of Latin American migrants and U.S.-born Latinos, has been critical in the effort to promote that city as "multicultural."[23] Latinos and new Latin American migrants have been credited for halting the population decline that Newark faced since the 1960s. In fact, the Latino population grew substantially, even in the 1970s and 2000 when the city's overall population declined. North Broadway and the Ironbound, the two neighborhoods where I conducted fieldwork, reflect the effects of Newark's crisis, from its depopulation to the steady economic deterioration, but they are also noted for their role in the possible resurgence and repopulation of the city, with their steady stream of newcomers from Latin American and Caribbean countries.[24]

As a Cuban client at one of the local Portuguese bakeries once told me, with evident neighborhood pride, when she was trying to figure out if I spoke Spanish or Portuguese: "Aquí se habla de todo menos inglés [Here everything is spoken but English]." Rather than a political statement about language learning, she was hinting at how the Ironbound was a poster for what Charles Hale calls "neoliberal multiculturalism"—neoliberal politics that do not negate but selectively recognize ethnic claims in order to safeguard dominant relations in the nation.[25] The image of a multicultural Newark, in its intention to eradicate or at least dissipate the city's predominantly Black demographics, draws on Latinos to interrupt long-held associations between Blackness and aggression. Moreover, this multicultural image simultaneously homogenizes and culturalizes groups of Latin and Caribbean Americans across nationalities. The present work, with its focus on Puerto Ricans and Brazilians, aims to highlight such distinctions and convergences.

As colonial subjects, Puerto Ricans have become equivalent or at least more proximate to African Americans in the imagination of many Latin American migrants. In October of 2005, for instance, the Brazilian consul in New York advised the Brazilian community of Danbury to "keep their distance from the cucarachos [cockroaches in Portuguese]" because "Brazilians do not need to participate in a story that is unrelated to them, the West Side Story," in reference to the violence associated with Puerto Rican gangs in the film.[26] Likewise, in areas like Framingham, Massachusetts, one of the cities with the highest Brazilian concentration in the United States, Brazilian migrants are credited with "revitalizing" an area that had deteriorated due to the lack of "entrepreneurial spirit" of old-time Puerto Rican residents, who have in turn been associated with welfare "abuse" and criminality.[27] These are important distinctions in how populations become racialized differently in response to the circumstances of their arrival, forms of capital they carry, and the relationship between the United States and particular countries of origin.

Spatial differentiations connect places like the Ironbound to their putative opposite—the ghetto, the 'hood, the no-go areas where the urban "underclass" resides.[28] Thus, representations of space and place involving metaphors that reflect dominant ideologies reinforce difference and by default devalue places associated with racialized people, but with some deal of variety even within racially marked populations, as is the case of majority–minority cities.

## The Poetics of Newark

In *The Country and the City*, Raymond Williams eloquently demonstrates how the contrast between "the country" and "the city" is an enduring modernist form through which "we become conscious of a central part of our experience and of the crises of our society."[29] Poets, novelists, and essayists—in Williams's case, those of eighteenth-century England—represent the city as a symbol of capitalist production, labor, and exploitation, or as the "dark mirror" of the country. By tracing the development of this city-versus-country duality in his cultural analysis, Williams shows that the country and city are inextricably related (and even constitutive of one another), when one looks at the historical, lived experience of a community as distinct from the institution and organization of the society. Structures of feeling arose from a given state in capitalism that requires the pursuit of a hegemonic cultural configuration to justify and organize productive forces and relations of production. The country as idyllic served, therefore, to explain the city's corruption as a consequence of a social malaise and cultural deficiency.

Just as suggested in Williams's cultural analysis, poets, playwrights, novelists, and even social scientists have played a critical role in documenting the urban–suburban divide in Newark in ways that sediment structures of feeling and the hegemonic cultural configuration Williams references. Williams identifies the novels he analyzes as "knowable communities," in the sense that authors depict people and their relationships in essentially knowable and communicable ways that place the country and the city within a single tradition.[30] Two Newark writers who have come to occupy a premiere role in documenting such "knowable communities" are novelist Philip Roth and anthropologist Sherry Ortner. Without going in depth into either of their prolific literary and social scientific production, I want to show that, epistemologically, these authors allow us to focus on the relationship between emotional performance and political authority, and to examine their respective positionality as former Newark residents.

Philip Roth's literary reputation has been advanced partly through the proposition that he has "universalized his Newark cityscape comparable to Joyce's Dublin or Faulkner's Yoknapatawpha County."[31] As Schwartz pointedly argues, however, Roth's Newark renders the Jewish neighborhood of his childhood as representative of the city, particularly of what Roth views as the city's golden era, in ways that remain disturbingly uncritical of race: "the hard-edged, thoughtful, and ironical realist, becomes a conservative 'utopian'—too much caught up in the interplay between his liberal, civil rights conscience and his sentimentalizing of Weequahic [the Jewish neighborhood of his late-1940s adolescence]."[32] As Roth recalls his driving through the streets of Black Newark in a 1998 interview, he considered Newark as an "intensive-care case" and added: "Over the years I went back to visit by myself, walk around. When it became too dangerous to walk by myself I'd go with somebody.... I was mesmerized by the destruction of this place.... And I knew all the streets and I knew what they had looked like and I knew how people lived."[33]

Roth's willingness to stereotype postriot Newark as a crime-ridden, burnt-out city of Blacks, in contradistinction to the nurturing Jewish urban community life of his youth, and Roth's own ideological contradictions, provide important analytical tools for examining how perspectives on Newark's history have always required a deeply emotive, racialized narrative. While Roth understands that apartheid flourished in Newark, he "does not make the connection between the enclave that was Weequahic and the exploitation of Black immigrants," nor does he recognize that industrial decline began much earlier than the 1960s or that once wartime manufacturing ended, the Black community was left with no work and "inhabiting one of the most congested and run-down ghettos in the country."[34]

Both Philip Roth and Sherry Ortner link anecdotal accounts to bigger historical events to add meaning to the individual lives of their predominantly Jewish literary characters and anthropological informants respectively. In a methodologically innovative ethnography, Ortner examines the lives of the members of the Weequahic High School Class of '58 in the decades following their graduation.[35] Although a couple of years apart, both Roth and Ortner attended the same high school and lived in the same neighborhood. In "Comment: High School Classmates Revisited: Sherry Ortner and Philip Roth," Jonathan Schwartz examines the intersection of anthropology and fiction in Newark through a comparison of these authors' publications.[36] What I would like to accentuate here is the centrality of a particular kind of emotional landscape that has all but vanished in contemporary descriptions of Newark: nostalgia, loss, sadness, and longing poignantly characterize the lives that Roth and Ortner depict, albeit in different ways.

While Roth's longing is rooted in the public space (e.g., the built environment, the way life used to be lived in terms of neighborhood), Ortner notes that, for her upper- and upper-middle-class former classmates, the recollections are reflective of a public sphere that has become more intimate as private matters of sexuality (and perhaps a sexual angst associated with high school class reunions), morality, and family become key issues to be projected onto one's memories.[37] The family and friendship groups become primary sites to negotiate the usage of the city. As the world of 1950s Newark broadens with increasing population heterogeneity, the role of the city's Jewish population grows smaller symbolically. The possibility for attaching one's identity to the urban landscape is challenged in light of the documented vulnerability experienced by these upwardly mobile, future suburbanite Jewish social actors.[38] The nostalgia and grief that both Roth and Ortner note are, therefore, the emotional underside of a process through which the group subjectivity that had constructed multiple meanings and levels of access to the city became delimited by a racial reconfiguration that rendered particular urban sites no longer accessible.

The prominent public role and national recognition conferred to the Newark-based works of Phil Roth and Sherry Ortner, while undoubtedly well deserved, should be considered in light of the knowledge production and perspectives that have been invisible in literary and anthropological representations of what Raymond Williams refers to as "knowable communities" and "structures of feeling" in contemporary Newark.[39] Particularly pertinent are the works of African

American playwright and poet Amiri Baraka and Puerto Rican social worker Hilda Hidalgo.[40] These authors' works enable a closer understanding of emotional transformations behind historical moments. Baraka's and Hidalgo's perspectives supply phenomenological perspectives of the lives of two populations that are nearly absent from the works of Roth and Ortner: a politically militant African American contingency and a newly emergent population of Puerto Ricans arriving in Newark.

Amiri Baraka's work draws from an Afro-centric tradition in Black Power, Third World nationalism, and anti-colonial struggles to interpret Newark. It has been conventionally argued that the further back a person reflects, including a reflection on ancestral stories about running from a slave lynching a century ago, the less immediate is the sense of bodily fear and the more strategic those recollections become.[41] Nevertheless, Baraka's deployment of the past, while certainly mediated by a sense of distance, still becomes situated in a deeply phenomenological narrative of racial oppression that draws from a long canon of Black radicalism rooted in emotional and affective links to such a past. There is not a sense of longing for a preriot era or even a particular marking of a critical moment—for example, the riots—as a turning point.

Likewise, the little-known monograph by Hilda Hidalgo and her Rutgers students, published barely three years after the riots), prominently features riots and disturbances, not to distinguish a nostalgically saturated era from a context of postriot decay, but rather to portray critical historical moments in the consolidation of a Puerto Rican community in Newark.[42] Among the Puerto Ricans whom Hidalgo describes, the formation of an institutional life of social agencies, and the socialization of emotions through the development of not-for-profit organizations, played a major role in how people interpreted community and evaluated community-building success. While Hidalgo considered the riots an "epidemic of anger," she situated the incident in the context of a longer history and memories of fear and danger.[43] Such fear and danger were so deeply a part of Newark's preriot fabric that they no longer required words to articulate their existence. A structure of feeling operated as a complex blend of short- and longer-term memories for Hidalgo's informants—Puerto Ricans being chased by Italians with knives down Branch Brook Park and absentee Jewish landlords that hoped their properties would burn down so they could collect insurance. Heightened emotion, drawing on such memories, came to define the ensuing days of spontaneous violence.

The fears of the time are most easily catalogued when transformed into stories told to serve various purposes including plain information, serious reflection, personal anguish, or even entertainment. In contradistinction to the narratives of longing and nostalgia so central to Roth's novels and Ortner's informants, Hidalgo highlights how newly arrived Puerto Rican informants were always entangled with others and infected by the social exchange of feelings, dispositions, satisfactions, and deprivations that were woven into historically enduring narratives that have remained outside the purview of dominant literary and social scientific accounts. Taken together, the works of Baraka and Hidalgo offer great insight into the transformation of Newark's emotional landscape in the mid- and late twentieth century, when the city ceased to be a promised land for Blacks and Puerto Ricans.

## Conclusion

One's sense of place is the product of a particular proximity and familiarity with the environments of one's routine circulation; nevertheless, these practices of everyday life also consist of minuscule details that may be overlooked due to their apparent insignificance, as noted in Ana Tereza Botelho's and Migdalia Rivera's remarks in the beginning of this essay.[44] Neither the individual subjective affiliation nor the collective inhabitation of proximate spaces can be reduced to a simple "sense of community" in any romantic sense. Individual and collective identities are connected to place, although rarely to a single place and never in a pure and unmediated way.

In the context of Newark, there was at times a sense that too much emotional restraint might be socially dangerous, that an emotional openness should allow people to know where they stood in relation to one another, and that this openness was preferable over too much restraint. Thus, the display of strong emotion was not only a public act, but also a social act and "the emotion, its display, and its domestication [usually by others] were all inseparably bound together in a single processual whole"; these were at times collaborative, social, communal efforts of other-control, so that self-control was not always the idiom of civility or the fundamental of a moral order, unless it was done in alignment with neoliberal goals. In this sense, emotions like "anger" were in fact "civic emotions."[45]

Neoliberal efforts in Newark have in fact highlighted the distinction within the city, as the case of a criminalized North Broadway and a quaint Ironbound suggests. Not surprisingly, these neighborhood characterizations, rather than centering on economics, tend to focus on the culturally dominant ethno-racial groups in each area and culture—or, rather, the viability of a particular culture and sometimes individual life histories—to be commercialized or showcased. A prevalent idea was that Newark, and Puerto Rican North Broadway and Brazilian Ironbound, were a product not of the capitalist or neo-capitalist system but rather of some putative sickness or hard work, respectively. That Puerto Ricans needed to be disciplined through military recruitment, and Brazilians needed to exploit their cultural excess became tacit expectations that aligned with proposed "renewal" projects. Therefore, as a city, Newark cannot be treated as a discrete spatial unit in which neighborhoods are mere physical and institutional arrangements; neighborhoods are proxies for racial and class distinctions and views of stability, community, and commercial viability and, more often, of crime, decay, and waste. Social relations, in a most fundamental way, were regional relations. Labels like "protective Italian mafia lords," "defective southern Blacks," "degenerate Puerto Rican poor," "Jewish deserters," and "hardworking Portuguese" have great emotional resonance in a city with such extreme social and economic inequalities.

Puerto Ricans in North Broadway and Brazilians in the Ironbound carved their respective positions in the context of a meta-sentiment of aggression associated with Newark. Historical conceptions and contemporary productions of space continue to inform perspectives on "renewal," "renaissance," "good areas," and "bad areas" to generate enduring narratives of heroism that continue to shape racial formations in Newark, although in decidedly context-specific (or even neighborhood-specific) ways.

Despite the array of reasons, which usually involved several forms of neoliberal maneuvering on behalf of private developers or government projects, Latino and Latin American youth marked those movements of everyday uncertainty regarding one's living conditions that existed among young Puerto Rican and Brazilian women in Newark. Evaluations of behavioral and emotional propriety, which often involved judgment on the affective capabilities of the new populations one encountered, were always altering one's immediate space, sense of safety, and perception of mobility opportunities. Bus rides, empty lots, sites of demolition and reconstruction, a new Starbucks that rendered a neighborhood safe for latte, or a Dunkin Donuts that intruded upon old-world-style cafés were structures that provided a particular engagement with, and readings of, social difference.

In April 2006, the Ironbound Improvement District organization hired off-duty police officers to "address student rowdiness" on Ferry Street, the main commercial artery of the neighborhood. The organization was concerned about "large numbers of students from East Side High School harassing shoppers, littering, and damaging property on Ferry Street as they wait to catch buses in their way home after school to other parts of the city."[46] The emphasis on how these students "did not belong" or "did not live" in the Ironbound appeared throughout the organization's communiqué; in the Ironbound, out-of-placeness almost invariably suggested "Blackness" so that the bodies criminalized on the streets—those who interrupted neoliberal commercial activity and social mobility aspirations and the well-being of the shoppers"—were those of young men of color. As hinted at in this chapter's opening quotes, seemingly spontaneous tension or outright hostility in Newark cannot be disentangled from a preceding historical moment. This is particularly the case when such moments highlight the prominence of race as excessive and violent, while predicating the success of urban renewal and personal safety on the establishment of a neoliberal-friendly, emotional style ensconced in a politics of respectability, personal responsibility, and profound policing.

## Notes

1. Eva Illouz, *Saving the Modern Soul: Therapy, Emotions, and the Culture of Self Help* (Berkeley: University of California Press, 2008).
2. Fred R. Myers, "Emotions and the Self: A Theory of Personhood and Political Order among Pintupi Aborigines," *Ethos* 7, no. 4 (1979): 343–370.
3. Ana Y. Ramos-Zayas, "Delinquent Citizenship, National Performances: Racialization, Surveillance, and the Politics of 'Worthiness' in Puerto Rican Chicago," *Latino Studies* 2 (2004): 26–44.
4. Raymond Williams, *Marxism and Literature* (London: Oxford University Press, 1977).
5. Ana Y. Ramos-Zayas, *Street Therapists: Race, Affect, and Neoliberal Personhood in Latino Newark* (Chicago: University of Chicago Press, 2012).
6. Tom Hayden, *Rebellion in Newark: Official Violence and Ghetto Response* (New York: Random House, 1967).
7. Julia Vitullo-Martin, "Gateway Newark," *New York Times*, October 22, 2006.
8. Ramos-Zayas, *Street Therapists*.
9. Andrew Jacobs, "Two Miles in Newark That Run from Long Decline to Rebirth," *New York Times*, January 5, 2007; Julia Vitullo-Martin, "Gateway Newark," *New York Times*, October 22, 2006.
10. Carly Rothman, "Newark Welcomes Its New Starbucks, and 40 Travel Agents," *Star-Ledger*, July 17, 2008.
11. The reconstruction of downtowns across the United States involved a neglect of manufacturing, warehousing, and freight-handling operations, and a shift in attention and resources to the construction of financial firms, government agencies, hotels, restaurants, entertainment, and cultural venues. See "Director Named for Newark Development," *New York Times*, March 9, 2000.
12. David K. Shipler, "The White Niggers of Newark: Mirror Images of America's First Black City," *Harper's Magazine* 245, no. 1467 (1972): 77–83, 79.
13. Michael Novak, *The Rise of the Unmeltable Ethnics: Politics and Culture in the Seventies* (New York: Macmillan, 1972).
14. Shipler, "The White Niggers of Newark," 81.
15. Philip L. Fetzer, "Reverse Discrimination: The Political Use of Language." *T. Marshall L. Rev* 17 (1991): 293.
16. Shipler, "The White Niggers of Newark," 82
17. Shipler, "The White Niggers of Newark," 81.
18. Shipler, "The White Niggers of Newark," 82.
19. See William B. Helmreich, *The Enduring Community: The Jews of Newark and Metrowest* (New Brunswick, NJ: Transaction, 1999), 32. During this time, Jewish business owners transferred their stores to Blacks in the postriot era in what came to be known as Project Transfer. These businesses for the most part failed and were eventually transferred to a new flow of immigrants from Latin America, the Caribbean, and Africa. This period is immortalized in Philip Roth's character of Seymour Levov, the quasi-all-American Jewish boy in *American Pastoral*, who upon returning from the Marines takes over his father's Newark Maid glove factory. After envisioning a paternalistic rage against the upheaval and Black workers' "refusal to work hard," the factory relocates to Puerto Rico in 1973 where labor is willing and plentiful and presumably "less contentious."
20. Sabrina Marie Chase, "Mujeres ingeniosas [Resourceful women]: HIV+ Puerto Rican Women and the Urban Health Care System" (PhD diss., Rutgers University, 2005), 63.

21  See Fox Butterfield, "Newark Held an Angry and Anguished City," *New York Times*, April 12, 1971.
22  Ramos-Zayas, *Street Therapists*.
23  Brian Donahue's "Diverse New Jersey," *Star-Ledger*, May 31, 2002, notes that, amid the largest immigration boom in U.S. history, the percentage of foreign-born residents living in New Jersey rose from 12.5 to 17.5 percent between 1990 and 2000. Significantly, during the 2000–2001 school year only 58 percent of Newark public school students spoke English at home, while 25 percent spoke Spanish and 6 percent spoke Portuguese.
24  These areas are comparable when it comes to accessibility to public transportation (they are walking distance from NJ Transit stations and bus lines), percentage of owner-occupied housing units (25.6% for the Ironbound and 22.1% for North Broadway), and even the preponderance of townhouse-like edifices, which are leading criteria for assessing the occupied homes. In the 2000 Census, 72 percent of the Ironbound population self-identified as White; under 6 percent was considered Black or African American. In North Broadway, 39 percent of the population was considered White and 24 percent was Black.
25  Charles R. Hale, "Neoliberal Multiculturalism: The Remaking of Cultural Rights and Racial Dominance in Central America," *PoLAR* 28 (2005): 10.
26  Leila Suwwan, "Para consul, hispánicos so cucarachos," *Folha de São Paulo*, October 21, 2005.
27  Teresa Sales, *Brasileiros longe de casa* (Sao Paolo: Cortez Editora, 1998).
28  Audrey Kobayashi and Linda Peake, "Racism out of Place: Thoughts on Whiteness and an Antiracist Geography in the New Millennium," *Annals of the Association of American Geographers* 90, no. 2 (2000): 392–403.
29  Raymond Williams, *The Country and the City* (London: Chatto and Windus, 1973), 289.
30  Williams, *The Country and the City*, 163.
31  Robert Stone, "Waiting for a Lefty," *New York Review of Books*, November 5, 1998, 38; see Larry Schwartz, "Roth, Race, and Newark," *Cultural Logic: A Journal of Marxist Theory and Practice* 8 (2005), https://ojs.library.ubc.ca/index.php/clogic/article/view/191860/188829.
32  Schwartz, "Roth, Race, and Newark," 1.
33  Roth cited in Schwartz, "Roth, Race, and Newark."
34  Schwartz, "Roth, Race, and Newark," 15.
35  Sherry B. Ortner, *New Jersey Dreaming: Capital, Culture, and the Class of '58* (Durham, NC: Duke University Press, 2003).
36  Jonathan Schwartz, "High School Classmates Revisited: Sherry Ortner and Philip Roth," *Anthropology Today* 14, no. 6 (1998): 14–16.
37  Lauren Gail Berlant, *The Queen of America Goes to Washington City: Essays on Sex and Citizenship* (Durham, NC: Duke University Press, 1997).
38  Helmreich, *The Enduring Community*.
39  Raymond Williams, *The Country and the City*, vol. 423 (New York: Oxford University Press, 1975).
40  The works of Philip Roth, Amiri Baraka, anthropologist Sherry Ortner (*New Jersey Dreaming*), and social worker Hilda Hidalgo (*The Puerto Ricans of Newark, NJ* (Newark, NJ: published by author, 1970)) provide a critical example of how structures of feeling are complicated by authorial positionality.
41  Darryl Forde, *African Worlds: Studies in the Cosmological Ideas and Social Values of African Peoples* (London: James Currey, 1997).

42  Hilda A. Hidalgo, *The Puerto Ricans of Newark, NJ*.
43  Puerto Rican Convention of New Jersey Conference Papers, "Structure for Change," 1971. In the Hilda Hidalgo Papers at the Newark Public Library Subseries I. A: Speeches, Addresses and Conference Proceedings (1969–1999, undated), Box 1, Folder 3
44  Murray Forman, *The Hood Comes First: Race, Space, and Place in Rap and Hip-Hop* (Chicago: Wesleyan University Press, 2002).
45  Peter Just, "Going through the Emotions: Passion, Violence, and 'Other-Control' among the Dou Donggo," *Ethos* 19, no. 3 (1991): 288–312, 299, 301.
46  Ironbound Development Corporation 2006, "IBID Hires Off-Duty Police Officers to Address Student Rowdiness on Ferry Street," April 6, 2006, www.goironbound.com, last accessed, October 15, 2011.

# Part 2
# Histories

# 6
# Peruvians in Paterson, New Jersey, 1920-1950

## GIANNCARLO MUSCHI

Peruvians began moving to Paterson in large numbers during the 1960s creating the basis for the emergence of a prosperous community by the end of the twentieth century. With almost 150,000 inhabitants, today Paterson is home to approximately 30,000 Peruvians, who, together with African Americans, Puerto Ricans, and Dominicans, constitute most of its population.[1] However, before the great wave of Peruvian migration to the area, a small group had already settled in the city as early as 1920. At that time, the city was mostly populated by White Americans and Europeans who worked in the city's textile industry. This small group of Peruvian newcomers adjusted to this industrial and multiethnic context in the Silk City.[2] Although their migration experience has received little attention by scholars, this early group of Peruvians outlined patterns of migration and socioeconomic adaptation that help us understand the later development of Paterson's Peruvian community.

The literature about Peruvian migration to Paterson often reiterates inaccurate historical information about the start of this flow of workers, often without supporting evidence.[3] These studies maintain that the first Peruvian migrants arrived when textile workers from Lima moved to New Jersey after U.S. factories operating in Peru sponsored their relocation to its subsidiaries around 1930.[4] To date, there is no evidence to substantiate the relationship between specific employers and sponsored migration. In fact, as I will show here, the Peruvians who arrived in Paterson between 1920 and 1950 followed the trading routes established by U.S. corporations with investments in Peru and independently decided to settle in the Silk City.

This chapter chronicles the lives of this early cohort of Peruvian migrants. It contextualizes the origins of this migration as a response to the expansion of U.S. capitalism in Peru and the development of shipping routes that served as migration channels to the United States. The chapter reconstructs this early migration and adjustment process of these migrants with information about their socioeconomic background, identity, and families. It also examines how these Peruvians endured the critical context of the Great Depression and World War II and their involvement in labor union activism. Finally, the chapter describes the connection between this first group of Peruvians and Puerto Ricans, Cubans, and a younger generation of compatriots that began arriving during the early 1960s.

## Trading Routes, Migration, and Settlement

Commercial relations and transportation routes established at the end of the nineteenth century created a pathway for the movement of workers between the United States and Peru.[5] Merchant lines played a pivotal role in the development of trade with the East Coast of North America. Grace Line, a pioneer in scheduled steamship service, initiated the movement of commodities and people with the opening of the New York–Callao route in 1893.[6] Following the inauguration of the Panama Canal in 1914, Grace Line expanded steamship service between New York and several Peruvian ports, increasing the transportation of products and people between the two countries.[7] Other shipping companies, such as the Compañía Peruana de Vapores also participated in this trade during the first decades of the twentieth century. American employees used these commercial routes to work for U.S. companies in Peru. For instance, in 1920, George M. Dunning traveled from Paterson to Peru to erect the new locomotives operated in the Talara–Negritos railway, owned by a subsidiary of the Standard Oil Company of New Jersey.[8] Similarly, Peruvian workers employed by U.S. corporations began to travel to the East Coast of the United States, which eventually resulted in an ongoing migration flow of Peruvians to the New York and New Jersey area.

The 1900 and 1910 U.S. Censuses counted fewer than fifty people born in Peru living in New Jersey. Most of these Peruvians were born from European ancestors, while others were sons or daughters of U.S. citizens who lived and worked in Peru.[9] Their Peruvian-born children eventually returned to the United States as adults. Additionally, female Peruvians migrated to the United States with their American husbands who worked for U.S. companies established in Peru.[10] Among this stream of migrants came Emma Rensch, the daughter of an English citizen who married a Peruvian woman in Lima. In 1883, Rensch moved to New

York and later to Passaic, a city located six miles from Paterson, where she became a well-known resident for her participation in civic organizations and aid societies.[11] Other Peruvians migrated to New Jersey at the beginning of the twentieth century to serve as skilled or semiskilled workers, many of them merchant seamen working on U.S. and Peruvian vessels that decided to settle permanently in the United States.[12] None of these Peruvians lived in Paterson, and these were isolated cases that did not reflect any migration trends.

According to the 1930 U.S. Census, of the 138,513 inhabitants residing in Paterson, 42,612 were foreign born, most of them Europeans. There were 12,404 Italians, 5,716 Polish, 3,462 Germans, and 3,392 Russians, the major immigrant groups in the area. The native White population of 92,815 consisted mostly of U.S.-born citizens of European background. There were only 106 Central and South Americans, among them fewer than a dozen Peruvians.[13] By the mid-1920s the first Peruvians began settling in the area as a consequence of the booming textile industry that made Paterson one of the most prosperous cities in the eastern United States. Immigration and naturalization records demonstrate that Manuel Cuentas, Frank Maraví, Ricardo Tello, Luis de la Flor Cosío, Manuel Tarazona, Victor Tarazona, Carlos Dulanto, and Carlos Cubillas were the first Peruvians who settled in Paterson.[14]

They were between twenty and thirty years old, single, and unskilled male laborers. None of these migrants had worked as textile factory workers before arriving at the United States and, in general, they came from working-class families with unstable economic conditions. Instead, most of them entered the United States as seamen working in merchant vessels traveling mostly between ports in Peru, New York, and Europe.[15]

As many working-class Peruvians at the time, they did not complete formal schooling and worked in seafaring and other manual occupations from a young age. For instance, Manuel Tarazona and Carlos Cubillas began working as teenagers for Compañía Peruana de Vapores.[16] Likewise, Ricardo Tello reported working as a mechanic in Peru when he arrived in New York in 1925.[17] From this first group of Peruvians, Luis de la Flor Cosío and Carlos Dulanto declared upon arrival that they had been students in Peru. However, one year later they ended up working as seamen for U.S. or European vessels.[18] As other unskilled workers in Peru, they earned low wages and had few opportunities for economic advancement in the home country.

These migrants were from diverse cities in Peru, principally from main ports in the chain of commerce that connected the Peruvian coast with the rest of the world, but most of them were from Lima, the capital city located only six miles from the port of Callao. Others, such as Manuel Tarazona and Carlos Cubillas, were from Salaverry, another important port located in northern Peru.[19] The only Peruvian of this group who was born in the Andes was Manuel Cuentas, from Huancané, a remote city in Lake Titicaca with commercial connections to Brazil and Bolivia.[20] In sum, except Manuel Cuentas, they all came from coastal

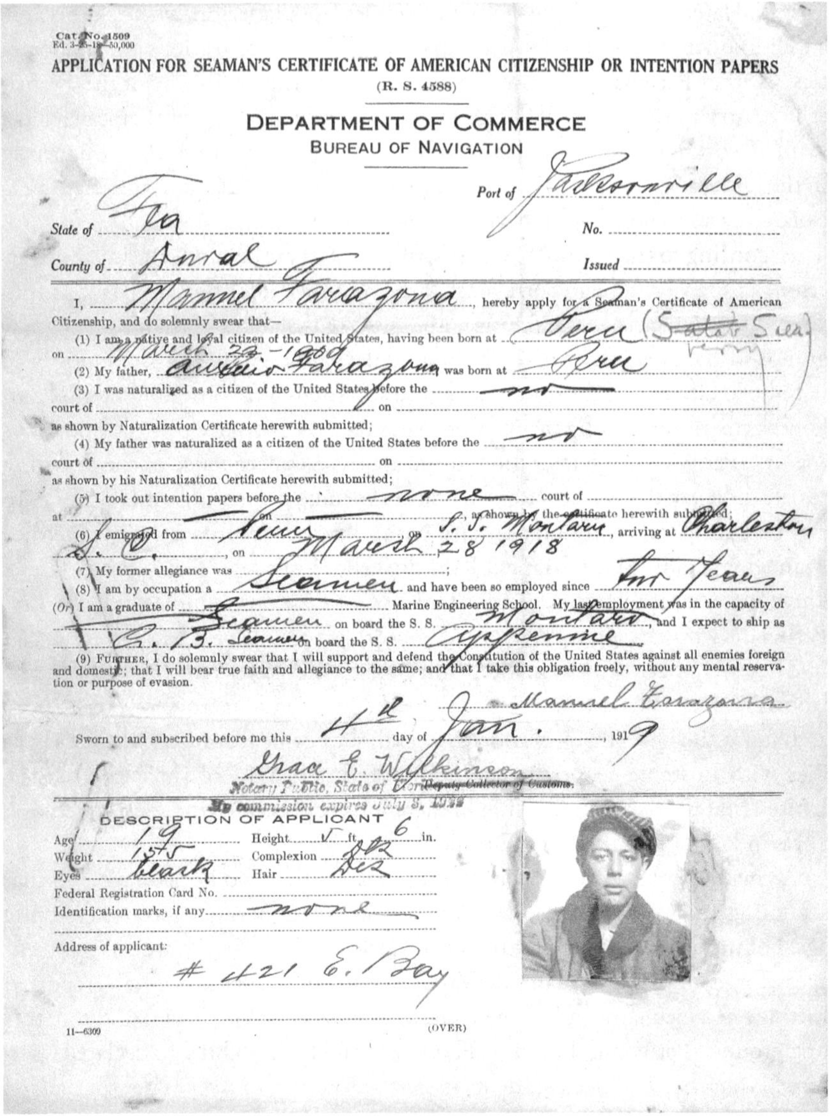
Cat. No. 1509
Ed. 3-25-18—50,000

APPLICATION FOR SEAMAN'S CERTIFICATE OF AMERICAN CITIZENSHIP OR INTENTION PAPERS
(R. S. 4588)

DEPARTMENT OF COMMERCE
BUREAU OF NAVIGATION

Port of Jacksonville

State of Fla No.

County of Duval Issued

I, Manuel Tarazona, hereby apply for a Seaman's Certificate of American Citizenship, and do solemnly swear that—

(1) I am a native and loyal citizen of the United States, having been born at Peru (State ~~Statr~~ Sea) on March 23 - 1900

(2) My father, Antonio Tarazona was born at Peru

(3) I was naturalized as a citizen of the United States before the no court of on as shown by Naturalization Certificate herewith submitted;

(4) My father was naturalized as a citizen of the United States before the no court of on as shown by his Naturalization Certificate herewith submitted;

(5) I took out intention papers before the none court of at on , as shown by the certificate herewith submitted;

(6) I emigrated from Peru on S. S. Montara, arriving at Charleston S. C., on March 28 1918

(7) My former allegiance was Seamen;

(8) I am by occupation a Seamen and have been so employed since Two Years

(Or) I am a graduate of Marine Engineering School. My last employment was in the capacity of Seamen on board the S. S. Montara, and I expect to ship as O. S. Seaman on board the S. S. Appenine

(9) Further, I do solemnly swear that I will support and defend the Constitution of the United States against all enemies foreign and domestic; that I will bear true faith and allegiance to the same; and that I take this obligation freely, without any mental reservation or purpose of evasion.

Manuel Tarazona

Sworn to and subscribed before me this 4th day of Jan., 1919

Grace E. Wilkinson
Notary Public, State of Florida ~~Deputy Collector of Customs.~~
My commission expires July 8, 1922

DESCRIPTION OF APPLICANT

Age 19 Height 5 ft. 6 in.
Weight 155 Complexion Dk
Eyes Dark Hair Dk
Federal Registration Card No.
Identification marks, if any none

Address of applicant:
# 421 E. Bay

11—6309 (OVER)

FIGURE 6.1 Manuel Tarazona's document showing first arrival at the United States in 1918 as a seaman. (Source: Ancestry.com)

urban centers that experienced the influx of international circulation of people, goods, and cultural forms that shaped views of mobility in its inhabitants. Thus, imaginings of modernity and international mobility in these cities may have stimulated the migration expectations of these Peruvians.[21]

As seafarers, they had the opportunity to visit many cities in Europe and the United States where they were exposed to the advances of modern societies, which contrasted with Peru's conservative customs. During the 1920s, the country was dominated by a traditional elitist society that looked to the modernism and cosmopolitism of cities such as Paris, London, and New York as models to emulate. The idea of living in Europe and the United States signified for many Peruvians a life of progress and development.[22] Members of the upper and upper-middle classes had the opportunity to live or study in these cities and experience a modern way of life. But working-class Peruvians considered this lifestyle foreign and out of reach. The benefits of capitalism and modernization, instead of improving their way of life, produced widespread uncertainties, distress, and dislocations in the working classes.[23] While landholders, mine owners, and trading companies were making profits, salaries of factory workers, artisans, and petit merchants remained unchanged for decades.[24] The socioeconomic aspirations of working-class Peruvians at the turn of the twentieth century thus help explain why Peruvian seamen chose to settle in the United States. Most of them were part of the working class in Peru, yet maritime work allowed them to experience city life abroad and piqued their interest in becoming part of a cosmopolitan culture that allowed for higher incomes.

Peruvians used different pathways to settle in Paterson during the 1920s. Most of them deserted the vessels in which they were employed in order to remain in the United States.[25] Their journey to permanent settlement in Paterson followed a pathway that began with a short residence in New York City. Some Peruvians moved to the Silk City through marital relationships with American or European women with family ties in Paterson.[26] Others moved by themselves looking for better living and working prospects. Overwhelmed by low wages and crowded living conditions of large cities like New York, these migrants followed the economic opportunities available to them in the Silk City.[27]

Having worked as seafarers, they had the skills to incorporate into Paterson's textile industries as mechanics or manual laborers. In the first article chronicling the flow of Peruvians to Paterson published by a local newspaper in 1972, Victor Tarazona recalled his arrival to the Silk City. "It was a cold morning of February [1926]. I was needing a job and I found it at the turn of the corner of the first block I walked."[28] Tarazona's experience demonstrates that, in addition to family ties, the abundance of factory jobs was overwhelmingly the reason that made migration to Paterson attractive. In 1927, its peak year, the silk industry employed 48.5 percent of Paterson's wage workers, while the textile industry as a whole employed 77.3 percent.[29] Although there was a slight decline in work opportunities during the Great Depression, for several decades thereafter jobs were still available for skilled and unskilled workers in the hundreds of local factories that produced textiles and other related products.

These Peruvians found their way in a mostly Anglo society without relying on the support of kinship ties or a community of conationals to facilitate their incorporation and adaptation. Although some of them knew each other from their time at sea and settled relatively near one another, there is no evidence of the establishment of any Peruvian social and economic organizations. Instead,

Peruvians developed close relationships with Americans and Europeans who helped them in their socioeconomic adjustment to the new setting. They married American or European women, forging ties with their spouses' families, a strategy that facilitated their incorporation into the local silk industry as dyers, weavers, or finishers.[30] There were also other job opportunities for these migrants. For example, Manuel Cuentas worked as a telephone installer for Western Electric Co. and Ricardo Tello worked in construction in 1930.[31] This labor environment defined their incorporation into the working class of Paterson.

Most of these Peruvians earned the same weekly wage as lower-middle-class families in Paterson. The average wage by 1930 for an unskilled factory worker was $10 to $12 per week.[32] For instance, with a weekly wage of $11 as a silk worker, Victor Tarazona was able to provide for his wife and two children.[33] Likewise, Ricardo Tello earned $12 per week working thirty-four hours as a dyer helper.[34] Thus, as unskilled immigrants and with few contacts in the city, they found occupations in the least desirable jobs receiving low weekly wages. Their membership in the working class was also reflected in their patterns of home ownership. During the 1920s, it was difficult for factory workers to own their own home. Like other immigrants, Peruvians mostly rented apartments or lived as tenants in boarding houses owned by Americans or European immigrants.[35]

Peruvians navigated their first years in Paterson trying to find economic and personal stability, which allowed them to marry and form families. For example, Manuel and Victor Tarazona married Americans with whom they had children before 1930.[36] Through marital liaison, some of these Peruvians became U.S. citizens. Nonetheless, those that settled in the United States by the late 1920s maintained an alien immigration status for several years after arrival even though many of them married U.S. citizens and would have had a pathway to citizenship. In terms of social adaptation, although most Peruvians tried to adjust into Paterson's multiethnic community, some struggled to navigate the new environment. For instance, in 1928, Manuel and Victor Tarazona were arrested for stealing $100 worth of goods from Phoenix Piece Dye Works, the factory in which they were employed.[37] Likewise, Carlos Dulanto was accused of using a counterfeit $20 bill to pay for goods.[38] These kinds of illegal practices infringed upon local regulations and often opposed the laws of the receiving country. However, in general, the first Peruvians in Paterson experienced a smooth labor and social incorporation that was restrained by the working and economic instability generated in the 1930s.

## Making It in Paterson

The stock market crash of 1929 and the consequent economic depression impacted wages, labor opportunities, and the relatively comfortable lifestyle of Paterson's industrial workers. Of the 915 factories operating in the city in 1929, only 568 were active in 1933. During these four years, the average number of employed workers fell from 32,686 to 20,160, while total wages paid dropped from $44 million in 1929 to $17.5 million in 1933. By 1934, workers in the textile industry represented more than 30 percent of the people listed on the relief rolls.[39] During the Great Depression, some Peruvians lost their jobs or enrolled in state-sponsored employment programs. Ricardo Tello reported being unemployed in the census of 1930.[40] Victor Tarazona enrolled in the Workers Progress Administration program, the employment agency created by the U.S. government to provide jobs for the unemployed.[41] Other Peruvians, such as Manuel Cuentas, sought out better opportunities in other cities in New Jersey. In 1930, he moved to Montclair and began working for a local electric company.[42] Most Peruvians workers endured adverse socioeconomic conditions while earning a living. However, for some migrants, the Great Depression constituted an opportunity. For example, Carlos Dulanto became involved in community and civic associations. In 1934, Dulanto was appointed as the president of the Wayne Township Unemployment Association, an institution that collected money, clothing, and food to help local jobless workers' families. He was also chosen as a trustee for Franklin D. Roosevelt Democratic Club, an organization that endorsed the nomination of democratic candidates for the senate and state government.[43] These experiences lead Dulanto to labor activism in the following years.

Other Peruvians such as Luis de la Flor Cosío and Carlos Cubillas settled in Paterson during the worst days of the Great Depression. The scarcity of industrial jobs in New York prompted them to look for opportunities in the remaining industries of the Silk City. In fact, by 1935, a series of political and economic state reforms progressively resolved Paterson's economic woes.[44] It gradually recovered its position as an important center for silk manufacture and continued to attract immigrants.[45] By the eve of World War II, most Peruvians in Paterson were able to improve their economic conditions.

During the 1940s some Peruvians decided to naturalize as a way to achieve better labor opportunities and social benefits. Becoming a U.S. citizen was also a personal project most of them pursued after settling in the United States. For many migrants, obtaining U.S. citizenship and, if possible, assimilating into the White mainstream society, was evidence of becoming true Americans. The case of Ricardo Tello illustrates how some Peruvians tried to anglicize themselves by adopting new names. After marrying into a German family, Ricardo Tello changed his name to Richard Hobteld. Naturalization records show that he racially identified himself as Spanish Dutch by 1940.[46] These changes in identity reveal that some of the first Peruvians tried to align themselves with ethnic groups less affected by racial prejudice and more associated with whiteness as a way to facilitate assimilation.

Before the United States entered World War II in December 1941, the U.S. government required all men between the ages of twenty-one and forty-five years old to register for the draft. Those selected were required to serve at least one year in the armed forces.[47] All Peruvians living in Paterson registered for the draft but were not selected to serve.[48] Since most of them were at least forty years old and heads of households, they were not likely to be selected for military conscription. For the most part, Peruvians navigated these years working in the factories of Paterson. The war created an economic boom for New Jersey's business and manufacturing sectors as factories transitioned from producing civilian merchandise to military goods. In Paterson, silk and textile industries ran overtime producing materials for army uniforms and parachutes.[49] The war economy increased full-time production, improved workers' salaries, and reduced unemployment in the Silk City.

This economic context afforded the group of Peruvians more confidence in their economic stability. They maintained their jobs and continued working in silk factories for a long time. Other Peruvians, such as Victor Tarazona, found positions in other occupations. Tarazona began working as a cook in Paterson's renowned Alexander Hamilton Hotel and remained in that occupation for three decades.[50] During the 1940s, some Peruvians became more involved in local union activities. For instance, in 1943, Carlos Dulanto became the president of the Plastic Workers Union at Mack Molding Co., the company for which he worked. This business received the Army–Navy "E" Award ("Excellence in Production"), a banner in recognition for producing materials for the war. Before a group of six hundred employees, Dulanto received the "E" pin on behalf of all employees of the union.[51] In the same year, he and 350 employed members of the union voted to affiliate themselves with the Workers of America, Congress of Industrial Organizations. In the following years Dulanto led the union to maintain harmonious labor relations with the company.[52]

After World War II a period of anti-communism known as the Red Scare altered the tone of U.S. politics and of the society in general. The federal government orchestrated raids on alleged radical centers throughout the country searching for national and foreign communists promoting subversive actions. Most U.S. citizens were released after arrest, but immigrants were deported.[53] In Paterson, active members of local unions, such as Manuel Tarazona, were prosecuted and incarcerated for a period of time. Described by a U.S. immigration officer as a Congress of Industrial Organizations labor organizer for the Fur Workers Union and the Dye Workers Union, Tarazona faced the possibility of deportation in 1949, accused of being a member of an organization advocating the overthrow of the government by force.[54] Although Tarazona filed a petition to become a U.S. citizen in 1920, he did not complete the process. Tarazona later returned to Peru and reentered the United States illegally as a seaman in 1924. For this reason, in 1949, he was sent to Ellis Island and held there for deportation in default of $4,000 bail.[55]

One year later, a federal judge ordered the release of sixteen detained aliens from Ellis Island, including Tarazona, who had been arrested on false claims. The bond was posted by the Civil Rights Congress. However, Tarazona was rearrested in 1951, accused of being free on "tainted" bail posted by this organization. He was promptly released after his wife obtained a writ of habeas corpus, once again avoiding deportation. The following year, Tarazona spoke at a rally organized by the Paterson Chapter of the Civil Rights Congress. In this meeting he recounted how the government's attacks on civil rights had affected him.[56] Thus, after being prosecuted by the federal government for suspicious subversive activities, Manuel Tarazona continued participating in events organized by local workers' organizations, demonstrating his commitment to union activism.

Peruvians in Paterson led a relatively stable working-class life during the postwar period. Industrial occupations provided Peruvians adequate economic resources to afford rent, groceries, and some luxuries. In the 1950s some of them bought cars and became homeowners in Paterson. Ricardo Tello bought a second home in the exclusive area of Skyline Lakes in Wanaque, New Jersey, among other properties in Paterson.[57] Economic stability encouraged some Peruvians, such as Victor Tarazona, to participate in charity campaigns. Tarazona and other co-workers in the Alexander Hamilton Hotel were instrumental in establishing a payroll deduction for employees in order to collaborate with the United Community Chest campaign, showing their interest in contributing to the welfare of the city.[58]

Some of these Peruvians married, divorced, and remarried in the United States. In spite of these destabilizing personal changes, postwar prosperity allowed them to raise their children in a relatively stable household environment.[59] Their children adopted North American customs and values, although some of them later reconnected with their father's culture. For example, Victor Tarazona's son became a Spanish teacher in a local high school after serving in the Korean War.[60] In fact, most sons and daughters of these Peruvians became skilled workers or were the first in their families to pursue a professional career. For instance, Cubillas's daughter worked as an optometrist in a local corporation and Tello's daughters became nurses.[61] Peruvian migrants in the postwar period also hosted extravagant weddings for their daughters: the events were published in local newspapers, evidencing an upward mobility trend.[62]

Immigration scholars have demonstrated that Europeans and Puerto Ricans in the United States communicated and traveled back and forth between their places of origin and destination, establishing transnational ties that were central to the building of migrant communities in New York and surrounding areas.[63] There is evidence that this pattern of mobility was replicated by the first Peruvians living in Paterson. Some of them returned to Peru to visit their families right after settlement in the United States while working as seamen for U.S. or European companies. Others waited until becoming citizens to visit Peru as tourists.[64] Immigration records also demonstrate that Peruvians invited family members to visit the United States. For instance, in October 1960, Maria Tarazona, Victor Tarazona's sister, had declared Paterson as her destination on an airline passenger list. However, her visit was not permanent, and she eventually returned to Peru.[65] The migration of Talalca Tello is the only case identified in which earlier migrants encouraged relatives from Peru to come and settle in Paterson.

Talalca Tello migrated to Paterson in 1949 to live with her uncle Ricardo Tello. Before migrating, she took courses at a university in Peru while working as a secretary for a U.S. company. In order to improve her English, she convinced her uncle to sponsor her trip to the United States.[66] "I always had the dream to come to America. Besides, my uncle was delighted to have somebody from the family," Talalca Tello remembers.[67] At arrival, she expected to find a job as bilingual secretary but, as other Peruvians, Tello ended up working as a manual laborer in a local factory. She experienced discrimination at work and in other public spaces. "At the beginning, people in New Jersey said my accent was beautiful, but later when Puerto Ricans began to arrive it wasn't nice anymore," declares Tello, exemplifying how intolerance toward Latinos affected her experience during the 1950s.[68] After registering in evening English classes and attending the Spencer Business College, she found a job that allowed her to apply her skills. Talalca Tello worked as a secretary for two local companies before marrying a Belgium migrant. Tello and her family moved to California in the 1960s, where she became an important activist for Mexican farmers and Latino migrants.[69]

Although the migration of Talalca Tello demonstrates that some Peruvians pulled family members from the home country, the first Peruvians in Paterson principally maintained only weak contact with their families, mainly because of the distance between Peru and New Jersey and the cost of the journey. In contrast to European, Puerto Rican, and Mexican migrants that came in large numbers to the United States during the same period, Peruvians did not create extensive migrant networks. There is no evidence of a direct connection between this early group of migrants and the flow of Peruvians that began to settle in Paterson during the 1960s, those who would eventually form a more organized system of migration. However, the first Peruvians in Paterson outlined patterns of migration and socioeconomic incorporation that were utilized by subsequent flows of conationals who settled in Paterson. In the next decades, with improvements in transportation, Peruvian migrants began to arrive by plane to New York and then moved to Paterson, finding jobs in local industries, as conationals did in previous decades.

## Conclusion

The first Peruvians in Paterson worked as blue-collar laborers until retirement in the late 1960s. After more than forty years of industrial work, they fulfilled their goal of crafting their own future in America. "[I feel] very happy living here. I am not a big shot, but now I am retired and live decently. I have no complaints of this wonderful country. I love it and I love the democratic system," expressed Victor Tarazona in an interview given in 1972 to a recent Peruvian migrant that worked in a local newspaper.[70] This account demonstrates Tarazona's sense of accomplishment regarding his decision to make a living in the United States. He was content to live a life without luxury, but also without significant hardship. Additionally, he enjoyed being part of what he saw as a fair society where he earned a regular income after retirement, a social benefit that semiskilled workers could not attain in Peru. Most importantly, Tarazona was one of the few Peruvians from this first wave of immigration that witnessed the development of the Peruvian enclave in Paterson, organized by a new group of migrants who began arriving during the 1960s.

The migration experience of the first Peruvians in Paterson was structured by a society shaped under North American and European norms. Traces from Latin America, and particularly from Peruvian culture, were nonexistent during most of their lifetime in the Silk City. However, the migration trajectory of some migrants from this group intersected with the arrival of the Hispanic populations that settled in Paterson during the postwar period.[71] The cultural proximity in terms of language, music, food, and socialization patterns facilitated contact with Puerto Ricans, Cubans, and later a younger generation of Peruvian migrants. Carlos Cubillas remarried a Puerto Rican woman and lived in Puerto Rico until his death in 1976.[72] Manuel and Victor Tarazona, who passed away in 1975 and 1986, respectively, witnessed the arrival of new waves of Peruvian migration that prompted celebrations of Peruvian heritage in Paterson.[73] Thus, the first ethnic businesses and institutions developed by young conationals allowed some of these first Peruvians an opportunity to reconnect with their native culture.

The European character of the city to which the first group of Peruvians arrived has gradually faded. In the second half of the twentieth century, African Americans, Latinos, and migrants of other ethnicities changed Paterson's demography and altered the city's physical appearance. New waves of compatriots were less motivated to assimilate into the mainstream Anglo society and more inclined to form their own institutions. This new generation of Peruvian migrants established the first businesses and ethnic organizations in the area that supported the arrival of family and friends. Although the migration experience of the first Peruvians in Paterson is quite different from the process that their conational contemporaries experienced, they established preliminary migration and settlement patterns that reverberated across successive generations of Peruvian migration.

## Notes

1  The official 2010 U.S. Census count of approximately ten thousand Peruvians living in Paterson does not include the vast number of undocumented immigrants, which,

according to officials from the Peruvian consulate of Paterson, may be up to three times as high as the official number. Scholar Michael Francesco has analyzed the large difference in numbers between the U.S. Census and the estimates of the Peruvian consulate by measuring the number of Peruvians casting absentee votes in Peruvian elections from New Jersey and emigration data from Peru. In this sense, a more reasonable estimate for the number of Peruvians in Paterson begins to approach to thirty thousand, an estimation that has already been circulating through mass media. See 2010 U.S. Census Bureau, Summary File 1 Data for Passaic County, Paterson city, 30. https://www.nj.gov/labor/labormarketinformation/assets/PDFs /census/2010/sf1/mcd/sf1_pas/paterson_sf1.pdf; Michael G. Francesco, "Peruvians in Paterson: The Growth and Establishment of a Peruvian American Community within the Multiethnic Immigrant History of Paterson, New Jersey," *Journal of Urban History* 40, no. 3 (2014): 497–513; Jayed Rahman, "Paterson's Peruvians Celebrate Unveiling of Sign for Peru Square," *Paterson Times*, November 28, 2016, http://patersontimes.com/2016/11/28/patersons-peruvians-celebrate-unveiling-of -sign-for-peru-square/.

2 At the turn of the twentieth century, the well-known Silk City was one of the most important textile centers in the country and one of the sites of American labor movement. See "Working in Paterson: Occupational Heritage in an Urban Setting," Library of Congress, https://www.loc.gov/collections/working-in-paterson/about -this-collection/, acessed July 5, 2024. The following books study Paterson's labor movement: Ann Huber Tripp, *The I.W.W. and the Paterson Silk Strike of 1913* (Chicago: University of Illinois Press, 1987); Steve Golin, *The Fragile Bridge: Paterson Silk Strike, 1913* (Philadelphia: Temple University Press, 1988).

3 See the works of Teófilo Altamirano, *Los Que Se Fueron: Peruanos en Estados Unidos* (Lima: Pontificia Univ. Católica del Perú, Fondo Ed, 1990); Karsten Paerregaard, *Peruvians Dispersed: A Global Ethnography of Migration* (Lanham, MD: Lexington Books, 2010); Larissa Ruiz Baia, "Rethinking Transnationalism: Reconstructing National Identities among Peruvian Catholics in New Jersey," *Journal of Interamerican Studies and World Affairs* 41, no. 4 (1999): 93–109.

4 See Altamirano, *Los Que Se Fueron*, 12. Latino migration literature explains that state-sponsored labor programs initiated massive migration from Mexico and Puerto Rico; however, there is no evidence of this pattern of migration in the Peruvian case. For a comprehensive study of Latino migration to the United States, see Juan Gonzales, *Harvest of Empire: A History of Latinos in America* (New York: Penguin, 2011). Likewise, some scholars have cited this argument in their investigations but have included footnotes mentioning the lack of archival research to support this claim. See Ulla D. Berg, *Mobile Selves: Race, Migration, and Belonging in Peru and the U.S.* (New York: New York University Press, 2015), 27; Ulla D. Berg and Karsten Paerregaard, *El Quinto Suyo: Transnacionalidad y Formaciones Diasporicas en la Migración Peruana* (Lima: Instituto de Estudios Peruanos, 2005), 14.

5 Immigration scholarship explains that the expansion of capitalism and international commerce from capitalist to noncapitalist nations prompted the movement of labor in the opposite direction. See, for example, Douglas Massey, Joaquín Arango, Graeme Hugo, Ali Kouaouci, Adela Pellegrino, and J. Edward Taylor, "Theories of International Migration: A Review and Appraisal," *Population and Development Review* 20 (1993): 699–752. For more information about the movement of workers between the United States and Peru see Cynthia McClintock and Fabian Vallas, *The United States and Peru: Cooperation at a Cost* (New York: Routledge, 2003), 12–13.

6   "Preparing for Opening of the Panama Canal in Eighteen Months by Building Steamships," *New York Herald*, January 28, 1912; W. R. Grace & Co. Records 1828–1986, box 122, series VII, Rare Book and Manuscript Library, Columbia University Library.
7   For a complete examination of the political and economic influence of W. R. Grace & Co. in Peru, see Lawrence A. Clayton, *Grace: W.R. Grace & Co. the Formative Years, 1850–1930* (Ottawa, IL: Jameson Books, 1986); Florencia E. Mallon, *The Defense of Community in Peru's Central Highlands: Peasant Struggle and Capitalist Transition, 1860–1940* (Princeton, NJ: Princeton University Press, 1983), 129, 185; Marquis James, *Merchant Adventurer: The Story of W.R. Grace* (Wilmington, DE: Scholarly Resources), 1993.
8   Gary Vereau, "Conexión histórica entre Paterson y el Perú," *Peruvian Parade Inc.*, Thirtieth Aniversary, Edición Especial #30, Julio 28, 2016, 39.
9   1900 U.S. Census, 1910 U.S. Census, digital image, s.v. "Birth Place: Peru/ Residence: New Jersey," Familysearch, http://familysearch.org, accessed July 5, 2024.
10  "Emergency Passport Applications, Argentina thru Venezuela, 1906–1925," digital image, s.v. "Peru, Consular Registration Certificates, compiled 1907–1918," Ancestry.com, http://ancestry.com, accessed July 5, 2024.
11  "Mrs. Rensch Passes Away," *Daily News*, August 29, 1930, 1, digital image, s.v. "Emma Rensch/1890–1930," Newspapers.com, http://newspapers.com, accessed July 5, 2024.
12  Atlantic merchant practices at the end of the nineteenth century brought thousands of European seafarers to the New World who initiated large-scale immigration. See Maria Borovnik, "Are Seafarers Migrants? Situating Seafarers in the Framework of Mobility and Transnationalism," *New Zealand Geographer* 60, no. 1 (April 2004): 36–43. A similar pattern of initial migration occurred between Peru and the East Coast of the United States. The 1930 Census of Merchant Seamen indicates that a group of eleven Peruvian seafarers working on U.S. and European vessels manifested residing in New Jersey. See "1930 Census of Merchant Seamen," digital image, s.v. "Peru and New Jersey," Ancestry.com, http://ancestry.com, accessed July 5, 2024.
13  1940 U.S. Census of Population and Housing, "Foreign-Born White, by Country of Birth, by Sex, for the City of Paterson, 1940 and 1930," 931, 934, Census.gov, http://www.census.gov, accessed July 5, 2024.
14  Manuel and Victor Tarazona were not related. See Victor Tirado, "Peruvians into Paterson Is on Upswing," *The News*, October 31, 1972, 9, Family Search.org, http://familysearch.org; see also 1920 U.S. Census, 1930 U.S. Census, and 1940 U.S. Census, s.v. "Birth Place: Peru/ Residence: New Jersey," Family Search.org, http://familysearch.org, accessed July 5, 2024.
15  "Passenger Lists of Vessels Arriving at New York, New York, 1820–1897, Year: 1922," digital image, s.v. "Peru," Ancestry.com, http://ancestry.com, accessed July 5, 2024; "Passenger Lists of Vessels Arriving at New York, New York, 1820–1897, Year: 1927," s.v. "Peru," Ancestry.com, http://ancestry.com, accessed July 5, 2024.
16  "Application for Seaman's Protection Certificates, 1916–1940," digital image, s.v. "Manuel Farasona [sic]," Ancestry.com, http://ancestry.com, accessed July 5, 2024; "Statement of Master of Vessel Regarding Changes in Crew Prior to Departure," digital image, s.v. "Carlos Cubillas," Ancestry.com, http://ancestry.com, accessed July 5, 2024.
17  "New York, New York Passenger and Crew Lists, 1909, 1925–1957," digital image, s.v. "Ricardo Tello," Familysearch.org, http://familysearch.org, accessed July 5, 2024.

18  "California, Index to San Francisco Passenger Lists, 1893–1934," digitial image, s.v. "Luis Eduardo de La Flor Cosio, 1920," Familysearch.org, http://Familysearch.org, accessed July 5, 2024; "New York Passenger Arrival Lists (Ellis Island), 1892–1924," digitial image, s.v. "Carlos A. Dulanto, 1920," Familysearch.org, http://familysearch.org, accessed July 5, 2024.
19  "Application," s.v. "Manuel Farasona"; "Statement of Master," s.v. "Carlos Cubillas, http://ancestry.com, accessed July 5, 2024.
20  "New York, New York Passenger and Crew Lists, 1909, 1925–1957," digital image, s.v. "Manuel Cuentas, 1931," Familysearch.org, http://familysearch.org, accessed July 5, 2024.
21  Berg, *Mobile Selves*, 35.
22  See Fanni Muñoz, *Diversiones Públicas En Lima, 1890–1920: La Experiencia De La Modernidad* (Lima: Pontificia Univ. Católica del Perú, 2001).
23  Carlos Contreras and Osmar Gonzales, *Perú: La Apertura Al Mundo* (Madrid: Fundación Mapfre, 2015), 245.
24  Peter Blanchard, *The Origins of the Peruvian Labor Movement, 1883–1919* (Pittsburgh, PA: University of Pittsburgh Press, 1982), 3, 104.
25  "Index to Alien Crewmen Who Were Discharged or Who Deserted at New York, May 1917–Nov 1957," digital image, s.v. "Birth Place: Peru, 1910–1950," Familysearch.org, http://familysearch.org, accessed July 5, 2024.
26  "New York, New York Passenger and Crew Lists, 1909, 1925–1957," s.v. "Ricardo Tello."
27  "New York Passenger Arrival Lists (Ellis Island), 1892–1924," s.v. "Carlos A. Dulanto."
28  Tirado, "Peruvians," 9.
29  James B. Kenyon, *Industrial Localization and Metropolitan Growth: The Paterson–Passaic District* (Chicago: University of Chicago, 1960), 62.
30  Frank Maraví, for instance, worked as a weaver in a local silk mill. See 1930 U.S. Census, Paterson, Passaic, New Jersey, digital image, s.v. "Frank Maraví," Familysearch.org, http://familyseach.com, accessed July , 2024. Manuel and Victor Tarazona worked as foreman and finisher, respectively. See "Three Men Charged with Dye Works Theft," *Morning Call*, November 12, 1928, 15, digital image, s.v. "Manuel Tarazona/1920–1973," Newspapers.com, http://newspapers.com, accessed July 5, 2024.
31  1930 U.S. Census, Paterson, Passaic, New Jersey, s.v. "Manuel Cueritas [sic]," Familysearch.org, http://familysearch.org, accessed July 5, 2024; 1940 U.S. Census, Paterson, Passaic, New Jersey, digital image, s.v. "Richard Hobteld," Familysearch.org, http://familysearch.org, accessed July 5, 2024.
32  Stewart Bird, *Solidarity Forever: An Oral History of the IWW* (Chicago: Lake View Press, 1985), 67.
33  1940 U.S. Census, Paterson, Passaic, New Jersey, digital image, s.v. "Victor Tarazona," Familysearch.org, http://familysearch.org, accessed July 5, 2024.
34  1940 U.S. Census, s.v. "Richard Hobteld."
35  1930 U.S. Census, Paterson, Passaic, New Jersey, digital image, s.v. "Birth Place: Peru/Residence: Paterson," Familysearch.org, http://familysearch.org, accessed July 5, 2024.
36  1940 U.S. Census, Paterson, Passaic, New Jersey, digital image, s.v. "Manuel Tarazona," Familysearch.org, http://familysearch.org, accessed July 5, 2024; 1940 U.S. Census, s.v. "Victor Tarazona"; 1940 U.S. Census, s.v. "Richard Hobteld."
37  "Three Men Charged," 15.
38  *Morning Call*, November 9, 1935, 23, digital image, s.v. "Charles Dulanto/1920–1975," Newspapers.com, http://newspapers.com, accessed July 5, 2024.

39  Edith B. Wallace, *"An Incorporation of the Adventurers": A History of the Society for Establishing Useful Manufactures, Paterson "Silk City" and Its People, and the Great Falls of the Passaic River* (n.p.: National Park Service, U.S. Department of the Interior, December 2019), 221–222, https://www.nps.gov/pagr/learn/historyculture/upload/Paterson-Great-Falls-Historic-Resource-Study-2020-Final508-2.pdf.
40  1930 U.S. Census, Paterson, Passaic, New Jersey, s.v. "Richard Hobteld," Familysearch.org, http://familysearch.org, accessed July 5, 2024.
41  1940 U.S. Census, s.v. "Victor Tarazona."
42  1940 U.S. Census, Montclair, Essex, New Jersey, digital image, s.v. "M. F. Cuentas," Familysearch.org, http://familysearch.org, accessed July 5, 2024.
43  *Morning Call*, December 11, 1933, 10, digital image, s.v. "Charles Dulanto/1920–1975," Newspapers.com, http://newspapers.com, accessed July 5, 2024; "New Democratic Club Is Organized Here," *Morning Call*, March 27, 1934, 10, digital image, s.v. "Charles Dulanto/1920–1975," Newspapers.com, http://newspapers.com, accessed July 5, 2024.
44  Wallace, *Incorporation of the Adventurers*, 221.
45  African Americans also began migrating in mass from the south after World War II. See Giles R. Wright, *Afro-Americans in New Jersey* (Trenton: New Jersey State Library, 2000).
46  Richard H. Teld, Petition for Naturalization, April 8, 1940, vol. 103, 29401–29700, Passaic County Clerk's Office, Public Records Electronic Search System, http://records.passaiccountynj.org/PRESS/Clerk/ShowDetailsPB.aspx. Similarly, Carlos Dulanto and Louis de la Flor changed their first names to Charles and Louis respectively.
47  For an account of the adoption of the draft in World War II, see J. Garry Clifford and Samuel R. Spencer Jr., *The First Peacetime Draft* (Lawrence: University Press of Kansas, 1986).
48  "United States World War II Army Enlistment Records, 1938–1946," digital image, s.v. "Birth Place: Peru/ Residence: New Jersey," Familysearch.org, http://familysearch.org, accessed July 5, 2024.
49  Joel Schwartz, *The Development of New Jersey Society* (Trenton: New Jersey Historical Commission, Department of State, 1997), 58.
50  Tirado, "Peruvians," 9.
51  "Mack Molding Gets "E" Award," *The News*, January 27, 1943, 9, digital image, s.v. "Charles Dulanto/1920–1975," Newspapers.com, http://newspapers.com, accessed July 5, 2024.
52  "Mack Employees Honor Union Pair," *Morning Call*, October 14, 1949, 28, digital image, s.v. "Charles Dulanto/1920–1975," Newspapers.com, http://newspapers.com, accessed July 5, 2024.
53  See John Earl Haynes, *Red Scare or Red Menace? American Communism and Anti-Communism in the Cold War Era* (Chicago: Ivan R. Dee, 2000).
54  "Held as Red Alien," *The Record*, November 30, 1949, 4, digital image, s.v. "Manuel Tarazona/1920–1975," Newspapers.com, http://newspapers.com, accessed July 5, 2024.
55  "Alien Union Aide Seized: Fur Workers Organizer Faces Deportation as Communist," *New York Times*, November 30, 1949, 28, digital image, s.v. "Manuel Tarazona/1920–1975," Newspapers.com, http://newspapers.com, accessed July 5, 2024.
56  See Edward Ranzal, "16 Detained Aliens Freed in Bail; Szigeti Is Detained on Ellis," *New York Times*, November 18, 1950, 1, digital image, s.v. "Manuel Tarazona/1920–1975," Newspapers.com, http://newspapers.com, accessed July 5, 2024;

Russel Porter, "U.S. Rounding Up 39 to Void Their Bail, Posted by Red Fund: Aliens on Way to Ellis Island," *New York Times*, August 3, 1951, digital image, s.v. "Manuel Tarazona/1920–1975," Newspapers.com, http://newspapers.com, accessed July 5, 2024; "Jersey Alien Freed on Bail after Writ," *Courier-News*, August 18, 1951, 9, digital image, s.v. "Manuel Tarazona/1920–1975," Newspapers.com, http://newspapers.com, accessed July 5, 2024; "Civil Rights Rally Planned for May 2," *The News*, April 21, 1952, 3, digital image, s.v. "Manuel Tarazona/1920–1975," Newspapers.com, http://newspapers.com, accessed July 5, 2024.

57 "Richard Hobteld, Native of Peru," *Herald-News*, February 13, 1968, 4, digital image, s.v. "Richard Hobteld/1920–1975," Newspapers.com, http://newspapers.com, accessed July 5, 2024.

58 "Hotel Workers Up Chest Aid 600 Percent," *The News*, October 30, 1954, 11, digital image, s.v. "Victor Tarazona/1920–1986," Newspapers.com, http://newspapers.com, accessed July 5, 2024.

59 *Herald-News*, June 21, 1961, 39, digital image, s.v. "Carlos Cubillas/1930–1975," Newspapers.com, http://newspapers.com, accessed July 5, 2024.

60 Vincent C. Tarazona, Obituary, January 7, 2015, Findagrave.com, https://www.findagrave.com/memorial/143315454/vincent-c-tarazona.

61 "Miss Cubillas Is Engaged to Richard Ebish," *The News*, February 15, 1967, 29, digital image, s.v. "Carlos Cubillas/1930–1975," Newspapers.com, http://newspapers.com, accessed July 5, 2024; "Miss Hobteld Is Wed to Edward Daehnke," *Morning Call*, October 7, 1947, 8, digital image, s.v. "Richard Hobteld/1925–1968," Newspapers.com, http://newspapers.com, accessed July 5, 2024.

62 "Miss Cubillas Is Engaged to Richard Ebish" and "Miss Hobteld Is Wed to Edward Daehnke."

63 See Nancy Foner, *From Ellis Island to JFK: New York's Two Great Waves of Immigration* (New Haven, CT: Yale University Press), 2002.

64 "Pan American Grace Airways: Passenger Manifest," digital image, s.v. "Charles Dulanto," July 5, 1956, Ancestry.com, http://ancestry.com, accessed July 5, 2024.

65 "Florida, U.S., Arriving and Departing Passenger and Crew Lists, 1898–1963," digital image, s.v. "Maria T. Tarazona," October 7, 1960, Ancestry.com, http://ancestry.com, accessed July 5, 2024.

66 Tala DeWynter, interview by Sandra Nichols, July 9, 2007, audio, 1:49:19, St. Helena Historical Society, https://shstory.org/tala-dewynter/.

67 "Una carrera dedicada a recién llegados," *Napa Valley Register*, November 23, 1991, 5, digital image, s.v. "Tala Dewynter/1949–2007," Newspapers.com, http://newspapers.com, accessed July 5, 2024.

68 "Una carrera dedicada a recién llegados."

69 "Talalca Tello, Gaston Dewynter United in Marriage," *The News*, April 19, 1951, 24, digital image, s.v. "Tala Dewynter/1949–2007," Newspapers.com, http://newspapers.com, accessed July 5, 2024; "Tala DeWynter-Area 5," *Napa Valley Register*, April 2, 1973, 6, digital image, s.v. "Tala Dewynter/1949–2007," Newspapers.com, http://newspapers.com, accessed July 5, 2024.

70 Tirado, "Peruvians," 9.

71 For more information about Puerto Rican and Cuban migration to New Jersey, see Isham B. Jones, *The Puerto Rican in New Jersey: His Present Status* (Newark: New Jersey State Department of Education, 1955); Yolanda Prieto, *The Cubans of Union City: Immigrants and Exiles in a New Jersey Community* (Philadelphia: Temple University Press, 2009).

72 Tirado, "Peruvians," 9. See also *The News*, November 6, 1961, 40, digital image, s.v. "Carlos Cubillas/1920–1975," Newspapers.com, http://newspapers.com, accessed July 5, 2024.

73 "Manuel Tarazona, Ex Textile Worker," *The News*, October 21, 1975, 29, digital image, s.v. "Manuel Tarazona/1918–1973," Newspapers.com, http://newspapers.com, accessed July 5, 2024; "United States Social Security Death Index," digital image, s.v. "Victor Tarazona," FamilySearch.org, https://familysearch.org, accessed July 5, 2024.

# 7
## "A Recoger Tomates"

Puerto Rican Farmworkers
in the Garden State,
1940s–1980s

ISMAEL GARCÍA COLÓN AND
WILLIAM SUÁREZ GÓMEZ

Although the history of Puerto Ricans stateside is largely a recounting of urban experiences, migrant farmworkers have played an important role in community formation and agricultural production. Many contemporary Puerto Rican communities in small towns and cities in the Northeast resulted from farm labor migration that began in the 1940s. Vineland, Perth Amboy, and Camden are some of the places where Puerto Rican migrant farmworkers settled from the 1940s through the 1980s. At the peak of their migration, in the late 1960s, more than ten thousand Puerto Ricans toiled in New Jersey's agricultural fields during the harvest season.[1]

Even though the presence of Puerto Rican seasonal migrant farmworkers was important to the development of agriculture and the prosperity of the mid-Atlantic region, scholars and local historians have largely ignored their histories.[2] Accordingly, Puerto Rican history in New Jersey has not been examined extensively, and the role of New Jersey in the history of Puerto Rican migration has long been ignored in favor of New York and new destinations in central

Florida. Despite this oversight, New Jersey was the first migratory stop of many Puerto Ricans who eventually moved to New York City, Philadelphia, and even the Midwest and western United States. Newark and Camden, and the proximity of Philadelphia, Baltimore, and New York City, made the state the region's agricultural hub. As Carmen Teresa Whalen points out, the Puerto Rican government filled 93,155 contract farm jobs in New Jersey between 1952 and 1965, representing 50 percent of the contracts.[3] New Jersey was the center of Puerto Rican seasonal migration to stateside farms.

The Puerto Rican presence in southern New Jersey dates to the first decades of the twentieth century, but migrant workers became visible during the midtwentieth century. One of the first organized farm labor recruitments to this region happened at Seabrook Farms in the early 1940s as part of the federal War Manpower Commission programs during World War II. Gloucester County, in southern New Jersey, was also home to one of the largest labor camps in the Northeast, owned by the Glassboro Service Association (GSA). The Glassboro labor camp, a former U.S. Civilian Conservation Corps camp, became a point of reference for thousands of farmworkers from the 1940s through the 1990s.[4] Most of these migrants arrived to take temporary jobs from April to October, harvesting vegetables and fruits and taking care of orchards and nurseries.

This chapter argues that U.S. policies on migratory labor and labor recruiters made New Jersey the first and principal destination for Puerto Rican farm labor migration. Moreover, local histories of migration and settlement intersected with policies on food production, labor migration, citizenship, and colonial self-rule in Puerto Rico. During the late 1940s, the labor regulations of the U.S. Employment Service, Puerto Rican migration to the U.S. Northeast, the creation of a migratory infrastructure, and growers' reliance on seasonal migrants shaped New Jersey as the main destination of Puerto Rican farmworkers.[5]

After the 1930s, New Jersey farms relied heavily on migratory labor. By 1945, New Jersey's agricultural production was still composed mainly of family farms, with 27,550 farms producing $205,500,000 worth of vegetables, potatoes, tree fruits, and berries. As use of pesticides and the mechanization of agriculture, as well as World War II and industrialization in the cities, eliminated much of the local agricultural labor force, these farms came to rely on temporary labor for intensive agricultural production.[6]

Puerto Ricans were the first large Spanish-speaking migrant group in New Jersey, contributing to the Latinization of New Jersey's farm labor force. One of the principal studies of Puerto Rican farmworkers was *El emigrante puertorriqueño*, by Luis Nieves Falcón (1975), which surveyed farmworkers and residents of farming communities in New Jersey as well as return migrants in Puerto Rico during the early 1970s. Nieves Falcón concentrated on the migratory policies of the Puerto Rican government without elaborating on developments at the federal level and the historical processes in the United States that impelled Puerto Ricans to migrate. Nevertheless, *El migrante puertorriqueño* documents an important moment in the early 1970s when the migrant flow was at its highest.[7] Gloria Bonilla-Santiago's work focused on the challenges of labor organizing among Puerto Rican farmworkers.[8] Other important works that consider Puerto Ricans on New Jersey farms are Carmen Whalen's *From Puerto Rico to Philadelphia* (2001) and Olga Jiménez de Wagenheim's "From Aguada to Dover" (2005). Both authors explain the processes of migrating from the rural towns in Puerto Rico to farms in New Jersey and to eventual settlement in Philadelphia and Dover, New Jersey. This chapter builds on these studies by examining how New Jersey, the Garden State, became a part of the settlement of Puerto Ricans stateside.

## Farm Labor Regimes

The U.S. invasion of Puerto Rico in 1898 incorporated the population into the stateside labor market by granting free entrance to U.S. territorial jurisdictions, initially as nationals and then, after 1917, as U.S. citizens. Although individuals could migrate on their own, by the mid-twentieth century migrant labor contracting had become an important source for employment. U.S. federal guest-worker policies restricted, allowed, and shaped Puerto Rican labor migration according to the needs of growers and the pressures of nativists and labor organizations. During and after World War II, the rise of guest-worker programs shaped Puerto Rican officials' ideas about the creation of a farm labor program.[9] In the early to mid-1940s, small numbers of Puerto Ricans arrived to work on southern New Jersey farms, contracted by those farms through the federal War Food Administration and private labor recruiters. In addition, colonial policies of self-government granted to Puerto Rico from 1948 to 1952 facilitated the development of the Puerto Rico Farm Labor Program (FLP). Puerto Rican officials succeeded in inserting themselves within the federal government to lobby for the hiring of Puerto Ricans.

Some migrant workers arrived in New Jersey because of family and friendship connections. For example, in 1926 Gloria Romano, from Manatí, Puerto Rico, arrived in Vineland, where a friend got her a factory job.[10] However, the Great Depression stopped the flow of migrants through personal networks. In the 1940s, Puerto Ricans traveled to southern New Jersey to work in agriculture in three different waves: the first wave comprised workers who arrived as part of the War Manpower Commission's and the War Food Administration's contracting efforts in Puerto Rico on behalf of farms and canneries. The second wave, from 1945 to 1948, was carried out by private labor contractors, and the third wave developed as workers arrived through the FLP beginning in 1947. These three waves of hiring and transporting Puerto Ricans to New Jersey built the foundation for large-scale labor migration during the 1950s.

The arrival of Puerto Ricans occurred in the context of an evolving farm labor regime. Since the United States seized Puerto Rico in 1898 overpopulation has been a concern for officials. Several governors attempted to use migration to decrease unemployment and poverty. The U.S. Employment Service took Puerto Ricans to states and territories during World War I, and in the 1920s some Puerto Ricans were recruited to work in Arizona. These experiments ended in disaster with migrants abandoning their jobs because of abuses, underpaid work, and difficult living and working conditions. U.S. citizenship, granted in the Jones Act of 1917, impeded their deportation, a powerful tool available to farmers to squelch labor dissent and control their labor force.[11] As a result, southwestern farmers rejected using Puerto Ricans as replacements for Mexicans.

In the 1930s, the Great Depression facilitated the availability of workers in U.S. agriculture, and New Deal policies began to regulate farm labor through child labor protections and labor-camp housing laws. Social reformers in the U.S. Farm Security Administration also attempted to improve labor conditions. In southern New Jersey, farmers recruited and transported Italian and Polish immigrant workers from the Philadelphia area, and African Americans from the South. During World War II, this massive source of low-cost labor from the cities virtually disappeared, although some German and Italian prisoners of war worked in New Jersey agriculture. As labor costs increased, growers argued that shortages required them to resort to guest workers. In response, the War Manpower Commission and the War Food Administration facilitated the creation of the Emergency Labor Supply Program, which oversaw guest workers from Mexico, British Caribbean territories, and Canada and expedited the incorporation of Puerto Ricans as farmworkers in the continental United States.[12]

The Naturalization Act of 1940, which granted birthright citizenship to Puerto Ricans, increased their undesirability as farmworkers. Nevertheless, Puerto Rico governor, Rexford G. Tugwell (1941–1946), began to lobby federal authorities intensively for the use of Puerto Rican workers despite growers' opposition. Unemployment in Puerto Rico remained high at this time because the blockade of the Caribbean by German submarines affected the territory's economy. Tugwell emphasized U.S. citizenship and equal opportunity to pressure federal agencies to include Puerto Ricans in the wartime effort, and Puerto Ricans soon began to arrive as farmworkers in southern New Jersey; in 1944 they were included in the War Food Administration and the Emergency Labor Supply Program. Approximately one thousand Puerto Ricans worked for Seabrook Farms in Bridgeton, in the canneries of the Campbell Soup Company in Camden, and for the Edgar F. Hurff Company in Swedesboro.[13] These companies were known for the harvesting and processing of tomatoes, which is one of the reasons Puerto Ricans referred to farm labor migration as "going to pick tomatoes" (*a recoger tomates*). Many of these migrants established themselves in rural towns near the farming areas, often bringing their relatives and returning to Puerto Rico with news of jobs and to recruit relatives and friends.

At the end of the war, the economic boom of northeastern manufacturing industrial centers, particularly in Philadelphia and New York, were attractive magnets for Puerto Ricans. In addition, the expansion of air transportation after the war and the strategic location of airports in Philadelphia, Newark, and New York City relative to southern New Jersey expanded considerably the commercial and social ties between the region and Puerto Rico. At the same time, the government of Puerto Rico was trying to develop the economy through tax incentives for manufacturing industries and by promoting population control, tourism, and out-migration to reduce unemployment.

After the war, New Jersey's agricultural industry depended exclusively on migrant labor. The main sources of workers in previous decades had almost disappeared. The son of a farmer in Gloucester County who was assigned to Puerto Rico during the war alerted the farmers about the availability of Puerto Ricans to supply their farming needs, although these connections between Gloucester County and Puerto Rico had been operative since the early 1940s.[14] In 1943, Williard B. Kille, chair of the Farm Labor Committee of the Gloucester County Board of Agriculture, wrote to Governor Tugwell and B. W. Thoron, director of the U.S. Division of Territories and Island Possessions, requesting assistance in hiring and transporting Puerto Rican migrants to New Jersey farms.[15] In 1946, a group of farmers in Gloucester County, known as the Glassboro Service Association, brought in two hundred Puerto Ricans. These farmers together with other farmer associations established the Garden State Service Cooperative Association (GSSCA) in 1949 to coordinate operations with the government of Puerto Rico.[16]

In this context, private labor contractors landed in Puerto Rico making offers of higher wages. Samuel Friedman, a Puerto Rican residing in Philadelphia, began to contract Puerto Ricans to work in the canneries and on farms in New Jersey and Maryland. Friedman continued supplying the employers who had hired Puerto Ricans as part of the War Food Administration's efforts during the war. The private labor contractors hired and transported workers for the Gloucester County Agricultural Association in Glassboro, New Jersey, but controversies between workers, farmers, travel agencies, and labor contractors soon arose. Migrants complained about false promises, lack of work, low wages, the high price of food, and unsanitary living and working conditions. They began to ask for help from their families, the press, and elected officials. Many responded to their plea. Vito Marcantonio, the congressman representing the Puerto Ricans of East Harlem, New York, and officials from Puerto Rico investigated the situation. The problems with labor contractors led the Puerto Rican government to enact laws regulating migration.[17] In May 1947 the government of Puerto Rico enacted Public Law 89, regulating the recruitment of labor.

The first contingent of Puerto Rican contract workers arrived at the Glassboro camp for the 1947 harvest. Using Samuel Friedman's services as a labor contractor and intermediary, the government of Puerto Rico allowed the hiring of workers. Governor Jesús T. Piñero sent the Secretary of Labor, Fernando Sierra Berdecía, to observe the labor conditions of migrants stateside. Following Sierra

Berdecía's findings and recommendations, the government of Puerto Rico passed Public Law 25, establishing the Bureau of Employment and Migration. By 1949 the government had displaced the private contractors in favor of direct negotiations with farmers' associations and cooperatives.[18] In the following decade, the government established a powerful infrastructure for seasonal migration and farm labor and the GSSCA contracted most of the Puerto Ricans hired by farmers.[19]

## Regulating Migration to New Jersey

During World War II the activities of private contractors and the Emergency Labor Supply Program led the government of Puerto Rico to promote the idea of farm labor migration. Initially, farmers in New Jersey did not oppose the idea of hiring Puerto Ricans even though their U.S. citizenship made them less desirable than guest workers. It was later, in the 1950s, that farmers' associations attempted to replace Puerto Ricans with British West Indians.[20] However, the U.S. Department of Labor strongly backed the FLP. In 1949, Sierra Berdecía and Robert Goodwin, director of the U.S. Employment Service, the agency in charge of certifying the use of guest workers, signed a memorandum of understanding stipulating that the U.S. Employment Service considered Puerto Ricans as domestic workers to be given preference over guest workers.

The FLP recruited, transported, and facilitated the settlement of migrants. Initially, the government used private labor recruiters, but it later replaced them completely with its own office branches and personnel. In 1947, the first group of 1,300 workers sponsored by the FLP arrived in New Jersey and Pennsylvania. Two private employment agencies hired these workers and subcontracted them to farmers. These contracts, under which migrants were paid fifty-five cents per hour, were approved by the Puerto Rico Department of Labor (PRDL). In Washington Point, New Jersey, a farmer was so happy with the work performed by Puerto Ricans that he provided economic aid to migrants for settling with their families.[21]

After 1950, the federal government extended the Employment Security Act to Puerto Rico. The Bureau of Employment and Migration became the Bureau of Employment Security, and its Migration Division (MD) took charge of the FLP. The government opened an office in Camden (1950–1979) and another one in Keyport (1955–1993). The Camden office served southern New Jersey, Philadelphia, and eastern Pennsylvania, while the Keyport office oversaw central New Jersey. Both offices were established as the FLP grew, the hiring of Puerto Rican farmworkers increased, and the settling of migrant farmworkers into New Jersey communities occurred. The Camden office housed the field office of the MD in the 1950s, which handled transportation, contract negotiations, and problems between growers and workers. The location of the Camden and the Keyport offices was also related to two principal recruiters of workers in New Jersey: the

GSA in Glassboro and the Farmers' and Gardeners' Service Association in Keyport.[22]

The Glassboro and Keyport labor camps were important in supplying Puerto Rican migrant farmworkers to farmers. These two large camps served as centers of labor distribution from which workers were sent to farms with smaller facilities. The FLP in New Jersey was so important that the number of contract workers increased from 6,136 in 1952 to 9,589 in 1968. Estimates of noncontract workers and contract workers ran from ten to fifteen thousand migrants during this period.[23] The FLP's mission of finding employment for Puerto Ricans was successful in New Jersey.

The government of Puerto Rico issued the workers' contract, the terms of which they negotiated with farmers and farmers' associations. The contract stipulated that farmers and associations could deduct from workers' pay expenses for airfares, transportation, and food. In turn, employers were required to provide three hot meals a day, free housing, and a guarantee of 160 hours of work every four weeks. The government also added a requirement for personal injury and health insurance to protect workers.[24] Workers and farmers paid for the health insurance administered by institutions where migrants were assigned to work. However, there were often cases in which workers had to get medical help at their own expense because some local facilities refused to accept their insurance or treat them.[25] Most workers signed the FLP contract in Puerto Rico, but some workers arrived in New Jersey and signed the FLP contract directly with the GSA.

Employers had to meet the housing and labor standards set by the State of New Jersey and the federal government, and the FLP contract allowed MD's field officers to inspect labor camps and farms. The government of Puerto Rico also exposed employers to prosecution in Puerto Rican courts if they violated the contract. Nevertheless, most violations occurred without consequences until the late 1960s, when Puerto Rico Legal Services began to file suits in Puerto Rican courts on behalf of workers and against employers for failing to fulfill their contracts.[26]

In the 1950s and 1960s, the government of New Jersey and labor and community organizations praised the FLP contract for providing adequate wages to migrant workers. In 1959, New Jersey governor, Robert B. Meyer, argued before the U.S. Senate Sub-Committee on Migrant Farm Labor that the FLP's contract with growers' associations improved wage levels because it decreased the wage-depressing influence of British West Indians arriving with H-2 visas. They could not make demands on their employers by threatening to stop their work because their temporary immigrant status rendered them subject to deportation.[27] Wages under the FLP's contract fluctuated from forty-five cents in 1948 to seventy-seven cents per hour in 1959. By 1975, the wages of contract workers were around $2.30 per hour for harvesting vegetables, ten cents above New Jersey's minimum wage and fifty cents over the federal minimum wage.[28]

Disagreements between the government of Puerto Rico and farmers' associations were common. Both parties knew that the Puerto Rican government did not have the resources to confront agricultural corporations, farm bureaus, or cooperatives.[29] They also knew that confrontations between the governments of New Jersey and Puerto Rico would be unlikely. However, Puerto Rican officials surveilled the hiring of migrating workers without contracts. In 1961, after complaints by the PRDL, the Supreme Court of Puerto Rico issued arrest orders for two agents of the GSSCA for recruiting farmworkers in Puerto Rico without authorization and contracts. The government also surveilled airports and asked migrants about their destinations and jobs. Illegal recruiters were usually arrested by the police and referred to court.[30]

Would-be migrants had to pass a health examination, obtain a certificate of "good conduct" from their hometown police, and demonstrate agricultural work experience. Larger employers or recruiters like the GSSCA screened workers in Puerto Rico before hiring them, and employers would verify any prior experience as migrant farmworkers. In the case of the GSSCA, officials blacklisted workers whom they perceived as problematic or who owed money to their prior employer. In 1956, Petroamérica Pagán de Colón, director of the Bureau of Employment Security, recommended that local managers of the Puerto Rico Employment Service annotate information in the applications of migrant workers to avoid future referrals of workers who caused problems or owed money. She also wanted staff to record the addresses of relatives in Puerto Rico in case the government had to trace migrants to collect debts, and she instructed staff to remind workers of their responsibility for fulfilling their contracts.[31] Workers whom employers had found satisfactory were usually rehired for the following season.

In the early 1950s, the FLP flew workers in leased airplanes to Millville, New Jersey (see Figure 7.1). GSA staff transported migrants to its camp and provided hot meals and assigned jobs on specific farms within twenty-four hours of their arrival. At least 150 workers were stationed in the camp as a pool from which local farmers could draw on a day-to-day basis or in an emergency.[32]

A constant problem for employers was workers who left before the end of their contracts. In 1951, the GSSCA transported ten thousand workers to New York, New Jersey, and Pennsylvania but lost $35,000 on unpaid airfares. Some migrant workers disappeared as soon as they landed while others left in protest over labor conditions or unpaid wages.[33] Workers also complained about being underpaid by farmers. In one case in 1956, twenty-one workers left a farm because they rejected the retention by their employer of two cents out of twelve cents per bucket of tomatoes until the end of the harvest as part of their contract.[34] In another case, a sixteen-year-old minor taken from Puerto Rico by a labor recruiter who signed the FLP's contract directly with the GSA left his job after feeling sick. The worker arrived in New York City and after being found wandering on the streets was sheltered by the Spanish American Rescue Mission.[35] In July 1960 a

FIGURE 7.1 Chartered flight with Puerto Rican migrant farmworkers, circa 1948. (Courtesy of the Records of the Migration Division, Archives of the Puerto Rican Diaspora, Centro de Estudios Puertorriqueños, Hunter College, City University of New York.)

Puerto Rican official reported that a worker who had left a farm had started to look for trouble immediately after arriving. He left the same night he arrived, indicating, "I just came for the ride, they [the GSA] deserve to get stuck with my fare because they are a bunch of crooks." The official requested help in tracing this worker and others who left and in holding them responsible for the payment of their airfare.[36]

Even with these problems, New Jersey's farmers described Puerto Ricans as "more dependable, more responsible, and easier to work with than any other migrant." A farmer stated that "The boys are on the farm, they stay there, and are ready to work when you are.... The only thing we expect of these people is that they are good farm workers."[37] Their presence on New Jersey farms demonstrates that despite the challenges these workers faced, they were reliable—and important for food production in New Jersey.

## Experiences in the Fields and Labor Camps

Migrant farmworkers experienced New Jersey through their lives and work in the fields and camps. Farmworkers usually toiled the fields from 6 A.M. to 6 P.M. and even longer hours at the peak of the harvest. Working days were from Monday through Saturday, though sometimes workers finished at midday on Sundays. Workers spent most of their time in the fields and little time in the labor camps. In 1957, New Jersey had registered 2,590 migrant camps and fields comprising 1,086,000 acres. Gloucester and Cumberland counties alone had a total of 1,030 camps, 39 percent of all the camps in New Jersey. These camps housed 8,400 Puerto Ricans at that time, of whom around 2,500 arrived without FLP contracts (see Figure 7.2).[38]

Workers found it hard to adapt to life in labor camps. Lack of privacy and closeness to their coworkers characterized their lives, and farmworkers often felt lonely so far away from home.[39] Many migrants reported feeling stranded or depressed; others felt that they lived in a prison. In 1964, Puerto Rican officials reported the case of Jaime, a twenty-year-old farmworker who committed suicide after feeling homesick and despondent. Jaime shot himself in the head with a revolver. The farmer indicated that he had been a good worker but he was worried about personal problems involving his wife and girlfriend in Puerto Rico.[40] However, the majority of workers eventually adapted to migrant farmwork. Many saved money or sent remittances to their families in Puerto Rico.

Labor camps usually accommodated ten to fifteen workers, although some accommodated from fifty to three hundred. Camp housing usually consisted of barracks with bunk beds, and its condition caused a great deal of bad publicity for the government of Puerto Rico, farmers, and the migrant farmworkers themselves. Despite the federal law that required flush toilets in the camps, many workers had to endure fetid latrines that sometimes overflowed into the camp water supplies. In some cases, rooms were very cramped, even below minimal living standards. Inadequately lighted and poorly ventilated rooms that lacked power sockets, beds, and/or heaters were frequently found. In some camps, a single toilet was used by more than twenty residents and emptied into a hideous cesspool less than one hundred feet away, drawing flies that infested rooms because of holes in the walls or lack of screens. The living conditions in farm labor

FIGURE 7.2. Glassboro Labor Camp in New Jersey, circa 1957. (Courtesy of the Records of the Migration Division, Archives of the Puerto Rican Diaspora, Centro de Estudios Puertorriqueños, Hunter College, City University of New York.)

camps throughout the 1970s were not much different from those in the camps of the 1940s.[41]

For many officials, if a worker was being paid, that was all that counted, but living in a squalid place among unknown people where basic needs, personal security, and property were compromised was not easy and it affected everyday life. Lack of minimal privacy, theft, substance abuse, bullying, bedbugs and/or body lice, poorly cleaned common areas, and unhygienic restrooms were common. For example, Florenzia, a thirty-six year old with a disabled husband and ten children, lived in one room of a labor camp crowded with their belongings and a broken refrigerator. Five of their children slept on the floor. They also experienced recurrent water shortages and poor access to sanitary services. The family earned $17.70 a week, equivalent to $124 today.[42]

The closeness of living quarters in the camps and the fact that working in the fields required long hours caused frequent conflicts between workers and employers. Although gambling and drinking in the camps were not allowed, reports by authorities and workers indicate that these activities were frequent. Camp staff and MD officials, concerned about providing workers with distraction from mental health problems, such as depression and personal conflicts, arranged recreation programs; most camps had a television set, a movie projector, and a ping pong table.[43]

Migrants, officials, and journalists often reported farmers' coercive measures. In Cumberland, Salem, and Gloucester Counties, there were reports of farmers intimidating migrant workers by threatening them with arrest and jailing on the slightest pretext, such as when migrants disputed their wages or criticized their living conditions. Multiple cases were handled by the farmworker division of Camden Regional Legal Services.[44] Towns in which farmers were very well known for their support for politicians and the communities where they lived received sympathetic attention from the local and state police, in addition to security. Sometimes using threats and intimidation, farmers advised anti-poverty institutions and their service providers to avoid going into South Jersey camps. As a result, many workers constantly lived in fear of being arrested and jailed for a simple call to the police. A migrant pointed out, "If you do not do what the farmer say, if you cause any trouble, he calls the police and you get arrested. Don't tell me about justice here. There is no justice for Puerto Ricans."[45] In the thirteenth Annual Migrant Labor Report from 1957, New Jersey State Police colonel, Joseph D. Rutter, reported that because over nineteen thousand citizens migrated to New Jersey from Puerto Rico and the Southern states, patrols maintained surveillance of camps.[46]

In the 1970s, the New Jersey State Migrant Labor Bureau reported to the press that the labor camps in the state were providing good conditions, even though this was far from reality. At the same time, some local health professionals, pastors, civil rights leaders, and anti-poverty officials were denouncing inhumane conditions, squalor, and deprivation in some camps. In 1971, a meeting between a delegation of seven senators from Puerto Rico and farmworkers is revealing of the workers' situation. Around thirty farmworkers alleged abuses at work, with some of them showing open sores on their feet. Some workers who feared reprisals stood silent.[47] Governor William T. Cahill denounced the harsh environment migrant farmworkers faced and acknowledged that New Jersey had failed to do enough on their behalf.[48] Still, Gabriel Coll, a Puerto Rican and director of the New Jersey State Migrant Labor Bureau, insisted on a television program in Philadelphia that "conditions in the camps were so good that he had stopped inspecting some of them."[49] Cases of document falsification, fake inspections, and corrupt inspections by officials were not rare.

Senators from Puerto Rico visited several farm camps to observe working and living conditions in those places and understand how medical support was being provided to workers. The delegation was also studying the working and living conditions of Puerto Ricans in other states. Senator Ernesto Carrasquillo, president of this special committee, intended to gather information on this visit to propose new legislation for the regulation of farm labor migration. Carrasquillo wanted to eliminate loopholes that allowed farmers to cheat Puerto Ricans of their wages and benefits and force them to live in inhumane labor camps. The committee's very first week of visits was dedicated to New Jersey, where twelve thousand Puerto Ricans were under contract to farmers.[50]

The Puerto Rican senators saw several migrant farmworkers in squalid camps where laborers complained bitterly of working and living conditions and a lack of adequate medical care. However, the supervising inspector of the New Jersey State Migrant Labor Bureau declared that he was under orders to prevent reporters from accompanying the senators inside the camps. A conflict between Carrasquillo and the supervising inspector revealed profound disagreements. Carrasquillo refused to accept the itinerary chosen by the inspector and the disclosure conditions imposed by the New Jersey State Migrant Labor Bureau, and this prompted the inspector to leave.[51]

Multiple deficiencies were found during the committee's visits to the camps. For instance, Jill Brothers owned four workers' camps in Salem County. The committee visited two. In the first one, they found a group of Puerto Rican men living in dilapidated shacks, complaining about the bad conditions. "This is worse than being in jail," one of them said. Another worker indicated that he had only earned $135 in a month (approximately $883 in 2021).[52] These living conditions and salaries were far below those set in the FLP's contracts, but these workers had come to New Jersey on their own, some of them with their families, without signing contracts through the PRDL. In the second Jill Brothers' camp, the Senate committee saw an old, dilapidated farmhouse that had been converted into a cooking, sleeping, and recreation center, with a grimy, bug-infested kitchen, a filthy dining table, lice-infested mattresses, and broken screens.[53]

New Jersey newspapers reported several contentious situations. Aggressive interactions between farmworkers and organizers, service providers, and public representatives occurred in the fields. These conflicts seemed to be isolated incidents, but, reading between the lines, they could be understood as farmers striking back against labor organizing and any kind of accountability. One case was against the Agricultural Workers Association (Asociación de Trabajadores Agrícolas) president while he was attempting to organize a group of ten workers in a camp. Someone attacked the Agricultural Workers Association leader, punching him twice in the face, according to the report, when he was talking to workers about union benefits. The report presented later in court revealed that the attacker worked for the GSA, the organization that represented the farmers in yearly contract negotiations with the Puerto Rican government.[54]

In New Jersey, public servants and federal anti-poverty officials were arrested on trespassing charges when they attempted to see migrant workers in the camps.[55] This led to an important case, *The State v. Shack*, in which the U.S. Supreme Court ruled, in 1971, that public representatives of any state agency must have access to labor camps to talk to and provide assistance to workers whenever they were not at work. However, years later, a physical attack was reported at Rosario-Sorbello and Son's farm. The foreman attacked Assemblyman Byron M. Baer after he and other public servants entered the farm to talk to workers. The politician accused the foreman of breaking his arm using a five-foot length of board, smashing the windshield and windows of the assemblyman's station wagon, and assaulting another official. While shouting in Spanish, "We're not people in a zoo just because we work on a farm," the foreman incited ten other workers to join in beating the officials. The incident happened in front of the camp as workers chased Baer and two other visitors to their cars parked near the Sorbellos' farmhouse. The attacker alleged that the victims had not identified themselves as public officials and were taking pictures of the workers and the farm without permission.[56]

A seventeen-year-old Puerto Rican farmworker returned one day to a migrant camp in New Jersey to pick up some back wages. The farmer complained to the police, and the youth was arrested on a charge of stealing. Unable to call anyone for help and having poor English skills, the young man was incarcerated in the Paulsboro jail, where he spent three weeks before his case came to light, during which time he was sexually assaulted.[57] Curiously, when the youth finally appeared before a magistrate, it turned out that the farmer had never issued a formal complaint. As a result, the judge dismissed the case. Federal court decisions were clear that a person could not be kept in jail for more than forty-eight hours without appearing before a magistrate. In Gloucester County, anti-poverty lawyers revealed that hundreds of migratory farmworkers in southern New Jersey had been jailed without seeing a judge after a reasonable period. Correctional officials refused to let anti-poverty lawyers counsel jailed migrants. Some reports suggest that it was not unusual to find migrant workers arrested who never formally appeared before a judge or had access to legal counsel. Although it was true that local courts met less frequently than those in cities and that many migrants could barely speak English or post a modest bail, the modus operandi adopted by the police was to jail them until the court met, which was often more than ten days after the arrest. In contrast, when New Jersey residents were arrested on similar charges, they were released without bail.[58]

Organizations such as the New Jersey Conference of NAACP (National Association of the Advancement of Colored People) charged repeatedly that farmers exploited Blacks and Puerto Ricans. In 1970, Irene Smith, the president of the New Jersey Conference of NAACP, stated that life on a southern plantation was "like a trip to the mountains compared with the life of a migrant farm worker in New Jersey." She added that "the Southern master took better care of his slaves because they were his year-round property. In New Jersey, the farmers work the blacks and Puerto Ricans to death for a couple of months and then get rid of them."[59]

A class-action suit was filed in 1972 on behalf of migrants by the Puerto Rican Legal Defense and Education Fund and the Camden Regional Legal Services' farmworkers division. Although probably based on actions conducted under the Puerto Rico governor, Luis A. Ferré (1968–1972), the case became more notorious under the ensuing governorship of Rafael Hernández Colón (1973–1976 and

1985–1992). This suit was the first to name New Jersey and Puerto Rican officials instead of individual growers. Michael Cohen, a federal district judge in Camden, reinstated the charges against officials for conspiring to deny migrants adequate housing. Activists also found that migrants working at Columbia Fruit Farm, near Hammonton, lived without proper living space, toilets, garbage disposal, and sewage facilities.[60]

Even with the poor living and labor conditions and experiences of discrimination and abuse that many Puerto Ricans experienced, the migratory flow continued to New Jersey farms. Unemployment, underemployment, and low wages in Puerto Rico made farm labor migration an option to improve their well-being. For some, migration became a regular back-and-forth between the islands and New Jersey. Others found the end of their journey in rural communities, small towns, and cities in the United States.

## Settling in New Jersey and Struggling for Labor Rights

Many Puerto Rican migrant farmworkers forged their whole lives migrating seasonally from rural areas of Puerto Rico to rural areas in the United States. Local and state officials and farmers usually wanted Puerto Rican workers with FLP contracts to return home after the harvest, but many began to settle in New Jersey's cities and small towns. By 1956, PRDL official Luisa Frías documented the cases of Félix Rodríguez Sampayo, who owned a restaurant serving migrants in Landisville, and Blas Meléndez, owner of a farm and truck business. She also reported that many of the migrants who arrived in 1944 to work for the Campbell Soup Company owned farms and houses in southern New Jersey.[61]

The Puerto Rican population increased from 4,055 in 1950 to an estimated 26,000 in 1954.[62] Many arrived as farmworkers—single men who, after settling and finding permanent jobs, brought their families. In the 1950s, Puerto Rican migrant farmworkers established communities in towns like Vineland, Perth Amboy, and Dover. Some migrants eventually found jobs in the service sector or factories, and some migrants moved to other states or big cities like Philadelphia, Boston, or Chicago, but only a minority of farmworkers ended up in New York City.[63]

From 1960 to 1970 the population of Puerto Ricans in New Jersey increased from 55,351 to 136,937 people. Most of these migrants from Puerto Rico or New York City were moving to urban areas as Puerto Ricans in rural areas numbered only 3,125 (5.65 percent of the Puerto Rican population) in 1960, and 5,349 in 1970 (3.91 percent).[64] In 1998, Octavio Negrón, an eighty-five-year-old resident of Landisville, reminisced about his experiences as a migrant farmworker in Florida and the northeast since 1946. Unlike many of his coworkers, Octavio settled in New Jersey in the 1960s. For Octavio, farmwork in the 1990s was no better than when he began working at fifty cents per hour because of its low wages and seasonal nature.[65]

Noncontract Puerto Rican migrant farmworkers were also arriving with their families. In 1960, the MD staff found thirteen families with twenty-two children in New Jersey. These families arrived first in Florida and trekked north as the harvest seasons changed. The MD's staff recruited their kids for migrant children's schools in New Jersey. Many of those seasonal migrant families settled in the state.

By the 1970s, the decrease in agricultural production reduced the number of seasonal migrants. During the food harvest of 1972, six thousand Puerto Ricans worked in the fields, housed in some of the fourteen hundred labor camps in New Jersey. Most of the workers arrived with contracts arranged by the FLP and the GSA, a group of six hundred farmers who hired 80 percent of Puerto Rican workers.[66] From the 1970s to the 1990s, Mexicans began to replace Puerto Ricans, who were finding more permanent jobs in factories, with better pay and less strenuous work than in agriculture. By then, even Octavio's children did not work in agriculture.[67]

In the 1980s, the active recruitment of Puerto Rican workers occurred in manufacturing. The New Jersey Labor Department's first major effort to recruit laborers from abroad involved searching for residents of Puerto Rico to work in factories to ease a shortage of assembly workers. The second major effort sought overseas workers from Ireland to fill vacant shore-area summer retail and resort jobs. However, manufacturers were not too enthusiastic about the idea of hiring Puerto Rican laborers instead of Irish; they were more interested in long-term workers with some basic skills. Although the state's manufacturers helped subsidize unemployment compensation for migrant farmworkers, they could not to afford to house migrants in areas where factories were concentrated.[68]

Criticism of farmers by labor organizations in the manufacturing sector was common. In 1966, Joel R. Jacobson, the president of the New Jersey State Industrial Union Council, publicly condemned growers for exploiting migratory farmworkers. He urged the governor to support contracts with wages of $1.30 per hour (equivalent to $10.15 in today's money), plus basic benefits, including transportation and health services. The GSSCA offered $1.20 per hour without any benefits, transportation, or health benefits. The New Jersey State Industrial Union Council's view was that farmers could afford to pay decent living wages with some basic protections, as is expected in advanced nations.[69]

The settlement of Puerto Ricans in New Jersey was facilitated and supported by local communities, labor, and religious organizations. A small group of churches, under the New Jersey Council of Churches, took the lead in helping Puerto Rican farmworkers in the 1950s. At that time, 15 percent of Puerto Rican workers in New Jersey were estimated to be illiterate (see Figure 7.3). The assistant pastor of the Memorial Presbyterian Church in Dover, Armando Divas, devoted six evenings a week to the educational, spiritual, and recreational needs of some of the seven thousand farmworkers. Other clergymen, from Cape May to High Point, offered similar services, and enthusiastic parishioners, usually

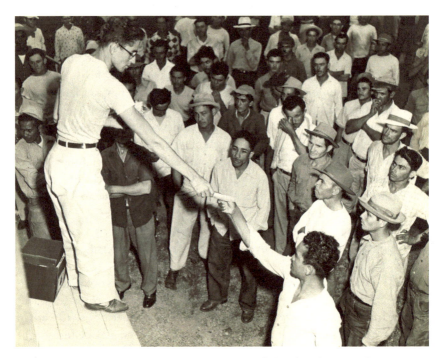

FIGURE 7.3. Jaime Quiñones, working for the Council of Churches, distributes letters to workers in the Rath Camp, circa 1950s. (Courtesy of the Records of the Migration Division, Archives of the Puerto Rican Diaspora, Centro de Estudios Puertorriqueños, Hunter College, City University of New York.)

women, helped with these goodwill activities. Reports highlighted that the participants, all men ranging in age from twenty to fifty years old, were active and highly motivated. This was not just an opportunity to learn to read and write but also to interact with others in a nonworking environment. After-class events were organized by the parishioners; sometimes they played music to motivate workers to sing. From time to time they watched a motion picture projected onto the side of a barn. These classes allowed some of the workers to discuss their personal and spiritual problems with the clergymen. However, workers were moved through the camps relatively quickly, limiting the learning possibilities of each migrant.[70] Eventually, disagreements between organizations and farmers developed. In an interview, Carleton E. Heritage, former director of New Jersey Farm Services, said that these organizations could do a great deal of good but, for some reason, they were not consulting with the growers about problems they felt needed attention.[71]

Service programs developed by institutions helped both Puerto Rican farmworkers and growers. For instance, the Ecumenical Farmworkers Ministry (Ministerio Ecuménico de Trabajadores Agrícolas), founded by the Catholic and Episcopal churches and other religious organizations, exposed the reality of migrant workers in Connecticut and New Jersey.[72] However, the economic power and political influence were more on the side of farmers than with religious organizations. New Jersey Puerto Ricans were also forming community organizations that helped migrant farmworkers, such as the Puerto Rican Action Committee of Salem County, which was established by migrants who had settled in southern New Jersey. It organized a festival to honor migrant workers and highlight their problems.[73]

In the late 1970s, after the dissolution of the Ecumenical Farmworkers Ministry, the Agricultural Workers Association played an important role as the first farmworkers' association in the region, attempting to unionize the mostly Puerto Rican farmworkers along the U.S. East Coast. Among the states of Delaware, New Jersey, New York, Massachusetts, and Connecticut, the organization represented around two thousand Puerto Ricans.[74] Their goal was to grow, to represent a much larger portion of the sixty thousand migrant workers who came to the United States each year from Puerto Rico.

Other organizations joined this effort, such as the American Civil Liberties Union of New Jersey, which sponsored legal services for farmworkers and denounced employers' housing and civil rights violations. However, a few years later their project initiatives were transferred to the Agricultural Workers Support Committee (Comité de Apoyo a los Trabajadores Agrícolas, CATA).[75] Organizers and twenty-nine workers established CATA in Vineland during the fall of 1979 and began immediately to fight for workers fired in favor of workers with H-2 nonimmigrant work visas and to contest the efforts of agricultural employers to lower the minimum wage for farmworkers below the federal rate. By the mid-1980s, CATA had a membership of sixteen hundred workers and a budget of over $120,000. The U.S. Catholic Conference Campaign for Human Development, Protestant churches of the Ecumenical Review Board, several foundations, and labor organizations, together with the American Civil Liberties Union of New Jersey, sponsored the funding of CATA. The organization also ran literacy campaigns and labor education training on health, safety, and legal rights. It negotiated agreements with farmers and engaged in litigation against abusive crew leaders, employers, and managers. CATA established the first medical plan for migrant workers in New Jersey and won changes in unemployment compensation and the use of pesticides. In 1985, CATA established a labor union, the Agricultural Workers Organizing Committee (Comité Organizador de Trabajadores Agrícolas, COTA), which won the right to represent migrant workers at the Levin Farm in southern New Jersey. This labor union fought to organize twenty to forty thousand migrant farmworkers in New Jersey and Pennsylvania, and its services and efforts on behalf of farmworkers continue to the present day.[76]

The case of the Levin Farm is important in the history of New Jersey farmer–worker relations. For five years migrant farmworkers had been earning $3.35 for twelve to fourteen hours of work per day, without overtime pay. The labor camp where they were housed was described as squalid and without laundry facilities, and workers were endangered by the improper use of pesticides. Workers had trouble applying for compensation and unemployment benefits.[77] Fifteen migrant workers formed a union on this farm. The owners, Saul and Isaac Levin, were incarcerated in 1985 for refusing to comply with a court order that forced them to recognize the union. This was the first time that a court or agency had ever directed farm employers to recognize a farmworkers union in the Northeast United States. However, the Levin brothers preferred to go to jail and bulldoze their farm before recognizing the workers' rights.[78]

The Levin brothers asserted that they would not sign an agreement because they would not cultivate their land that year, but COTA found that they were using nonunionized workers. COTA asked the court to force them to negotiate; because of the possibility of going back to jail, they agreed.[79] In 1986, the agreement between COTA and the Levin Farm consisted of a $3.80 hourly wage, round-trip airline tickets, employment security until October 15 of that year, payment of five cents per hour by workers for health insurance, and an increase in wages beginning in September. The New Jersey Farm Bureau grew concerned that labor organizing would lead to strikes that put pressure on the farmers—and threatened the $3 billion generated by this industry.[80] Indeed, the agreement with Levin Farm influenced other farms. Farmers began to raise wages from $3.35 to $3.65 per hour, offer round-trip tickets, and improve housing.

This important case validated workers' protection under New Jersey's Constitution (Art. 1, No. 19). The main farmer, Saul Levin, was ordered by a judge to bargain in good faith with the fifteen workers. After weeks of being threatened by the Levin farmers with replacement if they were unionized, fourteen farmworkers continued. This group of workers was eventually advised by the New Jersey State Board of Mediation. Finally, by a unanimous vote, COTA was recognized as their exclusive bargaining agent. After this incident, COTA formally established its activities in Glassboro, New Jersey, raising sufficient support from workers so that farmers began to raise salaries and provide better working conditions. To hinder COTA's efforts, farmers found ways to increase their requests for foreign guest workers; after 1986, under the new H-2A visa program, they began decreasing their hiring of Puerto Ricans in favor of guest workers, complaining that the FLP's contract was too onerous. Employers also began to replace Puerto Rican farmworkers with undocumented Mexicans.[81]

By the early 1990s, the FLP was a small and limited supplier of migrant farmworkers to the GSA. The government of Puerto Rico had begun dismantling the FLP program in 1989 when it eliminated its stateside offices.[82] In 1993, negotiations between the GSA and the government of Puerto Rico stalled as officials refused the organization's proposed reduction of benefits and rights under the contract. GSA planned to raise the fee for meals and shelter from $6 to $8 and reduce the number of hot meals per day from three to two. In 1993, the FLP was terminated, and the GSA hired Mexican seasonal migrant workers.[83]

## Conclusion

Between the late 1950s and the late 1980s, multiple reports highlighted the large contribution of Puerto Rican farmworkers to New Jersey agriculture. In 1962, the president of the New Jersey Farm Bureau observed that the state's farmers were finding a tight labor market.[84] The Puerto Rico Farm Labor Program represented the difference between having enough hands to harvest the state's multi-million-dollar fruit and vegetable crops and losing those crops. By 1964, the Associated Press reported that 43,760 Puerto Rican farmworkers had come to New Jersey under FLP work agreements from 1951 to 1964, helping to harvest tomatoes, corn, asparagus, potatoes, and much more, harvesting more than $830 million worth of Garden State crops.[85] The contributions of Puerto Rican migrant farmworkers are undeniably important to agricultural production and the establishment of Puerto Rican and Latinx communities in New Jersey.

After decades of experiencing deplorable conditions in the labor camps and fields of New Jersey, Puerto Ricans became disposable and replaceable. In the late 1970s and 1980s farmers responded to migrant farmers' unionization efforts by recruiting guest workers and undocumented immigrants. Around the same time, factories began to expand their recruitment of Puerto Rican migrants to ease a shortage of unskilled assembly workers.[86] The New Jersey Department of Labor encouraged businesses statewide to tap Puerto Rican farmworkers in the southern counties for factory positions that typically paid $5 to $6 an hour (equivalent to $11.48 per hour today). Thus, immigrants replaced gradually Puerto Ricans in New Jersey agriculture.

The arrival of thousands of Puerto Rican migrants to rural New Jersey in the twentieth century demonstrates how U.S. officials and farmers enabled and controlled the mobilization of labor from many parts of the world to satisfy the needs of food producers. New Jersey farms' reliance on migratory labor during the twentieth century, together with U.S. guest-worker policies, the development of air transportation along the U.S. Eastern Seaboard, and the geographical location of New Jersey between the metropolises of New York and Philadelphia, created the ideal conditions for Puerto Rican migration. The emergence and consolidation of farmers' cooperatives like the GSA and the GSSCA, and the power they exerted over farmworkers and labor regulations, illustrate how the influx of Puerto Rican farmworkers transformed New Jersey agriculture. In addition, changes in U.S. colonial policy in Puerto Rico during the 1940s and 1950s allowed the insular government to develop a project that included migration as one of its pillars of modernization. The government of Puerto Rico established an infrastructure of migration that included the staff and offices to hire, transport, educate, and supervise Puerto Rican migrant farmworkers.

This chapter has described briefly the histories of Puerto Rican farm labor migrants to New Jersey, most of which are absent from the majority of the state's historical narratives. The Puerto Rican experience in New Jersey agriculture is relevant to understanding the Latinization of the farm labor force and the histories of other Latinx groups, including urban Puerto Ricans. Puerto Rican histories are embeded within the myths of the reliability or laziness of certain groups over others, and the ethnic succession or segmentation in certain economic niches that employers deploy to lower labor costs. Immigration and colonial migration policies contribute to maintaining these social inequalities based on citizenship, immigration status, gender, race, and ethnicity.

## Notes

1 Ismael García Colón, "We Like Mexican Laborers Better: Citizenship and Immigration Policies in the Formation of Puerto Rican Farm Labor in the United States," *CENTRO Journal* 29, no. 2 (Summer 2017): 171.
2 The exceptions are Carmen Teresa Whalen, *From Puerto Rico to Philadelphia: Puerto Rican Workers and Postwar Economies* (Philadelphia: Temple University Press, 2001) and Olga Jiménez de Wagenheim, "From Aguada to Dover: Puerto Ricans Rebuild Their World in Morris County, New Jersey, 1948–2000," in *The Puerto Rican Diaspora: Historical Perspectives*, ed. Carmen Teresa Whalen and Víctor Vázquez-Hernández (Philadelphia: Temple University Press, 2005), 107.
3 Whalen, *From Puerto Rico to Philadelphia*, 74–75.
4 Isham B. Jones, *The Puerto Rican: His Present Status* (Newark, NJ: Department of Education, 1955), 14.
5 The research for this chapter includes archival research on the history of stateside Puerto Rican farm labor migration. García Colón carried out extensive archival research at the U.S. National Archives and Records Administration, the Archives of the Puerto Rican Diaspora at the Center for Puerto Rican Studies, Hunter College, New York (hereafter Centro Archives), and the Archivo General de Puerto Rico (AGPR), San Juan. We also rely on published sources, including newspaper articles and government reports.
6 New Jersey Department of Labor and Industry, *First Annual Report, 1945* (Trenton: State of New Jersey, 1949), 1–2.
7 Luis Nieves Falcón, *El emigrante puertorriqueño* (Río Piedras: Editorial Edil, 1975).
8 Gloria Bonilla-Santiago, "A Case Study of Puerto Rican Migrant Farmworkers Organizational Effectiveness in New Jersey" (PhD diss., City University of New York, 1986); Gloria Bonilla-Santiago, *Organizing Puerto Rican Migrant Farmworkers: The Experience of Puerto Ricans in New Jersey* (New York: P. Lang, 1988).
9 Ismael García Colón, *Colonial Migrants at the Heart of Empire: Puerto Rican Workers on U.S Farms* (Oakland: University of California Press, 2020).
10 Martín Pérez, "Living History, Vineland, New Jersey," in *Extended Roots: From Hawaii to New York, Migraciones Puertorriqueñas a los Estados Unidos*, ed. Oral History Task Force (New York: Centro de Estudios Puertorriqueños, City University of New York, 1984), 20.
11 Edwin Maldonado, "Contract Labor and the Origins of Puerto Rican Communities in the United States," *International Migration Review* 13, no. 1 (Spring 1979): 106.
12 Charles H. Harrison, *Growing a Global Village: Making History at Seabrook Farms* (New York: Holmes and Meier, 2003), 19, 30–31, 109.
13 Cindy Hahamovitch, *The Fruits of Their Labor: Atlantic Coast Farmworkers and the Making of Migrant Poverty, 1870–1945* (Chapel Hill: University of North Carolina

Press, 1997), 178, 186, 196; Whalen, *From Puerto Rico to Philadelphia*, 52–53; Jones, *Puerto Rican*, 13.
14   Bonilla-Santiago, "Case Study," 76–78.
15   Willard B. Killie to Rexford G. Tugwell, September 27, 1943, file 9-8-116, box 1138, classified files, 1907–1951, Office of Territories, Record Group 126, U.S. National Archives and Records Administration; Willard B. Killie to B. W. Thoron, November 15, 1943, file 9-8-116, box 1138, classified files, 1907–1951, Office of Territories, Record Group 126, U.S. National Archives and Records Administration; García Colón, *Colonial Migrants*, 56.
16   "Operation Breadbasket," reprinted from the *Great Silver Fleet News*, September–October 1955, file Div. Orientación, box 111, Correspondencia General, A. Monroy, D-G, Tarea 61-55, AGPR; see García Colón, *Colonial Migrants*, 137.
17   Vito Marcantonio to Lewis B. Schwellenbach, U.S. Secretary of Labor, reprinted, *Liberación*, September 4, 1946; "Farm Labor Probe Asked," *People's Voice*, September 14, 1946, 6.
18   Petroamérica Pagán de Colón to Estella Draper, June 23, 1949, file Correspondencia Personal 1949–50, box 163, Correspondencia de la Oficina de la Directora, 1948–50 A y la E, Tarea 61-55, Fondo Oficina del Gobernador, AGPR.
19   Consumers' League of New York, Migrant Labor in NYS, special newsletter, supplement for June 1957, 20–21, file C.L. Publications-Migrant Labor Miscellaneous, box 12, collection 5307, Consumers' League of New York City Records, Kheel Center for Labor-Management Documentation and Archives, Cornell University (Kheel Center), New York.
20   Charles Grutzner, "Alien Farm Labor Is Barred in State...," *New York Times*, April 5, 1950, 32.
21   Fernando Sierra Berdecía, Report to Jesús T. Piñero, "Migración a de trabajadores puertorriqueños a los Estados Unidos," November 17, 1947, box 454, Tarea 96-20, Fondo Oficina del Gobernador, AGPR.
22   Migration Division, Puerto Rico Department of Labor (PRDL), *Annual Report, 1966*, Annual Reports, 1953–1992, boxes 2733–2739, Agency Reports, 1939–1992, Administration, Migration Division, Centro Archives.
23   García Colón, "We Like Mexican Laborers Better," 171.
24   Michael Lapp, "Managing Migration: The Migration Division of Puerto Rico and Puerto Ricans in New York City, 1948–1968" (PhD diss., Johns Hopkins University, 1990), 178–181.
25   Ronald Sullivan, "Puerto Ricans Check Jersey Farm Camps," *New York Times*, September 13, 1971, 39.
26   Donald Janson, "Jersey Is Pressed on Migrant Pact: Puerto Rico Also Involved in Negotiations with the U.S on Working Conditions," *New York Times*, July 23, 1973, 63.
27   Robert B. Meyer, "Statement by Governor Meyer to U.S. Senate Sub-Committee on Migrant Farm Labor," Trenton, NJ, November 30, 1959, 3, file 14 New Jersey (State of), box 36, collection 5307, Kheel Center.
28   Donald Janson, "Migrants to Get Record Pay Raises: Puerto Rican Farm Hands in Jersey," *New York Times*, March 21, 1975, 77; Migration Division, PRDL, "Annual Report, 1953" and "Annual Report, 1959," Annual Reports, 1953–1992, boxes 2733–2739, Agency Reports, 1939–1992, Administration, Migration Division, Centro Archives.
29   Jim Hazel, "Islanders Fare Better Than U.S. Counterparts: Puerto Ricans on the Move-V," *News Journal (Evening Journal)*, May 19, 1961, 25.
30   Migration Division, PRDL, "Puerto Rico Cracks Down on Illegal Recruitment of Farm Workers, Orders Arrest of Agents of Largest Mainland Recruitment

Association," press release, March 13, 1961, file 19 Garden State Service Cooperative Association, Incorporated-Trenton, NJ, box 938, subject and resource files, Farm Labor Program 1948-1993, Migration Division, Centro Archives.
31 Jones, *Puerto Rican*, 15; Petroamérica Pagán de Colón, Memorandum to Gerentes..., reclutamiento de trabajadores para Glassboro Service Association, Inc., durante el mes de abril, March 23, 1956, file Visitas a las oficinas locales División de Operaciones, 1958, serie 11 Correspondencia de la División de Migración, 1958, Tarea 63-37, AGPR.
32 Jones, *Puerto Rican*, 15.
33 Jones, *Puerto Rican*, 15.
34 Alfonso Soto Franco, Memorandum, Viaje oficial a los Estados Unidos, November 5, 1956, 8, file Organización y personal, box 2254, Tarea 96-20, Fondo Oficina del Gobernador, AGPR.
35 Social Services Section, Migration Division, PRDL, Case #2285, 1951, file 4, 2269-2296, 3/17-5/30/1951, box 2264, case files, Social Services, Migration Division, Centro Archives.
36 Ervin Villanueva, Inter-Office Report to Anthony Vega, Re Employer Relations, August 2, 1960, date reported activity 29 July 1960, file 8 New Jersey Office—Inter-Office Reports, 1960, box 886, Reports, Farm Labor Program 1948-1993, Migration Division, Centro Archives.
37 Hazel, "Islanders Fare Better," 25.
38 New Jersey Department of Labor and Industry, *13th Annual Bureau of Migrant Labor Report, 1957*, 3, 6, box 2 of 4, Migrant Labor and Child Care Records of the Office of Economic Opportunity (ca. 1961-1974), series B1529-97, New York Department of Agriculture and Markets, New York State Archives.
39 "Migrants Propel N.J. Farm Season," *Philadelphia Inquirer*, July 25, 1993, B4.
40 Newspaper clipping, circa June 1964, file 12 New Jersey Inter Office Reports, 1964, box 886, Reports, Farm Labor Program 1948-1993, Migration Division, Centro Archives.
41 Ronald Sullivan, "Jersey's Migrants: A Hardly Human Existence," *New York Times*, August 23, 1970, section E5.
42 Sullivan, "Jersey's Migrants," E5.
43 Jones, *Puerto Rican*, 15.
44 Ronald Sullivan, "Court Abuse of Migrants Charged in South Jersey," *New York Times*, August 17, 1970, 1.
45 Sullivan, "Court Abuse of Migrants," 1.
46 New Jersey Department of Labor and Industry, *13th Annual Bureau of Migrant Labor Report, 1957*, 12.
47 Sullivan, "Court Abuse of Migrants," 1; Sullivan, "Puerto Ricans Check Jersey Farm Camps," 39.
48 Ronald Sullivan, "Aid for Migrants Urged by Cahill: Governor Recommends Plan for the Farm Workers," *New York Times*, November 8, 1970, 68.
49 Sullivan, "Puerto Ricans Check Jersey Farm Camps," 39.
50 Sullivan, "Puerto Ricans Check Jersey Farm Camps," 39.
51 Sullivan, "Puerto Ricans Check Jersey Farm Camps," 39.
52 Sullivan, "Puerto Ricans Check Jersey Farm Camps," 39.
53 Sullivan, "Puerto Ricans Check Jersey Farm Camps," 39.
54 "Hearing Date Set in Farm Assault," *Courier-Post*, November 7, 1974, 26.
55 Sullivan, "Jersey's Migrants," E5.
56 Donald Janson, "Baer, Injured at Migrant Camp, Accused of Trespassing at Farm," *New York Times*, July 18, 1974, 74.

57  Sullivan, "Court Abuse of Migrants," 1.
58  Sullivan, "Court Abuse of Migrants," 1.
59  Sullivan, "Jersey's Migrants," E5.
60  Donald Janson, "Governor of Puerto Rico Must Face Migrant Trial," *New York Times*, November 20, 1975, 87.
61  Luisa Frías de Hempel, Memorandum to Luis Muñoz Marín, Viaje oficial a los Estados Unidos, November 16, 1956, file Organización y personal, box 2254, Tarea 96-20, Fondo Oficina del Gobernador, AGPR.
62  Jiménez de Wagenheim, "From Aguada to Dover," 107.
63  Arthur C. Gernes, "Implicaciones de la emigración puertorriqueña al continente fuera de la ciudad de Nueva York," *Revista La Torre* 4, no. 13 (January–March 1956): 100.
64  U.S. Census Bureau, *Puerto Ricans in the United States: Social and Economic Data for Persons of Puerto Rican Birth and Parentage* (Washington, DC: GPO, 1963), 7–9; U.S. Census Bureau, *1970 Census of Population: Puerto Ricans in the United States* (Washington, DC: GPO, 1973), 1–2.
65  Phil Joyce, "A Lifetime of Working," *Philadelphia Inquirer*, November 25, 1998, B2.
66  Donald Janson, "Migrant Workers Uniting to Fight Job Abuse," *New York Times*, August 14, 1972, 29; Ronald Sullivan, "Study Criticizes Migrant Camps: Says Puerto Rican Laborers Are Degraded in Jersey," *New York Times*, August 27, 1972, 38.
67  Joyce, "Lifetime of Working," B2.
68  Mark Dillon, "State Would Help Recruit Puerto Ricans: Trade Groups' Fault Ideas to Ease Labor Shortage," *Asbury Park Press*, June 29, 1988, D13, D18.
69  United Press International, "Jersey Growers Hit on Migrant Workers," *Morning Call*, March 21, 1966; United Press International, "Farmers Accused of Exploiting Migrants," *Daily Journal*, March 21, 1966, 1.
70  "Migrant Schools DOT Jersey Farms: Ministers and Young Helpers Spend Many Hours Teaching English to Puerto Ricans," *New York Times*, August 19, 1954, 25.
71  Hazel, "Islanders Fare Better," 25.
72  "M.E.T.A. Gets $25,000 from Two Churches," *Hartford Courant*, April 1, 1973, 25.
73  Puerto Rican Action Committee, Salem, New Jersey, undated letter to Friends Interested in Helping Puerto Rican Communities, file 5 Miscellaneous, 1971–74, box 3001, subject files, Administration, Migration Division, Centro Archives.
74  "Hearing Date Set in Farm Assault," 26.
75  Donald Janson, "Effects of Jersey's Farm Strike Are Spreading," *New York Times*, September 1, 1980, B2.
76  Ángel Domínguez, "Sembrando," *Siembra* 3, no. 1 (June 1985): 4, in file 9 Comité de Apoyo a los Trabajadores Agrícolas (CATA)—Comité Organizador de Trabajadores Agrícolas (COTA) undated, 1983–1994, box 177, series XIII-Media Unit, Centro Records, Centro Archives; CATA, Farmworker Support Committee Narrative, [1985?] file 9, box 177, series XIII-Media Unit, Centro Records, Centro Archives.
77  CATA, "An Evening of Solidarity with Puerto Rican and Latino Farmworkers," [1985?], file 9, box 177, series XIII-Media Unit, Centro Records, Centro Archives.
78  Tom Torok, "Migrants' Union Is Supported: 2 Farmers Jailed for Ignoring Order," *Philadelphia Inquirer*, August 27, 1985, 1.
79  CATA, "Histórico convenio entre COTA y farmers," *Siembra* 3, no. 1 (1985): 3, file 9, box 177, series XIII-Media Unit, Centro Records, Centro Archives.
80  CATA, "Preocupación en el "Farm Bureau" con el convenio," *Siembra* 3, no. 1 (1985): 3, file 9, box 177, series XIII-Media Unit, Centro Records, Centro Archives.

81  Keith Talbot to Felipe del Valle, José A. Santiago, and Apolonio Collazo, RE Freedom of Information Request September 29, 1988, file 1 Correspondence-Claims, 1988, box 465, Correspondence, Farm Labor Program 1948–1993, Migration Division, Centro Archives.
82  Since the late 1950s, the Migration Division oversaw the FLP until 1989, when the Puerto Rican government transformed it into the Department of Puerto Rican Community Affairs in the United States: this was then abolished by the government of Puerto Rico in 1993. García Colón, *Colonial Migrants*, 217–221.
83  "NJ Farms Shift to Mexican Workers," *Philadelphia Inquirer*, June 30, 1993, A8.
84  Associated Press, "Puerto Rico Farm Workers Due in States," *Daily Register*, March 22, 1962, 16.
85  Associated Press, "Exhibit at NJ Farm Show in Trenton: Farm Show Will Portray the Role of Puerto Rican Labor," *Vineland Times Journal*, January 22, 1964, 6.
86  Dillon, "State Would Help," D13, D18.

# 8
# Puerto Ricans in New Jersey

## Migration, Settlement, and Work, 1940s-1980s

ALDO A. LAURIA SANTIAGO

Puerto Rico, once one of Spain's two colonial territories in the Caribbean, was invaded and occupied by the U.S. government in July 1898 in the context of U.S. intervention in the Cuban War of Independence (1895–1898). Since then, the country has remained an unincorporated U.S. territory, ruled in different ways but consistent in its colonial relationship with the U.S. government. This chapter will examine how Puerto Ricans, initially considered "naturals" of the United States and eventually granted U.S. citizenship in 1917 ended up living and forming a significant part of the State of New Jersey. The chapter introduces the migration and settlement of large numbers of people from Puerto Rico, their creation of a multigenerational "ethnic group," and their survival, work, and social struggles as they became part of New Jersey from the 1950s to the early 1980s. The website that accompanies this volume will contain additional narratives of civil rights, education, and political struggles as well as stories of struggles with police and local political elites from the 1960s to the 1990s.

## Puerto Rican Paths to New Jersey, 1940s–1980s

Today, people of Puerto Rican descent constitute about 5 percent of New Jersey's population. This large demographic includes at least three generations with diverse relationships to each other and to Puerto Rico. There are people who migrated, recently or half a century ago, as children or adults having been born or raised in Puerto Rico. There is also a second generation, born or raised in New Jersey and quite sizable after 1960. These second-generation Puerto Rican–identified New Jerseyans, in turn, have produced offspring who now constitute a third generation born in the last few decades, and often born to ethnically mixed parentage. These groups exist as distinct individual trajectories or experiences within the community but also often coexist within families. Yet they all have roots in the core dynamics that brought Puerto Ricans to New Jersey cities, towns, and suburbs in large and accelerating numbers between the 1950s and 1980s.

The rapid expansion of the Puerto Rican-identified population in New Jersey came after World War II, growing from about 5,600 in 1950 to 456,000 in 2020 (see Table 8.1 and Table 8.3).[1] The most dramatic period of growth was between 1960 and 1970 when the population grew from 43,568 to 136,937—a tripling in a mere ten years. The growth rate continued high through 1990 when the Puerto Rican-descent population, now including a sizable second generation, reached 320,133. By then New Jersey had established itself as the state with the second largest Puerto Rican-descent population, a position that would be lost to Florida in the early 2000s. By 2020, the population had continued to grow and reached nearly half a million, reflecting a steady but slower rate of growth since 2000 (see Figures 8.4 and 8.5 distribution by census tract).[2] Despite these numbers Puerto Ricans in New Jersey remain strikingly absent from both the mainstream and Puerto Rican studies literatures.

Puerto Ricans (or at least people born in Puerto Rico) have had a presence in New Jersey since the early days of the establishment of U.S. colonial rule in Puerto Rico in 1898. The census counts a small number of Puerto Rico-born residents in New Jersey in the decennial censuses from 1910 to 1940, with a slight decrease during the 1930s. Around the start of World War II (1940) there were nearly eight hundred in the state. This should not be surprising considering that New York City already had a Puerto Rico and U.S.-born Puerto Rican population of about two hundred thousand in 1940 and that New Yorkers often moved to New Jersey for industrial employment, better housing, as well as for suburban or rural settings.

Puerto Rican paths to New Jersey were diverse and closely related to the state's own economic and social conditions and opportunities over the decades. Little is known about the few Puerto Rico-born residents before 1940 (875 in 1930).[3] Some were the children of U.S. residents of Puerto Rico (merchants, technicians, colonial government officials, lawyers, soldiers) who returned to the United States after service or employment on the island. The state appears in some of

## Table 8.1
## Puerto Rican population in New Jersey, 1910-2020

| Year | Puerto Rican population | Percent change | Percent U.S. born | Percent of total NJ population | Rural nonfarm | Rural farm |
|---|---|---|---|---|---|---|
| 1910 | 101 | | | | | |
| 1920 | 580 | 474 | | | | |
| 1930 | 875 | 51 | | | | |
| 1940 | 780 | −11 | | | | |
| 1950 | 5,640 | 623 | | 0.12 | | |
| 1955 | 18,000-37,000 est. | | | | | |
| 1960 | 55,351 | 881 | 27.7 | 1.9 | | |
| 1970 | 136,937 | 214 | 39.0 | 1.9 | 5,349 | 289 |
| 1980 | 243,540 | 78 | | 3.3 | | |
| 1990 | 320,133 | 31 | | 4.1 | | |
| 2000 | 366,788 | 15 | | 4.4 | | |
| 2010 | 434,092 | 18 | | 4.9 | | |
| 2020 | 455,615 | 5 | | 4.9 | | |

SOURCES: ancestry.com; born in Puerto Rico only, 1910-1950; U.S. Bureau of the Census, United States Census of Population: 1950-1955, estimates: Division Against Discrimination of the Department of Education, Annual Report, 1955; "More than 30,000 Puerto Ricans Live in State," *Keyport Weekly*, October 6, 1955; Isham B. Jones, *The Puerto Rican in New Jersey: His Present Status, July 1955* (Newark: New Jersey, State Department of Education, Division Against Discrimination, 1955), 9-10; includes seasonal variation of 4,600 contract and 3,700 noncontract migrant farm workers. Bureau of the Census. *Puerto Ricans in Continental United States:* (Washington, DC: U.S. Department of Commerce 1953); United States Commission on Civil Rights, *Puerto Ricans in the Continental United States: An Uncertain Future: A Report* (Washington, DC: U.S. Commission on Civil Rights, 1976); Carlos Vargas Ramos, "Migration and Settlement Patterns in Puerto Rico, 1985-2005" *Policy Report* 2, no 1, (Center for Puerto Rican Studies, 2008); Socialexplorer.com.

the earliest narratives and sources that form part of the record of the Puerto Rican presence in New York. Cigar maker, labor leader, socialist, and memoir-writer Bernardo Vega described how soon after he migrated to New York, he found work in the Gillespie munitions plant in Middlesex, New Jersey, in 1918, the same that exploded a few weeks later.[4] That same year, a Puerto Rico newspaper that documented the early success of middle-class migrants noted how the young merchant Armando López Landrón, brother of one who would become one of Puerto Rico's most important labor lawyers, based his business in Jersey City from where he departed to join the U.S. Army and train in Puerto Rico.[5] A few years later, in 1927, the New York Spanish language press, which always kept an eye on the larger metropolitan area outside of the city, reported the presence of Puerto Ricans and Spaniards who shared the Bayonne Hispanic Club, drawing people from Jersey City and Elizabeth to a dance with 380 people.[6] More notably, a political leader who would later help transition Puerto Rico to more democratic colonial government, the "commonwealth," and served as Puerto Rico's elected governor for sixteen years, resided (and bought a house) with his mother and young family in pastoral West Englewood in the early 1920s, from where he developed his journalism work.[7]

Far more is known about the arrival of hundreds of contracted Puerto Rican workers, mostly men, during World War II (1943–1945). Recruited by the federal War Manpower Commission's operations in Puerto Rico and later directly through the government's employment services, nearly one thousand contracted workers joined one chemical and two food processing plants in addition to thousands of others who spread out from their arrival in the Jersey docks to shipyards, steel plants, naval bases, and other heavy industrial sites from New Orleans to Connecticut. Some of the workers became the core of the Puerto Rican presence in southern New Jersey including Camden and helped populate Philadelphia after the war. Others returned to Puerto Rico after their contract expired.[8] Workers arrived usually in the Weehawken dock, where one boat the SS *George Washington*, brought 885 workers for work in different sites throughout New York, Pennsylvania, Ohio, and New Jersey. Ship transport in those days was on complex military/civilian convoys and via the Guantanamo naval base.[9] Gilbert Ramirez, a Spanish-speaking employee of the War Manpower Commission, recalls meeting them at the docks with a pointed message:

> I boarded the ship and the purser arranged for me to greet the men over the public address system as they lined the rails waiting for the order to disembark. I spoke in Spanish. After greeting them in the name of the government of Puerto Rico and Governor Tugwell, I said that in addition to improving their own condition this was an opportunity for them to help the war effort and help Puerto Rico; that if they proved to be efficient and satisfactory thousands of others unemployed in Puerto Rico might be given similar opportunities; that by gaining a good reputation as a worker and as a citizen each of them would be doing a service of incalculable value to his island; that some things would seem strange and perhaps not to their liking at first but their welfare and the success of the undertaking depended on their willingness to learn and to adjust themselves.

The same staff person reported that on-ship conditions had not been ideal, were cramped and boring, with most of the time spent gambling, and the transport cost, despite wartime conditions, was too expensive. A twenty-one-car train of the Central Railroad of New Jersey met this group of workers and transported them to Philadelphia for further transit to Swedesboro and Camden, and to other points in Pennsylvania, Maryland, Ohio, and Indiana, with a significant contingent moving to work for the B&O train line.

In New Jersey at least two hundred of these men were recruited in multiple waves to work in CALCO, a division of American Cyanamide—a chemical dye manufacturer in Bound Brook New Jersey (and now a superfund cleanup site).[10] A few hundred worked in Swedesboro, at the Edger F. Hurff company cannery. Camden's Campbell canning plant, one of the largest in the world employing five thousand people during World War II, was among the first to receive wartime contract workers, when an intensified demand for processed food production met with wartime labor scarcity. Forty men arrived with the first contract, and soon four hundred Puerto Ricans were at work, establishing the first wave of migrants in Camden. Wages at Campbell were considered good and allowed Puerto Ricans to send money back home at a time when unemployment on the island was extremely high.

The Campbell's contract was monitored by both the War Manpower Commission and the U.S.-appointed "insular" government in Puerto Rico with multiple on-site visits that included Jesus T. Piñero, soon to be the first Puerto Rican to be appointed governor of Puerto Rico by the U.S. government (1946). When they visited the plant in June 1944, they met with the workers to hear complaints and investigate conditions. Workers reported satisfaction with the food, communications in Spanish, and their ability to save money. They were paid 66.5 cents an hour (more than twice the federal minimum wage), which was considered a decent industrial wage during the war.[11] Workers trained in a highly mechanized assembly line that processed chickens, vegetables, and tomatoes into canned soup. Typically, the men were willing to work hard for what they considered decent wages, but critical pieces for these contract workers were living quarters, quality of life, and quality of food. The biggest complaints came from the railroad workers, while canning plants did not generate many complaints as the scale of the operation allowed for selected Puerto Ricans to work as translators and cooks. Also critical was the speed of remittances from their wages to Puerto Rico, which moved from monthly to weekly based on their demands. The most challenging issues involved adjustment, mental health, and culture.[12] Reverend Enrique Rodriguez of the First Church of Spanish People wrote to Piñero complaining that among the workers at Hurff in Swedesboro some wanted to return to Puerto Rico, New York City, or Philadelphia and did not know how.[13]

The Campbell plant continued to provide employment to many Puerto Ricans in Camden into the 1980s. Maria Flores, who worked at Campbell's in the 1970s and 1980s remembered the productivity awards she received for "jobs well done" in the company newsletter. In 1989 the plant, like many other factories in the state during the 1980s, was closed. At that time Flores was paid $10/hour, three times the minimum wage for that year.[14]

After World War II ended, New Jersey farms began to recruit workers from Puerto Rico, something that many farmers had sought during the war but was not supported by federal rural labor policies. Farm laborer streams began in 1946 or 1947 through private contacts and contractors for seasonal workers. (See chapter 7 in this volume.) But in 1947 the Puerto Rico Labor Department established that the only form of legal contracting would be through the government-negotiated contract with farmers associations in New Jersey and other northeastern states.

The contract formalized wage, work, and benefit conditions for most seasonal workers and outlawed private or individual recruitment in Puerto Rico. Once the contract was in place five to ten thousand seasonal migrants from Puerto Rico traveled to work in the state's farms from the late 1940s to the 1980s. During the harvest season, the Puerto Rican population in New Jersey expanded by five thousand to twenty thousand people, when migrant farmworkers arrived and lived in the state for three to six months.[15] And from these seasonal migrants a more permanent sediment remained in New Jersey, continuing their work on farms and living in rural towns, or moving to work in factories.[16] Initially, in the late 1940s and early 1950s the Puerto Rican presence was centered in the state's central and southern rural areas. Soon after migrant farmworkers settled permanently, this small but growing group of residents (about 5,600 rural Puerto Rican residents in 1970) produced communities in a few small towns in southern New Jersey.[17] Permanent settlement proceeded slowly because most of these workers returned home to their rural communities in Puerto Rico, most with savings that they invested in the family economy, land purchases, or home construction. Many of these migrants were committed to agricultural work and used the savings from work in New Jersey to make their rural lifestyles in Puerto Rico more viable.

The Puerto Rican populations of Camden and rural southern New Jersey were distant from the industrial areas of northeastern New Jersey, where most Puerto Ricans who migrated to the state after the mid-1950s resided and worked. In the pre-New Jersey turnpike days, the social distance from southern New Jersey to Newark was far longer than it is today. Even in these early years, settlement expanded to new, more disperse areas in south and central Jersey including small towns that had their own local industrial economy. Dover, a center of farmworker residences, had factories, iron mines and foundries.[18] Puerto Ricans reached even more peripheral counties. By the late 1950s surveys found about two thousand Puerto Ricans living in Ocean, Atlantic, and Cape May Counties in coastal southern New Jersey, most of them farmworkers who had already transitioned to industrial work.

The immediate postwar years and booming industrial economy also brought other migrants to New Jersey. In 1949, a short-lived Puerto Rico government live-in domestic worker training program sought to place young women in affluent households in the United States. In the New York area most were recruited to Scarsdale, but a few ended up in New Jersey as well. Puerto Rico Labor Department staff mediated and negotiated solutions to work and pay disputes, including cases in Bayonne and Ridgewood.[19] Staff carried out confidential interviews with all the women and facilitated improvements in their conditions or changed their placement, suggesting improvements in the training and program management to the office in Puerto Rico.

By the early 1950s the vast majority of Puerto Ricans in the state had arrived through secondary migration from New York City, expanding dramatically in

Table 8.2
Puerto Rican population in New Jersey municipalities, New York City, 1960-1980

|  | 1955 | 1960 | 1970 | 1980 |
|---|---|---|---|---|
| New York City |  | 615,574 | 817,712 | 860,552 |
| Newark | 3,200 |  | 27,663 | 39,732 |
| Jersey City | 2,500 |  | 16,325 | 26,830 |
| Paterson | 2,000 |  | 12,036 | 24,326 |
| Camden | 5,000 |  | 6,566 | 14,799 |
| Passaic | 6,853 |  |  | 10,539 |
| Vineland | 400 |  |  | 8,976 |
| Union City |  |  |  | 8,103 |
| Hoboken |  |  | 10,047 |  |
| Perth Amboy | 4,000 | 5,000 |  | 11,025 |
| Dover |  |  |  |  |
| Trenton |  | 1,000 |  |  |
| Swedesboro | 40 |  |  |  |
| Elizabeth |  |  |  | 7,675 |

SOURCES: U.S. Bureau of the Census, *Puerto Ricans in Continental United States* (Washington, DC: U.S. Department of Commerce 1953); United States Commission on Civil Rights, *Puerto Ricans in the Continental United States: An Uncertain Future: A Report* (Washington, DC: U.S. Commission on Civil Rights, 1976); Howard G. Brunsman, U.S. Census of Population: 1960. *Puerto Ricans in the United States: Social and Economic Data for Persons of Puerto Rican Birth and Parentage*. Washington, D.C.: U.S. Department of Commerce, Bureau of the Census, 1963;
"Puerto Ricans in New Jersey, The United States and Puerto Rico, 2014," Center for Puerto Rican Studies, New York, 2015; Carlos Vargas Ramos, "Migration and Settlement Patterns in Puerto Rico, 1985-2005" *Policy Report* 2, no 1, (Center for Puerto Rican Studies, 2008); *U.S. Census Bureau, Puerto Ricans in the United States* (Washington, D.C.: US Census, 1973); Isham B. Jones, *The Puerto Rican in New Jersey: His Present Status, July 1955* (Newark: New Jersey, State Department of Education, Division Against Discrimination, 1955), 9, table iii 1955 estimates.

the mid-1950s. Added to this was some direct migration from Puerto Rico, especially for family unification and through chain migration recruitment (a large share of the Perth Amboy industrial workers came from one town in Puerto Rico). Observers in New York City had already noted in the late 1940s how Puerto Ricans who could afford it began to move to New Jersey to "comprarse sus casitas" (buy their little houses).[20]

Because of the region's integrated industrial economy on both sides of the Hudson, the Puerto Ricans' presence expanded primarily in the cities most proximate to Manhattan with Camden and its southern New Jersey farmworker hinterland as the principal exception. Initially movers from New York City settled in the core industrial centers of Paterson, Perth Amboy, Jersey City, Newark, Camden, Hoboken, Passaic, and Union City, each of which had Puerto Rican populations between seven thousand and twenty-eight thousand by 1970 (see Table 8.2 for the population by municipality).

However, by the 1970s, as the community's migration and work trajectories became more complex and diverse, and as the impact of emerging deindustrialization and urban decline were felt in the entire region, Puerto Ricans' movement also shifted and both New Yorkers and established New Jersey residents began to move toward towns and suburbs. For a steady stream of migrants from New York City during the 1970s, the availability of more affordable housing and better schools were forces attracting more Puerto Ricans to the state. All the same, through the turn of the twenty-first century, the vast majority of Puerto Ricans in New Jersey lived within a relatively short distance of Manhattan and the Bronx (see Figure 8.1 and Figure 8.4 to compare the census tract change in the population).

In general, New Jersey attracted Puerto Ricans because of its jobs, wages, schools, and quality of life conditions, although compared to New York City wages and union power in many industries were weaker. As early as 1960 the community showed a diversity of incomes and educational levels, including a significant middle-income sector. In 1960, 63 percent of Puerto Rican families in New Jersey were above or well above the poverty threshold for family incomes (about $3,000/yearly), while a large minority earned below poverty-level incomes (see Table 8.4 for a detailed breakdown of income and Table 8.6 for city-specific income data).

Except among the poorest inner-city population, New Jersey Puerto Ricans persistently showed higher incomes and educational levels than their peers in New York (see Table 8.8). Despite significant diversity within these averages, New Jersey encouraged migrant flows from the New York City residents with higher educational levels and industrial skills. All the same, low-income work in the context of declining industrial wages through the 1980s created a significant challenge for many Puerto Ricans, with New Jersey experiencing a milder version of the community's national-level poverty crisis of the mid-1980s.

During the 1980s, when the Puerto Rican population in the state expanded by nearly eighty thousand people, the community's demographics also became more diverse including an impoverished inner-city working class and a growing middle class—the product of out-migration from New York and the second generations' own educational accomplishments (see Table 8.7). Puerto Ricans now lived in many different settings as the state's economic growth shifted to growing suburbs and small towns. Is the economic and educational mobility that emerged since the mid-1980s a product of New Jersey conditions or of selective migration? Probably both, but further research is needed. The data are clearest on the in-migration selectivity.[21] In the only detailed study of migration from New York to New Jersey, out-migrants from New York to the outlying areas outside the city in the 1990s were disproportionately second generation, had higher education rates, and white-collar employment, and were older and already had significantly higher incomes, homeownership rates, and lower poverty levels.[22]

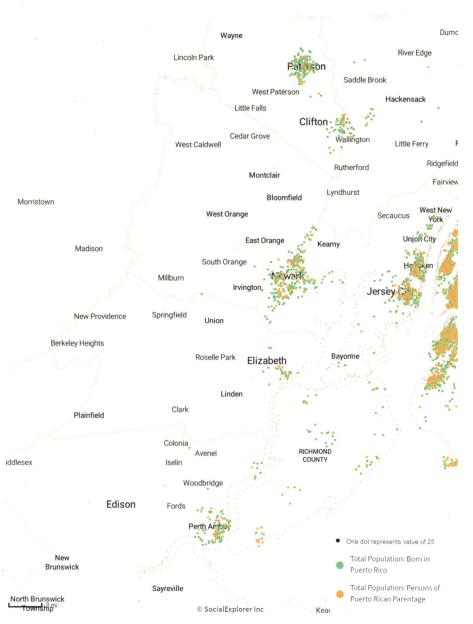

FIGURE 8.1  Puerto Rican and U.S.-born population by census tract, 1960. (Source: Social Explorer, based on data from the U.S. Census Bureau.)

## Settlement and Integration

There are few sources that discuss the arrival and adjustment of Puerto Ricans in the early years to northeastern New Jersey towns and cities. A few locally produced oral histories give insight into how Puerto Ricans experienced arrival in the 1950s. Puerto Ricans who moved to Hoboken from New York noted the ethnic geography of the city in the 1950s: Italians, Jews, Germans, and Irish. Angel Padilla arrived in Hoboken from Brooklyn in 1955 to join his father at age fifteen years.[23] Relatives at Fort Dix served as a guide for his family. Padilla recalls that the arrival of Puerto Ricans united Irish and Italians against them who "started picking on the Puerto Ricans... lots of conflicts"—the violent landscape of working-class youth in American cities. These White ethnics called them "spiks" and often refused to rent apartments to Puerto Ricans.

In Hoboken, Catholic priests helped negotiate discrimination and conflicts in times of crisis. Father Eugene Zwahl, a Franciscan priest, helped facilitate rentals. Zwahl was the center of the Spanish-speaking community in this period, and church attendance on Sundays provided a routine of contact and community formation despite the small frictions and hostilities between ethnic groups that were common in the 1950s. Through the church the early Hoboken community raised funds for family emergencies for rent and food and organized trips, and a Spanish mass in 1965 helped remove Puerto Ricans from contact with others who did not welcome them to "their" services. A Spanish American Catholic Center opened in 1955 uniting other Spanish speakers and provided a locale for services, celebrations, and sports. Padilla describes the emergence of local politics in Hoboken as an uphill battle against the Italians. Padilla noted proudly how Puerto Ricans slowly entered local governance in Hoboken—Ralph Castillo, a police officer, was the first to run for councilman, and other Puerto Ricans soon followed. Padilla himself moved to Jersey City from Hoboken in 1980 to pursue his goal of owning a house, which he paid off in ten years.

Tom Olivieri provides another early story of Puerto Rican arrival and settlement.[24] Tom could pass as Italian. The grandson of a Corsican immigrant to Puerto Rico (like thousands of other Puerto Ricans of Corsican descent), Olivieri came to Hoboken via New York in 1949 as a boy. His father was a World War II veteran (who was "truly bilingual") and worked for the federal government.[25] Settlement in Hoboken was facilitated by an uncle who had already migrated in the early 1940s. Uncle Eddie helped them get an apartment. Tom's father became a manager for the heating system in multiple buildings, as well as a superintendent. The building's Jewish owner and Tom's father became good friends.

Most of the Puerto Ricans in Hoboken worked at the Tootsie Roll factory through three daily shifts, with husbands and wives often working in the same plant. Neighborhood blocks quickly became majority Puerto Ricans by the late 1950s. Olivieri recalls how quickly ethnic conflicts expanded after Puerto Ricans

**UNEMPLOYMENT BLUES**—Four members of the St. Peter's Spanish-American Catholic Information Center, 161 Newark Ave., Jersey City, gather for a homemade jam session—Puerto Rican style—to while away the idle hours created by unemployment. The Rev. Joseph Faulkner, S.J., center director, listens attentively while guitarists David Rivera and Peter Torres play for Angel Ortiz and George Rivera.

FIGURE 8.2 "Unemployment Blues," newsclip, *Jersey Journal*, March 18, 1958.

became a large minority in Hoboken and his family's distinction as "not black" who spoke a "different" language. Olivieri also remembers the subtle hostilities, including from a teacher who asked, "Tommy, what's wrong with these Puerto Ricans?" Olivieri found it ironic that the ethnic group most similar to Puerto Ricans were the most hostile—in his experience Italians "were the most prejudiced." Conflicts for youth involved "real fighting" and getting beat up over turf disputes and access to the public pool on North Street. Olivieri served in the military for three years and then married in 1963 while working for a typewriter company on Canal Street. Once married, his family moved to Eastern Parkway in Brooklyn, a Jewish neighborhood. After being laid off they moved back to Hoboken, and he became a billing and shipping clerk for a garment manufacturer.[26]

Ethnic origins and identities were embedded in most social relations. Olivieri remembers renting an apartment from a Jewish landlord who treated him nicely. But his successful search for a larger apartment only encouraged him to resent the discrimination that he knew he was being exempted from for passing as Italian. These experiences led Olivieri to eventually become a tenants' rights activist, challenging landlords and rental agencies to rent to Puerto Ricans and to move people to Model Cities housing.[27]

Table 8.3
1960 Puerto Rican population by County

| Atlantic | 922 |
| --- | --- |
| Bergen | 2,001 |
| Burlington | 1,467 |
| Camden | 4,012 |
| Cape May | 1,573 |
| Cumberland/Sussex/Hunterdon | 371 |
| Essex | 10,364 |
| Gloucester | 558 |
| Hudson | 14,911 |
| Mercer | 2,013 |
| Middlesex | 4,710 |
| Monmouth | 1,685 |
| Morris | 714 |
| Ocean | 571 |
| Passaic | 7,139 |
| Salem | 227 |
| Somerset | 316 |
| Union | 1,649 |
| Warren | 148 |
| Total | 55,351 |

SOURCE: New Jersey Research Reports, *New Jersey Population: Nativity and Parentage* (Trenton, NJ: Department of Conservation and Economic Development, 1960).

## Early Community Organizing

In 1955 local leaders in Hoboken convened a coalition and a public meeting in a church with the Puerto Rican community to assess their needs. A local detective and a Catholic priest who spoke Spanish led the effort. The city had just hired a Spanish-speaking worker from Puerto Rico in the Health and Welfare Department as a way of improving access to services; but the community's early organizing efforts helped identify other needs and demands.[28] The meeting led to the inauguration of the Puerto Rican League of Hoboken, and bodega owner Juan Lopez was elected as its president. Multiple committees were created out of its initial membership of four hundred. Lopez stated that his goal was to find acceptance and expressed awareness of how "the habit among Puerto Ricans of standing on sidewalks and apartment building stoops conversing loudly" exacerbated resistance to the Puerto Rican presence in neighborhoods.[29]

Priests continued to play a role in initial organizing efforts in these early years. In North Hudson, Rev. Michael Feketie initiated a mass in Spanish at a Union City Catholic church, Our Lady of Mount Caramel Chapel. He was one of two clergy assigned to work with the rapidly growing Puerto Rican population. His associate, an Argentinian Jesuit, declared that their job was to organize the people not just for religious purposes but for larger community needs.[30] Starting in 1955, church authorities in Union County under the Diocese of Newark and Paterson began to work with Puerto Rican migrants by providing sermons in Spanish, covering their affairs in their newspaper (*The Advocate*), providing spaces for meetings, and opening a social center. Joseph Faulkner, a Jesuit priest, led the programs in the region and fought stereotypes and attacks on Puerto Ricans (see Figure 8.2 for an illustration of Faulkner's work).[31]

At other times, city officials stepped up to ask for help. In Hoboken, the Welfare and Health Department asked for help from Puerto Rico's Labor Department Migration Division office in New York and called for the hiring of a Puerto Rican representative to help D'Amelio, the director, with the community's needs, especially the poor housing conditions, overcrowding, and lack of welfare services. His inquiry grew out of an anti-polio program in which he visited many Puerto Ricans' homes and found deplorable conditions, while blaming the landlords and the community's lack of information. Three representatives of the Migration Division joined him in a meeting. Participants suggested that the city hire social workers and other Spanish-speaking staff.[32]

A similar process took place in Jersey City, with early Puerto Rican settlement building alliances with supporters as well as facing resistance and hostility. Father Faulkner was the most consistent and visible defender of Puerto Ricans and an organizational catalyst. He wrote a weekly column about the Puerto Rican community for the *Jersey Journal* through the 1960s. His job, as he saw it, was to bridge the community with local leaders and local institutions. Faulkner explained to English-speaking readers the origins of the migration and how

Puerto Ricans were adjusting. He considered their strides to be fast with progress on every front in the seven or eight years that the population had been developing in Jersey City. The community already had its own small businesses, including specialized shops for religious articles, food, and musical instruments, as well as hometown societies, storefront Protestant churches, and a Catholic center. Practicing professionals included a doctor, and two hundred Puerto Ricans had already purchased their houses in downtown Jersey City. Faulkner was in contact with and collaborated with the Migration Division in New York, and he explained to his readers that jobs attracted Puerto Ricans to the area.[33]

In the early 1960s Faulkner noted an important upsurge in Puerto Rican organizing in Jersey City and Hudson County. He emphasized the need for internal solidarity within the Puerto Rican community despite the advances since the 1950s.[34] In one column he rejected the practice of using the phrase "the Puerto Rican problem" to address a complex situation.[35] He also rejected the insistence by some that Puerto Ricans assimilate, give up their culture, language, and identity to become "real Americans."[36] He also supported Black–Puerto Rican unity, acknowledging the racial and color diversity within the Puerto Rican community and within that diversity their need and right to fight for civil rights.[37]

In his column Faulkner explained the work that he and his Puerto Rican colleagues carried out as a way of promoting acceptance in the larger community. He demonstrated an uncommon knowledge of the migration process and island cultural patterns and history. He explained Puerto Rican attitudes toward color, the importance of identity, respect, culture, and language for Puerto Rican people and how what he called "double citizenship" presented problems for Puerto Rican migrants as citizens of the United States but, culturally, citizens of two countries. He also explained the problems that Puerto Rican children faced with language and learning, a concern that would soon become the community's principal focus. Faulkner was no stranger to the sort of police abuse often experienced by young working-class Puerto Ricans, especially men. In one incident the police entered his community center and assaulted a young man. The police returned to arrest the youth and went through the center's files. Police denied the priest's allegations.[38] Yet Faulkner thought that all these conditions would improve with the growth of second-generation children—he did not foresee the turmoil and militancy of the next fifteen years.

As the population grew, both conflicts and collaborations became more frequent and complex. When a Puerto Rican was killed by another Puerto Rican in a brawl in Union City, New York Migration Division officials held meetings with leaders in Hudson County to offer support services for the community. As often was the case in the Migration Division's interventions, officials predicted that conflict was the product of resistance against Puerto Ricans and would further enable those who were hostile or rejected the community. A meeting with

# Eight Groups Back Meyner

Eight Puerto Rican organizations in Hudson County today endorse Gov. Robert B. Meyner for reelection.

Jerry Forman, chairman of the Spanish American Democratic Club of Hoboken, said his group and seven others supported Meyner at a meeting of the Commonwealth of Puerto Rico Independent Association, 61 Erie St., Jersey City.

He listed the others as the Commonwealth of Puerto Rico Independent Association; Puerto Rican League of Union City; Puerto Rican League of Hoboken; Puerto Rican Civic Association, Puerto Rican Cooperative Commoncial Inc., Downtown Spanish Democratic Club and Puerto Rican Benevolent Association, all Jersey City.

FIGURE 8.3 "Eight Groups Back Meyner," newsclip, *Jersey Journal*, October 18, 1957.

local officials would focus especially on housing needs, as the community was seen to have jobs and be nearly completely self-sufficient (!) allaying predictable fears that Puerto Ricans were relying on welfare as a means of support.[39] Yet at the same time savvy politicians knew to seek electoral support from the growing Puerto Rican community. Gubernatorial candidate Robert Meyner boasted of having the support of eight Puerto Rican organizations in Hudson County in 1957 (see Figure 8.3).[40]

The community's narratives of arrival and settlement share elements but also present significant diversity. Consider the contrast between these trajectories of the 1950s and Eva Rosas Amirault's story.[41] Eva migrated to marry in the early 1970s. She had trained as a teacher in Puerto Rico and after joining her sister in Plainfield began work at a bilingual day-care center and soon at a Head Start program, becoming the director in 1978. In an interview she acknowledged that migration was hard even for Latinos with a university education who had to struggle to gain accreditation for employment for their degrees from Puerto Rico institutions. Yet, overcoming delays and obstacles, she and others became principals in many community-serving organizations during the 1970s.

As in other cities in the United States, community groups responded to the arrival of Spanish-speaking Puerto Ricans in the 1950s and 1960s with various support services. Churches provided initial points of entry into local community networks. Teachers and school systems served in a murkier terrain of educating children who often did not speak English. Diverse service establishments and liberal politicians welcomed Puerto Rican migrants through efforts at integration and problem solving.

In Perth Amboy school principal and head of the Human Relations Commission Gilbert Augustine delivered a speech at the National Education Association convention in Atlantic City in November 1958 explaining their efforts to integrate "our new neighbors."[42] Citing the United States failure to "treat all citizens as equals, regardless of race, color, religious belief or national origin," Augustine described his twelve years of experience as an ally of Puerto Ricans. He noted that they had started at the bottom of the socioeconomic ladder already traversed by other immigrant groups but are U.S. citizens and entitled to rights and privileges. He explained how Puerto Ricans wanted recognition and called for an end to common exploitation and criticisms, justifying the rebellious response when recognition was denied them. Augustine channeled Perth Amboy's history of diversity and rights, as home of the first Black to vote under the Fifteenth Amendment and recipient of an award in 1952 from the national conference of Christians and Jews.

Augustine's view of the Puerto Rican experience was consistent with liberal views on the community's initial struggles, which emphasized obstacles as transitional and conditional. The speed with which Puerto Ricans arrived in Perth Amboy meant that, within five years, five thousand people competed for scarce housing, producing confusion, frustration, and resentment. Local newspapers emphasized how "Puerto Ricans getting into trouble" when they sought entertainment on weekends.[43] Often confrontations and police "riots" developed from attempts by Puerto Rican men to socialize with non-Puerto Rican local women. A shift to gender balance and family orientation once men settled into jobs and apartments ended this sort of conflict within just a few years, encouraged as well by the growing number of Puerto Rican homeowners. Yet these changes did not necessarily solve the interethnic politics and conflicts underlying the experience of Puerto Ricans in all these towns and cities. Language remained the principal initial barrier to full participation in larger communities and created obstacles to promotion at work as well. Local authorities noted how problems continued with high rents for low quality housing and discrimination against renting to large families.

Augustine provided a model of the familiar template in support of Puerto Rican newcomers. This model, promoted actively by the Migration Division in New York City, included adult education in English. Augustine, like many others during this period, noted how the most hostile aspect of American nativism focused on language: "Most continentals are appalled at the fact that Puerto Ricans, citizens of the United States of America, do not speak the English language prior to migrating to our shores."[44] Puerto Rican leaders also identified language as an important issue, perhaps with more practical goals in mind. Perth Amboy moved to offer a night program with fifty people in attendance every evening. With help from the Rutgers Institute of Management and Labor Relations they provided a bilingual course on labor–management relations, as well as leadership workshops in Spanish. Membership in established voluntary organizations like Parent-Teacher Associations, the YMCA, athletic groups, and church groups was actively promoted. This sort of attention also meant that teachers, like Mary Therkelsen, with Augustine's support, provided additional lessons in English to young Puerto Rican children in the Shull School.[45]

By 1958, Hudson County Puerto Ricans organized in various branches of the Liga Puertorriquena announced that they would be supporting political campaigns instead of just civic action as a way of enhancing Puerto Rican empowerment. The league had fifteen chapters in New Jersey and held a congress in Newark in 1958.[46]

## Early Antidiscrimination Efforts

During the 1950s and early 1960s the Puerto Rican presence in statewide issues also emerged, as local activists and allies counted on the powerful voices of New York City-based allies. Various controversies took place during these years mostly involving the conditions and treatment of farmworkers but also anti-Puerto Rican statements and actions by officials as well as the inclusion of Puerto Ricans in the state's antidiscrimination efforts, legislation, and work.

As in a few other states in which liberal politics were dominant in the postwar years, after Congress's decision to let the wartime Fair Employment Practice Committee lapse, New Jersey developed its own antidiscrimination legislation. The initial law came in 1945 with a focus on public facilities, housing, and work and eventually integrated education and services.[47] The Division Against Discrimination, initially operating within the Department of Education could carry out field investigations, receive complaints, pursue lawsuits, and enforce remedies. Initially focused on Italian, Jewish, and Black discrimination and on desegregating schools, by the mid-1950s the division began to take note of and include materials and cases on Puerto Ricans. The division sponsored a survey of Puerto Ricans in twelve cities and how their special conditions with color, language, and culture were worthy of attention and support as U.S. citizens. Antidiscrimination pamphlets were translated into Spanish and the division worked with Puerto Rican organizations to distribute copies.[48] The division also collaborated actively with Puerto Rico's Migration Division offices in Camden and New York and encouraged collaborations with the Spanish-language press and radio programs.[49] In 1958 the commission responded to a complaint brought by two Puerto Rican workers against both the employer and the union that claimed to represent them. Like in many large unionized shops, a large share of the workers was Puerto Rican (55%). The union was forced to improve its communication and accessibility including printed material in Spanish, while Puerto Rican leaders agreed to deepen their engagement with the local's activities.[50]

State antidiscrimination work during the 1950s focused on specific characteristics of the community and the obstacles and special problems faced in many arenas. The report acknowledged, even then, that many had jobs that paid acceptable working-class wages, but that many in more marginal positions were highly exploited. The report recognized the many, many problems emerging from language issues (in courts, with police, in social services), exploitation (in quality of housing, purchases of appliances, cars, and furniture), lack of knowledge or information, color-based discrimination, and access to healthcare services.[51]

But it was the community itself, with its allies in New York City and Puerto Rico, that responded most effectively to its own needs, even as it leveraged allies and supporters within New Jersey. Perhaps the first highly visible conflict involving Puerto Ricans in New Jersey was the Judge Lloyd controversy in 1956. When partaking in a Monmouth County grand jury investigation of poor housing conditions, Judge Lloyd stated that Puerto Rico "is one of the filthiest places I have ever seen" and that Puerto Ricans were "imported" into the United States. He named Puerto Ricans as creators of slums "in hovels and they live in exactly the same state you have mentioned here."[52] The New Jersey State Congress of Industrial Organizations (CIO), Puerto Rican groups in New York City and New Jersey, and the Spanish-language press in New York City demanded his firing immediately in a series of articles, press releases, meetings, and protests in both New York and New Jersey.[53]

New Jersey's governor responded with support for the Puerto Rican community's response: "it's a rather sad commentary when a judge of our courts is pointing to an area for criticism when we're engaged as a national power to preserve democracy in a free world."[54] Other responses in the New Jersey press blamed the United States for any poor conditions in Puerto Rico, as a U.S. colony taken from Spain, explaining the attraction of jobs and wages for rural workers as seasonal migrant workers in New Jersey agriculture: "we must not let the Puerto Ricans be made a political football by groups and people who seek to make capital out of miseries of the minorities.... All over the world we are spending money to improve conditions in backward countries. Why not spend a little of it at home? Here. In Monmouth County. Why not a state subsidized housing project, not only for the Puerto Ricans, but for all the people living in rural slums."[55] The Lloyd controversy connected with local resistance to the presence of Puerto Rican farmworkers, which began as soon as they arrived in the late 1940s, as well as calls for investigations of conditions, exploitation, and abuse from multiple sources within and outside the state.

## A Mature Community Emerges

In its 1964 Annual Report, the Migration Division painted a rich portrait of the community and its development. Having opened multiple service offices (Camden, Keyport, and Hamburg, Pennsylvania) with multiple staff, the Migration Division had moved from simply supporting its farm labor program to reproducing the employment, education, and community organizing functions familiar to its New York office. The office assigned a full-time community organizer and other support staff to help connect the emerging Puerto Rican organizations in New Jersey. The office continued to work with the young Consejo de Organizaciones Puertorriqueña de New Jersey (New Jersey Council of Puerto Rican Organizations), a younger coalition that mirrored its much larger cousin in New York City, a product of Migration Division organizing efforts. The Consejo mediated disputes and made demands for social services, like court interpreters and the hiring of Puerto Ricans in critical employment service office positions. Both the Consejo and the Migration Division worked to support new organizations of small groups or to revive moribund groups, like the Lakewood Hijos de Borinquen club, which catered to the many local farmworkers, and the Club Los 7 Amigos in Atlantic City. The Consejo and the Migration Division were also involved in helping small business owners in Hudson County organize voter registration, and county-level coordinating committees (Hudson County, Perth Amboy). Participant organizations reported on their parades (Puerto Rico day in Hoboken, Keyport and Camden, Commonwealth constitution day in Newark, statewide Puerto Rican parade—Passaic), cultural events (theater in Hoboken and Camden), wrestling club (Passaic), vaccination campaigns (Newark, Passaic), evening English classes in local schools (Newark, Keyport, Woodbine, Perth Amboy), training sessions with police (Newark), youth leadership training (Camden), and parents and educational organizations (Trenton and Camden). Local veteran organizations in Hoboken, Jersey City, and Camden were supported in their efforts to create a statewide organization. In New Brunswick, the Club Familia Puertorriqueña organized its annual picnic fair on the Rutgers campus.[56]

The Migration Division also supported the creation of a Civil Rights Committee in Jersey City in the face of multiple police abuse cases. On another front, the Migration Division and the Consejo worked to push for employment opportunities and training. In Camden, local AFL-CIO (American Federation of Labor and Congress of Industrial Organizations) unions created a training program for youth in printing and electrical work. In Woodbine, the coalition secured hospital worker training for seven youth. Worker training was, and would increasingly be, the focus of Migration Division work in the 1960s. The division worked to connect Puerto Rican workers with emerging federal programs including the MDTA (Manpower Development and Training Act of 1962), achieving over one thousand job-training referrals, in addition to their regular work helping Puerto Ricans find jobs.

The division staff also worked more quietly behind the scenes, meeting with state and local administrators. In that year alone they held nearly two hundred meetings with public entities and one hundred with private agencies. None of this includes the work done administering, managing, and crisis interventions related to the agricultural workers program. They also lobbied the governor to produce the first statewide "learn English" program in New Jersey, which funded evening classes for adults.

By the late 1960s, Puerto Ricans in New Jersey were poised to enter more firmly positions of leadership that often bridged their community with local and state government. Puerto Ricans gained a presence and experience in different local and county governance. These years posed tremendous challenges to Puerto Rican leaders, the urban poor, and local, state, and federal governments that promised reform and delivered limited improvements. Soon a more militant narrative would emerge in which youth, especially male youth, pushed for power, response, entitlement, or protest in varied ways but often including more militant demand-making and confrontations, including a considerable number of riots and urban revolts.

## Jobs and Unions: Puerto Ricans in the New Jersey Industrial Economy

Central New Jersey's industrial economy was already in decline after nearly a century of growth when Puerto Ricans started arriving in large numbers in the 1960s. Yet this did not mean that they could not find work, supportive unions, improved wages, and higher skill work. Subject to the cycles of growth and recession, for Puerto Ricans in New Jersey industrial/manufacturing employment was even more important than in New York City. New York had a more diversified economy, with significant employment in industrialized services, and other areas that were not as prominent in New Jersey. In New Jersey, many food processing and garment plants were connected to the larger New York economy and used New Jersey as a platform for "exports" across the Hudson River. The southern and central parts of the state were important food production and farming centers but stood in contrast with the massive industrial activity of Hudson and Union Counties (see Table 8.5).

For some communities, industrial employment was a very local experience. The ring of small and large cities in the area combined working-class housing near the locations of industrial plants. In Hoboken, as in other smaller industrial cities, a few large employers played a dominant role in the local labor market. The Sweets Company of America, which manufactured tootsie rolls, employed hundreds of workers and hired many Puerto Ricans. Hoboken, like Jersey City, had an industrial waterfront that connected transport to garment and food processing plants including Rego Electric, Lipton Tea, Hostess Cake, Wonder Bread, and Van Leers Chocolates.

Cities like Paterson and Newark were industrial centers in their own right and not so dependent on connections to New York City. To the familiar industries of household goods, electrical products, metalworks, food production, and garments, fundamental to the larger New York City economy, New Jersey added additional strengths in chemicals, textiles, farm-product processing, and other areas.

As in New York City, most production workers in manufacturing and industrialized services in New Jersey were unionized and pay rates and conditions were determined by union contracts. As the European immigrants who had provided the labor in these plants aged, Puerto Ricans (and soon enough Cubans) found many opportunities for manual labor. For most Puerto Ricans in this period finding work was not as challenging as securing better wages and upgrading skills and rank.

As shown in other contexts, discrimination at work was less important than the conflicts and discrimination faced within residential communities and with government services. Factories gladly hired Puerto Ricans and, in many cases, provided for stable decades-long employment. Besides existing gender differences and hierarchies in the labor market, Puerto Ricans faced two challenges: the lack of skill of many workers—especially those with rural origins—and, in this migrant-majority population, the lack of English-language skills.[57] Of course, most Puerto Rican workers sought to improve their language and work skills, but often found additional obstacles and discrimination on the way out of the lowest work categories. Observers found that many Puerto Ricans got stuck in the lowest pay jobs because they could not communicate with foremen and other workers, and thus had to rely only on union wage increases.[58] This pattern encouraged the hiring of large numbers of Puerto Ricans at the lowest level of plant work as a way of facilitating the use of a common language.

One industrial plant in Perth Amboy sought candidates for its foreman training program, positions that paid more than $5,000 a year, nearly twice the wage of production-line workers. A Puerto Rican industrial truck operator showed promise but because of his language skills could not be offered the position despite interest from the employer. Some employers expressed support for hiring Puerto Ricans in any job within the limitations of their verbal and written knowledge of English. Others, the subject of various complaints with the Civil Rights Commission, refused to hire Puerto Ricans in any job category. One Puerto Rican community leader expressed that the hiring agencies, presumably including the government's own Employment Service, did the most discriminating and that workers often thought that they were better off finding employment on their own.[59]

During this early period, the vast majority of Puerto Ricans working in Perth Amboy occupied a marginal position in the workforce, more likely to be laid off first. In the mid-1950s they worked in food, clothing, stone, leather, and metals factories (82% of all workers, 51% of the men in metalwork). Unemployment and low wages were correlated with low educational levels and English skills.[60] Most of these workers were in low skill work categories, and income ranged from $35 to $65 a week. Their marginality coupled with the availability of higher wages explains the second most common complaint by employers, that Puerto Rican workers quit their jobs more frequently individually or in groups.[61] In Perth Amboy nearly half of the Puerto Rican workers were unionized with modest involvement in union business, and no participation in elected union roles yet.[62]

Needless to say, in the mid-1950s, very few Puerto Ricans in New Jersey worked in white-collar jobs, except for the small number of small business owners and professionals. In New York there were already significant numbers of second-generation Puerto Ricans who had moved into white-collar and administrative/clerical employment, but this demographic was small in New Jersey at this time and would not emerge until the late 1960s.[63]

Puerto Ricans could easily find unskilled and semiskilled jobs with decent pay, but these groups were vulnerable to cyclical downturns especially if they were of recent hires and had no seniority rights, which could result in higher unemployment cycles for the youngest men. In the mid-1950s, Puerto Rican veterans also reported not being able to find work in New Jersey that matched their skills and their training although, over the longer term, veterans fared better than others in employment and wages.[64] The 1958 recession was felt in the Hudson County area, with reports of extensive layoffs. In Jersey City, Joseph Faulkner, director of the Spanish American Community Center at Newark and Barrow found that two thousand Puerto Rican workers, nearly 40 percent of the downtown male population, could not find work in summer of 1957 and into early 1958. He pointed to how many had responded by taking courses, learning English, and earning a general equivalency diploma (GED) during evening study. Faulkner's center provided support services and served as a clearing house for hiring by various employers. He emphasized how Puerto Ricans relied on unemployment and relief as a last resort because of the stigma attached to these practices.[65]

Early sample surveys of Puerto Rican factory workers in 1955 found that 66 percent of Puerto Rican workers were in skilled and semiskilled positions, while 33 percent were skilled or supervisory. Reports found a pattern in which larger factories that employed hundreds of workers preferred Puerto Rican workers.[66]

Puerto Ricans might have been concentrated in the familiar counties in central New Jersey but, as early as 1956, 140 industrial companies surveyed in the coastal south employed 151 Puerto Rican workers among its 8,807 (about half of the firms employing Puerto Ricans were unionized). The vast majority of them were men, indicating likely origins in the farm labor program. The few women worked in garment and food processing, with the men in food processing and machine operators. Garment workers were in high demand and secured marginal wage gains by moving from one employer to another.[67]

Puerto Ricans with English skills and technical training could gain mid-level positions in the industrial economy and many quickly moved into higher pay positions during the 1960s and early 1970s. Eleuterio Martinez, an activist in Hoboken's community, was a foreman at Emersion Radio factory in Jersey City. When the employer closed the plant in 1970, he found work at Emerson's Puerto Rico plant.[68]

The Puerto Rican stories of engagement with factories, their owners, the labor movement, and the legal and political aspects of fighting for better conditions abound. Art Metalcraft Plating in Camden was owned by two brothers and their wives. When its all-Puerto Rican workers sought to join a union in 1961, the leaders Manuel Rodriguez, Juan Delgado Gomez, and Juan Rodriguez, were all fired. A mass walkout resulted, and all fourteen workers signed union cards. Teamsters local 676 began to picket the plant in support of their efforts. The National Labor Relations Board (NLRB) ruled that the union vote should be recognized, and the workers reinstated.[69]

In a Hoboken spring factory in March 1957 a group of mostly Puerto Rican workers fought to reinstate fired workers. The seventeen workers had few skills in English but were savvy about their legal and labor rights. As part of a larger trend in the region at fighting union corruption they took on both their union and the employer. They moved the NLRB to order the workers reinstated (Hector Figueroa, Adrian Gomez, Ramiro Gomez, Francisco Rivera, Ana Lydia Gomez, Celestino Olmeda, Francisco Garcia, Praxedes C. Gonzales, Ana Noboa, Gilberto Torres, and Herman Gomez) and to decertify local 21 of the Industrial Production and Novelty Workers AFL. The "ghost" local held a contract with the employer. Their managers were in constant turnover, had no office, and were nonresponsive. Hector Figueroa, the only worker with significant English skills, filed a successful complaint against the ghost union. Workers walked out and the employer claimed he could not negotiate with workers directly because of the union contract. The effects of the larger anti-mobster movement in this period were critical to this effort, radiating out of the New York City mayor's office and the Central Labor Council.[70]

In Jersey City, Father Faulkner noted years later how corrupt union practices continued to affect Puerto Rican workers and had made some of them resistant to supporting the labor movement. Puerto Rican workers paid union entry and membership fees but received no benefits and labor bargaining based on collusion between employers and corrupt union leaders.[71]

Work disputes were as common as work itself. In 1955, seventy-five Puerto Rican workers mobilized the press and especially New York's Hispanic establishment to support their strike of eleven months. They worked in the quarries of Kingston, New Jersey. Led by Efrain Nieves, Quintin Soto, and Juan Santiago, all from Newark, they held a press conference to denounce their firing as leaders that sought unionization into the AFL Hod Carriers local 734, which won the NLRB-sponsored election. The case dragged on forever as the employer resisted recognizing the union and the men "suffering all the hardships imaginable."[72] Employers used communist flags and signs claiming "viva Albizu" (referring to imprisoned Nationalist leader Albizu Campos) to smear the workers and invite the FBI (Federal Bureau of Investigation), whose agents interviewed the workers but did not intervene. Employers used strikebreakers against them.

Supporters including Migration Division Joseph Monserrat representing the Council of Spanish American organizations visited the workplace and rallied in support, coordinating the donation of food, clothes, and arranging for press coverage of the conflict.[73]

Typically, work was not hard to find and there was little discrimination in industrial hiring, but employer pressure for low wages was always present.[74] Movement away from the lower levels of the factory floor took time. By 1970, through combined effects of second-generation changes and selective migration from New York City, Puerto Ricans showed significant changes in their occupational structure.[75] Factory operatives had declined from 62 percent to 55 percent, white-collar employment had nearly doubled, while farm labor employment declined by two thirds. The Puerto Rican upper-middle class had expanded by 50 percent but still represented a minority of the community (4.8% to 6.5%), with other higher income categories (craftsmen, white collar) increasing from 16 percent to 25 percent—the most significant change in this period.[76]

Interestingly, even as early as 1960, Puerto Rican family incomes in eastern-central New Jersey were diverse (see Tables 8.4, 8.6, and 8.9). Always lower than those of the general population (which included well established immigrant communities as well as the entire local, national, and global business owning elites of the state, most of whom were White), the majority clustered above the poverty line of $3,500. In these three metropolitan areas (Jersey City, Passaic, Newark), each of which included highly urbanized counties with cities and smaller towns, there were both patterns and variations to how well Puerto Rican families were doing. Jersey City had a higher proportion of higher income people with 24 percent earning more than $7,000 but it also had the largest lower income percentage with 9.5 percent earning less than $2,000. All three regions had significant bulging in the middle of the income scale with about 25–28 percent, which would represent high working class and middle-class incomes ($5,000–$7,000). These numbers also represent diversity within the family units as some families might have three income earners and some only one, as well as variations in the number of dependents. In a study that compared the incomes of Puerto Ricans and Cubans in Hudson County, for example, the modestly higher Cuban incomes could be attributed to the multigenerational character of the households in which Cubans were more likely to have an income-earning grandparent in the household.[77]

In the core industrial areas, Puerto Ricans became a very large presence in the larger manufacturing plants. In Edison, the Fedders factory employed 1,500 Puerto Ricans out of a labor force of 2,300, plus several hundred Cubans and all the local Dominican men. The company also had plants in Puerto Rico. By 1970, the union leadership had become Puerto Rican and Cuban. The Fedders plant shrank its operations in New Jersey through the late 1970s and 1980s. A seven-month strike of the 2,500 production workers in all Fedders plants lasted until October 1972. By this time the labor force was nearly completely Puerto Rican

## Table 8.4
## Puerto Rican family incomes by group, household type, birth, 1960

|  | Total | Puerto Rico born | U.S. born |
|---|---|---|---|
| All families | 30,344 | 28,247 | 2,097 |
| Less than $1,000 | 1,811 | 1,733 | 78 |
| $1,000 to $1,999 | 946 | 903 | 43 |
| $2,000 to $2,999 | 1,711 | 1,577 | 134 |
| $3,000 to $3,999 | 2,799 | 2,697 | 102 |
| $4,000 to $4,999 | 2,972 | 2,802 | 170 |
| $5,000 to $5,999 | 3,498 | 3,324 | 174 |
| $6,000 to $6,999 | 3,031 | 1,813 | 218 |
| $7,000 to $7,999 | 2,431 | 2,280 | 151 |
| $8,000 to $8,999 | 2,079 | 1,954 | 125 |
| $9,000 to $9,999 | 1,733 | 1,613 | 120 |
| $10,000 to $11,999 | 2,951 | 2,699 | 252 |
| $12,000 to $14,999 | 2,184 | 1,928 | 256 |
| $15,000 to $24,999 | 1,881 | 1,645 | 236 |
| $25,000 or more | 317 | 279 | 38 |
| Median income | $6,473 | $6,387 | $7,858 |
| Mean income | $7,389 | $7,275 | $8,922 |
| Female head | 5,746 | 5,381 | 365 |
| Less than $1,000 | 952 | 923 | 29 |
| $1,000 to $1,999 | 473 | 449 | 24 |
| $2,000 to $2,999 | 957 | 862 | 95 |
| $3,000 to $3,999 | 1,302 | 1,254 | 48 |
| $4,000 to $4,999 | 731 | 666 | 65 |
| $5,000 to $5,999 | 352 | 314 | 38 |
| $6,000 to $6,999 | 263 | 245 | 18 |
| $7,000 to $7,999 | 151 | 144 | 7 |
| $8,000 to $8,999 | 154 | 141 | 13 |
| $9,000 to $9,999 | 72 | 64 | 8 |
| $10,000 to $11,999 | 175 | 159 | 16 |
| $12,000 to $14,999 | 73 | 73 | – |
| $15,000 to $24,999 | 87 | 83 | 4 |
| $25,000 or more | 4 | 4 | – |
| Median income | $3,377 | $3,364 | $3,719 |
| Mean income | $3,862 | $3,845 | $4,122 |

SOURCE: Nathan Kantrowitz and Donnell Maynard Pappenfort, *Fact Book for the New York-Northeastern New Jersey Standard Consolidated Area: The Non-White, Puerto Rican, and White Non-Puerto Rican Populations* (New York: Graduate School of Social Work, New York University, 1960).

and Black and was actively participating in picket lines.[78] In 1974, the company laid off 400 workers but the union, International Union of Electrical Workers (IUE) local 483, managed to place most of these workers in other Fedders factories, based on seniority.[79]

The Fedders plant in Edison specifically suffered the same fate as most other large factories shuttered in the corporate search for cheaper labor and mechanized plants. It went from three thousand employees in the mid-1960s to six hundred in 1979. By 1982, only 170 production workers remained at Fedders, and the company was organizing a transfer of 100 of their positions to Illinois. The IUE local led by President Jesse Montanez, sought arbitration to enforce a clause in the last contract that would keep the company from doing this in exchange for lower wage demands.[80] In 1992, Fedders closed its two remaining plants in New Jersey laying off six hundred workers.[81] The deindustrializing trend was brutal to the Puerto Rican community, especially older migrants who, while veterans of New Jersey's industrial economy, had few options for decent wages.

As in the Fedders plant, industrial unions played a very big role in their economic well-being between the 1950s and 1970s. Puerto Ricans encountered industrial unions as soon as they entered the factories of New Jersey. Puerto Ricans had a strong presence in Teamsters locals, International Union of Electrical Workers (IUE) and remaining UElocals of the United Electrical, Radio and Machine Workers (UE), and the International Ladies' Garment Workers' Union (ILGWU). As early as 1948, New York City labor, left, and civil rights activist Gilberto Gerena Valentin, like many others young Puerto Rican workers from New York City, spent some time working in an Elizabeth factory (Emerson) as a television cabinet wood polisher. He became a local organizer for the IUE.[82]

Puerto Rican Angel Roman also worked as an organizer for IUE local 485 in Brooklyn, which organized many New Jersey factories. When the Fedders plant moved in a merger to Edison in 1967, the union and organizers followed. He was assigned there because of the large number of Spanish-speaking workers. Roman continued working as an organizer assigned to service twenty shops and do work among the unorganized in Brooklyn as well. Union political conflicts in the main office in Brooklyn resulted in his removal from membership organizing, eventually leading to his dismissal.[83]

Another runaway plant that had closed its plant in New York and moved to North Bergen was Spun-Jee, manufacturer of women's garments. In New York, their plants had been represented by the International Ladies' Garment Workers' Union local 62, but when they moved to New Jersey and reorganized as James Textile Corp. in 1963 they refused to recognize the jurisdiction of the local. In 1968, the International Ladies' Garment Workers' Union local began to organize its fifty-five workers again from its local 148–162. Like many small manufacturing plants, these businesses were often family owned. In this case three siblings owned this plant. In response to union organizing, they began a fellowship at the Fashion Institute of Technology in Manhattan in production management for a child of their workers. The employers refused to recognize the signed union cards and fired four workers involved in the drive. The organizers worked with Wendell Moyd and Joaquin Gutierrez holding meetings and encouraging the signing of union cards. They in turn recruited signatures. Most of the workers were Puerto Rican and many did not speak English. A meeting followed at a restaurant in which seventeen workers signed the bilingual cards in support of the union, securing the success of the campaign. Puerto Ricans were foremen at the plant including Sam Colon in the cutting section. An internal conflict ensued with Gregorio Rodriguez and Eulogio Rodriguez. Colon, as an agent of the employer, was found to violate the right to organize. Joaquin Gutierrez was ordered back to his job. They won the jobs back and union representation in an NLRB case.[84]

Puerto Rican struggles for employment and better conditions also intersected with civil rights-based demands for inclusion. Minority employment in publicly funded construction, especially housing and hospitals, became an issue. Starting in the late 1950s the presence of all-White construction crews in urban construction projects triggered these movements. Throughout the 1960s, African Americans and Puerto Ricans worked to pressure construction unions to admit, and construction contractors to hire, minorities. In the early 1960s, the Citizen Negotiating Committee sent Newark mayor Addonizio a plan for hiring; the mayor had appointed this committee in 1963. The plan, which specifically referred to Blacks and Puerto Ricans, called for immediate hiring especially in city-controlled projects, data gathering, admission into training and apprentice programs, review of test criteria by unions, the proposal contained guidelines for enforcement and legal sanctions in the court system, and the local and state human rights commissions.[85] In Newark, the construction of the Rutgers Medical School in 1970 led to protests and demands for the hiring of Blacks and Puerto Ricans. The Black and Puerto Rican Construction Coalition demanded from the U.S. Labor Department that they halt the federally funded construction project to guarantee entry level and trained positions to members of their communities. This struggle would be an uphill and persistent battle for these communities throughout the 1970 and 1980s.[86]

Discrimination in construction trades and unions was as common and was at the root of this problem in New Jersey as in New York City. Local and federal agencies responded to pressure for inclusion. In 1970 a federal district judge ordered Sheet Metal Workers local 10 to admit minority apprentices. Big jobs and spending in the construction of the new Newark airport prompted the lawsuit supported by the federal labor department. Newark was one of U.S. Secretary of Labor James P. Mitchell's eighteen target cities. The efforts were supported by local Black and Puerto Rican activists, including the urban coalition, in various construction projects, with the support of the port authority.[87]

Soon after, the State Division on Civil Rights moved against the electrical construction industry for discrimination in its hiring. Four union locals and Fluoro Electrical were under investigation for completely excluding Blacks and Puerto Ricans. Locals 52, 262, 581, and 675 of the International Brotherhood of Electrical Workers as well, where of 1,500 members only 2.5 percent were

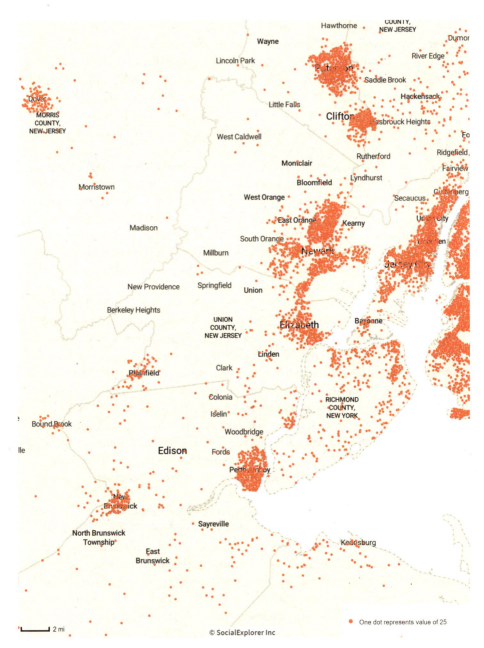

FIGURE 8.4　Puerto Rican population by census tract, 1980. (Source: Social Explorer, based on data from the U.S. Census Bureau.)

non-White.[88] Discrimination was not restricted to construction work. Some large employers also developed a culture of discrimination despite the large presence of Puerto Rican and Black workers in the industrial labor market. In Newark, Black brewery workers and their allies called for a national boycott of Budweiser. They listed twelve demands, which included hiring more Black and Puerto Rican workers and providing resources to Newark's community projects. Pickets were organized for Hight Street. The coalition explained how in Newark, a city that was 65 percent Black and 10 percent Puerto Rican, the Anheuser-Busch brewery only hired 7 percent "minority" workers.

Wage enforcement was another arena in which civil rights demands intersected with working-class issues. In New Jersey, Spanish-speaking enforcers of the federal Wages and Hours Division arrived in 1970. Mexican American Marshal Mendez began working to investigate wage theft and other violations in New Jersey industrial establishments. Mendez, who came from San Antonio, Texas, had worked organizing farmworkers. In Newark he collaborated with Puerto Rican leaders to identify complaints against employers. Based in Newark, the office had already recovered $700,000 in wages. Black, Spanish-, and Portuguese-speaking workers were most affected by violations. In first few months of 1970 the office recovered an additional $250,000 in Newark alone, mostly among low-wage workers.[89]

One suit filed in federal court against four employers and a union in Vineland in 1974 was representative of how Puerto Ricans fared in many of the dispersed, smaller workplaces. In Camden, four factories were accused of underpaying Puerto Rican workers (50 percent of their workforce) and not promoting them to high paying jobs or protecting their seniority rights.[90]

Puerto Ricans faced other more subtle forms of discrimination. State unemployment payment policy in New Jersey discriminated against those who moved into higher unemployment areas. Of the nearly 3,300 rejected claims in New Jersey, 97 percent involved Puerto Ricans who moved back to Puerto Rico. A Legal Services lawsuit on behalf of Puerto Rican cannery workers successfully challenged this policy in court.[91]

In the context of the industrial economy, civil rights were critically connected to labor rights, employment, and the economic well-being of the community. By the early 1970s, Puerto Ricans had become sufficiently organized, visible, and confident that Puerto Rican civil rights leaders demanded that Governor Byrne name a Puerto Rican to be the next director of the State Division of Civil Rights, arguing that "blacks have had the position for too long." Jack Hora, chairman of the Commission for Puerto Rican Rights noted how only Black leaders had been appointed to the commission, "denying an equal opportunity" for a Puerto Rican. Previously the Cahill administration had promised a Puerto Rican deputy director but did not fulfill its promise.[92]

Unlike New York City, which had a highly active, centralized, and politicized union movement (and Central Labor Council with Hispanic participation since the 1930s), New Jersey unions were more fragmented and had no clear political center, with less commitment to the civil rights agenda so present in most New York City industrial unions. Missing also were the strong leftist factions and activists that had been so important in the formation of New York City class politics. In New Jersey, union officials could hide more effectively from antidiscrimination efforts from local members, state government, and federal authorities. The contrast was clear in the experience of the International Brotherhood of Electrical Workers, which in New York had led a progressive incorporation of Hispanics and Blacks since the 1940s and more dramatically in the 1960s, while the International Brotherhood of Electrical Workers (IBEW) in Elizabeth was sued in the Federal District Court by fourteen Cuban Americans for its near total absence of Blacks and Hispanics.[93]

The mid-1970s were difficult for industrial workers and urban Puerto Rican communities in general. The growing deindustrialization trend intersected with the OPEC (Organization of Petroleum Exporting Countries) oil embargo crisis and the 1973–1975 recession, while urban centers became decrepit and underserved. Community and social service leaders, in place since the war on poverty began in the early 1960s, mobilized to respond to the crisis. The Puerto Rican Veteran's Association carried out a field study in 1974 that provides significant insights into the conditions of the community in Hudson, Essex, Passaic, and Middlesex Counties, with a random sample of 5,089 people interviewed.[94] Hudson County Puerto Ricans reported very high youth unemployment, which quickly reduced family incomes and raised the poverty rate. Data for this working-class area showed that one in four Puerto Rican families were poor and eligible for public assistance but only 20 percent received welfare, this even though women had a very high rate of participation in the workforce.[95] Youth in urban schools faced the biggest obstacles with higher education than their elders but also higher unemployment levels. They also dropped out of high school at very high rates (46 percent, although part of this is accounted for by return migration to Puerto Rico).

The following summer John Goetsch, research director for the Puerto Rican Congress of New Jersey, applied to the state's Department of Community Affairs for a larger follow-up survey to examine the growing "economic woes" of Puerto Ricans in Hudson and the state. The Congress was alarmed that the earlier survey found that English acquisition and a U.S.-based education for high school graduates did not help Puerto Rican youth find work as it had in previous decades. Data indicated also that concentrations of New Jersey residents that originated in one same town in Puerto Rico had better economic indicators including youth unemployment.[96]

All the same, the New Jersey community's economic experience through the 1970s developed through a bifurcating path, with most workers receiving low pay and often uncertain incomes, high youth unemployment, lack of advancement, and slow improvement, especially compared to New York City. This was noted

Table 8.5
Occupation of employed persons by ethnicity (%), New Jersey

| Occupation | 1960 Puerto Ricans | 1970 Puerto Ricans | 1970 Blacks | 1970 Whites |
| --- | --- | --- | --- | --- |
| Professional, technical, and kindred workers | 2.7 | 4.2 | 8.3 | 16.7 |
| Managers, administration, and non-farm | 2.1 | 2.3 | 2.2 | 9.4 |
| Sales and clerical | 7.7 | 13.2 | 18.3 | 28.9 |
| Craftsmen | 8.2 | 11.3 | 9.3 | 14.2 |
| Operatives, laborers | 62.1 | 55.2 | 38.9 | 20.6 |
| Service workers | 10.1 | 11.1 | 22.1 | 9.5 |
| Farmers and agricultural workers | 5.7 | 1.7 | 0.9 | 0.6 |

SOURCE: US Census, *1970 Census of Population. Characteristics of the Population, New Jersey* (Washington DC: Bureau of the Census, 1973); US Census, *1960 Census of Population. Characteristics of the Population, New Jersey* (Washington DC: Bureau of the Census, 1963).

by the U.S. Civil Rights Commission report on Puerto Ricans in 1976, when the economic downturn was already being felt and the community was losing some of the gains it had accumulated in the 1950s and 1960s. The commission noted how compared to New York the community's income distribution was more polarized with a larger, higher income middle class and a poorer inner-city core. The commission's survey was not promising. Of Puerto Ricans in New Jersey, 68 percent had low paying jobs, with the worst conditions among the large clusters living in urban centers like Newark, where more than 78 percent had low incomes and held semiskilled or skilled jobs. Federally funded programs like the Comprehensive Employment and Training Act and the United States Employment Service, which elsewhere were critical of the ability of low-income workers to find improved jobs and training for existing jobs, were found to be inadequate in New Jersey. One United States Employment Service job trainer described their preparedness as "a crime."[97] In Camden, one student described how school counselors "generalize and tell me that my people are dumb, that we make good dishwashers. We can't manipulate our minds, but we're good with our hands, and we are docile."[98]

Around the same time PACO (Puertorriqueños Asociados for Community Organization), a Jersey City social service agency founded in 1970, and Perfecto Oyola conducted a survey of Puerto Ricans in that city, one of the poorest communities in New Jersey.[99] They found that the average Puerto Rican earned $5,500 in 54.5 weeks of work ($458 monthly) enough for the majority to be above poverty level but still including many whose incomes were not enough to meet their needs. The study responded to the need for more data on these urban communities in the late 1960s and early 1970s as anti-poverty programs and federal agencies provided at least the hope of improvements in services if not higher incomes. The survey included 1,500 adults, half of whom were in labor unions,

## Table 8.6
## Distribution of Puerto Rican family incomes in New Jersey urban areas (Standard Metropolitan Statistical Area), 1960

|  | Newark |  | Jersey City |  | Paterson |  |
|---|---|---|---|---|---|---|
| All families | 2,831 | 100% | 2,032 | 100% | 3,188 | 100% |
| Under $1,000 | 162 | 5.7% | 192 | 9.5% | 178 | 5.6% |
| $1,000 to $1,999 | 189 | 6.7% | 131 | 6.4% | 277 | 8.7% |
| $2,000 to $2,999 | 461 | 16.3% | 268 | 13.2% | 526 | 16.5% |
| $3,000 to $3,999 | 660 | 23.3% | 340 | 16.7% | 628 | 19.7% |
| $4,000 to $4,999 | 414 | 14.6% | 312 | 15.4% | 579 | 18.2% |
| $5,000 to $5,999 | 285 | 10.1% | 205 | 10.1% | 334 | 10.5% |
| $6,000 to $6,999 | 245 | 8.7% | 196 | 9.6% | 246 | 7.7% |
| $7,000 to $7,999 | 120 | 4.2% | 124 | 6.1% | 191 | 6.0% |
| $8,000 to $8,999 | 101 | 3.6% | 85 | 4.2% | 110 | 3.4% |
| $9,000 to $9,999 | 57 | 2.0% | 53 | 2.6% | 41 | 1.3% |
| $10,000 and over | 137 | 4.8% | 126 | 6.2% | 78 | 2.4% |

SOURCE: Nathan Kantrowitz and Donnel Maynard Pappenfort. *Fact Book for the New York-Northeastern New Jersey Standard Consolidated Area: The Non-White, Puerto Rican, and White Non-Puerto Rican Populations* (New York: Graduate School of Social Work, New York University, 1966).

with many working in Manhattan, Hoboken, or Newark. The vast majority rented their apartments at an average of $105 a month.[100]

After the late 1970s, and because of lingering low wage industrial employment, Puerto Rican populations continued to expand in the industrial cities of the Hudson corridor. In Newark, Paterson, Jersey City, Perth Amboy, and Hoboken, the Puerto Rican population continued to expand through the early 1980s even as total population for these urban centers declined, some of them dramatically (see Table 8.7). A pattern of succession was at work, also, with newer and younger arrivals occupying the lower rungs of the declining wage and housing markets and older families moving to improved housing and jobs in other areas, a pattern that would continue into the twenty-first century.

Poverty caused by declining wages and employment opportunities rates in urban areas for Puerto Ricans increased dramatically, so inner cities became even poorer as those who could find better conditions elsewhere moved. In most New Jersey cities, Puerto Ricans who remained in inner cities experienced increasing poverty rates, nearly doubling in some cities, as higher income people moved out.[101] The data presented by Santiago and Galster suggested that even in this period of declining wages for industrial work, if families had two incomes even if both were in manufacturing, income levels were sufficient to keep the family out of poverty, indicating that the real crisis was of unemployment and lack of full-time work opportunities or the inability to work because of parenting responsibilities or parental abandonment. Female-headed households were critical in

Table 8.7
Puerto Rican poverty rates in selected U.S. and
New Jersey cities, 1970 and 1980

| City | 1970 | 1980 |
|---|---|---|
| Allentown, PA | 24.3 | 44.8 |
| Boston, MA | 40.0 | 57.5 |
| Bridgeport, CT | 20.0 | 36.8 |
| Buffalo, NY | 31.0 | 39.0 |
| Chicago, IL | 23.4 | 26.4 |
| Detroit, MI | 12.6 | 6.8 |
| Gary, IN | 12.5 | 11.2 |
| Hartford, CT | 48.6 | 46.9 |
| Honolulu, HI | 13.1 | 28.2 |
| Lancaster, PA | 30.8 | 28.3 |
| Lorain-Elyria, OH | 11.4 | 33.7 |
| Los Angeles, CA | 14.8 | 16.3 |
| Miami, FL | 18.6 | 23.2 |
| New Haven, CT | 25.6 | 51.1 |
| New York, NY | 29.7 | 41.1 |
| Philadelphia, PA | 30.6 | 35.9 |
| Reading, PA | 36.3 | 55.4 |
| Rochester, NY | 14.6 | 36.3 |
| San Francisco, CA | 12.8 | 15.7 |
| Springfield, MA | 24.0 | 50.5 |
| Atlantic City, NJ | 34.8 | 64.3 |
| Jersey City, NJ | 25.7 | 34.8 |
| Long Branch, NJ | 11.3 | 36.1 |
| New Brunswick, NJ | 18.5 | 48.4 |
| Newark, NJ | 30.2 | 44.2 |
| Paterson, NJ | 20.7 | 39.1 |
| Trenton, NJ | 21.7 | 33.3 |
| Vineland, NJ | 27.2 | 42.7 |

SOURCE: George Galster and Anna M. Santiago, "Explaining the Growth of Puerto-Rican Poverty, 1970–1980," *Urban Affairs Review* 30, no. 2 (December 1994): 249–274, 253.

this crisis of poverty and accounted for nearly all the increase as well as increased segregation within declining urban areas.

This meant an increase in poverty during the period of decline and restructuring of the northeastern United States' manufacturing sector, 1975–1990. In 1970, 25 percent of Puerto Rican households in New Jersey lived below the poverty line and by the 1980s the numbers increased further before they declined in the 1990s.[102] Yet, according to Alice Colón-Warren's research, median family incomes of Puerto Ricans in New Jersey ($6,500 in 1970, $10,500 in

## Table 8.8
## Puerto Rican median family income in New York and New Jersey, 1970 and 1980

|  | 1970 New York | 1980 New York | 1970 New Jersey | 1980 New Jersey |
|---|---|---|---|---|
| Total | $5,697 | $9,654 | $6,458 | $10,510 |
| Husband/wife household | $6,781 | $14,557 | $7,284 | $15,699 |
| Female head of household | $3,191 | $4,913 | $3,380 | $4,631 |
| Female head as percent of husband/wife | 47 | 34 | 46 | 29 |
| Puerto Rican income as percentage of total | 53 | 47 | 56 | 46 |

SOURCES: Alice Colón-Warren, "Impact of Job Losses on Puerto Rican Women in the Middle Atlantic Region, 1970–1980," in *Puerto Rican Women and Work: Bridges in Transnational Labor*, ed. Altagracia Ortiz (Philadelphia: Temple University Press, 1996), 108; Bureau of the Census, *1970 Census of Population*, vol. 1, *Characteristics of the Population*, chapter D. "Detailed Characteristics," part 34 "New York," part 32 "New Jersey" (Washington, DC: Bureau of the Census, 1973); Bureau of the Census, *1980 Census of Population*, vol. I, *Characteristics of the Population*, chapter C, "General Social and Economic Characteristics," part 34 "New York," part 32 "New Jersey" (Washington, DC: Bureau of the Census, 1984).

1980—$32,000 in 2020 dollars) were higher than in New York state in 1970 and the approximately 10 percent gap continued in 1980 (see Table 8.8).[103]

Yet in the period of economic recovery that followed the crisis of the late 1970s and early 1980s, New Jersey, compared to other states, produced better economic outcomes for both its established Puerto Rican communities and those moving in from New York. According to Gilbert Marzan, Puerto Ricans in New Jersey had very high employment levels, with the highest wages and lowest poverty levels of any state with a large concentration of Puerto Ricans (Florida, New York, Illinois) for 1990. Its industrial economy held more Puerto Rican adult males in industrial, and precision, manufacturing, repair, and employment than New York state, 37 percent and 18 percent, versus 25 percent and 16 percent, with far fewer Puerto Ricans in service work. In education, Puerto Ricans in New York and New Jersey were very similar, with about 26 percent of the adult men having some college education or higher. Yet more than half the Puerto Ricans in New Jersey resided in suburbs compared to only 13 percent in New York state.[104]

By the early 1960s, the Puerto Rican community in New Jersey had diversified its work, regional, and income profiles and had engaged with supporters and local political activism. In these decades the community simultaneously established roots but also experienced constant patterns of change and significant internal diversity as it expanded from 50,000 to 450,000 people. In the first decades of engagement with New Jersey, its struggles focused on gaining access to jobs and housing, usually with the limited help of local allies and against significant obstacles and hostility. By the 1970s, the community was closely tied to the fate of the region's industrial economy and labor movements but also to the quality of the state's educational systems and access to them for often

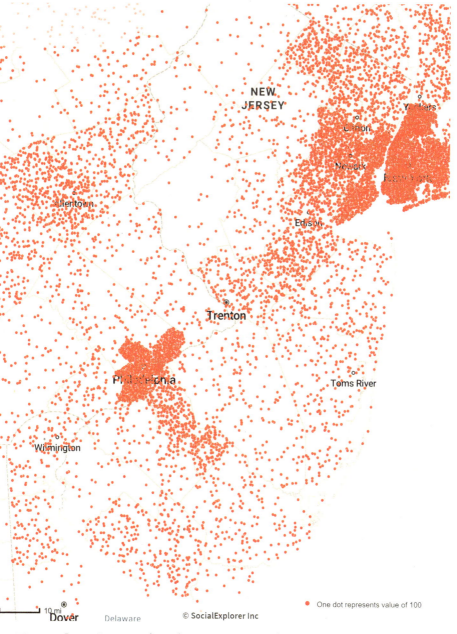

FIGURE 8.5  Puerto Rican population by census tract, 2022. (Source: Social Explorer, based on data from the U.S. Census Bureau.)

marginalized and predominantly working-class people. Between the 1960s and the 1980s the community developed even stronger social and political mobilizations (these are treated in the websites that accompany this volume).

## Notes

1. Census categories change over time. Any earlier data refer to Puerto Rico born or, if so identified, U.S.-born second generation. Not until the 1980 Census would the third generation appear when ethnic self-identification became part of the data. Later categories refer to ethnic self-identification.
2. American Community Survey, 2021, SocialExplorer.com.
3. For details on these numbers, see Daniel Lopez's inventory of data sources ("Puerto Rican Migrant Farm Workers in Mercer Camden Counties," typescript, 2021.
4. Bernardo Vega and César Andreu Iglesias, *Memoirs of Bernardo Vega: A Contribution to the History of the Puerto Rican Community in New York* (New York: Monthly Review Press, 1984), 19; Randall Gabrielan, *Explosion at Morgan: The World War I Middlesex Munitions Disaster* (Charleston, SC: History Press, 2012).
5. "Puerto Rico en Nueva York," *La correspondencia*, September 23, 1918.
6. "Sociedades Hispanas," *La Prensa*, September 20, 1927.
7. A. W. Maldonado, *Luis Muñoz Marin: Puerto Rico's Democratic Revolution* (San Juan: Universidad de Puerto Rico, 2006), 62; Carmelo Rosario Natal, *La Juventud de Luis Munoz Marin: Vida y Pensamiento, 1898–1932* (San Juan: Editorial Edil, 1989), 137.
8. Carmen Teresa Whalen, *From Puerto Rico to Philadelphia: Puerto Rican Workers and Postwar Economies* (Philadelphia: Temple University Press, 2001); Lorrin R. Thomas and Aldo A. Lauria-Santiago, *Rethinking the Struggle for Puerto Rican Rights* (New York: Routledge, 2018); Edwin Maldonado, "Contract Labor and the Origins of Puerto Rican Communities in the United States," *International Migration Review* 13, no. 1 (April 1979): 103–121; John N. Stinson Fernández, "Hacia Una Antropología de la Emigración Planificada: El Negociado de Empleo y Migración y el Caso de Filadelfia," *Revista de Ciencias Sociales* 1 (June 1996): 112–155.
9. Report the Arrival of Puerto Rican Workers at Weehawken, New Jersey, May 9, 1944, War Manpower Commission, United States National Archives (USNA).
10. "Annual Report of the Commissioner of Labor, 1944–1945" (San Juan, 1947); Thoron to Gutwell, November 8, 1944, Office of Territories Classified File, 1907–1951, file 9-8-116, box 1138, Record Group (RG) 126, USNA.
11. "Puerto Ricans working for Campbell Soup Co.," June 21 1944, Office of Territories Classified File, 1907-1951, RG 126, File 9-8-116, Box 1138, USNA.
12. Puerto Rican Labor Camps, press release by Gabriel Guerra Mondragon, July 6, 1944, War Manpower Commission, USNA.
13. Reverend Enrique Rodriguez, Minister of the First Church of Spanish Speaking People, to Jesus T. Pinero, 1945, Bureau of Insular Affairs, USNA.
14. "Plant's Closing Disrupts a Dream," *Philadelphia Inquirer*, September 17, 1989; Daniel Sidorick, *Condensed Capitalism: Campbell Soup and the Pursuit of Cheap Production in the Twentieth Century* (Ithaca, NY: ILR Press/Cornell University Press, 2009).
15. In 1955, Jones found that the seasonal agricultural population increased the Puerto Rican population in the state by about 9,000 at a time when the entire population was estimated to be about 26,000, bringing the total to 34,500. Isham B. Jones, *The*

*Puerto Rican in New Jersey: His Present Status, July 1955* (Newark: New Jersey, State Department of Education, Division Against Discrimination, 1955), 10.
16 Stewart M. Meyers, New Jersey Division on Civil Rights, *Minority Group Workers in Industry* (Trenton: State of New Jersey, Department of Education, Division Against Discrimination, 1956).
17 Olga Jimenez de Wagenheim, "From Aguada to Dover: Puerto Ricans Rebuild Their World in Morris County, New Jersey, 1948 to 2000," in *The Puerto Rican Diaspora: Historical Perspectives*, ed. Carmen Teresa Whalen and Víctor Vázquez-Hernández (Philadelphia: Temple University Press, 2005), 106–127.
18 Jimenez de Wagenheim, "From Aguada to Dover," 111.
19 "Experiment with Domestic Help from Puerto Rico Successful," *Daily Argus* (Mount Vernon), July 22, 1949; Estrella Draper to Petroamerica Pagan de Colon, August 10, 1949, Migration Division, Department of Labor, Archivo General de Puerto Rico.
20 Gilberto Gerena Valentin, Oral Histories, Center for Puerto Rican Studies.
21 "Middle Class Hispanics Heading for Greener Pasture," *New York Times*, May 20, 1979.
22 Gilbert Marzan, Andres Torres, and Andrew Luecke, "Puerto Rican Out-Migration from New York City: 1995–2000," May 2008; Andres Torres and Gilbert Marzan, "Where Have All the Puerto Ricans Gone?" in *Latinos in New York: Communities in Transition*, ed. Angelo Falcon, Sherrie Baver, and Gabriel Haslip-Viera (Notre Dame, IN: University of Notre Dame Press, 2017).
23 Angel Padilla, *We Were Not as They Thought: Recollections of Angel Padilla* (Hoboken, NJ: Hoboken Oral History Project, 2010).
24 Tom Olivieri, *When People Got Together and There Were Feasts: Recollections of Tom Olivieri* (Hoboken, NJ: Hoboken Oral History Project, 1975).
25 Olivieri, *When People Got Together*.
26 Olivieri, *When People Got Together*.
27 Model Cities was a federal experiment in a comprehensive, urban, anti-poverty program that integrated governance, housing, and services all in the same place.
28 "Problem Study: Priest, Hoboken Detective Plan Puerto Rican Program," *Jersey Journal*, September 1, 1955.
29 "Puerto Rican Understanding Groups Goal," *Jersey Journal*, October 6, 1955.
30 "Spanish-Speaking's Priests Map North Hudson Program," *Jersey Journal*, July 10, 1959.
31 "The Puerto Rican, Why He Came," *The Advocate*, June 14, 1963, 11:25.
32 "Aid Sought for Puerto Rico Population," *Jersey Journal*, October 9, 1960; "Puerto Rican Study Set in Hoboken," *Jersey Journal*, September 20, 1960. For more details on the Migration Division, an office of Puerto Rico's Labor Department that helped migrants once in New York City, see Aldo A. Lauria Santiago, *The Migration Division and Its Work*, 2018; Edgardo Meléndez, *Sponsored Migration: The State and Puerto Rican Postwar Migration to the United States* (Columbus: Ohio State University Press, 2017).
33 "Puerto Rican Community Making Fast Adjustment," *Jersey Journal*, May 13, 1960; "Migration Division Aids Many Puerto Rican Units," *Jersey Journal*, October 15, 1963; "Migration Unit Workshop is Effective Weapon," *Jersey Journal*, October 29, 1963; "Strength Through Unity, Basic Ethnic Principle," *Jersey Journal*, November 5, 1963; "Community Life: Goals Charted in All Phases," *Jersey Journal*, November 12, 1963.
34 "Puerto Rican Now Feels Confidence in Himself," *Jersey Journal*, December 3, 1963.

35 Prejudice in New Form Aimed at Puerto Ricans," *Jersey Journal*, April 21, 1964.
36 "Puerto Ricans Resent Concepts of Inferiority," *Jersey Journal*, May 19, 1964.
37 "Civil Rights Struggle Affects Puerto Ricans," *Jersey Journal*, June 9, 1964.
38 "Illegal Search, Brutality Charged by Fr. Faulkner," *Jersey Journal*, March 1, 1965.
39 "Labor Official, Board to Meet," *Jersey Journal*, September 21, 1955.
40 "Eight Groups Back Meyner," *Jersey Journal*, October 18, 1957.
41 Eva Rosas-Amirault, interview by Claudia Flores, October 27, 2007, Latinos in Conversation, Plainfield Public Library, https://plainfieldlibrarynj.contentdm.oclc.org/digital/collection/p17109coll15/id/46.
42 Gilbert P. Augustine, "Our New Neighbors: The Puerto Ricans." Paper presented at New Jersey Economics Association Convention, Atlantic City, 1958.
43 Augustine, "Our New Neighbors."
44 Lauria Santiago, *The Migration Division and Its Work*.
45 "Class in English helps Puerto Ricans to Adjust," November 17, 1958, clippings file, Perth Amboy Public Library.
46 "Puerto Ricans Enter Politics," *Jersey Journal*, June 5, 1958.
47 *The Anti-Discrimination Law of 1945: Together with Amendments and Supplements Thereto* (Newark, NJ: Division Against Discrimination, 1949).
48 Division of Civil Rights, Annual Report, New Jersey: State of new Jersey, 1961.
49 Brian Almutt, "Another Victory for the Forces of Democracy: The 1949 New Jersey Civil Rights Act," *Pennsylvania History: A Journal of Mid-Atlantic Studies* 85, no. 3 (2018).
50 "Division against Discrimination," Annual Report, New Jersey, 1958.
51 Jones, *Puerto Rican*, 46–47.
52 "Gobernador Destituye al Juez Lloyd," *El Diario de Nueva York*, January 18, 1956; "Judge's Removal Upheld in Jersey: State Supreme Court Rules Unanimously Lloyd Had Not Acquired Tenure," *New York Times*, September 25, 1956.
53 "Judge Lloyd," *Long Branch Daily Record*, January 18, 1956.
54 Augustine, "Our New Neighbors."
55 "Our Puerto Ricans," *Freehold transcript/Monmouth Inquirer*, January 26, 1956.
56 Migration Division NJ–PA Region, "Annual Report 1963–64," Records of the Office of the Government of Puerto Rico in the United States, Center for Puerto Rican Studies.
57 Studies have consistently shown that English-language skills correlate positively with income and employment categories for Puerto Rican men, both migrants and second generation.
58 Augustine, "Our New Neighbors."
59 Jones, *Puerto Rican*.
60 Frederick Tobias Golub, "Some Economic Consequences of the Puerto Rican Migration into Perth Amboy, 1949–1954," 1955, MA Thesis, Rutgers University.
61 Golub, "Some Economic Consequences," 11.
62 Golub, "Some Economic Consequences," 14.
63 Jones, *Puerto Rican*.
64 Jones, *Puerto Rican*; Thomas F. Ryan, "Problems Associated with the Assimilation of Puerto Ricans into American Industry with Particular Reference to Employment in New Jersey" (thesis, Newark State College, 1969), 61; Golub, *Some Economic Consequences*, 9.
65 "Jersey City Puerto Rican Colony in Job Crisis," *Jersey Journal*, March 18, 1958.
66 Jones, *Puerto Rican*; Golub, "Some Economic Consequences."
67 Meyers, *Minority Group Workers in Industry*.

68 "First Puerto Rican Candidate Leaving Hoboken for Job," *Jersey Journal*, July 18, 1970.
69 Art Metalcraft Plating Co., Inc., 133 NLRB, no. 48 (1961).
70 Springs, Inc., 121 NLRB, no. 119 (1958); Aldo A. Lauria-Santiago, "Puerto Ricans, the Labor Movement and the Fight against 'Exploitation,' 1956–1965, 2018.
71 "Corrupt Unions Exploit Puerto Rican Labor," *Jersey Journal*, September 7, 1965.
72 Monthly Bulletin, Labor Advisory Committee on Puerto Rican Affairs, June 1955, Transport Workers Union, box 28, folder 15, Tamiment Library and Robert F. Wagner Labor Archives, New York University.
73 "Obreros boricuas denuncian son víctimas de atropellos," *El Diario*, July 19, 1955, Transport Workers Union, Tamiment Library and Robert F. Wagner Labor Archives, New York University.
74 "Drop-Out Rate Decreasing," *Trenton News Tribune*, February 2, 1971.
75 Puerto Rican Congress and Hector Rodriguez, *Socio-Economic Profile of N.J.'s Puerto Ricans* (Trenton, NJ: Puerto Rican Congress of New Jersey, 1972).
76 Puerto Rican Congress and Hector Rodriguez, *Socio-Economic Profile*, Table 4.
77 Guadalupe Martinez, "Cubans in New Jersey" (thesis, Rutgers University, 2013).
78 "Talks to Start in 7-week-old Fedders Strike," *Newark Star-Ledger*, April 14, 1972; "Jersey Labor to Aid Strikers at Fedders," *Newark Star-Ledger*, March 29, 1972.
79 "Fedders Employees face mass Layoffs in Edison," *Newark Star-Ledger*, Wednesday, March 6, 1974.
80 "Union Acts to Prevent Fedders Job Transfer," *Newark Star-Ledger*, Thursday, June 17, 1982.
81 "Fedders to close 2 N.J. Plants," *Trenton Evening Times*, Friday, August 21, 1992.
82 Gilberto Gerena Valentin, folder 3, IV#14, Oral Histories, Center for Puerto Rican Studies.
83 International Union of Electrical Workers, Local 485 WAG 137, Tamiment Library and Robert F. Wagner Labor Archives, New York University; Amalgamated Machine and Metal Local 485, NLRB, no. 36 199 (1972), Tamiment Library and Robert F. Wagner Labor Archives, New York University.
84 James Textile Corp., 184 NLRB, no. 70 (1970).
85 Memo from the Citizen Negotiating Committee to the Union Negotiation Committee, no date, Rise Up North/Newark(https://riseupnewark.com/).
86 "Bias Charge Could Stop U.S. Projects in Essex," *Sunday Star Ledger*, March 15, 1970.
87 "U.S. Legal Action Expected in Trade Union Bias Probe," *Newark Star Ledger*, December 6, 1970.
88 "State Finds Bias in Electrical Firms and Union Locals," *Newark Star Ledger*, April 15, 1971.
89 "U.S. Crackdown on Exploitation of Minorities," *Newark Star Ledger*, November 1, 1970.
90 "Bias against Puerto Ricans Charged," *New York Times*, February 8, 1974.
91 "Jobless Aids Rules Challenged," *Newark Star Ledger*, April 14, 1974.
92 "State Pressed on Rights Job for Puerto Rican," *Newark Star Ledger*, June 27, 1974; "Shape Up Process: Brewery Workers Plan Demonstration," *New Jersey Amsterdam News*, October 2, 1971.
93 "Hispanics Sue Union for Bias," *Newark Star Ledger*, November 4, 1976.
94 Puerto Rican Congress of New Jersey, *The Puerto Rican Experience: A Manpower Research Study*, Trenton: The Congress, 1974.
95 "Finding Jobs Is Frustrating for Puerto Ricans, Says Study," *Jersey Journal*, May 30, 1974.

96 "Ask Funds for Puerto Rican Survey," *Jersey Journal*, July 17, 1974.
97 United States Commission on Civil Rights, *Puerto Ricans in the Continental United States: An Uncertain Future: A Report* (Washington: U.S. Commission on Civil Rights, 1976).
98 United States Commission on Civil Rights, *Puerto Ricans*.
99 See "Helping the Community since 1970," Puertorriqueños Asociados for Community Organization, https://pacoagency.org/our-history/.
100 "Jersey City Survey Shows Puerto Ricans Earn $5,500," *Jersey Journal*, September 13, 1971.
101 Anna M. Santiago and George Galster, "Puerto Rican Segregation in the United States: Cause or Consequence of Economic Status?" *Social Problems* 42, no. 3 (1995): 361–389, appendix.
102 Puerto Rican Congress and Hector Rodriguez, *Socio-Economic Profile*.
103 Alice Colón-Warren, "The Impact of Job Losses on Puerto Rican Women in the Middle Atlantic Region, 1970–1980," in *Puerto Rican Women and Work: Bridges in Transnational Labor*, ed. Altagracia Ortiz (Philadelphia: Temple University Press, 1996), table 4.1.
104 Gilbert Marzan, "Regional Variation in Socioeconomic Status among Mainland Puerto Rican Males: A Comparative Analysis" (diss., State University of New York at Albany, 2001).

# 9
# A Century of Cuban Music in New Jersey

BENJAMIN LAPIDUS

During her notorious visit to the *Dick Cavett Show* in 1973, the Cuban singer La Lupe (Lupe Victoria Yolí Raymond), also known as La Yiyiyi, offers her host a golden basket of *torticas de morón* (shortbread cookies) from a Cuban bakery in Union City, New Jersey. Wearing a gold lamé jumpsuit and channeling the Yoruba orisha (ancestral spirit) Ochún, La Lupe places the basket in her lap and tells Cavett she has a surprise for him:

> The surprise is that I know you like cookies and I brought you Cuban cookies, torticas de morón and I want you to try them because they're very good. . . . You know they make it for you in Union City, we have like a big community, like a 150,000 Cuban people, we live there. And we have bakeries, laundries, you know like a little Cuba. They make it for you with love so take it, you know Cuban cookies. ¡Torticas de morón, mantecaditos caballero con salsa, con sabor, ahi nama, la moral no es alta pero abundante! (Cuban shortbread cookies, butter cookies, sir, with salsa, with flavor, there it is, humble but from the heart.)[1]

And just like that, with the *dulzura* (sweetness) and seductive glamour that characterizes the female orisha Ochún, La Lupe proudly paid tribute to her Cuban community of Hudson County, New Jersey, on national television.

Although La Lupe's estimates of the Cuban community's size were exaggerated, this encounter is but one of many examples of the extensive and dynamic cultural and musical connections between Cuba and New Jersey since the 1920s and to this day.

## Cubanía and Latin Music in the Garden State

*Cubanía* (Cuban national identity) sometimes collides with Latin music history, particularly in the United States, in an ongoing debate about the term salsa, which some believe is used to obfuscate the Cuban origins of Latin music. Cubans are generally quick to point out that all of the instruments and song forms used in salsa are rooted in Cuban genres such as the bolero, *son*, mambo, among others. This debate tends to miss the numerous points of interethnic collaboration within musical groups based in New York City from the earliest days of recordings, well over 120 years ago. Innovations in arranging, recording, orchestration, subject matter, education, instrument construction, folklore, and other areas made by Puerto Ricans, Cubans, Jews, Panamanians, Colombians, Dominicans, African Americans, and other New Yorkers undeniably changed the sound of the music and made it something quite distinct and international.[2]

Many written histories of Cuban music performed and recorded in the United States take stock of musicians and musical activities in New York City but they have consistently overlooked New Jersey, New Jersey-based musicians, recording studios, venues, and events. In other publications I have considered Hudson County, Elizabeth, and Newark to be close enough to New York to be included in discussions of activities by New York-based musicians. Therefore, I had not dedicated much effort to differentiate between these locales and New York City in my own research. Events that happened in New Jersey have been misattributed to New York City possibly because New Jersey geography is unfamiliar to outsiders and New York is iconic in Latin music history. For example, some of the emblematic 1920s RCA Victor recordings were made by El Sexteto Habanero and Trio Matamoros in Camden, New Jersey. Considering all of this we can see that no matter what happened in New York City, New Jersey Cubans proudly expressed their musical cubanía and continued performing and recording a variety of Cuban music genres for largely Cuban audiences in a wide variety of settings within the Cuban community of Hudson County, as well as in Elizabeth, Newark, and elsewhere in the Garden State.

Cuban migration and musical history often follows settlement based on familial connections. This chapter provides an overview of how Cuban artists, through successive waves of immigration, established a rich legacy of Cuban music in New Jersey since the 1920s, never missing the latest musical trends. Today the area remains home to a who's who of Cuban folkloric and popular musicians who have been arriving since the 1990s, such as Ogduardo "Román"

Díaz, Mauricio Herrera Tamayo, Ariacne Trujillo Duran, Pedrito Martínez, Daymar Calvario, Manuel Alejandro Carro, Jorge Bringas, Lisandro and Igor Arias, Lino Fernández, David Oquendo, Yuniel Jiménez, Julian Chang, José "Pepito" Gómez, and many others who continue to arrive.[3]

Recording studios, such as those owned by the musicians/engineers Guido Díaz, Juan Wust, Julio "Chino" Moreno, and others, have produced albums for some of the biggest names in Latin music.[4] This chapter will focus primarily on the area of West New York, Union City, and North Bergen, which has served as a major focal point for a variety of Cuban genres including Afro-Cuban religious music (*santería* and *palo*) and secular music such as *rumba, punto guajiro/música campesina, son montuno*, and *charanga*.

## A Brief History of the Cuban Community of Hudson County

Cubans first started settling in Union City in the 1940s and 1950s and tended to come from the small town of Fomento and other nearby parts of Villa Clara, the present day province of Las Villas.[5] One family in particular, the Rodríguezes, had visited Miami during their honeymoon in 1949 and were invited to come visit Union City by Florence Colarusso, a woman the couple had met in Miami; finding success, many of the couple's friends and family followed them from Fomento to New Jersey.[6] Prieto points out that subsequent Cuban refugees came from Villa Clara in greater numbers than from Havana even after the revolution, which further confirms "a chain migration effect."[7]

During the 1950s, Fidel Castro visited the Cuban community of Union City, which supported his struggle to overthrow the Batista government.[8] Looking at musical programs from the late 1950s and as late as 1960, there are many Cuban social clubs and businesses that supported and advertised in events that championed the new government. One such event in Manhattan, a social dance for the Coronacíon de la Reina de la Reforma agraria cubana en los Estados Unidos y Sus Damas (Coronation of the Queen of the Cuban Agrarian Reform in the United States and her Court), was sponsored by Cuban American businesses, civic and political groups from Bridgeport, Connecticut, Newark and Passaic, New Jersey, and New York as well as the Cuban Consul in New York.[9]

With a massive influx of Cubans arriving after the Cuban Revolution, the total population of Cubans in Union City and West New York was 33,000.[10] Cuban refugees from the Mariel boatlift in 1980 brought the Cuban population to 45,719.[11] The *balseros* (Cuban rafters) of the early 1990s brough more Cubans to Hudson County while others from Union City and West New York moved to neighboring Bergen County. In addition, there were communities previously established in Elizabeth and Newark.

The generation of Cubans who arrived before the revolution had established bodegas, a travel agency, and a social club, El Liceo Cubano, which also served to help subsequent arrivals.[12] By the 1970s and 1980s, the community in and around Bergenline Avenue had expanded to include: "Cuban doctors, lawyers, engineers, public accountants, and piano, arts, and dance academias or schools.... Among the typical businesses were supermarkets, bakeries, restaurants, clothing stores, jewelry stores, travel agencies, florists, pharmacies, cigar manufacturers, and construction companies."[13] This is when the Cuban music scene had its greatest moments until it declined after the 1990s along with the larger Cuban population. As the Cuban population aged, many left for other parts of New Jersey or Florida. In addition, large numbers of Central American, Dominican, and Puerto Rican arrivals settled in the community and their musical tastes differed from their Cuban neighbors.

Other important social clubs that sponsored musical events were affiliated with particular towns and municipalities in Cuba like Camajuaní, Caibarién, Sancti Spiritus, and Güines, as well as El Club Amigos e Hijos de Fomento.[14] The social club Tertulias de Antaño offered "counseling and social activities" for seniors such as annual dances that hired many local Cuban musicians.[15] Similarly, the Cuban Lions club, the Masonic Lodge, and the National Association of Cuban American Women of New Jersey also sponsored dances and banquets with live musical performances by numerous local Cuban bands.

## Early Recordings of Cuban Music in New Jersey: Sexteto Habanero and Trio Matamoros

Among the first known activities of Cuban music in New Jersey are the recordings made by El Sexteto Habanero and El Trio Matamoros in Camden. El Sexteto Habanero traveled from Havana on Friday, August 27, 1926, arrived in New York aboard the SS *Metapan* on August 31, 1926, and after checking into the Hotel Pennsylvania, "they board a train for an hour and a half to Newark, New Jersey and then Camden, New Jersey to be the first Cuban on Sextet to record electronically outside of Cuba, [recording] 12 sones for RCA Victor."[16]

Cuban son was an important source for much of the Latin music that was to be performed and recorded subsequently in New York and the United States, but these sessions also demonstrate how Cuban and other Latin American and Caribbean music was recorded in the New York and New Jersey area before ever being recorded in the countries of origin.[17] An expert in Cuban *sextetos*, Michael Avalos believes that the studio quality was potentially superior to the New York locales as evidenced by these recordings.[18] Less than two years later, in May 1928, another important Cuban musical group, El Trío Matamoros, also recorded in Camden, New Jersey, songs that are still performed to this day.[19] Thus, the early arrival of these two iconic exponents of Cuba's national musical genre, the son, demonstrates the long-standing connection between the cutting edge of Cuban musical performance and the Garden State.

## The Performance of Cuban Music in New Jersey before and after the Cuban Revolution

These recordings were not the only Cuban musical activities that took place in New Jersey before the large influx of Cubans. A review of English-language newspaper advertisements and articles from before 1959 shows a significant number of performances by other internationally known Cuban musicians, in addition to frequent coverage of Cuban music and culture. What follows is a snapshot of this coverage.

In the 1930s, a number of bands performed throughout New Jersey as well as on local radio broadcasts. Around May 26, 1931, the Hermanos Castro Orchestra accompanied the American dance team of David and Hilda Murray at the Regent Theater.[20] Antobal's Cubans performed live at 8:30 p.m. on July 15, 1933, for Asbury Park-area listeners of radio station WEAF.[21] On May 26, 1933, the Delta Phi Fraternity sponsored a supper dance at Ben Mardin's Riviera featuring Don Carlos and his marimba band.[22] Interestingly, an April 3, 1936, article about Afro-Cuban *ñanigos*, associated with the all-male *abakuá* secret society, appeared in the *Central New Jersey Home News* of New Brunswick, New Jersey, on April 3, 1936, portending performances of abakuá music and dance at La Esquina Habanera in Union City that would take place more than sixty years later.[23] Finally, an article from the *Keansburg News* on May 20, 1938, interviews José Negret about his performance with The Havana Stars (Las Estrellas de Habana) at the Rhumba Bar on the Keansburg boardwalk. Negret explains: The essence of dancing is rhythm which explains why, after a number of years of scattered popularity, the rhumba is fast becoming the great dancing vogue of the United States. For rhythm is the very soul of rhumba. Dancers who have difficulty following the timing of other music find it easy to keep in step with the rhumbas [sic] rhythmic beat, the steps of the ballroom form of the rhumba are not intricate. However, dancers feel a lost-in-the-rhythm sensation which many say surpasses that of all other dances."[24] Beginning in the 1920s, when the son was exported from Cuba and performed internationally it was labeled rhumba or rumba. Negret's description of his music actually refers to the son and not rumba which is played with three drums, claves, and *guaguá* (a wooden block or cylinder percussed with two sticks). Rumba was not marketed as rumba until the 1940s and 1950s. Almost sixty years later, Afro-Cuban rumba would also be the featured music on Sunday nights at La Esquina Habanera, Las Palmas, and other Union City venues in the late 1990s and beyond.

New Jersey newspapers in the 1940s showed more local Cuban musical activity including lectures on music as well as numerous summer performances. On Wednesday, February 24, Pedro Sanjuan, the Spanish composer and founder of the Havana Philharmonic Orchestra gave a lecture in Spanish on Cuban music at the New Jersey College for Women that was sponsored by the Círculo

FIGURE 9.1 *From left to right*: José Curbelo Sr. (kneeling bottom left, bass and violin), Mechita Verella (left of José Curbello), José Curbelo (standing, piano, director), Carl Orich (right of Curbelo, saxophone), Tito Rodríguez (third from right, vocals), Ben Pickering (smiling with eyes closed behind Tito Rodríguez, trumpet), Irwin Applebaum (right of Tito Rodríguez, trumpet). (Courtesy of the Cuban Heritage Collection, University of Miami Libraries, Coral Gables, Florida.)

Español on Gibbons campus.[25] In July 1944, Mario and Vincio performed "Spanish and Cuban music" at Ellinson's Café on Broadway in Long Branch.[26] Throughout July 1945, José Curbelo and "His Society Music featuring the Dynamic Marga" performed nightly at Ross Fenton Farm in Asbury Park.[27] In the summer of 1949, Curbelo and other performers such as Bobby Escoto, Mechita, Arturo, and Rodrigo Arturos also performed for dancers at the West End casino on Ocean Avenue, West End, and at the Stockton Hotel, Sea Girt.[28]

Throughout the 1950s, Cuban music continued to have a strong presence. Local press coverage continued to reflect its consumption by a largely non-Cuban and non-Latino audience. This coincides with the general trend of Latin music being embraced and consumed by non-Latino dancers in the New York area at the time. This also meant that the bands performing Cuban music were often made up of Cubans and/or Puerto Ricans, as well as musicians from other ethnic groups. A February 17, 1950, advertisement for Club Scandia in Garwood, New Jersey, demonstrates this in announcing "Prince (Stoney) Martin, the Cuban dancer, [with] music by Pat DiFabio and his Kings of Rhythm."[29] Interestingly, Cuban composers had press coverage in mainstream non-Latino newspapers further demonstrating the appeal and influence of Cuban music in New Jersey. The death of Cuban composer Eliseo Grenet was announced in the *Central New Jersey Home News* on Sunday, November 5, 1950.[30] A November 18, 1950, article from *The Record* of Hackensack, New Jersey, discusses Gilberto Valdés as being named composer of the year by the American Friends of Latin Music.[31] Valdés's score for Katherine Dunham's Broadway show *Bal Negre* is mentioned as is the fact that he was living at 2 East Park Place in Rutherford, New Jersey.[32] The Puerto Rican bandleader, Pupi Campo, was quite active in the 1950s and he and his "rumbas" are advertised performing at the gala opening of Bill Miller's Riviera on May 1, 1951, "at the foot of the George Washington Bridge" in Fort Lee, New Jersey.[33] Campo is also listed as performing on the same bill as Sammy Davis, Jr. and others at the Riviera, Thursday, July 16, 1953.[34] Finally, *The Record* also announced a performance by Campo at the Paramount Theatre in New York City.[35] The *Montclair Times* informs readers that "a Cuban music festival will be televised from Havana as the first 'live' pickup from outside the continent. TV signals will be beamed to an airplane circling midway between Havana and Miami for transmission to the NBC network telecast—November 13th."[36] And, on August 7, 1954, *The Record* reprinted a feature article from the *Saturday Review* all about Pérez Prado and his performance at the Waldorf-Astoria.[37] Thus, frequent and widespread non-Latin press coverage of Cuban composers and performers, as well as didactic events in local New Jersey newspapers prior to the major influx of Cubans post-1959 demonstrates how mainstream Cuban music had already become and how this set the stage for what came next.

After the Cuban Revolution (1959) coverage of Cuban music in New Jersey's English-language print media expanded. In the 1960s the coverage shifted from non-Cuban to Cuban performers. In August 1960, the Teaneck Jazz Festival featured a concert by Chuck Miesmer's Afro-American Drum Sextet, which "specializes in Afro-Cuban music."[38] A program of Cuban music with a lecture by Dr. Gracella Campos and a performance by musicians was offered by "The Women's Association of the Presbyterian Church in Berry Hall" as announced in the *Millville Daily* on Saturday, April 14, 1962.[39] In July 1962, the Jamaican drummer, Montego Joe, played and spoke about the *bongó* and Cuban music to a crowd of young people at the First Reformed Church in Ridgewood, New Jersey.[40] A 1963 article on recent recordings of Latin music covered Machito, Tito Puente, Mauricio Smith, and Frank Anderson, among others in *The News*.[41]

By the mid-1960s, the shift to covering locally based Cuban performers was complete. Xavier Cugat's television performance on Saturday, September 25, 1965, was listed in the *Morning Call*.[42] Mongo Santamaria's performance at the Second Quaker City Jazz Festival was announced in the *Courier Post* on Friday, September 15, 1967.[43] The death of Fernando Ortiz, the founding father of Cuban folklore studies was announced in the *Central New Jersey Home News* on Friday, April 11, 1969.[44] José Ignacio Lanza's programs were listed in the *Daily Journal* on Saturday, April 12, 1969.[45] A June 22, 1969, article about Rutgers receiving money from the Ford Foundation to "make possible the taping of the outstanding collection of Afro-American and Afro-Cuban music" at the Jazz Institute ran in the *Central New Jersey Home News*.[46]

In the 1970s, New Jersey news coverage of Cuban musicians included pieces about long-established performers as well as newcomers. A performance by Mongo Santamaria and his quintet at Branch Brook Park in Newark was announced on Saturday, August 14, 1971, in *The News*.[47] The actual concert took place on Sunday, August 15, 1971, and performances by Mongo Santamaria, Chico O'Farrill, and others were reviewed.[48] The *Asbury Park Press* ran a listing for Mongo Santamaria at the Rainbow Grill on Sunday, July 2, 1972.[49] A radio "program of Cuban music both traditional and popular" on WBAI was listed in *The Record* on Tuesday, August 1, 1972.[50] The March 9, 1974, television listings in the *Courier-News* listed a program "Rachel, La Cubana, Opera story of beautiful exciting Cuban music hall star."[51] "An Evening with Machito and Graciela" was announced in the November 17, 1974, television listings of *The Record*.[52] The *Asbury Park Press* ran an article about the history and roots of salsa that included comments from Cuban singer and composer Rudy Calzado, June 27, 1976.[53] Journalist John Curley wrote about the difficulty in presenting Latin music in Paterson, New Jersey, when he covered Mongo Santamaria's upcoming concert as well as others promoted by Angelo Jordan in the *Morning News* on Friday, April 28, 1978.[54] On Wednesday, August 30, Tito Puente and Machito played a concert at the Meadowlands Family Fair as announced in the *Ridgewood News*.[55]

Around this time Irakere, one of the most important and long-lasting groups in postrevolutionary Cuba, performed at the Capitol Theatre in Passaic on March 23, 1979, as part of a thirty-city U.S. tour, which was filmed by CBS Records, ultimately earning them a Grammy award.[56] In December 1980, the *Central New Jersey Home News* also covered the new season of the New Jersey public television program *Imágenes Latinas*, which included a show dedicated to the Newark-based charanga group, Charanga Casino.[57] Rutgers hosted a concert by Machito and his orchestra on April 10, 1979, as well as a lecture by musicologist Isabelle Ortiz on "the origins and development of Afro-Cuban music" on April 12, 1979.[58] On Friday, February 22, 1980, the *Courier Post* in Camden, New Jersey, ran an article on musical happenings in Atlantic City with a photo of Mongo Santamaria who was playing at Billy's Pub in the Park Place Hotel.[59] The *Daily Register* had a listing for Santamaria, "a major exponent of authentic Afro-Cuban music," performing at Club Bene in Sayreville on Friday, August 29, 1980.[60] The *Herald-News* announced an outdoor concert at Rutgers by Machito on October 4, 1980.[61] The same paper offered a review of Machito's concert on October 7, 1980, while announcing performances by Nosotros and Son de la Loma.[62] Mongo Santamaria continued to perform in New Jersey later in his career as seen in an announcement for an engagement at Newark Symphony Hall at the end of February 1988.[63]

In the 1970s and 1980s different facets of Cuban music were covered in local English-language media and Cuban performers can be seen enjoying high profile performance opportunities in non-Cuban and non-Latin venues. This coverage included articles about lectures on Cuban music, interviews with musicians, reviews of concerts, and announcements of performances. However, the prevalence of Cuban music press coverage in English-language media does not reveal fully what was happening in the Cuban community. One must explore the Spanish-language press for a deeper understanding.

## Cuban Music on "the Strip": Bergenline and Beyond

Between the 1960s and the 1980s local and internationally known performers were active in the clubs in and around Bergenline Avenue known locally as "the strip"; Spanish-language newspaper advertisements from the 1970s show a lively and dynamic scene that featured Cuban music and catered largely to a Cuban audience. This is distinct from venues in New York City, which aimed to bring audiences of all types. The strip of clubs ran roughly from Thirty-Second to Forty-Eighth Street, but there were additional venues nearby.[64] A who's who of iconic musicians who had well-established careers in Cuba and who were internationally known gave nightly performances at these venues. Guitarist Benny Díaz can be seen in advertisements from many different venues before he and others began performing regularly at his own club, Mi Guitarra, located at 4809 Bergenline Avenue.[65]

Mariana Merceron, Facundo Rivero, Tony García (piano), Kike ("the king of the maracas"), and others performed regularly at El Pavo (1313 Summit Avenue).[66] In January 1979, Catalino's Steakhouse (4319 Bergenline Avenue) featured vocalist Vicentico Valdés and would also have regular performances by Gladys Ibañez "El bombón cubano" and weekly appearances by the composer/musician Arty Valdés.[67] Ibañez was married to Guillermo Azcuy, the owner of the Broadway Sandwich Shop (Fifty-First Street and Broadway). When they moved the business to another location, Azcuy partnered with famed Chilean vocalist Lucho Gatica to open a venue upstairs called La Terraza (Forty-Fifth and Broadway), which featured regular live performances of Cuban music. La India de Oriente also performed Friday to Sunday for the month of December at Catalino's in 1981.[68] The bassist Lázaro Prieto, best known for his work with Arsenio Rodríguez, is listed as the musical director for the vocalist Kristian's performances at Catalino's.[69]

In another advertisement, Georgina Granados is listed as the headlining act for the grand reopening of Catalino's also with Lázaro Prieto handling the musical direction.[70] Nico Membiela, Tongolele, and her musical accompanist Joaquin, the *conguero*, performed at El Nuevo Kibú Night Club (3331 Palisade Avenue).[71] El Nuevo Kibú also featured the vocalist Orlando Contreras and the duo Mayra y Silvio.[72] The Habana Madrid (Bergenline and Seventy-First Street) was another venue that featured regular shows with Rolando Martín, María Magdalena, and Arty Valdés.[73] The Cuban American vedette, Ruby Sandrell, who left Marianao at the age of eight years and attended New Jersey public schools, also performed regularly at the Habana Madrid.[74] Cine Tony (1212 Summit Avenue), a local movie theater in Union City, also featured live musical performances, such as those following the showing of the film *La Cuba del ayer*, sponsored by the Colegio Nacional de Periodistas Cubanos (Exilio) Delegación de New Jersey.[75] La Choza (Bergenline and Fourteenth Street) featured the Hermanas Cano Combo, vocalist/percussionist Virgilio Martí, and Orlando Contreras "La voz romántica de Cuba" performing throughout May 1977.[76] Vocalist Alby Feliz performed at Club 38.[77] Vocalist and bandleader, Ernest "Chico" Álvarez, was a local resident from 1967–1977 and from 1980 on, who remembers live Cuban music at venues such as El Reloj (Twenty-Ninth Street and Bergenline), La Barraca (not the one in Manhattan), Le Frisón (Forty-Second and West Street), La Roca (Twenty-Second and West), El Mesón Español (Fifty-Seventh and John F. Kennedy Boulevard), La Milonga (4535 Bergenline Avenue), La Terraza (second floor of Broadway Sandwich Shop, Forty-Fifth and Broadway), a solo pianist who performed at El Palacio de Los Batidos (Forty-Eighth and Broadway), and music at Zelva Club (Manhattan Avenue in Hoboken).[78] Bandleader Felipe "Pipo" Martínez recalled live Cuban music at the Continental Pavillion (Manhattan Avenue), Royal Crest (Twenty-Third Street and West Street), Hudson Hall (Hudson between Sixtieth and Sixty-First), the Masonic Lodge (Forty-Seventh Street and Bergenline), Mi Bandera (Thirty-Second and Bergenline), El Elegante (Fairview, New Jersey), Los Violines, Embassy Hall, Park Theater, Saint Rocco's, and La Casa Gallega.[79]

There was really no limit to the quality of musicians who performed on the Bergenline strip. The strip was unique because there was no comparable area that had such a high concentration of venues in close proximity. Non-Cubans patronized these establishments, but the artistic direction was decidedly Cuban and not presented in advertising as salsa or pan-Latin music. There was a notable number of female performers in this scene. The vocalist Rita Elena led groups in the 1970s and there was a mostly female Cuban son group that was active in the late 1970s and early 1980s called Orquesta Camajuaní.[80] In an interview for the Smithsonian with Raúl Fernández, the legendary Cuban bassist and composer Israel "Cachao" López recalled that he played in a quartet with Charlie Palmieri, Miguelito Valdés, and Tito Puente that would play regularly in New Jersey in the early 1960s.[81]

Numerous Cuban artists including Hilda Lee, José Fajardo, Angelo Vaillant, Los Kimy, and others performed at a variety of large public events in Schuetzen Park (3167 John F. Kennedy Boulevard) that catered to Cuban audiences including the Cuban Festival.[82] According to an article in *La Tribuna*, close to one thousand people joined the Association of Sons and Daughters of Regla in Schuetzen Park to dance to the *comparsa* group, Los Guaracheros.[83] Lastly, the Mad Bull was another venue that frequently featured Cuban charanga groups. In sum, Cuban music was everywhere in Hudson County, even seen in advertisements with musical notation and lyrics for local businesses such as

Nino and Braulio's Palisade Furniture Warehouse (5505 Palisade Avenue) in West New York.[84]

The focus on Cuban performers and audiences was unique to New Jersey. There was nothing comparable in New York City largely because of the numbers of Cubans in New Jersey compared to the numbers of Puerto Ricans, Dominicans, and other groups in New York City. This is not to say that there was no interethnic collaboration in the New Jersey scene but Cuban music in New Jersey was not marketed as salsa by the performers and the venues during this time. Meanwhile, salsa music and bands were exploding across the river in New York City and beyond.

While the Bergenline strip may have been the local center of the Cuban musical universe at one time, there were a number of venues beyond Hudson County in Newark and Elizabeth that also featured Cuban music and catered to the local Cuban communities. Conjunto Caribe performed regularly at the Capri Night Club (511 Elizabeth Avenue) in Elizabeth, New Jersey.[85] The Capri also hosted Virginia Blanco another vedette, accompanied by Conjunto Caribe.[86] Charanga 76 and Orquesta Fantasy played the Baile de Las Flores, the coronation of the queen and her court sponsored by the Cuban Lions Club of Newark, which was held at the Salones de Singer in Elizabeth, New Jersey, on May 21, 1977.[87] Rosendo Rosell and Anibal del Mar performed at the Liberty Theater also in Elizabeth.[88]

In Newark Xonia y Oscar performed regularly at the Olde Office Lounge (Twenty-Two Wilson Avenue) and the Living Room (Jackson and Clover Street) hosted Conjunto Los Azabaches.[89] Newark was also home to the Latin Grammy-winning Cuban composer José "Chein" Dámaso García (1953–2014) who "wrote hit songs for the Latin market such as 'Bailando', 'Tu me vuelves loco', and 'Experiencia religiosa' performed by Enrique Iglesisas, Jose Feliciano, Boys II Men, Thalia, and Carlos Santana."[90] Finally, Ñico Membiela "La voz del recuerdo" performed at El Liborio Restaurant in Union, NJ and Grupo Caribe performed regularly at Fandango (1664 Stuyvesant Street) in Union, NJ.[91]

Considering the aforementioned vitality of the Cuban music scene in New Jersey, it is worth looking at specific protagonists who made important contributions as pioneers, mentors, and local success stories. These musicians are seldom recollected in written histories of Latin music in the United States despite their standing in the local Cuban community of Hudson County and their active performance and recording careers.

## A Family of Cuban Bands Based in New Jersey, 1960s–1990s

While the internationally known Cuban composer Osvaldo Farrés made his home in New Jersey along with Celia Cruz and other superstars,[92] the local New Jersey scene served as an incubator for young Cuban-born and Cuban American performers, most of whom had come from Cuba as young children or young adults.[93] One of the earliest groups formed in Union City was the Jersey Cuban

FIGURE 9.2 Advertisement from *La Tribuna* for Clubs on the Bergenline strip.

FIGURE 9.3 Advertisement from *La Tribuna* for Clubs on the Bergenline strip.

FIGURE 9.4 Advertisement from *La Tribuna* for Clubs on the Bergenline strip.

FIGURE 9.5 Advertisements from *La Tribuna* for Clubs on the Bergenline strip.

Boys. Led by the Matanzas-born Jorge "Papito" Sánchez (1949–), a former child singing sensation who performed all over Cuba at the age of five years, the group came together in the mid-1960s and performed in New Jersey and New York. They shared bills with Joe Cuba, Pete Rodríguez, Joselito, and many Mexican artists at New York City venues such as El Teatro Puerto Rico, Manhattan Center, and the Cheetah until their split in 1966.[94] After the split, one of the bandmembers, trumpeter Omar Junco, formed another group called Havana Brass, which included some members of the Jersey Cuban Boys. When Junco, a U.S. Army reservist, was called to Germany, the members of Havana Brass staged a mutiny and formed Orquesta Riviera. The band recorded three albums. The first featured vocalist Frank Hernan and Puerto Rican cuatro virtuoso Yomo Toro (1970), Manolo Vega held the vocal chair on the second album (1974), and Baby González was the vocalist on the third album (1975).[95] Eventually Orquesta Riviera would be led by Lázaro "Orlando" Espinosa and Leonardo Freide, and featured Roberto Lugo as the lead vocalist. In the 1980s, Espinosa would go on to form Charanga Kreación with Jorge González. The band got its name from the fact that González used a synthesizer keyboard instead of a violin section, it was *una creación* (creation).[96]

When Omar Junco returned from Germany, he formed the big band Casino International, which served as a training ground for generations of musicians in the area. Born in Matanzas, Omar Domingo Junco (1934–2014) joined the Eighty-Second Airborne as a paratrooper in the 1950s. A contractor who did roofing and siding by day, he served as a father figure for many young musicians. He would take players from local high schools like Memorial, Union Hill, and North Bergen and recruit them to play in his big band performing throughout the state at all kinds of venues: quinceañeras, weddings, and private events. Many musicians such as Junco's protégé Waldo Fernández—who led his own group, Conjunto Son Moderno—Oscar Oñoz, Marcos Quintanilla, Robert "Duffy" Mier (leader of Conjunto Crema), Freddy Luciano, George Rivas, Albert Fernández, Mark and Jeffrey López, Leonel "Papo" Ortega, and others would go on to work with Mark Anthony, Celia Cruz, Tito Puente, and other artists.[97] A man with a big heart and a penchant for show business, Junco performed under the name Omar de Junco and wore an Elvis Presley wig during live performances. Since he loved Lawrence Welk and Benny Moré he had music stands made with the initials CI for Casino International.[98] Junco's daughter Mimi vividly remembers that the young band members wore pink polyester suits with bow ties as well as pastel pink, blue, mint green, and canary yellow tuxedos, rumba jackets with gold sequined sleeves, and yellow mustard pants with bright blue belts. Many of these were purchased at discount and were out of style for at least ten years, if not more, when the band wore them at performances.[99] For trumpeter Oscar Oñoz, "people would be laughing at the clothes that we were wearing, green and dark brown tuxedos, [but] you joined that band, [and] you learned all the styles. We played big band charts: mambo, son, pasodobles, boleros, merengue and each gig paid $25–30."[100] The band lasted twenty-five years and its impact and legacy for Cuban music in New Jersey and beyond remains important and largely overlooked.

Two other bands and musicians who moved between them came out of this scene in the 1970s. The first was Orquesta Realidad and the second was Orquesta Zodiacal led by vocalist Pancho Hernández, known locally as Pancho Mangos. Another important band from this era was Charanga 76 led by Felipe "Pipo" Martínez, which featured the flute player Andrea Brachfeld and the vocalists Hansel and Raúl. Additionally, the Cuban percussionists Ignacio Berroa, Gabriel "Chinchilita" Machado, and Ángel "Mandarria" Pérez performed regularly in New Jersey as members of La Típica Novel. The group even traveled to perform for Cubans who lived in Cuba and still worked at the U.S. Naval Base in Guantánamo, Cuba, with the flautist Nestor Torres around 1982.[101]

The bandleader, vocalist, and graphic artist, Chico Álvarez, also performed on the strip and released a number of recordings.[102] Finally, the group Los Jimaguas, centered around the twin brother percussionists Freddy and Santi Nieto, featured the vocalist and barber Mariano Sánchez who had been the former singer of Gloria Matancera in Cuba.[103] When Los Jimaguas broke up Lázaro "Orlando" Espinosa and other musicians joined forces with the brothers to form Orquesta Zodiacal.

FIGURE 9.6   On the boat to Guantánamo: *left to right*, Eddie Drennon (violin), Nestor Torres (yellow jacket), Gabriel Machado (percussion), Willy Ellis (piano), Ángel Pérez. (Courtesy of Gabriel Machado.)

FIGURE 9.7 U.S. soldiers with Gabriel Machado, Alberto González (vocals), Ángel Pérez, Victor Gallo (Fania Records), Alfredo Goykuria (bass, kneeling), Gerónimo González (violin), Marco Motroni (director/vocals, with knife). (Courtesy of Lazaro "Orlando" Espinoza.)

FIGURE 9.8 Gabriel Machado and Ángel Pérez. (Courtesy of Judith "Mimi" Junco.)

FIGURE 9.9 Orquesta Riviera, 1970s. (Photo courtesy of Lázaro "Orlando el Niño" Espinosa.)

With a mix of musicians who arrived in the 1960s as well as those who came during the 1980 Mariel boatlift, alongside Puerto Ricans and musicians from other countries, the groups did not limit themselves to playing traditional music but used a variety of approaches to modernizing their sound. They performed for Cuban and non-Cuban Latin audiences. Nevertheless, as progressive as some of their music might be, they did not use the term salsa to describe their music and stuck to easily recognizable Cuban labels such as *típica*, charanga, conjunto, or *orquesta* when naming and promoting their groups. These specific labels indicated the instrumentation of the group and could also imply particular genres of Cuban music. A number of Cuban and Cuban American musicians in Hudson County also played in rock bands such as Safari and Scorpio that offered a mix of Latin music and rock akin to Carlos Santana.[104]

## Punto Guajiro/Música Campesina in Hudson County

A sizable share (32.8 percent) of the Cuban immigrant population of Union City and West New York came from Villa Clara and other rural areas.[105] In Villa Clara, Spanish-influenced cultural traditions have thrived. Musicians and *trovadores* (poets) steeped in the Cuban musical genre of punto guajiro or *música campesina* (country music) were among the many early arrivals from Villa Clara. In this style, poets improvise *décimas*, ten-line poems of eight syllables with a

FIGURE 9.10  Orquesta Zodiacal, 1970s. (Photo courtesy of Lázaro "Orlando el Niño" Espinosa.)

rhyme scheme of ABBA ACCDDC, while they are accompanied by string instruments such as the Cuban *tres*, *laúd*, and guitar, as well as light percussion such as the claves, *güiro*, and sometimes bongó. According to bandleader, Leonel "Papo" Ortega, there was a great amount of punto guajiro performed in the area starting in the 1960s particularly for community gatherings of people who arrived Villa Clara and surrounding areas.[106] He remembers his father performing at a place on Thirty-Fourth and Palisade when he was a child. Ortega's family included a number of musicians and trovadores such as his aunt Maria Julia Torres "La Londra de San José" and his uncle Sergio Sorí Brito. Ortega remembered that the first organized punto guajiro events were performed once a month at La Logia on Sixtieth Street, but also at El Recreo Bar (Hudson Avenue and Fifty-Second Street).

Another punto guajiro gathering would take place at the Park Café and was sponsored by two nonmusicians, the Caro brothers, who had a garage near the Park Café on Sixty-First and Park Avenue. Another punto guajiro trovador, Severino García "El Primo," and some of his colleagues were in the linoleum and carpet business and once a month on Sundays they would open the back of their store on Forty-Third and Bergenline to gather and play punto guajiro. These were informal but planned events for people who liked punto guajiro. They were not featured in the dance-oriented nightclubs on the Bergenline strip.

The culmination of the New Jersey punto guajiro scene was called El Parnaso Campesino and, in the 1990s, I attended some of their performances at El Cucalambé, a bar on Bergenline Avenue as well as a gathering with musicians

A Century of Cuban Music in New Jersey • 217

Una fiesta campesina en el corazón del Norte; en ocasión de la visita del Sr. Benito Díaz, padre de Divina Santana, esposa de Diosdado. Aparecen en la foto de izquierda a derecha: Rubén García, Divina Santana, Ramón Cintra, Antolín Díaz, Benito Díaz, Diosdado Santana, Ismael García, Raúl Pérez, Nery Pérez y abajo sentados: Sergio Sorí y Paco Hernández.

Poetas y músicos del Parnaso Campesino

FIGURE 9.11   El Parnaso Campesino. (Courtesy of Leonel Ortega.)

and trovadores from Miami, Puerto Rico, and New Jersey that was held once a month on Sundays at Las Palmas. El Parnaso was founded by Ortega's uncle, Sergio Sorí Brito, and Diosdado Santana Delgado, and included Marino González, Rubén García, Celestino García "El Primo," Divina Santana, Ramón Cintra, Antolíin Díaz, Benito Díaz, Ismael García, Raúl Pérez, Nery Pérez, Paco Hernández, and others.[107] Sorí and Santana would write entire letters of décimas to each other while one resided in New Jersey and the other in Miami.

A collection of their décima letters entitled *Raíces Campesinas diálogos poéticos entre: Diosdado Santana y Sergio Sorí* (Country peasant roots: poetic dialogues between Diosdado Santana and Sergio Sorí) was published in 2002. This epistolary collection covers a wide range of topics including their feelings about the terrorist attack on the World Trade Center on September 11, 2001.[108] Today, the once vibrant punto guajiro scene has largely disappeared as the trovadores and musicians associated with this scene have passed on or moved away to Florida or other parts of New Jersey.

## Rumba and Afro-Cuban Music at La Esquina Habanera

The demographics of the Cuban community in Hudson County started to change with the Mariel boatlift and the arrival of the balseros in the early 1990s and with it the musical styles.[109] Those migrants brought the latest Cuban musical information and the most accurate Afro-Cuban ritual practice to the Northeast.[110] The more established Cuban community reached out to help the Mariel refugees. With this wave there was an influx of Afro-Cubans when the population of Cubans of color in New Jersey had previously been considerably small compared to White Cubans. Prieto indicates that prior to 1980, "only 1.9% were non-white in Union City and West New York."[111] Nancy Raquel Mirabál notes that, "The recent migrations of Afro-Cubans again reconfigured a language of race, sexuality, culture, and gender that was not always understood or employed and among community making Cuban exiles."[112]

A large number of musicians arrived as part of the Mariel boatlift of 1979 including Regino Tellechea, Daniel Ponce, Felipe García Villamil, Ignacio Berroa, Roberto Borrell, Orlando "Puntilla" Ríos, Geradro "Taboada" Martínez, Juan González, Fernando Lavoy, Gabriel Machado "Chinchilita," Los Kimi, and others brought new sounds and energy to the Bergenline strip.[113] Some also made contributions as educators in New Jersey and New York City.[114] Some achieved success integrating themselves into the music scene, but others had problems adjusting to the new setting.[115]

In the early 1990s, the new migratory wave of Cuban balseros (rafters), brought increased numbers of Afro-Cuban musicians who played contemporary Cuban popular musical genres such as *timba* (Cuban popular dance music of the 1990s) and another group of rumberos and ritual drummers. In March 1996, a Cuban restaurant on Summit Avenue and Fourteenth Street called La Esquina Habanera began to feature weekly rumba performances on Sunday nights as well as Afro-Cuban ritual music.[116] A number of scholars such as Berta Jottar and Lisa Maya Knauer have written extensively about the scene, interactions between Cubans and non-Cuban rumberos and ritual drummers, and even made documentaries about the protagonists.[117] During this time I attended a performance dedicated to *abakúa* music and dance performed by Pedrito Martínez, Román Díaz, and other musicians, as well as other events dedicated to Santa Barbara/

Changó and other orishas. Although the scene at La Esquina Habanera was covered in the press, documentaries, and other media, the venue was much more than a popular Cuban music venue that enjoyed popularity well after the heyday of clubs profiled earlier during the first wave of migration. As the Grammy-nominated musician David Oquendo explained to Yolando Prieto:

> There is no other place like La Esquina Habanera. When I met Tony Zequeira (the owner), I said to him, "we have to do something, we have to open up a place where we can promote the rumba. We have to transmit our cultural roots to Cubans in the United States. I am not a businessman, I am a musician, but if you want to go along with the idea, let's start this club." Tony agreed, and it's been three years already! We have a group Raíces Habaneras (Havana Roots), which plays wonderful music there. When new musicians come from Cuba, they visit this place and immediately feel at home. The rumba was always discriminated against in Cuba, even now. It was the music of poor people, of black Cubans. Not many people valued it. For that reason, our job is to educate Cubans here to appreciate the rumba, which is the mother of all Cuban rhythms.[118]

Oquendo and Raíces Habaneras would eventually record an album that was nominated for a Latin Grammy award in 2003.[119]

This shift in musical focus, from son and punto guajiro to rumba, Afro-Cuban ritual music, and timba was the next iteration of some of the processes that Christina Abreu discusses in her book on music and race among Cuban musicians in New York in the period of 1940–1960.[120] Over time, the community supporting punto guajiro has moved out of Hudson County or passed on while younger Cubans and new Cuban arrivals to Hudson County tend to support Cuban popular music and Afro-Cuban genres. There are no second-generation Cuban American musicians carrying on the tradition of punto guajiro in Hudson County. In addition, the overall numbers of Cubans in Hudson County have declined due to an influx of Central American and Dominican immigrants, changes in U.S./Cuba immigration policy, as well as gentrification. The end result is that today there is more Cuban music performed in the area of New York City than in Hudson County's glory days of Cuban music and cubanía.

## Conclusion

This overview of Cuban music in New Jersey demonstrates its presence in its multiple variations and genres since at least the 1920s, if not earlier. To this day, a variety of Cuban genres continues to be cultivated and can be heard by Cuban musicians throughout the state and beyond. However, the high concentration of Cuban musical activity and performance venues that had found a home in the densely populated area of Union City and West New York has declined significantly. Local government entities still sponsor public events with Cuban music, but they continue to decrease. The large punto guajiro scene has all but disappeared and there is no longer a dedicated space for the weekly performance of rumba that La Esquina Habanera once held.

Both of these discrete scenes provided important spaces for groups within the local Cuban community. Despite this largely Cuban patronage and musical focus, non-Cuban musicians, particularly Puerto Ricans and Dominicans, among others, participated in Cuban musical groups in New Jersey and vice versa: as has happened for over one hundred years in the Greater New York metropolitan area. Puerto Rican trovadores have even participated at punto guajiro events in New Jersey. However, much of the decrease in Cuban musical activity can be attributed to the rising cost of real estate and the Cuban American population shifting away from Hudson County, as well as the influx of new non-Cuban migrants from Latin America and the Caribbean. The flow of Cuban music in New Jersey parallels the flow of Cuban people to the region and is also bound to factors of race, identity, and economics in both Cuba and the United States. Future scholarship should examine and explore the depth and breadth of this little discussed and important site of Cuban music that is often left in the shadow of Latin music history that often focuses only on New York City.

## Notes

1 "La Lupe 'The Queen of latin Soul' en Dick Cavett Show," Accessed January 13, 2021. https://youtu.be/5wCPNvP2osg.
2 This is the central thesis of my book, *New York and the International Sound of Latin Music, 1940–1990* (Jackson: University Press of Mississippi, 2021).
3 Prior to the 1990s, New Jersey has been the home base for countless other Cuban musicians such as Celia Cruz, Fernando Lavoy, and Juan González (Los Soneros), Ernest "Chico" Álvarez Peraza, Paquito D'Rivera, El Conjunto Crema, Conjunto Son Moderno, Charanga 76, Charanga Creación, Orquesta Zodiacal, Orquesta Riviera, Orlando Contreras, Cano Sisters, Facundo Rivero, Regino Tellechea, Oscar Oñoz, Gabriel Machado, Juan Pablo Torres, and other musicians who arrived prior, during, and after the Cuban revolution. Forty-Third Street and Bergenline Avenue in West New York is also called Celia Cruz Way.
4 Cuban Dreams, *A Reunion: The New York Sessions*, Compact Disc. Pimienta/Universal Records 245360549-2, 2004. The Buena Vista Social Club even recorded an album in Wust's studio in 1998 on the same night that they performed at Carnegie Hall in 1998. Under the direction of trombonist and arranger Juan Pablo Torres, this recording featured members of the Buena Vista Social including Ibrahim Ferrer, Pio Leiva, Manuel "Guajiro" Mirabal, Orlando "Cachaito" Lopez, along with U.S.-based Cuban-born musicians such as Oscar Oñoz, Gabriel "Chinchilita" Machado, Alfredo Valdés, and Elsa Torres. I played Cuban tres on three tracks. During the week prior to this recording and the concert at Carnegie Hall, a number of the Buena Vista Social Club musicians even showed up to jam at the Hard Grove Café in Jersey City.
5 Yolanda Prieto, *The Cubans of Union City: Immigrants and Exiles in a New Jersey Community* (Philadelphia: Temple University Press, 2009), 21–22.
6 Prieto, *Cubans of Union City*, 23.

7   Prieto, *Cubans of Union City*, 28.
8   Prieto, *Cubans of Union City*.
9   Lapidus, *New York and the International Sound of Latin Music*.
10  Prieto, *Cubans of Union City*, 26.
11  Prieto, *Cubans of Union City*, 26.
12  Prieto, *Cubans of Union City*, 39–40.
13  Prieto, *Cubans of Union City*, 44–45.
14  Prieto, *Cubans of Union City*, 55.
15  Prieto, *Cubans of Union City*.
16  Ávalos, Michael. Facebook post, September 5, 2020. Text of Facebook post: Un Viernes, Agosto 27, hasta un Martes, Agosto 31 de 1926- una embarcación de 5 días- el Sexteto Habanero embarca el buque S.S. Metapan desde La Habana a Nueva York. La lista de buque alista los siguientes pasajeros: Rafael Zequeira (por supuesto, Rafael "el Picher" Hernández Zequeira, clavero), Guillermo Castillo (director y guitarrista), Carlos Godinez (tresero), Agustín Gutiérrez (bongosero), Gerardo Rivero (por supuesto, Gerardo "el Principe" Martínez Rivero, contrabajista); no viajan Felipe Neri Cabrera (maraquero) o su manager- Ángel García, residente de Calle San José 55 en La Habana- en esta embarcación. Se hospedan en el hotel más grande del mundo en ese entonces, el Hotel Pennsylvania en la Séptima Avenida entre calles 32 y 33, construido en 1919 de 22 pisos y con 2,200 habitaciones. Situado en el centro de Manhattan a cruzar la calle en la Penn Station, embarcan un tren por una hora y media hacia Newark, New Jersey y después Camden, New Jersey para ser el primer Sexteto Cubano de Sones de grabar electrónicamente fuera de Cuba, un Jueves y Viernes (2 y 3 de Septiembre de 1926), quizás la sesión más importante del Son Cubano. En el Studio #3 en Camden, New Jersey el Sexteto Habanero graba en 8 horas (1:30-4:40 de la tarde, 9:30-11:45 de la mañana, y 12:30-3:05 de la tarde) 12 Sones para la RCA Victor. Desde el Hotel Pennsylvania, los integrantes del Gran Sexteto Habanero podían coger el tren #1 hacia el Teatro Apolo en Harlem. (Foto tomada por Michael Ávalos); https://www.facebook.com/photo/?fbid=1862543230588955 &set=a.125757029108625.
17  The twelve songs recorded on these dates were "Cabo de guardia, siento un tiro" (M. Corona and G. Castillo), "Se fue" (Ernesto Lecuona), "Quisiera ser mi estrella" (Gerardo Martínez), "Tres lindas cubanas" (Guillermo Castillo), "Soy tu queta" (Sexteto Habanero), "Carmela mía" (Gerardo Martínez), "La sabia naturaleza" (Carlos Valdés Brito), "Y Tú? ¿Qué has hecho?" (Eusebio Delfín), "Andar, andar" (Ernesto Lecuona), "Galán, galán" (Guillermo Castillo), "Yo no tumbo caña" (unknown), and "Caballeros, silencio" (Guillermo Castillo).
18  Michael Ávalos, personal communication, January 21, 2021. Ávalos also points out that the Camden recordings are not as thin sounding as the first electrical recordings of a Cuban sextet done in New York in 1926. He posits that it could have been because of the position or inclusion of the trumpet.
19  The RCA recording ledger notes for Trio Matamoros at Studio #3 in Camden show that on May 28, 1928, the "Trio Composed of Miguel Matamoros, Tenor & 1st Guitar) [first voice in *largo, guia* in *montuno*], Rafael CUETO, Guitar Acc. [accompaniment] [first voice in montuno] & SIRO Rodríguez, Baritone & Claves" (second voice in largo and montuno) recorded "Promesa" (Cuban capricho), "Juramentos" (bolero), "Son de la Loma" (son) from 3:15–5:10 P.M. On May 29, they recorded "Olvido" (bolero), "Mujer celosa" (son), "El beso" (bolero), "Tito me rompió la máquina" (son), "Visiones" (capricho), and "Luz que no alumbra" (bolero) from 9:00 A.M. to 12:00 P.M. "Mata y Beby" (bolero), "Pobre bohemia" (bolero), "Mi ropa" (bolero), "Mariposita de

primavera" (habanera), and "El que siembra su maiz" (son) were recorded the same day from 1:00 P.M. to 4:15 P.M. Finally, on May 31, 1928, the trio recorded "Santiaguera" (bolero), "Regálame el ticket" (son), "Elixir de la vida" (bolero), "El voto y la muser" (bolero), "Canción triste" (criolla), and "¿Porque pasaron?" (capricho) between 9:30 A.M. and 12:30 P.M. "RCA Recording Ledger Notes for Trio Matamoros," courtesy of Michael Ávalos. Trio Matamoros, "RCA Recording Ledger Notes," May 28, 29, 31, 1926.

20 "Regent. Vaudeville," *The Morning Call* (Paterson, NJ), Tuesday, May 26, 1931, p. 18.
21 "454m-WEAF-660Kc," *Asbury Park Press* (Asbury Park, NJ), Saturday, July 15, 1933, p. 5.
22 "Delta Fraternity to Have Supper Dance," *The Morning Call* (Paterson, NJ), Friday, May 19, 1933, p. 20.
23 "Voodoo Dancers Hold Rites in Havana Streets," *Central New Jersey Home News* (New Brunswick, NJ), Friday, April 3, 1936, p. 3.
24 "Rhumba Bar Engage Havana Stars," *Keansburg News* (Keansburg, NJ), Friday, May 20, 1938, p. 7.
25 "N.J.C. Lists Lecture at Tea: Spanish Composer to Speak on Cuban Music Next Wednesday," *Central New Jersey Home News* (New Brunswick, NJ), Thursday, February 18, 1943, p. 18. Sanjuan's wife had recently joined the school's faculty.
26 "Ellinson's Café," *Daily Record* (Long Branch, NJ), Saturday, July 15, 1944, p. 1.
27 "Ross Fenton Farm, Under New Management," *Daily Record* (Long Branch, NJ), Friday, July 13, 1945, p. 12.
28 "Nightclubs," *Asbury Park Press* (Asbury Park, NJ), Saturday, July 2, 1949, p. 9.
29 "Club Scandia," *Courier-News* (Bridgewater, NJ), Friday, February 17, 1950, p. 23.
30 "Cuban Composer Dies," *Central New Jersey Home News* (New Brunswick, NJ), Sunday, November 5, 1950, p. 3.
31 "Composer of 1950," *The Record* (Hackensack, NJ), Saturday, November 18, 1950, p. 20.
32 "Composer of 1950," *The Record*, 20.
33 "Bill Miller's Riviera," *The Record* (Hackensack, NJ), Thursday, July 16, 1953, p. 29.
34 "Bill Miller's Riviera," *The Record*, 39.
35 "Paramount Theater," *The Record* (Hackensack, NJ), Friday, November 13, 1953, p. 37.
36 Ralf Hardester, "TV Today and Tomorrow," *The Montclair Times* (Montclair, NJ), Thursday, October 20, 1955, p. 21.
37 "Personality of the Week: Perez Prado," *The Record* (Hackensack, NJ), Saturday, August 7, 1954, p. 30.
38 "Hot, Cool Jazz Climaxes Teaneck Summer Series," *The Record* (Hackensack, NJ), Wednesday, August 24, 1960, p. 34.
39 "Program on Cuba," *The Millville Daily* (Millville, NJ), Saturday, April 14, 1962, p. 3.
40 "Church Swings to Jazz Tunes," *The Record* (Hackensack, NJ), Monday, July 30, 1962, p. 21.
41 "Outstanding," *The News* (Paterson, NJ) Friday, March 8, 1963, p. 17.
42 "An Evening with Xavier," *The Morning Call* (Paterson, NJ), Saturday, September 25, 1965, p. 59.
43 "2nd Quaker City Jazz Festival," Courier-Post (Camden, NJ), Friday, September 15, 1967, p. 18.
44 "Cuban Folklore Authority Dies," *Central New Jersey Home News* (New Brunswick, NJ), Friday, April 11, 1969, p. 31.
45 "Channel 47 Programs," *The Daily Journal* (Vineland, NJ), Saturday, April 12, 1969, p. 17.

46 "Rutgers Study Aided by $89.000 Ford Grant," *The Central New Jersey Home News* (New Brunswick, NJ), Sunday, June 22, 1969, p. 14.
47 "Highlights, Concerts," *The News* (Paterson, NJ), Saturday, August 14, 1971, p. 12.
48 "Concert with a Latin Beat," *The Herald-News* (Passaic, NJ), Friday, August 13, 1971, p. 8.
49 "Mongo Santamaria," *Asbury Park Press* (Asbury Park, NJ), Sunday, July 2, 1972, p. 73.
50 "WBAI Announcement," *The Record* (Hackensack, NJ), Monday, August 1, 1972, p. 12.
51 "10:30," *The Courier-News* (Bridgewater, NJ), Saturday, March 9, 1974, p. 27.
52 "Television Listing," *The Record* (Hackensack, NJ), Sunday, November 17, 1974, p. 148.
53 Augustin Gurza, "Latin Music Surges Out of Nowhere," Asbury Park Press (Asbury Park, NJ), Sunday, June 27, 1976, p. 53.
54 John Curley, "Paterson Armory: It's Music to People Who Count," *Morning News* (Paterson, NJ), Friday, April 28, 1978, p. 1.
55 "Meadowlands Family Fair," *The Ridgewood News* (Ridgewood, NJ), Sunday, August 27, 1978, p. 88.
56 "Irakere—Full Concert—03/23/79—Capitol Theatre (Official)," accessed March 2, 2021, https://youtu.be/VapQAWxEGzo.
57 "'Imagenes' Begins New Season," *Central New Jersey Home News* (New Brunswick, NJ), Sunday, December 21, 1980, p. 86. The same story was also run as "Imagenes Latines [*sic*] to Begin on Dec. 21," *Asbury Park Press* (Asbury Park, NJ), Wednesday, December 10, 1980, p. 46.
58 "Dead Jazz Musician Honored with Series," *Asbury Park Press* (Asbury Park, NJ), Thursday, February 22, 1979, p. 71. Ortiz "Lecture" *Courier-News* (Bridgewater, NJ), Tuesday, April 10, 1979, p. 16.
59 "Get Hot in Atlantic City," *Courier-Post* (Camden, NJ), Friday, February 22, 1980, p. 48.
60 "Mongo Santamaria at Bene," *The Daily Register* (Red Bank, NJ), Friday, August 29, 1980 p. 14.
61 "Machito and His Orchestra," *The Herald-News* (Passaic, NJ), Friday, October 3, 1980, p. 34.
62 "Machito's Jazz Opens Hispanic Culture Fest," *The Central New Jersey Home News* (New Brunswick, NJ), Tuesday, October 7, 1980, p. 10.
63 "Entertainment Calendar," *The Central New Jersey Home News* (New Brunswick, NJ), Sunday, February 21, 1988, p. 60.
64 Ernest "Chico" Álvarez, personal communication, December 31, 2020.
65 "Mi guitarra," advertisement, *La Tribuna*, April 19, 1986, p. 18.
66 "Pavo Nightclub," advertisement, *La Tribuna*, August 5, 1977, p. 38.
67 "Catalino's Steakhouse," advertisement, *La Tribuna*, August 5, 1977, p. 38; "Catalino's Steakhouse," *La Tribuna*, January 5, 1979, 31. After an introduction by pianist Facundo Rivera, Ibañez can be seen dancing to the musical accompaniment of Virgilio Martí in the Álvarez Guedes film *Bla, bla, bla . . .* (1978).
68 "Catalino's Steakhouse," advertisement, *La Tribuna*, December 20, 1981, p. 22.
69 "Catalino's Steakhouse," advertisement, *La Tribuna*, April 20, 1982, p. 17.
70 "Catalino's Steakhouse," advertisement, *La Tribuna*, February 20, 1982, p. 17.
71 "El Nuevo Kibú," advertisement, *La Tribuna*, April 20, 1982, p. 16.
72 "El Nuevo Kibú," advertisement, *La Tribuna*, February 20, 1982, p. 16.
73 "The Habana Madrid," *La Tribuna*, May 5, 1977, p. 41.
74 Emilio Santana, "Recorriendo Bergenline," *La Tribuna*, April 20, 1977, p. 14.

75 "Gran Show Artístico Musical, Cine Tony," *La Tribuna*, April 20, 1977, p. 35.
76 "La Choza Bar Night Club," *La Tribuna*, April 20, 1977, p. 39. The Cano Sisters were both active musicians in Havana's female band scene that took place at the Aires Libres. See Patrick Dalmace, "Orquesta Renovación," accessed March 10, 2021, https://www.montunocubano.com/Tumbao/biogroupes/renovaction,%20orquesta,.htm.
77 "Arte y espectáculos en 'La Tribuna'," *La Tribuna*, December 20, 1983, p. 18.
78 Ernest "Chico" Álvarez, personal communication, December 31, 2020.
79 Felipe "Pipo" Martínez, personal communication, January 4–6, 2021.
80 Felipe "Pipo" Martínez, personal communication, September 11, 2021; Julio "Chino" Moreno, personal communication, September 15, 2022.
81 Raúl A. Fernández, *From Afro-Cuban Rhythms to Latin Jazz*, (Berkeley: University of California Press, 2006), 79.
82 "Festival Cubano," *La Tribuna*, April 19, 1986, p. 26; Benjamin Lapidus, "Chinita Linda: Portrayals of Chinese and Asian Identity and Culture by Chinese and non-Chinese in Spanish Caribbean Dance Music." *Chinese America: History and Perspective, Journal of the Chinese Historical Society of America* (2015): 17–28.
83 "Encuentro reglano en El Schuetzen Park," *La Tribuna*, April 20, 1982, p. 17.
84 "Nino and Braulio's Palisade Furniture Warehouse," *La Tribuna*, April 19, 1986, 34.
85 "Capri Night Club," *La Tribuna*, April 20, 1977, p. 39.
86 "Capri Night Club: Virginia Blanco," *La Tribuna*, May 5, 1977, p. 43.
87 "Baile de Las Flores," *La Tribuna*, May 5, 1977, p. 8.
88 Emilio Santana, "Recorriendo Bergenline," *La Tribuna*, May 5, 1977, p. 35.
89 "Old Office Lounge" and "The Living Room," advertisement, *La Tribuna*, October 5, 1978, p. 39.
90 "Jose "Chein" Damaso Garcia," Carolina Cremation, accessed March 3, 2021, https://carolinacremation.com/obituary/jose-chein-damaso-garcia-concord.
91 "Fandango," advertisement, *La Tribuna*, April 19, 1986, p. 10.
92 "Osvaldo Farres, Cuban Composer, Interviewed by Gilda Miros,"accessed March 12, 2021, https://youtu.be/1i47tSmzPwA.
93 "Madrecita, canción de Osvaldo Farrés," *La Tribuna*, May 3, 1986, p. 7.
94 Jorge "Papito" Sánchez, personal communication, January 26, 2021.
95 Orquesta Riviera, *No dejes camino por vereda*. West Side Records LPS-2019, 1970, LP; Orquesta Riviera, *Orquesta Riviera con Manolo Vega*. West Side Records LPS-2034, 1974, LP; Baby González con La Orquesta Riviera, *Concinando Salsa*. Cotique Records CS-1081, 1975, LP.
96 Lázaro "Orlando" Espinosa, personal Communication, January 11, 2021.
97 Judith Noemi "Mimi" Junco, personal communication, January 12, 2021.
98 Junco, personal communication .
99 Oscar Oñoz, personal communication, January 10, 2021.
100 Oñoz, personal communication.
101 People who worked in Guantánamo from the Cuban side also attended the performances.
102 Lapidus, *New York*, 18–23.
103 Los Jimaguas, *Igualitos y con sabor*. Mericana Records XMS-121, 1973, LP.
104 Moreno, personal communication.
105 Eleanor Meyer Rogg and Rosemary Santana Cooney, *Adaptation and Adjustment of Cubans: West New York, New Jersey* (Bronx NY: Fordham University, 1980), 18–19.
106 Leonel "Papo" Ortega, personal communication, January 14, 2021.

107 Diosdado Santana and Sergio Sorí, *Raíces Campesinas diálogos poéticos entre: Diosdado Santana y Sergio Sorí.* (N.P.: 2002), i–iii.
108 Santana and Sorí, *Raíces Campesinas diálogos poéticos entre,* 42–43.
109 Ramón Grosfoguel and Chloé S. Georas, "Latino Caribbean Diasporas in New York," in *Mambo Montage: The Latinization of New York City,* edited by Agustín Laó-Montes and Arlene Dávila, 97–118. New York: Columbia University Press, 2001.
110 Lapidus, *New York,* 279–322.
111 Prieto, *Cubans of Union City,* 28.
112 Nancy Raquel Mirabal, "Scripting Race, Finding Place: African-Americans, Afro-Cubans and the Diasporic Imaginary in the United States," in *Neither Enemies nor Friends: Latinos, Blacks, Afro-Latinos,* edited by Anani Dzidzienyo and Suzanne Oboler (New York: Palgrave Macmillan, 2005), 189–207.
113 Lapidus, *New York,* 279–322. Paquito D'Rivera also arrived during this time and was active with these musicians, but did not arrive via the Port of Mariel.
114 Lapidus, *New York,* 316–319.
115 Lapidus, *New York,* 279–332.
116 "Raices Habaneras—Da Me La Mano"; Heddy, *Dame la mano.* Dir. Heddy Honigman. (Amsterdam: Pieter Van Huystee Film and Television/Vrijzinnig Protestantse Radio Omroep [VPRO], 2004); "Rumba Night Union City Club Showcases Folkloric Cuban Music on Sundays," *Hudson Reporter,* February 14, 2002, https://archive.hudsonreporter.com/2002/02/14/rumba-night-union-city-club-showcases-folkloric-cuban-music-on-sundays/; "Rumba Rhythm Union City Man Makes Documentary about Cuban Tradition," *Hudson Reporter,* April 2, 2004, https://archive.hudsonreporter.com/2004/04/02/rumba/rhythm-union-city-man-makes-documentary-about-cuban-tradition/.
117 Lisa Maya Knauer, "Audiovisual Remittances and Transnational Subjectivities," in *Cuba in the Special Period: Culture and Ideology in the 1990s,* edited by Ariana Hernández-Reguant (New York: Palgrave Macmillan, 2009), 159–177; Berta Jottar, "Central Park Rumba: Nuyorican Identity and the Return to African Roots," *Centro Journal* 23, no. 1 (Spring 2011): 5–29; Berta Jottar, "From Central Park, Rumba with Love!" *Voices: Journal of New York Folklore* 37 (Spring–Summer 2011), http://www.nyfolklore.org/pubs/voic37-1-2/rumba.html; Berta Jottar, "Zero Tolerance and Central Park Rumba Cabildo Politics," *Liminalities: A Journal of Performance Studies* 5, no. 4 (November 2009): 1–24; Lisa Maya Knauer, "The Politics of Afrocuban Expression in New York City," *Journal of Ethnic and Migration Studies* 34, no. 8 (November 2008): 1257-1281; Lisa Maya Knauer, dir. *The Cuban Americans.* WLIW21, public televisión, 2000. VHS; Arístedes Falcón Paradí, dir. *Rumba Clave Blen Blen Blen.* Paradí Productions, New York, 2013. DVD.
118 Prieto, *Cubans of Union City,* 52–53.
119 Raíces Habaneras, *Raíces Habaneras.* P&A Records/Universal Music Latino, 2002, Compact Disc.
120 Christina Abreu, *Rhythms of Race: Cuban Musicians and the Making of Latino New York City and Miami, 1940–1960* (Chapel Hill, NC: University of North Carolina Press, 2015).

# Part 3
# Experiences

# 10
# Mexican Immigrants Fighting for Educational Justice

Community Activism to Save a New Brunswick Public School

LILIA FERNÁNDEZ

Mexican immigrants have become a significant and fast-growing part of New Jersey's Latino population in the past two decades. As of the 2019 American Community Survey, they and their children were estimated to be the third-largest Spanish-speaking group in the state after Puerto Ricans and Dominicans, respectively, numbering approximately 225,484 people. In cities such as Paterson, Passaic, New Brunswick, Lakewood, and Bridgeton, they make up more than half of the Latino population and provide an important source of labor and tax revenues.[1] Yet political leaders and policymakers have tended to ignore the relatively young and largely immigrant community when it comes to local fiscal and policy decisions. In cities like New Brunswick, where most Mexican-born residents are undocumented and therefore ineligible to vote, they routinely find themselves politically disenfranchised and marginalized, to say nothing of the anti-immigrant and anti-Mexican sentiments that permeate the public sphere. They endure this neglect and hostility despite the fact that they provide essential labor in the area's landscaping and construction companies, warehouses, and other businesses and despite providing substantial rental income to local property owners. Moreover, although they constitute more than a quarter of the city's population, their children along with those of other Latinos make up 90 percent of public school pupils. Nonetheless, the school district's own reporting to the state reveals that it is not providing those students an adequate education.[2]

This chapter examines this marginalized community's unprecedented grassroots struggle to defend its children and their educational rights—specifically the historic leadership role that Mexican immigrant parents played within a larger coalition to save a local school from demolition. In early 2020, city and business leaders announced plans to shutter New Brunswick's highest-performing public school, Lincoln Annex (serving grades four to eight), and temporarily relocate its 750 children to classrooms in a converted warehouse, so that New Jersey's largest hospital chain, Robert Wood Johnson Barnabas Health, could acquire and demolish the property to expand its facilities. The plans, concocted behind closed doors for more than a year, then fast-tracked for approval with minimal community input, sparked fierce opposition from parents and allies. As one researcher described it, "the planning and decision-making processes of the redevelopment have been both opaque and non-participatory."[3] Many residents—including immigrant parents whose children would be impacted by the school closure—as well as Rutgers University students and faculty were outraged to learn that leaders planned to displace low-income Latino children and disrupt their education for "the greater good" of creating a new cancer treatment center when one already existed a block away.[4] The conflict raised critical issues about how New Jersey's immigrant Latino communities, especially its growing Mexican sector, have become central figures in battles over urban redevelopment, educational equity, and political power.

While some of the Mexican immigrant activists had been engaged in immigrant rights struggles with the state and federal government in the past, primarily through groups like Cosecha New Jersey, New Labor, and to a less extent, Make the Road New Jersey, they gained considerable knowledge about the workings of local government, the long-standing educational neglect of Latino children in local public schools, and the municipal corruption that Latino and African American residents have endured for decades under a self-dealing Democrat-controlled city and county government. I draw on my own participation in community and school-board meetings, protests, and other activities as part of the Coalition to Defend Lincoln Annex, as well as news coverage of the school struggle, public records, interviews with key coalition members, and court documents that formed the basis of a lawsuit against the school district. Ultimately, I conclude that while the city's elites have effectively subordinated and marginalized the Mexican community, activist residents managed to mobilize a formidable and visible resistance to demand dignity and respect for their children. Immigrant parents making their voices heard represented a coming of age for this population as they asserted a consciousness of their rights as people who contribute to the local economy regardless of their immigration status, and they asserted their children's right to an equitable and just education. While they were unable to stop the sale of the school, they did force the political establishment to recognize them as a rising constituency and to make significant concessions in response to community pressure.

## "The Hub City": New Brunswick's Changing Economy and Demographics

For nearly two centuries after its founding, New Brunswick was an almost exclusively White city; its racial homogeneity only changing in the 1940s as African Americans began migrating northward during the Great Migration. Black Americans' growing numbers, however, and exaggerated fears about their presence, provoked racist opposition from White residents and predictably resulted in violent racial conflicts from the late 1960s to the early 1970s. In 1967, as nearby Newark and Plainfield, New Jersey, burned, New Brunswick barely averted an uprising.[5] Still, White anxieties over African American newcomers motivated some Whites to move out, while Puerto Ricans, who began arriving in the 1950s, increasingly replaced them. The Black population grew from an estimated 10.2 percent of the city in 1950, to 22.7 percent by 1970, and up to 28.5 percent by 1980. By then, non-Hispanic Whites had declined from 76 to 51.4 percent and Hispanics (of any race) made up 11 percent. Over the next three decades, non-Hispanic Whites continued to decline to less than 27 percent, while African Americans also declined to 14 percent, and Latinos became the largest segment of the city at nearly 50 percent (see Table 10.1). Nevertheless, a White elite retained control of city hall and the county political establishment, with token representation from middle-class African Americans and Latinos who work for city government, serve on county bodies, or sit on the local school board.[6]

New Brunswick has been anchored for decades by three major institutions and employers—Rutgers University (the main campus of the state's flagship public institution of higher education), the pharmaceutical giant Johnson & Johnson, and a hospital sponsored by Johnson & Johnson's charitable foundation, the Robert Wood Johnson University Hospital, part of a statewide RWJBarnabas Health chain. Rutgers is a major landowner here, with facilities stretching beyond city limits across the Raritan River to the neighboring township of Piscataway. As a result, thousands of Rutgers's fifty thousand students make up a significant number of part-time residents, not only in campus dormitories but in private rental housing, where landlords welcome the steady income that student financial aid loans or parents' checkbooks supply.

In the first half of the twentieth century, the city was home to manufacturing and retail firms that provided desirable, stable employment for working-class residents. But starting in the 1950s, the construction of federal interstate

Table 10.1
New Brunswick population (in percentages and total numbers) 1950–2020

|  | 1950 | 1960 | 1970 | 1980 | 1990 | 2000 | 2010 | 2020 |
|---|---|---|---|---|---|---|---|---|
| White | 89.6 | 84.5 | 75.9* | 51.4 | 49.2 | 32.9 | 26.8 | 26.7** |
|  | 34,774 | 33,917 | 31,795 | 21,301 | 20,521 | 15,981 | 14,789 | 14,756 |
| Black or African American | 10.2 | 15.5 | 22.7 | 28.5 | 27.3 | 20.7 | 14.0 | 16.2*** |
|  | 3,959 | 6,222 | 9,509 | 11,811 | 11,387 | 10,055 | 7,725 | 8,953 |
| Hispanic (of any race) | n.a. | n.a. | n.a. | 11.7 | 19.3 | 39.0 | 49.9 | 46.8 |
|  |  |  |  | 4,849 | 8,050 | 18,943 | 27,535 | 25,864 |
| Total population | 38,811 | 40,139 | 41,891 | 41,442 | 41,711 | 48,573 | 55,181 | 55,266 |

SOURCE: Data compiled from Social Explorer and U.S. Census Bureau, 1950–2020.
* May include Hispanics who identified racially as "White" in the 1970 census.
** In 2020, this category was labeled as "White alone," meaning it did not include those who identified as White and Hispanic or those who identified as "two or more races."
*** In 2020, this category was labeled as "Black alone," meaning it did not include those who identified as Black and Hispanic or those who identified as "two or more races."

highways, suburbanization, and the creation of regional shopping malls began to eclipse New Brunswick's economic vitality and contribute to its decline. By the 1960s and 1970s, previously thriving downtown businesses began losing customers to those outlying shopping centers and many permanently closed their doors, while young home seekers opted for more spacious suburban living in new housing developments outside the city. As one report concluded, "between 1965 and 1979 [New Brunswick lost] seven department stores; 83 percent of its smaller quality retail establishments; more than 3,000 white-collar jobs ... six major industrial plants; and 2,000 industrial jobs."[7] Popular narratives have characterized such urban decline as an inevitable or lamentable consequence of demographic change. Yet scholars have aptly documented that various other factors prompted manufacturing flight throughout the Northeast and Midwest in the mid-twentieth century, including the search for nonunionized, cheaper labor and lower taxes.[8] Moreover, ethnic minority newcomers in subsequent decades—the city's growing Latino population—actually revitalized the city's commercial corridor by opening new small businesses catering to the immigrant community.[9]

Facing an expanding non-White population and shrinking tax base, city officials and corporate leaders pursued a "meds and eds" model of urban revitalization, one aimed at removing low-income African American and Puerto Rican residents, especially those in federally subsidized public housing, and replacing them with expanded educational and medical facilities and middle-class housing.[10] Johnson & Johnson, for example, agreed to keep its headquarters in New Brunswick if the city pursued a redevelopment plan centered around public–private partnerships approved by its principals. After consulting with a private revitalization company, the American City Corporation, in the mid-1970s, city officials created two entities to promote and carry out their urban renewal agenda—the Development Corporation of New Brunswick (DEVCO) and New Brunswick Tomorrow. Their boards would be made up primarily of Johnson & Johnson executives, other business leaders, and select community representatives. Moreover, the city now faced the challenge of catering to the competing interests of a largely commuter workforce in local workplaces (Johnson & Johnson, the hospital, Rutgers) and an economically marginalized, increasingly African American and Puerto Rican resident population.[11]

From the beginning, neighborhood leaders criticized the public–private initiative charging that slum clearance and the construction of upscale amenities did not address the economic needs of its most vulnerable residents. Instead, critics claimed, DEVCO seemingly pursued plans meant to enrich private companies and "clean up" the city's image without doing anything to improve conditions for the poor. Such plans included constructing modern office buildings, a new $60 million Johnson & Johnson headquarters designed by I. M. Pei, a since-demolished shopping center, a major hotel, a highway expansion, and, by the 1990s, upscale housing for single or childless white-collar professionals who the city sought to lure back with luxury living and tax breaks.[12] As a result of such market-rate development, New Brunswick is marked by sharp inequality—a small, middle class of predominantly White professionals in some sections, just blocks away from impoverished Latino and African American residents. Indeed, ten years after the American City Corporation's redevelopment recommendations, a Rutgers urban planning professor noted that "there had been little 'trickle-down' to the residential neighborhoods."[13] Some middle-class African Americans and Latinos have certainly benefited from the newer housing, but the broader racial and economic segregation produced by such neoliberal urban renewal and "revitalization" leaves no doubts about where the city has chosen to invest and what areas it has neglected.[14] Ironically, as one community activist noted, poor people are often used as "a main factor in drawing federal money to the city," yet rarely are they actual beneficiaries of such funding.[15]

Since 2010, at least half of New Brunswick's population has been Hispanic, nearly half of whom live in poverty and precarious, overcrowded conditions. Many are recent immigrants from Mexico, the Dominican Republic, and Honduras. Indeed, the city is home to over seventeen thousand immigrants, more than 84 percent of them from Latin America, with 64 percent having entered the United States since 2000. A minority of older Puerto Ricans, many of whom have secured economic mobility through government or social service employment, represent the Latino middle class.[16] They tend to live in newer housing compared to more recent immigrants and African Americans in areas marked by low median household incomes, high poverty rates, and severe overcrowding in dilapidated rental units. As of the 2018 American Community Survey, population density in those neighborhoods averaged from twenty-two to twenty-eight thousand people per square mile, one of the densest in the state after Hudson and Union Counties in northern New Jersey. In comparison, New Brunswick's White, middle-class census tracts measure population density closer to 9,200 people per square mile. In the three densest tracts, Latinos make up 68–79 percent of residents, with 74–85 percent of them being renters. They experience high poverty despite high labor participation rates. Among men aged sixteen years and older, 70–88 percent were in the labor market as of 2019, although nearly a quarter of households earned less than $20,000 a year. Looking at a slightly higher income threshold, 42–54 percent of households earned under $35,000 annually. Between 35 percent and 42 percent of households with children under eighteen years of age live below the poverty line. Among the foreign born, 55–73 percent of immigrants entered the United States since 2000, meaning they are likely of child-bearing age and may have U.S.-born children.[17] In sum, this is a community of relatively young immigrant families who struggle to make ends meet. As older immigrants and their children achieve some degree of economic stability, many move to surrounding suburbs like North Brunswick or Somerset where they find more spacious housing, less crowding, and better municipal services.

## New Brunswick's Public Schools

The local school district has witnessed a dramatic growth in its student body over the last four and half decades. In 1974, New Brunswick Public Schools (NBPS), had only 5,577 students—the result of family outmigration from the city and White parents' opting for private schools after the fifth grade.[18] By 2019, the district served over ten thousand pupils, 99.8 percent of whom were identified as "economically disadvantaged." While Latinos make up half of the city's population, they are an astonishing 91 percent of NBPS students while another 7.4 percent are African American. In 2022, NBPS advertised that two-thirds of its students "speak one of 41 languages other than English at home," implying that the city is a "melting pot" of sorts. A closer inspection of its records, however, reveals that 76 percent of students come from Spanish-speaking households, while only 0.5 percent of its student body—fifty-one students—speak a language other than Spanish or English at home.[19] Why the district does not highlight that Spanish is the predominant language at home for three-fourths of its students is a mystery.

The district operates thirteen schools, including nine neighborhood elementary schools, a middle school, a high school, a health sciences high school, and a vocational training high school in an industrial park made possible through a public–private partnership. It also hosts a daycare program for students with young children, as well as adult education programs. NBPS provides employment to "nearly 2,000 certified teachers and professional support staff." Many of those

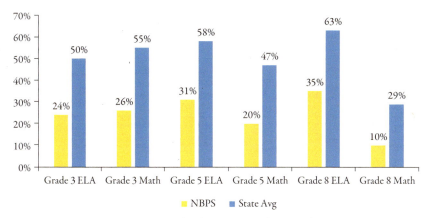

FIGURE 10.1 New Brunswick Public Schools District, academic performance on state English Language Arts and Math standards and New Jersey academic performance on state English Language Arts and Math standards. (Source: "NJ School Performance Report," Official Site of the State of New Jersey, April 2024, https://rc.doe.state.nj.us/.)

employees seem to come from outside the city, while 62.5 percent of the 778 teachers and 45.5 percent of administrators are White. Only 20 percent of teachers and 25.5 percent of administrators are Latino.[20]

District data clearly show that students consistently fail to meet state standards for academic proficiency. Since the educational policy shift from emphasizing academic "achievement" or "proficiency" (reaching state or federal norms in subjects such as math and reading) to measuring academic "growth" (the degree to which students demonstrate learning) NBPS has claimed its students are meeting state targets for "typical" student growth standards. Yet in raw scores they still fall severely behind in meeting the English Language Arts (ELA) section of the New Jersey Student Learning Assessment. Only 24 percent of third graders met or exceeded the New Jersey Student Learning Assessment's ELA expectations (see Figure 10.1). At higher grades, they continue to fall far below state ELA standards. In math, students perform even worse. At the sixth and eighth grades, for example, only 10–11 percent of students met or exceeded state standards. At all grades, students are lagging and demonstrate severe deficiencies. Additionally, although the state's four-year high school graduation rate has been above 90 percent from 2017 to 2019, the district's rate has hovered between 68 and 78 percent in that same period.[21]

Rates of postsecondary schooling are equally dismal. Eighty-four percent of district tenth and eleventh graders took the Preliminary SAT in the 2019–2020 school year, but their scores averaged far below state "college readiness" benchmarks (see Table 10.2). Only 31 percent reached that standard in reading and writing, while a mere 16 percent did so in mathematics. Only 47 percent of high school seniors took the SAT. Among those who took the SAT or the ACT, most

## Table 10.2
## New Brunswick Public School District college readiness

| Exam type | District average score | State average score | College readiness benchmarks | District–student scores at or above benchmark (%) | State–student scores at or above benchmark (%) |
|---|---|---|---|---|---|
| PSAT10/NMSQT—reading and writing | 406 | 476 | Grade 10: 430<br>Grade 11: 460 | 31 | 61 |
| PSAT10/NMSQT—math | 421 | 473 | Grade 10: 480<br>Grade 11: 510 | 16 | 39 |
| SAT—reading and writing | 484 | 536 | 480 | 48 | 69 |
| SAT—math | 485 | 536 | 530 | 32 | 52 |

SOURCE: Adapted from "New Brunswick School District Performance Report 2019–20," 15. Official Site of the State of New Jersey, accessed July 15, 2024, https://rc.doe.state.nj.us/district/detail/23/3530/demographics?lang=EN

fell far below the state benchmark once again. Less than 24 percent of 2019 graduates were planning to attend a four-year college. There is no available data on what proportion of NBPS graduates complete a college degree.[22]

These statistics paint a portrait of a troubled school district where students face enormous challenges and where teachers and staff fail to help them meet basic academic standards. A high poverty rate and lack of English proficiency at home undoubtedly contribute to these academic deficiencies, but racial and class segregation likely exacerbate lower educational achievement. The lowest child poverty rate in the city registers at 23 percent in one outlying census tract—home to many government employees and white-collar professionals who have few children in the public schools. That well-manicured neighborhood counts the mayor and past school-board president among its residents. Its local school, Woodrow Wilson Elementary, has newer facilities, built in 1998, and the smallest student body but highest per-pupil expenditure in the city.[23] Schools in census tracts where 45–56 percent of children lived in poverty as of 2019, such as Roosevelt, Lincoln, Lincoln Annex, Livingston, Lord Stirling, Paul Robeson, and Redshaw serve much needier students, some in substandard facilities. Roosevelt and Livingston school buildings, for example, are over one hundred years old and lack basic amenities such as air conditioning during sweltering summer days. The district has renovated or built new schools in the past decade, such A.C. Redshaw, and Paul Robeson. In the case of Redshaw, however, it took over ten years to complete, as the state financing authority ran out of funds causing ongoing construction delays. Students from schools undergoing renovation have been relocated to 40 Van Dyke Street, a warehouse building converted for classroom use, that is rented from a real estate developer who also owns the office building that houses the mayor's private law firm. While the school district officially calls it a "swing space" and adamantly claims that it is not a warehouse, the building sits in an industrial park and resembles the other warehouse buildings around it. Thus, in some cases, students have spent much of their elementary education in an industrial facility that has been retrofitted for school use.[24] Due to these and many other district shortcomings, families with resources and knowledge opt for nearby private or charter schools. Those with means move out of the district altogether to surrounding towns with larger tax bases and better-performing schools.

## Demolishing a Promising School

In a school district with such challenging conditions, parents and community members were bewildered to learn in late 2019 that city officials proposed, and the school board ultimately agreed to, the closing, sale, and demolition of Lincoln Annex—one of the newest and best performing schools in the city. Numerous districts around the country have witnessed permanent school closures since 2009 when the federal government proposed closing five thousand of the nation's lowest-performing schools. In the case of Lincoln Annex, however, it was not targeted for low performance or enrollment but rather its desirable location. NBPS planned to sell its facilities and relocate students to its industrial swing space while it constructed a new and purportedly "better" school elsewhere. As the public controversy over the closure wore on, the district began emphasizing the current school's inadequacies as justification to shutter it. Regardless of the reason for school closings, research shows that these events disrupt children's education, affect their well-being, and often have other unanticipated impacts.[25]

The Lincoln Annex School consisted of two separate buildings constructed in 1960 and 1970 and connected by an enclosed walkway. The site had previously operated as St. Peter's Catholic School. For decades, many of the city's well-heeled families who opted out of public schools sent their children there. Indeed, St. Peter's counts many local government officials and even some celebrities among its most famous alumni. It closed its doors in 2010, however, as enrollments declined, likely because middle-class residents no longer had school-age children and younger Latino families could not afford the school's tuition.[26] In 2014, the Catholic Diocese of Metuchen sold the facilities to NBPS for $13 million. The school district spent an additional $8 million on renovations, including installation of rooftop solar panels, finally opening the buildings in the fall of 2016. From an environmental perspective, repurposing the solid facilities of a former Catholic school was a sound decision.

The school sat directly across the street from the Robert Wood Johnson University Hospital (see Figure 10.2), previously known as Middlesex General

FIGURE 10.2 Map of the former Lincoln Annex School and its surroundings. Note the solar panels on the buildings' roofs. (Source: Google Maps satellite view.)

Hospital. In 1986, RWJ Hospital acquired the public county hospital and turned it into a private not-for-profit facility, in addition to acquiring other hospitals around the state.[27] While the surrounding area had once been home to a vibrant residential district, the hospital gradually demolished much of the housing over the years as it expanded its footprint, erecting more buildings and parking garages.[28] The area to the northwest, closer to Rutgers University, is home to a great deal of student rental housing, where Rutgers students share single-family homes and two-flat apartments with one another. The Lincoln Annex School thus sits in a transition zone of sorts, on the border between private student housing to the northwest, the large hospital complex and new upscale high-rise apartments to its northeast, and the commercial and residential heart of the immigrant community to the southeast.

Families welcomed the new Lincoln Annex School (grades four to eight)—named so because it was essentially an overflow site for the severely overcrowded Lincoln School (formerly K-8, now K-3) several blocks to the north, near the Rutgers campus. Lincoln Annex also hosts the district's Gifted and Talented program in a "Self-Contained Full-Day Placement for students who meet the established criteria." The program served the top 10 percent highest performing children in all the district's elementary schools. The school also enrolled children living in the surrounding neighborhood.[29] The improved facilities and the Gifted and Talented program proved motivating for students and their families. In the 2018–2019 academic year, students met the ELA and math growth standards and did particularly well in ELA for economically disadvantaged students. Moreover, female students exceeded the district's ELA median while male students surpassed the district's math median. Though the school did not meet some federal accountability targets or state testing expectations, students in the sixth and seventh grades who had spent two to three years in the new school were the only ones to have met or exceeded ELA state expectations. In math, students again struggled but English-language learners seemed to perform well. The school also had a lower-than-average rate of chronic absenteeism compared to the rest of the district. Academic performance at Lincoln Annex appeared mixed in its first three years, and students faced many of the same district-wide challenges. Still, the school showed signs of promise.[30]

In early June 2019, executives of Robert Wood Johnson University Hospital, DEVCO, and Rutgers Health, along with New Brunswick mayor James Cahill and others (12 men in total) posed in suits for a photo after announcing plans for a new $750 million cancer center.[31] Over the next eight months, officials refused to publicly disclose where the cancer center would be located, although internal emails between the Rutgers Cancer Institute of New Jersey and DEVCO officials obtained through an OPRA (Open Public Records Act) request revealed that they had already decided as early as May 2019 on the Lincoln Annex site. These emails also showed they were aware that this would be a delicate matter.[32] This was the first moment of subterfuge in the city's development plans—the failure to inform the public that it would be sacrificing a newly renovated, high-performing public school for a hospital expansion project.

While the city already counts with the Rutgers Cancer Institute of New Jersey—located across the street from the Robert Wood Johnson University Hospital and accessible by a pedestrian bridge—hospital and city leaders emphasized the new "freestanding" building was an extraordinary step in advancing cancer treatment for central New Jersey patients. They cited state health statistics that fifty thousand New Jerseyans receive cancer diagnoses every year. Perhaps because of the state's history of widespread industrial, chemical, and oil-refining operations, New Jersey has the tenth highest incidence of cancer in the United States. Still, a 2016 news report highlighted ten existing treatment facilities in New Jersey, some of them branches of New York City institutions and others affiliated with other New Jersey medical centers, including the Rutgers Cancer Institute of New Jersey.[33] Critics noted that there are many options in the state and there was hardly a pressing need for yet another facility. Moreover, not all of these New Jerseyans seek out or need extensive treatment. The plan for a new cancer center seemed a calculated move to capture greater market share from its primary competitor in the state, the Hackensack Meridian medical network, and from facilities in New York City, where many New Jersey residents opt to receive care from one of the nation's six leading cancer centers.[34] Ironically, in the midst of the growing Lincoln Annex controversy, even New Jersey governor Phil Murphy, a former Goldman Sachs investment banker, who announced he had a cancerous tumor on his kidney in February 2020, opted for treatment in New York City over a facility in his own state.[35]

## Fighting for Lincoln Annex

Parents and community members began to hear rumors in the fall of 2019—only three years after Lincoln Annex had opened—that the school was slated to be the site of the new RWJBarnabas Health and Rutgers Health cancer center. Mayor James Cahill, who rarely makes public appearances despite being in office for thirty years, had reportedly let the information slip at an event of the city's immigrant project, Proyecto Esperanza, earlier that summer. Few discussed the matter, however, and, thus, no one quite understood the implications of his comments. By fall, however, parents began asking questions as a local reporter spread word of the news. Parents and residents questioned school-board members at their monthly public meetings in October, November, December, and January but board members repeatedly denied knowledge of any such plans and insisted this was simply hearsay. They maintained that they had not received any formal proposal to sell the school and refused to comment further. By February, supporters of the school formed the Coalition to Defend Lincoln Annex, made up of Lincoln Annex parents and students, community residents, Rutgers student organizations (from the Mexican American Student Association, the student assembly, the National Association for the Advancement of Colored People, to Students for Palestine), as well as leftist, environmental, and immigrant rights groups in the state such as Movimiento Cosecha,[36] Lazos America Unida, New Labor, Escuelas Dignas, New Jersey Work Environment Council, Democratic Socialist Alliance, and others. The Rutgers faculty and graduate student union, AAUP-AFT (American Association of University Professors/American Federation of Teachers), also joined the coalition and issued a public statement opposing the plans.[37]

Parents, community members, and allies began voicing their opposition to the potential closing of the school through leafleting, public protests, press conferences, attending municipal government meetings open to the public (city council, planning board, Middlesex County Freeholders), and raising awareness in the community by doing "sound blasts" with loudspeakers on a truck much like political candidates often do in Latin American countries before an election. On February 4, the mayor finally announced publicly that the school had been selected as the site for the cancer center. Cahill also indicated that a replacement school would be built at 131 Jersey Avenue, a former industrial site on the outskirts of town. Parents and community members immediately highlighted the surrounding area's dangers—a heavily trafficked street, abandoned and decaying factory buildings, industrial contamination, and nearby homeless encampments. They attended the local planning board meeting at City Hall on February 5 to register their opposition to the plan during the public comment session. The room was filled to capacity with nearly one hundred people and an overflow crowd that spilled into the hallway. Some Lincoln Annex schoolchildren even provided testimony, pleading with board members not to close their school

Mexican Immigrants Fighting for Educational Justice • 241

FIGURE 10.3 Lincoln Annex children in line to give public comment at the New Brunswick City Planning Board meeting, urging board members not to approve the cancer center plans on their school site, February 5, 2020. (Photo courtesy of the author.)

(Figure 10.3). Two days later on February 7, the school district finally announced that it had received a proposal from DEVCO to purchase the Lincoln Annex buildings.[38] Although Robert Wood Johnson University Hospital owns land throughout the city, it insisted on the school's site and adjoining private properties for its new facility.[39] In addition, Mayor Cahill starred in several professionally produced promotional videos touting the benefits of the cancer center and explaining that the hospital was giving students a much better state-of-the-art school in exchange. The videos circulated on social media, garnering strategic praise from White and Black residents who supported the cancer center, and provoking scorn from Latino and Black community members who opposed the project. When the superintendent summoned Lincoln Annex parents for a meeting with school-board members at the 40 Van Dyke swing space, aimed at convincing parents of the benefits of the cancer center, they opened the gathering by playing the Cahill videos. Coalition members worked hard to attract news coverage from the New York City Univision affiliate and New Jersey news outlets, who began reporting on the school-closing controversy in nightly news broadcasts.[40]

By then, coalition members had begun investigating the environmental status of the proposed new school location through public records requests. They quickly discovered the site's history of heavy contamination with underground oil tanks, chemicals, and carcinogens that so thoroughly seeped into the soil and groundwater that the owner had spent ten years trying to remediate unsuccessfully. The New Jersey Department of Environmental Protection requires property owners to cap such toxic brownfields with a thick layer of asphalt, but the site had been abandoned for so long that its asphalt cap was deeply cracked in many places, making it a hazard even to breathe the surrounding air.[41] The realization that the mayor, hospital officials, cancer center executives, and school board deemed this an acceptable alternative for New Brunswick children further outraged parents and community members. Many pointed out the hypocrisy of displacing children to a potentially *cancer-causing* site in order to build a brand-new cancer *treatment* center. Others wondered if middle-class White children would be relocated to such a derelict site. In response to the environmental concerns, DEVCO and school officials reassured the public that they had built many projects on brownfields around town before (including the high school), and that they knew how to remediate appropriately.[42] This offered plan opponents little comfort.

Hundreds of parents, children, community residents, Rutgers students, faculty, and union members gathered in front of the school—in full view of the hospital—for a rally and march to the Rutgers Board of Governors meeting on February 18, 2020. The crowd wound its way through the city's main thoroughfares, even drawing out residents from side streets who could hear the chants and came out to support the cause. Once on the Rutgers campus, protestors gathered in front of Winants Hall, the administrative building known as Old Queens, and heard parents and allies denounce the plans and defend the schoolchildren. Those who planned to attend the Board of Governors meeting then began moving inside. The Board of Governors and university administrators witnessed an unprecedented scene—the public-seating gallery was filled with immigrant parents and their children. One by one, their names and those of other coalition members were called from the speakers' sign-up list. Parents and children explained their opposition to the plan; faculty and union members registered their objection to Rutgers's role in the school's displacement and emphasized the detrimental effects of school closings and disruptions to children's education. Board officials acknowledged they had never been confronted with such a large and emotional public response.[43] They certainly had never been addressed by the local Mexican immigrant community and its children.

The coalition maintained its momentum, organizing, publicizing, and encouraging community members and allies to attend the February 24 school-board meeting the following week. Over two hundred parents, students, community members, and supporters filed into the New Brunswick High School auditorium to voice their opposition to the plan and speak during the public comments segment of the meeting. People held signs and placards defending children's education and their right to their existing school. When board president Diana Solis announced that only those who had signed up on the speakers' list *before* the start of the meeting would be allowed to speak, parents and community members erupted in protest. The board's attorney George Hendricks ordered security officers to remove two members of the public from the auditorium. Solis then abruptly ended the meeting. Outraged and in disbelief, members of the audience slowly began leaving. They were unaware, however, that the board had quietly moved into closed session. Although a vote on the school's sale had not been listed on the published agenda, one board member, Edward Spencer, reportedly scribbled a motion by hand to approve the sale of the school. Returning to the empty auditorium after most of the public had left, the board then voted in its reconvened public session to approve the sale of Lincoln Annex.[44] The elected officials entrusted to represent the interests of local schoolchildren had sided with the city's powerful elite.

By early March, faculty activists held an emergency meeting with Rutgers students on campus to explain the Lincoln Annex struggle and enlist their support in the fight. Students were clearly moved by the issue, and many signed up to volunteer, register to vote for the next school-board election, or otherwise support the cause. Beyond spreading the word through social media, faculty stressed the importance of ousting three Board of Education members in the upcoming April 21 elections. But then, just as the movement was gaining momentum, the COVID-19 pandemic struck. As cases in New York City and northern New Jersey rose quickly, Rutgers university administrators announced on March 11 that the campus would be shutting down completely and instruction would move online. In subsequent days, the governor announced a statewide curfew and shutdown of all public facilities. As one Rutgers planning student noted, "The COVID-19 pandemic has only made it easier for public officials to further silence opposition to the redevelopment plan."[45] The campaign lost its ability to gather people in public and governmental agencies shifted to telephonic or video public meetings. And in a city of more than fifty-five thousand residents, school-board incumbents retained their seats in a contest where a shockingly low number of voters cast ballots.

Community members did not give up their fight, however. They continued educating fellow residents, meeting, discussing next steps, and preparing for a lawsuit. Allies continued building public support for the parents and students. One of the obstacles to the school's sale lay in a deed restriction that the Catholic Diocese of Metuchen had attached to the property when it sold it to NBPS. Originally, it included a lengthy morality clause that prohibited the property from being used for anything that defied church doctrine (pornography stores, abortion clinics, gun shops, etc.). Its final amended rider, however, simply stated that the property must be used as a public educational or administrative facility for fifty years after the 2014 sale.[46] Parents, children, and allies appealed to the Bishop of Metuchen, writing letters asking him to enforce the deed restriction and save their school. Since the diocese was concurrently in negotiations with RWJBarnabas Health over merging its own St. Peter's Hospital with the RWJBarnabas Health network, however, the matter of the school's deed restriction became a sort of bargaining chip for the diocese. It could choose to overlook the deed restriction if RWJBH gave it favorable terms in the purchase of St. Peter's Hospital.

Hoping to enforce the deed restriction, coalition members contacted Latino Justice (formerly known as PRLDEF, the Puerto Rican Legal Defense and Education Fund) about potentially filing suit against the diocese to enforce the deed restriction and therefore save the school. Several parents and a community resident (the author) volunteered to serve as plaintiffs. Latino Justice and several private law firms then filed the lawsuit, *Maria Juarez et al. v. New Brunswick Board of Education et al.* in May 2020, two months after the state had been hit by the growing COVID-19 crisis, as a last hope effort to challenge the school's sale. The assigned judge, Arthur Berman, took weeks to hear the case (remotely via videoconference) and ultimately kept the case in limbo by dismissing some complaints and holding others in abeyance. The judge was subsequently forced to resign over misconduct in another unrelated case, and the lawsuit was transferred to another judge, one whose father had been an attorney for NBPS just several years prior. The attorney who now represented the school district, an African American, was also married to an NBPS administrator. Such family connections and conflicts of interest reflect the tight-knit, closed network and self-dealing of local governments and their allies.[47]

By summer 2020, the coalition circulated flyers highlighting twenty-two RWJBarnabas Health and Rutgers Health executives who earned salaries of at least $1 million a year. The highest paid executive drew an astonishing $5.3 million in 2018 for running a nonprofit, tax-exempt hospital chain. The campaign aimed to educate the public about the economic inequality of the struggle—a group of powerful millionaires fighting against low-income Latino children and their families.[48] The coalition also managed to organize a couple of car caravans but, otherwise, the campaign against the school closing shifted entirely to social media and chat groups. By early 2021, the lawsuit plaintiffs learned that their suit had failed. The judge dismissed the case and, although Latino Justice tried twice to appeal, the appellate court declined to hear arguments both times.

## Lessons Learned

On January 21, 2021, district superintendent Aubrey Johnson announced the sale of the "former" Lincoln Annex School and informed parents that "construction that will provide your children with an exceptional, state-of-the-art educational facility will begin this spring, on our property at 50 Jersey Avenue."[49] The failure to save their neighborhood school was a profound disappointment for the affected families and coalition allies. Still, the struggle to save Lincoln Annex provided community residents and activists critical political lessons. And it managed to secure significant concessions from the city's leaders.

First, although the initial public announcement stated that Robert Wood Johnson University Hospital would be "donating" $25 million for a replacement school, coalition members questioned whether that would be enough to build the school.[50] Eventually, RWJ Hospital raised its offer to $55 million. It is not clear if this will cover all construction costs, but city leaders, hospital executives, development principals, and school district administrators were forced to respond to community pressure and will have to be accountable for the full cost of the new school.

Second, the coalition succeeded in forcing the district and DEVCO to reconsider the deeply contaminated original replacement site at 131 Jersey Avenue. The alternative location at 50 Jersey Avenue, about half a mile north was also under New Jersey Department of Environmental Protection monitoring and had unknown levels of groundwater and soil contamination. While the new site also has environmental hazards and gets heavy vehicular traffic, it represents a significant improvement over the previous site. Architectural sketches of the proposed new school identify it as a K-8 facility, meaning that it will house more than just grades four to eight as Lincoln Annex did. This suggests that the current Lincoln School (K-3), in sore need of rehabilitation and updates, will likely be next in line for closing and demolition, and that its children will be relocated to the new school. This will push the poor farther away from the Rutgers campus, the hospital facilities, and the upscale housing that developers continue building in that area.

Third, while school-board president Diana Solis had publicly announced that the district would only provide busing to the temporary warehouse school for students who live more than two miles away (though most children live just under two miles from the location), the district and DEVCO agreed to provide busing for all children, a valuable concession to low-income and working parents who often lack transportation or resources to get their children there every day.

Finally, perhaps the most important accomplishment of the coalition's work was the empowerment of immigrant parents and community residents and the signal to local officials that residents will not tolerate "business as usual," particularly when it negatively impacts community children. Spanish-speaking parents with limited English-language skills, many of them undocumented, gained confidence in speaking out at public meetings in defense of their children. They took enormous risks in doing so. But they also saw that hundreds of Rutgers faculty and student allies, as well as community activists, stood with them in demanding respect for their children's well-being. The coalition took a clear and visible stand in defense of the immigrant community's dignity and rights. Residents may have lost the battle, but they and their children will be forever changed after launching a major campaign to defend themselves and confront the city's powerful elite.

## Notes

1. In 2000, Mexicans surpassed Dominicans in population and were second only to Puerto Ricans, the state's largest Spanish-speaking group for decades. Social Explorer Tables (SE), C2000, U.S. Census Bureau and Social Explorer. The 2019 five-year American Community Survey estimates, however, projected that Mexicans were the third largest population. "ACS 2019 (5-Year Estimates)," Social Explorer, accessed July 15, 2024, https://www.socialexplorer.com/tables/ACS2019_5yr/R12827874. See also Richard Brand, "The Second Great Wave: Hispanic Immigrants Are Changing the Face of Central Jersey," *New York Times*, May 28, 2000, NJ1; Tania Mota, "Mexican Settlement in New Jersey," ArcGIS Online, accessed July 15, 2024, https://www.arcgis.com/apps/MapJournal/index.html?appid=b121f349ecc74f2491 42a328d67e9a43. On New Brunswick, see Tania Mota, Luz Sandoval, and Laura Sandoval, "A Latino History of New Brunswick," accessed July 15, 2024, https://www.youtube.com/watch?v=JSSsroeZbno; Rutgers-New Brunswick, video, https://latcar.rutgers.edu/about-us/the-latino-new-jersey-history-project.
2. The *Abbott v. Burke* cases beginning in 1981 charged that the state's tax funding system disadvantaged poorer school districts and was, therefore, unconstitutional. The New Jersey Supreme Court agreed and the state has since reformed its school funding. This has failed to remedy educational disparities in poorer districts. See "Abbott v. Burke," Supreme Court of New Jersey, accessed July 15, 2024, https://www.nj.gov/lps/newsreleases06/abbott-brief-4.06.pdf.
3. Leah Ripley Hunt, "Spatial and Procedural Justice in Urban Planning: A Case Study of the Lincoln Annex School Redevelopment" (Honors thesis, Edward J. Bloustein School of Planning and Public Policy, Rutgers University, May 2020).
4. To protect parents, especially those who are undocumented, their names are not used here.
5. Chris A. Rasmussen, "Recalling the 1967 New Brunswick Protests," My Central Jersey, July 14, 2017, https://www.mycentraljersey.com/story/news/history/new-jersey/2017/07/14/recalling-1967-new-brunswick-protests/428509001/; Erin Jerome, "50 Years Later, New Brunswick Looks Back on Summer of 1967," *New Brunswick Today*, July 29, 2017, https://newbrunswicktoday.com/2017/07/29/50-years-later-new-brunswick-looks-back-on-summer-of-1967/; Kevin Coyne, "Remembering the 1967 Riot That Wasn't," *New York Times*, July 29, 2007; Chris Rasmussen, "'A Web of Tension': The 1967 Protests in New Brunswick, New Jersey," *Journal of Urban History* 40, no. 1 (January 2014): 137–157.
6. Social Explorer Tables (SE), Census 1980, U.S. Census Bureau and Social Explorer. Although 1950 census data notes that African Americans made up around 4 percent of Middlesex County, the city had a somewhat larger concentration given its factories and other employers. For more, see David Listokin, Dorothea Berkhout, and James Hughes, *New Brunswick New Jersey: The Decline and Revitalization of Urban America* (New Brunswick, NJ: Rutgers University Press, 2016).
7. Cited in Listokin et al., *New Brunswick New Jersey*, 85.
8. See, for example, William M. Adler, *Mollie's Job: A Story of Life and Work on the Global Assembly Line* (New York: Touchstone, 2000); Jefferson Cowie, *Capital Moves: RCA's Seventy-Year Quest for Cheap Labor* (New York: New Press, 2001); Jefferson Cowie, *Stayin' Alive: The 1970s and the Last Days of the Working Class* (New York: New Press, 2012).
9. Richard J. H. Johnston, "New Brunswick Weighs Future Amid Mounting Frustrations," *New York Times*, June 1, 1970, 37; Alfonso Narvaez, "New

Brunswick: Its Ills Are Almost Manageable," *New York Times*, November 24, 1972, 78; Joseph F. Sullivan, "New Brunswick Warns City Workers of Layoffs to Hold Down Realty Taxes," *New York Times*, January 1, 1976, 39; Peter Parisi, "French Street's Revitalization Taking Random, Eclectic Course," *Home News*, July 1, 1984. On how Latino immigrants have revitalized Chicago and Dallas, see Andrew Sandoval-Strausz, *Barrio America: How Latino Immigrants Saved the American City* (New York: Basic Books, 2020).

10  Joseph Picard, "New Brunswick Plan Debated," *New York Times*, June 28, 1987, NJ10.

11  Listokin et al., *New Brunswick New Jersey*, 100–101. American City Corporation, *Trends, Issues and Priorities in the Revitalization of New Brunswick, New Jersey* (Columbia, MD: American City Corporation, 1975). For news coverage from the period, see Rudy Larini, "Hospital the Cure for What's Ailing French Street?" *Home News*, July 22, 1979; "New Brunswick Tomorrow: Five Years of Progress, 1980 Annual Report," New Brunswick: 1980; New Brunswick Tomorrow, City of New Brunswick, NJ; "Corporate-City Alliance Has Helped Rebuild New Brunswick," *New York Times*, August 21, 1984, B4. For a boosterish account that credits corporate and local government policies for the city's "transformation," see Listokin et al, *New Brunswick New Jersey*. For a critical view of public–private partnerships, see Jason R. Hackworth, *The Neoliberal City: Governance, Ideology, and Development in American Urbanism* (Ithaca, NY: Cornell University Press, 2007). On the link between education and neoliberal governance, see Pauline Lipman, "Economic Crisis, Accountability, and the State's Coercive Assault on Public Education in the USA," *Journal of Education Policy* 28, no. 5 (September 2013): 557–573.

12  Listokin et al., *New Brunswick New Jersey*, 114; Walter H. Waggoner, "Financing Is Set in New Brunswick to Build $6 Million Office Building," *New York Times*, April 14, 1977, 49; Walter H. Waggoner, "Johnson & Johnson Expanding in Jersey: Planning $50 Million," *New York Times*, April 7, 1978, 13; Bill D. Ross, "J&J's New Brunswick Tract: 16 Transactions," *New York Times*, July 14, 1974, 60; Joseph Sullivan, "Poor Opposing New Brunswick Project: 'Suburbanizing' the City," *New York Times*, August 13, 1979, B1; Carl Faith, "A Plan to Revivify New Brunswick," *New York Times*, October 7, 1979, NJ32; Morris Levine, letter to the editor, *New York Times*, October 21, 1979, NJ34; Abraham Wallach, "New Brunswick Tomorrow: It Won't Happen Overnight," *New York Times*, November 4, 1979, NJ34; Lisa Wood, letter to the editor, *New York Times*, November 18, 1979, NJ41; Maureen Nevin Duffy, "New Brunswick: Today and Tomorrow," *New York Times*, September 6, 1981, NJ36; Orrin T. Hardgrove, "In Defense of New Brunswick Tomorrow," *New York Times*, October 11, 1981, NJ44.

13  "Corporate-City Alliance."

14  Marian Courtney, "Benefits for People Sought in New Brunswick Revitalization," *New York Times*, October 14, 1984, 5; Joseph Picard, "New Brunswick's Changing Face Stirs Controversy," *New York Times*, August 30, 1987, 11; Orrin Hardgrove, letter to the editor, *New York Times*, September 13, 1987; Rachel Garbarine, "For New Brunswick: A Surge in Housing," *New York Times*, January 3, 1988.

15  Picard, "New Brunswick Plan Debated."

16  "ACS 2019 (5-Year Estimates)," "Place of Birth of the Foreign-Born Population." For a history of the early Puerto Rican community, see Otilio Colón, "A Brief History of the Hispanic Community in New Brunswick, 1948–1980: A Tercentennial Project," Special Collections, Alexander Library, Rutgers University, New Brunswick.

17  "ACS 2019 (5-Year Estimates)" for New Brunswick census tracts 53, 56.02, and 58.

18 American City Corporation, *Trends, Issues, and Priorities*, 44.
19 "New Brunswick School District Performance Report 2019–20," Official Site of the State of New Jersey, accessed January 28, 2022, https://rc.doe.state.nj.us/district/detail/23/3530/demographics?lang=EN; "About New Brunswick Public Schools," New Brunswick Public Schools, accessed January 28, 2022, https://www.nbpschools.net/overview.
20 Conversation with unnamed Lincoln Annex schoolteacher, February 2020; "New Brunswick School District Performance Report 2019–20," https://www.nbpschools.net/overview.
21 The district also struggles with chronic absenteeism—more than 11 percent of all students miss more than 10 percent of all school attendance days, and these rates are even higher for prekindergarten children and high schoolers, of whom 20 percent are chronically absent. "New Brunswick School District Performance Report 2019–20."
22 The minority of White students in the district seemed to fare much better on these standardized tests. Data from State of New Jersey, Department of Education, "New Brunswick School District," 2019–2020, accessed July 15, 2024, https://rc.doe.state.nj.us/district/detail/23/3530/postsecondary?lang=EN.
23 Data from NJ Department of Education, "2019–20 Per Pupil Expenditures by Source with Average Daily Enrollment," accessed July 15, 2024, https://homeroom4.doe.state.nj.us/audsum/PpeReport?&did=3530&fileformat=html&reportname=PERFORMREPORT&fy=20. In 2019, Wilson School was targeted for improvement for its smattering of White students, who were reportedly underperforming. "New Brunswick School District Performance Report, 2019–20."
24 Former NBPS and Rutgers student, Jenifer Garcia interview, July 13, 2022, Andy Urban. Accessed July 15, 2024, https://lincolnannex.org/jennifer-garcia/.
25 School closures of both public and parochial schools often stir up community opposition and are met with resistance. See, for example, Robert McClory, "Schools Contest Closing Orders in Chicago," *National Catholic Reporter*, March 25, 2005, 4a; Dara N. Sharif, "Urban Academy to Close," *New York Amsterdam News*, February 10, 2011, 35, 38; Lesli A. Maxwell, "Chicago School Closure Battle Echoes in Other Cities," *Education Week* 32, no. 33 (June 5, 2013): 10–11. For a firsthand account of the impact of school closures on receiving schools, see Roy Chan, "Closing the Gap: The Human Impact of D.C. Public School Closings," *Harvard Kennedy School Review* 9 (March 2009): 24–28. See also Jennifer Ayala and Anne Galletta, "Documenting Disappearing Spaces: Erasure and Remembrance in Two High School Closures," *Peace and Conflict* 18, no. 2 (May 2012): 149–155; Jin Lee and Christopher Lubienski, "The Impact of School Closures on Equity of Access in Chicago," *Education and Urban Society* 49, no. 1 (January 2017): 53–80; Sally A. Nuamah, "The Paradox of Educational Attitudes: Racial Differences in Public Opinion on School Closure," *Journal of Urban Affairs* 42, no. 4 (May 2020): 554–570.
26 St. Peter The Apostle, "Parish History," accessed July 15, 2024, https://stpeternewbrunswick.org/parish-history; Charles Kratovil, "St. Peter's Buildings Will Once Again Serve as School for City Kids," *New Brunswick Today*, May 15, 2015, https://newbrunswicktoday.com/2015/05/15/st-petersbuildings-will-once-again-serve-as-school-for-city-kids/.
27 Star-Ledger Staff, "Glimpse of History: Robert Wood Johnson attends 1958 dedication ceremony at Middlesex General Hospital," May 1, 2011, https://www.nj.com/news/local/2011/05/glimpse_of_history_middlesex_g.html. Middlesex General became the teaching hospital for Rutgers Medical School in 1977. In 1986, with the name change of the hospital, the school was also renamed the Robert Wood Johnson

Medical School. Robert Wood Johnson Medical School, "Our History," accessed July 15, 2024, https://www.rwjms.rutgers.edu/about_rwjms/history.
28  See maps in *The Sanborn Building and Property Atlas of New Brunswick, N.J.* (Pelham, NY: Sanborn Mapping and Geographic Information Service, 1989).
29  See New Brunswick Public Schools, "Gifted and Talented Program," accessed July 15, 2024, https://www.nbpschools.net/Page/855. New Brunswick Public Schools, "Gifted and Talented Program Guide," accessed July 15, 2024, https://docs.google.com/document/d/e/2PACX-1vQqkV48WwEZ7K5TU059Y5dbUtffcT9woAJDzhp19fL9pY1Hc26qdarx_auxxrcyk6KHtpF3hdOp9ZWn/pub.
30  "Lincoln Annex School Performance Report, 2018–19," Official Site of the State of New Jersey, accessed January 29, 2021, https://rc.doe.state.nj.us/schoollist.aspx?district=3530&distName=NEW%20BRUNSWICK%20CITY&year=2018-2019.
31  RWJ Barnabas Health, "RWJBarnabas Health and Rutgers Cancer Institute Announce New $750 Million State-of-the-Art, Free-Standing Cancer Pavilion in New Brunswick," accessed June 3, 2019, https://www.cinj.org/rwjbarnabas-health-and-rutgers-cancer-institute-new-jersey-announce-new-750-million-state-art-free.
32  Emails between Christopher Paladino, president of DEVCO, and Steven Libutti, head of Rutgers Cancer Institute of New Jersey, Wednesday, May 29, 2019, obtained through Open Public Records Act (OPRA) request.
33  https://www.njspotlight.com/2016/12/16-12-04-the-list-where-to-find-world-class-cancer-care-in-new-jersey/. Still, the fact that a healthcare reporter identified ten distinct treatment centers throughout the state suggests that New Jersey is not lacking in facilities and that there is not a pressing need for yet another one.
34  U.S. News Staff, "Top 7 Cancer Hospitals in New York," April 24, 2019, https://health.usnews.com/conditions/cancer/ny-cancer-hospitals.
35  Michael Levenson, "Phil Murphy, New Jersey Governor, Says He Has a Kidney Tumor," February 22, 2020, https://www.nytimes.com/2020/02/22/nyregion/governor-phil-murphy-cancer.html.
36  Movimiento Cosecha has been a key leader among New Brunswick and other New Jersey immigrant communities in fighting for the right to drivers' licenses, for example, as well as pandemic relief funds for essential workers who are undocumented and did not qualify for state funds earlier.
37  Madison McGay, "Rutgers Cancer Institute of New Jersey May Build on School Site," *Daily Targum*, October 17, 2019; Madison McGay, "New Brunswick Community Continues to Speak Out against Selling of Lincoln Annex School," *Daily Targum*, January 28, 2020. Nick Muscavage, "Activists Oppose Potential Sale of New Brunswick School for Rutgers-RWJ Cancer Expansion," *Bridgewater Courier News*, January 17, 2020, https://www.mycentraljersey.com/story/news/local/development/2020/01/17/new-brunswick-activists-fight-school-sale-rutgers-cancer-institute/4489346002/. Hayley Slusser and Madison McGay, "Members of New Brunswick Community Announce Formation of Coalition to Defend Lincoln Annex School," *Daily Targum*, February 6, 2020. Nick Muscavage, "Rutgers Groups Oppose New Brunswick School Demolition for Cancer Institute Expansion," *Bridgewater Courier News*, January 31, 2020, https://www.mycentraljersey.com/story/news/local/development/2020/01/31/rutgers-union-opposes-new-brunswick-school-demolition-nj-cancer-institute/4620016002/. Bob Makin, "Rutgers Cancer Institute's $750M Expansion Includes $55M New Brunswick School," January 4, 2020, https://www.mycentraljersey.com/story/news/education/college/rutgers/2020/02/04/rutgers-cancer-institute-nj-expansion-includes-new-brunswick-school/4656390002/. Flyers. NBPS has closed other schools in the past, such as the

Washington School, in the heart of the immigrant community, torn down to build an RWJ Hospital health clinic, and the historic Bayard School, torn down during the redevelopment of the Hiram Square Market area. Doris E. Brown, "Historic School Education in New Brunswick to Celebrate 100th Anniversary Thursday," *Home News*, January 11, 1953; Sullivan, "Poor Opposing New Brunswick Project," B1.

38  Madison McGay, "Cahill Announces Potential Plans to Build New Public School in New Brunswick," *Daily Targum*, February 5, 2020. Hayley Slusser, "Parents, Community Members Continue to Organize against Destruction of Lincoln Annex School," *Daily Targum*, February 13, 2020. New Brunswick Public Schools, "Facility Upgrade Projects / Blanquita Valenti School," accessed July 15, 2024, https://www.nbpschools.net/Page/2295.

39  For a map of RWJ Hospital property in New Brunswick, see Hunt, "Spatial and Procedural Justice," 29.

40  Hunt, "Spatial and Procedural Justice," 35–36. Although Mayor Cahill counts on the loyalty of a number of African American city employees or mid-level officials, community resident Danielle Moore, an African American mother, has been a longtime opponent of many city plans and a vocal critic on many issues affecting the welfare and well-being of local residents. Univision Nueva York, "Padres de familia rechazan los planes de demoler la escuela Lincoln Annex en Nueva Jersey," Univision, February 11, 2020, https://www.univision.com/local/nueva-yorkwxtv/padres-de-familia-rechazan-los-planes-de-demoler-la-escuela-lincoln-annex-ennueva-jersey-video.

41  New Jersey Department of Environmental Protection, documents in author's possession.

42  NBPS has constructed other schools, such as Lord Stirling and the high school, on highly contaminated sites. Winnie Hu, "$187 Million Public School, Under a Cloud in New Jersey," *New York Times*, April 8, 2007.

43  News 12 Staff, "Parents, Teachers March to Prevent Sale of New Brunswick School," News 12 New Jersey, February 18, 2020, http://newjersey.news12.com/story/41716077/parents-teachers-march-today-to-prevent-sale-of-new-brunswick-school; David Hutter, "Rutgers Board Hears Protests against Planned RWJBarnabasHealth Expansion" NJBiz, February 18, 2020, https://njbiz.com/rutgers-board-hears-protests-planned-rwjbarnabashealth-expansion/; NJTV, "Plan to Tear Down School to Build Cancer Center Sparks Protest in New Brunswick," NJ Spotlight News, February 18, 2020, https://www.njtvonline.org/news/video/plan-to-tear-down-school-to-build-cancer-center-sparks-protest-in-new-brunswick/; Univision Nueva York, "Padres de familia salen a marchar para evitar la demolición de una escuela en Nueva Jersey," Univision, February 18, 2020, https://www.univision.com/local/nueva-york-wxtv/padres-de-familia-salen-a-marchar-para-evitar-la-demolicion-de-una-escuela-en-nueva-jersey-video; Univision Nueva York, "Pese a oposición de la comunidad, superintendente planea seguir con el plan de demoler una escuela en New Brunswick," February 22, 2020; WRSU Radio, "Board of Governors Protest," Facebook, February 18, 2020, https://www.facebook.com/Wards5and6/videos/819647021883225/; Bob Makin, "Lincoln Annex School Supporters March on Rutgers University Board of Governors," *Home News Tribune*, February 18, 2020; Hayley Slussler, "Coalition to Defend Lincoln Annex School Marches to Rutgers Board of Governors Meeting," *Daily Targum*, February 19, 2020; Mike Kennedy, "Protesters in New Brunswick, N.J., Object to Hospital Expansion That Would Claim Elementary School Site," *American School and University*, February 20, 2020.

44 "New Brunswick Board of Education Meeting—2/25/2020," *New Brunswick Today*, accessed July 15, 2024, https://www.youtube.com/watch?v=6jdVYpRZyE8; Brianna Kudisch, "Parents Slam District for Plan to Knock Down School to Make Way for Cancer Center," NJ.com, February 26, 2020; Univision Nueva York, "Cara a cara entre padres de familia y empresarios por demolición de una escuela en New Brunswick," Univision, February 25, 2020, https://www.univision.com/local/nueva-york-wxtv/cara-a-cara-entre-padres-de-familia-y-empresarios-por-demolicion-de-una-escuela-en-new-brunswick-video; Hayley Slusser, "New Brunswick Board of Education Holds Meeting on Lincoln Annex School, Faces Legal Obstacles," *Daily Targum*, February 27, 2020; Hayley Slusser, "New Brunswick Board of Education Approves Long-Range Facilities Plan to Replace Lincoln Annex School," *Daily Targum*, March 25, 2020.

45 Ashley Balcerzak, "Murphy Imposes Statewide Curfew; Shuts Down Casinos, Bars and Restaurants," NorthJersey.com, March 16, 2020; "Governor Murphy Announces Statewide Stay at Home Order, Closure of All Non-Essential Retail Businesses," Official Site of the State of New Jersey, March 21, 2020, https://www.nj.gov/governor/news/news/562020/20200320j.shtml; Hunt, "Spatial and Procedural Justice," 45.

46 Madison McGay, "Coalition to Defend Lincoln Annex Holds Press Conference, Attends New Brunswick Planning Board Meeting," *Daily Targum*, March 9, 2020; Daniel Han, "Rutgers Cancer Institute of NJ Expansion Approved by New Brunswick Planning Board," My Central Jersey, March 10, 2020, https://eu.mycentraljersey.com/story/news/local/middlesex-county/2020/03/10/rutgers-cancer-institute-plan-okd-new-brunswick-nj-planning-board/5011650002/; Hayley Slusser, "Lincoln Annex School Advocates Voice Concerns as City Council Passes Ordinance in Support of Hospital Expansion," *Daily Targum*, April 2, 2020; Hayley Slusser, "New Brunswick Board of Education Passes Resolutions to Prepare for Sale of Lincoln Annex School," *Daily Targum*, April 29, 2020; Hayley Slusser, "Community Comes Together to Preserve Lincoln Annex School," *Daily Targum*, May 4, 2020; Univision, "Una frase en el título de propiedad podría evitar la demolición de una escuela en Nueva Jersey," February 21, 2020, https://www.univision.com/local/nueva-york-wxtv; Univision, "Obispo de New Brunswick se niega a hablar de la demolición de una escuela, pese a que él puede evitarla," February 24, 2020, https://www.univision.com/local/nueva-york-wxtv; Bob Makin, "Rutgers Cancer Institute Expansion Could Be Impacted by Lincoln Annex School Deed Restriction," *Home News Tribune*, February 24, 2020.

47 Nick Muscavage, "Middlesex County Judge Facing Ethics Complaint in Property Dispute Case," *Bridgewater Courier News*, October 23, 2020. As noted previously, the warehouse where the children were to be sent to school was rented from a commercial landlord who also rented office space to the mayor's private legal practice. And the new replacement school site was owned by the chair of the Robert Wood Johnson University Hospital Board of Directors.

48 Charlie Kratovil, "Million Dollar Men: RWJ Execs Rake in Millions," *New Brunswick Today*, February 17, 2020, https://newbrunswicktoday.com/2020/02/17/million-dollar-men-rwj-execs-rake-in-millions/.

49 Superintendent Aubrey Johnson, "January Update Letter," January 21, 2020, https://www.nbpschools.net//site/default.aspx?PageType=3&DomainID=1555&ModuleInstanceID=4761&ViewID=6446EE88-D30C-497E-9316-3F8874B3E108&RenderLoc=0&FlexDataID=6337&PageID=2295.

50 Interestingly, the hospital never announced a price it would be *paying* to purchase the existing school site.

# 11
# Forgotten Voices

## Gender and Social Networks in Paterson's Peruvian Community

ELENA SABOGAL

Manuela Callegari arrived in Paterson in 1963. She was just nineteen years old and already had three small children, the youngest only two months old. A resident of Paterson for over sixty years, Manuela raised her eight children there and worked at the Shulton factory in Clifton. In an interview titled "Why Paterson, New Jersey, Is Famous in Lima, Peru" that was published by *The Atlantic* in 2016, her former husband, Guillermo, shared reminiscences of his initial days in Paterson.[1] The article did not mention Manuela, who joined him a year after his arrival. Although Guillermo has been interviewed numerous times about his early experiences and his role in making Paterson the "cuna de los peruanos en Estados Unidos," (cradle of Peruvians in the United States) the voices of Manuela and other Peruvian women have yet to be heard.

Manuela was a friend of the Sibori sisters, who had migrated to Paterson by themselves in 1965. Matilde Sibori opened one of the first Peruvian restaurants, La Flor de la Canela, in the 1970s. The restaurant was located on the corner of Market Street and Mill Street. This area became an important symbol of pride for Peruvians after the determined multiyear efforts of four Peruvian women and one man led the city of Paterson to designate Mill, Market, Main, and Cianci

Streets as Peru Square in 2016. As one of the women spearheading this effort, Nelly Celi, stated, "This is something important to us, it gives recognition to a group of people who came to Paterson, settled, and contributed here."[2] However, her group's efforts to pass this ordinance were not publicly recognized by local government or Peruvian authorities during Peru Square's inauguration ceremony, nor did the current owners of the businesses located in the area mention any of the early pioneer women's contributions. Yolanda Sibori, Matilde's sister, told me during an interview, "I could not believe that my sister was not given a posthumous recognition during the ceremony for her contributions to our community."[3] This silence about the presence of women and their contributions to the city of Paterson has limited our understanding of the social and gendered dynamics of Peruvian migration to this New Jersey city.[4]

This chapter focuses on the unrecognized roles of women and their contributions to the development of Paterson's Peruvian community. With few exceptions,[5] the academic literature about Peruvians in New Jersey has centered primarily on the arrival and contributions of Peruvian men in Paterson, and gender has not been a central focus of analysis.[6] Although a few articles have focused on the emergence and continuity of various cultural and religious organizations and associations that brought visibility to the Peruvian community in Paterson,[7] the analysis has not been "engendered."

The importance of gender cannot be understated. Migration scholars have established how gender structures migration and provides an insight into how identity and social relations are negotiated.[8] These processes are not static, and they also interact with place. Psychologist and scholar of gendered violence Ingrid Palmary and colleagues explain that "although the overall context is the same for men and women, a focus on gender illuminates accounts and positions (of both women and men) that would otherwise remain invisible and highlights the significance of gender (whether visible or not) in the responses that are made to migrants."[9] Applying this to the present context, a study of the role of women and their social networks in Paterson can provide a more nuanced understanding in our knowledge about Peruvian migration to Paterson. Women's voices have been overlooked, but their gendered experiences and roles in the growth of the community provide alternative narratives of Peruvian migration and Paterson as an immigrant city.

## The Presence of Women in Contemporary Peruvian Migration

During the second half of the twentieth century, Peruvians began to migrate across the globe.[10] Their international migration in the 1960s and early 1970s coincided with a period of internal migration from rural areas to Lima and the implementation of policies that gave women access to education in Peru. This led to better chances for women to participate in the Lima labor market and their increased involvement in neighborhood and community associations, where they took a central role. Gains made by women in Peru during the 1960s and 1970s were reversed in the 1980s and 1990s when the impact of neoliberal policies together with political turmoil caused by Shining Path, a newly emerging terrorist group, created a climate of economic instability and insecurity in the country. Although both genders felt the impact of this political crisis in Peru, it led to an important change in the female population's sociopolitical situation by forcing women to take an active role in the formation of grassroots programs, such as popular kitchens, dining rooms, and glass of milk committees, to deal with the food crises.[11] Although women began to gain visibility through their work and participation in these new food security endeavors, they remained invisible in formal public spaces, with no presence in political leadership or government positions.

Under increasingly difficult social, political, and economic circumstances in Peru, women found they needed to find work outside their homes to contribute to their families' incomes. Unemployment, insecurity, a lack of educational opportunities, and insurgency within the country led to massive migration and turned Peru into a "nation of emigrants." By the 1990s, women comprised the larger percentage of Peruvian migrants.[12] Women began to migrate to places where they already had established networks, such as friends or family, in search of economic opportunities. While the United States was the primary destination, Peruvians also chose to migrate to other countries based on access to resources and social networks.[13]

As stated by Giancarlo Muschi (chapter 6 in this volume), Peruvians began to arrive in Paterson in the 1920s. By the late 1960s, Paterson had become a preferred destination for migrants from Peru. The influx of Peruvians in the 1960s and 1970s coincided with the end of Paterson's industrial era, when factories were closing, Paterson's industrial boom had begun to fade away, and Europeans were leaving the city in large numbers.[14] The establishment of the Peruvian community in Paterson followed a pattern similar to prior immigrant communities who arrived to work in the silk mills surrounding the city.[15] Although the city was already in economic decline, the promise of manufacturing jobs appealed to Peruvian immigrants. The first generation of mostly working-class Peruvian men to arrive in New Jersey came in search of the American dream: a comfortable lifestyle, the promise of homeownership, a car, and dollars in the bank, all aspirations that were attainable only by the middle and upper classes back home in Peru.[16] In the 1960s, less than one hundred Peruvians lived in Paterson.[17] There is no record of how many of those migrants were women.[18]

Upon their arrival in Paterson in the 1960s, Peruvians found an established Puerto Rican community that was instrumental in opening doors to help them find employment, at times serving as translators, given the Peruvians' limited English-speaking skills. An article in the *Paterson News* reported in 1972 that "after the Puerto Rican community [Peruvians] are the largest Spanish speaking group in the area."[19] Peruvian migration was not a result of U.S. military intervention in their country of origin, unlike other Latino populations who settled in Paterson, such as Puerto Ricans and Dominicans; however, economic ties between Peru and the United States did shape the earliest migrations (see Muschi, chapter 6 in this volume).[20]

The women who participated in my study had understood that what awaited them in New Jersey was not going to be easy, and they spoke of the many challenges they encountered. With limited English, they initially joined men in the slowly declining manufacturing industry, but with no experience in these jobs, they had to learn to fend for themselves. Rosa, an influential and well-respected businesswoman within the community who had worked in a factory for more than ten years after her arrival in New Jersey in the early 1970s, stated: "Like everyone who arrives, I worked in a factory working two shifts. Since I arrived, Paterson was the place where you found a job. It was the place where you encountered many Peruvians. Paterson was the place where you saw for the first time the inside of a factory and learned how they functioned." In search of better economic opportunities, many women had taken the initiative to migrate by themselves. Celia, who arrived on her own in the early 1970s, explained that gendered networks were already in place that facilitated her journey to Paterson. A former friend—a woman who had migrated to New Jersey many years before Celia—provided the ticket, found her a place to live, and provided contacts for work. Because the demand for labor was still strong in nearby factories, Celia initially worked at a factory making bags, but soon she found a better-paying job as a machine operator in another Paterson factory. Several years later, she found an even better-paying job at the Shulton Perfume Factory in nearby Clifton, where she worked until it closed in the 1990s.

Although migration provided increased economic independence and an opportunity to redefine their traditional roles, Peruvian women were still responsible for taking care of their households.[21] Rosa and her husband initially rented a room in a house in Paterson, which they shared with two single women and three single men. While they all shared the food expenses, the women were still in charge of cooking for the household. Women generally experienced long nights, arriving home after working in the factories to cook for their families or others and take care of the children, while also attempting to learn English on their own. Rosa reminisced that it was here in Paterson, working at a factory, that she began to value and compare herself not only to other women, but also to men because she was doing the same work as the men with almost no training. She had found a job in a factory setting up a machine that made drilling equipment, a job that she would not have been hired to do in Lima. Even though the Peruvian men rarely spoke about the accomplishments of women, migration affected gender dynamics, especially when female migrants began to make inroads into public spaces.

## The (In)Visibility of Peruvian Women in Paterson's Public Spaces

Peruvian society is patriarchal, and gender inequality continues to be pervasive. There are different gender expectations for men and women. Being a wife and a mother are seen as intrinsic aspects of women's identities.[22] Within the private realm of their households, women's roles center on fulfilling the needs of their husbands and children, while the men are at work and in control of public spaces. In mainstream Peruvian culture, "definitions of masculinity are identified with domination in the public sphere, authority in the family and control of female sexuality."[23] There is general agreement regarding what constitutes appropriate manhood, although men can emphasize certain aspects more than others, depending on their regional culture, class, social status, or generation.[24]

Migration disrupts traditional roles and ideologies. Research conducted by Pierrette Hondagneu-Sotelo shows that "traditional family patriarchy weakens, [and] immigrant women assume more active public and social roles" within their communities.[25] Migrant Peruvian women in Paterson embraced the challenge of having more active roles in public spaces and becoming financially independent in the new society.

However, men's and women's experiences are also conditioned by established culturally expected roles.[26] Cooking, a task that had been traditionally and almost exclusively reserved for women in the past, became the gateway that provided Peruvian women an opportunity to start new businesses in the Paterson community. Many of the interviewed women fondly remembered the opening and success of restaurants owned by entrepreneurial women who, in their traditional roles as nurturers, were able to provide a taste of home in public venues for men who were living alone.

The contributions of Peruvian businesswomen in the literature on migration have been reported only in passing. Ingrid Palmary and her colleagues suggest that including gendered accounts can highlight the contributions made by women, which are ignored in most of the literature.[27] Peruvian women have been largely (in)visible in studies about migration to Paterson. They are usually referred to simply as the mothers, sisters, or wives of the men who are interviewed. On the other hand, these men are very vocal about their own contributions, explaining in detail their "rags to riches" experiences of migration, as detailed in various studies.[28] A case in point is the migration story of Carlos Vera, the current owner of the first Peruvian rotisserie chicken restaurant in Paterson. While recounting his story to one of these researchers,[29] Carlos stated that his sister first opened the restaurant Panchito's, encouraged him to migrate to Paterson, and provided him with support. However, Carlos referred to her only as "my sister." In fact, her name was Isabel Vera, and missing from Carlos's narrative was how Isabel managed to buy that first restaurant and a second one called El Zaña before selling Panchito's to Carlos. Isabel died in 2019; a family member remembered her on social media as a strong woman and a brave warrior. Through her efforts,

Isabel laid the foundation for other members of her family to migrate to Paterson.[30]

A common practice among the migrant Peruvian women was selling home-cooked food in their homes, outside factories, and in parks where Peruvian migrants gathered. This laid the groundwork for subsequent restaurant openings years later. Although local Peruvian community papers carried obituaries to honor Maria Elena Machado, known as "la pionera de las peñas y jaranas" in Paterson through her restaurant Lima de Antaño, which had opened its doors in 1972, and Matilde Sibori, who opened La Flor de la Canela, we know very little about other such women.[31] For example, many interviewees spoke of Teresita Rojas, who was the first woman to sell the traditional *anticuchos* (beef heart skewers) and *picarones* (Peruvian donuts) in a small garage on the corner of Market and Mill Streets that Matilde rented to her. In 2000, Matilde sold her property to Delia Cortez, who opened the restaurant La Tia Delia.[32] Many also fondly recalled a woman referred to as Señora Faride who provided daily meals for many of the newly arrived Peruvians. However, we know very little about the beginnings, sacrifices, and efforts of any of these women or others who pursued similar paths.

With the arrival of more Peruvians in the 1980s and 1990s, new markets and ideas began to emerge. Flor Morales, a successful businesswoman, and her husband, with whom she worked shoulder to shoulder, were the first to import Peruvian products. The couple formed the Peruvian Import Company in 1978, which introduced a variety of products to Paterson that offered the authentic taste of home. Today, their company exports to various countries around the world. Inka's Foods ("Of the good . . . the best!") and Doña Isabel are two of the brands that offer authentic Peruvian flavor for cooking typical dishes, as well as various frozen products.

As noted by M. Cristina Alcalde, gender hierarchies are as pervasive in Peruvian cuisine as they are in other facets of Peruvian life, and there is a broad tendency in Peruvian gastronomy that privileges masculinities.[33] Nevertheless, the work and efforts of these pioneer women blossomed in the city of Paterson, and the growing appreciation of Peruvian cuisine by the public has contributed to Paterson's becoming a culinary destination. According to data compiled by Bernardo Muñoz Angosto, director of the Trade Commission of Peru in New York, by 2020 there were twenty-nine Peruvian restaurants in Paterson and over 165 in New Jersey.[34] Thus, Paterson became a cultural enclave for Peruvians and, by the 1980s, with the opening of migrant businesses and the ongoing arrival of new migrants, an area of the city became known as "Little Lima."

## Women Redefining the Symbols of Peruvian National Identity

Peru is a multicultural and heterogeneous country divided along geographical, linguistic, racial, ethnic, and class lines. The colonial legacy has influenced every aspect of the Peruvian experience and created a fractured country that has trouble defining its national identity because education, values, and traditions vary according to regions and socioeconomic status. These complexities led the Peruvian novelist and anthropologist Jose Maria Arguedas to question whether it was possible for Peruvians to identify with a common project that would allow them to move beyond their differences.[35]

The elite sectors in Peru do not acknowledge that social hierarchies are in place, that geographical spaces are delineated along racial, class, and gendered lines, and that discrimination is constantly experienced by indigenous peoples and other minorities. Marisol de la Cadena has identified this as "silent racism" in Peruvian society.[36] Marco Avilés argues that, among the elite, there continues to be a colonial mentality that sees people from the Amazon or the Andes or any Peruvian citizens who are not from Lima as "other."[37] There is an urgent need for open dialogue to expose racism, discrimination, and the living situations of the indigenous, Afro-descendants, and ethnic minorities.[38] Furthermore, Sulmont and Callirgos[39] argue that these hierarchical relationships between different ethnic and racial groups have prevented the indigenous population from having the same rights as well-to-do Peruvians.[40] National identity therefore remains unresolved because a multiplicity of Peruvian voices are silenced through discrimination and lack of integration.

Because Peru is a nation with multiple identities within its boundaries, migrants who leave Peru to go abroad bring the established social hierarchies with them and then attempt to construct and negotiate an "imagined" national identity based on the one tangible element that they unequivocally have in common: their Peruvian nationality. Historian Cecilia Mendez argues that "nationality is very emotional because we feel it as our own; these are our experiences, our family ... that is why it is so powerful to belong to a nation. It matters because it has to do with a community."[41] However, as Vazquez del Aguila notes, "migration creates displacement and multiple dislocations that challenge Peruvian racial and social hierarchies, ... creat[ing] new social spaces for re-negotiating [gender,] race and social hierarchies that are more difficult to overcome in Peruvian society."[42] Arriving in Paterson with a strong sense of national pride, new immigrants embrace a commitment to keep Peruvian values alive by forming voluntary associations to reimagine and affirm their shared sense of national identity.[43] The formation of such associations had characterized earlier internal migration in Peru and had empowered women from rural backgrounds to take leadership roles in the urban environment.[44] In his pioneering studies of Peruvian migration, Teofilo Altamirano argues that the fundamental objective of creating voluntary associations abroad was immigrants' commitment to demonstrating their love of being Peruvian and to show unity despite complex internal regional and cultural differences.[45] Peruvian associations in Paterson—whether religious, cultural, or regional—have consistent overriding themes and share similar goals: to establish a connection to their country of origin, to pass on various cultural values and traditions, to provide a positive image of their country abroad, and to highlight or recognize the achievements of and contributions of Peruvian immigrants to the community. With a strong tradition of welcoming immigrant populations from around the world, the officials and institutions that Peruvians encountered in Paterson supported the establishment of immigrant associations.

The first Peruvian associations organized in Paterson were religious *hermandades* (brotherhoods). The Hermandad de Damas y Caballeros de San Martin de Porres, housed at the Cathedral of St. John the Baptist in Paterson, was founded in 1975. The Hermandad del Señor de los Milagros at Our Lady of Lourdes followed in 1976. These two brotherhoods imported their icons from Peru and hold annual processions to honor them. They also have similar structures. Traditionally, male devotees carry the icon during the processions, while female devotees participate as *sahumadoras* (incense carriers) and *cantoras* (singers).[46] Both traditions can be traced back to colonial times. The cult of the Señor de los Milagros (Lord of Miracles) has African roots but over time has become embraced by all Peruvians, regardless of race, ethnicity, or class and, as such, it has become a symbol of Peruvian national identity. These religious associations "highlight how the process of identity construction is mediated by religion" and provide migrants a space to "negotiate and reconstruct their identity."[47]

Changes in voluntary religious associations in Paterson have included changes in the roles and position of women. One of the women I interviewed told me that she became involved with the community after attending her first Lord of the Miracles procession ten years after her arrival in Paterson. By 1994, she had become the first woman to preside over this association and allow women to carry the platform of the Lord of Miracles during the procession. Even today, this honor is reserved only for men in Peru. As the interviewee explained, "I went to my first procession and from there I got involved with the community until I became president of the Brotherhood of the Lord of Miracles of Paterson. It was in that year, 1994, when I, along with 42 women, carried the platform with the image of the Lord for the first time. It was such a privilege that this started here, because in Peru women do not carry it. Paterson in many ways is great for the Peruvian community."[48]

In research on religious brotherhoods in Paterson, Larissa Ruiz Baia learned from a male member of the brotherhood that there was disagreement within the brotherhood regarding whether women were physically capable of carrying the icon. After much debate, women were permitted to carry the image, thus opening the path for other migrant Peruvian women to take a more prominent role in the ceremony. Today most brotherhoods in New Jersey allow women to participate in their processions as carriers, and some associations in Elizabeth, Clifton, and Paterson consist exclusively of women.[49]

Through their involvement in religious associations, migrant Peruvian women in Paterson were able to empower themselves and start their own new traditions.

They negotiated a role and a level of equality not yet available to women in their country of origin. In Lima, women continue to play a subordinate role as sahumadoras and singers in the main Lord of the Miracles procession. Yet today, outside of Peru, the Lord of the Miracles, an image representing a mestizo nation with an Afro-descendant tradition, has become a symbol of national identity embraced by all Peruvians, a "letter of introduction of the Peruvian people to the world," and a path to empowerment for these women in Paterson.[50]

As the number of Peruvians grew in Paterson, migrants formed other associations to teach cultural traditions to children.[51] Yolanda Esquiche along with her husband and other educators founded the Peruvian Teachers Association, which met on Saturdays at her house with the purpose of passing on Peruvian history and culture to second-generation Peruvian American children. Other associations focused on traditional dances, sports, and regional interests. It is important to note that these efforts were voluntary and not compensated. During my interviews, women were more likely to emphasize their contributions and accomplishments in terms of their children's success; they felt proud of the sacrifices they made to send their children to school and happy that they had become professionals and did not experience the hardships they themselves had endured. Unlike men, these women were more reluctant to talk about their own involvement in and contributions to the community. They were generally humble and did not promote their own achievements but instead advised me to meet and interview the male leaders of the community who over the years had become the community's recognized spokespersons. Multiple researchers and journalists have documented this male-dominated narrative.

In Peruvian society, public life provides an opportunity for men to achieve visibility, prestige, and respect.[52] Becoming a leader of an association is an aspiration and a significant honor, particularly if the association is influential and well respected within the community.[53] Once elected, a leader's priority is to carry out sociocultural activities for the promotion of Peru.[54] Altamirano has pointed out that associations have leaders who are democratically elected and that, contrary to popular belief, many of the leaders are women. While describing women as active participants of cultural associations and keepers of Peruvian values and identity, he also stated that "there were many women's groups or committees that operated in parallel with the newly formed associations" and maintained that ladies' committees comprised the members' wives.[55] Unfortunately, however, Altamirano did not make clear which associations operated in parallel, what the women's roles in these organizations were, or how women contributed to the leadership of the newly formed associations.

The Peruvian Parade, Inc., in Paterson sheds some light on the roles women play in the community associations discussed by Altamirano. This is the largest and perhaps best-known Peruvian community association in the city and has a very active and influential presence in the community. It was founded in 1986, almost a decade after the first religious associations were formed. As one of the founders told me, its emphasis was on celebrating and showcasing Peruvian cultural traditions, following the example of the Paterson Puerto Rican Day Parade and Festival established in 1972. To realize this dream, the founders of the Peruvian Parade, all male, counted on the support of the first Latina to serve as councilwoman in the city of Paterson, Maria Magda, a pioneer woman of Puerto Rican descent who was elected to office in 1984.

However, although established with the support of a Latina council member, the Peruvian Parade, Inc., continues to operate in a male-dominated manner in terms of leadership and events. The association holds annual elections, but in its thirty-seven years of existence, only once—in 2001–2003—was a woman, Maria del Pilar Rivas, elected president. Rivas was born in Piura and migrated to New Jersey in the late 1970s, where she became a successful businesswoman, opening first a bridal shop and later a bakery before dedicating time to the community. In an interview, Rivas described her leadership experience as very challenging because a former president of the association confronted her and told her that a woman should not oversee the parade. Evidently, she was contesting a space that was culturally perceived as belonging only to men. She felt compelled to demonstrate to the former president and the rest of the community that she could successfully lead the association. She told me, "As women, everything is more difficult because we are questioned and challenged, so in the end I was very proud of the success of the parade and because it was a major accomplishment for me as a woman." As a woman, Rivas had managed to position herself as a community leader and was proud of her ability to bring national pride to her community.[56]

## Peru Square: The Connection to Home and a New Path to Women's Empowerment

Maria del Pilar Rivas has worked tirelessly throughout the years to overcome gender barriers and become a vocal leader of the Peruvian community in Paterson. The founder of several associations, she has been listed as a "Notable Peruvian American" in *Multicultural America: An Encyclopedia of the Newest Americans*.[57] Although she has never held an elected office, she has been identified as a businesswoman and politician but not recognized in her role as a community leader.[58] Well known in Paterson, her most recent initiative was Peru Square, mentioned at the beginning of this chapter. In 2009, Puerto Rican mayor Joey Torres appointed Rivas as deputy mayor, an honorary position in the city of Paterson. The role of the deputy mayor is to act as a cultural liaison between the mayor and the appointee's community and, in her new role, Rivas discussed the idea of designating a street in Paterson as Peru Lane with Mayor Torres. At the time, her idea did not go anywhere, but she did not let this initial disappointment deter her. Years later, in 2015, she put together the group of three women and one man who would undertake her "Peru Street" dream. She convened Patricia Quispe, Nelly Celi, Cristina Tone, and Daniel Gutierrez, all well-known and active members of the Peruvian community, and invited them to join her in making this dream come true. To the team this was "hacer patria," or their way of showing that their love for Peru superseded any individual benefit.[59] The team adopted this goal as their own and collected over 650 signatures throughout the community, submitted a petition to the city's authorities, and lobbied the city of Paterson for this designation.

On April 21, 2016, the city of Paterson designated the area situated between Mill, Market, Main, and Cianci Streets as Peru Square. The designation was announced at a regular session of the city council in Paterson City Hall, which was packed with members of the community. Patricia Quispe said that the best part of this emotional moment was when the team members hugged each other and felt their tears streaming down their faces because of what they felt was an enormous accomplishment. The announcement was followed by a celebratory buffet donated by various Peruvian restaurants from Market Street. However, the euphoria of the announcement did not last long. The Peruvian community was divided over who deserved to receive credit for the designation of Peru Square. Rivas and her team accused Councilwoman Maritza Davila of taking undeserved credit for their work. However, it was only in her role as an elected official in the city of Paterson that Davila introduced the resolution designating Peru Square.

The inauguration of Peru Square took place months later, on a Sunday morning in November, but none of the originators of the idea were invited to the event. A picture published in the *Paterson Times* shows Mayor Joey Torres, the Peruvian consul Vitaliano Gallardo, Carlos Vera, the current owner of Panchito's Restaurant who had just been appointed as the city's Peruvian American deputy mayor, and two council members. The gender composition of this lineup could not be more telling. There were four men and one woman on the podium, the reverse gender composition of the group who had worked so hard for this idea since its inception.

The hour-long ceremony was marked with absences and moments of silence. Councilwoman Maritza Davila, whose father was a Peruvian immigrant, presided over the ceremony, briefly mentioned the names of two of the team members, and asked for a moment of silence in memory of the recent passing of Delia Cortez, the former owner of the restaurant Tia Delia. Earlier, one of the four women on the original team, Nelly Celi, had spoken to the Peruvian news outlets in Paterson, expressing the team's upset over not being recognized as the originators of the initiative for the creation of Peru Square. The controversy over who deserved credit for the creation of Peru Square divided the community in half, resulting in Mayor Andre Sayegh issuing two formal proclamations in the naming of Peru Square.[60]

Rivas has continued to work toward making Peru Square a place of which all Peruvians can be proud. Through a campaign called "limpiando la casa," or "cleaning the house," she recruited members of the community to help her clean the streets in front of the businesses in Peru Square. Identifying Peru Square as "the house" extended the act of cleaning beyond the domestic sphere, into the public space. Symbolically, this redefined women's traditional role, done in the privacy of their homes, to include a public space that connected them to a home far away, the *patria*. According to Rivas, her goal was not personal, but community oriented. She wanted to beautify Peru Square as a way to show pride in her national identity. She said that "as a Peruvian, it was important to me to achieve this honor for all Peruvian immigrants so they can feel proud of their legacy in Paterson." Rivas has encountered multiple roadblocks in her journey as a community leader in a place that has traditionally recognized only men in that role. Her contributions have been minimized by those studying the Peruvian community in Paterson because of the lack of a gender lens in most of the published research about this community.

Maria del Pilar Rivas does not give up. On June 27, 2021, she organized the third flag-raising ceremony to commemorate an important event: Peru's bicentenary, which took place on July 28, 2021. In attendance were Mayor Andre Sayegh, Councilwoman Lilisa Mims, and Yvan Solari, consul of Peru in Paterson. During the ceremony, Rivas emphasized that her work and that of her team had aimed to leave a Peruvian legacy by creating a space that could be claimed by all Peruvians. In spite of the continuing tensions that arose from the naming of Peru Square, the event was well attended by community leaders, and it was clear that Rivas was finally being recognized for her work on behalf of the community.[61]

The untimely passing of Nelly Celi on July 29, 2021, will likely bring the community together in recognition of her many accomplishments as a community leader in Paterson. Her contribution to the naming of Peru Square along with the entire team's efforts, may finally be acknowledged.

## Conclusion

Despite gains in contested spaces, gender dynamics in Paterson have scarcely changed. Peruvian men, and some women, continue to validate the idea that males belong in public spaces, while females guard cultural traditions and values and occupy mostly subordinate roles in those spaces. Even when women have succeeded in leadership positions within the community or in business, the broader community rarely acknowledges their work and contributions. In Paterson, the female struggle for visibility and power continues.

The creation of new associations founded and led by women in Paterson has added visibility to women as community leaders. To develop a better understanding of the Peruvian community, we need to make an effort to highlight female initiatives and contributions, which male-dominated narratives have obscured for too long, and to acknowledge that Peruvian women also see Paterson as a place of opportunity and pride. Like men, they hold themselves and others to very high standards, validating their efforts and their sense of belonging, and see their contributions to the community as a way of honoring their country as proud Peruvians.

## Notes

This chapter is based on my field-based research in Paterson between 2016 and 2019. I conducted over one hundred in-depth formal and informal interviews with Peruvian immigrants who arrived in New Jersey between 1962 and 2000. As a Peruvian myself, I was welcomed into the community and became an active participant observer, attending multiple social, political, cultural, and religious events to understand how identity is shaped by the politics of gender, place, and belonging.

1. Maria-Pia Negro-Chin, "Why Paterson, New Jersey, is Famous in Lima, Peru." *The Atlantic*, May 18, 2016.
2. As quoted by Fausto Giovanny Pinto, "Paterson Residents Want Area Designated as 'Peru Square,'" NJ.com, April 26, 2016. The other members of the Peru Square initiative were Maria del Pilar Rivas, Patricia Quispe, Cristina Tone, and Daniel Gutierrez.
3. Matilde died in 2018.
4. Other pioneer women include Maria Chinchay, Maria Elena Machado, and Yolanda Esquiche.
5. Larissa Ruiz Baia, "Rethinking Transnationalism: Reconstructing National Identities among Peruvian Catholics in New Jersey," *Journal of Interamerican Studies and World Affairs* 41, no. 4 (Winter 1999): 93–109; Ulla D. Berg, "¿Enmarcando la 'peruanidad'? La poética y la pragmática del performance público entre los migrantes peruanos en Nueva Jersey," in *El quinto suyo: Transnacionalidad y formaciones diaspóricas en la migración peruana*, ed. Ulla D. Berg and Karsten Paerregaard (Lima: Instituto de Estudios Peruanos, 2005), 37–68; Ulla Berg, *Mobile Selves: Race, Migration, and Belonging in Peru and the U.S.* (New York: New York University Press, 2015).
6. Rua Teófilo Altamirano, *Los que se fueron: Peruanos en Estados Unidos* (Lima: Pontificia Universidad Católica del Perú, 1990); Karsten Paerregaard, *Peruvians Dispersed: A Global Ethnography of Migration* (Lanham, MD: Lexington Books, 2008); Arthur Holland Michel, "The Peruvians in Paterson, 1956–1970: In Northern New Jersey, Two Histories Intersect and a Community Germinates," senior project, Division of Social Studies, Bard College, New York, May 2013; Gianncarlo Muschi, "From Factory Workers to Owners: Informality, Recurseo and Entrepreneurship in the Formation of the Peruvian Community of Paterson, New Jersey 1960–2001" (PhD diss., University of Houston, May 2019).
7. Ruiz Baia, "Rethinking Nationalism"; Michael G. Francesco, "Peruvians in Paterson: The Growth and Establishment of a Peruvian American Community within the Multiethnic Immigrant History of Paterson, New Jersey," *Journal of Urban History* 40, no. 3 (2014): 497–513; Berg, "¿Enmarcando la 'peruanidad'?"

8 Sarah J. Mahler and Patricia R. Pessar, "Gender Matters: Ethnographers Bring Gender from the Periphery toward the Core of Migration Studies," *International Migration Review* 40, no. 1 (Spring 2006): 27–63.
9 Ingrid Palmary, Erica Burman, Khatidja Chantler, and Peace Kiguwa, eds., *Gender and Migration: Feminist Interventions* (London: Zed Books, 2010), 3.
10 Paerregaard, *Peruvians Dispersed*; Ayumi Takenaka, Karsten Paerregaard, and Ulla Berg, "Introduction: Peruvian Migration in a Global Context," *Latin American Perspectives* 37, no. 5 (2010): 3–11.
11 Cecilia Blondet and Carmen Montero, "La situación de la mujer en el Peru, 1980–1994," Documento de Trabajo No. 68 (Lima: Instituto de Estudios Peruanos, 1994).
12 Altamirano, *Los que se fueron*; Michael G. Durand, "The Peruvian Diaspora: Portrait of a Migratory Process," *Latin American Perspectives* 37, no. 5 (September 2010): 12–28; Instituto Nacional de Estadística e Informática (INEI), *Migración Internacional Peruana: Una Mirada Desde las Mujeres*. (Lima, April 2012), accessed July 10, 2023, https://www2.congreso.gob.pe/sicr/cendocbib/con4_uibd.nsf/1558A4 FABBDC106805257CD3007056D9/$FILE/1_pdfsam_Peru_Migracion _internacional_peruana.pdf.
13 See Paerregaard, *Peruvians Dispersed*, for a geographical mapping of Peruvian global migration.
14 Thomas Y. Owusu, "Economic Transition in the City of Paterson, New Jersey (America's First Planned Industrial City): Causes, Impacts and Urban Policy Implications," *Urban Studies Research* 2014 (2014): 1–9.
15 Altamirano, *Los que se fueron*.
16 Altamirano, *Los que se fueron*.
17 Muschi, "From Factory Workers."
18 Prior to the 1960s, the majority of Peruvian migrants worldwide were men (68.7%), but by the 1960s a shift began to emerge. Data collected by the Instituto Nacional de Estadística e Informática in 2012 showed that women comprised more than half of Peruvian migrants worldwide reaching 56.5 percent during the decade 1991–2000, coinciding with the social and political turmoil in their home country.
19 Victor Miguel Tirado, "Flow of Peruvians into Paterson Is on Upswing," *Paterson News*, November 3, 1972, 9.
20 See Altamirano, *Los que se fueron*, 26–29.
21 Sherry Grasmuck and Patricia Pessar, *Between Two Islands: Dominican International Migration* (Berkeley: University of California Press, 1991); Pierrette Hondagneu-Sotelo, ed., *Gender and U.S. Immigration: Contemporary Trends* (Berkeley: University of California Press, 2003).
22 Norma Fuller, *Dilemas de la femineidad: Mujeres de clase media en el Perú* (Lima: Pontificia Universidad Catolica del Peru, 1993).
23 Norma Fuller, "The Social Constitution of Gender Identity among Peruvian Males," in *Changing Men and Masculinities in Latin American*, ed. Matthew C. Gutmann (Durham, NC: Duke University Press, 2003), 134–152.
24 Fuller, "Social Constitution."
25 Pessar, "Engendering Migration," 29–30.
26 Cecilia Menjivar, *Fragmented Ties: Salvadoran Immigrant Networks in America* (Berkeley: University of California Press, 2000).
27 Palmary et al., *Gender and Migration*.
28 Altamirano, *Los que se fueron*; Paerregaard, *Peruvians Dispersed*; Holland Michel, "Peruvians in Paterson"; Muschi, "From Factory Workers."

29 Muschi, "From Factory Workers."
30 Based on conversations with Yolanda Sibori and Maria Ambrosio, Matilde Sibori's sister and daughter.
31 A *peña* is a bar/restaurant where people go to listen to Afro-Peruvian creole music. A *jarana*, a tradition with colonial roots, is a party with creole music.
32 I had lunch at La Tia Delia many times since arriving in New Jersey in 2007 and tried to interview Ms. Cortez. Despite encouragement from her family to meet with me, she never agreed to an interview.
33 M. Cristina Alcalde, *Peruvian Lives across Borders: Power, Exclusion, and Home* (Champaign: University of Illinois Press, 2018).
34 Bernardo Muñoz Angosto, "Relación de Restaurantes Peruanos del Consuldo General del Perú en Paterson" (New York: Trade Commission of Peru, 2020).
35 Gonzalo Portocarrero, *Racismo y mestizaje* (Lima: SUR, Corporación de Estudios Sociales y Educación, 1993), 258.
36 Marisol de la Cadena, "Silent Racism and Intellectual Superiority in Peru," *Bulletin of Latin American Research* 17, no. 2 (1998): 143–164.
37 Marco Avilés, *De Dónde Venimos los Cholos* (Lima: Seix Barral, 2016).
38 COVID-19 laid bare the country's inequalities and the wealth disparity between various sectors of society: access to life-saving medical care has not been available to poor citizens.
39 David Sulmont and Juan Carlos Callirgos, "¿El país de todas las sangres? Race and Ethnicity in Contemporary Peru," in *Pigmentocracies: Ethnicity, Race, and Color in Latin America*, edited by Edward Telles (Chapel Hill: University of North Carolina Press, 2014), 126–171.
40 The 2021 Peruvian election has brought to the forefront the upper classes' unwillingness to even consider an indigenous president. Racism has become visible in social media in memes and derogatory comments about President Pedro Castillo.
41 Cecilia Méndez, Conversación con Cecilia Mendez *La Periódica*, December 7, 2020, (my translation). Accessed August 2, 2021, https://laperiodica.pe/conversacion-con-cecilia-mendez.
42 Ernesto Vazquez del Aguila, *Being a Man in a Transnational World: The Masculinity and Sexuality of Migration* (London: Routledge, 2015), 32.
43 Although many Peruvian immigrants initially came from Lima, my interviews with community members and records at the Peruvian Consulate in Paterson show that Peruvians in New Jersey trace their roots to every region of Peru.
44 See Altamirano, *Los que se fueron*; Rua Teófilo Altamirano, *Liderazgo y Organizaciones de Peruanos en el Exterior: Culturas Transnacionales e Imaginarios sobre el Desarrollo* (Lima: PromPeru y Pontificia Universidad Católica del Perú, 2000); Paul L. Doughty, "Life Goes On: Revisiting Lima's Migrant Associations," in *Migrants, Regional Identities and Latin American Cities*, edited by Teofilo Altamirano and Lane Ryo Hirabayashi (American Anthropological Association, 1997), 67–93; Karsten Paerregaard, *Linking Separate Worlds: Urban Migrants and Rural Lives in Peru* (Oxford: Berg Publishers, 1997); Blondet and Montero, "La situación."
45 Altamirano, *Los que se fueron*, 64.
46 Ruiz Baia, "Rethinking Transnationalism"; Karsten Paerregaard, "In the Footsteps of the Lord of Miracles: The Expatriation of Religious Icons in the Peruvian Diaspora," *Journal of Ethnic and Migration Studies* 34, no. 7 (September 2008): 1073–1089; Francesco, "Peruvians in Paterson."
47 Ruiz Baia, "Rethinking Nationalism," 93–94.
48 According to Ruiz Baia, the first time women carried the saint's image was in 1995.

49　Ruiz Baia, "Rethinking Nationalism."
50　Ruiz Baia, "Rethinking Nationalism"; Julia Costilla, "Una práctica negra que ha ganado a los blancos: símbolo, historia y devotos en el culto al Señor de los Milagros de Lima (siglos XIX-XXI)," *Anthroplogica* 34, no. 36 (2016): 149–176, 167 (my translation).
51　Miguel Esquiche, "Peruvian Teachers Association," in *First Golden Book* (NJ: Peruvian Parade, 1991), 40.
52　Fuller, "Social Constitution."
53　Altamirano, *Liderazgo y Organizaciones*.
54　Altamirano, *Liderazgo y Organizaciones*.
55　Altamirano, *Liderazgo y Organizaciones*, 61 (my translation).
56　In "¿Enmarcando la 'peruanidad'?" Berg provides more comprehensive insight into the challenges faced by Maria del Pilar Rivas during her tenure as president of the Peruvian Parade, Inc. See also Berg, *Mobile Selves*.
57　Erika Busse-Cárdenas and Rodrigo Lovatón Dávila, "Peruvian Immigrants," in *Multicultural America: An Encyclopedia of the Newest Americans*, ed. Ronald H. Bayor (Santa Barbara, CA: Greenwood, 2011), 1785–1793, 1795–1799.
58　Busse-Cárdenas and Lovatón Dávila, "Peruvian Immigrants."
59　"Hacer patria" has both objective (geographical) and subjective (love and respect for the country) components, but for the Peruvians who were interviewed in my study, it implies the idea of working together toward achieving a common goal for the overall good of the country. They felt that, as representatives of Peru in New Jersey, it was their job to make sure that the name of the country would be held up high. See "¿Qué significa hacer patria en el Perú?" *Servindi*, July 31, 2014, https://www.servindi.org/actualidad/109856.
60　One, named "Peru Square Business and Community Association," was created by Maria del Pilar Rivas in 2016, and another, named "Peru Square Business Association," was founded by Carlos Vera in 2018.
61　In June 2022, Maria del Pilar Rivas was appointed Deputy Mayor for the City of Paterson for the second time by Mayor Andre Sayegh.

# 12
# "La Iglesia Católica es Mi Comunidad"

## A Union City Latinx Destination from Arrival to Old Age

MELANIE Z. PLASENCIA

It is a cold rainy Sunday, but that does not stop a crowd of older (sixty-five years plus) Latinxs from making their way to Holy Family Church in Union City, New Jersey.[1] Elaine, one of those seniors, rushes to enter the church. She yells out from under her plastic bag-turned-umbrella to another senior, Garcia, holding open the church door a few feet away, "Is there a seat for us in the front?!" Pushing against the wind to hold the door open, Garcia replies, "yes, there is, come! Hurry!" I rush in right after Elaine, and we walk together on the side of several pews to reach Elaine's regular seat directly in front of the priest who will celebrate mass. Older Latinxs like Elaine and Garcia are willing to compromise their health, traveling long distances through bad weather, even on foot, to be in community with their congregation.

Older Latinxs like Elaine and Garcia migrated to the United States in search of a better life. They arrived at different historical moments; Elaine came in the 1950s from Ponce, Puerto Rico, to seek employment in New York City's factories, and Garcia in the 1980s from Guayaquil, Ecuador, to marry the love of his life. Elaine chose Union City based on the recommendation of a friend from the factory who lived in Hoboken, while Garcia's decision was at his son's bequest. Both Elaine and Garcia found refuge in the Catholic church. For many Latinx immigrants, the Catholic pan-Latinx churches in Union City, New Jersey, became a place of refuge and support as they adapted to life in the United States.

This chapter focuses on the Catholic church in Northern New Jersey and the local and regional dynamics of Union City in transforming the state and city into a "center of migration" for Latinx immigrants during their arrival and even today in old age.

## Arrival to Old Age

Historically, the church has been seen as a key institution that supports the assimilation of its members and their adaptation to life in the United States. Research on the role of religion in migration processes, such as the work of Milton Gordon, has long articulated the importance of the church for assimilating European immigrants but, in recent times, the church's role has shifted from being seen as "a facilitator of immigrant assimilation . . . [to] an enabler of immigrant incorporation, transnational social life, and ethnic resilience and affirmation."[2] Scholars, such as David A. Badillo, show that Latinx immigrants have constructed a new meaning for the church, a "new immigrant church" that maintains their connections to the homeland and creates community in the new place that considers their ethnic identity and cultural needs.[3]

But while we understand the history and role of the church for Latinx immigrants, very few studies have explored how this plays out in old age, with much of the research focused on middle-aged adults and children coming of age in the United States. Most of this research has focused on youth participation, with little attention to older adults and their integral role in the church.[4] This is despite the fact that American Catholics are aging, while older Latinxs continue to be the largest foreign-born aging population in the United States and make up a large proportion of the Catholic population in the U.S.[5]

## Sources and Methods

This chapter is based on ethnographic fieldwork in Union City, New Jersey. From 2015 to 2017, I spent several days every week interacting with older Latinxs in locations in Union City where they congregate socially or to receive services. I also conducted in-depth interviews with fifteen older Latinxs in Holy Family Church's rectory and came to know them as devout Catholics belonging to this church. They spent much of their time attending church or volunteering in the service of the church. They described themselves and were described by other older Latinxs in the community as "los católicos"/the Catholics. Los católicos allowed me to observe and participate in their daily experiences and be in community with them as their "adopted granddaughter."

The interviews, conducted in Spanish and English, lasted approximately sixty to ninety minutes each and included questions about their migration to the United States and Union City, New Jersey. I also asked about the church's significance in their lives and if the church played an active role in their sense of community. When I asked older Latinxs about how they found social support, many brought me to and reflected on the church, often describing Holy Family Church as their second family and second home in Union City.

My ethnographic notes and information gleaned from church archives illuminate the important role of the Catholic church in Union City, and the Archdiocese of Newark, in supporting and creating a Latinx church for immigrants from their arrival to the United States into old age. This chapter is divided into two parts. Part One, discusses arrival, and shares how the Archdiocese of Newark and the Catholic churches of Union City supported Latinx immigrant arrival to the county and city. Part Two, is about the older Latinx community, and discusses the church's role in the lives of Latinx immigrants who are now in *la tercera edad* (the third stage in life). Together, both parts articulate the role of the Catholic church in cultivating a Latinx community in the state of New Jersey and supporting its members across their life course as they age in the community and their adopted nation.

## Part One: New Arrivals and the Church

> The history of the urban Union City is a revolving door of immigrant groups—first the Irish, Germans, Italians and Armenians, then the Cubans, and in the last five years, Central and South Americans.
> —Wehrwein, 1985[6]

Churches are a primary form of ethnic organization. As an immigrant-receiving institution, the U.S. Catholic Church has evolved with subsequent waves of immigrants, contributing to its social and political richness. From European immigrants to Puerto Rican laborers, Cuban exiles, and Central and South American communities escaping war and poverty in their countries, each community has found a home in the Catholic church in New Jersey and, more specifically, Union City.

The first waves of immigration to the area were mainly from Europe, including Italian, Polish, Irish, and Dutch immigrants. In an interview, Father Riley, a former priest of Holy Family Church, shared that these immigrant groups often came with priests from their home country, establishing "national parishes" in their respective communities and enclaves. For example, Holy Family Church was established by German immigrants in 1857 and thus became a national parish for that community, led by Father Greiff. Churches in each community were based on national origin and met the needs of the ethnic community, while also promoting their assimilation into U.S. society. Churches were seen as way stations, and there was a belief that immigrants would move elsewhere for permanent settlement, which played largely into the church's assimilationist role. After World War II, when Puerto Ricans and Cubans arrived, many European immigrants moved beyond Union City's urban enclave to more spacious areas of New Jersey, including Essex and Bergen Counties, partly in response to the area becoming more ethnically and racially diverse.[7] White flight, or the mass exodus of Whites from urban spaces, left Union City open for new settlements.

Union City is often described as a Cuban-created enclave; however, church accounts show that Puerto Ricans were the first Latinxs to occupy the community as early as the 1940s.[8] Puerto Rican farmworkers came to work as seasonal laborers on farms across central Pennsylvania, New Jersey, and upstate New York.[9] In New Jersey, they gravitated to churches in Camden and Trenton. Shortly after, they moved to urban areas in Hudson County, New Jersey, including Newark, where there was "cheap housing and a market for unskilled labor."[10] Some Puerto Ricans arrived in Jersey City and Hoboken to work in factories such as Tootsie Roll and Maxwell House,[11] while other Puerto Ricans settled in the neighboring community of Union City to work in the embroidery factories that shaped the area into the "embroidery capital of the world." By the 1950s, the Archdiocese of Newark recognized the growing population of Puerto Ricans in the area and began training priests in the Spanish language.

In 1959, the Catholic church became involved in Cuban migration to the United States. "The American church perceived communism as a prime enemy of Christianity, [and] the exiles' rejection of it [communism] made them come across as people who had given up their homeland in order to practice their faith in freedom."[12] Cubans arriving in New Jersey were attracted by factory work and received government support to settle in New Jersey and Florida. One reason they settled in Union City was the aid the church provided, which offered "spiritual aid and religious formation but also guidance and support with social services."[13] One organization, Cubans in Exile, worked under the Catholic Community Services Agency to provide support to the community of North Hudson County.[14] Furthermore, organizations such as Catholic Charities provided Cuban refugees with funds and basic necessities, including clothes, housing, food, and job opportunities when they first arrived in the community.[15] With this support, incoming immigrants also received help in translating important documents. One church member, Alegria, shared that upon arriving in Union City from Cuba, Catholic Charities awarded her a sum of money ($250) to help her get settled. Other Latinxs were introduced to the church when they arrived by family and friends or worked in the church, which welcomed them as recently arrived immigrants and community members.

Two main parishes in Union City and West New York that aided the Cuban population and hosted Cuban refugee programs were St. Augustine and St. Joseph of the Palisades.[16] So too did St. Anthony's, St. Rocco's, and Holy

Family Church.[17] These churches provided employment assistance, found housing, and translated important documents.[18] During this time, St. Augustin's parish developed a Hispanic ministry with Rev. Michael Feketie, who studied Spanish in Puerto Rico.[19] By 1960, more Latinx-created initiatives came to the Catholic church in Union City, including La Legion de Maria, a prayer group in the name of the Virgin Mary. Seven years later, a statue of Our Lady of Charity was commissioned in Spain and brought to Union City. It became a symbol of the Cuban Catholic community that prompted an annual procession that became "a continuity of the faith, a bastion of hope, and a symbol of promise of the return home they [Cubans] longed for."[20]

With time, Cubans became a vital ethnic force in the church as many of the first waves were educated and could speak English.[21] They were also mostly White, allowing their easy integration into the existing church structure and racial composition. Moreover, "they had the education, the stability, the enthusiasm and the determination to structure a community within a church."[22] During this time, Union City was described as "Havana on the Hudson," as the only larger U.S. Cuban population was in Miami. Like previous European immigrants, Cubans traversed the urban landscape and attained upward social mobility that moved them to the suburbs of New Jersey and the state of Florida.

In the 1980s, New Jersey churches saw a growth in the undocumented Latinx population, specifically from the Dominican Republic and Central and South America, which caused a new shift in the demographics and needs of church communities.[23] The economic and social inequities and political instability in Latin America and the Hispanic Caribbean led to this new migration. Many newly arrived immigrants gravitated to established Puerto Rican and Cuban areas with a high Spanish-speaking presence. Central and South Americans, in particular, were drawn to the area for reasons similar to those of Puerto Ricans decades ago: low cost of living and job opportunities. Due to this growth in the Latinx population, the Archdiocese of Newark and, by extension, the state of New Jersey became the first diocese to have a vicar (a specialized member of the clergy) for Hispanics.[24]

### The Archdiocese of New Jersey's Plan for Latinx Immigrants

The archdiocese's response to this growing and changing Latinx population was its plan called La Presencia Nueva: Knowledge for Service and Hope, a study of Hispanics in the Archdiocese in Newark, modeled after the U.S. Bishops National Pastoral Plan for the Hispanic Ministry in 1980. Father Riley said that the "spark" for this plan emerged from Sister Lourdes Torro, a trinitarian nun dedicated to supporting Latinx youth, evangelization, and social justice.[25] Specifically, the Archdiocese of Newark's La Nueva Presencia focused on the area with the largest local Latinx Catholic population, Hudson County. The plan detailed information regarding the Latinx population by incorporating "demographics, socio-ecological, sociological, anthropological and historical data ... to facilitate

Table 12.1
Estimated percent Hispanic of Total Catholic population The Archdiocese of Newark, 1980, 1985

|  | Percent of Total Hispanic Population | |
|---|---|---|
| County | 1980 (%) | 1985 (%) |
| Total Archdiocese | 17 | 23 |
| Bergen | 5 | 6 |
| Essex | 19 | 25 |
| Hudson | 39 | 49 |
| Union | 13 | 17 |

SOURCE: Office of Research and Planning, 1986

informed and intelligent mission projects for the Roman Catholic Church of Newark."[26] In the first pages, the words of Rev. Theodore E. McCarick set the tone of the plan and its mission: "At every level—ministerial formation, evangelization, spirituality, family needs, youth, and social justice—the church of Newark wants to include the Hispanic community and truly be a Church for all people."[27]

Perhaps the plan's most important aspect was its articulation of the state of New Jersey as a "center of migration." The plan demonstrated the growing presence of Latinxs since the 1950s and mapped out the area's most important counties for Hispanic ministry (see Table 12.1). This area included Hudson County with its "large concentrations of Hispanics in Hudson County cities: Union City, West New York, Hoboken and Jersey City."[28] According to the report, Latinxs numbered "over 365,000 of the region's population, with 80% of these belonging to the Catholic faith, comprising of almost half of the Catholic population in Hudson County."[29] The church predicted that one of every three Latinxs would turn to the Catholic ministry for their faith practices.[30] At the time, the Catholic community consisted of Puerto Ricans (41%), Cubans (24%), Colombians, Ecuadorians, Hondurans, Mexicans, and other Central and South American ethnic groups (see Table 12.2).[31]

When I interviewed Father Riley on October 25, 2021, he discussed his participation in La Presencia Nueva and his role in supporting the emerging Latinx population in New Jersey.[32] Father Riley has served as an accredited representative of a recognized agency on behalf of immigrants during deportation proceedings for several decades. He now serves the immigrant community as a monsignor, an honorary title bestowed upon him by the archbishop due to his work with the Latinx and immigrant community. During his fifty-six years as a priest, Father Riley has worked with parishes in Union City, Garfield, Lyndhurst, and Newark. He also became the coordinator of the Hispanic Apostolate in Newark, New Jersey. In Newark, Father Riley helped cultivate a Spanish ministry that welcomed ministers from outside the country to speak to and serve

## Table 12.2
### The six largest Hispanic groups in the Archdiocese of Newark, by total numbers of persons and by percent of total Hispanics

| Hispanic group | Numbers | Percent of Hispanics in archdiocese (%) |
| --- | --- | --- |
| Puerto Rican | 118,800 | 41 |
| Cubans | 73,200 | 25 |
| Colombians | 12,520 | 4 |
| Ecuadorians | 9,360 | 3 |
| Dominicans | 7,380 | 3 |
| Spaniards | 6,740 | 2 |
| Other countries | 65,500 | 22 |
| Total | 293,500 | 100 |

SOURCE: Presencia Nueva—Pastoral Agents (Hispanic Study), box 9, 17. Archdiocese of Newark Office of Research & Planning, ADN 0063. The Monsignor Field Archives & Special Collection Center.

Spanish-speaking people. He also received a grant from the Conference of Catholic Bishops for the Campaign for Human Development to open an agency to represent people in immigration hearings who could not afford a lawyer.

Additionally, Father Riley was at the forefront of recognizing the evolving demographics of the Catholic Latinx church in New Jersey. He acknowledged the differences in experiences and conditions of each Latinx immigrant population. In our interview, he remarked: "Each country has a different history, not just a language, but the whole style of evangelization." Both La Nueva Presencia and grassroots community efforts on behalf of immigrants by priests such as Father Riley sought to articulate the importance of understanding the diversity within the Latinx category to bolster the role of the Catholic church in Latinx New Jersey (see Figure 12.1).

Focusing on New Jersey and Union City highlights the importance of understanding state and regional contexts and how they come to shape the possibilities of the church. A regional approach to understanding the Latinx Catholic community also builds on the theological literature, which has established that there are social, political, and economic contexts that shape church differences throughout the United States and "useful contrasts within Latinx urban Catholicism emerge from examinations of differences in origin, destination, and socioeconomic status, as well as religious and social conditions in city life."[33] For example, there are contrasts between Catholicism on the East and West Coasts. The American West developed its own basis for the church that did not include ethnic terms since their incoming community members migrated from the East and Midwest of the United States and included many people who were cutting ties with their ethnic communities.[34] In fact, the Catholic church of the American West excluded Mexican Americans and even developed Catholic schools that

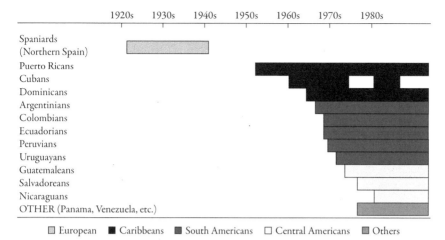

FIGURE 12.1  Main waves of Hispanic immigrants and Puerto Ricans migrants into the Archdiocese of Newark by decade, 1920s to 1980s. (Source: Presencia Nueva—Pastoral Agents (Hispanic Study), Box: 9, 195, Archdiocese of Newark Office of Research & Planning, ADN 0063. The Monsignor Field Archives & Special Collection Center.)

were located near European communities, limiting the chances of Latinx members attending.[35] Additionally, theologian Stevens-Arroyo argues that unique historical moments and social identities have influenced the regional dimensions of the church, such as the civil rights of the 1960s and 1970s, which ushered in an immigrant church for Latinxs that differed from the needs and concerns of European origin groups.[36] Badillo explains that the formation of religion and church in San Antonio, Texas, differs substantially from the meaning and creation of Latinx churches in Miami and also in Chicago, to show how church plays a unique role based on geography, histories of reception, modes of urban living, racial/ethnic composition, and communal needs.[37]

### Growing Old in Union City and the Church

The Catholic church's efforts have aided in establishing Union City, New Jersey, as a pan-Latinx destination. In Union City, 91 percent of the population is foreign born, and 77 percent of adults are Spanish speaking.[38] A few years ago, Union City was declared a "sanctuary city" to protect immigrants from potential deportations.[39]

## Part Two: Holy Family Church and the Older Latinx Community

While part one of this chapter showed how Union City and the Catholic church became an immigrant-friendly destination for Latinxs, part two turns to meaning-making and cultural and institutional practices of the Holy Family Church in Union City and its support of older Latinxs. Specifically, I ask: Now that older Latinx immigrants have decided to remain in the United States, what role has the Catholic church served and continues to serve in their lives? And how might the church's support differ in old age? I discuss how Holy Family met older Latinxs' critical needs as older adults through social support, festivities, and shared common purpose, which made the church a significant staple in the older Latinx community of Union City, New Jersey.

Older Latinxs who arrived and were supported by the church during their arrival, and cultivated a community within the church, now have new experiences that require them to readjust and readapt to life in the United States. Gerontological literature shows that spiritual and religious needs change and increase with age.[40] Old age is filled with newfound life transitions and institutional encounters that older Latinxs might not have experienced prior to reaching *la tercera edad*. In the case of older Latinx immigrants, they must learn to navigate a plethora of challenges, including ongoing language barriers, navigating health and medical care, making major end-of-life decisions, confronting the loss of relationships, greater distance from younger relatives who move beyond the enclave, while also coming into their newfound status as family matriarchs and patriarchs. They might also find themselves navigating financial constraints due to limited retirement savings and facing age, racial, and ethnic discrimination and nativist sentiments daily.

Many older Latinxs have remained in Union City as their children have moved elsewhere. Most older Latinxs have decided to stay in a community where they can navigate to their culturally competent medical doctors, pharmacies, and other places important for their health and well-being rather than move to an unknown place. In sum, they want to remain in a community that possesses an *ambiente tranquilo* and that speaks to their social and cultural needs (i.e., speaking the Spanish language, culturally competent care from health professionals, and events that cater to their Latinx senior population).[41] In fact, a majority of older Latinxs in Union City criticize the idea of moving to the suburbs or a rural location where many basic necessities would be out of their reach and require a car or other forms of transportation, thus jeopardizing their independence.[42] Many also indicated that leaving their local community would mean leaving their church family and, in turn, increase feelings of social isolation in old age.

In Union City, several social service organizations, including the church, have supported Latinx seniors. Save Latin America, a nonprofit organization in Union City, has worked to support the health and well-being of all Latinxs and has also led senior-based activities on end-of-life planning, diabetes prevention, and seeking health practitioners in the community. Another integral place for older Latinxs is the city's senior center located in City Hall. This office coordinates events for older Latinxs, including trips to Amish Country, to see the Rockettes and Atlantic City. Five office employees provide transportation to seniors for medical appointments. They also offer Medicaid and Medicare support, furniture referrals, energy assistance program applications, and translation of documents for older Latinxs. The robust activity and modes of assistance within this small office make it an invaluable part of older Latinx community and life.

Among older Latinxs in my study, the Catholic church was one of the main reasons they remain in the community rather than move with family or to a more affordable area. This comes as no surprise since scholars have shown that part of what makes an age-friendly community (i.e., a community that is navigable and supportive regardless of age) are churches and places where spirituality and religiosity are explored.[43] This can be as beneficial as promoting physical and social support in making an age-friendly community, given that spirituality and religion are also influential in people's daily lives.

Presently, Holy Family Church is a predominantly Latinx institution with a large Ecuadorian and Peruvian population.[44] There is an English-speaking mass, but most of the church is Latinx, mainly representing middle-aged and older Latinx immigrants (sixty-five years old and older). It is estimated that of the nine hundred families in Holy Family, six hundred are Spanish speaking, while three hundred are English speaking.[45] The church's population of older adults is due to factors including few youth programs (although there are Confraternity of Christian Doctrine classes). Furthermore, several religious groups at the church cater to the aging population, including La Legion de Maria (The Legion of Mary) and Cursillistas, who go on communal retreats for religious renewal.

Gerontological literature shows us that a majority of older Latinxs attribute their positive health and well-being to their faith and sense of religiosity.[46] A study on older Latinxs within a church-based institution found they "identified faith and religious beliefs as dominant sources of well-being and often indicated that without faith, well-being was not an achievable state."[47] Another study of older Latinxs' experiences growing old in the United States found that religiosity and spirituality influenced their attitudes about growing old.[48] Furthermore, a study conducted among Mexican American widows found that "frequent church attendance was associated with a slower increase in depressive symptoms during widowhood."[49] In sum, existing research highlights a strong connection between religiosity and faith in overcoming challenges among older Latinxs.

## Communal Support

Older Latinxs expressed a desire to age in community and at Holy Family Church due to the strong social support they received at church. The church provided an opportunity to meet with friends, for example, after the Spanish Mass on Sunday, where church members would head to the Lyceum to lunch together. For older Latinxs, after-church activities allowed them to relax and *desahogar*, or unburden, themselves through conversation.

Samuel, an immigrant from Colombia who arrived in the 1980s, discussed the importance of attending church, especially in having someone to talk with outside of his home. He found that many of his family members were too busy to spend time with him, including his daughter, who was raising her four children. As a result, he relied on the church as his community to ease his feelings of isolation. One Sunday, Samuel shared why Holy Family Church is important to him: "Oh, we talk about everything. Our health, the government. Oh politics, ayayaye [figure of speech]. We also talk about the sick, the kids, the accidents, and good things too!" This range of conversation shows how older adults who are church members share in the holy gospel but also cultivate an intimate space where personal matters, and even politics, are discussed.

Holy Family Church provided an opportunity to have conversations, to let go of the stresses that come with growing old and reckon with the legacy of the hard journey of migrating to the United States. One day during lunch, a woman who wished to remain anonymous, described to other church members, the challenges she endured with an abusive husband, and the will to survive that led her to travel to the United States. Her abusive husband had told her that if she left him, he would hurt her, which provoked her to escape with her children from Central America. Like this woman, many of the older Latinxs at church were aware of each other's migration stories and, as a result, often lent a compassionate ear, along with words of wisdom and hope. In this case, when the woman shared her story, her friends from church responded gratefully and with spiritual conviction, "you are here now, thank the Lord," while other church members also repeated, "gracias a Dios [thank the Lord]." Moments like these, intertwined with notions of religiosity, affirmed church members' experiences and furthered their communal bonds.

Another example of communal support among older Latinxs at Holy Family Church are the experiences of Carla and Karina. During a coffee before church at the local Dunkin Donuts, Carla describes how the church helped her to forget her husband's passing: "I didn't have a place to go, and I wasn't feeling good with what was happening in my life at the time. I became a friend of Karina's, and she started bringing me to the church. Now I go more than once a day at 12 P.M. and also back at 6 P.M." Similarly, another senior began coming to church in later life: "I was just sitting there in front of my television with nothing to do. Elaine told me to come to church, and at first, I wasn't interested because I had only been to English-speaking mass, but when she introduced me to Spanish-speaking mass, I became more involved."

Many older Latinxs described their relationships and time spent in church as ways to age meaningfully. Conception, a migrant from El Salvador, shares, "we talk about our kids, our grandkids, our sickness because everything is hurting at this age, and we pass the time very good." Conception, who is close to her biological family, tells her children and grandchildren that Sundays belong to her, "I tell my family, Sundays are mine. I leave my home very early in the morning and don't come back until 4 p.m." When I follow up with Conception to ask how she passes the day at church, she responds happily, "I am just talking. It's a fun way to pass time." But it is evident that Conception guards this time sacredly because she sees it as a meaningful part of her weekly routine.

Other older Latinxs saw the church as a place to find tangible support for their survival. During a fundraiser, Mari shared with me the importance of the church for her as an immigrant who is having a tough time finding food. "I would not go back to Mexico even if it is tough to live here. No. We did not have much there, and I've been here since I was a child. [In] Mexico, there was not much food. I cannot complain because here [at church], they always tell me to come [get food]. I do not get hungry. I try not to go hungry." Other older Latinxs shared similar perspectives—they had been through a lot and felt that the church recognized this and offered them support wherever possible.

Many older adults who expressed feeling lonely and without familial support would attend the church lunch and stock up on four to five foam plates of food for a dollar each to last throughout the week. For example, many single seniors who could not afford the rising rents in the area lived in makeshift apartments without a kitchen. Sometimes seniors like Johan had just a microwave to warm up meals in his studio. As a result, many older Latinxs relied on the church community food for home-cooked meals. Church members also made *colectas* for older Latinxs to help pay their rent on time or buy weekly groceries. Often, the priest would also offer financial assistance.

Aviana, an immigrant from Colombia, arrived to care for her sister's young daughter and was later left to age on her own. She shares with me that priests have been foundational to her survival, especially Father Riley, who met with Aviana to review her immigration case and offer different avenues for her to seek U.S. citizenship. Father Riley and other church members care for Aviana and remain involved in the precarious situations of their congregation.

Alma, another undocumented senior from Ecuador, resides in her daughter's home. She shares with me her journey to the United States, as well as her connection to and role in the church. Church is both a place to get a meal and connect with fellow Latinx congregants. It also provides stress relief as she often wants to give her daughter privacy at home. When I ask Alma why she attends church on Saturdays and Sundays, she shares that it is a place where she can find family, "I see my friends every seven days, or you can say every Saturday in the Legion of the Virgin Mary . . . that is where they are . . . they are more like my sisters than just friends."

Many older Latinxs described other church members as their second family. Several participants even described the church members as brothers and sisters. When I asked Margarita, alongside her mother, who migrated in the 1980s, why they chose to stay in the community rather than return to their home country, they said, "We have found a family here [at church]. She [her mother] is [also] a part of the family here... the priests are very united, and they are like family too." In addition to describing the church as a family for her and her mother, who have no other relatives in the country, Margarita also describes clergymen as family members because they offered a listening ear and support members through personal issues, but also immigration ones (as was the case for Aviana). This is echoed in the gerontological literature, which shows that church leaders have the capability to improve the well-being of older church members and are a critical reason why older adults continue to attend church.[50]

While parishes like Holy Family can be seen as new immigrant churches with "little pieces of the homeland," there were also racial and political differences among older Latinxs in the church.[51] An undocumented older Latina, Ramona, is alone in the United States and worked for a wealthy family nearby. For Ramona, the church members are her family and, while there are sometimes differences, she continues to take part in the community. "You know I consider myself a feminist. But here, there are different perspectives, different walks of life. Traditional views about the role of the man and the woman. Even so, they are still my [church] family." Ramona regards the disagreements that occur as part of being in a family, where you still remain close and have strong ties. There were also political divides within the church that became more apparent in small groups of two or three people. In these more intimate spaces, some Latinxs, particularly older Cubans, supported Donald Trump, while other older Latinxs saw his presidency as being against their immigrant community. These differences created subtle tensions but were not publicly discussed among the larger group, given the need to keep peace within the church.

### Festivities

The "new immigrant church," cultivated by a now older generation of Latinx immigrants, includes supporting Latinx identity and culture but also creating local events and addressing community needs.[52] For older Latinxs, the church has become a space of participation where they can carry out their traditions and share with other generations in the church. In Holy Family, the community has come together to create a well-known predominantly Latinx event in Union City, called the International Festival. One of the first festival presidents was Father Legarra, who saw the festival as a way to cultivate a diverse Latinx community, "our parish community is enriched with a very strong presence of people from different countries in Latin America... there is a remarkable spirit of collaboration among the different ethnic groups."[53] The festival's objective was to celebrate cultural traditions from different Latinx and cultural communities and integrate the largely immigrant community into U.S. customs. The festival is noted in flyers and newspaper clippings as an opportunity to offer a moment of nostalgia for the homeland for its church members, while sharing cultural traditions with younger family members (see Figure 12.2).[54]

FIGURE 12.2  Image of a flyer for the International Festival, Holy Family Church. (Source: Holy Family Church, Union City, Facebook photo, August 18, 2018, https://www.facebook.com/holyfamilychurchunioncity/photos/a.546502622129853/1772992586147511/.)

Older Latinxs have played vital roles in organizing the International Festival from its origins to the present day. Many have participated by performing Celia Cruz music for the audience, collecting tickets for the purchase of food, or offering their ethnic dishes for sale to fundraise for church repairs. Like other immigrant groups, older Latinxs have cultivated a space for themselves that gives purpose and meaning in later life.

Older Latinxs also volunteered their time throughout the year for the highly anticipated International Festival as well as for other ongoing events. One older Latina shared the importance of cooking. "We make food there [at the rectory], or at home and bring it for the church.... I bring a huge amount of arroz morro and chicken. We pass the time really good." Alejandra, from El Salvador, shared that one of her weekend activities included making food for church events, especially for events where different Latinx cultures were highlighted, "When the Salvadorans cook, they make pupusas. I belong to the *lectores* [church readers] group, but I help them [the Salvadorans] too when I can." Alejandra shared that she felt that the time she spent cooking for the events at the church positively impacted her mental health, stating, "I am in church so much that I do not have time to be depressed.... I also do volunteer work there. I cook and pass out the tickets for food on Sunday.... I also go to the rectory and help out."

At the church lyceum, older Latinxs played games on their phones, drank coffee, sold raffle tickets, and discussed how they could get food donated to cook for upcoming events. In an interview, Elaine shares that many conversations at church are about cooking and selling food for events; several older adults did indeed discuss cooking and selling food for the church. In one conversation, Conception mentions that they only sold a little food the week before. Elaine responds that it was because there was no catechism that day, and the kids did not come with their parents to buy empanadas and donuts. My ethnographic notes show that the conversation ends with a discussion on what should be sold next time, with Margarita suggesting that they sell seafood or ground beef since it is cheap to buy in bulk and easy to make, while Conception chimes in that selling ground beef would be greasy and unhealthy to sell. These conversations took on a gendered dimension as women were largely responsible for cooking weekly for the church.

### Volunteerism and Shared Purpose

Volunteerism has been shown to support older adults' social engagement and mental health.[55] Furthermore, studies show that providing informal, tangible support to fellow church members "is associated with better health but only for study participants who were more deeply committed to their faith."[56] Church volunteer work makes seniors like Lali feel "useful" and "good inside." Many seniors in the community worked as volunteers to support the church's mission to help the poor and needy. Furthermore, their interactions with others in need helped put their lives into perspective. Volunteering was a way of life for older Latinxs in retirement. They were drawn to the church for a sense of involvement that could offer a distraction from their daily lives. With limited opportunities for Spanish-speaking community building beyond the walls of the church, older Latinxs turned to Holy Family to find culturally relevant opportunities. As volunteers from church-based religious organizations, they visited nursing homes and hospitals, gave the eucharist in homes of disabled or sick individuals, and led prayers for the recently deceased. These activities gave them a shared purpose, tied by their mutual culture, religion, and faith in God.

Abran shares that he dedicates his time to serving the sick: "I give the communion to three floors of the nursing home and to people who are sick at home." Other seniors spent their time praying the rosary for the sick at the hospital or homebound. Older adults also create week-long prayer groups for those recently passed to make sure the soul of the deceased reaches heaven. Additionally, seniors embarked on trips to other churches in Pennsylvania and Maryland and went on retreats with one another to pray for several days straight. These activities of prayer and volunteer work cultivated a deep sense of contributing to the community and to those in need among the church participants. It was common for older Latinxs to say goodbye to one another by saying, "the sick need me right now. We will see each other later," or "I need to head out; I need to visit the sick."

Events such as the Legion of Mary occurred at church and reified a sense of community engagement and community formation among older Latinxs. Conception, a very social senior involved in the church, explained:

> For me, the church is the most important place.... I meet with my friends at church on Sundays... we talk and eat together at church. We do a lot of blah blah blah and eat. I also have a group for breakfast; I am part of the lectors that read the bible. There are 25 of us. Every few months, we read, and we do breakfast one at a time. There is a group of lectors, the minister who gives the body and blood of Jesus Christ. There is a Legion of Maria group, a Mexican group, and a Peruvian group; every group is different. Last Sunday was my turn [to cook for the church]. I was part of the lector group. And when we are not in charge, we just hang out and eat together after mass.

These frequent activities referenced by Conception demonstrate that the church is a socially engaging and dynamic space that keeps Latinx seniors active. Many seniors spent more than just Sunday in church, like Mariluz, who shares: "In my free time, I do volunteer work in the nursing home for the church, I go to my doctor's visits, I walk, go to the store, spend time with my sister, take part in the Legion at church, clean the house, iron, I never get bored." While many of Mariluz's activities are typical tasks such as going to the doctor, visiting family, and cleaning her home, volunteer work through the church was equally important to her daily life. Lali from the Dominican Republic shared a similar perspective about the church, "One passes the time well here, and every Sunday we get together and make food, and sell it, and one feels useful, and one is helping for the Lord's projects. It feels really nice."

## Conclusion

For Latinx seniors in Union City, participation in the church is both impactful and meaningful, as they grow old in the United States. For them, the church is a place that offers a second family, activity, festivity, and shared purpose. However, the church would not exist as a safe space for the Latinx community into old age without the role of the Archdiocese of Newark, which shaped New Jersey and, by extension, Union City into a Latinx Catholic immigrant community.

My study of the Holy Family Church demonstrates that previous shifts within the church from "national parish" to "new immigrant church" will now shift from focusing on assimilation and incorporation upon arrival to considering old age and the end of life for Latinxs in New Jersey. While older Latinxs have not been structurally supported through specific programs for seniors, such as those run by the city, the church must consider the emergence of an aging Latinx population. An older Latinx population that today survives from its support and service and is also crucial to the very survival of the church as a community institution. Older Latinx fundraising and labor feed the parish and keep the faith alive and moving forward in Union City, New Jersey.

## Notes

The author wishes to express gratitude to Briana Lo Sardo, the archivist of the Archdiocese of Newark, for her assistance in locating pertinent sources for this chapter. The author would also like to extend appreciation to all the interviewees who generously shared their insights and contributed to this chapter.

1. In accordance with the Gerontological Society on Aging's Reframing Aging Initiative and to support inclusive images of aging, I use "older adult" and "older people" instead of "elderly." I use "seniors" since some older adults referred to themselves as seniors within the community. To protect the privacy of my research participants, all names have been changed.
2. Milton Myron Gordon, *Assimilation in American Life: The Role of Race, Religion, and National Origins* (New York: Oxford University Press, 1964); Pierrette Hondagneu-Sotelo, *God's Heart Has No Borders: How Religious Activists Are Working for Immigrant Rights* (Berkeley: University of California Press, 2008), 8.
3. David A. Badillo, *Latinos and the New Immigrant Church* (Baltimore, MD: Johns Hopkins University Press, 2006).
4. For research in this area, see Carolyn Chen and Russell Jeung, *Sustaining Faith Traditions: Race, Ethnicity, and Religion among the Latino and Asian American Second Generation* (New York: New York University Press, 2012) and Felipe Hinojosa, *Apostles of Change: Latino Radical Politics, Church Occupations, and the Fight to Save the Barrio* (Austin: University of Texas Press, 2021).
5. Michael Lipka, *A Closer Look at Catholic America* (Washington, DC: Pew Research Center, September 14, 2015), https://www.pewresearch.org/fact-tank/2015/09/14/a-closer-look-at-catholic-america/; Nobuko Mizoguchi, Laquitta Walker, Edward

Trevelyan, and Bashiruddin Ahmed, "The Older Foreign-Born Population in the United States: 2012–2016," U.S. Census Bureau, ACS Reports, ACS-42 (Washington, DC: U.S. Government Printing Office, 2019), https://www.census.gov/content/dam/Census/library/publications/2019/acs/acs-42.pdf. Cary Funk and Jessica Martínez, *Fewer Hispanics Are Catholic, so How Can More Catholics Be Hispanic?* (Washington, DC: Pew Research Center, May 7, 2014), https://www.pewresearch.org/fact-tank/2014/05/07/fewer-hispanics-are-catholic-so-how-can-more-catholics-be-hispanic/.
6   Peter Wehrwein, "Union City's Past Reveals Diversity," *Union City Reporter*, October 1, 1985, Union City Public Library Archive.
7   Troy J. Simmons, "Treasured Windows Help Illuminate Faith Legacy," *Catholic Advocate*, March 5, 2008, Holy Family Church Archive.
8   "Presencia Nueva—Pastoral Agents (Hispanic Study)," 1988, box 9, p. 196, Archdiocese of Newark Office of Research & Planning, ADN 0063, Monsignor Field Archives & Special Collection Center; Asterio Velasco and Church of the Holy Family, Union City, NJ, *Una Huella Profunda: Pinceladas Históricas De La Parroquia De San José Y San Miguel, Union City, New Jersey (1851–1997)*, 39.
9   Jay P. Dolan and Jaime R. Vidal, eds., *Puerto Rican and Cuban Catholics in the U.S., 1900–1965*, Notre Dame History of Hispanic Catholics in the U.S. 2 (Notre Dame, IN: University of Notre Dame Press, 1994), 112.
10  "Presencia Nueva—Pastoral Agents," 196, 214.
11  "Presencia Nueva—Pastoral Agents," 214.
12  Dolan and Vidal, *Puerto Rican and Cuban Catholics*, 4.
13  Velasco and Church of the Holy Family, *Una Huella Profunda*, 40.
14  "Presencia Nueva—Pastoral Agents," 196, 222.
15  Yolanda Prieto, *The Cubans of Union City: Immigrants and Exiles in a New Jersey Community* (Philadelphia: Temple University Press, 2009), 28.
16  Prieto, *Cubans of Union City*, 28.
17  "Presencia Nueva—Pastoral Agents," 199.
18  Prieto, *Cubans of Union City*, 28.
19  "Presencia Nueva—Pastoral Agents," 224.
20  Velasco and Church of the Holy Family, *Una Huella Profunda*, 9.
21  "Presencia Nueva—Pastoral Agents," 199.
22  "Presencia Nueva—Pastoral Agents," 199.
23  "Presencia Nueva—Pastoral Agents," 205; Velasco and Church of the Holy Family, *Una Huella Profunda*, 41.
24  Velasco and Church of the Holy Family, *Una Huella Profunda*, 21.
25  William Reilly, phone interview with author, October 25, 2021.
26  "Presencia Nueva—Pastoral Agents," 1.
27  "Presencia Nueva—Pastoral Agents," foreword.
28  "Presencia Nueva—Pastoral Agents," 5.
29  "Presencia Nueva—Pastoral Agents," 5.
30  "Presencia Nueva—Pastoral Agents," 2.
31  "Presencia Nueva—Pastoral Agents," 3.
32  Case studies of Latinx immigrants in the Archdiocese of Newark's Nueva Presencia were from Father Riley's parish.
33  Badillo, *Latinos*, 208.
34  Richard D. Alba, Albert J. Raboteau, and Josh DeWind, *Immigration and Religion in America: Comparative and Historical Perspectives* (New York: New York University Press, 2009), 14.

35 Alba et al., *Immigration and Religion in America*, 15.
36 Anthony M. Stevens-Arroyo, Allan F. Deck, and Jay P. Dolan, "The Emergence of a Social Identity among Latino Catholics: An Appraisal," in *Hispanic Catholic Culture in the U.S.: Issues and Concerns* (Notre Dame, IN: University of Notre Dame Press, 1994), 80.
37 Badillo, *Latinos*.
38 U.S. Census Bureau, "QuickFacts: Union City City, New Jersey," July 1, 2019, https://www.census.gov/quickfacts/unioncitycitynewjersey.
39 Hannington Dia and Staff Writer, "Union City Becomes a Sanctuary City," *Hudson Reporter*, February 19, 2017, https://hudsonreporter.com/2017/02/19/union-city-becomes-a-sanctuary-city-2/.
40 Robert C. Atchley, *Spirituality and Aging* (Washington, DC: Johns Hopkins University Press, 2009); Jeanne M. Hilton and Stephen L. Child, "Spirituality and the Successful Aging of Older Latinos," *Counseling and Values* 59, no. 1 (2014): 17–34.
41 Melanie Z. Plasencia, "Age-Friendly as Tranquilo Ambiente: How Sociocultural Perspectives Shape the Lived Environment of Latinx Older Adults," *The Gerontologist* 62, no. 1 (January 14, 2022): 110–118.
42 Plasencia, "Age-Friendly."
43 Noelle L. Fields, Gail Adorno, Karen Magruder, Rupal Parekh, and Brandi J. Felderhoff, "Age-Friendly Cities: The Role of Churches," *Journal of Religion, Spirituality and Aging* 28, no. 3 (July 2, 2016): 264–278.
44 Hilda Benitez, Holy Family Church Secretary, conversation with author, November 3, 2021.
45 Benitez, conversation.
46 Vladimir Melkumyan, "Religiosity and Religious Coping and Mental Health Outcomes among Evangelical Latinos" (DSW diss., Capella University, 2020); Ann W. Nguyen, "Religion and Mental Health in Racial and Ethnic Minority Populations: A Review of the Literature," *Innovation in Aging* 4, no. 5 (August 8, 2020); Yewoubdar Beyene, Gay Becker, and Nury Mayen, "Perception of Aging and Sense of Well-Being among Latino Elderly," *Journal of Cross-Cultural Gerontology* 17, no. 2 (June 1, 2002): 155–172; Hilton and Child, "Spirituality."
47 Rosalba Hernandez, Mercedes Carnethon, Frank J. Penedo, Lizet Martinez, Julia Boehm, and Stephen M. Schueller, "Exploring Well-Being among US Hispanics/Latinos in a Church-Based Institution: A Qualitative Study," *Journal of Positive Psychology* 11, no. 5 (September 2, 2016): 511–521, 515.
48 Beyene et al., "Perception of Aging."
49 Maria A. Monserud and Kyriakos S. Markides, "Changes in Depressive Symptoms during Widowhood among Older Mexican Americans: The Role of Financial Strain, Social Support, and Church Attendance," *Aging and Mental Health* 21, no. 6 (June 3, 2017): 586–594, 592.
50 Vern Bengtson, Camille Endacott, and Samantha Kang, "Older Adults in Churches: Differences in Perceptions of Clergy and Older Members," *Journal of Religion, Spirituality and Aging* 30, no. 2 (April 3, 2018): 154–178.
51 Badillo, *Latinos*, xviii.
52 Badillo, *Latinos*, 202.
53 Melissa McNally, "Parish Commemorates 150 Years of Warmly Welcoming Immigrants," *Catholic Advocate*, October 24, 2007.
54 Francisco Legarra, "Festival Internacional," *New Jersey Católico*, n.d., Holy Family Church Archive.

55 Kimberly J. Johnson, Kenzie Latham-Mintus, and Judith L. Poey, "Productive Aging via Volunteering: Does Social Cohesion Influence Level of Engagement?" *Journal of Gerontological Social Work* 61, no. 8 (November 17, 2018): 817–833; Fengyan Tang, EunHee Choi, and Nancy Morrow-Howell, "Organizational Support and Volunteering Benefits for Older Adults," *The Gerontologist* 50, no. 5 (October 1, 2010): 603–612.

56 Neal Krause, "Church-Based Volunteering, Providing Informal Support at Church, and Self-Rated Health in Late Life," *Journal of Aging and Health* 21, no. 1 (February 1, 2009): 63–84.

# 13
## Parque Oaxaca/Jotería

Trans Latina History in New
Brunswick from Urban Renewal
to the Coronavirus Pandemic

DANIELA VALDES

When Mercedes Martínez lay in bed, alone, fighting the wretched symptoms of COVID-19 merely blocks away from the renowned Robert Wood Johnson University Hospital in New Brunswick, New Jersey, she began seeing "demons," as she described her hallucinations: "During the nights, from the very high fever that I had, I began seeing demons. I saw very strange things. I cried, I cried, very, very hard... I thought I was going to die."[1] Martínez is an undocumented Mexican trans woman living in New Brunswick, New Jersey.[2] Her adopted home is known as the Healthcare City, home to five nationally recognized hospitals, global biotechnology, and internationally recognized medical research institutes.[3] Martínez, however, cannot access any of these facilities without risking possible detention and deportation. Moreover, her expired Mexican documents do not reflect her chosen name but the masculine name her parents gave her at birth. Instead of going to the doctor in her own city, she travels to an LGBTQ (lesbian, gay, bisexual, transgender, and queer/questioning) clinic in Queens, New York, for her medical needs. But traveling to Queens proved impossible during the first wave of the pandemic when Martínez fell ill. In her small apartment across Parque Oaxaca she relied on homemade teas of cinnamon, mint, chamomile, and ginger, and food drop-offs from her friends to survive the disease.

Like most of the Mexican, Central American, and broader Latinx immigrant community in New Brunswick, Martínez lives in the shadow of the Healthcare City, only steps away from cutting-edge research and medical facilities but largely unable to access that care.[4] Centered on interviews with an undocumented Mexican trans woman, Mercedes Martínez, and a formerly undocumented Guatemalan trans woman, Lissa Méndez, this study examines how the coronavirus pandemic impacted trans immigrants in the city of New Brunswick.[5]

This chapter is divided into three sections. The first section sketches a portrait of New Brunswick, New Jersey, which I call a "Latino city." Census statistics show that, as of 2015, a majority of residents were Latinx, mostly from Mexico.[6] More significantly, calling New Brunswick a Latino city places it in conversation with scholars of postwar Latino urbanism who have examined how Latinx immigration has affected and, in some cases, reversed a decline in commercial, public, and social activity caused by the "urban crisis," the transformation of postwar cities by White flight, racial violence, deindustrialization, and suburbanization.[7] The second section narrows in on the social world of trans immigrants in New Brunswick through the lens of two working-class trans women.[8] Although individual experiences are never entirely representative of a larger group, this chapter recognizes the value of individual voices. Trans immigrants face the same economic and racial marginalization as their non-trans counterparts, in addition to suffering injustices at the hands of those peers. Anti-trans violence pervades U.S.-based Latinx communities, fueled in part by the idea that the undocumented, immigrant, or Latinx community might be more acceptable to the nation-state if it displayed signs of "respectability," heteronormativity, and traditional mainstream behaviors.[9] Trans workers thus face a unique type of economic vulnerability shaped by race and gender nonconformity that intensifies the disposability of their labor, rendering them a type of "industrial reserve."[10] The third section examines how the coronavirus pandemic exacerbated existing economic, social, and health crises among Latinx trans immigrants in New Brunswick. Trans individuals often rely on makeshift support networks to supplant an estranged biological family. The coronavirus pandemic exhausted these networks, temporarily halting the forms of mutual aid that kept them connected. Moreover, for undocumented trans individuals, the fear of deportation and lack of health insurance often prevents them from accessing critical health care, a reality that was exacerbated as COVID-19 began to rapidly spread. Finally, during one of the worst pandemics in recent history, trans immigrants were cut off from gender-affirming care, which risked deepening the existing mental health crisis in the population and prevented them from accessing one of the most viable ways to minimize the violent responses to gender nonconformity trans people often face.

Trans immigrants in New Brunswick value their privacy and safety. Though often willing to share their stories, they do not want to draw attention to themselves. Exact estimates of the size of the community would require a "long haul" research study.[11] Furthermore, the term community may imply more stability among a group of people who may actually be quite mobile, forced to move between different cities and towns in the United States and across international borders. Rather than drawing generalized conclusions about trans immigrants in New Brunswick, both my execution and my analysis of these oral histories urge scholars to consider the value of individual voices in their approach to studying the coronavirus pandemic. Oral histories with trans immigrants serve as a type of *testimonio*, or testimony, in which subjects become active social agents in the production of knowledge.[12] The archiving of these stories on the Voces Oral History Center YouTube page invites researchers of the pandemic to consider the emotional impact of this historic event, incapable of being captured by statistics alone. Moreover, trans people are traditionally examined through a focus on identity. I instead analyze them as gender nonconforming and racialized workers burdened by a unique set of material conditions whose explication is necessary to understanding how gender normativity, as reproduced in families, churches, the workplace, or the state, is a foundational category of being, that every day powerfully marks who lives and who dies.

## New Brunswick, New Jersey: The Healthcare City in Crisis

Known as the Healthcare City, New Brunswick, New Jersey, is home to world renowned hospitals and medical research institutions. However, the city's residents live in segregated communities where socioeconomic status determines access to quality health care. Examining trans immigrants' experiences reveals entrenched patterns of neglect and the social, economic, and health disparities in New Brunswick's history. To examine the experiences of trans immigrant women in the "Latino city" of New Brunswick, this section provides a brief sketch of the city's postwar political economy.

Two trends transformed New Brunswick in the post-1960s period: a redevelopment plan created by private–public partnerships and Latin American—most significantly Mexican—immigration.[13] The "revitalization" of New Brunswick began in 1968 following civil unrest, stalled during the 1970s, ramped up in the 1980s, and continues to this day. The most prominent promoters of redevelopment have been private–public partnerships in the form of nonprofits like New Brunswick Tomorrow and DEVCO (New Brunswick Development Corporation). Although the organizations in charge of planning and carrying out urban redevelopment always included community members on their boards, criticisms emerged quickly and never abated. When redevelopment ramped up in the 1980s, Puerto Rican barrios had already nurtured several generations. Despite their protests, the construction of a large Hyatt Hotel in downtown New Brunswick in

1982 replaced the main Puerto Rican neighborhood and displaced the community.[14] Mexican immigration intensified in its wake, eventually leading to an increase in the total population of the city and the reintroduction of commercial activity in abandoned downtown areas like French Street. These two main trends fomented competing visions of the city among residents who fought for access to public space in a geography shaped by economic and racial divisions. Today, one end of the city centers on Parque Oaxaca, a small public plaza that immigrants from the most prominent Latinx community in the city renamed. In recent history, the southern Mexican state of Oaxaca has emerged as a newly important sending state.[15] Filled with small bodegas and Mexican restaurants, the area around Parque Oaxaca remains largely separate from the more upscale end of the city that is home to Rutgers University, the largest state employer in New Jersey and headquarters of Johnson & Johnson, a multinational pharmaceutical giant that grossed $100 billion in 2019.[16] This economic (and racial) segregation, and especially the inability of undocumented immigrants to access the resources available in their own city, virtually ensured extreme hardship during the COVID-19 crisis.

Since the pandemic began, media outlets have provided analyses of the disproportionate impact on Latinx communities across the United States. In New Jersey, where Latinx people make up 19 percent of the total population, they accounted for nearly 30 percent of COVID-19 patients.[17] This does not take into account those who may not have sought or received health care, like many undocumented immigrants, or those who did not register a positive COVID-19 test. In neighboring New York City, officials reported that COVID-19 was killing Latinx people at 1.6 times the rate for White non-Hispanics.[18] In addition to suffering the physical consequences of the disease, Latinx immigrants account for a large segment of the essential workforce and of the industries hit hardest by the pandemic. With the largest concentration of undocumented immigrants in the country, the New Jersey–New York metropolitan area mirrors national trends.[19]

On March 16, 2020, New Jersey's governor Phil Murphy signed Executive Order No. 104 directing all nonessential businesses to close and for residents to stay home. Without simultaneously offering economic aid, this created a dire situation for undocumented immigrants in New Brunswick unable to access public assistance. "A lot of people lost their jobs," remembers Dr. Lilia Fernández, then an associate professor in the Latino and Caribbean Studies and History Departments at Rutgers University.

Only three other states, Illinois, New York, and California, issued stay-at-home orders in March 2020. When businesses shut down and individuals were forced to stay home, many people were left without enough money to meet their basic needs. Soon, local WhatsApp groups—an app popular within immigrant communities in the United States—began sharing requests for food, clothing, and cash assistance.[20] Because many immigrants in New Brunswick work in the service sector, construction, landscaping, or warehouses and were ineligible for stimulus checks or unemployment, the community as a whole began to suffer.

New Brunswick is located in Middlesex County, a region shaped by race, ethnic, and class inequality. In 2017, the median household income in New Brunswick was a little over $38,000. In the surrounding wealthy suburbs where many hospital and university employees live, the median income is upward of $100,000.[21] More startling, the city had a poverty rate of 34.2 percent in 2018, triple the county's rate of about 11.8 percent.[22] According to residents, New Brunswick is "a city of sharp contrasts."[23] Half of New Brunswick residents are of Latin American descent, and Mexicans alone account for more than a quarter of the city's total population. Undocumented immigrants are more likely to live in the poorest areas of the city, like Mercedes Martínez, who resides in a census tract with a median income of $43,385.[24]

These stark statistics provide quantitative support for the frustration and neglect felt by the trans immigrant community. In Martínez's words, "Trans women in the state where I live, here in New Jersey, there is no support. There is no support for us. We are forgotten. We are suffering in this respect as trans women. I feel abandoned. I feel forgotten."[25] In addition to feeling neglected by the state, trans immigrants also find themselves unable to count on their own community for acceptance. For example, Méndez works as a taxi driver and is well known in New Brunswick. For several years, she has lived openly as a trans woman, and her cisgender peers have witnessed her gender transition. She nonetheless described animosity by her taxi clients, which suggests a reality shaped by not only a lack of respect but also a lack of safety: "Almost the majority of people here know me. The entire Latinx community, almost. The town of New Brunswick knows me. And I noticed how they looked at me. . . . Discrimination always persists. Even though I look like this, beautiful, precious, like a young lady, they still refer to me as a man."[26] (See Figure 13.1).

At the onset of the coronavirus pandemic, then, a compounded set of obstacles shaped trans Latinx immigrant lives as members of a group devalued by the city and sidelined within their own community.

## Las Chicas Trans: The Social History of Trans Latinx Immigrants in New Brunswick

Since Transgender Day of Remembrance began in 1999, much attention has rightfully been drawn to the high rates of murder of trans women of color in the United States.[27] The Trans Murder Monitoring Project suggests that "aggregated data indicates that Black and migrant trans women of color are more vulnerable and frequently targeted." Lissa Méndez's and Mercedes Martínez's oral interviews color in a picture that these striking statistics can only sketch. This section uses their oral interviews to examine the social world of trans immigrants in New Brunswick, illustrating the conditions of economic and social precarity in which

FIGURE 13.1  Lissa Méndez during her oral history interview. (Photo courtesy of Rutgers Oral History Archives, Rutgers University)

they live. Trans immigrants lived on the margins of the broader Latinx community prior to the pandemic, leaving them acutely vulnerable to the economic fallout. As more and more experienced income loss and economic insecurity, the methods they used to support and uplift one another quickly fell apart, although new formations have emerged in their wake.

Lissa Méndez was born in a small rural town in Guatemala in 1991 to members of the peasant working class. She experienced gendered violence from a young age as members of her family and her community physically punished her for embracing her femininity. She recalled:

> I never had a normal childhood . . . I was discriminated against. . . . I never played with boys because anytime I wanted to, they rejected me, they ignored me or beat me. There was a time that lasted about six months where I didn't leave my house. I didn't go anywhere because they always beat me. . . . I couldn't defend myself because it wasn't just one person, it wasn't just one youth. Sometimes they were older than me, but never just one, rather it was a group of three, four, or five and, well, I felt unprotected in that moment. So, I couldn't act. I couldn't defend myself out of fear, fear of being beaten, out of

fear. I always felt that fear in me. That is why I sought refuge in my own house. I never left. I dedicated myself to helping with the chores around the house so I never had to leave.[28]

Although she sought refuge in her home, she did not always find it. Méndez grew up in an abusive household where her father beat her mother and her mother beat her. Neither could she count on her sister to protect her. Méndez recollected how:

Sometimes my sisters would tell me they were ashamed of me. In fact, during that time of abuse I told my sister about what was happening. I told her not to tell my mom at that moment because my mom was a very violent person.... She hit me really hard and, well, I was afraid of her, I was terrified of her. And, well, she told her, and what my mom did was hit me, she hit me so hard that... I had a fever until the next day.[29]

Descriptions of her homelife help explain why Guatemala, along with Honduras and El Salvador, is one of the top three countries with the highest rates per capita of LGBTQ asylum seekers in the United States.[30] None of these countries allow trans people to change their names or gender markers on their official documents, a practice that helps reduce the threat of violence that comes from living openly gender nonconforming, nor do they have civil nondiscrimination provisions in employment or housing.[31] Institutions that are designed to nurture and protect individuals, such as the family and the church, often become the center of violence. Thus, when Méndez's sister declined an opportunity to migrate to the United States with a friend, Méndez asked her mother to send her instead. At sixteen years old, Méndez boarded a train in Chiapas, Mexico, traversing the rough terrain of the Sierra Madre for three months before arriving in the United States. Young, inexperienced, and with few resources at her disposal to plan ahead, she simply focused on fleeing.[32]

After arriving in the United States, she moved in with her father in Missouri who had migrated a few years earlier. She attended high school, where she began learning English, and landed a job as a custodian at Target. The anti-queer violence that caused Méndez to flee Guatemala did not subside in the United States. In high school, North Americans and other Latin Americans bullied her. She moved to Trenton, New Jersey, in part to escape her situation in Missouri. She finally sought help in New Jersey from a social worker who connected her with immigration lawyers and guided Méndez through a successful asylum case:

I sought help ... because I was suffering from domestic violence and one time I sought help for therapy or something like that and a social worker approached me ... and he says, "We're going to try to help" ... It was a really rough process. Believe me. There were negative people who told me ... "What are you doing?

This is a waste of time"... Sometimes I had to walk in the cold, the snow, for an hour to wait for a bus, an hour there to be able to go see my lawyer. And I did it, walking and everything, and thank God I accomplished it and I feel happy because everything that I've set my mind to, thank God, I've been able to achieve.[33]

The asylum process provided Méndez with permanent residency, affording her stability and safety unavailable to the country's eleven million undocumented immigrants. However, in a more abstract way, it also enacted a type of ontological and archival erasure. As a "sexile," the physical violence and distress Méndez withstood as a child for expressing socially unacceptable levels of femininity motivated her migration.[34] The judge granted her asylum, however, on the assumption that she was a gay man persecuted for her sexuality, not on the basis of her gender or gender expression.[35] As she explained:

I think that... the law and the judge and everything about migration is based on your sexuality. Because if we talk about sexuality, I think that in the LGBT community, we are enclosed... in the letters LGBT... we, ourselves, gays, lesbians, we enclose ourselves in the same language. And well in that moment... it was written [on my papers] that I was a gay man, let's say, because at that moment I didn't have information about what it is to be trans and everything, but with time I looked for information... and I came to realize that, in reality, I was me, in other words, I was and was always a trans person.

Shortly after receiving asylum, Méndez obtained a driver's license that eventually led her to New Brunswick, where she began working as a taxi driver. In New Brunswick, she met other trans women who introduced her to resources to continue her gender transition and became part of a larger trans Latinx community, including Mercedes Martínez who also fled as a teenager from Chiapas, Mexico, arriving in New Brunswick in the 1990s.

New Brunswick's trans immigrant community developed, in part, through its connection to the late Lorena Borjas, a Mexican transgender woman and activist who lived in Jackson Heights, Queens, from 1980 until her passing from COVID-19 in March 2020. As a friend of Martínez, Borjas helped connect her with transition-related resources in New York City and provided a model for the kind of support Martínez would offer the trans community in New Brunswick prior to the pandemic.[36] For example:

Before the pandemic, we organized events to help each other as trans women. We organized events. We organized dances to collect funds... if, unfortunately, a trans person died, we could have the funds to help her family or send her body back to her home country. Because... there is no support... for us girls. So instead, we look for ways to support each other.[37]

Martínez and her friends organized shows open to the public, helping to form bonds between cis and trans immigrants. The broader immigrant community often admired and complimented Martínez for the way she portrayed Paulina Rubio, Thalía, Alejandra Guzmán, Diana Reyes, and other popular Latin American artists, something she enjoyed: "I felt really happy. Really pleased. I liked it and, besides, I could help other people ... make them feel happy in that moment, have a good time and also, they paid me to give performances. So, I helped financially the people who needed it."[38]

Martínez participated actively as an entertainer, but she also occupied a sort of mother role in the community. Although organizing was a team effort, when funds were collected at the end of the event, Martínez took charge of distribution. Each person contributed monies for drinks, food, and trinkets so they could sell items, charge for performances, and raise funds. In the two years leading up to the pandemic, they organized five successful events. A trusted member of the community, Martínez took care of event expenses, after which she distributed remaining funds to trans women in need.

As her story shows, trans women in New Brunswick found creative ways to thrive under difficult conditions. The creativity extends to the realm of health and hormones as well. When another Mexican trans woman, Diana Gonzales, lived in New Brunswick, for instance, she purchased hormones to facilitate her vision for her womanhood in the small *tienditas*, or bodegas, that pepper the streets of the Mexican side of the city.[39] In nearby Newark, Jenesys Alicea, a Puerto Rican trans woman, began her hormone therapy through a network of "traveling trans clinics" organized by Ceyenne Doroshow, a Black Trinidadian trans movement leader based in New York City.[40] Although trans immigrants display innovation and self-determination, they ultimately remain beholden to a city infrastructure largely neglectful of their needs.

Both Méndez and Martínez travel hours to have their basic health needs met despite being surrounded by resource-rich medical institutions capable of providing care. For Méndez, access to trans health care in the Healthcare City is either nonexistent or prohibitively expensive. She said:

> New Jersey doesn't support me at all. I'll tell you why. Because the main support for my sexuality, what is medicine ... psychologically, in every way I'm supported by Philadelphia ... New Jersey is more complicated ... there aren't many centers here. ... In Pennsylvania, in Philadelphia, injection prices vary a lot. For example, over there they can run you $100, whereas here they cost me almost $300. ... Medicine in New Jersey is extremely expensive.[41]

Martínez argues similarly. Since becoming friends with Lorena Borjas, Martínez made use of the extensive network of LGBTQ clinics in New York City even though she has always resided in New Brunswick. Members of her biological family with whom she is close live in New Brunswick, and she has managed to find a good landlord and steady employment as a factory worker. Despite living in the city for more than twenty years, she typically travels two and a half hours to Queens to access medical care. She described her situation: "In the state of New Jersey there are no places that support you as a trans woman. There are none, none in New Brunswick. This is why I tell you that I feel, that we feel forgotten. We feel like we don't matter and it's a really sad thing. That is why I have to go to New York because over there in New York, they give me all the support I need as a trans woman."[42]

Martínez and Méndez live in a city that boasts about its outstanding institutions while failing to care for its most vulnerable residents at its own doorsteps. The lack of adequate local medical care for these women emerges not only from a disinvestment in undocumented communities but also from the nature of trans health care itself, which is characterized by economic inaccessibility and geographic dispersal.[43]

Trans immigrants in New Brunswick face barriers to health while also being part of the essential workforce. In fact, undocumented transgender workers in New Jersey constitute an "industrial reserve," an essential yet disposable racialized workforce relegated to the lowest-paying positions without benefits or paid leave.[44] Attending to the variety of employment in trans immigrant life will help widen the range of spaces where the public sees trans women working, living, and striving, and hopefully challenge nefarious stereotypes that feed their criminalization. Of necessity, much of the public discourse surrounding trans women's labor participation centers on sex work.[45] Trans women are often profiled as sex workers when interacting with law enforcement or by the public at large.[46] As the Mexican American trans activist Bamby Salcedo described, "There is a stigma attached to trans people—especially trans women of color—that basically everywhere we are and everywhere we go, we get criminalized. We are constantly assumed to be sex workers and drug addicts."[47]

The reality is that trans women are not a homogeneous group and labor in a variety of positions. Often, their employers hold the ability to dismiss them without prior notice. At Parque Oaxaca, mostly male immigrant and migrant day laborers congregate to wait for daily work in construction, landscaping, and other informal jobs.[48] Martínez prefers to wait for job offers over the phone, and she routinely accepts calls from agencies looking for workers for warehouses. Martínez lives "al día, al día," day to day, completely dependent on the labor agencies to notify her when employment is available and on friends who carpool. Although she was out of work at the time of our interview, previously she worked at a chocolate factory and a clothing factory. Unlike Martínez, Lissa Méndez does not work in the industrial sector though her trans roommate does. Still, Méndez concurred that most trans women in New Brunswick work in factories.[49] She labors as a taxi driver, but her work history also paints a portrait of working-class trans migrant life steeped in the historical labor patterns of undocumented immigrants.[50] In the past, Méndez worked as a roofer in construction.

When she lived in Trenton, New Jersey, she worked in a factory that manufactured military defense, automotive, and aerospace products. When she lived in New York, she became certified to work as a nursing assistant. These various experiences demonstrate the wide variety of working-class employment available to Latinx trans women and their important role in the economy. Trans immigrants share the burdens of the tenuous nature of their employment with their cis immigrant counterparts. However, transphobia compromises their sense of belonging in the community and, as a result, the strength and cohesiveness of the workforce overall. For example, although Martínez is generally content with factory work, she has been subject to anti-trans discrimination from her coworkers. She described one warehouse where her supervisors prohibited her from using the women's bathroom:

> I was discriminated against in a factory where I used to work because they didn't permit me to use the women's bathroom. The boss didn't want me to go inside the women's bathroom because, since I am a trans woman, he wanted me to bring him papers certifying that I was a woman who was totally trans. I suffered a lot in this respect. I suffered a lot because I felt denigrated. I felt a sad presence for being the way I am, and I felt discriminated against.[51]

Although Latinx people often shun trans immigrants, there exist important cultural elements that have nurtured the growth of the community in the small city of New Brunswick. Three nearby larger cities, New York, Newark, and Philadelphia, have large trans populations and institutional resources, and yet New Brunswick retains a vibrant trans immigrant community. Gonzales speculates that this is due to the large Oaxacan cultural influence on the city's immigrant community. Oaxaca is home to sixteen indigenous groups of people, the largest of whom are the Zapotec and Mixtec.[52] These indigenous groups "have a relationship with the Mexican state that differs from that of non-indigenous, or mestizo, migrants."[53] Likewise, "as indigenous peoples, they bring with them cultural and political resources for identity formation, political organizing, and community building that mestizo Mexicans do not share."[54] A cultural resource that seems to be prevalent in New Brunswick is an awareness of, and even a positive association with, gender-variant people through popular knowledge of *muxes*—a third gender category of people within the Zapotec culture.[55] In general, muxes are valued members of their communities, although they may still face ostracism. They are known, in part, for undertaking the important responsibility of caring for their parents in their old age.[56] Although the women interviewed for Voces of a Pandemic did not indicate having ties to indigenous communities, Gonzales suggested that popular knowledge of gender variance among people from Oaxaca and their significant influence on the broader immigrant community in New Brunswick may play a role in fostering some community acceptance for trans women, allowing a trans immigrant community to thrive. Thus, oral interviews with trans immigrant women from New Brunswick suggest the presence of cultural formations with avenues for inclusion and belonging in addition to, or perhaps in spite of, the persistent class, race, and gendered antagonism that shapes the city. These latter elements, however, ultimately played a more significant role in shaping the impact and outcome of the coronavirus pandemic on trans Latinx immigrants.

## The Impact of the Coronavirus Pandemic on the Trans Latinx Community of New Brunswick

When coronavirus began spreading in New Jersey in March 2020, Rutgers campuses quickly shut down as medical researchers and scientists began investigating ways to address the impending health crisis. Rutgers's RUCDR Infinite Biologics, the world's largest university-based biorepository, developed the first at-home saliva test for coronavirus to be authorized by the Food and Drug Administration in early May 2020.[57] Rutgers Medical School was also selected as a site for a COVID-19 vaccine clinical trial in September 2020. In fact, Rutgers's research and public health outreach efforts to combat COVID-19 were so numerous that the university created an exclusive COVID-19 center to serve as an institutional hub for both research and information dissemination.[58] Although Rutgers mobilized hundreds of thousands, if not millions, of dollars to conduct research on the pandemic, virtually no institutional resources were directed toward New Brunswick's immigrant and undocumented residents by the university or the city's political establishment, reinforcing the perception of an entrenched pattern of neglect.

Because Martínez does not see a doctor in New Brunswick, when she began experiencing COVID-19 symptoms seeking professional medical advice was out of the question.[59] Martínez contracted COVID-19 during the first wave of the pandemic after visiting a friend in his home. Her harrowing account belies the trauma caused by the disease:

> I went to visit him and he had the symptoms and he went to the hospital and didn't tell me he had the symptoms. I went to visit him and that's when I entered his house and his room and I felt chills throughout my body, something really ugly and different came over me. And that's when I caught it. And that's when it all started. . . . I spent fifteen days sprawled on my bed . . . two months locked at home. I didn't go out for anything.[60]

Martínez's experiences fit the term "long-haulers," coined to describe patients whose COVID-19 symptoms lasted weeks or months.[61] Some long-haulers suffer from preexisting conditions, like Lissa Méndez, who has asthma.[62] Martínez did not have preexisting conditions, but like 50 percent of the long-haulers surveyed in a recent medical study, Martínez was never tested.[63] Her symptoms persisted for months to the point that, when she returned to work, she kept taking medication to manage her pain every day. When I asked her about her recovery at the time of our interview, she said: "My body doesn't feel the same. Now I feel like I have pain in my body, in my back. My head hurts. These are things that leave grave side effects. There are side effects. I'm not 100 percent back to how I was before."[64] Martínez suffered long-term physical and mental health consequences, which include the trauma of isolation, thinking she might die without anyone knowing, "me duermo y amanezco muerta," having experienced confusing hallucinations as well as extreme stress from not knowing how she would be able to pay for her food, electricity, water, or rent.

As of September 2020, polls indicated that at least 72 percent of Latinx households faced serious financial problems during the pandemic.[65] Even before this, 23 percent of Latinx households were identified by researchers as being food insecure.[66] Lissa Méndez was among them. Shortly after arriving in the United States, she worked the night shift at a Target but did not earn enough to be able to afford both rent and food:

> I was charged with cleaning the store, picking up the garbage, the boxes, and I didn't have enough money. Sometimes, all the way at the end of the store, there was a pizza shop that made small pizzas, personalized pizzas, and sometimes the last ones that wouldn't sell were thrown in the store's trash. Well, I didn't have enough money. So, what I did at night was go pick up those small pizzas and eat them because sometimes I didn't have enough for food.[67]

Although Méndez found more economic stability after moving to New Brunswick, it remained insubstantial. Like the fifty-four million Americans facing food insecurity during the pandemic, she found herself "short on food."[68] Likewise, when Martínez's symptoms began to appear, her first thoughts revolved around housing and food: "My first thought was, How am I going to pay the rent? How am I going to buy my food? I didn't have the strength to cook. I didn't have the strength to do absolutely anything. I didn't want anything. I didn't want anyone to talk to me. I isolated myself. . . . It was very traumatic, to be honest."[69]

When Martínez caught COVID-19 she was not working. The factory that employed her closed after Governor Murphy's stay-at-home order. She had been out of work for one month before she got sick and for two months afterward until she recovered enough to search for a new job. At the time of our interview, Martínez had recently found employment in a cosmetics factory, where she worked alongside three other trans women. She spent eight hours on her feet each day assembling packages and was allotted one lunch break and two fifteen-minute breaks. Her feet fatigued easily, "se cansan mucho los pies," and she began taking Tylenol each day to deal with the chronic pain. The eviction moratorium issued in mid-March gave Martínez temporary relief from the consequences of being unable to pay her rent. Still, even after she returned to work, she continued to worry about how she would put food on the table: "Before [the pandemic] I did have my food, but now I don't."[70] Martínez, in her words, was "not prepared" to be out of work for so long. She survived primarily with the help of her family and friends: "Well, with the help of my friends, they gathered enough so that I could pay rent. I asked to borrow money from my brothers to pay rent. And well my girlfriend helped me as well. She helped me pay my bills. Light, water, rent, and my cell phone which is indispensable during these times."[71]

Martínez was fortunate that her brothers were able to assist her with her rent, since both she and her siblings send remittances to their parents in Chiapas, Mexico. Martínez's parents are eighty-two and eighty-three years old and have no retirement income. They depend on their sons and daughters and, in particular, Martínez, since she has no children. After Martínez lost her income, her parents "suffered as well." In April 2020 the World Bank predicted a 20 percent drop in migrant remittances, leaving not only individual families like Martínez's vulnerable but also entire governments in trouble, as remittances often account for a significant portion of a country's gross domestic product.[72] Martínez's experiences make evident that trans undocumented immigrants are important and valuable members of their communities who contribute financially and socially to the well-being of others despite the enormous obstacles placed in their way.[73] They also suggest, however, that trans immigrants occupy spaces of unique vulnerability in the United States that can have rebounding effects in their countries of origin during moments of crisis.

In addition to dealing with the physical consequences of the disease, trans people like Martínez also faced anxiety as a result of new restrictions on access to hormones during the pandemic. She lamented, "It has affected me greatly. I haven't been able to go to get my hormones." Access to hormones can profoundly shape the direction of a trans person's life and can significantly contribute to mental well-being and economic security. Trans people experience disproportionate mental health crises compared to the non-trans population. The National Transgender Survey found that 39 percent of respondents experienced psychological distress, compared to only 5 percent of the U.S. population. Hormone therapy can provide peace of mind for trans people, which has been linked to better mental health outcomes.[74] Méndez alluded to the detrimental effects of the coronavirus through interruptions in her own transition: "At that moment I found myself in a situation in terms of my transition. I was not doing very well, I was . . . living through the changes and accommodating myself to being depressed and so . . . it hit me really hard and it was really difficult, really difficult."[75]

Equally important, hormone therapy, or "living through the changes," also helps trans people minimize public scrutiny of their bodies and reduce the threat of violence in a heteronormative culture by allowing them to blend into the general population.[76] As Toby Beauchamp explains, "Surveillance of gender-nonconforming people centers ... on the perceived deception underlying transgressive gender presentation."[77] Gender nonconformity is viewed as dangerous, deceptive, and dishonest. Martínez described how the police view her and her friends, "they look at us like we're odd."[78] Moreover, surveillance of trans bodies hinges on the degree and perceptibility of gender transgressiveness, whether through facial recognition technology, identity documents, or on the street. In a society that normalizes responding to gender nonconformity through murder, incarceration, deportation, or termination from employment, consistent hormone use can function as a social safety net, offsetting the high rates of unemployment and poverty among the population. Indeed, trans Latinx workers report unemployment more than three times the rate of the population as a whole (21% versus 5%), and trans workers of all ethnic and racial groups are nearly four times more likely than the general population to have a household income of under $10,000 (15% versus 4%).[79] Being unable to access hormones or having transitions interrupted during the pandemic contributed an additional layer of hardship not only through affecting a deeply personal sense of self but also by jeopardizing the ability to move through public settings safely, avoid discrimination or encounters with the police, and stay employed. These effects could have been mitigated if local healthcare institutions served the immigrant trans community that surrounds them.

Access to hormone therapy alone does not prevent anti-trans violence or discrimination. After Méndez became a permanent resident, she obtained an identification card with her name and female gender marker. In contrast, Martínez's undocumented status makes that all but impossible. As a result, every time she uses her identification card, whether to get a vaccine or to apply for public assistance, she risks exposure, discrimination, and misgendering in addition to the threat of deportation. Churches, which comprise the most numerous and popular form of nonprofit public aid in New Brunswick, often discriminate against trans people through the enforcement of onerous requirements reflective of cisheteronormative values. As Martínez described her experience:

> The organizations that offer help have many identity requirements, like when you say you are trans, they don't want to help you. Organizations with fundraiser events for example. Because there are churches that don't accept us when you tell them, I am a trans woman—I have always spoken the truth. I have always said what I am. I have nothing to hide. Why? Because I, my name is Mercedes. So, yes, my name is different than what shows on my ID.[80]

Fortunately, during the pandemic Martínez managed to obtain aid from two local groups that do not discriminate against trans people. Mil Sonrisas (which means "one thousand smiles") is a local grassroots collective that distributed food and clothing to residents during the coronavirus pandemic and to Central Americans after Hurricane Eta in November 2020. Martínez also received a small cash grant from New Brunswick Mutual Aid, a group formed by María Juárez, Dr. Lilia Fernández, Miguel Romero-Trejos, and another local activist who collected and distributed $23,000 to the local community. When they called Martínez to follow up on her application and determine her eligibility, they discovered that she had listed herself by her masculine legal name but also gave her feminine chosen name as an alternative. Group members subsequently recognized and decided to respect her transness, identifying and addressing her only by her chosen name.[81]

Although Méndez also applied to New Brunswick Mutual Aid after her work as a taxi driver dramatically declined, she did not qualify. So many people from New Brunswick applied for funds that the group quickly decided to limit their criteria to single mothers, undocumented individuals, victims of COVID-19, and the elderly. They disqualified those who received public assistance and eventually those who did not live within city limits.[82] The elaborate criteria the group developed indicated the level of need as well as the concentration of hypervulnerable immigrants in New Brunswick. Instead of mutual aid, Méndez found support from a romantic partner who worked in construction. At the time of our interview, she felt confident about her relationship and his ability to support her financially. Weeks after, when we reconnected on the phone, the relationship had turned physically abusive, and she was actively searching for other forms of help. The prevalence of intimate partner violence against trans people is well documented.[83] Because trans people are often cut off from a central support system—the family—they often must create a patchwork of friends, lovers, ex-lovers, and, if able, professionals to survive crises or simply navigate life's challenges. When compared to the legal and emotional ties that often bind biological family members, trans people's support networks are characterized by instability, vulnerability, and uncertainty.[84] Although Méndez lives free from the fear of deportation, she bears the burden of economic pain shared by Martínez and faces the uphill battle of building the stability necessary to rise out of a state of constant survival.

## Conclusion

Conducting interviews with Latinx immigrants living through the global coronavirus pandemic resulted in an important archive that future researchers will use to examine the crisis. Rarer still are the interviews with undocumented and low-income trans Latinx immigrant women, who do not often appear in official records. Elevating trans Latinx immigrant voices in scholarship on race and inequality promises to produce new knowledge that challenges the representation of trans people in broader society and contests understandings of history that erase their presence. These oral histories also encourage scholars to examine the nature of place or geography, class, and race in producing variability among trans populations. In New Brunswick, New Jersey, despite trans women's contributions in labor, entertainment, and international economies, most live in the shadow of a city unwilling to prioritize them. Their ingenuity in surviving poverty, however, self-determination in the face of hostility and neglect, and ability to blossom into autonomous individuals with chosen names and realized selves, demonstrate resilience and a will to go on that we may all draw strength from.

## Notes

This is a modified version of an article previously published in the *US Latina and Latino Oral History Journal* (University of Texas Press, 2021). Thank you to Mercedes Martínez, Lissa Méndez, and all the other individuals interviewed for sharing their stories. Thank you to Maggie Rivas-Rodriguez and Lilia Fernández for inviting me to work on the Latino New Jersey Oral History Project and for reading and editing drafts of the article on which this chapter is based. Thank you to Joseph Kaplan for pointing out the Healthcare City, and for all our generative conversations. Special thanks to my mother, Carmen Arenas, for always editing my translations and raising me bilingual in the first place. My utmost gratitude to my advisors Lilia Fernández and Donna Murch for their unwavering support and for modeling the kind of scholar I wish to become.

1 Mercedes Martínez, interview with the author. Mercedes Martínez is a pseudonym to protect her identity.
2 This chapter defines *trans* and *transgender* as someone who does not live as, or identify with, the gender or gender role they were assigned at birth. For an analysis of terminology, see Susan Stryker, Paisley Currah, and Lisa Jean Moore, "Introduction: Trans-, Trans, or Transgender?" *Women's Studies Quarterly* 36, nos. 3–4 (2008): 11–22.
3 "We Are the Healthcare City," New Brunswick City Center, November 15, 2021, https://www.newbrunswick.com/pub/listing/the_healthcare_city.
4 My use of the ethno-racial term *Latinx* reflects an approach to Latinx studies that centers the critical contributions of Black, indigenous, and queer and gender nonconforming people from the Latin American diaspora. In the context of New Brunswick, *Latinx* reflects a pan-ethnic group of mostly Spanish-speaking immigrants and children of immigrants, mostly from Mexico, shaped by and spatially grouped together through shared social conditions relating to language, immigration, class, ethnicity, and race. Although race statistics on the Hispanic/Latinx demographic are inadequate, I reprint the 2017 American Community Survey five-year estimates to give more context on New Brunswick's demographics: American Community Survey Data, US Census Bureau, accessed July 15, 2024, https://datausa.io/profile/geo/new-brunswick-nj/#:~:text=Population%20%26%20 Diversity&text=In%202022%2C%20there%20were%201.5,third%20most%20 common%20ethnic%20groups. Hispanic categorized as white comprised 43.4% of the population. Hispanics categorized as Black or African American comprised 1.17%. Hispanics categorized as multiracial comprised .76%. Hispanics categorized as some other race comprised 7.46% of the population. Hispanics categorized as Asian comprised .12% of the population. Lastly, Hispanics categorized as American Indian or Alaskan Native comprised only .0546%. These statistics, especially the first and last categories, seem incongruent with the lived experiences of many people in the Latino/a/x diaspora. Providing examples of individual voices not captured by statistics broadens this picture. For example, Lissa Méndez described her race as

*Morena* (dark-skinned people on a spectrum from Brown to Black), and Miguel Romero-Trejos, also interviewed for the Latino New Jersey Oral History Project and cited in this chapter, described embracing the term *Indian* in adulthood after kids used the word to taunt him in his youth. He does not belong to an indigenous community.

5   Mercedes Martínez is a pseudonym. Lissa Méndez and all other names are not pseudonyms.

6   American Community Survey data list the Hispanic population of New Brunswick as 55.8 percent in 2015. Mexicans alone accounted for 28.44 percent of the total population. The second two largest Hispanic groups among the total population were Central American (9.5 percent) and Dominican (9.36 percent). All census data was obtained through Social Explorer and the US Census Bureau.

7   Although some scholars, such as Sandoval-Strausz, have argued that Latinx immigration "solved" the "urban crisis," I do not make that claim. New Brunswick experienced an increase in Latinx population in the post-1970s period, but the problems of the urban crisis remained despite public–private initiatives. See A. K. Sandoval-Strausz, *Barrio America: How Latin Immigrants Saved the American City* (New York: Basic Books, 2019).

8   My use of *social* follows the methods developed by social historians who examine the everyday life experiences and material conditions of non-elite people over an extended period of time and who spearheaded the use of oral histories to derive new insight into traditional narratives.

9   Indeed, as Eithne Luibhéid explains, immigration control measures along the border have historically reproduced social hierarchies, including those of gender and sexuality, thus incentivizing immigrant communities to self-police gender expression. Before the 1952 McCarran-Walter Act, those deemed "undesirable" or likely to become a public charge, including gender and sexually transgressive people, were denied entry at the border. Under the McCarran-Walter Act, homosexual exclusion became subsumed into the provision that barred entry by "psychopathic personalities." See Eithne Luibhéid, *Entry Denied: Controlling Sexuality at the Border* (Minneapolis: University of Minnesota Press, 2002).

10  I find the term *industrial reserve* useful in exploring how race, ethnicity, and the coercive nature of gender nonconformity shape the tenuous nature of the trans immigrant working class. See Joe Trotter, *Black Milwaukee: The Making of an Industrial Proletariat, 1915–45* (Urbana: University of Illinois Press, 1985), 148.

11  Linda Shopes, "Commentary: Sharing Authority," *Oral History Review* 30, no. 1 (Winter–Spring 2003): 105–108.

12  In populations that are semiliterate, that have inherited rich oral traditions, or that are often left out of the official record, testimonios are a political imperative. Horacio Roque Ramírez became one of the first oral historians to pay attention to trans Latinx people. My own methods follow his call for "a shared queer authority." See Nan Alamilla Boyd and Horacio Roque Ramírez, *Bodies of Evidence: The Practice of Queer Oral History* (Oxford: Oxford University Press, 2012), especially chap. 10.

13  For an overview of Mexican immigration, see Douglas S. Massey, Jorge Durand, and Nolan J. Malone, *Beyond Smoke and Mirrors: Mexican Immigration in an Era of Economic Integration* (New York: Russel Sage Foundation, 2002). For a history of redevelopment in New Brunswick, see Eric Schkrutz, "Urban Development in the City of the Traveler: The Story of New Brunswick and Why It May Never Resolve Its Identity Crisis," Honors thesis, Rutgers, The State University of New Jersey, April 2011.

14 In 1980, Puerto Ricans comprised only 8 percent of the city's population but 67 percent of all Latines. Martin Perez, "A Latino History of New Brunswick," September 1, 2019; Latino New Jersey Oral History Project, https://www.youtu.be/JSSsroeZbno?si=KxIc55x0NL-GhXp8.

15 For a recent history of Oaxaca, see Lynn Stephens, *We Are the Face of Oaxaca: Testimony and Social Movements* (Durham, NC: Duke University Press, 2013). For information on the Oaxacan community in New Brunswick, see Rutgers University Center for Latin American Studies, *Transnational New Brunswick = New Brunswick transnacional: A Project in Engaged Anthropology = Un proyecto de antropología comprometida* (New Brunswick, NJ: Rutgers University, Center for Latin American Studies, 2010).

16 Jason Hackworth explains how urban renewal in the 1980s and 1990s began demolishing public housing and low-income neighborhoods to attract commercial businesses to the downtown area that had relocated in the 1960s and 1970s. See Jason Hackworth, "State Devolution, Urban Regimes, and the Production of Geographic Scale: The Case of New Brunswick, New Jersey," *Urban Geography* 21, no. 5 (May 2013): 450–458.

17 Maanvi Sing and Mario Koran, "'The Virus Doesn't Discriminate but Governments Do': Latinos Disproportionately Hit by Coronavirus," *Guardian*, April 18, 2020, https://www.theguardian.com/us-news/2020/apr/18/the-virus-doesnt-discriminate-but-governments-do-latinos-disproportionately-hit-by-coronavirus.

18 Lissandra Villa, "'We're Ignored Completely,' Amid the Pandemic, Undocumented Immigrants Are Essential but Exposed," *Time*, April 17, 2020, https://time.com/5823491/undocumented-immigrants-essential-coronavirus/.

19 Jeffrey Passel and D'Vera Cohn, *20 Metro Areas Are Home to Six-in-Ten Unauthorized Immigrants in US* (Washington, DC: Pew Research Center, March 11, 2019), https://www.pewresearch.org/short-reads/2019/03/11/us-metro-areas-unauthorized-immigrants/#:~:text=Most%20of%20the%20United%20States,estimates%20based%20on%20government%20data.

20 Miguel Romero-Trejos, interview by Leo Valdes, June 18, 2020, New Brunswick, videotaped teleconference, Latino New Jersey Oral History Project, Voces of a Pandemic Collection, Rutgers Oral History Archive (ROHA) at Rutgers University.

21 The suburb of Somerset is only a twenty-minute drive from the Rutgers University campus and as of 2017 had a median household income of $106,046 (American Community Survey Data 2017 Fiver Year Estimates, United States Census Bureau, accessed July 15, 2024, https://data.census.gov/table/ACSST5Y2017.S1901?q=Somerset%20County,%20New%20Jersey%20Income%20and%20Poverty). Whereas the median household income in New Brunswick in 2017 was $38,413 (American Community Survey Data 2017 Fiver Year Estimates, United States Census Bureau, accessed July 15, 2024, https://data.census.gov/table/ACSST5Y2017.S1901?q=New%20Brunswick%20city,%20New%20Jersey%20Income%20and%20Poverty).

22 Leah Ripley Hunt, "Spatial and Procedural Justice in Urban Planning: A Case Study of the Lincoln Annex School Redevelopment," 29. Honors thesis, submitted to the Edward J. Bloustein School of Planning and Public Policy, Rutgers University, May 2020.

23 Lilia Fernández, "Voces of a Pandemic," videotaped teleconference interview by Carie Rael, New Brunswick, July 30, 2020, Latino New Jersey Oral History Project, Rutgers Oral History Archive at Rutgers University (hereafter Lilia Fernández, Voces of a Pandemic, ROHA); Samuel O. Ludescher, "New Brunswick and the

Street with Two Faces," *Medium*, April 26, 2017, https://medium.com/nj-spark/new-brunswick-and-the-street-with-two-faces-5e05aa7fa4dd.
24 American Community Survey Data 2017 Fiver Year Estimates, United States Census Bureau 2022, accessed July 15, 2024, https://data.census.gov/table/ACSST5Y2017.S1901?g=1400000US34023005300.
25 Martínez, interview.
26 Lissa Méndez, interview by Leo Valdes, August 11, 2020, New Brunswick, videotaped teleconference, Latino New Jersey Oral History Project, Voces of a Pandemic Collection, ROHA.
27 Transgender Day of Remembrance began in 1999, organized by the trans advocate Gwendolyn Ann Smith to honor the memory of Rita Hester, a Black trans woman murdered in 1998. The Trans Murder Monitoring Project reported that twenty-seven trans people had been murdered in the United States by November 20, 2020, while the Human Rights Campaign reported thirty-seven by the same day. This indicates a variation in who is being counted as trans, where the Human Rights Campaign includes a broader group of gender nonconforming people. As of the time of this writing, the Human Rights Campaign reported a staggering forty-four trans people had been murdered in 2020.
28 Méndez, interview.
29 Méndez, interview.
30 NBC News filed a Freedom of Information Act request to obtain data on LGBTQ people who sought asylum between 2007 and 2017. See Tim Fitzsimons, "Trump Proposals Threaten LGBTQ Asylum-Seekers' Hopes of Refuge in the US," *NBC News*, August 20, 2020, https://www.nbcnews.com/feature/nbc-out/trump-proposals-threaten-lgbtq-asylum-seekers-hopes-refuge-u-s-n1236736.
31 "Human Rights Violations against Transgender Women in Guatemala," 122nd Session of the Human Rights Committee, Geneva, March–April 2018, https://tbinternet.ohchr.org.
32 Méndez, interview.
33 Méndez, interview.
34 First defined by Manuel Guzmán as "the exile of those who have had to leave their nations of origin on account of their sexual orientation," the term has been expanded and refined by Horacio Roque Ramírez, Yolanda Martínez-San Miguel among others. See Manuel Guzmán, "*Pa la escuelita con mucho cuidado y po la orillita*: A Journey through the Contested Terrains of the Nation and Sexual Orientation," in *Puerto Rican Jam: Essays on Culture and Politics*, ed. Frances Negrón-Muntaner and Ramón Grosfoguel (Minneapolis: University of Minnesota Press, 1997), 209–228; Horacio N. Roque Ramirez, "'That's My Place!': Negotiating Racial, Sexual, and Gender Politics in San Francisco's Gay Latino Alliance, 1975–1983," *Journal of the History of Sexuality* 12, no. 2 (2003): 224–258; Yolanda Martínez-San Miguel, "Female Sexiles? Toward an Archeology of Displacement of Sexual Minorities in the Caribbean," *Signs* 36, no. 4 (2011): 813–836. See also the beautiful graphic novel on the life of Adela Vásquez, a Cuban trans woman and activist based in San Francisco: Jaime Cortez, *Sexile* (Los Angeles: AIDS Project Los Angeles and Institute for Gay Men's Health, 2004).
35 Sara McKinnon discusses similar cases in her book, although her emphasis is on how gay cis men and male-assigned asylum seekers have more "rhetorical license" upon which to claim asylum than cis women refugees. Sara S. McKinnon, *Gendered Asylum: Race and Violence in US Law and Politics* (Urbana: University of Illinois Press, 2016).
36 Mercedes Martínez, in conversation with author.

37  Martínez, interview.
38  Martínez, interview.
39  Diana Gonzales, in conversation with author. Gonzales is a trans woman who was born in Mexico City in 1971 and emigrated to New Jersey in 2000. She lived in New Brunswick from 2008 to 2010.
40  Jenesys Alicea, by Leo Valdes, June 12, 2019, oral history interview, ROHA. See also Leo Valdes, "Queer Latinx New Jersey," Story Map, Esri Geospatial Cloud, https://www.arcgis.com/apps/MapJournal/index.html?appid=a7e457433688403ba2eb307f9dbc9f95.
41  Méndez, interview.
42  Martínez, interview.
43  Hil Malatino, *Trans Care* (Minneapolis: University of Minnesota Press, 2020), especially chap. 5.
44  Historians first applied the term *industrial reserve* to describe the early stage of the proletarianization of African American workers in the first half of the twentieth century. From "peasants to proletariat," in short. Joe Trotter expanded the term to include Black unemployed city workers. The fragile nature of the industrial reserve meant that Black workers were last hired, first fired, used as strikebreakers, and forced to remain below a job ceiling. I borrow and repurpose this term to describe the undocumented trans urban experience in New Brunswick from a historical perspective. See Trotter, *Black Milwaukee,* especially chap. 5. To understand how undocumented Mexican immigration emerged from an agrarian working class deemed "surplus labor" in post-1964 Mexico, see Ana Minian, *Undocumented Lives: The Untold Story of Mexican Migration* (Cambridge, MA: Harvard University Press, 2018).
45  Current trans activists argue for the decriminalization and destigmatization of sex work to combat violence against trans women, and I join them in these efforts. See Kaniya Walker, "To Protect Black Trans Lives, Decriminalize Sex Work," *ACLU News & Commentary*, November 20, 2020, https://www.aclu.org/news/lgbtq-rights/to-protect-black-trans-lives-decriminalize-sex-work.
46  The U.S. Transgender Survey found that 33 percent of Black transgender women, 30 percent of multiracial women, 25 percent of Latina women, and 23 percent of American Indian women said that an officer assumed they were sex workers in the past year. Respondents were only allowed to select one racial/ethnic category, so Latinx people may be represented across these figures. See Sandy E. James, Jody L. Herman, Susan Rankin, Mara Keisling, Lisa Mottet, and Ma'ayan Anafi, *The Report of the 2015 US Transgender Survey* (Washington, DC: National Center for Transgender Equality). In New Jersey, 66 percent of trans people reported having faced mistreatment by law enforcement. See New Jersey Transgender Equality Task Force, "Addressing Discrimination against Transgender New Jerseyans, New Jersey Transgender Equality Task Force Report and Recommendations," November 20, 2019, https://www.gardenstateequality.org/wp-content/uploads/2023/02/Transgender_Equality_Task_Force_Final.pdf.
47  Bamby Salcedo, "Validation through Documentation: Integrating Activism, Research, and Scholarship to Highlight (Validate) Trans Latin@ Immigrant Lives," in *Queer and Trans Migrations: Dynamics of Illegalization, Detention, and Deportation*, eds. Jack Cáraves and Bamby Salcedo (Urbana: University of Illinois Press, 2020), 172.
48  Parque Oaxaca has also been called Parque Jotería ("faggot park") because queer workers congregate in the park as well. Teresa Vivár, local activist with New Labor, in conversation with author.

49 Méndez, interview.
50 For a sociological study on the conditions that create a class of disposable immigrant labor, see Tanya María Golash-Boza, *Deported: Immigrant Policing, Disposable Labor, and Global Capitalism* (New York: New York University Press, 2015). For a historical study of Mexican labor in the United States, see Zaragosa Vargas, *Proletarians of the North: A History of Mexican Industrial Workers in Detroit and the Midwest, 1917–1933* (Berkeley: University of California Press, 1993).
51 Martínez, interview.
52 For a history of recent social movements in Oaxaca and the centrality of oral testimony in empowering communities and maintaining indigenous traditions, see Stephens, *We Are the Face of Oaxaca*.
53 Michael Kearney, "Transnational Oaxacan Indigenous Identity: The Case of Mixtecs and Zapotecs," *Identities: Global Studies in Culture and Power* 7, no. 2 (2000): 175.
54 Kearney, "Transnational Oaxacan Indigenous Identity," 176.
55 For an ethnography of the *muxe*, see Marinella Miano Borruso, *Hombre, mujer y muxe' en el Istmo de Tehuantepec* (Córdoba: Plaza y Valdés, 2002).
56 Alfredo Mirandé, "Hombres Mujeres: An Indigenous Third Gender," *Men and Masculinities* 19, no. 4 (2016): 384–409.
57 "Coronavirus News: Rutgers Develops 1st FDA Authorized At-Home Saliva Test for COVID," *ABC Eyewitness News NY,* May 8, 2020, https://abc7ny.com/coronavirus-test-at-home-saliva-rutgers-university/6164163/.
58 Neal Buccino, "Rutgers Creates COVID-19 Center to Fight Pandemic," *Rutgers University Foundation News*, March 27, 2020, https://support.rutgers.edu/news-stories/rutgers-creates-covid-19-center-to-fight-pandemic.
59 The U.S. Transgender Survey found that 33 percent of trans patients who saw a healthcare provider had at least one negative experience related to being transgender. See also Susanna D. Howard, Kevin L. Lee, Aviva G. Nathan, Hannah C. Wenger, Marshall H. Chin, and Scott C. Cook, "Healthcare Experiences of Transgender People of Color," *Journal of General Internal Medicine* 34, no. 10 (2019): 2068–2074.
60 Martínez, interview.
61 UC Davis Health, "COVID-19 'Long-Hauler' Patients Search for Answers and Help," *UC Davis Health* (blog), October 22, 2020, https://broadcastmed.com/infectiousdiseases/1164/news/covid-19-long-hauler-patients-search-for-answers-and-help.
62 Méndez, interview.
63 Rita Rubin, "As Their Numbers Grow, COVID-19 'Long Haulers' Stump Experts" *Journal of the American Medical Association* 324, no. 14 (September 2020): 1381–1383; Martínez, interview.
64 Martínez, interview.
65 Nicole Acevedo, "COVID-19's Economic Impact on Latino Families Is 'Much Worse' Than Expected, Poll Finds," *NBC News*, September 17, 2020, https://www.nbcnews.com/news/latino-families-much-worse-expected-n1240293.
66 Ashley L. Munger, Tiffani D. S. Lloyd, Katherine E. Spiers, Kate C. Riera, and Stephanie K. Grutzmacher, "More Than Just Not Enough: Experiences of Food Insecurity for Latino Immigrants," *Journal of Immigrant and Minority Health* 17, no. 5 (2015): 1548–1556.
67 Méndez, interview.
68 Bridget Balch, "54 Million People in America Face Food Insecurity during the Pandemic: It Could Have Dire Consequences for Their Health," *Association of American Medical Colleges News*, October 15, 2020, https://www.aamc.org/news

-insights/54-million-people-america-face-food-insecurity-during-pandemic-it-could-have-dire-consequences-their.
69  Martínez, interview.
70  Martínez, interview.
71  Martínez, interview.
72  The lockdown limited the capacity of money-transfer operators that migrants rely on, highlighting for advocates the need for the digitization of these services. "World Bank Predicts Sharpest Decline of Remittances in Recent History," press release, April 22, 2020, https://www.worldbank.org/en/news/press-release/2020/04/22/world-bank-predicts-sharpest-decline-of-remittances-in-recent-history.
73  Indeed, Martínez joins a long immigrant tradition of sending remittances to support families and economies in home countries affected by U.S. imperialism. See Minian, *Undocumented Lives*, esp. chap. 5.
74  Hillary B. Nguyen, Alexis M. Chavez, Emily Lipner, Liisa Hantsoo, Sara L. Kornfield, Robert D. Davies, and C. Neill Epperson, "Gender-Affirming Hormone Use in Transgender Individuals: Impact on Behavior Health and Cognition," *Current Psychiatry Report* 20, no. 110 (2018): 110.
75  Martínez, interview.
76  This is, of course, also a burden. No one should be punished for gender nonconformity, either in behavior, expression, or through identity documents.
77  Toby Beauchamp, *Going Stealth: Transgender Politics and US Surveillance Practices* (Durham, NC: Duke University Press, 2019), 9. For a historical analysis of the criminalization of queer people and the tropes used to represent them, see Joey L. Mogul, Andrea J. Ritchie, and Kay Whitlock, *Queer Injustice: The Criminalization of LGBT People in the United States* (Boston: Beacon Press, 2011).
78  This could also be interpreted as "they look at us like we're suspicious" in the context of the dialog.
79  The unemployment rate is derived from the U.S. Transgender Survey. The income statistic is derived from a report produced in 2013, which found the unemployment rate of trans people to be twice the national average. As more labor statistics on trans people emerge, we will gain a fuller picture. For the 2013 report, see Movement Advancement Project, National Center for Transgender Equality, Human Rights Campaign, and Center for American Progress, "A Broken Bargain for Transgender Workers," September 2013, https://www.lgbtmap.org/transgender-workers.
80  Martínez, interview.
81  Fernández, personal communication.
82  Romero-Trejos, interview.
83  Studies have found ranges between 31 percent and 55 percent of trans people reporting intimate partner violence, such as a study conducted in Lima, Peru. See Ellen C. Murphy, Eddy R. Segura, Jordan E. Lake, Leyla Huerta, Amaya G. Perez-Brumer, Kenneth H. Mayer, Sari L. Reisner, Javier R. Lama, and Jesse L. Clark, "Intimate Partner Violence against Transgender Women: Prevalence and Correlates in Lima, Peru (2016–2018)," *AIDS and Behavior* 24, no. 6 (2020): 1743–1751. For a recent U.S.-based study, see Xavier L. Guadalupe-Diaz, *Transgressed: Intimate Partner Violence in Transgender Lives* (New York: New York University Press, 2019).
84  In their recent book Hil Malatino examines the practice of "care labor and care ethics" among trans communities. Nonetheless, as they write, "the mere necessity of this work also points to the fact that the most fundamental networks of care that enable us to persist in our existence are often threadbare, or, sometimes, nearly nonexistent." Malatino, *Trans Care*, 41–42.

# Part 4
# Institutions

# 14

## Reverse Diasporas

Immigrant Detention,
Deportation, and Latinx
Communities in New Jersey
and South America

ULLA D. BERG

New Jersey is home to a large and diverse immigrant population. With 23.4 percent of New Jersey's residents being foreign born, the state has the second highest percentage of foreign born of any U.S. state only superseded by California. Close to half of New Jersey's foreign-born population (46.9%) are from Latin America.[1] While most have U.S. documentation, the state also counts a significant undocumented population at 440,000 in 2019.[2] Despite that, New Jersey saw a decline of around ninety thousand in the number of undocumented migrants over the past decade—almost entirely due to a large drop in new arrivals from Mexico, but also due to deportations—and the state continues to have one of the highest percentages in the United States of undocumented migrants in relation to the overall state population.[3] How the undocumented population fare in the state is shaped by federal and local immigration policies, and the particularities of each person's migration trajectory and family and social history, but it also depends to a great extent on where they live. Those who have been swiped up in operations carried out by U.S. Immigration and Customs Enforcement (ICE) in the state and deported to their countries of citizenship now constitute a "reverse diaspora" of New Jerseyans far beyond the borders of the state.[4]

For a long time, New Jersey was a textbook example of what migration scholars have called a "patchwork approach" to immigration enforcement.[5] This term characterizes a situation in which some cities and towns actively seek to deter undocumented migrants from settling in their jurisdictions by allowing their local law enforcement agents to affiliate with federal enforcement programs such as section 287(g) of the Immigration and Nationality Act (INA) which enable local law enforcement agents to perform specified immigration functions whereas others actively seek to limit such cooperation with ICE in the detention of undocumented migrants.[6] In New Jersey, this has resulted in a local geography where some townships and municipalities are known as being "immigrant friendly," sometimes also referred to as sanctuary cities or towns, whereas others are known as "anti-immigrant towns" eager to champion nativist, xenophobic, and anti-immigrant municipal ordinances and unwilling to acknowledge the many contributions undocumented migrants make to local economies and communities in the state.[7] Cities like New Brunswick, Newark, North Bergen, Plainfield, Trenton, Union City, Camden, Hoboken, Jersey City, and a few others, have been known to work intently to limit local law enforcement's cooperation with ICE. In contrast, Sussex County and a smaller number of municipalities including Parsippany-Troy Hills (Morris County), Middletown (Monmouth County), Freehold Township (Monmouth County), and Jackson (Ocean County) have long voiced open opposition to discouraging cooperation with ICE agents operating in New Jersey.[8]

New Jersey's patchwork situation came to a partial halt in 2018 when former New Jersey state attorney Grubir Grewal issued the Immigrant Trust Directive, a directive designed to limit the "types of voluntary assistance that New Jersey's 36,000 law enforcement officers may provide to federal immigration authorities."[9] The directive applies to state and local police officers, correctional officers working in state prisons and county jails, as well as state and county prosecutors. It was intended to reduce the reluctance in immigrant communities to cooperate with local law enforcement out of fear that they could be handed over to ICE.[10] While the directive was mostly embraced by the state's immigrants, activist communities argued that it did not go far enough to stop immigration detention in the state. For example, the directive did not apply to local law enforcement agencies who were acting under active Intergovernmental Service Agreements with the federal government. The latter was the case of Bergen, Essex, and Hudson County jails, which, by the time the directive was issued, were holding hundreds of ICE detainees awaiting adjudication in New Jersey- and New York City-based immigration courts.[11] It also did not prevent ICE from carrying out enforcement operations in New Jersey without the cooperation from local authorities.[12] In a statement issued after a sweeping immigration raid in late January 2020, ICE threatened local New Jersey law enforcement with increased ICE activity in the state as retaliation over the directive: "Any local jurisdiction thinking that refusing to cooperate with ICE will result in a decrease in local immigration enforcement is mistaken. These jurisdictions that choose to not cooperate with ICE are likely to see an increase in ICE enforcement activity as ICE has no choice but to conduct more at-large, targeted enforcement actions."[13]

This chapter tells the story of how shifting immigration policies and practices over time have affected New Jersey's immigrant communities, particularly those from Latin America, and how they continue to shape the lives of Latinx families and communities in the state and far beyond its boundaries in migrants' countries of citizenship. The chapter is organized in two main sections. The first section offers an overview of enforcement policies and practices in New Jersey situating it within the post-9/11 U.S. security state as a curious archipelago of immigrant-friendly and anti-immigrant localities. The second section offer different voices of South American migrants who have passed through one or more of the state's detention facilities before they were either released back to their families and communities in New Jersey or deported back to their countries of citizenship. These include transnationalized families affected by immigration detention in New Jersey and deported New Jerseyans struggling to find their place in their South American countries of citizenship.

In the chapter, I draw on ethnographic interviews conducted intermittently between 2015 and 2020 with deported migrants in Peru and Ecuador whose lives were upended by detention and deportation and their families in New Jersey.[14] I also draw on research and activist work with different local organizations and advocacy groups including First Friends of New Jersey and New York. Finally, during the pandemic, I was the principal investigator on a research project about the spread of COVID-19 in New Jersey's detention centers, which taught me a great deal more about the intricacies of detention systems and processes in the state.[15] My aim here is to show that while detention and deportation primarily target noncitizens, the lived experiences and economic, social, and emotional repercussions of what Peutz and DeGenova call "the deportation regime" extend way beyond the targeted noncitizens themselves.[16] These individuals are members of families, employed in local businesses, some have U.S.-citizen children in local schools, they worship in local churches and temples, and are in all ways except one full members of their local communities in the state. Understanding how the deportation regime has shaped and is shaping everyday life in Latinx communities in New Jersey offers a critical lens on the key themes of poverty, racism, labor exploitation, violence, police brutality, and marginalization and, in doing so, challenges the official narratives the state often likes to tell about itself.

## A Brief History of Immigration Detention in New Jersey

On August 20, 2021, New Jersey's governor Phil Murphy signed a bill into law that barred county and privately run jails from entering into, renewing, or extending already existing agreements with ICE.[17] The bill ended a decade-long profit-making practice in which county governments rented out bedspace in local county jails to the federal government to hold migrants awaiting adjudication in New Jersey and New York immigration courts. The bill was a historic win for immigrant communities and their advocates in the state who had long argued that immigration detention creates existential insecurities in New Jersey's immigrant population by separating people from their loved ones and violating important civil and human rights. The law was part of a broader political agenda of a democratic governor to court the present and future Latinx vote by working with New Jersey's immigrant communities to broaden how they can contribute to the state's economy and to civil society. These efforts included, for example, a bill (A4743) from December 2019 allowing "all New Jerseyans without regard to immigration status" to apply for a New Jersey driver's license and another bill (S2455) signed into law in August 2020, which for the first time allowed immigrants in the state to obtain professional or occupational licenses regardless of status.[18] These initiatives also illustrate how in the eyes of democratic politicians "Latinx" and "immigrant" are often conflated. That said, New Jersey is not an unequivocally immigrant-friendly place, and the state has a long and troubled history with immigration detention.

New Jersey was home to the first dedicated immigration detention facility in the world—Ellis Island Immigration Station—which opened in 1892 and remained open until 1954.[19] After the closure of Ellis Island and until the 1980s, very few migrants spent time in detention as part of their regular immigration process. This began to change in the 1980s and immigration detention in the United States increased from about two thousand noncitizens detained at any given time in the 1980s to over fifty-thousand a day by fiscal year 2019.[20] This swelling of the immigration detention system is intimately linked to the boom in the prison industry in the 1980s and the war on drugs with its harsh mandatory minimum sentencing policies.[21] Mandatory detention laws, which allow the government to hold noncitizens facing deportation without right to a bail hearing pending removal proceedings, were first introduced in 1988 and expanded several times throughout the 1990s. The most sweeping expansion came in 1996 with the Antiterrorism and Effective Death Penalty Act and the Illegal Immigration Reform and Immigrant Responsibility Act. These "1996 laws," as they are often referred to, expanded the list of crimes making someone subject to mandatory detention and deportation to include nonviolent drug and many other charges.[22] This increasing application of criminal law in immigration law contexts has been referred to as "the crimmigration crisis" by legal scholar Juliet Stumpf, a crisis that laid the legal ground to continue to build and expand the system of mass detention we know today.[23] The 1996 laws also targeted certain asylum seekers as subject to removal, artificially creating a need for more detention space, and revoked the discretion of immigration authorities to release noncitizens from detention.[24] A consequence of the 1996 laws was the creation of ample profit opportunities both for private prison companies and for municipal governments across the United States who used immigration detention to generate income for their state. This has been the story of New Jersey, which has long served as a leading provider of detention space in the United States.[25]

Elizabeth Detention Center (EDC) was the first private for-profit facility in New Jersey to come under contract in 1993 with the now defunct Immigration and Naturalization Service (INS). When opened, the facility counted around one hundred Latinxs among its detainee population of around three hundred.[26] The detention center was operated by the private for profit company Esmor Correctional Services of Melville, L.I., and it was surrounded by controversy from the beginning.[27] Conditions were so poor at the privately run facility that detainees soon organized an uprising inside.[28] The uprising, which took place in 1995, is described at length in *Do They Hear You When You Cry* (1999) by Fauziya Kassindja, an asylum seeker from Togo who spent sixteen months in detention before she finally was granted asylum.[29] Kassindja tells the story of how one night in EDC she and her cellmate Sylvia woke up to glass shattering, metal slamming against metal, men shouting and women screaming, and fire alarms going off. In her account, the riot in Esmor was staged by the men in the detention center and went on for about six hours until law enforcement threw a grenade into the barricades built by the detainees and subsequently stormed the facility. After the riot, the detainees at Esmor were transferred to other facilities in the area. Most of the women were sent to Hudson County Correctional Center which, back then, was frequently running over capacity. Kassindja recalls in her book how they were received with curiosity but also disdain by the inmates at Hudson who hooted at the refugee women when the incident appeared on the evening news: "Hey! That your prison? Why'd you bust it up?"[30] Kassindja did not exactly have an answer at the time, but she later writes:

> As for why, I found out later that INS was asking the same question. They investigated and did a report—"The Elizabeth, New Jersey, Contract Detention Facility Operated by ESMOR Inc. Interim Report"—which was published just over a month of the riot.... The report says that during the review, prior to the "disturbance," the assessment team interviewed some twenty-four detainees, as well as various guards and other Esmor and INS personnel. I don't know who the detainees were. I never heard about anybody being interviewed—unless you counted women, I'd heard being videotaped that day in my dorm while Miss Jones listened to every word they said. Most people, like those women, like me, would have been too afraid to speak honestly even if they had been interviewed. But somebody talked—a lot of people, it seems—because the report contains a

huge, long list of problems and complaints, most of which I knew about firsthand or had heard about from other refugees. In fact, virtually every horror I had experienced there was accurately described in the report.[31]

Esmor was later removed as the contractor for the Elizabeth facility, which was taken over by the Corrections Corporation of America. Hudson County, New Jersey, where Kassindja and other asylum seekers were transferred after the 1995 riot in EDC, signed its first contract with INS the year after (the same year the 1996 laws were passed). Bergen County Jail soon followed Hudson County's lead and signed in 1997 its first contract with INS. Then came 9/11 and the Bush administration began ramping up immigration enforcement arguing that this was necessary to fight terrorism. The Department of Homeland Security was created along with a series of agencies and programs related to immigration enforcement and over the next decade astronomical budgets were directed into "protecting the homeland."[32] The high demand for detention space created by these combined institutional reforms was further solidified when the Obama administration authorized ICE to expand the Bush-era program known as Secure Communities, piloted and then established in 2008, which facilitated the sharing of arrest data and fingerprints between local law enforcement agencies and ICE.[33] If this database crossing resulted in a fingerprint match, ICE could issue a detainer request for local police to hold the targeted individual in jail for up to forty-eight hours until they could arrange for pick up, even if the person was not being charged with a crime. With the extension of the reach of immigration enforcement through local police departments, it is not surprising that many people apprehended under Secure Communities include those suspected of a variety of nonviolent crimes including traffic violations and immigration offenses. Nor is it surprising that these arrests mirror existing racial and ethnic inequalities in policing that disproportionally affect Black and Latinx communities.

When Secure Communities was established in 2008, Essex County signed its first contract with ICE and, after only three years, Essex became ICE's largest holding pen in New Jersey. ICE's detainer requests in New Jersey peaked in 2009, but then declined steadily until 2015, only to rise again when Secure Communities after having been discontinued was reinstated after Trump's election.[34] During the Obama administration's expansion of immigration detention, Essex County signed a five-year contract in 2011 more than doubling its capacity to hold a total of 1,250 ICE immigration detainees. Eight hundred beds were made available at Essex County Correctional facility itself and up to 450 beds were available at the nearby privately run and former halfway house, Delaney Hall.[35] The ICE contract with Delaney Hall, which was run by Community Education Center, Inc.—a public–private partnership with close ties to former New Jersey governor Chris Christie—was issued after a fraud bidding process and the deal was from the beginning surrounded by controversy.[36] The Delaney Hall contract was finally terminated after a labor conflict in 2016 and a settlement was reached between Essex County, Community Education Center, Inc., and the New Jersey Department of Labor, which ordered the two employers to pay $4.8 million in back wages and benefits to 122 detention center employees.[37]

After Trump's election, his January 2017 executive order greatly expanded who would be detainable under the law and New Jersey, like elsewhere in the country, witnessed an increase in ICE activity.[38] ICE arrests of migrants with no criminal records more than doubled in New Jersey in 2017 as a direct consequence of the Trump administration's decision to also include migrants and asylum seekers with no criminal convictions in the government's enforcement priorities.[39] This period also saw a steep increase in the immigration court backlogs, which had already grown substantially under President Obama.[40] Communities and advocates across the Garden State protested the Trump administration's draconian policies and took many kinds of direct and indirect action to end immigration detention in New Jersey. Advocates cited years of complaints of medical neglect and poor conditions in detention that negatively affected the physical and mental health of detainees. These claims were backed up by government reviews of the facilities. For example, a Department of Homeland Security Office of Inspector General report found "egregious violations of detention standards" at the Essex facility, including overly restrictive segregation, inadequate medical care, unreported security incidents, and significant food safety issues.[41] Hudson County Correctional Facility also had a long and troubled record of medical neglect and deaths in custody—over seventeen deaths since 2013. Mounting public outrage over deaths at the jail accelerated after the death of Carlos Bonilla, a father of four, due to medical neglect, and led Hudson County to seek to terminate its five-year, $29 million contract with CFG Health Systems.[42] In November 2020, freeholders in Hudson County voted to extend their contract with ICE for another ten years walking back promises made in 2018 to phase out the contract with ICE in 2020. The vote went through despite massive public protest and advocacy by members of the Abolish ICE NY–NJ coalition.[43] However, this vote would not be the last word on the matter.

When COVID-19 hit, New Jersey became an early epicenter of the pandemic. Public protest to abolish immigration detention using the hashtags #AbolishICE and #FreeThemAll intensified. On May 15, 2020, four detainees in EDC at risk of serious illness and death from the virus filed a class-action lawsuit demanding the immediate release of all immigrants locked up there. One of the plaintiffs, Hector García Mendoza (age thirty), had been detained at EDC since March 2020. He shared a dorm with dozens of other detained men, some of them ill from COVID-19, and he reported on the living conditions with no space to socially distance.[44] García who suffered from asthma had experienced chest pain and shortness of breath, but the medical staff had refused him adequate treatment. The lawsuit also sought to stop ICE from admitting new people into EDC and from unilaterally transferring people from EDC to other immigration jails

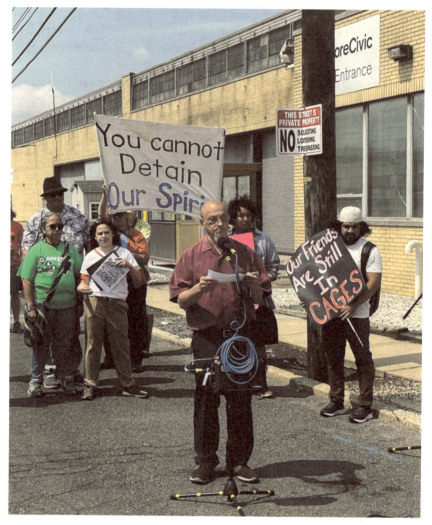

FIGURE 14.1 "Make EDC History." Protesters in front of Elizabeth Detention Center, June 17, 2023. (Photo courtesy of Ulla D. Berg)

and prisons around the country. García himself was deported after the suit was filed and since disappeared.[45]

After the filing of the COVID-19 lawsuit and after months of pressure from advocacy groups, the Elberon Group, CoreCivic's landlord at the EDC site, announced that it would terminate its lease with CoreCivic. In response, ICE announced that the agency would refuse to leave the premises until their lease with CoreCivic expired in 2027.[46] Then, on May 3, 2021, Elberon filed a lawsuit alleging that CoreCivic had breached its contract by failing to follow local and federal safety regulations to stop the spread of COVID-19.[47] EDC had at that time seen more COVID-19 cases than other ICE facilities in the region, and both security and medical employees had died from the virus.[48] Despite ongoing litigation, CoreCivic was able to renew its contract with ICE until August 2023. But it also turned out that they did not have the last word.

Ongoing organizing efforts of pro-immigrant advocates and the families of detainees and mounting public pressure finally introduced a wrench in the wheels of the deportation machine in the state. In August 2021, Governor Murphy, who had complied with several court-mandated medical and judicial releases during the pandemic to assist facilities in reducing their populations, signed a bill into law barring New Jersey's county and privately run jails from entering into or renewing already existing agreements and contracts with ICE.[49] The bill, however, did not annul the existing contracts with ICE including the new ten-year contract in Hudson County signed in 2020 despite massive public opposition. Local elected officials, who had begun to worry about their reelection, soon came under pressure to back down from the deal with ICE. The county soon announced that no detained migrants would be held at the jail after November 1, 2021. Essex County Jail, in turn, had already announced in April 2021 that it would not renew its contract with ICE set to expire in August that same year and when the contract expired the jail transferred its detainee population to other facilities amidst intense public protest and campaigns.[50] Bergen County Jail was the last of New Jersey's jails to announce that they would no longer hold ICE detainees at their jail.[51]

Advocates and family members of detained migrants had hoped that ICE would release their loved ones under supervision or on their own recognizance as their cases proceeded through the hugely backlogged immigration courts. ICE denied most of these requests and instead proceeded to transfer detainees out of the state, further away from their families, citing public safety as the main reason.[52] This critical juncture in the history of ICE's presence in New Jersey became an important lesson for community advocates: banning contracts with ICE in one state does not solve the problem of immigrant detention if migrants are just transferred to other states further away from their families and support network. It only displaces the issue to other jurisdictions who are willing to enter, renew or even expand their contracts with ICE. These interstate transfers removing people from both family support and legal counsel were often a step further toward deportation as an inevitable outcome of detention, an outcome that affects New Jersey families and the state's economy in multiple ways.

## Transnational Communities and Deportation in New Jersey and Beyond

Scholars in the social sciences have documented the multiple and immediate effects of detention and deportation on Latin American migrant families and communities, which include significant loss of income and frequent descent into poverty, and disruption to care and living arrangements, in addition to the deep emotional scars and social costs of family separation. Sociologist Joanna Dreby has written about how undocumented migrant women in New Jersey become "suddenly single mothers" when their husbands are detained and deported back to Mexico.[53] Similarly, Tanya Golash-Boza has noted how traditional family roles and expectations are disrupted, and that young children risk becoming "abruptly adult" with the deportation of a parent or close relative.[54] Luis Zayas has focused on deportation's short- and long-term consequences for children's mental health.[55] All of these issues affect Latinx communities and families in New Jersey, many of whom are mixed status.

Benjamin was born in a small town in the province of Cañar in southern Ecuador but migrated to New Jersey in 2005 to work and provide for his wife and two children who had remained in Cañar. The children were two years and a few months old at the time their father left. For ten years, Benjamin lived a productive life in the Garden State contributing to the state's economy by working and paying taxes. In 2013, Benjamin's wife joined him in Newark. They decided that it was best for the children to stay in Ecuador with their grandparents and to send for them later. This plan, however, never materialized. In 2014, Benjamin was involved in a car accident in New Jersey, which ended with ICE putting a detainer on him because of his undocumented status. He was deported to Ecuador in 2015 after an unsuccessful attempt at fighting his deportation. His wife was working in a flower shop in Newark at the time and in the process of applying for U.S. residency. The family decided that she should stay in Newark and attempt to complete the legalization process, so that she could later petition for Benjamin and the children and bring them to New Jersey.[56]

Benjamin's unexpected deportation is an example of the forced transnationalization of New Jersey's immigrant families as a result of excessively harsh and draconian immigration laws in the United States. Benjamin's deportation—and the deportation of others like him—brings significant hardship upon New Jersey's mixed-status families. Aside from the huge social and emotional costs of family separation, it also hurts the state's economy: families suffer from lost wages, businesses lose valuable customers, and employers must deal with the costs associated with worker turnover.[57] Benjamin's wife is now the family's main breadwinner, and she sends small monthly remittances from her job as a florist in Newark to sustain her family back in Ecuador. While Benjamin has now been back in Ecuador for close to seven years, a significant portion of his life and family is still in New Jersey. Aside from his wife, Benjamin's father and multiple cousins also still live in New Jersey. Benjamin still hopes to return to New Jersey, this time with his children, to reunite with his wife and extended family in the Garden State.

Not all arbitrary detentions like Benjamin's end with deportation. But immigration detention—even for those New Jerseyans who remain in the state—can have devastating social and economic consequences. During the pandemic, I met Felix at a public hearing in Newark organized by Essex County Correctional

Facility Civilian Task Force established by ordinance to address growing complaints from detainees before and during the pandemic about unsafe and unhealthy conditions for inmates and migrants in detention.[58] Felix survived the virus in Essex County Correctional Facility and was released on bond with the help of local immigration advocates. He showed up at the hearing with his attorney to make his voice heard.

Felix was born in Ecuador but had lived in North Newark since he was fifteen years old. He was detained in early 2020 before the onset of the pandemic for violating a reentry ban after a prior deportation almost twenty years earlier. A father of six, Felix had a lot of financial responsibilities. His family's livelihood was greatly affected by the wage loss they endured from his nine months in detention, in addition to the economic losses they had suffered due to the pandemic. Felix's wife, who worked as a beautician, lost her job when her workplace shut down during the lockdown and she had to move in with Felix's mother along with their three youngest children. Aside from the loss of income there were other losses too. Felix recounts:

> It's pretty hard. Even my two kids graduated this year, and I missed it. I'm never gonna have that again. You know, my son graduated from a technical school. My daughter graduated high school and she went to college. Those little things, those small things, they look small but they're not. And I would not be there, you know. My other kids ... I missed all their birthdays. You know. Just everything. I missed nine months of their lives and I'm never gonna get that back. No matter what I do. It's gone; that time I was supposed to be there, and I wasn't there. That's one thing I'm never gonna forgive.

When Felix was released, he was enrolled in an electronic monitoring program and had to always carry with him a cellphone with a GPS tracker. He was not allowed to work and contribute to sustain his family and he had to stay within the perimeters of the city of Newark. Anthropologist Carolina Sánchez Boe has noted how electronic monitoring often feels like an extension of the carceral condition to those subjected to it, and with significant consequences for privacy and a migrant's human rights.[59] Felix's story illustrates just how devastating the effects of immigration detention—even when not resulting in deportation—can be on New Jersey families. The sense of having lost valuable time and access to livelihood opportunities is, in many ways, as sociologist Golash-Boza has noted, similar to the collateral consequences of incarceration.[60] Contrary to those deported to their countries of citizenship, long-term New Jersey residents like Felix who were able to get out on bond and return to their families on electronic monitoring, still struggle to reestablish themselves as full members of their families and their Garden State communities.

Latin American migrants, like Benjamin and Felix, and U.S.-born Latinxs are often members of the same families and communities. It is therefore not necessarily productive to distinguish too rigidly between these two groups when studying the effects of detention and deportation on the everyday life of families and communities in the Garden State. Many Latinx, including those with citizenship from birth, such as Puerto Ricans, are themselves less affected by legal immigration issues; however, they may have an undocumented family member, a family member who overstayed a visa, or a family member who never naturalized and who is arrested for a deportable offense. Thus, while the deportation regime targets noncitizens, the repercussions of enforcement actions go beyond the "detainable" and "deportable" individuals themselves.[61]

Despite its broad sanctuary statute, New Jersey's undocumented migrants live their daily lives with the awareness of the risk of deportation. Those who are confident that their status will protect them, might not see themselves at risk of deportation before it is too late. This was Christian's experience. Christian was born in the port city of Callao in Peru, but joined his parents in Paterson, New Jersey, as a young child. Growing up in Paterson with two working parents and little supervision, he spent a lot of time by himself as a teenager. He dropped out of high school in tenth grade from what he called "one of the worst schools in Paterson." Christian had three younger U.S.-citizen brothers who were all born in New Jersey. Coming of age in Paterson he had numerous encounters with the criminal justice system. "I've been on probation since I was 15," he tells me in 2018 over lunch in Callao's largest mall. "I used to get into fights and stuff like that when I was a minor, so I was always on probation. Always. When I turned 18, probation again. Then came those felonies." One of the felony charges was from a domestic violence incident with the mother of his first child when he had just turned eighteen years old (he became a father at age seventeen years and later had two more kids). His family bailed him out several times, but Christian also served a few shorter sentences for drug transactions and for not keeping up with child support. In the eyes of many, including some of his own family members, he lived a questionable life.

In 2010, ICE knocked on Christian's door one afternoon and told him they had a detainer to take him into immigration custody. This was during the Obama administration when deportations from the United States were at an all time historic high.[62] Christian tells me: "They didn't knock, they was sittin outside in the car, then they just pulled up and said 'What's your name?' I said my name's Christian. They said 'come on, we're lookin for you, let's go.' Then they told me, 'no, you got two felonies that's deportable, you gotta go.'" He first thought it was a bad joke. Since high school Christian had seen other youth from his school in Paterson go in and out of juvenile or jail and never thought that his own situation would be any different. However, as a green card holder who had never naturalized, his situation was indeed different. The prospect of being sent to another country, which he no longer saw as his own, was a sobering but highly distressing realization. Christian, who was taken into custody by ICE that day because of an open drug charge, spent eight and a half months in jail before he was deported to Peru. He was transferred around for a lot for reasons not clear to him and this was in itself taxing: "I did a few months in Bergen, then a few months in Essex, and then a few months in Hudson. It was awful. You gotta start all over each time."

Christian's mother came to visit him every weekend in jail, but she was upset and sad about the situation. The family hired a lawyer but there was apparently no easy way to win the case. On January 3, 2011, Christian was deported to Peru. When he arrived in Lima his grandmother and one of his U.S.-citizen brothers from New Jersey were there to receive him, but they returned to New Jersey shortly after and left him on his own in the empty and abandoned family home in Callao. Christian did not have any job skills, did not speak Spanish, and had no extended family left in Lima. When I first met him, it was over seven years since his deportation. He did not yet feel at ease in Peru and was still dependent on his mother's financial support: "I really try not to have a lot of friends around cause out here they got different mentalities. Different cultures. Different everything. Cause over here they're trying a win. They try to see what they can get outta you. And I'm not here to give anybody anything, I'm here to get, not for people to get me. I can't trust nobody unless they come from your way. A lot of grimy people out here." When I asked him what his hope for the future was, he answered: "I'm just tryin a get back to Jersey, that's it."

Christian had decided to wait in Peru for his ten-year reentry ban to expire so he could apply for a pardon and attempt to return to the United States legally. Other deported migrants did not have that kind of time or patience. This was the situation of JZ who had grown up in Newark's North Ward since age nine years. His parents had migrated there from Lima in the 1990s to join a large extended family in New Jersey, which now included his grandmother, her seven children, and their spouses, and around twenty-five cousins, nieces, and nephews. Most of the foreign-born family had naturalized and became citizens long ago but, despite being eligible, JZ had never bothered to take the citizenship test. He was blissfully unaware that the lack of citizenship could come back to haunt him. Like many other Black and Latinx youth who are pushed out of an underserved public education system and funneled into the criminal justice system, JZ also had a story of entanglement with the criminal justice system.[63] After serving a nine-month prison sentence for charges of possession and eluding and then subsequently losing his immigration case, JZ was first deported in 2005.[64] He tried to reenter the United States shortly after but was caught at the U.S.-Mexico border and sentenced to four years of federal prison because of his attempt at reentry after deportation. When deported after completing his sentence in federal prison, JZ knew he had to stay in Peru. He could not risk another long prison sentence by attempting to return again even though he was on his own in Lima. He began working as a barber and soon became popular for the urban haircuts and styles he had learned in the United States. JZ later formed a family of his own in Lima, which helped him get back on his feet emotionally.

However, he confided, despite growing used to life in Lima and having considerable success at his job, his heart is still in Jersey: "Sometimes it's still like, man, I wish I could take that plane and go back. I've lived in the U.S. my whole youth. I left a lot of love and people over there."[65]

The stories of people like Benjamin, Felix, Christian, and JZ are not typically part of the narratives that New Jersey politicians, institutions, mainstream media, and even residents with upwardly mobile aspirations tell about themselves and about the Garden State. Nevertheless, this "reverse diaspora" of deported New Jerseyans is very real and a part of the everyday lives across borders of many New Jersey families and communities. It is an outcome of complex social and legal histories of migration, poverty, underserved public schools, social exclusion, racism, and lack of a clear path to legalization affecting and shaping the lives of immigrant and Latinx communities in the Garden State.[66] While recent years have seen the passage of state anti-detention laws and the termination or pausing of contracts with ICE in three of the state's detention facilities setting an important example for the rest of the country, New Jersey is far from done with the task of protecting and caring for its Latinx and immigrant residents so that New Jersey's communities and future generations can feel secure and included.

## Notes

1. "New Jersey: Demographic and Social," Migration Policy Institute, July 1, 2020, https://www.migrationpolicy.org/data/state-profiles/state/demographics/NJ.
2. "Profile of the Unauthorized Population: New Jersey," Migration Policy Institute, July 1, 2020, https://www.migrationpolicy.org/data/unauthorized-immigrant-population/state/NJ.
3. "U.S. Unauthorized Immigrant Population Estimates by State, 2016," Pew Research Center, February 5, 2019, https://www.pewresearch.org/hispanic/interactives/u-s-unauthorized-immigrants-by-state/.
4. Christin Hess, "What Are 'Reverse Diasporas' and How Are We to Understand Them?" *Diaspora: A Journal of Transnational Studies* 17, no. 3 (Summer 2014): 288–315.
5. Doris Marie Provine, Monica W. Varsanyi, Paul G. Lewis, and Scott H. Decker, *Policing Immigrants: Local Law Enforcement on the Front Lines* (Chicago: University of Chicago Press, 2016), 9.
6. See "The 287(g) Program: An Overview," American Immigration Council, July 8, 2021, https://www.americanimmigrationcouncil.org/research/287g-program-immigration.
7. See, for example, Robyn Magalit Rodriguez, *In Lady Liberty's Shadow* (New Brunswick, NJ: Rutgers University Press, 2017) and Carolina Alonso Bejarano, Lucia López Juárez, Mirian A. Mijangos García, and Daniel M. Goldstein, *Decolonizing Ethnography* (Durham, NC: Duke University Press, 2019).
8. David Matthau, "What Towns in New Jersey Are Considered Sanctuary Cities?" New Jersey 101.5, February 1, 2015, https://nj1015.com/what-towns-in-new-jersey-are-considered-sanctuary-cities/.
9. Attorney General Law Enforcement Directive No. 2018-6 v2.0. Attorney General Gurbir S. Grewal, Office of the Attorney General, State of New Jersey,

September 27, 2019, https://www.nj.gov/lps/dcj/agguide/directives/ag-directive-2018-6_v2.pdf.

10 The Trust Directive was embraced by Democrats but soon came under critique by Republicans who falsely argued that Governor Murphy was providing "sanctuary" to immigrants committing crimes in New Jersey.

11 Sara R. Tosh, Ulla D. Berg, and Kenneth Sebastian León, "Migrant Detention and COVID-19: Pandemic Responses in Four New Jersey Detention Centers," *Journal on Migration and Human Security* 9, no. 1 (2021): 44–62.

12 For example, ICE arrested fifty-four individuals in an enforcement action in New Jersey that ran from September 21, 2019, to September 25, 2019, and targeted individuals with prior immigration detainers. During the week of January 27, 2020, ICE conducted a similar raid in New Jersey and arrested 115 people mainly from Mexico, Central America. See Anthony Zurita and Monsy Alvarado, "ICE Sweep Leads to Over 100 Arrests in New Jersey," *NorthJersey.com*, February 6, 2020, https://eu.northjersey.com/story/news/new-jersey/2020/02/06/ice-arrests-nj-see-over-100-people-detained/4677716002/.

13 "ICE Arrests Brazilian National Wanted for Homicide in Home Country during NJ Enforcement Efforts," U.S. Immigration and Customs Enforcement, February 4, 2020, https://www.ice.gov/news/releases/ice-arrests-brazilian-national-wanted-homicide-home-country-during-nj-enforcement.

14 A total of ninety deportees were interviewed for the project. Of these, fifty-five interviews were conducted in Ecuador and thirty-five in Peru. The interviews in Ecuador were done in collaboration with my colleague Gioconda Herrera from FLACSO-Ecuador and with research assistance from Rosa Guamán Morocho and Lucía Pérez Martínez. The interviews in Lima and Callao were completed with research assistance from Miguel Morales. I am grateful for research support from the Wenner Gren Foundation for Anthropological Research and the School of Arts and Sciences at Rutgers University.

15 This research project titled "Migrant Detention, Deportation, and COVID-19 Transmission: Public Health and Safety Challenges in New Jersey" was supported by the Rutgers Center for COVID-19 Response and Pandemic Preparedness. The findings are documented in Tosh et al., "Migrant Detention and COVID-19," and in Ulla D. Berg, Sarah Tosh, and Kenneth Sebastian León, "Carceral Ethnography in a Time of Pandemic: Examining Migrant Detention and Deportation During COVID-19," *Ethnography*, February 28, 2022.

16 Nathalie Peutz and Nicholas De Genova, *The Deportation Regime. Sovereignty, Space, and the Freedom of Movement* (Durham, NC: Duke University Press, 2010).

17 New Jersey Assembly Bill 5207, New Jersey Senate, August 20, 2021. For a link to the statute, see https://legiscan.com/NJ/text/A5207/id/2434104. See also Dustin Racioppi and Mary Ann Koruth, "NJ Jails Can No Longer Contract with ICE to Hold Federal Immigrant Detainees," *NorthJersey.com*, August 20, 2021, https://www.northjersey.com/story/news/new-jersey/2021/08/20/nj-jails-ice-federal-detainees-banned-murphy-law/8212074002/.

18 New Jersey Motor Vehicle Commission, "NJMVC to Begin Scheduling Appointments for Driver Permits Regardless of Immigration Status 1 May," press release, April 29, 2021, https://www.nj.gov/mvc/press/archives/2021/042921.htm. See also "Governor Murphy Signs Legislation Expanding Access to Driver's Licenses," State of New Jersey, December 19, 2019, https://www.nj.gov/governor/news/news/562019/20191219a.shtml; Nieto-Muñoz, "New Driver's License for Undocumented Immigrants Takes Effect Saturday. Here are all the details," NJ.com, January 13,

2021, https://www.nj.com/news/2021/04/new-drivers-license-for-undocumented-immigrants-takes-effect-saturday-here-are-all-the-details.html; "Governor Murphy Signs Legislation Expanding Access to Professional and Occupational Licenses," State of New Jersey, September 1, 2020, https://nj.gov/governor/news/news/562020/approved/20200901c.shtml.

19  César Cuauhtémoc García Hernández, *Migrating to Prison: America's Obsession with Locking Up Immigrants* (New York: New Press, 2019).

20  American Civil Liberties Union, *Justice-Free Zones: U.S. Immigration Detention Under the Trump Administration* (n.p.: American Civil Liberties Union, 2020), https://www.hrw.org/sites/default/files/supporting_resources/justice_free_zones_immigrant_detention.pdf. See also U.S. Immigration and Customs Enforcement, *U.S. Immigration and Customs Enforcement Fiscal Year 2020 Enforcement and Removal Operations Report* (Washington, DC: ICE, 2020), https://www.ice.gov/doclib/news/library/reports/annual-report/eroReportFY2020.pdf.

21  The private prison company Corrections Corporation of America built its first immigrant detention center in 1983. Corrections Corporation of America was rebranded as CoreCivic in 2016. It is the world's largest owner of private prisons and the second-largest private prison operator after GEO Group. See "CoreCivic Inc," American Friends Service Committee, accessed February 15, 2022, https://investigate.afsc.org/company/corecivic.

22  Patricia Macías-Rojas, "Immigration and the War on Crime: Law and Order Politics and the Illegal Immigration Reform and Immigrant Responsibility Act of 1996," *Journal on Migration and Human Security* 6, no. 1 (2018): 1–25.

23  Juliet Stumpf, "The Crimmigration Crisis: Immigrants, Crime, and Sovereign Power," *American University Law Review* 56 (2006): 367. See also César Cuauhtémoc García Hernández, "Creating Crimmigration," *Brigham Young University Law Review* 2013, no. 6 (2014): 1457.

24  Nancy Morawetz, "Understanding the Impact of the 1996 Deportation Laws and the Limited Scope of Proposed Reforms," *Harvard Law Review* 113, no. 8 (2000): 1936–1962.

25  See Deirdre Conlon and Nancy Hiemstra, "'Unpleasant' but 'Helpful': Immigration Detention and Urban Entanglements in New Jersey, USA," *Urban Studies* 59, no. 11 (2022): 2179–2198.

26  R. Bustamante, "Fiscalia De Union Pedira El Cierre De Esmor: Cerca De 100 Hispanos Entre Los 300 Prisioneros Del Tenebroso Lugar," *El Diario La Prensa*, June 22, 1995.

27  John Sullivan, "Operator of Immigration Jails Has a History of Troubles," *New York Times*, June 20, 1995.

28  Ashley Dunn, "US Inquiry Finds Detention Center Poorly Run," *New York Times*, July 22, 1995.

29  Kassindja coauthored the book with her lawyer and friend Layli Miller Bashir, *Do They Hear You When You Cry* (New York: Random House, 1999).

30  Kassindja, *Do They Hear*, 284.

31  Kassindja, *Do They Hear*, 285–286. For the original report see "The Elizabeth, New Jersey Contract Detention Facility Operated by ESMOR Inc., Interim Report, Executive Summary," Office of the Commissioner, Immigration and Naturalization Service, U.S. Department of Justice, July 20, 1995, https://archive.org/stream/758481-ins-report-esmor/758481-ins-report-esmor_djvu.txt.

32  These include ICE, U.S. Citizenship and Immigration Services, and U.S. Customs and Border Protection.

Reverse Diasporas • 329

33 "Removals Under the Secure Communities Program," TRAC (Transaction Records Access Clearinghouse) Immigration, July 1, 2020, https://trac.syr.edu/phptools/immigration/secure/.
34 Erika J. Nava, "Working with ICE: A Costly Choice for New Jersey," New Jersey Policy Perspectives, November 13, 2018, https://www.njpp.org/publications/report/working-with-ice-a-costly-choice-for-new-jersey/.
35 Richard Khavkine, "Essex County Signs New 5-Year Agreement That Could Increase Number of Immigrant Detainees, Generate $50M Annually," NJ.com, August 13, 2011, https://www.nj.com/news/2011/08/essex_county_signs_new_5-year.html.
36 Chris Megerian, "Essex County Immigrant Detention Center a House of Controversy," NJ.com, September 22, 2011, https://www.nj.com/news/2011/09/essex_county_immigrant_detenti.html#:~:text=The%20center%20has%20become%20a,civil%2C%20not%20criminal%2C%20violations.
37 Jessica Mazzolla, "122 Workers at Immigration Detention Facility Get $4,8M Settlement," NJ.com, October 5, 2016, https://www.nj.com/essex/2016/10/48m_in_backpay_will_go_to_immigrant_detention_faci.html.
38 Erika Nava, "Working with ICE: A Costly Choice for New Jersey," New Jersey Policy Perspectives, November 13, 2018, https://www.njpp.org/publications/report/working-with-ice-a-costly-choice-for-new-jersey/.
39 Carla Astudillo, "ICE Arrests of N.J. Immigrants without Criminal Records More Than Doubled in 2017," NJ.com, March 1, 2018, https://www.nj.com/data/2018/03/ice_arrested_more_than_twice_as_many_non-criminals.html.
40 However, it is during the Biden administration that the immigration court backlogs have reached their highest, with a total of 2,097,244 pending cases at the end of fiscal year 2023. The reason is due to a reopening of old cases and delays due to COVID-19, but mostly it is because of newly issued Notices to Appear to migrants arriving to the United States. At the end of May 2021, New Jersey had 71,720 pending cases. See "Historical Immigration Court Backlog Tool - Pending Cases and Length of Wait by Nationality, State, Court, and Hearing Location," TRAC (Transaction Records Access Clearinghouse) Immigration, July 1, 2023.
41 U.S. Department of Homeland Security, Office of Inspector General (DHS-OIG), *Concerns about ICE Detainee Treatment and Care at Four Facilities*, OIG-19-47 (Washington, DC: DHS-OIG, June 3, 2019), https://www.oig.dhs.gov/sites/default/files/assets/2019-06/OIG-19-47-Jun19.pdf. See also DHS-OIG, *Issues Requiring Action at the Essex County Correctional Facility in Newark, New Jersey*, OIG-19-20 (Washington, DC: DHS-OIG, February 13, 2019), https://www.oig.dhs.gov/sites/default/files/assets/2019-02/OIG-19-20-Feb19.pdf.
42 Bonilla v. Hudson County, Civil Action No. 2:19-CV-13137.
43 Freedom for Immigrants, "Hudson County Freeholders Shamefully Vote to Renew 10-Year Multimillion-Dollar Contract with ICE," Freedom for Immigrants, November 25, 2020, https://www.freedomforimmigrants.org/news/2020/11/25/hudson-county-freeholders-shamefully-vote-to-renew-10-year-multimillion-dollar-contract-with-ice.
44 This information was confirmed by others who participated in a study I conducted on the spread of COVID-19 in New Jersey's detention centers with two Rutgers colleagues, Sarah Tosh and Kenneth Sebastian León. See Tosh et al., "Migrant Detention and COVID-19."
45 Matt Katz, "ICE Detainee Who Sued His Jailers Was Swiftly Deported. Now He's Missing," *Gothamist*, May 28, 2020.

46  In October 2020, however, activists learned that ICE had been soliciting information on a federal contracting site for a new detention center in the New York City metropolitan area, and another in New Jersey or Pennsylvania, both with capacities of up to nine hundred detainees.
47  Giulia McDonnell Nieto del Rio, "ICE Quietly Extends Elizabeth Detention Center Contract with CoreCivic," Documented, August 13, 2021, https://documentedny.com/2021/08/13/ice-quietly-extends-elizabeth-detention-center-contract-with-corecivic/.
48  ICE maintains a live database to monitor the COVID-19 positive cases. On October 14, 2022, ICE reported a total of 214 COVID-19 positive cases for EDC since the beginning of the pandemic (see "ICE's Enforcement and Removal Operations Post Pandemic Emergency COVID-19 Guidelines and Protocols," July 13, 2023, https://www.ice.gov/coronavirus#detStat). ICE's official case counts, however, have been disputed by advocates as severe undercounts, especially in the early months of the pandemic where testing was limited. See Nina Siulc, "Vera's New Prevalence Model Suggests COVID-19 Is Spreading through ICE Detention at Much Higher Rates Than Publicized," Vera Institute of Justice, June 4, 2020, https://www.vera.org/news/covid-19-1/veras-new-prevalence-model-suggests-covid-19-is-spreading-through-ice-detention-at-much-higher-rates-than-publicized.
49  ICE actively litigated some of these court orders. In November 2020, ICE rearrested in a single day eighty-eight of the 2,261 county jail inmates who had been released from New Jersey prisons in an effort by lawmakers to reduce the prison population and curb the spread of the virus. See Raymond G. Lahoud, "ICE Arrests 88 Inmates Released from New Jersey Prisons," *National Law Review* 10, no. 322 (2020), https://www.natlawreview.com/article/ice-arrests-88-inmates-released-new-jersey-prison.
50  Matt Katz, "New Jersey County Ends Lucrative and Controversial Jailing of ICE Detainees," *Gothamist*, April 28, 2021, https://gothamist.com/news/new-jersey-county-ends-lucrative-and-controversial-jailing-ice-detainees.
51  Giulia McDonnell Nieto del Rio, "Bergen County Will No Longer Detain Immigrants for ICE," Documented, October 7, 2021, https://documentedny.com/2021/10/07/bergen-county-will-no-longer-detain-immigrants-for-ice/.
52  Giulia McDonnell Nieto del Rio, "ICE Denies Release Requests, Sending Detained Immigrants across the Country," Documented, October 25, 2021, https://documentedny.com/2021/10/25/are-detained-immigrants-a-public-safety-threat-ice-says-yes-as-transfers-continue/.
53  Joanna Dreby, *Everyday Illegal: When Policies Undermine Immigrant Families* (Oakland: University of California Press, 2015).
54  Tanya Golash-Boza, "Punishment beyond the Deportee: The Collateral Consequences of Deportation," *American Behavioral Scientist* 63, no. 9 (2019): 1331–1349.
55  Luis H. Zayas, *Forgotten Citizens: Deportation, Children, and the Making of American Exiles and Orphans* (New York: Oxford University Press, 2015).
56  Part of my research with deported migrants in Cañar was carried out with Dr. Gioconda Herrera with whom I have coauthored several articles. See, for example, Ulla D. Berg and Gioconda Herrera, "Transnational Families and Return in the Age of Deportation: The Case of Indigenous Ecuadorian Migrants," *Global Networks* 22, no. 1 (2021): 36–50; Gioconda Herrera and Ulla D. Berg, "Vulnerability and (Im)mobilities: U.S. Deportation and Post-Deportation Lives among Ecuadorian Transnational Families," in *Handbook of Transnational Families Around the World*, ed. Javiera Cienfuegos, Rosa Brandhorst, and Deborah Fahy Bryceson (New York: Springer, 2023), 299–311.

57 Erika J. Nava, "Working with ICE: A Costly Choice for New Jersey," New Jersey Policy Perspectives, November 13, 2018, https://www.njpp.org/publications/report/working-with-ice-a-costly-choice-for-new-jersey/.
58 I later interviewed Felix for a joint project with two Rutgers colleagues on the spread of COVID-19 in New Jersey's detention centers. See Berg et al., "Carceral Ethnography."
59 Carolina Sanchez Boe, "Expanding Penal Landscapes into Immigrant Communities: Digital 'Alternatives' to Detention in the USA," Faculty of Law Blogs/ University of Oxford, March 29, 2023, https://blogs.law.ox.ac.uk/border-criminologies-blog/blog-post/2023/03/expanding-penal-landscapes-immigrant-communities.
60 Golash-Boza, "Punishment beyond the Deportee."
61 Nicholas P. DeGenova, "Migrant 'Illegality' and Deportability in Everyday Life," *Annual Review of Anthropology* 31 (2002): 419–447; Nicholas De Genova, "Detention, Deportation, and Waiting: Toward a Theory of Migrant Detainability," *Gender a výzkum* 2, no. 1 (2019): 92–104.
62 Daniel E. Martínez, Jeremy Slack, and Ricardo Martínez-Schuldt, "The Rise of Mass Deportation in the United States," in *The Handbook of Race, Ethnicity, Crime, and Justice*, ed. Ramiro Martinez Jr., Meghan E. Hollis, and Jacob I. Stowell (Hoboken, NJ: John Wiley, 2018), 173–201.
63 Victor M. Rios, *Punished: Policing the Lives of Black and Latino Boys* (New York: New York University Press, 2011). See also Gilberto Rosas, *Barrio Libre: Criminalizing States and Delinquent Refusals of the New Frontier* (Durham, NC: Duke University Press, 2012).
64 Eluding, or attempting to flee, from the police, can become a second-degree offense in New Jersey if the attempt to elude creates a risk of death or serious injury to another person.
65 I have shown elsewhere how the post-deportation lives of ex-U.S. residents, like Christian and JZ, continue to be deeply entangled with, and imperiled by, the very institutional structures and disciplinary regimes that produced their precarity and led to their banishment from the United States. See Ulla D. Berg, "The Afterlife of US Disciplining Institutions: Transnational Structures of (Im) Mobility among Peruvian Deportees," in *Critical Dialogues in Latinx Studies*, ed. Merida Rúa and Ana Ramos-Zayas (New York: New York University Press, 2021), 392–403.
66 Hess, "What Are 'Reverse Diasporas.'"

# 15
# Latinx LGBTQ Students and Placemaking in School

## Voguing and Ball Culture at Elizabeth High, 1989–1994

YAMIL AVIVI

Queer youth students of color have faced marginality in high schools across the United States due not only to their race and class but also their sexual and gender nonheteronormative orientations, or orientations that do not follow sexual mores aligned with middle-class sensibilities that privilege whiteness and heterosexuality. Triple marginality can lead to invisibility or hypervisibility, whereby queer youth of color are threatened, silenced, and made to feel vulnerable on school grounds. Alternatively, students may take it upon themselves to organize spaces of support and belonging for queer youth of color. This chapter offers an analysis of the courage, leadership, and collective action of Latinx and Black queer youth who contested the homo- and transphobia that were displayed at Elizabeth High School in Elizabeth, New Jersey, when, for example, in 1989, an out African American transgender student who cross-dressed, wore blouses off the shoulder, palazzo pants, and either teased out weaves or box braids all put in a bun, was brought into the principal's office and threatened with suspension for dressing too eccentrically and causing "distraction" in the classroom. The student told the principal, "You don't like it? I'll sue you."[1] As a second example, a high school fashion show in 1991 was discontinued after queer students at the first annual event sang the lyrics "Sexuality! Let Your Body Be Free!" from an underground house music hit these LGBTQ youth danced to in New Jersey metro nightlife venues.[2] In the late 1980s and mid-1990s, New Jersey metro queer musical subcultures and scenes at underground parties, including underground gay balls and commercialized nightclubs, emboldened queer youth of color, such as those who went to Elizabeth High, to organize everyday spaces of support and belonging at their school amidst an adverse environment that kept such students at the margins.

Along with the marginalization of LGBTQ students, the high school faced a decline in overall student academic performance and attendance. In 1986, Elizabeth High School had been performing well and was certified by the state as a majority-White high school in contrast to other urban high schools in New Jersey that were not.[3] According to the 1990 Census, Hispanics were the majority ethnic group compared to Asians and Blacks and at par with the town's White population.[4]

By 1991, Elizabeth High School had become majority–minority, with a largely Hispanic population of first- and second-generation working-class immigrant students. According to the *Elizabeth Daily Journal*, "Of 4,147 students at the four-year school, slightly more than half [were] Hispanic."[5] That year, the paper published a series of articles investigating students' truancy and violence, and the administration's grade inflation.[6] The stigma the school received is not surprising in light of this reporting on truancy of a majority student-of-color population.[7] Despite the transition from a White-majority to a Hispanic-majority student population by 1991, the need for a revised curriculum that addressed the students' social needs and identities was left unexamined as a possible reason for the truancy and violence. Instead, the paper printed stories about enforcement measures like "zero tolerance" and better student attendance.

As such, the 1991 reporting and other newspaper articles about student life at Elizabeth High School never raised explicit questions about how issues of race and identity and changing demographics needed attention or how providing accurate resources for students could lead to better attendance and school performance. Unsurprisingly, this reporting included nothing about the growing LGBTQ youth of color student population that I documented through ethnographic interviews with former students who attended the school during the late 1980s and early mid-1990s. While truancy was a problem, the reporting did not explain the reasons for it. As this chapter explores through interviews with former students, LGBTQ youth in particular cut school because they did not see themselves reflected in the curriculum or feel accepted by the school administration. Even more, bullying and violence were part of their everyday life in the high school. What must be told is the story of the defiant presence and mobilization of the courageous coming out of LGBTQ and questioning youth of color from the late 1980s into the mid-1990s, with help from the queer musical and dance subcultures and scenes they enjoyed in metro New Jersey, including Newark and New York City. These students created spaces of support within the school during a time before the arrival of gay and straight alliances.[8]

This chapter has three sections. In the first, I introduce some of the queer of color youth attending the high school and offer a general overview of the queer subcultures they belonged to or looked up to and how those scenes influenced their personalities and ways of dressing. This section begins with a description on research methodology and arrives at how some of these LGBTQ students were outed by peers but then assumed this identity with courage. In the second section, I explore how LGBTQ students of color and their allies describe their experiences at Elizabeth High School where they faced homo- and transphobic silencing and violence. Students recall getting hardly any support from the school faculty and administration while in their process of questioning, coming and being out, or expressing themselves. In the final section, I show how these youth created their own placemaking amidst this repression within the school that engendered support for each other when there was almost no other support available. I examine moments when these students interfaced with the rest of the high school through their placemaking. By "placemaking" or oppositional placemaking in the school, I am referring to how these LGBTQ students created spaces within the homo- and transphobic school environment to engender a sense of dignity, belonging, and inclusion for themselves among a homo- and transphobic student body and school environment. Specifically, I argue that Latinx LGBTQ youth tapped into the queer Black subculture capital of a translocal New Jersey gay, voguing, and house music subculture referred to as the "ball scene"—as depicted in *Paris Is Burning* (1990) and *Pose* (2018–2021)—through which they challenged the school's repressive environment.[9] They did so by participating in a ball network of voguing dance and eccentric dress competitions that exuded a student oppositional culture of critical multiculturalism, cultural excess, and tolerance.

Inspired by ball subculture, these LGBTQ students confronted the bullying and rigid structure of the school and of mainstream education by affiliating with Newark- and New York City-based LGBTQ fraternal families, referred to as "house families," with last names like Jourdan, Labeija, Xtravaganza, Ninja, Corey, Prestige, Fields, and Latoomuch. These families competed with each other through voguing and costuming competitions in Newark, New York City, or local, student-organized Elizabeth balls. Voguing was a dance form using "model [striking and photoshoot] poses and also influenced by Ancient Egyptian hieroglyphics and gymnastic moves," and its origins were "in the ballrooms of 1980s New York birthed by the black and Latinx queer communities of Harlem. . . . Trans, gay and queer contestants would compete for trophies and the reputation of their 'house family' by walking categories, including Executive Realness or Town & Country . . . that were . . . glorifying and subverting ideals of [White] beauty, sexuality, and class."[10] Danny Tiberius Ninja Infiniti (class of 1992), one of the former students interviewed and featured throughout this chapter and a longtime member of the LGBTQ ballroom scene, explains that "Even while there was rivalry among the house families, the ballroom community as a whole will support and defend all those within it when needed," as was the case among students of different house families within Elizabeth High School. This helped them survive their time there and facilitated their coming into their full selves.

## Ethnographic Interviewing and Self-Reflexivity: Remembering Our Lives Then

Through recorded and unrecorded ethnographic interviews with twenty-five former Elizabeth High School students, I demonstrate just how pioneering, vibrant, and resilient these youth were at a time when the school was highly homo- and transphobic and provided no support or resources for them. Based on the transcriptions of recorded interviews and the fieldnotes of unrecorded and recorded conversations, I critically examine Elizabeth queer Latinx youth students' lived experience and the placemaking they engaged in when mainstream society viewed them as lesser and expendable. Further, like Henry Giroux, who posits in *The Terror of Neoliberalism* that the future of working-class African American and Latino youth is dim because a significant number of these students discontinue(d) or disappear(ed) from school due to zero-tolerance and prison-like policies, Jose Muñoz argues that those in power (educators, administrators, and politicians) view(ed) LGBTQ youth of color as unentitled to a future and therefore unworthy within the school environment.[11] LGBTQ students' and their allies' experiences and perspectives provide an alternative narrative of individual and group agency and placemaking that has been only minimally documented in high school yearbooks, programming, and newspaper reporting.

My local positioning as a brown-skinned cisgendered gay Latino who came of age in Elizabeth and nearby Hillside in the early 1990s and struggled to come out at a nearby parochial high school in Roselle allows me to draw from my own experience in this self-reflexive ethnography.[12] For example, I frequented several of the same local and New York City venues as these LGBTQ youth to enjoy house music and queer nightlife subcultures of the time. My ethnographic interviews and fieldwork also reflect a multisited ethnography of a queer Latinx youth lived experience in Black-centered and queer subculture scenes in local Elizabeth, Newark, and New York City that complicate views of them being contained and ordered by nationalist racial projects that privilege heteronormativity.[13] Instead, this ethnography illustrates how these LGBTQ youth forged spaces and placemaking inspired by queer Black epistemologies that defied White supremacist racial projects.

### Boldly Out(ed), Private, or "Shy": LGBTQs of E-High, 1989–1995

Student leaders, like the late Andre "Angel" Melendez (class of 1989), Danny Tiberius Ninja Infiniti (class of 1992), and "Jean Paul Fields" (class of 1992), were pioneering queer student leaders of Colombian descent.[14] Other queer student leaders included Erin Jourdan (class of 1990), Shahid Grandeur (class of 1991), Tyrone Prestige (class of 1993), Geraude Scarface Jourdan and Walter Jourdan (class of 1993) who were of African American descent, Dennis Andromeda Corey (class of 1993) of Polish and Cuban descent, Ricky Xtravaganza (class of 1992) of Puerto Rican descent, and Denasia Labeija (dropped out) of Puerto Rican descent. According to Danny, these students "were the most talked about queers in Elizabeth High School." Danny explains that out of four thousand students, there were ten who were out or "outed" while at least another fifteen were either in the process of coming out or were in the closet and "dealing with their demons." Despite this, the school did nothing to create an LGBT-tolerant high school. These student leaders helped other students come out, grow connected within the translocal queer house and ball and dance scenes in NY, Newark, and Elizabeth, and become a part of the queer collectivity within the school. Danny adds, "Some [of the visibly out] were shyer than the others at recruiting into houses." Danny, Jean, and others remained at the high school after the departure of Angel, who developed a high profile in the club kid scene that unfortunately ended in his murder in 1996.[15]

Before the gay house networks appeared within the school, students suspected of being LGBTQ or those who were out faced isolation or experienced bullying, which included intimidation, name calling, and even physical violence. Angel, a queer misfit with a high mohawk, thin moustache and beard, broken-in combat boots, black fitted jumpers, and a vintage 1970s leather jacket with metal studs around the collar, was an older upperclassman who frequently came to school only around lunch. Angel skipped school a lot and focused instead on going to CBGB's in the East Village to hear live punk bands, walking in ball competitions and clubbing in the New York City LGBTQ-friendly nightlife dance scenes, and building an entourage of followers among his younger classmates. While Angel was a punk misfit, others were hypervisible and vulnerable to verbal and physical bullying and violence. According to Danny Tiberius Ninja Infiniti, his fellow underclassman friend Dennis Andromeda Corey was made fun of as a freshman in the lockers after gym class because he was effeminate, and his chest was overdeveloped. At the time, Danny, who was in with the boys, was not out and went along with the jeers painfully in silence. "Yo! That guy's a fag! He's a fuckin' girl." They said it loud enough so he could possibly hear. Danny, in fact, had been having downlow sexual relations with one male masculine friend called "Phantom Ninja" who refused to come out to please his mother and who was planning to have children and enlist in the military. Danny also had sexual relations with multiple females, maintaining a "pretty boy" masculine image before officially coming out. He explained, "Yet, [at the time I was in the closet] if I didn't follow along, those guys would think there's something wrong with me."

Not very long after, Erin Jourdan, an eccentric and pioneering African American student who cross-dressed, wearing blouses and palazzo pants, and who had long hair and appeared to be transgender, outed Danny to other classmates, and when it got around the school, the intimidation at first was great, especially in the locker room. He began changing in a separate area of the locker room to avoid confrontations. "No one bought the story that I was bisexual and so I felt like I had no other choice but to identify as gay." It is hard to imagine that Danny would be one of the most prominent out gays in school soon after, with Jean Paul Fields's support and guidance; yet, they would become best friends and briefly date during high school.

More students like Danny began to assume their LGBTQ identity loudly through the vibrant nightlife in metro New Jersey. Erin Jourdan, who outed other students for the sake of not standing alone as an open transgender student in school, also outed Jean Paul Fields, who was going clubbing already and mentored Danny and others to develop eccentric styles within the school and when they went to clubs like New York City's Limelight, Red Zone, The Building, and Sound Factory. "Jean would say to me, 'if you're gonna turn it, honey,' [you got to look your fiercest by building your queer persona] to get into these clubs.'" "We went shopping to the Salvation Army and bought clothing items like a silver blouse, a pocketbook, and bell bottoms that made me look like a femme queen—even though I identified as bisexual—yet I had fun dressing up flamboyantly after a while and it was fun." These styles were not unfamiliar to Danny since he had interacted with Black cross-dressed dancers and voguing years before in Elizabeth dance party venues like the Police Athletic League, the Elks Lodge, or even out on the street in broad daylight. Danny explains that even though he had been bisexual all along, being affiliated with and assuming this flamboyant gay and gender fluid culture of dance and eccentric dress was "fun," despite making him be perceived not as a bisexual who also liked women but as an effeminate gay who dressed up. During school hours, Danny's queer yet "composed" outfits were often tight jeans, a blazer, and combat boots with his signature hoop earrings on both ears.

Another student, Ernie (class of 1991), a Puerto Rican, straight-acting student on the high school wrestling team, clandestinely hung out with these youth when they went out to the clubs. In the midst of dealing with coming out and maintaining an image of a straightlaced jock on the wrestling team with his military buzz cut, Ernie confided in Danny and Jean Paul his struggles with his own homosexuality. Danny explained, "Ernie loved the queer scene and enjoyed going out and dressing up with us, but when he was in school, he was like, shhhhhh don't tell [any]body [*laughing*]."

## Out(ed) and Unapologetically Loud: Dressing the Part and Placemaking through Nightlife and Ball Culture Subcultures Within the School

Elizabeth High School, New Jersey's third largest at the time, experienced a surge of queer youth of color collectivity and eccentricity between 1990 and 1995. LGBTQ students at school dressed provocatively, cross-dressing, exuding androgyny, or expressing misfit and countercultural ideals. They honed their queer personas in school, too, and made themselves notable. They referred to themselves and were referred to by classmates as "club kids," who were known to go to all-night queer-affirming dance parties that involved dressing up and showing up to school without sleep and in their costumes from the night before, with sweat stains from dancing and reeking of cigarette smoke. They frequented queer-empowering and affirming dance scenes and underground translocal house music scenes at venues including Sound Factory (New York City), Zanzibar (Newark), and Underground Dreams (Elizabeth), and queer nightlife parties spearheaded by the mostly White and glamourous club kids at the Limelight, Club USA, Palladium, and Tunnel. One straight male, Bert (class of 1994), who eventually became an ally, commented on the eccentricities of these youth: "These guys were in high school and they were already gay. A lot of them were flamboyant. Club kids wearing platform shoes and fuckin' neon puff platform shoes. You know black and white bobby socks. Shit like that.... Guys wearing little pig tails or whatever those things are on each side." LGBTQ youth of color who identified with an urban gay subculture, exuded styles, street talk, and groupings that ran contrary to heteronormative codes at Elizabeth High School. Despite the potential for homophobic intolerance, violence, and bullying, these displays of embodiments, eccentricity, language, and groupings of gender and sexual variance were a "posturing of a bold and fearless character" and "uncompromising incorrigibility" that challenged the school's dominant heteronormative culture.[16]

One LGBTQ Latina ally, Marie (class of 1994), raves about Jean Paul Fields over his leadership and boldness. Outed leaders like Jean Paul and Danny moved forward with their gay personas in school and after a while exuded a confidence that made even homophobic male students think twice before bullying them. I asked her who she thought the most popular kid was and she responded that it was Jean Paul: "First of all, because he was like a club kid so he was very, very extravagant, very eccentric gay and didn't give a shit.... He was like, you know I don't care! I'm not gonna let anybody bully me. If I want to go to the prom with another guy I'm going to, you know, and people recognized that and nobody messed with him."

Marie describes here how Jean Paul's defiant attitude allowed him to successfully navigate dominant spaces that attempted to silence and potentially bully him. She says that "nobody messed with him." According to her, he was the most popular kid and achieved respect from both heteronormative and nonheteronormative students for his boldness and sense of individuality. Marie does not describe his "eccentricities" and "extravagance" as being looked down upon but as being regarded as elements of character and leadership that he proudly embodied in the dominant space and culture of the school. Similarly, Ernie said of Danny that "if someone tried to mess with Danny, he would probably pull out a knife from his bookbag. Danny didn't take shit from no one." Ernie conveys Danny's fearless bold and leader-like character, which everyone in school knew would not easily yield to symbolic violence.[17]

Elizabeth queer youth in the high school gained entry into long-standing, vibrant, translocal gay and majority-Black houses or gay gangs of "fraternal family networks" in Newark and New York City. To this day, many are either still in those same houses or acknowledge and represent their lineage if they moved to another house. These youth were engaged with not only the queer nightlife scenes but also the metro New Jersey ball culture, which became a way of surviving in school amidst their growing hypervisibility. LGBTQ youth in the high school were associated with different Newark- and New York-based families with fraternal family last names like Jourdan, Corey, Ninja, Fields, and Latoomuch. While they were in competing houses, they maintained a ball subculture within the school. For example, even though Danny was a Ninja, he shares that "Walter Jourdan and his other Jourdan family members walked me down the school hallway in school after [I gave] a presentation on ball culture" to class. Ball culture within the school challenged the invisibility and disempowerment of queer youth students of color vis-à-vis school bullying and lack of support by the school administration.

When Danny and Jean Paul left Elizabeth High School, Dennis Andromeda Corey (class of 1993) would maintain the LGBTQ support network among the students. The once picked on, shy, and ridiculed Dennis in the locker room would become, as Danny explained, "the mother to other students who gelled the community of LGBTQ students and supported others either coming out at that time or who needed support." Dennis, who enjoyed goth music, often painted his nails black, and wore black lipstick. He donned his strong matriarchal presence with gothic black outfits.

## Experiences within a Heterosexist School Environment: Queer Latinx Students Speak

According to my interviewees, violence and bullying against LGBTQ students occurred frequently in all forms in the high school. In *Get That Freak: Homophobia and Transphobia in High School* (2010), Rebecca Haskell and Brian Burtch show that educational institutions are "key sites that impart social norms" and that educators and faculty frequently downplay most homo- and transphobic bullying of LGBTQ students as "gentle violence" and often fail to regard the aggression and harm to students who embody sexual and gender difference in a heteronormative school culture.[18] Homophobic students monitored, policed, and disciplined LGBTQ students to "quietly reinforce" the school public's dominant worldviews (of traditional gender roles, heterosexuality, and reproductive family values), which in effect enacted symbolic violence or the view that "heterosexuality [is] the only or at least the normal, sexual orientation . . . and imposed on others" in various forms.[19] In essence, such students, along with teachers and administrators, defend or are complicit with a heteronormative curriculum of homo- and transphobia. As a result, LGBTQ students would cut class and/or not perform well at the high school or would even drop out.

### More on Bullying in the High School and Its Consequences

Danny recalls that an underclassman female student who was questioning her sexuality ended up leaving school: "There was one girl [in the high school] that she was just suspected of being gay. . . . She dropped out by the time she was 15 because they put dyke on her locker." This student dropped out because of her ordeals with homophobia and potential violence. Danny's reflection is premised on the reality that the high school was not doing much to protect its growingly open and questioning LGBTQ minority youth. As a result, students may have dropped out or been close to doing so because of the repressive, heterosexist environment of the school.

In another incident, Katia (class of 1993), an LGBTQ ally, painfully recollects a bullying incident she witnessed as a senior when an effeminate gay male student was harassed: "[H]e was totally getting bullied in the hallway because he was getting followed . . . and he was being mocked . . . and you know he was . . . by himself." Katia's witnessing of how others "mocked" this gay student refers to the disciplining and policing of sexual and gender differences that were "lessons (often referred to as the hidden curriculum), teaching [students] which behaviors and associated identities are valued and which are not."[20] As part of the hidden curriculum, such bullying acts are quietly and frequently committed and downplayed as normal teasing and left unreported; yet, symbolic violence is fulfilled. These incidents offer another look at vulnerable moments LGBTQ students experienced and how they were silenced and dehumanized. Yet, I showed earlier in this chapter how LGBTQ students often prevented such degrading and potentially violent moments; for example, with Danny being walked by other LGBTQ youth to and from class. That is, LGBTQ students began walking with others in the school hallways or staying in groups for protection from moments like the ones Katia described.

### On Silent/Silenced Teachers and Counselors

Most of my interviewees did not express any memory of faculty at Elizabeth High School being unusually supportive, vocal, or nurturing of LGBTQ students, which would have helped alleviate the stigma and discrimination LGBTQ students of color faced in school.

Students like Ernie, for example, suffered greatly from the lack of guidance and mentorship from openly gay and ally teachers, counselors, and administrators at the high school. Here, he explains several circumstances, including coming out, that led to his truancy during the 1991 truancy scandal among Elizabeth High School students:

> There were a series of problems that came up.... I came out in November of 1991.... My grandfather had died prior to that. There were just a lot of things going on through my head and I found myself cutting a lot of class. A lot of times it was just to go downtown and go to Broad Street or just go back home and just going back to sleep because I was so tired from the night before.... I ... had to go to summer school before attaining my high school diploma because I had failed two classes due to absenteeism in class. I was never there.... Nobody ever addressed it until two weeks prior ... when I was told I wouldn't be graduating unless I went to summer school. It was just amazing to me. Two weeks prior [to graduating].

Ernie describes personal circumstances that include grappling with his sexuality as a questioning and closeted student until he eventually came out in November 1991. He was on high school sports teams, and his ability to incorporate well among the boys and perform a heterosexual masculinity covered his questioning homosexual orientation at the time. Because there were no specialized counseling or support services or teachers that could help him through that difficult time, he turned to Danny, one of the openly gay students in the high school, for support. Ernie explained the difficult "things going on through my head" during that period while he was coming to terms with his sexuality. For instance, he constantly worried that his father would commit suicide because his only son was gay and therefore an embarrassment to the family.

The fact that there were no specialized support services or teachers to help Ernie through this difficult time suggests that his truancy was a consequence of the symbolic power of heterosexuality that perpetuated ongoing silencing and even bullying due to homophobia and transphobia. Those moments when Ernie felt depressed without any support at school harmed his attendance and performance the most. Giroux describes how conservative rhetoric about citizenship often leaves it up individuals to solve their own problems, including sexism, AIDS, and other social problems deemed not a school's "social responsibility."[21] In effect, Giroux explains here how such individual responsibility proposed by conservatives unburdens teachers and school staff over what Danny calls, "interacting [meaningfully with us] ... guiding us [on our everyday lives and struggles]" as a "practice of social responsibility." Rather, it suggests the silence of high school faculty over these "individual problems" such youth faced.

### Silencing Black Queer Expression: A Fashion Show Cannot Go On

Danny recounted a fashion show organized by the arts workshop teacher in his junior year in which several LGBTQ students participated, including him. This art teacher was the closest to being a student LGBTQ ally based on her engagement with many LGBTQ students for the production of the fashion show, which included voguing. Danny recalls the fashion show's success, saying, "We turned it! We packed the house... there were hundreds of kids screaming our name!" He explains that the administration did not approve the same show the following year because, in the first, Danny and other LGBTQ students began chanting repeatedly before a school audience at the end of the show, "Let your sexuality be free! Dance with me baby!" The disapproval of this show reflects the administration's prevention of any further pro-LGBTQ- and Black-centered collectivism, rhetoric, and further influence ("Dance with me baby!") from spreading within the student population. Therefore, gay and ally teachers likely felt too threatened to pursue any genuine familiarity with LGBTQ students because it was strongly looked down upon within the school environment.

Along with that, the school administration was likely worried about parents getting the idea that the school had endorsed students' vocalizing about being sexual and "let[ting] your sexuality be free," especially with the risk of teenage pregnancy and HIV/AIDS. Even more, Danny recalled to me that his friends' parents during high school called his and other parents to inform them that their LGBTQ son or daughter was immorally influencing their child with homosexuality. Therefore, it is imaginable that those same parents would be up in arms if they found out that their son's or daughter's teachers and school administration were influencing or supporting active homo- and transgender sexuality. In effect, a lack of strong teacher or school support led such students to feel isolated, without open and professional engagement, especially doubly and triply marginalized LGBTQ students.

## Building Community Amidst Repression: Queer Youth Families and Voguing within the School and Placemaking

### Fraternal Family: Houses and Placemaking in the School

Among the most vital LGBTQ spaces formed at the high school were the gay houses. Elizabeth High queer students were involved in translocal gay houses that bonded them for support and protection, especially from high school bullying, street violence, and family rejection. These gay houses built their own family-like structures outside "ideal" family values of heteronormativity where LGBTQ members could thrive and be who they were across gender and sexuality in relation to other members. The queer house fraternal family structure developed critical collective action that empowered out and questioning queer youth to confidently face their straight tolerant and intolerant peers, teachers, and administrators more openly and assertively. These Elizabeth African American and Latinx LGBTQ students borrowed such fraternal family/kinship structures derived from a largely inner-city African American and Latinx local gay subculture in the ballroom culture that they also adopted in their everyday lives for community, support, and loving relationships.[22]

However, these students not only borrowed from this translocal ballroom culture of houses, but were also recruited by different existing houses, resulting in there being various fraternal family lineages among these peers. Danny shared that while his queer peers were affiliated with different houses, they were still united against LGBTQ violence: "We stuck together as far as LGBTQ violence [in school and on the street] but we were rivals on the runway and dance floor [referring to ballroom competitions and any given night at a nightclub]." Danny explained that "Fields, Labeija, Xtravaganza, Ninja, Ebony, Prestige, and Corey were NY houses to have membership in Newark, Elizabeth, and other parts of NJ.[23] The Shade and Jourdan houses were NJ-based." Virtually all these houses recruited queer youth of color, including students from Elizabeth High School who built their fraternal families, networking, and talent for voguing ball competitions.

Danny further explained that as one of the first upperclassmen students to be out, he not only became a leader like Jean Paul Fields, but they both became gay mothers in this queered/counterhegemonic family structure to support and protect LGBTQ underclassmen, as presented in *Pose* (2018–2021) and the film *Paris Is Burning* (1990). Marlon Bailey suggests that this was actually a queered matriarchy, drawing on the input of one of his interviewees, Tim'm T. West, who suggests that "calling a biological man your mother was sort of a radical revision of motherhood" and reclaims an accepting, all-embracing, and loving maternal figure as he/she/they are.[24] This "mother" role is symbolic and celebratory of what Ferguson describes as the matriarchy and queer political economy of African American and Latinx working-class communities that were often stigmatized and pathologized within larger surrounding local and mainstream culture.[25]

Therefore, a queered matriarchy or patriarchy of these fraternal family networks practiced by these students challenged traditional gender and sexual roles and familial expectations within heteronormative immigrant and U.S. mainstream contexts. I asked Danny if he was ever a mother or father in the house, and he explained:

Yes, I [am]! Several of my children [today] were my children [then]. They came to me because they didn't have anybody to look up to and what's interesting about it is that they were all different from one another (a plurality) in other words, I had a girl come up to me. She's like, "I'm having these feelings and I think I really like girls. I think I'm a lesbian but I can't come out. I was born and raised in the Pentecostal church." And she became my daughter.... And then one of my sons [Ernie], you would never think that he was the typical, stereotype of what a homosexual is, because he didn't vogue, he didn't dress up like a girl, he didn't mix gender clothes, or do any of that flavor and stuff... and he was the ultra masculine, all American, Hispanic boy and he came up to me and said I need to talk to you. He's my gay son until this day. And then I had others that were not so masculine but not so feminine and also were male and they also were my children. A lot of them looked up to me because they didn't have anyone to go to.

Danny discusses the support and mentoring he offered to LGBTQ youth within the oppositional space of the gay house, which they could not find in the school environment. For example, Ernie was a private person and did not pursue joining a house; yet Danny took on a father role for him. As a bisexual at the time, Danny could assume both roles in his ability to perform masculinity and femininity, while Dennis, for example, only assumed the motherly role. Danny performed the fatherly role of what Bailey termed masculine "butch queens" in the gay house and ball scene. Not all the out and questioning youth at the time became actual members of a house; yet, leaders like Danny, Dennis, and Jean took on parental roles for them.

These family/kinship ties helped the LGBTQ youth at Elizabeth High find belonging, strength, and pride by articulating their moral anxieties and deep hurt over a homophobic and heteropatriarchal society and moral upbringing to house mothers or fathers (and other members). The leaders improvised a kind of loving mentorship and empathy that helped "children" achieve "acceptance [of] ourselves," as Danny explained, at school and in their everyday lives. In discussing his "daughter" whose family was Pentecostal, Danny reflected on the pain surrounding the moral upbringing of these youth: "A lot of us came from conservative and religious families... [for example, a] Pentecostal mom does not let her son be out and claim his homosexuality.... Although, we [within the house] learned to accept ourselves... we showed to the world or to Elizabeth, NJ that we were proud of who we were, deep inside a lot of us were hurting and... numb[ed] ourselves." Despite dilemmas these youth faced within the school and in society at large, their queer family at Elizabeth High School became both an immediate source of support and an organized response to society's heteropatriarchal and moral tensions and hostilities.

Lucio describes how being part of a gay family was instrumental in feeling supported and safe from tensions and hostilities that could erupt into verbal attacks, violence, and bullying. He described the agency and familial networks that gay students organized for themselves in this way:

> I think that we had it pretty good. Fortunately, I had my gay family, my gay mother. My gay grandmother, you know, we kind of called ourselves that... because, um, we wanted to let it be known. It's better to be like in numbers, you know? To be in numbers, you know to have more people. To be united.

I know like my gay mother, one of my friends that I met in high school. He was already out. People knew of him. . . . As far as we can trace it back, she's one of the first persons that came out in the high school [*interrupted*]. . . . She led the way and then came my gay mother and my gay aunt. . . . By the time I rolled by they became friends of mine. Everybody in the high school respected us. The high school respected us.

Lucio describes how gay students used a (nonheteronormative) family structure as a survival network to engender an empowered sense of belonging and "unity" among gays and allies within the school grounds. By the time Lucio arrived in high school, the leaders or mothers who were upperclassmen had developed these familial and supportive structures to help the underclassman. Ultimately, because the queer matriarchy ("my gay mother and gay grandmother") organized "[us] in numbers," Lucio saw that it had accomplished a placemaking within the school to the effect that a significant degree of "respect" and incorporation was gained by his high school years ("Everybody in the high school respected us"). Lucio emphatically suggests that these groupings gained more respect from the rest of the high school student body, which helped to significantly reduce bullying and other forms of violence, including symbolic violence.

## Voguing and Placemaking

The family structures within the school prevented gay youth in the high school from being alone and therefore vulnerable to school violence. In essence, these gay house structures within the school were student-led minoritarian spaces. Such spaces critically interfaced with other students, especially while voguing, as indicated by several heterosexual interviewees—in the school hallways, cafeteria, local dance music parties, and events like Elizabeth High School's "Hugs Not Drugs" in 1991.[26] The voguing could include battle dancing, a nonviolent rivalry between houses, or even among family members within a house, that was settled on the dance floor or even the school floor, especially in local ball competitions.

Pop star Madonna's "Vogue" production in 1990 became a record-setting hit and brought voguing from the gay ball culture to the mainstream—recognized in the series *Pose*—which helped this urban queer dance form to gain broader, mainstream appeal, with straight boys practicing to vogue after watching it on the popular Club MTV show of that time. The familiarity created through mainstream images of voguing on television and radio was an advantage for local Elizabeth queer youth in their quest for placemaking in different contexts particularly the school. Elizabeth High School student, Rodney, aka DJ Rodney RodWone Rios, an ally who was friendly with Danny and other LGBTQ students, shares his own view and experience: "Voguing was popular back then cause they didn't make it so gayish [as in the actual ballroom scene]. You know like you had Madonna videos. It was more mainstream, so it was more accepted like you didn't think, 'oh, he's voguing, that's gay!' Even straight kids were voguing. I was voguing back then and I'm straight. . . . It kind of blended in. It wasn't like cause you're voguing, you're gay."

Rodney suggests that bringing voguing to the mainstream reduced the social stigma attached to the dance form itself. However, the LGBTQ student voguers at E-High and ballroom community members were portraying this dance form and urban Black queer cultural repertoire outside Madonna's whitewashed mainstream production. Their everyday experience and struggles and their learned epistemology and exposure of voguing as an Afrocentric underground form allowed them to share with and educate their peers, tolerant and intolerant alike. Schijen writes, "Voguing was a tool for ball-goers to tell their stories"—in this case, their stories of struggle and their motivations with sexual and gender nonconformity, which they shared with their classmates and to crowds at parties amidst the pervasive heterosexist mainstream in school and society at large in Elizabeth and metro New Jersey.[27] These youth spent free time within the school and whenever they could to work on their techniques to gain admiration within their houses and the ball community and beyond for their skills. Danny, Erin Jourdan, and Jean Paul Fields were voguing at house parties and nightlife venues in Elizabeth, Newark, and New York City before and at the time Madonna released her hit song. Danny recalls also "battling" with Jean Paul Fields at Elizabeth High's "Hugs Not Drugs," a public concert in the school's auditorium: "I remember . . . [the crowd] was mostly heterosexual and again I remember me and Jean would battle and we would have a crowd and a girl named Hope, aka Dominatrix Ninja . . . [who] was a biological female she could vogue her ass off, I mean she was doing splits on the floor and everything. She was tango dancing and straight people loved it because I was able to maneuver her and I threw a little tango into it. You know what I'm saying? And I was doing contortions."

Danny explains vividly through his, Hope's, and Jean's queer cultural repertoire of voguing and playful battling that they were able to gather a crowd of "straight" goers who "loved" it. In other words, this crowd stayed engaged with them, which built a sense of connection and/or familiarity as they introduced their viewers to their local, queer, Black cultural repertoire and voguing performance, inviting them to a critical diversity of acceptance and tolerance that challenged the disenfranchisement and expendability of queer of color youth.

Voguing among LGBTQ youth in the high school was common and grew visible. Katia explains,

> In Elizabeth High School you have 4,000 kids so anything and everything was in there. Umm for the most part they respect that and the majority of the kids didn't really seem to care! They enjoyed having them around. They laughed at it. It was great. . . . [Many] straight boys had no problems hanging out with them because they were sure of who they were. You know but you had some other ones who were a little bit more on the I guess ignorant side or not even

ignorant, they were kids, they were not exposed to that.... Most of the kids are products of their environment and are from certain neighborhoods that don't get exposed to many things and then they go to Elizabeth High School [*laughing*] back then especially where you had Madonna Vogue. Kids voguing in the courtyard, I mean, it's like what the hell! Back then it was a whole show, it was fun, it was cute, you know!

Unlike the experience where she witnessed the bullying of a gay male student, discussed earlier, Katia describes here a moment that shows tolerance from the heterosexual student body. She mentions LGBTQ youth voguing in the school's courtyard, putting on a "show" for other students to watch. Katia notes how these voguers were now associated with Madonna's "Vogue" and how their eccentric catwalking, pops, dips, spins, and contortions were less threatening yet displayed "a whole show" that engendered awareness in heteronormative students. Even while voguing after the release of Madonna's video and her numerous voguing performances, these LGBTQ youth disidentified with the mainstream form "as a survival strategy that work[ed] within and outside the dominant [school environment] simultaneously" and were performing their local underground version instead.[28] These youth were not only dancing or expressing themselves but doing the "cultural labor . . . to not only survive but also to enhance the quality of their lives" by pushing their placemaking and LGBTQ identities and knowledge of queer Black and ballroom cultures within the school and incorporating themselves rightfully among normative and homo- and transphobic students.[29]

These youth were not simply reproducing what was familiar on mainstream television (as in Madonna's video productions, for example) but were more importantly engaging in their own self-production ("a whole show"), cultural knowledge (urban LGBTQ Brown and Black ball subculture), and relentless self-expression of local subjectivity and existence in the school environment (placemaking). Danny reminds me that this placemaking is not only about finding a place in the school. For example, in referring back to Katia's view that this "[whole show] was cute," I wrote in my fieldnotes Danny's response after I shared her view with him. He said, "It wasn't cute that Walter and me vogued in the courtyard, it was a battle." In effect this placemaking involved everyday ballroom community dynamics and rivalries that not only centered the struggle to self-pave a place in school but also involved students living out their ballroom personas and LGBTQ identities unfiltered during school hours. The student voguers at the high school were voguing and placemaking to live out their cultural difference "as they were" and challenged the dominant ideologies around sexual, gender, and racial norms within the educational environment at Elizabeth High that excluded them.

In conclusion, queer Latinx student life at Elizabeth High was shaped by the cross-racial, nondivisive affirming spaces of empowerment, solidarity, and healing that students created. These spaces of empowerment and placemaking—in particular the fraternal family structures—changed students' experiences of Elizabeth High from one of invisibility and bullying to one of boldness and hard-won inclusion within the student body. This chapter offered a look into the organizing and cultural work of these students' groupings, voguing, and costuming that interfaced with all students at Elizabeth High proudly and unapologetically. These students achieved courageous acts of oppositional placemaking "as they were," challenging the expendability of the queer, anti-assimilationist, and non-White(ned) other. They taught their peers about critical racial and sexual diversity, democracy, and tolerance. These youth passionately came together in those years to offer an alternative of nonnormative racial, gender, and sexual tolerance that welcomed all in the high school for an equal shot at a public education.

## Notes

1   This is Erin Jourdan who you will read about more later in the text. See under subheading: Boldly Out(ed), Private, or "Shy": LGBTQs of E-High, 1989–1995.
2   Blake Baxter, "Sexuality," Incognito Records, *Sexuality*, 1988, vinyl.
3   See Nancy Shields, "City High School Kids' Scores Make the Grade," *Elizabeth Daily Journal*, June 28, 1986; Peter K. Mitchell, "Elizabeth's School System, Certified, Sitting Pretty," *Elizabeth Daily Journal*, June 18, 1986; Deborah Yaffe, *Other People's Children: The Battle for Justice and Equality in New Jersey's Schools* (New Brunswick, NJ: Rivergate Books, 2007).
4   According to the 1990 Census, Elizabeth had a population of 110,002. Hispanics totaled 43,050, or 39.1 percent of the population. The Latinx student body included Cubans, Puerto Ricans, Colombians, Salvadorans, Peruvians, Ecuadorians, Hondurans, and Nicaraguans.
5   "Dropouts, Low Scores Plague Elizabeth High," *Elizabeth Daily Journal*, February 18, 1991.
6   Andrew S. Harris and Dana Coleman, "Class Absentees Get Credit," *Elizabeth Daily Journal*, April 1, 1991; Andrew Harris, "Elizabeth High Violence Common: Journal Reporter Discovers Discipline Is Almost Non-Existent," *Elizabeth Daily Journal*, February 18, 1991; Dana Coleman, "Elizabeth High Gets Tough on Truants," *Elizabeth Daily Journal*, April 1, 1991.
7   The Latinx student body is described in footnote 4. The non-Latinx Black student body included African Americans and Haitians. These students included mainly first-, 1.5-, and second-generation immigrants. The White student body included multigeneration Italian Americans, Irish Americans, and Portuguese Americans. Many were also racially and ethnically mixed.
8   Melinda Miceli, *Standing Out, Standing Together: The Social and Political Impact of Gay-Straight Alliances* (New York: Routledge, 2005).
9   Sarah Thornton, *Club Cultures: Music, Media and Subcultural Capital* (New York: Polity Press, 1995); *Paris Is Burning*, directed by Jennie Livingston (Encino, Academy Entertainment, 1990); *Pose*, directed by Steven Canals, Brad Falchuk, and Ryan Murphy (West Hollywood, Color Force, 2018–2021).
10  Sarah Schijen, "An Investigation into the History of Voguing," *Vogue*, June 5, 2019, vogue.com.au/culture/features/an-investigation-into-the-history-of-voguing/image-gallery/838a1a2765bc616979caf34e79dfac74.

11  Henry A. Giroux, *The Terror of Neoliberalism* (Boulder, CO: Paradigm, 2004); Jose Muñoz cited in Kat Rands, Jess McDonald, and Lauren Clapp, "Landscaping Classrooms toward Queer Utopias," in *Utopia: A Critical Inquiry into Queer Utopias*, ed. Angela Jones (London: Palgrave Macmillan, 2013), 149–174.
12  Ruth Behar, "Introduction: Out of Exile," in *Women Writing Culture*, ed. Ruth Behar and Deborah A. Gordon (Berkeley: University of California Press, 1995); Norman Denzin, *Interpretive Ethnography: Ethnographic Practices for the 21$^{st}$ Century* (Thousand Oaks, CA: Sage, 1997); Kamala Visweswaran, *Fictions of Feminist Ethnography* (Minneapolis: University of Minnesota Press, 1994).
13  On multisited ethnography, see Julio Cammarota, "The Gendered and Racialized Pathways of Latina and Latino Youth: Different Struggles, Different Resistances in the Urban Context," *Anthropology and Education Quarterly* 35, no. 1 (2004): 60–61; George E. Marcus, "Ethnography in/of the World System: The Emergency of Multi-Sited Ethnography," *Annual Review of Anthropology* 24 (1995): 95–117; Ana Y. Ramos-Zayas, *Street Therapists: Race, Affect, and Neoliberal Personhood in Latino Newark* (Chicago: University of Chicago Press, 2012), 37–38. On nationalist racial projects, see Michael Omi and Howard Winant, *Racial Formation in the United States: From the 1960s to the 1990s* (New York: Routledge, 1994).
14  Most names of the former students who I interviewed in Elizabeth and the surrounding area in 2013–2014 have been changed to preserve their privacy, such as "Katia," "Ernie," "Lucio" and "Bert." Only the late Andre "Angel" Melendez is an actual name, while the others are their house names (i.e., Danny Tiberius Ninja Infiniti or Erin Jourdan) or DJ names (i.e., Rodney RodWone Rios), and not their legal/actual names. Read more about gay ball house lineages under subheadings Out(ed) and Unapologetically Loud: Dressing the Part and Placemaking through Nightlife and Ball Culture Subcultures Within the School and Fraternal Family: Houses and Placemaking in the School. Danny is a second-generation Latinx of Colombian and Cuban descent.
15  Yamil Avivi, "Remembering Andre 'Angel' Melendez: Rave Subculture's Contested/Conflicted Memory of a Racially Motivated Murder," in *Researching Subcultures, Myth, and Memory*, ed. Bart van der Steen, and Thierry P. F. Verburgh (London: Palgrave Macmillan, 2020), 143.
16  Nicholas De Genova, "The Queer Politics of Migration: Reflections on 'Illegality' and Incorrigibility," *Studies in Social Justice* 4, no. 2 (2010): 103.
17  See discussion of symbolic violence in subsection Experiences within the Heteronormative School Environment: Queer Latinx Students Speak.
18  Rebecca Haskell and Brian Burtch, *Get That Freak: Homophobia and Transphobia in High Schools* (Black Point, NS: Fernwood, 2010), 92, 94–95.
19  Haskell and Burtch, *Get That Freak*, 94–97.
20  Haskell and Burtch, *Get That Freak*, 91.
21  Henry Giroux, "The Politics of Insurgent Multiculturalism," in *Critical Multiculturalism: Uncommon Voices in Common Struggle*, ed. Barry Kanpol and Peter McLaren (Westport, CT: Bergin and Garvey, 1995), 112.
22  Marlon M. Bailey, *Butch Queens Up in Pumps: Gender, Performance and Ballroom Culture in Detroit* (Ann Arbor: University of Michigan Press, 2016); Livingston, *Paris Is Burning*; Canals et al., *Pose*.
23  Alvernian Prestige started the Prestige family in Philadelphia and developed a chapter in New York.
24  Bailey, *Butch Queens*, 109.

25 Roderick A. Ferguson, *Aberrations in Black: Toward a Queer of Color Critique* (Minneapolis: University of Minnesota Press, 2004).
26 In 1990 and 1991, Elizabeth High School administrators approved a house, hip-hop, and freestyle concert called "Hugs Not Drugs." Nightlife and radio promoters organized the lineup of this concert that included freestyle, hip-hop artists, Stevie B, Oh Snap, Dougie Fresh, Slick Rick, Two Without Hats, and Coro. DJ Master Flex, a DJ celebrity from Hot 97, and other known DJs of the time also performed and mixed at these events that raised awareness to encourage youth to not use or sell drugs and to avoid violence and gang culture.
27 Schijen, "Investigation."
28 José Muñoz, *Disidentifications: Queers of Color and Performance of Politics* (Minneapolis: University of Minnesota, 1999), 5.
29 Bailey, *Butch Queens*, 16–17.

# 16

# From Puerto Rican to Latino Studies at Rutgers University

Fifty Years of Student Activism

KATHLEEN LÓPEZ

In August 1969, Luis Angel Molina, one of three Puerto Rican students attending Rutgers College in New Brunswick, recalled, "My counselor told me to be a machinist. He said machinists make good money. I couldn't tell him that wasn't all that I was interested in." Sigfredo Carrión, a twenty-three-year-old student leader at Rutgers-Newark, said, "When I entered high school, they told me to take commercial courses. I didn't and I got into college." Keyport High School graduate Miriam Rivera—who would become a prominent attorney and community advocate—confirmed the push toward vocational training: "My counselor was very nice to me when I wanted to be a secretary. But when I mentioned college, she grew cold and wouldn't help."[1] By the time these students shared their experiences with the Newark *Star-Ledger*, the spark for expanded access to education for minority students in New Jersey had ignited. The following year, over forty Puerto Rican high school graduates began college in New Jersey instead of working on a factory assembly line.[2]

These transformations occurred amidst the urban unrest of the 1960s and 1970s, when inequalities in access to higher education for Blacks and Latinos/as became a focus for youth, educators, government officials, and local community activists in cities around the country. Growing awareness of social and economic disparities coalesced with the anti-war and civil rights movements. In 1968 at San Francisco State College, students formed multiracial coalitions to demand the admission of more minorities and a curriculum that reflected their own histories and cultures. This call reverberated across the nation as students sought expanded access to higher education and curricular reform to include Black, Chicano, Puerto Rican, Asian American, and Native American studies. As the movements took different turns according to local political and racial landscapes, they shared a philosophy of the interconnected struggles of Third World peoples against an imperialist and capitalist Western oppressor. In the northeast, Black and Puerto Rican communities became the foci of the struggles for representation on college campuses.[3]

This chapter examines the origins and development of the Puerto Rican student movement at Rutgers University within the context of civil rights and antipoverty campaigns and protests in New Jersey.[4] It demonstrates how Puerto Rican youth drew on their own experiences to promote educational access, academic innovation, and community engagement, and it traces the legacies of the movement for Latino/a studies today. While the chapter focuses on the first decade of Puerto Rican studies at Livingston College, it also addresses pioneering developments in Newark and Camden.[5]

## Puerto Rican Communities and Educational Access in New Jersey

As the first large-scale Spanish-speaking population in New Jersey, Puerto Ricans reshaped local landscapes while settling alongside older European immigrant communities and Blacks from the U.S. South who had migrated in search of better opportunities.[6] Puerto Ricans began arriving in the U.S. Northeast in large numbers after World War II, when they were recruited for agricultural and industrial work. While many Puerto Rican farm laborers returned home seasonally after the harvest, some relocated to urban areas to find more permanent jobs. By the 1950s and 1960s, Puerto Ricans resided in cities and towns across New Jersey, including Newark, Jersey City, Paterson, Perth Amboy, and Hoboken in the north and Camden and Vineland in the south. Many of them had initially settled in New York City and, by 1970, the Puerto Rican population in New Jersey claimed a growth rate of 150 percent.[7] The 1970 U.S. Census counted 135,676 Puerto Ricans in New Jersey (with 63,424 born on the mainland), which the government admitted reflected a significant undercount among urban minority populations.[8] By 1974, the Puerto Rican Congress of New Jersey estimated 325,000 Puerto Ricans in the state, 45,000 of them in Newark alone.[9]

The educators and students who initiated Puerto Rican studies on college campuses in the Northeast were a product of this postwar migration, either born on the island or of Puerto Rican ancestry, and many had experienced firsthand the deficiencies of public schools in preparing them for higher education. In the 1960s, the category "minority" generally referred to U.S.-born Blacks, and discussions of race relations centered on interactions with Whites. The marked increase in Puerto Rican migrants and their children changed these dynamics, at a time when upper- and middle-class Whites were moving to developing suburbs amidst deindustrialization and social unrest. Inadequate tax bases and low teacher salaries furthered the disintegration of urban schools.[10] Although the anti-poverty programs of the 1960s delivered some benefits for Blacks and Puerto Ricans, these gains were marginal in comparison to those for low-income Whites.[11] According to the 1970 Census, 24 percent of Puerto Rican families were categorized as below the poverty line, compared to 4.8 percent of White families.[12] Nationwide, Blacks and Latino/as encountered poverty, discrimination and barriers to employment, high rents for deteriorated housing, poor health care, and low educational levels, and Puerto Ricans generally remained at the bottom of these scales.[13]

Puerto Rican community leaders took inspiration from and worked alongside leaders of the Black movement. The 1969 Black and Puerto Rican Political Convention that helped to elect Mayor Kenneth Gibson in Newark represented such a community-based coalition. However, Puerto Rican activists also adapted strategies and tactics to serve the distinct needs of a Spanish-speaking migrant group within a U.S. colonial context, which at times produced conflict. A 1971 report by Rutgers University faculty Hilda Hidalgo noted that Puerto Ricans resent the fact that "when 'blacks and Puerto Ricans' are lumped together, the result is that blacks are served; *Puerto Ricans are left out.*"[14] Moreover, Puerto Ricans experienced a loss of "individual cultural identity" when grouped together with U.S. Blacks, and would benefit from "a tailor-made approach" to address their distinct cultural and linguistic backgrounds.[15] Puerto Ricans also faced divisions *within* their communities, based on color, class, and affiliation with the island or the U.S. mainland. Some objected, for example, that the 1969 coalition in Newark supported by Hilda Hidalgo and others did not fully represent the Puerto Rican community and was divisive because it excluded Whites.[16]

In a 1976 report on Puerto Ricans, the U.S. Commission on Civil Rights devoted an entire section to "the crisis in education" that addressed the high dropout rate, language and cultural differences, the achievement gap, low parent and community involvement, and the challenges of access to higher education.[17] Puerto Rican education leaders especially targeted the dropout rate and need for bilingual and bicultural programs. In Jersey City, for example, fewer than half of Puerto Rican students in elementary school continued on to high school. Felipe García, assistant dean of Livingston College, repeated a common refrain that Puerto Rican youth do not "drop out" of school, but rather are "pushed out" through a combination of lack of bilingual classes, a practice of routinely holding back students, and inadequate counseling.[18] A massive 1974 study found that statewide, 70 percent of Puerto Ricans aged eighteen to twenty-four years did not graduate high school.[19] High school students were often channeled toward a vocational rather than academic track, making them uncompetitive for college admission. Moreover, public school systems inadequately prepared minorities for entrance into these institutions and success once they were admitted.[20]

Despite the barriers, a handful of Puerto Rican students made their way to public universities in New Jersey by the late 1960s. In the aftermath of the 1967 Newark uprisings, state officials supported a range of programs to address the underlying conditions of the unrest, including some that focused on education. New Jersey's Educational Opportunity Fund (EOF) legislation passed in 1968, and still today provides financial aid, counseling, tutoring, and developmental coursework to "students from educationally and economically disadvantaged backgrounds" at participating institutions of higher education.[21] Another major source of support for Puerto Rican youth who dreamed of attending college was the national education and leadership organization ASPIRA, created in 1961 with affiliates in cities such as New York, Philadelphia, Chicago, and San Juan. The program focused on keeping students in school and encouraging them to pursue college through workshops on higher education, scholarships and loans, and careers. ASPIRA operated local clubs at high schools, and club members—known as *aspirantes*—learned about Puerto Rican history and culture to develop awareness "of what it means to be a Puerto Rican," according to Hilda Hidalgo, who led the Newark chapter that opened in 1969.[22]

## Puerto Rican Student Activism at the State University of New Jersey

For both Black and Puerto Rican youth, public universities had the potential to narrow the gap in future employment and earnings. The push for increased educational access went hand in hand with the development of a new curriculum. In the Northeast, City University of New York became the first home to programs in African American and Puerto Rican studies. Puerto Rican studies centered on a critique of traditional educational institutions that reproduced hierarchies and class divisions, legitimized colonization and exploitation, and controlled knowledge in the interests of a ruling elite. In New Jersey's public institutions of higher education, the Puerto Rican student movement embraced this mission and had two immediate goals: the recruitment and retention of Puerto Rican students and the development of programs in Puerto Rican studies.[23] Inspiration came from the Black Organization of Students that had formed at Rutgers-Newark in 1967 to pursue increased minority admissions, hiring of Black faculty and staff, and development of Black studies programs. On February 24, 1969, the Black Organization of Students protested and occupied Conklin Hall, a movement that captured national attention and amplified subsequent demands for educational access at the Camden and New Brunswick campuses.

A small group of Puerto Rican students at Newark supported the protestors and articulated their own set of conditions to university administrators through the newly formed Puerto Rican Organization.[24] The group was born when two Cuban women saw Sigfredo Carrión on campus and called out "Boricua!"; they subsequently discussed the need for Spanish-speaking students to collaborate with each other.[25]

Like their counterparts at City University of New York across the Hudson, Rutgers student activists decried inequalities in the public school system and demanded programs to assist Puerto Rican high school students prepare for college and learn about access to scholarships and loans. They implored the university to target a population of full-time Puerto Rican students proportionate to the urban Puerto Rican population in New Jersey. Moreover, as state university and private corporation expansion plans collided with poor urban areas in Newark, New Brunswick, and Camden, Black and Puerto Rican student leaders advocated for the protection of local communities and attention to the educational needs of minority youth.[26]

Rutgers-Newark Puerto Rican Organization leaders Sigfredo Carrión and Melba Maldonado embodied this commitment to the neighborhoods surrounding Rutgers University campuses. After graduating from high school in Puerto Rico in 1966, Maldonado moved to Newark with her family and worked for low wages in factories. She also engaged in community and political organization at a local church, which drew the attention of Carrión and other members of the Puerto Rican Organization. After Carrión encouraged Maldonado to apply to the university, she met with recently hired Puerto Rican advisor Maria De Castro Blake, who arranged for her to take an evening history course. This experience gave her the confidence that she was capable of college-level work.[27] Once enrolled at Rutgers-Newark, Maldonado volunteered alongside other Puerto Rican students to recruit students in New Jersey public high schools in cities such as Newark, Bloomfield, and Passaic. The Puerto Rican Organization also developed summer programs for potential students that extended to other Latino/a groups. "We had activities, we had movies, we had free lunch and basically we just wanted them to feel that they can come here and they can sit in these desks," Maldonado recalled, adding that when their requests to the administration failed, they resorted to more forceful tactics such as occupying buildings. By the time Maldonado graduated in 1975, there were about two hundred Puerto Rican students at Rutgers-Newark, some of whom continued outreach on tenant and welfare rights in poor neighborhoods and for Puerto Rican studies at the university. Both Carrión and Maldonado also protested at city hall during the Newark Puerto Rican riots of 1974.[28]

At the Rutgers-Camden campus, Puerto Rican student leader Gualberto (Gil) Medina participated in the Black movement for increased recruitment and representation, for a university that serves its community, as well as the anti-war Students for a Democratic Society. He mobilized others to support the student center takeover in 1969 and the renaming of the library after Paul Robeson. Like Carrión and Maldonado in Newark, Medina's activism extended to the surrounding urban neighborhoods in Camden.[29] In 1971, an incident of police brutality resulted in the death of a Puerto Rican man during a routine traffic stop. Medina led a protest at city hall, and afterward he was asked to help with negotiations. Decades later, he reflected on a moment that would remain forever etched in his mind. As Medina went store to store to apologize for the damage and looting, one of the owners stopped him and showed him tattoos on his forearms, explaining "I got these at Auschwitz. If we had stood up like you have, there never would have been an Auschwitz."[30]

## Puerto Rican Studies at Livingston College: An Engaged Interdisciplinary Curriculum

While courses and programs in Puerto Rican and Latino/a studies were eventually established at Newark and Camden, the New Brunswick campus of Rutgers University became home to the state's only Department of Puerto Rican Studies. The campus consisted of four distinct colleges, each with its own faculty and curriculum: Rutgers College (founded in 1766 as Queen's College), Douglass College (founded in 1918 as the New Jersey College for Women), the College of Agriculture and Environmental Science (founded as the land-grant Rutgers Scientific School in 1864 and renamed Cook College in 1971), and the new coeducational and experimental Livingston College, which opened in 1969.[31] In the wake of the 1967 Newark riots, Livingston College embraced a mission of social responsibility and solutions to urban problems and community development, along with new pedagogical models and diversification of the student body.[32] Dean Ernest Lynton emphasized that beyond the presence of more minority students, "the needs, the contributions, the desires of the black and the poor community must become as integral a part of our entire enterprise as traditionally has been the case for the needs, desires, and contributions of the white middle class."[33] Lynton further expressed that in much of the curriculum "it will be the urban student who is at an advantage through his background experience."[34] The new dean viewed minority students as a critical component of a solution, rather than a "problem" to be fixed.

In the summer of 1969, sixteen newly admitted Livingston College EOF students organized to make demands for Puerto Rican studies, along with support from the few Puerto Rican students already enrolled at Rutgers.[35] With the recent passage of the New Jersey EOF legislation and pressure from community and student activists, conditions were ripe for administrators and trustees to respond positively. Dean Lynton supported the establishment of a program in Puerto Rican studies at Livingston College in fall 1970, with Maria Josefa Canino Arroyo as founding coordinator and Vilma Cardona (Pérez) as part-time secretary.[36] Four Puerto Rican faculty affiliates from other departments formed the backbone of the program: Hilda Hidalgo and Edward Ortiz (Urban Studies and Community Development), poet and playwright Victor Fernández Fragoso (Comparative Literature), and Miguel Algarín (English), a founder of the Nuyorican Poets Café on the Lower East Side of Manhattan and the Nuyorican Literary Movement. For a program that began with only one full-time faculty line, this "critical nucleus" of experts and community activists at Rutgers sustained the department through its first decade, along with doctoral students hired as adjunct instructors in sociology, political science, and economics.[37] In 1973, Maria Canino became the first chair of the new Department of Puerto Rican Studies.

From the beginning, students took a leading role in shaping both the trajectory of the department and the social and academic experiences of Puerto Ricans on campus. Inspired by leftists movements and the Young Lords, they formed the Union Estudiantil Puertorriqueña (United Puerto Rican Students) and advocated for Puerto Rican representation in the general student congress.[38] Fifty students lived in the dormitory known as the Puerto Rican House, with sounds of Spanish language and salsa in the halls, rice and beans cooking in the small kitchen, and Puerto Rican flags and murals adorning the walls.[39] Alumni Margaret (Margie) Rivera recalls a collective sense among students of an opportunity "to begin to know more about our history and know more about ourselves." The Puerto Rican House became a center of "heavy duty conversations" and debates about campus events and world politics.[40] Three students served on the Puerto Rican Studies Committee, alongside three faculty and three staff members, to establish policies and direction for budget, curriculum, personnel, research, and programming.[41] The extraordinary level of student input into programming and even hiring became a distinctive feature of the department.

Interlocking goals of historical recovery, cultural affirmation, and interdisciplinarity undergirded the broader Puerto Rican studies project. The initial curriculum at Livingston College focused on the historical, political, economic, social, and cultural development of Puerto Rico and its diasporic communities in the United States, as well as the literary and artistic expressions of the Puerto Rican experience and linkages with the region.[42]

Beyond academic study, the program fostered innovative art and music that developed from immigrant and diasporic experiences. Victor Fernández Fragoso taught theater at Livingston College and founded the progressive troupe El Teatro Guazábara, which performed in New York and New Jersey. Fragoso envisioned theater as reaching "in two directions: inward, towards the community in order to survive through the preservation of its culture, and outward, trying to communicate with non-Puerto Rican communities."[43] Recurring themes included gender stereotypes, homosexuality, and Puerto Rican urban life in the 1970s and early 1980s.[44] In 1973–1974, students wrote and performed plays as they acquired skills in production, publicity, direction, and collaboration.[45] At times they performed in the streets without props to reach communities who did not have access to theater: "We were the chairs, we were the tables, we were the telephones," recalls alumni Mercedes Valle. Having grown up in an Italian neighborhood in Newark, Valle became more comfortable with her Puerto Rican identity through her participation in the theater troupe.[46]

An education in Puerto Rican studies extended beyond classroom walls through integrated fieldwork and community programs. Given the scarcity of academic materials on the Puerto Rican experience, the department produced new knowledge about it. In just the first few years, students and faculty embarked on several large-scale projects: surveying migrant farmworkers in South Jersey, tutoring at Trenton State Prison, interviewing Puerto Rican artists and curating an exhibit at El Museo del Barrio in New York City, recovering and cataloging historical documents related to Puerto Rico at the Library of Congress, and outreach in New Jersey public schools.[47]

The migrant farmworker study demonstrates how engaged scholarship generated new research in critical but neglected areas. By the late 1960s and early 1970s, over sixty thousand Puerto Rican agricultural workers migrated annually to the United States, living in camps or on farms and encountering discrimination from local residents.[48] Together with Puerto Rican community members who lived adjacent to migrant camps, Livingston College graduate and undergraduate students carried out fieldwork for eighteen months in 1971–1972 under the supervision of Luis Nieves Falcón, who eventually published the results as part of the book *El emigrante puertorriqueño* (1975).[49] The comprehensive study included interviews with workers, farmers, local residents, public officials, and community leaders, as well as migrants who had returned to Puerto Rico.[50] Student Elias Rivera reflected in his research field notes: "In many cases after being given permission to enter camps, we would be hassled verbally by the crewleader's bullys in order to discourage the migrants from cooperating with us."[51] When they did gain access, students would encounter up to one hundred men in a converted chicken coop, filthy outdoor bathrooms, and cigarettes and beer sold at inflated prices.

The prison education and outreach program responded to the high incidence of Latino/a incarceration. In 1972–1973, Maria Canino and five students regularly visited Trenton State Prison to tutor in remedial skills, teach Puerto Rican history and culture, and facilitate discussions of community issues. The following year the program expanded to four evenings each week through an independent study. It featured theater and music, including performances by folk singer and adjunct faculty Suni Paz. In a moving letter to the department, Eduardo Voluntud expressed the "awakening" he and fellow inmates experienced: "These beautiful brothers & sisters from Livingston college sang of our homeland and our heroes and we were struck dumbfounded. What sort of strange creatures were these to be proud of being a Puerto Rican?"[52] Despite the popularity and success of the program, it suffered from a lack of resources and relied heavily on fundraising and volunteer efforts, and it was ultimately terminated by the prison.[53]

Students and faculty sought to tear down the gates dividing Rutgers University campuses from the surrounding communities. In addition to leading the historical document project, faculty member Carlos Piñeiro coordinated an independent study on guidance and tutoring with New Brunswick High School Spanish-speaking students, who were primarily Puerto Rican.[54] Students also participated in clothing drives and Three Kings Day celebrations for local families in New Brunswick.[55] In just her second semester, Margie Rivera along with six other students received training and undertook fieldwork in Newark as part of a course led by Hilda Hidalgo on the Puerto Rican urban experience. Student interviewers—all Puerto Rican—administered a questionnaire in Spanish to collect information about demographics, family composition, and occupations, as well as attitudes toward educational and health services. The research agenda also included "surveying prices of typical Puerto Rican food items in supermarkets and 'bodegas' and visiting religious stores and observing what customers bought."[56] The published study provides an unparalleled in-depth portrait of Puerto Rican families in 1970 Newark.

The department promoted cultural and academic knowledge among the broader community in New Jersey and the Northeast. On a Sunday in April 1970, the Union Estudiantil Puertorriqueña held the first Puerto Rican cultural festival in New Jersey at Douglass and Livingston Colleges. It featured a talk by Arturo Díaz on Puerto Rican history and culture, a play by Piri Thomas, and folk dancers and singers, followed by *bizcocho* and Café Bustelo.[57] In 1967 Thomas had published *Down These Mean Streets*, which chronicled the hardship and discrimination he encountered as a dark-skinned youth growing up in El Barrio in New York City.[58] The festival became an annual event drawing hundreds of people from the around the state. In November 1974, the Union Estudiantil Puertorriqueña commemorated the "discovery" of Puerto Rico with three hundred New Brunswick community members at Bayard School, which was predominantly Black and Puerto Rican, through a theatrical production, "a historical narrative combined with music and dances of our Indian, Black and Spanish forefathers which made the audience of parents, teachers, and children of the inner city grammar school become aware of Puerto Rico."[59]

In addition to studying Puerto Rican history and politics, the department curriculum centered questions of what it meant to be Puerto Rican within a U.S. context. For many students who grew up in New York or New Jersey, it was the first time they studied their own history in an academic setting. Graduate student Reginald (Reggie) Morales commented that doing fieldwork in migrant communities in South Jersey allowed him to reflect on his identity as a Puerto Rican. Growing up on a naval base, he had spoken only English since the age of six years. When he attended Duke University and joined a fraternity, he recorded, "I was so far removed from my Latin American heritage that I no longer felt any attachment to it." While interviewing residents in South Jersey, Morales was shocked at the prejudice he encountered, including from children of Italians and Japanese.[60] Alumni Ivette Méndez, who entered Douglass College in 1971, shared the feelings of ostracization she experienced on a predominantly White campus and the importance of interaction with Black and Puerto Rican communities: "I recall being described ... all of us ... as educationally, culturally, and socially disadvantaged." Méndez became a founding member of the residential Casa Boricua and channeled her activism through the campus newspaper. She wrote about issues impacting Puerto Ricans, such as increased admissions and persistent stereotypes.[61] To reconnect students with their heritage, in March 1972 the department also organized an educational tour of Puerto Rico that prioritized those who had never been to the island.[62]

## Puerto Rican Studies and Challenges to Legitimacy

As Puerto Rican studies took root on all three campuses of the State University of New Jersey, minority student enrollments, faculty and staff hiring, and cultural programming blossomed.[63] Sustained pressure from community and government officials and support from EOF resulted in increased Black and Puerto Rican admissions to New Jersey's fifty-seven public and private colleges. From 1969 to 1972, the number of Puerto Rican students attending college in the state more than tripled to about two thousand (150 of them at Livingston College).[64]

Alongside this growth, Puerto Rican studies programs faced significant challenges in the 1970s, many of which continue through today. In a comprehensive 1974 report, the Puerto Rican Congress of New Jersey concluded that, despite increased admissions after 1969, Puerto Ricans comprised less than 2 percent of college students statewide.[65] By mid-decade amidst a university budget crisis, the department at Livingston College reported a state of "permanent struggle" in which the administration had "no real commitment to the existence and continuation of Puerto Rican Studies as an institutional program." The 1976 annual report put it bluntly: "The gains in the 60's have become threatened in the 70's."[66] The department confronted obstacles to student admissions, financial aid, and advising, as well as reductions in faculty and staff. Moreover, administrative response to an incident of police brutality against two Puerto Rican students and Black student opposition to a Puerto Rican dean divided the campus. The 1976 report ended on a self-critical but forward-looking note: "The present is one of struggle, the future will be ours."[67]

The struggle for the intellectual and social project of Puerto Rican studies manifested in continued actions throughout the 1970s. Puerto Rican students from Camden, Newark, and New Brunswick coordinated demands for a major protest of the administration at Old Queens during the spring semester of 1971.[68] Again in 1977 a group of about sixty students, faculty, and supporters assembled in front of President Edward J. Bloustein's office to condemn the university's failure to consistently recruit and retain Puerto Rican students and employees. The Puerto Rican Congress of New Jersey organized the protest, declaring "that

Puerto Ricans are concentrated in lower-paying jobs at the university and Hispanic faculty stand a poorer chance of being promoted than non-Hispanics." According to the congress, "a revolving-door policy" kept the proportion of Puerto Rican employees around 2 percent, and demonstrators urged the administration to implement an aggressive affirmative action plan.[69]

Activists also turned their attention to Puerto Rican representation in graduate and professional schools. At a press conference during the 1977 demonstration, Hilda Hidalgo proclaimed that anti-Puerto Rican bias was both overt and systemic. While not aimed specifically at Puerto Ricans, some practices disproportionately impacted Puerto Ricans. Hidalgo cited as examples the hurdles posed by the Graduate Record Exam and inability to subsist on low stipends offered to teaching assistants, as "Puerto Rican graduate students tend to be older and burdened by financial responsibilities." Moreover, "those wishing to write about Puerto Rican history or culture find themselves blocked by an academic establishment which regards the field as too parochial."[70] In July 1978, a group of community leaders and medical students and faculty charged the College of Medicine and Dentistry of New Jersey with racist hiring and admissions policies.[71]

Increased admissions of minority students to public institutions of higher learning proved to be just half the battle. Once students were admitted, ethnic studies programs and departments remained committed to their success through advising and accountability. Livingston College alumni Mercedes Valle commented on the faculty: "They stayed on us, and they made sure that we did well. They didn't just see you for class. If they had to come to your room and wake you up because you didn't go to class, they would show up in your room and knock on the door."[72] Carlos Piñeiro recalled doing precisely that when students failed to attend his morning seminar.[73] Students also learned to advocate for themselves in the face of adversity. Alumni Elizabeth Rivera (Jiménez) recalled an incident in which a chemistry professor deducted more points from her exam than a White classmate's exam. She reported the discrepancy to the dean, with the result that everyone who received a low or failing grade was able to retake the exam. "This professor had never been challenged in terms of his practice and now he was challenged," she said.[74] At the end of the spring 1977 semester, a student wrote a letter to document "an apparent discriminatory pattern" in which expository writing instructors from the English Department at Livingston College targeted Spanish-speaking students of Puerto Rican descent. In one case, the student wrote, the instructor "expressed to me that there was no way I could hope to pass the course because Puerto Ricans cannot improve." The student had brought her complaint to the English Department chair, who dismissed the conflict as resulting from "mutual misinterpretation."[75]

Rutgers's goal of recognition as a major public research university included a contentious plan for academic reorganization of the different colleges in New Brunswick and Piscataway, which presented a challenge to small interdisciplinary departments such as Africana studies and Puerto Rican studies. Opponents pointed out that centralization would remove oversight in admissions, financial aid, and scheduling from the individual colleges and, as a result, be less responsive to students. In the 1980s, as the target date for implementation neared, a coalition of Latino/a students, faculty, and staff in New Brunswick joined forces with other groups to oppose the plan and express their concerns. The plan for consolidation of interdisciplinary departments into a "Division of Area Studies" threatened such programs with disintegration. Billy Delgado, who represented both the Union Estudiantil Puertorriqueña and the Coalition to Protect the Colleges said, "We feel that as minority students with special needs, the Puerto Rican Studies Department needs to grow with reorganization rather than disappear."[76] While Puerto Rican studies retained its department status, the centralization plan ultimately resulted in the current structure of one university with multiple degree-granting schools by 2007.[77]

## From Puerto Rican to Latino/a Studies and Continued Activism

Over the past half century, Puerto Rican studies programs in the Northeast have responded to shifting demographics and broadened their scope to encompass Latino/a, Latin American, and Caribbean studies. In 1986, the department at Livingston College changed its name to Puerto Rican and Hispanic Caribbean Studies to highlight connections with the former Spanish colonies of Cuba and the Dominican Republic. A decade later, the department called a plenary meeting for majors and minors to discuss a further name change.[78] The potential removal of "Puerto Rican" from the department name faced vehement opposition from students, alumni, and Puerto Rican community leaders who expressed concern about the weakening of the mission of Puerto Rican studies. Highlighting the reach of the department, one letter from the Hudson County Office of Hispanic Affairs in March 1997 implored: "To include Puerto Ricans in the same category as all Caribbean Latinos constitutes a disservice to History, both Puerto Rico's and the United States', and a drawback in the struggle of this community that much too often must focus its efforts in defending past accomplishments rather than placing its energies into creating new opportunities."[79] It was not until 2006 that the department formally changed its name to Latino and Hispanic Caribbean Studies. By 2000, Puerto Ricans still comprised the largest Latino/a group in New Jersey, but most newer immigrants were from the Dominican Republic and Central and South America, while the Cuban population had slightly declined.[80] Today the Department of Latino and Caribbean Studies comprises scholars of different geopolitical and linguistic regions of the Caribbean and Latin American groups in the United States, with increased attention to gender and sexuality and the experiences of Afro-Latinx people in the Americas.[81]

Puerto Rican and Latino/a student activism has continued through the decades, although animated by different concerns and tempered by the institutionalization of ethnic studies programs. In 1988, for example, nearly six hundred students from around the country gathered at Livingston College for a three-day convention to form a national student activist organization. The meeting captured the range of student concerns in that era: Puerto Rican political status, housing for homeless, Native American land rights, as well as opposition to U.S. intervention in Central America, apartheid in South Africa, and the Central Intelligence Agency recruiting on college campuses.[82] Besides these national and global issues, Latino/a students joined broader undergraduate movements supporting gender equity and opposing tuition hikes.[83]

Despite the gains by minority students, racial discrimination persisted on campus. In fall 1987, the main New Brunswick campus newspaper ran a series that addressed several aspects of the issue, such as declining minority enrollments and affirmative action policies.[84] In 1989, as part of the commemoration of the twentieth anniversary of the Black student movement, the university offered a "Racism at Rutgers" mini course. Those who were dissatisfied with the course formed a coalition with the aim of fully realizing the goals of the 1969 uprisings. Puerto Rican Mayra Ramírez joined forces with Black student Denise Gayle to lead a group of about two hundred in putting a stop to racial slurs and discrimination and increasing minority faculty and staff.[85]

In addition to joining broader campus movements, Latino/a students formed new cultural organizations. In the 1970s, a handful of Cubans and Dominicans supported the Puerto Rican Student Union. As these student populations grew, they developed their own associations to address issues particular to their communities. More recently, the establishment of organizations such as the Peruvian Student Association and Mexican American Student Association reflects continued shifts in demographics.

Like the activists of the 1970s, Rutgers students continue to serve as liaisons for newer generations of college students and underrepresented populations who face obstacles. Growing up in a mostly Dominican and Puerto Rican neighborhood in Passaic, alumni Saskia Leo Cipriani (Livingston College, 2004) had difficulties adjusting to the academic and social environment at Rutgers. During her first semester as a transfer student from community college, she faced academic challenges and felt "lost" in a large, mostly White university. Cipriani became involved with Casa Boricua (the community residence established at Douglass College in 1972) and also joined the Rutgers-New Brunswick chapter of the Latina academic sorority Lambda Theta Alpha. Since their advent in the 1970s, Black and Latino/a fraternities and sororities have provided a critical academic and social support system for students, promoting scholarly excellence, empowerment, and political and community awareness and activism.[86] Once she took on leadership roles within these organizations, Cipriani recalls, "I found my voice. I found who I was. It was so empowering."[87] Today, Cipriani continues to mentor new student leaders through her role as assistant director of the Center for Latino Arts and Culture.[88]

In 2008, the Rutgers Future Scholars program brought an inaugural class of two hundred low-income, middle-school students from Newark, Camden, New Brunswick, and Piscataway to campus for summer enrichment, afterschool and Saturday workshops, and tutoring.[89] A decade later, Liandy Gonzalez—a first-generation EOF student from Paterson who describes himself as "a proud Afro-Boricua"—advised students in the program at Piscataway High School through a Mentoring as Public Service course.[90] The experience inspired him to pursue a master of arts in higher education while working as program coordinator for the TRIO Upward Bound Project at Montclair State University. Peer outreach and activism among current students extends to new immigrants in New Jersey. In fall 2016, students formed the organization UndocuRutgers to provide resources and support for undocumented immigrants at the university and improve their retention and graduation rates. The organization's founder and president, Carimer Andujar, had arrived in the United States from the Dominican Republic at the age of four years and was a recipient of Deferred Action for Childhood Arrivals, which allowed her to study and work. When Andujar was summoned for an interview with Immigration and Customs Enforcement and faced possible deportation, a broad range of students rallied behind her outside the federal building in Newark.[91]

Efforts to close the equity gap are ongoing, and Latino/a college enrollment and degree completion continues to increase. While their graduation rate from four-year institutions in New Jersey is higher than in the nation, they lag compared to other groups in New Jersey. In 2017–2018, for example, 27 percent of Latino adults held an associate degree or higher, compared to 52 percent of White adults.[92]

## Legacies of Puerto Rican Alumni

As a student in 1971, Elias Rivera kept in mind his purpose for attending college: "The only reason our parents left Puerto Rico was for economic advancement. They didn't come to wash dishes or to work in factories, as many of them ended up doing. When we graduate from Livingston, we can do one of two things. We can turn our backs on our people and be a success or we can return and work in and for our community."[93] In 1973, the Department of Puerto Rican Studies at Livingston College graduated its first class of seniors, all five of whom were double majors. Four of them continued with law or professional school, and the fifth worked for the Puerto Rican educational organization ASPIRA.[94] The impact of these first cohorts of Puerto Rican students outweighs their small numbers.

Today, several former student activists from all three Rutgers campuses hold prominent roles in politics, business, education, and the professions. They remain committed to the communities from which they came and influenced by their interdisciplinary training. Margie Rivera continued her work in recruitment, eventually becoming director of admissions at Livingston College. She reflected that her experiences on campus "awakened something that I didn't even know I had" and impelled her to "pay it forward" and "be supportive of others as they go through their trajectory."[95] Mercedes Valle, who grew up in Newark in the 1950s and 1960s, became a child psychologist for Newark public schools and assists new immigrant families in navigating the system. She commented: "I do a lot of work with Latino families, basically, to tell them their rights, to help them understand what they can and can't do in terms of resolving issues at school. Most of the population I have served here in Newark has been Latino, Dominicans, Puerto Ricans, Ecuadorians who come here and really don't know what a school district is like or what are their rights."[96] After finishing Rutgers-Newark, Sigfredo Carrión continued to work for local government in Essex County. Melba Maldonado, who is now executive director of La Raza Community Resource Center in San Francisco, learned from her experiences on campus and in Newark that "all poor people suffer" and about the need for mutual understanding across race and ethnicity.[97] After graduating from Rutgers-Camden in three years in 1971, Gil Medina continued with law school at Temple University, but not before promoting a program in Camden to assist Puerto Ricans with legal aid and education on interactions with landlords, merchants, police, and social welfare agencies and to advocate for improved housing, health care, and bilingual education that would ultimately benefit all Spanish speakers. In 1994, Medina became commissioner of the Department of Commerce and Economic Development in New Jersey. He has made a career of public service and is now executive vice president of CBRE Brokerage Services.[98]

In October 2016, Rutgers Puerto Rican alumni from the 1970s gathered in New Brunswick to share their experiences with current students as part of the campus-wide commemorations of the university's 250th anniversary. The student activists who demanded inclusiveness and diversity in education, and critiqued colonialism and the university structure, embodied the theme of "revolution" that permeated the campus-wide events. The Puerto Rican students of the 1970s—despite their limited numbers and resources—demonstrate the power of collective action to generate societal change, and their legacy continues with new generations of students today.

## Notes

1  William Slattery and Roger Harris, "Puerto Ricans: School Teaches English and Limited Expectations," *Star-Ledger*, August 6, 1969, 16.
2  "Agency Aids Puerto Ricans into College," *Jersey Journal and Jersey Observer*, August 6, 1970, 9.
3  For educational activism during the civil rights era, see *Amerasia Journal* 15, no. 1 (1989) on the Asian American student movement in California; Angela Rose Ryan, "Education for the People: The Third World Student Movement at San Francisco State College and City College of New York" (PhD diss., Ohio State University,

2010); and Kitty Kelly Epstein and Bernard Stringer, *Changing Academia Forever: Black Student Leaders Analyze the Movement They Led* (Gorham, ME: Myers Education Press, 2020). Perspectives on the field of ethnic studies can be found in Johnnella E. Butler, ed., *Color-Line to Borderlands: The Matrix of American Ethnic Studies* (Seattle: University of Washington Press, 2001). For the origins and development of Puerto Rican studies, see María E. Sánchez and Antonio M. Stevens-Arroyo, eds., *Toward a Renaissance of Puerto Rican Studies: Ethnic and Area Studies in University Education* (New York: Columbia University Press, 1987). For a recent retrospective view, see María E. Pérez y González and Virginia Sánchez Korrol, *Puerto Rican Studies in the City University of New York: The First Fifty Years* (New York: Centro Press, Center for Puerto Rican Studies, 2021), especially Pedro Cabán, "Remaking Puerto Rican Studies at 50 Years," 16–42.

4   For scholarship on student movements and Puerto Rican studies at Rutgers University, see Maria Josefa Canino Arroyo, "The 40th Anniversary of the Department of Latino and Hispanic Caribbean Studies" (lecture, Rutgers University, Piscataway, NJ, October 11, 2013), https://www.academia.edu/9366844/40th_Anniversary _Latino_and_Hispanic_Caribbean_Studies_Rutgers_and_250th_anniversary_of _Rutgers_University; Paul G. E. Clemens, *Rutgers since 1945: A History of the State University of New Jersey* (New Brunswick, NJ: Rutgers University Press, 2015); and *Scarlet and Black*, ed. Miya Carey, Marisa J. Fuentes, and Deborah Gray White, vol. 3, *Making Black Lives Matter at Rutgers, 1945–2020* (New Brunswick, NJ: Rutgers University Press, 2021). For Puerto Rican political and social activism within broader national struggles in the second half of the twentieth century, see Lorrin Thomas and Aldo A. Lauria-Santiago, *Rethinking the Struggle for Puerto Rican Rights* (New York: Routledge, 2019), especially Chapter 3, "Mass Mobilizations for Social Justice, 1966–1973."

5   This research is part of the Rutgers Latino and Caribbean Memory Project, a collaborative archival and oral history initiative within the Department of Latino and Caribbean Studies. We began this work in 2016 with the Aresty Research Assistant Program (co-principal investigators Carlos Decena, Kathleen López, and Yolanda Martínez-San Miguel and students Mina Afayee, Deandrah Cameron, Amanda Rivera, and Jonathan Vides), and we were later joined by Asela Laguna and Aldo Lauria-Santiago. The project is grateful for support in 2022–2023 from the Institute for the Study of Global Racial Justice through a grant awarded to the Latino Studies Research Institute and from the Latino New Jersey History Project. We thank Thomas Frusciano and Erika Gorder of Rutgers University Libraries Special Collections and University Archives (RUL-SCUA) and Paul Clemens of the Department of History. We also thank Carie Rael, contributor to the Latino New Jersey History Project and Scarlet and Black, for sharing digitized documents during the COVID-19 pandemic.

6   Other Spanish-speaking residents included Cubans, Dominicans, and South Americans. After the Cuban Revolution of 1959, Cuban exiles—initially mostly upper-middle class and professionals—concentrated in Union City and West New York.

7   Kal Wagenheim, *"Thorough and Efficient" Public School Education for Puerto Rican Children in New Jersey* (Newark, NJ: Puerto Rican Consortium for a Thorough and Efficient Education, 1974), 2.

8   The Puerto Rican Congress of New Jersey estimated the undercount to be "no less than 40 percent." Wagenheim, *Thorough and Efficient*, 3. The census reported a total Puerto Rican population on the U.S. mainland of 1,429,000 in 1970 (783,000 born in Puerto Rico and 646,000 on the mainland). U.S. Bureau of the Census, *1970*

*Census of Population. Subject Reports: Puerto Ricans in the United States* (Washington, DC: U.S. Government Printing Office, 1973), 11.
9   Zana Welborn and Dan Dolan, "Jersey's Puerto Ricans: High Hopes Turn into Squalid Nightmare," *Star-Ledger*, September 8, 1974, 1, 26.
10  Maxine N. Lurie, ed., *A New Jersey Anthology* (New Brunswick, NJ: Rutgers University Press, 2010), 375–378.
11  Thomas and Lauria-Santiago, *Rethinking the Struggle*, 87.
12  Wagenheim, *Thorough and Efficient*, 4.
13  For detailed data on income and education, see Kal Wagenheim, *Puerto Ricans in the Continental United States: An Uncertain Future* (Washington, DC: U.S. Commission on Civil Rights, 1976).
14  Hilda A. Hidalgo, *The Puerto Ricans of Newark, N.J.* (Newark: Aspira Inc. of New Jersey, 1971), 14, italics in original. While recognizing that Puerto Ricans encompassed a range of racial categories, community activists used the term "Puerto Rican" to differentiate their socioeconomic condition and cultural identity from that of U.S. Blacks and Whites.
15  Hidalgo, *Puerto Ricans of Newark*, 8.
16  "Convention Is Called 'Divisive,'" *Star-Ledger*, November 21, 1969, 18.
17  Wagenheim, *Puerto Ricans*, 92–143.
18  Paula Gilliland, "Puerto Rican Group Will Strive to Make Leaders," *Star-Ledger*, August 10, 1969, 22.
19  "Study Lists Puerto Rican Job Woes," *Jersey Journal and Jersey Observer*, May 30, 1974, 1, 14. The study was commissioned by the Puerto Rican Congress of New Jersey.
20  Clara E. Rodriguez, *Puerto Ricans: Born in the U.S.A.* (Boulder, CO: Westview Press, 1991), chap. 6 "Educational Dynamics."
21  "Educational Opportunity Fund," Official Site of the State of New Jersey, last updated April 17, 2024, https://www.nj.gov/highereducation/EOF/EOF_Eligibility.shtml.
22  "Agency Aids Puerto Ricans into College," 1, 13.
23  Josephine Nieves, "Puerto Rican Studies: Roots and Challenges," in Sánchez and Stevens-Arroyo, *Toward a Renaissance*; Canino, "40th Anniversary."
24  Sigfredo Carrión, Pablo Santana, and Jenny Díaz to Vice President Malcom D. Talbott, March 10, 1969, https://riseupnewark.com/wp-content/uploads/2017/02/Letter-from-Puerto-Rican-Organization-to-Malcolm-Talbott-March-10-1969.pdf; Richard P. McCormick, *The Black Student Protest Movement at Rutgers* (New Brunswick, NJ: Rutgers University Press, 1990); Clemens, *Rutgers since 1945*; Beatrice J. Adams, Jesse Bayker, Roberto C. Orozco, and Brooke A. Thomas, "A Second Founding: The Black and Puerto Rican Student Revolution at Rutgers-Camden and Rutgers-Newark," in Carey et al., *Scarlet and Black*, 3: 111–140.
25  Sigfredo Carrión, Panel 1, "Remembering the Rutgers Puerto Rican Student Movement of the 1970s," October 14, 2016, video livestream, https://livestream.com/rutgersitv/events/6428319.
26  Adams et al., "Second Founding," 112.
27  Melba Maldonado, Oral History Interview by Molly Graham, October 9, 2014, Rutgers Oral History Archives (unprocessed).
28  Sigfredo Carrión and Black community leader Amiri Baraka formed the People's Committee Against Police Brutality and Repression to negotiate with Mayor Kenneth Gibson. Nicole Torres, "Newark's 1974 Puerto Rican Riots through Oral Histories," *NJS: An Interdisciplinary Journal* 4 no. 2 (2018): 212–229, 226.

29 Clemens, *Rutgers since 1945*, 179.
30 Gualberto Medina, Panel 1, "Remembering."
31 Clemens, *Rutgers since 1945*, 40; "Our History," Rutgers School of Environmental and Biological Sciences, accessed April 19, 2021, https://sebs.rutgers.edu/about/our-history.php. Rutgers College became coeducational in 1971–1972.
32 For an in-depth examination of the goals and evolution of Livingston College that incorporates an architectural perspective, see Paul G. E. Clemens and Carla Yanni, "The Early Years of Livingston College, 1964–1973: Revisiting the 'College of Good Intentions,'" *Journal of the Rutgers University Libraries* 68, no. 2 (2016): 71–114. Livingston College was named after the first postcolonial governor of New Jersey, William Livingston.
33 Ernest A. Lynton to Lawrence Howard, May 29, 1968, Danforth Foundation, St. Louis, Missouri, box 1, folder 39, Office of the Dean of Livingston College (Ernest A. Lynton), RG 21/A0/04, Rutgers University Libraries Special Collections and University Archives (hereafter RUL-SCUA).
34 Ernest A. Lynton to William J. Kolodinsky, January 29, 1969, Director of Undergraduate Admissions, box 2, folder 39, RG 21/A0/04, RUL-SCUA.
35 Canino, "40th Anniversary," 5. Before 1969, only a handful of Puerto Rican students attended the New Brunswick campus, including several Douglass College women who were admitted from 1967 to 1969. Despite their isolation, Gloria Soto, Diane Maldonado, Diane Miranda, and Zaida Josefina "Josie" Torres became involved with cross-campus efforts to pressure the administration for more Puerto Rican students, faculty, and staff. For a detailed discussion of their experiences, see Kaisha Esty, Whitney Fields, and Carie Rael, "Black and Puerto Rican Student Experiences and Their Movements at Douglass College, 1945–1974," in Carey et al., *Scarlet and Black*, 3:74–103.
36 More than a secretary, Vilma Pérez served as the backbone of the department from 1970 through 1993. After leading the department from 1970 to 1974 and 1979 to 1989, Maria Canino continued to work as a scholar and advocate of education and public policy and is professor emerita in Public Administration, Rutgers-Newark.
37 Canino, "40th Anniversary," 6, 8.
38 Margaret Rivera, Panel 2, "Remembering."
39 Ronnie Lovler, "On Campus in New Jersey: Salsa Makes the Scene at Livingston College," *Sunday San Juan Star Magazine*, December 3, 1972; Margaret Rivera, Panel 2, "Remembering."
40 Margaret Rivera, Oral History Interview by Yolanda Martínez-San Miguel, March 6, March 20, and April 18, 2021, Rutgers Oral History Archives (unprocessed), conducted for the Rutgers Latino and Caribbean Memory Project.
41 "Annual Report 1970–1971, Puerto Rican Studies Departmental Review (October 1974)," box 1, Department of Puerto Rican and Hispanic Caribbean Studies, RG 16/B25/01, RUL-SCUA.
42 Canino, "40th Anniversary," 8; "Annual Report 1973–1974," box 1, Department of Puerto Rican and Hispanic Caribbean Studies, RG 16/B25/01, RUL-SCUA.
43 Consuelo Martínez-Reyes, "Gender, Homosexuality, the Diasporic Experience, and Other Key Themes in Víctor Fragoso's Theater," *Centro Journal* 19, no. 2 (2017): 104–133, 128.
44 Martínez-Reyes, "Gender, Homosexuality."
45 "Annual Report 1974–1975," box 1, Department of Puerto Rican and Hispanic Caribbean Studies, RG 16/B25/01, RUL-SCUA.

46  Mercedes Valle, Panel 2, "Remembering"; Mercedes Valle, Oral History Interview by Aziel Rosado, July 13, 2018, 5, Rutgers Oral History Archives, https://oralhistory.rutgers.edu/alphabetical-index/interviewees/2256-valle-mercedes.
47  "Annual Report, 1973–1974." Prominent organizations such as the John Hay Whitney Foundation, Ford Foundation, and National Endowment for the Humanities supported this community-engaged research, signaling growing awareness of the importance of minority issues.
48  Ismael García-Colón, *Colonial Migrants at the Heart of Empire: Puerto Rican Workers on U.S. Farms* (Berkeley: University of California Press, 2020), 3.
49  In 1971, the John Hay Whitney Foundation awarded Maria Canino a major grant of over $60,000 for the eighteen-month study of Puerto Rican farmworkers in southern New Jersey; "Annual Report 1973–1974"; Luis Nieves Falcón (1929–2014) was a sociologist at the University of Puerto Rico, lawyer, and lifelong advocate for Puerto Rican human rights and sovereignty.
50  "Report on the Activities of the Puerto Rican Migrant Study Project," August 25, 1972, Department of Puerto Rican and Hispanic Caribbean Studies, box 8, RG 16/B25/01, RUL-SCUA.
51  Elias Rivera Field Notes, box 8, RG 16/B25/01, RUL-SCUA.
52  Eduardo Voluntud to Department of Puerto Rican Studies, May 9, 1973, Livingston College, Department of Puerto Rican and Hispanic Caribbean Studies, box 6, RG 16/B25/01, RUL-SCUA.
53  "Annual Report 1973–1974."
54  Carlos Piñeiro was acting chair from 1974 to 1977 and served on the New Brunswick Board of Education. "Annual Report 1976–1977," Department of Puerto Rican and Hispanic Caribbean Studies, box 1, RG 16/B25/01, RUL-SCUA.
55  Rivera, Oral History Interview.
56  Hidalgo, *Puerto Ricans in Newark*, 17.
57  Debbie Brookmeyer, "Puerto Rican Day a First for State," *The Caellian*, April 10, 1970, 2.
58  Poet Martin Espada noted that, before its publication, "we could not find a book by a Puerto Rican writer in the English language about the experience of that community, in that voice, with that tone and subject matter." Joseph Berger, "Piri Thomas Dies at 83: Spanish Harlem Author," *New York Times*, October 20, 2011, B18.
59  "Discovery Day Celebrated," *Black Voice/Carta Boricua*, November 26, 1974, 1, 5. In 1970 Bayard students were classified as 5 percent White, 49 percent Black, and 46 percent Other (principally Puerto Rican), according to New Brunswick Board of Education Minutes from February 3 and April 7, 1970. Chris Rasmussen, "Creating Segregation in the Era of Integration: School Consolidation and Local Control in New Brunswick, New Jersey, 1965–1976," *History of Education Quarterly* 57, no. 4 (2017): 480–514.
60  "Reporte de Reggie Morales sobre las experiencias de campo del estudio," September 20, 1972, Department of Puerto Rican and Hispanic Caribbean Studies, box 8, RG 16/B25/01, RUL-SCUA.
61  At the 2016 symposium, Ivette Méndez read to the audience from a 1973 article she published about the efforts for Puerto Rican admissions to Douglass College. Ivette Méndez, "Increased Admissions by United Effort," *The Caellian*, December 13, 1973.
62  Memorandum from Maria Canino to Dean Ernest Lynton, March 13, 1972, Department of Puerto Rican and Hispanic Caribbean Studies, box 6, RG 16/B25/01, RUL-SCUA.

63 Clemens, *Rutgers since 1945*, 180.
64 Alfonso A. Narvaez, "Puerto Ricans at Colleges Triple," *New York Times*, October 14, 1972, 71.
65 Clemens, *Rutgers since 1945*, 174. A total of 1,598 Spanish-speaking students were enrolled in fifteen state colleges in 1972. Alfonso Roman, *Educational Opportunities and the Hispanic College Student: Final Report on Needs Assessment of the Processes, Programs, and Services Used to Enroll Spanish-Speaking Students in Higher Education in New Jersey* (Trenton: Puerto Rican Congress of New Jersey, 1974), 6.
66 "Annual Report 1975–1976," Department of Puerto Rican and Hispanic Caribbean Studies, box 1, RG 16/B25/01, RUL-SCUA. During the fiscal crisis of 1975, the City University of New York chancellor declared Puerto Rican studies programs to be "prime candidates for elimination," and programs and full-time faculty were subsequently cut. Nieves, "Puerto Rican Studies," 7.
67 "Annual Report 1975–1976."
68 Clemens, *Rutgers since 1945*, 177.
69 Dan Lazare, "Pickets Protest RU Failure to Hire Hispanic Employes [sic]," *Daily Home News*, 12 May 1977, 32.
70 Lazare, "Pickets Protest RU Failure."
71 Robert Steyer, "Puerto Rican Group Claims Bias at CMDNJ," *Star-Ledger*, July 6, 1978, 14.
72 Valle, Oral History Interview.
73 Carlos Piñeiro, Oral History Interview by Asela Laguna, January 18, 2021, Rutgers Oral History Archives (unprocessed), conducted for the Rutgers Latino and Caribbean Memory Project.
74 Elizabeth Jiménez, Oral History Interview by Yolanda Martínez-San Miguel, August 3, 2021, Rutgers Oral History Archives (unprocessed), conducted for the Rutgers Latino and Caribbean Memory Project.
75 Letter from Carmen Nelly Celpa, May 9, 1977, Department of Puerto Rican and Hispanic Caribbean Studies, box 1, RG 16/B25/01, RUL-SCUA.
76 Carmela Vetri, "Hispanics Fearful of Reorganization Plan," *Daily Targum*, October 23, 1980. Billy Delgado is a well-known attorney in Perth Amboy who entered the mayoral race in 2012.
77 Clemens, *Rutgers since 1945*, 40.
78 "What's in a Name?" flyer, Interdepartmental Correspondence 1996–1997, Department of Puerto Rican and Hispanic Caribbean Studies Archives (unprocessed).
79 Hudson County Office of Hispanic Affairs to Richard Foley, March 31, 1997, Dean of Faculty of Arts and Sciences, Rutgers University, Interdepartmental Correspondence 1996–1997, Department of Puerto Rican and Hispanic Caribbean Studies Archives (unprocessed). The letter was signed by the director of the Hudson County Office of Hispanic Affairs, the president of the Jersey City Borinquen Lions Club, the president of the Jersey City Puerto Rican Day Parade and Festival, and two trustees of the Jersey City Board of Education.
80 John R. Logan, "The New Latinos: Who They Are, Where They Are," Lewis Mumford Center for Comparative Urban and Regional Research, University at Albany, September 10, 2001, 8; Richard Brand, "The Second Great Wave: Hispanic Immigrants Are Changing the Face of Central Jersey," *New York Times*, May 28, 2000, NJ1, 10.
81 In 2016 the department changed its name again to the Department of Latino and Caribbean Studies.
82 Joan Verdon, "Uniting Student Radicals Anew," *The Record*, February 7, 1988, A23, 27.

83  Clemens, *Rutgers since 1945*, 45–46.
84  Andrew Harris Stevens, "Racism at Rutgers: An Ugly Issue Goes Ignored," *Daily Targum*, November 16, 1987, 1, 4.
85  Evelyn Apgar, "Challenge '89 Committed to Fighting Racism at RU," *Central Jersey Home News*, March 19, 1989, 15, B2.
86  In 1975, Lambda Theta Alpha was established at Kean University in Union, New Jersey, as the first Latina sorority in the nation, "It Began with a Vision," Lambda Theta Alpha Latin Sorority, accessed April 19, 2021, http://lambdalady.org/about-us/history/. The Rutgers-New Brunswick chapter was established in 1987.
87  Saskia Cipriani, Oral History Interview by Luz Sandoval and Aziel Rosado, June 20, 2019, 8, Rutgers Oral History Archives, https://oralhistory.rutgers.edu/alphabetical-index/interviewees/2267-cipriani-saskia-leo.
88  The Center for Latino Arts and Culture was established in 1992 with Isabel Nazario as founding director. It stemmed from the former Office of Hispanic Arts, an organization that promoted Latino/a New Jersey artists since 1976.
89  Rutgers Future Scholars, https://futurescholars.rutgers.edu/.
90  The service-learning course was developed by the Department of Africana Studies and is cross-listed with the Department of Latino and Caribbean Studies.
91  "Meet Carimar Andujar: Rutgers Student & Immigration Activist Who Faces Possible Deportation Today," *Democracy Now!*, May 9, 2017, https://www.democracynow.org/2017/5/9/meet_carimer_andujar_rutgers_student_immigration.
92  "Degree Attainment for Latino Students (2017–2018), United States," Latino College Completion: New Jersey, Excelencia in Education, www.EdExcelencia.org.
93  Lovler, "On Campus in New Jersey."
94  Clemens, *Rutgers since 1945*, 175. "Annual Report 1972–1973," box 1, Department of Latino and Hispanic Caribbean Studies, RG 16/B25/01, RUL-SCUA. The five students who double majored in Puerto Rican studies were Angelo Mercado (economics), Manuel Norat (political science), Charles Roche (political science), Luz Towns (psychology), and Mercedes Valle (political science).
95  Rivera, Oral History Interview.
96  Valle, Oral History Interview.
97  Maldonado, Oral History Interview. La Raza is "a bilingual, multi-service, non-profit organization dedicated to meeting the social service, immigration, educational, and leadership development needs of low-income families and individuals." See www.larazacrc.org.
98  The Legal Education and Action Program was initiated by the Puerto Rican Community Coalition and Camden Regional Legal Services. Richard Phalon Jr., "Aid Sought for Puerto Ricans," *New York Times*, May 19, 1974, 77; Ivette Méndez, "Immigrant Now in Charge of Developing State Commerce," *Star-Ledger*, February 6, 1994, 15.

# Notes on Contributors

YAMIL AVIVI has a PhD in American culture from the University of Michigan. His work focuses on the intersection of queer and Latino studies and he has written on Latino Muslims as well. He is currently a postdoctoral fellow at Penn State University.

JENNIFER AYALA is a professor of education at Saint Peter's University where she also directs the Center for Undocumented Students. She has a PhD in psychology from the City University of New York's Graduate Center. Her publications focus on education, community, and health education.

ULLA D. BERG is an associate professor in the Departments of Latino and Caribbean Studies and Anthropology at Rutgers University, New Brunswick. She has a PhD in anthropology from New York University. She is the author of *Mobile Selves: Race, Migration and Belonging between Peru and the US*.

GIOVANI BURGOS is an assistant professor in the Department of Sociology and Criminal Justice, Adelphi University. He has a PhD in sociology from Indiana University. His research interests center on the pathways that link structural disadvantages to the well-being of marginalized populations.

ELSA CANDELARIO is a professor of professional practice at the Rutgers University School of Social Work. She has an MSW from Columbia University. She served as member of the New Jersey governor's Blue-Ribbon Advisory Panel on Immigrant Integration and has also served as chairperson of the New Jersey Latino Health Advisory Committee.

**LAURA CURRAN** (PhD, University of California, Berkeley) is dean of the School of Social Work at the University of Connecticut. She was coprincipal investigator on a grant-funded project to create a certificate program to train social work students to work in Latino communities and oversaw development of courses focused on Latino populations.

**LILIA FERNÁNDEZ** is a professor in the Department of History at the University of Illinois, Chicago. Previously, she was the Henry Rutgers Term Chair in Latino Studies at Rutgers University in New Brunswick, NJ, and also served as a professor at The Ohio State University. She is a three-time Ford Foundation fellowship awardee and the author of *Brown in the Windy City: Mexicans and Puerto Ricans in Postwar Chicago*, as well as many other book chapters, articles and essays.

**ISMAEL GARCÍA COLÓN** is an anthropologist with a PhD from the University of Connecticut. He is a professor at the College of Staten Island and Graduate Center of the City University of New York. His most recent book is *Colonial Migrants at the Heart of Empire: Puerto Rican Workers on U.S. Farms*.

**BENJAMIN LAPIDUS** is a Grammy-nominated musician who has performed and recorded throughout the world as a bandleader and supporting musician. As a scholar he has published widely on Latin music, and he is a professor at John Jay College of Criminal Justice and the Graduate Center, City University of New York.

**JOHANA LONDOÑO** is an associate professor in the Department of Latino and Caribbean Studies at Rutgers, New Brunswick. Her PhD is in American studies from New York University. She is the author of *Abstract Barrios: The Crises of Latinx Visibility in Cities*.

**KATHLEEN LÓPEZ** is an associate professor in the Departments of Latino and Caribbean Studies and History at Rutgers University, New Brunswick. She received a PhD in history from the University of Michigan. She is the author of *Chinese Cubans: A Transnational History*. At Rutgers she co-coordinates the Latino Studies Research Initiative.

**ALDO A. LAURIA SANTIAGO** is a professor in the Departments of Latino and Caribbean Studies and History at Rutgers University New Brunswick. He has a PhD in history from the University of Chicago. His recent publications include *Rethinking the Struggle for Puerto Rican Rights* (coauthored by Lorrin Thomas). At Rutgers he directs the Center for Latin American Studies and the Puerto Rico Archival Collaboration, He also co-coordinates the Latino Studies Research Initiative.

Notes on Contributors • 375

WILLIAM SUÁREZ GÓMEZ is an assistant professor in the Department of Health Equity, Administration and Technology at Lehman College, City University of New York. Suárez holds an MS in Agricultural Science from the University of Puerto Rico-Mayaguez. His PhD is in International Development and Economics Studies from the University of Bradford in the United Kingdom.

GIANNCARLO MUSCHI is an adjunct professor of Latino Studies at St. Edwards University. He received his PhD in history from the University of Houston. His recent publications focus on Latino music and Peruvians in New Jersey.

MELANIE Z. PLASENCIA earned her PhD from the University of California, Berkeley. From 2021 to 2024, she was the Cesar Chávez Postdoctoral Fellow at Dartmouth College and is now an assistant professor of Sociology at Rutgers University, Newark. She completed her undergraduate studies in the Department of Latino and Caribbean Studies at Rutgers University.

ANA Y. RAMOS-ZAYAS is the Frederick Clifford Ford Professor of Ethnicity, Race, and Migration and professor of American studies and women's, gender, and sexuality studies at Yale University. She has a PhD in anthropology from Columbia University. Her most recent book is titled *Parenting Empires: Class, Whiteness, and the Moral Economy of Privilege in Latin America*.

ELENA SABOGAL is a sociologist with a PhD from Florida International University. She was formerly an associate professor and chair in the Department of Women's and Gender Studies at William Paterson University. Currently, she is a visiting scholar with the Center for Latin American Studies at Rutgers University. Her recent publications focus on Peruvian migration and Peruvians in the United States.

RAYMOND SÁNCHEZ MAYERS is professor emeritus at the Rutgers University School of Social Work. He was the founding director of the Latino/a Initiatives for Service, Training, and Assessment. He has a PhD from Brandeis University. His areas of interest include geographic information science, financial management for nonprofits, and issues related to Latinos.

ALEX F. TRILLO has a PhD in sociology from Stony Brook University (SUNY). He is an associate professor at Saint Peter's University. His recent publications focus on segregation and homicides in New York City and how homeless mothers create opportunities for mobility.

DANIELA VALDES is a PhD candidate in the Department of History at Rutgers University specializing in U.S.-based social movements and the carceral state.

Valdes's dissertation explores the political cultures of Black and Latinx trans/ nonbinary communities in the New York/New Jersey metropolitan area. Valdes is an oral historian and community researcher who collaborates with grassroots groups including the Rikers Public Memory Project and Movimiento Cosecha.

ANIL VENKATESH is an assistant professor in the Department of Mathematics and Computer Science Adelphi University. He has a PhD in mathematics from Duke University.

LYNA L. WIGGINS is professor emerita of urban planning at Bloustein School, Rutgers University. She has a PhD from the University of California, Berkeley. Wiggins's research interests focus on planning methods and computer applications in planning, particularly urban geographic information systems.

# Index

Note: Page numbers in italics denote a figure or table.

abakuá, 203, 218
Acevedo-Garcia, Dolores, 35
African Americans, 33–34, 50, 234; LGBTQ, 342; in Newark, 103–105; in New Brunswick, 232–233; women, 99–100
Afro-American Drum Sextet, 205
Afro-Cuban music, at La Esquina Habanera, 218–219
age patterns: on Bergenline Avenue, 84; demographics and, 16, 21. See also old age
aggression, 101
agricultural industry, in New Jersey, 137–138, 141–143, 149
Agricultural Workers Association, 146; Puerto Ricans in, 151
Agricultural Workers Organizing Committee (COTA), 151–152
Agricultural Workers Support Committee (CATA), 151
Alcalde, M. Cristina, 257
Alexander Hamilton Hotel, 124, 125
Algarín, Miguel, 357

Alicea, Jenesys, 296
Altamirano, Teofilo, 258, 260
alumni, Puerto Rican, 364–365
Álvarez, Chico, 213
Álvarez, Ernest, 208
American City Corporation, 233
American Civil Liberties Union (ACLU), 151
American Community Survey (ACS), 12, 233–234; data from, 37
American Cyanamide, 162
American Federation of Labor and Congress of Industrial Organizations (AFL-CIO), 177
Amtrak, 71n1
Andujar, Carimer, 364
anger, 109, 110
Annual Migrant Labor Report, 145
antidiscrimination efforts, 175–176
Antiterrorism and Effective Death Penalty Act, 316
Archdiocese of Newark, 272–273, *274*; immigration to, *281*
Aresty Research Assistant Program, 366n5

Art Plaza, 74n44
Art UC, 64, *65*
Arturos, Rodrigo, 204
Asbury Park, 204
Asian Americans, 16–17
ASPIRA, 354, 364
Atlantic City, 35
Augustine, Gilbert, 174
Avalos, Michael, 202
Avilés, Marco, 258
Azcuy, Guillermo, 207

Badillo, David A., 269
Baer, Byron M., 146
Bailey, Marlon, 343
ballroom scene, 335
ball subculture, 334
balseros, 201
Baraka, Amiri, 109, 110
Barrette, Michael, 63
barrioization, 59, 68, 70–71, 72n2
Bayard School, 359
Bayonne Hispanic Club, 161, 164
Beauchamp, Toby, 301–302
Ben Mardin's Riviera, 203
Berbary, Lisbeth A., 63
Bergen County, segregation in, 51–52
Bergen County Jail, 318

377

Bergenline Avenue, 202; age patterns on, 84; Bolivarian enclave on, 83–86; changes on, 94–95; clubs on, *210, 211*; conflict in, 90–93; Cuban music on, 207–209; Cubans on, 76, 79–83, 88–89, 91–92; diversity on, 77–79; Downtown, 79; education on, 84; geography of, 78–79; income on, 84–85; inequality on, 84–85; Puerto Ricans on, 76; residents of, 87–90; solidarity on, 86, 88–90, 93–94; Uptown, 79
Berman, Arthur, 244
Biden, Joe, 71n1
birthplaces, *13*
birth rates: demographics and, 16–17; teenage, 17–18
Bishops National Pastoral Plan, 272
Black Cubans, 70
Black Latinos, 36
Blackness, 99–100, 111
Black Organization of Students, 354
Black Panthers, 70
Black Power, 109
Black Pride, 103–104
Blake, Maria De Castro, 355
Bloustein, Edward J, 360
Boe, Carolina Sánchez, 323
Bolivarian enclave, on Bergenline Avenue, 83–86
Bonilla, Carlos, 319
Bonilla-Santiago, Gloria, 2, 136
Borjas, Lorena, 295, 296
"Born to Run," 67
Botelho, Ana Tereza, 98–100, 110
Bound Brook, 162
Branch Brook Park, 109
Brazilians, 110
Breezy Point, 61
Breul, Moritz, 61
Bridgeton, 16
British West Indians, 139
Broadway Sandwich Shop, 207
Brooklyn Heights, 66
Brothers, Jill, 146
*Brown v. Board of Education*, 50
bullying, 334; of LGBTQ people, 340

Bureau of Employment and Migration, 139
Bureau of Employment Security, 139
Burrill, Fred, 66
Burtch, Brian, 339
Bush, George W., 318
Buttigieg, Pete, 71n1

Cabrera, Abel, 104
Cadena, Marisol de la, 258
Cahill, James, 240, 241
Cahill, William T., 145
Caibarién, 202
CALCO, 162
California, 291–292
Callao, El, 324
Callegari, Manuela, 252
Camajuaní, 202
Camden, 11, 16, 134, 162, 165, 175; dissimilarity in, 38; Puerto Ricans in, 139–140
Camden County, 16
Camden Regional Legal Services, 145
Campbell, 162
Campo, Pupi, 205
Campos, Albizu, 181
Campos, Gracella, 205
Canino Arroyo, Maria Josefa, 2, 358, 368n36; grant awarded to, 369n49
*cantoras*, 259
Cape May, 149, 164
caregiving, 282
Caridad del Cobre, 90–91
Carlos, Don, 203
Carrasquillo, Ernesto, 145
Carrión, Sigfredo, 351, 355, 365
Casa Boricua, 360
Casino International, 212
Castillo, Pedro, 266n40
Castillo, Ralph, 168
Castle Island, 60
Catholic Church, 2–3, 69, 150–151, 269; Cubans in, 271–272; old age and, 275
Catholic Conference Campaign for Human Development, 151, 270
Celi, Nelly, 253, 262, 263
Celia Cruz Salsa Park, 78
Census Bureau, U.S., 11–13; data from, 37; on Mexican population, 246n1; on Paterson, 119; on Peruvians, 118–119, 127n1; on Puerto Ricans, *167, 186, 193*
censuses, 11–12, 14
Center for Latino Arts and Culture, 371n88
Central Americans: dissimilarity index for, *43, 47–48, 48*; isolation index for, *45*
Central Labor Council, 181
Central Railroad of New Jersey, 162
chain migration, 165, 201
Charanga 76, 209
Charanga Casino, 206
Cheung, Amy, 66
Chiapas, 294
Children's Health Insurance Program, 25
Christie, Chris, 318
Cine Tony, 208
Cipriani, Saskia Leo, 363
Círculo Español, 203–204
citizenship, 81, 86, 315; double, 172; neoliberalism and, 101; of Puerto Ricans, 159, 172
City Beautiful movement, 63
Civilian Conservation Corps, 135
Civil Rights Commission, U.S., 189
Civil Rights Committee, 177
Civil Rights Congress, in Paterson, 124–125
civil rights organizing, 50
Clemens, Paul, 366n5
Club Bene, 206
club kids, 336, 338
Club Los 7 Amigos, 177
Club MTV, 345
Coalition to Defend Lincoln Annex, 230
Cohen, Michael, 148
Colarusso, Florence, 201
Cold war, 80
Coll, Gabriel, 145
Colombia, 14–15, 278, 279
Colombians, 84
Colon, Sam, 185
colonialism, 160
Colón-Warren, Alice, 191
Columbia Fruit Farm, 148
coming out, 336–337

Commission on Civil Rights, 353
communism, 80; anti-communist actions in United States, 124
Community Education Center, Inc., 318
Congress of Industrial Organizations, 124, 176
Conjunto Caribe, 208
Consejo de Organizaciones Puertorriqueñas de New Jersey, 177
contract labor, 164
Contreras, Orlando, 208
CoreCivic, 320, 321
Corey, Dennis Andromeda, 336, 339, 342, 343–344
Corrections Corporation of America, 318
Cortez, Delia, 262
*Country and the City, The* (Williams), 106
COVID-19, 266n38; food insecurity and, 300–301; ICE monitoring, 330n48; long-haul symptoms, 299–300; Martínez on trauma from, 295–296; Méndez on, 300–301; in New Brunswick, 288–289, 291, 299–303; in New Jersey, 319–320; in New York City, 291–292; stay-at-home orders, 291; unemployment and, 291–292
crimmigration crisis, 316–317
Cruz, Celia, 209
Cuban Adjustment Act, 80
Cubanía, in New Jersey, 200–201
Cuban music: Afro-Cuban, 218–219; on Bergenline Avenue, 207–209; in New Jersey, 200–201; in 1950's, 204–205; in 1960s through 1990s, 209–218; press coverage of, 205–207; venues for, 207–208; from Villa Clara, 215–216
Cuban Revolution, 201, 205
Cubans, 2–3; on Bergenline Avenue, 76, 79–83, 88–89, 91–92; Black, 70; in Catholic Church, 271–272; in Hoboken, 68; in Hudson County, 201–202; income of, 182; incorporation of, 92; isolation index for, 42–43; migrants, 65, 80–81, 92; migration of, 200–201, 200–201`; as percentage of Hispanic population, *17*; segregation of, 51; in Union City, 68–69
*Cubans of Union City, The* (Prieto), 80
Cuban War of Independence, 159
Cubillas, Carlos, 123, 125, 127
Cuentas, Manuel, 119–120, 122
Cugat, Xavier, 205
Cumberland County, 15, 16, 36, 145
Curley, John, 206

Dámaso García, Jose, 209
dancers, 203
Davila, Maritza, 262
Decennial Census, 11; data from, 37
de facto segregation, 33
Deferred Action for Childhood Arrivals, 364
DeFino, Anthony, 82
DeGenova, Nicholas P., 315
deindustrialization, 70, 188
de jure segregation, 33
Delaney Hall, 318
Delgado Gomez, Juan, 181
Delia, Tia, 262
Democrats, 51; in Hudson County, 81–83
demographics, 11–12, *13*; age patterns, 16, *21*; birth rates and, 16–17; education and, 20–24; employment and, 20–24; family structure, 16–17; health insurance status and, 25–26; immigration and, 12–13; income and, 24–25; marriage rates and, 18–19; New Brunswick, 231–234; trends, 12–16
Denton, Nancy A., 33; on isolation index, 38
Department of Homeland Security, 318, 319
Department of Labor, U.S., 139

deportation regime, 315; in New Jersey, 321–326
Development Corporation of New Brunswick (DEVCO), 233, 239, 245, 290
Díaz, Arturo, 359
Diez, Javier Revilla, 61
DiFabio, Pat, 204
Dinzey-Flores, Zaire, 67
dissimilarity index: in Camden, 38; for Central Americans, *43*, 47–48, *48*; changes in, 38–39; for Dominicans, 47–48, *48*; formula for, 53; in New Jersey, *40*, *42*; percent change in, *47*; in Salem County, 38; segregation and, 30, 32–33, 37–38; for South Americans, *43*, *49*; in Sussex County, 39–40; trends in, 39–40, *47*; in Warren County, 39–40
Divas, Armando, 149
diversity, 11–12; on Bergenline Avenue, 77–79; horizontal, 77; integration conflated with, 53; in United States, 28–29; vertical, 77
Division Against Discrimination, 175
DJ Rodney RodWone Rios, 345
Dominicans, 16, 36, 42, 86; dissimilarity index for, 47–48, *48*; migrants, 84–85; as percentage of Hispanic population, *18*
Domino sugar factory, 66
Doña Isabel, 257
Doroshow, Ceyenne, 296
double citizenship, 172
Douglass College, 356, 369n61
Dover, 148
Dreby, Joanna, 322
dropout rates, 21
Duke University, 359
Dulanto, Carlos, 122, 124
*dulzura*, 199–200

economic crisis, 1970s, 192–193
Ecuador, 14–15, 268, 323
Ecumenical Farmworkers Ministry, 150–151
Edgar F. Hurff Company, 137, 162
Edison, 182–184

education: access to, 352–354;
activism, 365n3; attainment,
22; on Bergenline Avenue, 84;
demographics and, 20–24;
dropout rates, 21; postsecondary, 235–236; public schools,
234–237; of Puerto Ricans,
166–167, 174, 352–354; SAT
scores, 234–237; school
demolition, 237–239; student
activism, 354–356, 362–363.
*See also specific topics*
Educational Opportunity Fund
(EOF), 354
Elberon Group, 320
Elena, Rita, 208
Elizabeth Detention Center
(EDC), 317, 319; protests
against, *320*
Elizabeth High School: fashion
show at, 342; LGBTQ
people at, 332–339; placemaking in, 342–343; silenced
teachers at, 340–341; voguing at, 345–348
Ellis Island, 60, 124, 316
Embroidery Plaza, 65
*Embroidery Tree*, 66
Emergency Labor Supply
Program, 137
Emersion Radio, 180
*emigrante puertorriqueño, El*
(Nieves Falcón), 358
emotional intelligence, 100
employment, 23; demographics
and, 20–24; gendered
nature of, 23–24, *24*; high
rates of, 22–23; immigration
and, 21–22; of men, 23–24;
of Puerto Ricans, 192;
unemployment, 180; of
women, 23–24. *See also
specific topics*
Employment Security Act, in
Puerto Rico, 139–140
Employment Service, U.S.,
137
Episcopal Church, 150–151
equity gap, 364
Espada, Martin, 369n58
Esquina Habanera, La:
Afro-Cuban music at,
218–219; rhumba at, 218–219
Essex, 15
Essex County, 104, 318

Essex County Correctional
Facility Task Force, 322–323
ethnicity, 170; occupations by,
in New Jersey, *189*
evenness, 30–32
Executive Order No. 104, 291
exposure, segregation and,
30–33
exposure index, 33
exurbs, 35

Fair Employment Practice
Committee, 175
Fair Housing Act, 33
Fajardo, José, 208
family structure, demographics
and, 16–17
Farm Labor Program (FLP),
136, 139, 140, 152, 153, 158n82
farm labor regimes, Puerto
Ricans and, 136–139
Farrés, Osvaldo, 209
Fashion Institute of Technology,
64, 184
Faulkner, Joseph, 171, 172, 180
Fedders factory, 182–184
feelings, structure of, 101–102,
108–109
Feketie, Michael, 171, 272
Feliciano, Jose, 209
Feliz, Alby, 207
Fernández, Albert, 212
Fernández, Lilia, 291, 303
Fernandez, Lucio, 64–65
Fernández Fragoso, Victor,
357
Ferré, Luis A., 147
Ferry Street, 111
Fields, Jean Paul, 336–337, 338,
346
Figueroa, Hector, 181
First Friends of New Jersey and
New York, 315
Florida, Richard, 66
Fluoro Electrical, 185–186
food insecurity: during
COVID-19 pandemic,
300–301; Méndez on, 300
Ford Foundation, 205
Frías, Luisa, 148
Friedman, Samuel, 138–139
"From Aguada to Dover"
(Wagenheim, O.), 136
*From Puerto Rico to Philadelphia* (Carmen Whalen), 136

Frusciano, Thomas, 366n5
Fulop, Steven, 53

Gallardo, Vitaliano, 262
Galster, George, 190
Garcia, Felipe, 353
García Colón, Ismael, 154n5
Garcia Mendoza, Hector, 319
Garden State Service
Cooperation Association
(GSSCA), 138, 141, 149,
153
garment district, New York
City, 65
gated communities, 67–68
gateway, 60–64; architectural
definition, 63; defining,
58; etymology of, 62–63;
functions of, 59; keywords
approach to, 59–60; Latinx
experiences in, 68–71; New
York City as, 60–61; Union
City as, 59, 70–71
Gateway, The, 71n1
Gateway Development
Corporation, 58
Gateway National Recreation
Area, 61
Gatica, Lucho, 207
Gayle, Denise, 363
gender, 99–100, 293–294;
employment and, 23–24, *24*;
in indigenous communities,
298–299; migration and,
253–257, 295; in Peru, 257
gentrification, 40; in New York
City, 66–67; warehouse
conversion, 66
*George Washington, SS*, 162
Gerena Valentin, Gilberto,
184
Gerontological Society on
Aging, 284n1
*Get That Freak* (Haskell &
Burtch), 339
Gibson, Kenneth, 105
Glassboro, 140, *144*; Puerto
Ricans at, 138–139
Glassboro Service Association
(GSA), 135, 153
Gloucester County, 15–16, 145
Goetsch, John, 188
Golash-Boza, Tanya, 322, 323
Gonzales, Diana, 296, 298–299
Gorder, Erika, 366n5

Gordon, Milton, 269
Grace Line, 118
Granados, Georgina, 207
Great Depression, 118, 122; Puerto Ricans in, 137
Grenet, Eliseo, 204–205
Grewal, Grubir, 314
*guaguitas*, 78–79, 87, *87*
Guaracheros, Los, 208
Guarnaccia, Peter, 3
Guatemala, 294
Guatemalans, 21
Güines, 202
Gutierrez, Daniel, 262
Gutierrez, Joaquin, 184–185
Guzmán, Manuel, 307n34

Habana Madrid, 207
*hacer patria*, 267n59
Hackensack, 52
Hale, Charles, 105
Hall, Stuart, 59
Haskell, Rebecca, 339
Havana Brass, 212
Havana Philharmonic Orchestra, 203
Havana Stars, 203
Head Start, 173
health care: for LGBTQ people, 295–296; Méndez on, 295–296
health insurance status, demographics and, 25–26
Hendricks, George, 243
Heritage, Carleton E., 150
Hermanas Cano Combo, 208
*hermandades*, 259
Hernández Colón, Rafael, 147
Herrera, Gioconda, 327n14
Heyer, Gruel & Associates, 64
Hidalgo, Hilda, 2, 109, 354, 357, 361
High, Steven, 66
High Point, 149
high school diplomas, 20–21
Hijos de Borinquen, 177
Hispanic population: Cubans as percentage of, *17*; defining, 25n1; Dominicans as percentage of, *18*; Mexicans as percentage of, *19*; in New Brunswick, 233–234; percentages of, by county, *15*, *32*; total, in New Jersey counties, *46*; in United States, 12

Hispanic-Serving Institutions, 26n2
Hispanics in the Archdiocese in Newark, 272
HIV, 342
Hoboken, 62, 66, 170; community organizing in, 171–175; Cubans in, 68; Puerto Ricans in, 168
Hobteld, Richard, 123
Holy Family Church, 268; establishment of, 270–271; festivities in, 280–282; Latinx community in, 277; old age and, 275–284; shared purpose in, 282–284; volunteerism in, 282–284
homeownership, 166
homophobia, 339–340
Hondagneu-Sotelo, Pierrette, 256
Hondurans, 21
Honduras, 294
Hora, Jack, 187
hormone therapy, 301
house families, 334
Hudson County, 4, 15, 37, 61, 319; Cuban community of, 201–202; Democratic Party in, 81–83; *música campesina* in, 215–218; *punto guajiro* in, 215–218; residential segregation in, 30
Human Relations Commission, 174
Hurricane Eta, 302–303
hyper-barrios, 77
hypersegregation, 33

identity: cultural, of Puerto Ricans, 353, 367n14; national, of Peru, 257–261; of New Jersey, 1; self-identification, of Latinos, 93
Iglesias, Enrique, 209
Ignacio Lanza, José, 205
Illegal Immigration Reform and Immigrant Responsibility Act (IIRAIRA), 316
Illinois, 291–292
Immigrant Trust Directive, 314
immigration, 2, 5n2, 128n5; to Archdiocese of Newark, *281*; control measures, 305n9;

demographics and, 12–13; employment and, 21–22; to New Jersey, 139–143, 164, 273–274; to New York City, 60, 62; of Puerto Ricans, 134–135; regulation of, 139–143; sexuality and, 295; undocumented immigrants, 12–13, 279–280, 292, 313–314; to Union City, 270–271; waves of, *281*
Immigration and Customs Enforcement (ICE), 321; arrests by, 319, 321, 327n12; COVID-19 monitoring by, 330n48; deportations by, 324–325; migrants arrested by, 319, 321; in New Jersey, 314–315
Immigration and Nationality Act (INA), 314
Immigration and Naturalization Service (INS), 317
immigration detention: history of, 315–316; in New Jersey, 316–321
immigration enforcement: in New Jersey, 314; patchwork approach to, 314
income: on Bergenline Avenue, 84–85; of Cubans, 182; demographics and, 24–25; in New Jersey, 166; of Puerto Ricans, 166, 182, *183*, *190*
indigenous peoples, 298
industrialization, 135, 178
Industrial Production and Novelty Workers AFL, 181
industrial reserve, 308
inequality: on Bergenline Avenue, 84–85; in New Brunswick, 292
Institute for the Study of Global Racial Justice, 366n5
integration, diversity conflated with, 53
International Brotherhood of Electrical Workers (IBEW), 185–186, 188
International Festival, 280, *283*
International Ladies' Garment Workers' Union (ILGWU), 184

International Union of Electrical Workers (IUE), 183–184
Irakere, 206
Ironbound, 110–111, 113n24
Ironbound Improvement District, 111
isolation index, 33; of Central Americans, 45; of Cubans, 42–43; formula for, 53; Massey and Denton on, 38; of Mexicans, 44; in New Jersey, 40, 41, 44; percent change in, 47; of Puerto Ricans, 42–43; as segregation measure, 37–38; of South Americans, 45; trends in, 40, 42–43, 47
Italians, 109

Jacobs, Jane, 63
Jacobson, Joel R., 149
James, Sharpe, 103
Jersey City, 35, 53, 60, 62; Puerto Ricans in, 171–172
Jersey Cuban Boys, 212
*Jersey Journal*, 171
Jewish people, 104
Jimaguas, Los, 213
Jim Crow laws, 33
Jiménez de Wagenheim, Olga, 2, 136
John Hay Whitney Foundation, 369n49
Johnson & Johnson, 231, 233
Jordan, Angelo, 206
Jottar, Berta, 218
Jourdain, Erin, 336, 337
Jourdan, Geraude Scarface, 336
Junco, Omar, 212

Kassindja, Fauziya, 317
Keyport, 140
keywords, 59–60
*Keywords* (Williams), 59
*Keywords for Latina/o Studies*, 59–60
Kille, Williard B., 138
Kimy, Los, 208
Kingston, 181
Knauer, Lisa Maya, 218
knowable communities, 108–109
Korean War, 125

Labeija, Denasia, 336
labor: contract, 164; farm labor regimes, 136–139; of migrants, 297–298; migratory, 135–136; movement in Paterson, 124; noncontract, 149; rights in New Jersey, 148–152; of trans people, 297–298; unionization, 175, 179–182, 187–188
labor camps: privacy in, 143–144; Puerto Rican migrants in, 143–148
Laguna, Asela, 366n5
Lambda Theta Alpha, 371n86
language, 88, 174–175, 180
Latinization, 80
Latin music, histories of, 200
Latino/a studies, 2–5, 362–364
*See also specific topics*
Latino Justice, 244
Latino New Jersey History Project, 366n5
Latinx communities, 1–2, 86; conflict within, 90–92; defining, 304n4; gateway as experienced by, 68–71; in Holy Family Church, 277; identification of, 14; identities of, 76–77; LGBTQ people in, 294; national origin of, 14f; in New Brunswick, 289; respectability politics and, 289; segregation patterns, 35–36; shared purpose in, 282–284; solidarity of, 77; in Union City, 275–276. *See also specific topics*
Lee, Hilda, 208
Legion de Maria, La, 277
Legion of Mary, 282–283
Levin, Saul, 152
LGBTQ people, 288–289; Black, 342; bullying of, 340; community-building, 342–348; discrimination against, 339–340; at Elizabeth High School, 332–339; health care for, 295–296; in Latinx communities, 294; marginalization of, 332–333; violence against, 293–295
Liceo Cubano, El, 201–202

Lima, 119–120, 253–254, 325–326
Limelight, 338
Lincoln Annex School, 237–239; fighting for, 240–244
Lincoln Tunnel, 61, 64, 67, 69
linguistics, 83–84
Livingston College, 356–360, 362; Puerto Rican alumni, 364–365
Lloyd (Judge), 176
*Loft Living* (Zukin), 66
Long Island City, 66
López, Israel, 208
López, Jeffrey, 212
López Landrón, Armando, 161
Luciano, Freddy, 212
Lupe, La, 199
Lynton, Ernest, 356

Machado, Gabriel, 214
Mack Molding Company, 124
Madonna, 345, 347
Malatino, Hil, 310n84
Maldonado, Diane, 368n35
Maldonado, Melba, 355, 365
Mallet, Marie, 90
Manati, 136
Manpower Development and Training Act (MDTA), 177
Marcantonio, Vito, 138
Marco Designs, 66
Maria Arguedas, Jose, 258
*Maria Juarez et al, v. New Brunswick Board of Education et al*, 244
Marianao, 207
marriage rates, 22; demographics and, 18–19
Martí, Virgilio, 208
Martin, Prince, 204
Martinez, Eleuterio, 180
Martínez, Felipe, 208, 213
Martinez, Grisselle, 68
Martínez, Mercedes, 288, 292; on COVID-19, 295–296; on discrimination, 302–303; shows organized by, 295–296
Martinez, Ruben Orlando, 7
Marzan, Gilbert, 192
mass detention, 317
Massey, Douglas S., on isolation index, 38

McCarrick, Theodore E., 273
McKinnon, Sara, 307n35
Medicaid, 25
Medicare, 25
Medina, Gualberto, 355
Melendez, Angel, 336, 349n14
Membiela, Ñico, 207
Memorial Presbyterian
 Church, 149
men, employment of, 23–24
Mendez, Cecilia, 258
Méndez, Ivette, 360, 369n61
Méndez, Lissa, 289, 292, *293*, 293–294, 299; on COVID-19, 300–301; on discrimination, 302–303; on food insecurity, 300; on health care, 295–296
Menendez, Robert, 81–82
Menendez, Robert, Jr., 82
Merceron, Mariana, 207
*Metapan, SS*, 202
meta-sentiment, 101
Methodist Episcopal Church, 60
Mexicans, 16, 42, 229–230; Census data on, 246n1; isolation index for, *44*; in New Brunswick, 290–291; as percentage of Hispanic population, *19*
Meyner, Robert B., *173*
Miami, 69
Middlesex County, 15, 47–48
Mier, Robert, 212
Miesmer, Chuck, 205
migrants: deportation of, 325; Dominican, 84–85; farmworkers, 139–143, 148–152, 358; human rights violations against, 323; ICE arrest of, 319, 321; in labor camps, 143–148; labor of, 297–298; in Newark, 100–101, 105; Peruvian, 80–81, 92, 117–118, 125–127, 254–257, 259–260; Puerto Rican, 134–139, 161–164, 171–173; undocumented, 324; in Union City, 70
migration, 36; chain, 165, 201; challenges of, 173; of Cubans, 200–201; gender and, 253–257, 295; from New York City, 166–167; patterns of, 117–118, 166–167, 182, 200–201; Peruvian, 119, 125–126, 254–255; racialized, 63; regulation of, 139–143; religion and, 269–272; social hierarchies challenged by, 258; of Tello, 126; trading routes and settlement, 118–122; to Union City, 269. *See also* immigration
Migration Division, 174–176
Migration Policy Institute, 12–13
migratory labor, in New Jersey, 135–136
Mi Guitarra, 207
Miller, Bill, 205
Millville, 141
Mims, Lilisa, 263
Mirabál, Nancy Raquel, 218
Miranda, Diane, 368n35
Mitchell, James P., 185
Model Cities, 170
Molina, Luis Angel, 351
Monmouth County, 176
Monserrat, Joseph, 182
Montanez, Jesse, 184
*Montclair Times*, 205
Montego Joe, 205
Morales, Flor, 257
Morales, Miguel, 327n14
Morales, Reginald, 359
Moran, Robyn, 63
Mount Laurel, 50
Mount Laurel Doctrine, 51, 53
Moyd, Wendell, 184
multiculturalism, 105
Muñoz, Jose, 335
Muñoz Angosto, Bernardo, 257
Murphy, Phil, 239, 291, 316, 321
Murray, David, 203
Murray, Hilda, 203
Muschi, Giancarlo, 254
Museo del Barrio, El, 358
*música campesina*, in Hudson County, 215–218
Musto, William, 81–82
*muxes*, 298
Myers, Fred, 101

*ñanigos*, 203
National Association of the Advancement of Colored People (NAACP), 147

National Education Association, 174
National Labor Relations Board (NLRB), 181
National Park Service, 61
Naturalization Act, 137
Nazario, Isabel, 371n88
NBC, 29–30
Negret, José, 203
neoliberalism, 110, 233; citizenship and, 101; emotional regime in Newark, 102–103; racialization under, 101
Newark, 60, 71n1; African Americans in, 103–105; industrial employment in, 178; migrants in, 100–101, 105; neoliberalized emotional regime in, 102–103; poetics of, 106–110; Puerto Ricans in, 104–105, 108–109, 355; "slum clearance," 102
Newark International Airport, 62
Newark Renaissance, 101–102, 103, 105
Newark Symphony Hall, 206
New Brunswick, 229, 325; African Americans in, 232–233; COVID-19 in, 288–289, 291, 299–303; demographics, 231–234; economy of, 231–234; Hispanic population in, 233–234; inequality in, 292; Latinx communities in, 289; Mexicans in, 290–291; population of, *232*; poverty in, 292; public schools in, 234–237; Puerto Ricans in, 233–234, 290–291; school demolition in, 237–239; trans people in, 290, 292–303; undocumented immigrants in, 292; urban renewal, 233; White communities in, 231
New Brunswick Mutual Aid, 303
New Brunswick Public Schools (NBPS), 234–237
New Brunswick Tomorrow, 290
New Deal, 137

New Jersey: agricultural industry in, 137–138, 141–143, 149; COVID-19 in, 319–320; Cubanía in, 200–201; Cuban music in, 200–201, 209–218; demographics of, 3; deportation in, 321–326; dissimilarity index in, *40*, *42*; Educational Opportunity Fund, 354; ICE in, 314–315; identity of, 1; immigration detention in, 316–321; immigration enforcement in, 314; immigration to, 139–143, 164, 273–274; income in, 166; isolation index in, 40, *41*, *44*; labor rights in, 148–152; migratory labor in, 135–136; occupations by ethnicity in, *189*; population of Puerto Ricans in, 148, *161*; poverty in, 166; relative rankings of segregation in, *39*; residential segregation in, 50; segregation in, 36–37, *41*; total Hispanic populations in, *46*; undocumented immigrants in, 313–314; unionization in, 187–188; wages in, 140. *See also specific topics*
New Jersey Council of Churches, 149
New Jersey Department of Labor, 319
New Jersey Farm Bureau, 152
New Jersey Farm Services, 150
New Jersey State Industrial Union Council, 149
New Jersey State Migrant Labor Bureau, 145
New Jersey Transit, 78–79
New York City, 59, 164, 175; club culture in, 336–337; COVID-19 in, 291–292; garment district, 65; as gateway, 60–61; gentrification in, 66–67; immigration to, 60, 62; industrial employment in, 179; migration from, 166–167; Puerto Ricans in, *165*; tourism, 61–62; unionization in, 187–188
*New York Times*, 61
Nieto, Santi, 213

Nieves, Efrain, 181
Nieves Falcón, Luis, 135, 358
NJ Transit, 113n24
noncontract labor, 149
North Jersey Transportation Planning Authority, 61
Novak, Michael, 103–104
Nueva Presencia, la, 272, 274
Nuevo Kibú Night Club, El, 207
Nuyorican Poets Cafe, 357

Oaxaca, 298
Obama, Barack, 318, 319
Ochoa, Gilda, 77, 86
Ochún, 199
O'Farrill, Chico, 206
Office of Immigration Statistics, U.S., 12
old age, 269, 284n1; Catholic Church and, 275; communal support for, 277–280; Holy Family Church and, 275–284; shared purpose and, 282–284; in trans community, 298–299; Union City and, 275
Olivieri, Tom, 168
Oñoz, Oscar, 212–213
Open Public Record Act (OPRA), 239
Oquendo, David, 219
oral history, 290
Organization of Petroleum Exporting Countries (OPEC), 188
Orquesta Camajuaní, 208
Orquesta Fantasy, 209
Orquesta Realidad, 213
Orquesta Riviera, 212, *215*
Orquesta Zodiacal, 213, *216*
Ortega, Jose, 68
Ortega, Leonel, 212, 216
Ortiz, Edward, 357
Ortiz, Fernando, 205
Ortiz, Isabelle, 206
Ortner, Sherry, 108

Padilla, Angel, 168
Pagán de Colón, Petroamérica, 141
Palisades Cliffs, 65
Palladium, 338
Palmary, Ingrid, 256
Palmieri, Charlie, 208
Panama Canal, 118

Panchito's, 256, 262
Panero, Julius, 64
*Paris Is Burning* (film), 343
Park Avenue, 66–67
Park Performing Arts Center, 65
Parnaso Campesino, El, 216–217, *217*
Parque Oaxaca, 289, 291, 297
Passaic County, 4, 47–48, 119; segregation in, 51–52
Paterson: Census data on, 119; Civil Rights Congress in, 124–125; industrial employment in, 178; labor movement in, 124; Peruvians in, 117–126, 254–255, 256–257; public space in, 256–257; Puerto Ricans in, 254–255; religious communities in, 259–260
patriarchy, 345
Patterson, 52
Pavo, El, 207
Paz, Suni, 358
Pei, I. M., 233
Penn Station, 71n1
Pérez, Ángel, *214*
Pérez, Vilma, 368n36
Pérez Martínez, Lucía, 327n14
Perth Amboy, 15, 36, 134, 148, 174; industrial employment in, 179; Puerto Ricans in, 179–180
Peru, 119–120, 325; cuisine of, 257; gender in, 257; national identity, 257–261; socioeconomic conditions in, 253–254, 258
Peru Lane, 261
Peru Square, 261–263
Peruvian: migration, 119, 125–126, 254–255
Peruvian Parade, Inc., 260–261
Peruvians: Census data on, 118–119, 127n1; migrants, 117–118, 125, 254–257, 259–260; migration of, 119, 125–126, 254–255; in Paterson, 117–126, 254–255, 256–257, 258–259; women, 253, 256–257
Peruvian Teachers Association, 260
Peutz, Nathalie, 315
Philadelphia, 50
Pinto-Coelho, Joanna, 51, 90

Piñeiro, Carlos, 359, 361, 369n54
Piñero, Jesús T., 138
placemaking, 62–63, 74n44, 334; through ballroom scene, 338–339; in Elizabeth High School, 342–343; in Union City, 64–68; voguing and, 345–348
Plastic Workers Union, 124
Plaza of the Arts, 66, 78–79
police abuse, 172
*Policing the Crisis* (Hall), 59
politics, 4
*Pose* (series), 343, 345
postsecondary education, 235–236
poverty, 24–25; in New Brunswick, 292; in New Jersey, 166; in Puerto Rican communities, 190
Prado, Pérez, 205
Prestige, Tyrone, 336
Prieto, Lázaro, 207–208
Prieto, Yolanda, 80, 201, 219
prison education programs, 358
privacy, in labor camps, 143–144
Project Transfer, 112n19
Proyecto Esperanza, 240
Public Law 25, Puerto Rico, 139
public schools, in New Brunswick, 234–237
public signage, 83–84
public space, in Paterson, 256–257
public transportation, 87–88
Puente, Tito, 206, 208
Puerto Rican Action Committee, 151
Puerto Rican Congress of New Jersey, 366n8
Puerto Rican Legal Defense and Education Fund (PRLDEF), 147, 244
Puerto Rican Organization, 354–355
Puerto Ricans, 67, 86, 99–100, 111, 324, 356–360; in Agricultural Workers Association, 151; alumni, 364–365; on Bergenline Avenue, 76; in Camden, 139–140; Census data on, *167*, *186*, *193*; citizenship of, 159, 172; community organizing of, 171–175; cultural identity of, 353,

367n14; discrimination against, 175–176, 187; education of, 166–167, 174, 352–354; employment of, 192; farm labor regimes and, 136–139; in fields, 143–148; at Glassboro, 138–139; in Great Depression, 137; in Hoboken, 168; immigration of, 134–135; income of, 166, 182, *183*, *190*; integration of, 168–169; isolation index for, 42–43; in Jersey City, 171–172; in labor camps, 143–148; migrants, 134–139, 161–164, 171–173; in Newark, 104–105, 108–109, 355; in New Brunswick, 233–234, 290–291; in New Jersey, 160–167; in New York City, *165*; in Paterson, 254–255; in Perth Amboy, 179–180; population by county, *170*; population of, in New Jersey, 148, *161*; poverty in communities of, 190; Puerto Rican studies, 2, 35; segregation of, 51; settlement of, 168–170; student activism, 354–356, 362–363; in Union City, 69–70; unionization of, 179–180, 181–182; United States population, 366n8; urban experiences of, 134; as workers, 141–143; in World War II, 136, 162
Puerto Rican studies: challenges to legitimacy, 360–362; at Livingston College, 356–360; at Rutgers, 361–362
Puerto Rican Veterans Association, 188
Puerto Rico: colonialism in, 160; Employment Security Act in, 139–140; history of, 161–163; invasion of, 136, 159; Public Law 25, 139; United States and, 136
Puerto Rico Labor Department, 164
Puertorriqueñhos Asociados for Community Organization (PACO), 189
*punto guajiro*, in Hudson County, 215–218

Queens, 288–289, 295–297
Quiñones, Jaime, *150*
Quispe, Patricia, 262

racialization, under neoliberalism, 101
Racialized Place Inequality Framework (RPIF), *34*, 52; aims of, 34
racism, 34–35, 102–103; silent, 258; structural, 52–53
Rael, Carie, 366n5
*Raíces Campesinas diálogos poéticos entre* (Santana & Sorí), 218
Raíces Habaneras, 219
railroad, 162
Ramirez, Gilbert, 162
Ramírez, Mayra, 363
RCA Victor, 200
recession, 188
*Record, The*, 68
redlining, 33–34
Red Scare, 124
Reframing Aging Initiative, 284n1
refugees, 92
Regent Theater, 203
Rego Electric, 178
religion: migration and, 269–272
Rensch, Emma, 118–119
Republicans, 51
residential segregation: defining, 30–33; in Hudson County, 30; in New Jersey, 50; in Union County, 30
Rhees, Suzanne Sutro, 63
rhumba, 203; at La Esquina Habanera, 218–219
Ricky Xtravaganza, 336
Ridgewood, 164
Riley (Father), 273
Rivas, George, 212, 364
Rivas, Maria del Pilar, 261, 263
Rivera, Elias, 358
Rivera, Margie, 364–365
Rivera, Migdalia, 99, 110
Rivera, Miriam, 351
Rivero, Facundo, 207
Robert Wood Johnson University Hospital, 231, 237–238, 239, 241, 245, 288
Rodriguez, Eulogio, 184
Rodriguez, Gregorio, 184

Rodriguez, Juan, 181
Rodriguez, Manuel, 181
Rodríguez Sampayo, Félix, 148
Roman, Angel, 184
Romano, Gloria, 136
Romero-Trejos, Miguel, 303
Rosario-Sorbello and Son, 146
Rosas Amirault, Eva, 173
Ross Fenton Farm, 204
Roth, Philip, 107, 112n19
RUCDR Infinite Biologics, 299
Ruiz Baia, Larissa, 259
Rutgers, 11, 109, 174–175, 231, 299, 351, 355; Puerto Rican studies at, 361–362
Rutgers Cancer Institute of New Jersey, 239
Rutgers Future Scholars program, 364
Rutgers Latino and Caribbean Memory Project, 366n5
Rutgers Medical School, 185
Rutter, Joseph D., 145
RWJBarnabas Health, 231, 240, 243–244

Sacco, Nicholas, 70, 83
Safari, 215
*sahumadoras*, 259
Salem County, 16–17, 145; dissimilarity in, 38–39
Salvadorans, 21, 36, 278, 294
Sánchez, Jorge, 212
Sancti Spiritus, 202
Sandrell, Ruby, 207–208
Sandy Hook, 61
Sanjuan, Pedro, 203–204
Santamaria, Mongo, 205, 206
Santana, Carlos, 209, 215
Santana, Diosdado, 217–218
Santiago, Anna M., 190
Santiago, Juan, 181
SAT scores, 235–236
Sayegh, Andre, 262
Scarsdale, 164
Scholvin, Sören, 61
Schwartz, Jonathan, 107–108
Scorpio, 215
Seabrook Farms, 135, 137
seafaring, 120–121
Second Quaker City Jazz Festival, 205
Secure Communities, 318
segregation: in Bergen County, 51–52; of Cubans, 51; data on, 37–38; de facto, 33; de jure, 33; dimensions of, 30–31; dissimilarity index and, 30, 32–33, 37–38; documentation of, 51; evenness in, 30–32; exposure and, 30–33; exposure index, 33; geography and, 35; hypersegregation, 33; impact of, 52; indices, 32–33; 'isolation index, 33; isolation index as measure of, 37–38; in New Jersey, 36–37, *41*; in Passaic County, 51–52; patterns of, 35–36; of Puerto Ricans, 51; redlining, 33–34; relative rankings of, in New Jersey, *39*; results of study on, 38–50; study of, 33–36; trends in, *41*. See also residential segregation
self-identification, of Latinos, 93
Señor de los Milagros, 259–260
September 11, 2001, 218
Sexteto Habanero, El, 200, 202
sexuality, 332–333; migration and, 295 (*See also specific topics*)
sex work, 308n45; trans people and, 308n46
Shaw, Douglas, 60
Sheet Metal Workers, 185
Shining Path, 254
Shull School, 175
Shulton Perfume Factory, 255
Sibori, Matilde, 252
Sibori, Yolanda, 253
Sierra Berdecía, Fernando, 138
silent racism, 258
Silk City, 118, 121, 123, 128n2
Sinatra, Frank, 67
Singer, Audrey, 62
Sires, Albio, 82
"slum clearance," 102
Small Business Administration, 80
Soho, 66
solidarity: on Bergenline Avenue, 86, 88–90, 93–94; of Latinx communities, 77
Solis, Diana, 245
Somerset, 306n21
Sorí, Sergio, 217–218
Soto, Gloria, 368n35
Soto, Quintin, 181
Sound Factory, 338

South Americans: dissimilarity index for, *43*, *49*; isolation index for, *45*
Spanish American Community Center, 180
Spanish American Rescue Mission, 141–142
Spencer Business College, 126
Springsteen, Bruce, 67
Spun-Jee, 184
Stack, Brian, 70, 82–83
*State v. Shack*, 146
stay-at-home orders, COVID-19, 291
stock market crash, 1929, 122–123
St. Peter's Hospital, 243–244
strip, the. *See* Bergenline Avenue
structural racism, 52–53
student activism, 354–356, 362–363
Students for a Democratic Society, 355
Stumpf, Juliet, 316
suburbanization, 2–3, 35, 52
Sussex County, 16–17; dissimilarity index in, 39–40
Swedesboro, 137

Tarazona, Manuel, *120*, 123, 124, 125, 127
Tarazona, Victor, 122, 124, 127
teachers, at Elizabeth High School, 340–341
Teamsters, 181
Teaneck Jazz Festival, 205
Teatro Guazábara, 357
teen pregnancy, 17–18
Tello, Ricardo, 122, 123, 125, 126
Tello, Talalca, 126
Tertulias de Antaño, 202
Therkelsen, Mary, 175
Thomas, Piri, 359
Thoron, B. W., 137
Tia Delia, 262
Tiberius Ninja Infiniti, Danny, 335, 336
*timba*, 218
Tone, Cristina, 262
Tongolele, 207
Tootsie Roll, 168–169
Toro, Yomo, 212
Torres, Joey, 261
Torres, Zaida Josefina, 368n35

tourism, New York City, 61–62
trading routes, 118–122
Transgender Day of Remembrance, 292
Transgender Survey, U.S., 308n46
translanguaging, 84
Trans Murder Monitoring Project, 292
trans people, 288–289; discrimination against, 302–303; hormone therapy access for, 301–302; labor of, 297–298; in New Brunswick, 290, 292–303; old age and, 298–299; sex work and, 308n46; social history of, 292–299; surveillance of, 302; unemployment and, 310n79
Trenton, 298
Trenton State Prison, 358
Tribeca, 66
Trio Matamoros, 200, 202
Trump, Donald, 319
Tugwell, Rexford G., 137, 138
Tunnel, 338

Underground Dreams, 338
undocumented immigrants, 12–13, 279–280, 324; in New Brunswick, 292; in New Jersey, 313–314
unemployment, 180; during COVID-19 pandemic, 291–292; trans people and, 310n79
Union City, 268–269; Cubans in, 68–69; as gateway, 59, 70–71; immigration to, 270–271; migrants in, 70; migration to, 269; old age and, 275; placemaking in, 64–68; planning for, 62; Puerto Ricans in, 69–70; as sanctuary city, 275; social service organizations in, 276
Union County, 15–16, 47; residential segregation in, 30
Union Estudiantil Puertorriqueña, 357, 359
unionization, 175; in New Jersey, 187–188; in New York City, 187–188; of Puerto Ricans, 179–180, 181–182
United Electrical (UE), 184
United States: anti-communist actions in, 124; diversity in, 28–29; Hispanic population in, 12; nativism in, 174–175; Puerto Rican population in, 366n8; Puerto Rico and, 136
Universal Records, 220n4
Urban Enterprise Zone Program, 64, 67
urban planning, 63

Vaillant, Angelo, 208
Valdés, Gilberto, 205
Valdés, Miguelito, 208
Valdivia, Juliana, 81
Valle, Mercedes, 361, 365
Vazquez del Aguila, Ernesto, 258
Vega, Bernardo, 161
Vera, Carlos, 256, 262
Vera, Isabel, 256–257
Villa Clara, 201; Cuban music from, 215–216
Villa, Raúl Homero, 72n2
Vineland, 134, 136, 148
Virgen de Guadalupe, La, 90
Voces Oral History Center YouTube, 290
"Vogue," 345
voguing, 345–348
volunteerism, in Holy Family Church, 282–284

Wagenheim, Kal, 2
Waldorf-Astoria, 205

Wall Street, 61
warehouses, conversion of, 66
War Food Administration, 136, 138
War Manpower Commission, 136, 137, 162
Warren County, 46; dissimilarity index in, 39–40
W Developers, 66
Weehawken, 162
Whalen, Carmen Teresa, 135
WhatsApp, 291
White communities, 36–37, 50–51, 353; in New Brunswick, 231; White flight, 69, 103–106
whiteness, 105
Wichert, Arthur, 82
William Musto-Union City Museum, 79
Williams, Raymond, 59, 101, 106, 107
women: African American, 99–100; employment of, 23–24; empowerment of, 261–263; Peruvian, 253, 256–257
Woodbine, 177
Woodrow Wilson Elementary, 236
Workers of America, 124
Workers Progress Administration, 123
World War II, 123–124, 160; Puerto Ricans in, 136, 162

Young Lords, The, 69–70

Zaña, El, 256
Zanzibar, 338
Zapotecs, 298
Zayas, Luis, 322
zoning laws, 50
Zukin, Sharon, 66
Zwahl, Eugene, 168

Available titles in the Ceres: Rutgers Studies in History series

James M. Carter, *Rockin' in the Ivory Tower: Rock Music on Campus in the Sixties*
Thomas Gustafson, *American Anti-Pastoral: Brookside, New Jersey and the Garden State of Philip Roth*
Jordan P. Howell, *Garbage in the Garden State*
Aldo A. Lauria Santiago and Ulla D. Berg, eds., *Latinas/os in New Jersey: Histories, Communities, and Cultures*
Maxine N. Lurie, *Taking Sides in Revolutionary New Jersey: Caught in the Crossfire*
Jean R. Soderlund, *Separate Paths: Lenapes and Colonists in West New Jersey*
Camilla Townsend and Nicky Kay Michael, eds., *On the Turtle's Back: Stories the Lenape Told Their Grandchildren*
Hettie V. Williams, *The Georgia of the North: Black Women and the Civil Rights Movement in New Jersey*